CHILDHOOD PROGRAMS AND PRACTICES IN THE FIRST DECADE OF LIFE

A Human Capital Integration

Childhood Programs and Practices in the First Decade of Life: A Human Capital Integration presents research findings on the effects of a variety of early childhood programs and practices for young children and families and their implications for policy development and reform. Leading scholars in the multidisciplinary field of human development and in early childhood learning discuss the effects and cost effectiveness of the most influential model state and federally funded programs, policies, and practices. These include Head Start, Early Head Start, the WIC nutrition program, Child-Parent Centers, the Nurse-Family Partnership, and Perry Preschool, as well as school reform strategies, such as small classes and teacher training. This volume provides a unique multidisciplinary approach to understanding and improving interventions, practices, and policies to optimally foster human capital over the life-course.

Arthur J. Reynolds is a professor in the Institute of Child Development at the University of Minnesota and the director of the Chicago Longitudinal Study (CLS). He is also co-director of the Human Capital Research Collaborative (HCRC; formerly the Early Childhood Research Collaborative, ECRC). Reynolds investigates the effects and economic benefits of early childhood programs, and the Chicago study is one of the most extensive life-course studies of early experience. His interests include child development and social policy, evaluation research, prevention science, and school and family influences on educational success and adult well-being. His publications include *Success in Early Intervention: The Child-Parent Centers* (2000), *Early Childhood Programs for a New Century* (2003), several adult follow-up studies, and two cost-benefit analyses of the Child-Parent Center Program.

Arthur J. Rolnick is senior vice president and director of research at the Federal Reserve Bank of Minneapolis and an associate economist with the Federal Open Market Committee. He is also co-director of the HCRC. He has been a visiting professor of economics at Boston College, the University of Chicago, and the University of Minnesota. Most recently, he was an adjunct professor of economics in the MBA program at Lingnan College, Guangzhou, China, and at the University of Minnesota's Carlson School of Management. His research interests include banking and financial economics, monetary policy, monetary history, the economics of federalism, and the economics of education. Rolnick's essays on public policy issues have gained national attention, and his work on early childhood development has garnered numerous awards, including from Edutopia, the George Lucas Educational Foundation, and the Minnesota Department of Health.

Michelle M. Englund is a research associate and affiliate member of the Graduate Faculty in Child Psychology at the Institute of Child Development, University of Minnesota. Her research interests are in the areas of education and substance use. More specifically, her work in the area of education examines how relationships (with parents, peers, and teachers) influence educational success across development; her work on substance-use behaviors examines the developmental predictors of patterns of substance use in adolescence and early adulthood and of adult functioning resulting from the interplay between earlier development and substance use. Englund's research has been published in *Child Development, Development and Psychopathology, Addiction*, and the *Journal of Educational Research.* She is a co-investigator on the Minnesota Longitudinal Study of Risk and Adaptation.

Judy A. Temple is an associate professor in the Humphrey Institute of Public Affairs and the Department of Applied Economics and adjunct professor in the Institute of Child Development at the University of Minnesota. Previously, she was an associate professor of economics at Northern Illinois University, where she taught and conducted research in public economics. Her major interests are public economics, economics of education, early education, cost-benefit analysis, and policy evaluation. Temple's recent work focuses on evaluation of the long-term effects of early educational interventions. She conducted the economic analysis of the nationally recognized Child-Parent Center Program and is co–principal investigator in the CLS, which has followed 1,500 young children from low-income neighborhoods into adulthood. She has published articles in the *National Tax Journal, Southern Economic Journal, Journal of the American Medical Association*, and *Economics of Education Review.*

Childhood Programs and Practices in the First Decade of Life

A HUMAN CAPITAL INTEGRATION

Edited by

Arthur J. Reynolds
University of Minnesota

Arthur J. Rolnick
Federal Reserve Bank of Minneapolis

Michelle M. Englund
University of Minnesota

Judy A. Temple
University of Minnesota

CAMBRIDGE UNIVERSITY PRESS
Cambridge, New York, Melbourne, Madrid, Cape Town, Singapore,
São Paulo, Delhi, Dubai, Tokyo, Mexico City

Cambridge University Press
32 Avenue of the Americas, New York, NY 10013-2473, USA

www.cambridge.org
Information on this title: www.cambridge.org/9780521132336

First published 2010

Printed in the United States of America

A catalog record for this publication is available from the British Library.

Library of Congress Cataloging in Publication data

Childhood programs and practices in the first decade of life : a human capital
integration / edited by Arthur J. Reynolds . . . [et al.].
p. cm.
Includes bibliographical references and index.
ISBN 978-0-521-19846-2 (hardback) – ISBN 978-0-521-13233-6 (pbk.)
1. Child welfare – United States. 2. Children – Nutrition – United States.
3. Head Start programs – United States. 4. Early childhood education – United
States. I. Reynolds, Arthur J. II. Title.
HV741.C53585 2010
362.70973–dc22 2010006635

ISBN 978-0-521-19846-2 Hardback
ISBN 978-0-521-13233-6 Paperback

CONTENTS

CONTRIBUTORS

CHARLES M. ACHILLES, Seton Hall University.

W. STEVEN BARNETT, National Institute for Early Education Research.

HEATHER BARNEY, RAND Corporation.

CLIVE BELFIELD, Queens College, City University of New York.

JEANNE BROOKS-GUNN, Columbia University.

FRANCES A. CAMPBELL, Frank Porter Graham Child Development Institute, University of North Carolina at Chapel Hill.

RACHEL CHAZAN-COHEN, Administration for Children and Families, U.S. Department of Health and Human Services.

FLAVIO CUNHA, University of Pennsylvania.

MARIJATA DANIEL-ECHOLS, HighScope Educational Research Foundation.

BARBARA DEVANEY, Mathematica Policy Research.

MICHELLE M. ENGLUND, University of Minnesota.

ALEXANDRA FIGUERAS, National Institute for Early Education Research.

JEREMY D. FINN, The University at Buffalo–SUNY.

ELLEN FREDE, National Institute for Early Education Research.

DANIEL GERSHWIN, RAND Corporation.

WILLIAM T. GORMLEY JR., Public Policy Institute, Georgetown University.

JAMES J. HECKMAN, University of Chicago, American Bar Foundation, and University College Dublin.

KWANGHEE JUNG, National Institute for Early Education Research.

SHEILA NATARAJ KIRBY, RAND Corporation.

CYNTHIA ESPOSITO LAMY, Robin Hood Foundation.

VI-NHUAN LE, RAND Corporation.

HENRY LEVIN, Teachers College, Columbia University.

JOHN M. LOVE, Mathematica Policy Research.

ROBERT G. LYNCH, Washington College and Economic Policy Institute.

ELENA V. MALOFEEVA, University of Arizona.

ANDREW J. MASHBURN, Center for Advanced Study of Teaching and Learning, University of Virginia.

SEONG HYEOK MOON, University of Chicago.

DAVID L. OLDS, University of Colorado Denver.

SUH-RUU OU, University of Minnesota.

ROBERT C. PIANTA, Center for Advanced Study of Teaching and Learning, University of Virginia.

RODRIGO PINTO, University of Chicago.

HELEN H. RAIKES, University of Nebraska–Lincoln.

CRAIG T. RAMEY, Georgetown Center on Health and Education, Georgetown University.

GARY RESNICK, Harder+Company Community Research, San Francisco.

ARTHUR J. REYNOLDS, University of Minnesota.

ARTHUR J. ROLNICK, Federal Reserve Bank of Minneapolis.

PETER SAVELYEV, University of Chicago.

LAWRENCE J. SCHWEINHART, HighScope Educational Research Foundation.

CLAUDE MESSAN SETODJI, RAND Corporation.

GARY H. STERN, Federal Reserve Bank of Minneapolis.

ALLISON E. SURIANI, The University at Buffalo–SUNY.

JUDY A. TEMPLE, University of Minnesota.

ADAM YAVITZ, University of Chicago.

EDWARD ZIGLER, Yale University.

FOREWORD: THE ESSENTIAL ROLE OF YOUTH DEVELOPMENT

ROBERT H. BRUININKS
President, University of Minnesota

Since the earliest days of my career, issues of early childhood and youth development have been a passion of mine, so it is truly an honor to share a few of my thoughts with you. It is my sincere hope that the ideas that emerge here will yield positive results for children, youth, and families across the nation.

Too often when we see stories about children and youth in the media, or when I hear public discussion about kids, they're portrayed in a negative light. Consider this assessment by an educator of international renown, who said, "The children now love luxury; they have bad manners, contempt for authority; they show disrespect for their elders and love chatter in place of exercise."

Now, Socrates is widely regarded as a wise man ... but, in this case, he seems to be voicing a popular perspective that has continued to the present day. As 20th-century critic and essayist Logan Pearsall Smith put it, "The denunciation of the young is a necessary part of the hygiene of older people, and greatly assists in the circulation of the blood."

I have long been concerned about this consistent focus on what is wrong with America's kids and the seeming lack of public awareness and interest in the problems that many children and families are facing. These issues seem to be steadily losing ground in the competition for public attention. With an aging population that is increasingly more interested in personal health and public safety than in the welfare of "other people's children," as evidenced by trends in public spending, I fear that the erosion of public interest may continue. The stakes are very high for our society: We must continue to make the case that the development of our children is an important priority, and we must do more to give our children a healthy start.

Conversations about a healthy start for children often center on the "3 Cs": Connection, Competence, and Contribution. I've added a fourth C: Conviction. Discussing "at-risk" children and youth often conjures images of kids who live in poverty, and it cannot be denied that they are often our most vulnerable children. But I would argue that without these four things – strong connections, especially to engaged adults who are genuinely concerned for their well-being; core competencies that enable continued learning and socialization; a clear vision of their personal contribution, their worth to society, and their potential to make a difference; and the courage of their convictions and belief in themselves – without these four Cs, *all* children are potentially at risk. A middle-class child living in a well-to-do suburb who doesn't have these four things may actually face a greater likelihood of not reaching his or her full potential than the children of a working-poor family whose parents read to them every night before bed.

Improving outcomes for our children and youth requires us to take a fresh look at these problems and to identify alternatives to what isn't working and what hasn't worked in the past. And I'm especially excited to see the current focus on the cost effectiveness of early childhood programs – for better or for worse, this is often the deciding factor in what investments are made on behalf of our children.

I believe the University of Minnesota has an important role to play in identifying effective education and developmental programs for children and youth. In fact, in the spring of 2003, I delivered a similar address to a University-hosted Children Summit entitled "Starting Strong," which sought to spark ideas and generate consensus on how we might work together across organizations to improve the childhoods of Minnesota's next generations.

The summit was one of the early outcomes of an interdisciplinary initiative I announced in 2002: the Children, Youth, and Families Initiative. This initiative has been coordinated by the University's Children, Youth, and Family Consortium and chaired by professors Rich Weinberg and Marti Erickson. Their efforts were rooted in the idea that an individual's contributions to society can be traced directly to his or her formative years. In a few short years, this initiative has also resulted in:

- the Human Capital Research Collaborative – sponsored by the University of Minnesota and our colleagues at the Federal Reserve Bank of Minneapolis – which fosters policy analysis and multidisciplinary research on the benefits of investing in childhood development from birth to age 8
- the development of a campus-wide Center for Excellence in Children's Mental Health, which was key to developing our new Infant and Early Childhood Mental Health Certificate
- the Commission on Out of School Time, which researched and reported on the importance of quality out-of-school programming to youth development

These efforts build on the activities of a number of research centers and institutes throughout the University, including:

- The Center for Early Education and Development (CEED), which has worked to improve developmental outcomes for young children through applied research, training, and outreach since 1973
- The Irving B. Harris Training Center for Infant and Toddler Development, which became CEED's Harris Programs, providing training and continuing professional development opportunities to individuals and organizations serving infant and toddler populations
- The Konopka Institute for Best Practices in Adolescent Health – inspired by the pioneering work of Dr. Gisela Konopka, its goal is to disseminate reliable information pertaining to adolescent health to anyone in a position to help
- The Center for 4-H Youth Development, which offers out-of-school, research-based educational programs that nurture positive partnerships between youth and caring adults in safe learning environments

We've also made strategic investments to enhance learning and preparation, not only at the university level but also throughout the education system. Strategic initiatives to help Minnesota schools better prepare young people for college – such as the Consortium for Postsecondary Academic Success and the Minnesota P-16 Partnership – benefit all students in Minnesota but explicitly focus on helping students of color, low-income students, and students whose first language is not English.

The University of Minnesota has made significant strides to improve access to and affordability of higher education through record levels of private fundraising and careful allocation of internal resources. The groundbreaking Founders Free Tuition Program for low-income students, for example, is making the college dream a reality for thousands of young people each year who might not have otherwise had the opportunity. And not only have we raised roughly $200 million for the Promise of Tomorrow Scholarship Drive, but donors are finding new and creative ways to ensure both access and success.

The McGuire Scholars Program, for example, provides additional grant funding to students who benefit from the Founders Free Tuition Program. These additional grants cover 90% of the total cost of attendance. They also provide enhanced academic advising and a bridge program to facilitate the transition from high school to college. The program supported 77 students last fall and an additional 50 this year – and the results announced last month are compelling:

- Once enabled to focus on their studies, 95% of the students continue at the university for a second year (versus 88% of the general population).
- They also achieved higher than expected grades, despite somewhat lower ACT scores.
- In addition, nearly 75% of McGuire scholars are students of color, and 90% fall under federal Pell guidelines for low-income students, underscoring

our commitment to diversity and meeting the needs of underserved populations in Minnesota.

This combined strategy (Founders program plus McGuire program) has been effective in recruiting, retaining, and supporting the success of students through their critical first year of college and beyond. We are further analyzing these early numbers, but I suspect we may find that we are attracting the highest-caliber students in these underserved populations and that these students are outperforming not only their peers here but also those nationally!

Of course, research and education are only valuable when applied to real-world needs and societal problems. Our recent strategic positioning efforts have provided us with an opportunity to revitalize our land-grant mission. For example, University of Minnesota Extension has been reorganized to better meet the needs not only of our rural populations but of urban and suburban youth and families as well. The University Northside Partnership is a prime example of our urban agenda in action – a pilot opportunity to develop sustainable engagement focused on building human capacity, strengthening communities, and promoting urban health in neighborhoods bordering our campus.

The University also supports community youth initiatives such as STEP-UP (Short-Term Education Program for Underrepresented Persons), an innovative program that encourages young people to learn the value of work in a nurturing environment. These few examples illustrate our conviction that it is imperative for any outstanding public university, and all of us together, to celebrate and commit to our civic responsibilities to improve the lives and futures of our nation's children.

I see these efforts as part of a continuum of children and youth development from birth through postsecondary education. The early development – physical, mental, and emotional – of a child sets his or her direction for life, but development doesn't cease at age 6 or at age 16. At each new stage in life – beginning school, reaching puberty, moving to a new community – the ability to adjust and thrive is dependent on the quality of experiences and support that have brought him or her to that point.

In addition, getting our children and youth off to a strong start has lifelong implications for all of us. We live in an increasingly knowledge-based economy, and the need for a highly educated workforce is expected to grow during the course of this century, while the numbers of youth and working adults are expected to shrink. Children whose education, physical health, and mental health have not been attended to will likely be left behind, and each person who is left behind will contribute further to the scarcity of educated workers and engaged global citizens.

Today, in the midst of difficult financial times, some may suggest that it is time to lessen our commitment to the public good and turn our attention inward. I believe instead that we must strive to renew our commitment to, and our investment in, public service and public needs.

I referenced Socrates earlier; another ancient Greek thinker, Diogenes, is credited with saying, "The foundation of every state is the education of its youth." Today's children are tomorrow's parents, teachers, workers, and leaders, and the quality of their childhood experiences will have a direct bearing on their ability to contribute as adults. This nation's children must be nurtured before they arrive on our campuses or workplaces – or they will likely turn away from education toward a lesser future.

ACKNOWLEDGMENTS

This volume is part of the Human Capital Research Collaborative, a partnership of the University of Minnesota and Federal Reserve Bank of Minneapolis devoted to understanding the determinants of well-being and the effects of social programs on improving health and well-being. Many individuals, centers, and organizations made this volume possible. At the Federal Reserve Bank of Minneapolis, Rob Grunewald, Wendy Davis, Diane Wells, and Joan Gieseke were instrumental in planning, organizing, and providing technical support. We thank Rich Weinberg, Karen Cadigan, Sara Zettervall, and Karen Anderson in the Center for Early Education and Development at the University of Minnesota College of Education and Human Development for valuable assistance in planning and coordination. We are especially grateful to the centers and institutions that provided funding for the preparation of the volume and the conference on which it is based, including the Federal Reserve Bank of Minneapolis, the McKnight Foundation, and the University of Minnesota President's Initiative on Children, Youth, and Families, Center for Early Education and Development, and Consortium on Early Childhood Development.

1

Early Childhood Development and Human Capital

ARTHUR J. REYNOLDS, ARTHUR J. ROLNICK,
MICHELLE M. ENGLUND, AND JUDY A. TEMPLE

Since the Great Society era of the 1960s, hundreds of studies have documented positive effects of early childhood programs. Advances in knowledge have contributed not only to the development and improvement of programs but have also spurred expansion of services across the nation (Barnett, Epstein, Friedman, Sansanelli, & Hustedt, 2009; Zigler, Gilliam, & Jones, 2006).

These policy changes have been motivated by the synergy of three sets of findings. First, early childhood development (ECD) programs large and small, mostly focused on children ages 3 and 4, have demonstrated strong effects on school readiness, including language and literacy, numeracy, and socio-emotional skills (Camilli, Vargas, Ryan, & Barnett, 2010; Gormley, 2007; Karoly, Kilburn, & Cannon, 2005; Reynolds, Wang, & Walberg, 2003). Given the connection between school readiness and later performance, early education is a reliable strategy for enhancing child development outcomes. Second, ECD programs can affect broader well-being in ways ranging from preventing child maltreatment and crime to promoting health behavior (Campbell, Ramey, Pungello, Sparling, & Miller-Johnson, 2002; Reynolds et al., 2007; Schweinhart et al., 2005). Most other social programs do not show such broad and enduring impacts. Finally, ECD programs have demonstrated high levels of cost effectiveness by reducing the need for later remediation and treatment and increasing social benefits (Burr & Grunewald, 2006; Rolnick & Grunewald, 2003, 2007; Temple & Reynolds, 2007). Thus, they are widely considered to be more economically efficient investments than other social programs. Together, these findings have contributed to the high national priority placed on early education.

Increased attention to the early years of life also has sparked greater interest in prenatal to age 3 programs and services, which are increasingly viewed as central to optimal child and family outcomes (Olds, Sadler, & Kitzman, 2007; Sweet & Applebaum, 2004). Similarly, increased attention to the early years of life has strengthened interest in the transition to school and in the experiences in the early grades that can reinforce preschool gains and improve achievement (Bogard & Takanishi, 2005; Reynolds, 2003; Reynolds & Temple, 2008; Takanishi & Kauerz, 2008). Early childhood systems and practices that enhance the continuity of development over the first decade of life can promote well-being and have enduring effects over the life-course.

OVERVIEW: EARLY CHILDHOOD PROGRAMS AND HUMAN CAPITAL

To illuminate the expanding knowledge of the ECD field, this volume presents research findings on the effects of early childhood programs and practices in the first decade of life and their implications for policy development and reform. The contributors are leading researchers in the multidisciplinary field of human development and in early childhood learning. They describe effects and cost effectiveness of the most influential model, state, and federally funded programs, policies, and practices. The book is based on a national invitational conference that was held at the Federal Reserve Bank of Minneapolis in December 2007. The conference was sponsored by the Human Capital Research Collaborative (HCRC, Reynolds & Rolnick, 2009). The HCRC is a partnership of the University of Minnesota and the Federal Reserve Bank of Minneapolis dedicated to advancing knowledge on the identification, understanding, and use of cost-effective programs and policies from prenatal development to young adulthood.

ECD programs and practices are conceptualized as human capital investments. Investments of personal and financial resources in educationally enriching experiences and activities promote child well-being and can increase economic and social returns over the life-course. The focus on human capital is well tailored to multidisciplinary research and to public policy decision making. In addition, economic benefits relative to costs are a most relevant indicator for policy development. The value of public investments can be judged, at least in part, on efficiency. Moreover, a human capital perspective emphasizes the longer term effects of programs and practices. Demonstration of immediate and shorter term effects, although an important first step, is not the ultimate goal of most social programs. Indeed, long-term effects are a major focus of early childhood programs. A major question for social policy is whether short-term effects translate into long-term effects on adaptive life skills and behavior.

We define ECD broadly to include the first decade of life, including prenatal and infant development, early education and preschool, kindergarten, and early school-age programs and practices. This breadth maximizes the coverage of influential periods of development. Although it reports findings on achievement and other short-term outcomes, this volume emphasizes longer term effects and cost effectiveness.

HUMAN CAPITAL FRAMEWORK

As an organizing framework for the volume, human capital is a broad identifier for a variety of behaviors, skills, and attitudes that are instrumental for optimal learning and well-being. Originating from the work of moral philosopher Adam Smith (1776/1904), the concept of human capital in contemporary scholarship was developed and popularized by economists (Becker, 1964; Mincer, 1958; Schultz, 1961; Weisbrod, 1962). More recent contributions by, among others, Heckman (2000), Heckman and Krueger (2003), Karoly et al., (2005), Todd and Wolpin (2007), and Currie (2009) illustrate the expansion of the field. Applications to psychology (Foss & Spence, 1992) and public health (Victora et al., 2008) also have occurred within a human development perspective. The concept has been further broadened to social capital (Coleman, 1988), health capital (Grossman, 1972), and cultural capital (Bourdieu, 1977).

Historically, human capital emphasized the enhancement of education and training for economic success in the workforce. Becker (1964) contrasted general and specific human capital skills, with general skills (e.g., problem solving and communication) having greater transferability across contexts. Investment in educational enrichment to promote human capital skills in early childhood is believed to have a greater impact than later investment because positive early experiences are foundational to later learning and can reduce or prevent the occurrence of problem behaviors that require remediation or treatment. Given the high costs of treatment, early childhood investments also have the potential for greater levels of cost effectiveness (Heckman, Stixrud, & Urzua, 2006; Levin & McEwan, 2001; O'Connell, Boat, & Warner, 2009).

Our focus on human capital highlights the identification of effective and cost-effective programs for public policy as well as key elements of their benefits. To the extent that children's experiences in early learning are enriching and mutually reinforcing, continuity is maintained, and this continuity is an important condition for longer term effects. Encouraging continuity of experience also can yield synergistic effects of intervention. In addition to emphasizing investments that are made early in the life-course and that promote continuity, the human capital framework also values complementarity of services. Not only are effective programs implemented over different ages, they are also diverse in focus, with services ranging from parenting education to child-focused language instruction and combination programs that provide many services. Each type of program is part of a larger spectrum of services that address important goals. Thus, they are complementary rather than viewed as either-or alternatives or hierarchically.

Like other theoretical frameworks, including ecological systems theory (Bronfenbrenner, 1989) and the risk and protection model (Rutter & Rutter, 1993), human capital theory is a life-span perspective of well-being in which skills and experiences from one stage of development influence those in the next. Each framework also specifies the importance of timing, duration, and content of services in promoting child development outcomes. In addition to valuing the maintenance of continuity of experiences over time in improving well-being, human capital theory more directly emphasizes economically consequential indicators of well-being such as educational attainment, socioeconomic status, and crime prevention from which the return on investments can be readily estimated.

Given the similarities across theories, human capital provides an integrative framework for understanding the impacts of ECD programs and practices. In ecological systems theory, for example, human capital develops as personal resources of the child interacting with family and larger social contexts to promote well-being (Bronfenbrenner, 1989). Investments in educational enrichment have an impact to the extent that they facilitate proximal processes of development, which are the social interactions and learning experiences that directly strengthen learning. The more comprehensive the services, the larger and more enduring the impacts can be. From the perspective of risk and protection (Rutter & Rutter, 1993), human capital investments are viewed as a process of building protective factors defined as individual, family, school, or broader levels of support that compensate or buffer child risks and vulnerabilities from poverty to family dysfunction. The dosage and quality of enrichment help initiate a chain of protective mechanisms that lead to cumulative advantages over time in educational, social, and psychological development. As in the human capital and ecological models, the earlier that services are provided in age-appropriate and meaningful ways, the larger the impact on well-being.

VOLUME THEMES

Based on the human capital and related perspectives, the chapters integrate four critical themes in the field. The first is children's stage of development. The focus is on the entire period of early learning from prenatal development to early school-age transitions. Not only are the intervention approaches matched to children's ages, they are also representative of the major contexts of learning, including family, center, school, and community. Among the interventions covered are WIC, the Nurse-Family Partnership, Early Head Start and Head Start, Child-Parent Centers, Perry Preschool, kindergarten programs, teaching practices, and the Tennessee STAR class-size reduction program. Although the principle of developmental continuity addresses the importance of alignment between programs across ages in yielding synergistic effects, the expectations for even the best ECD programs and experiences should be realistic. As cautioned by Zigler, Styfco, and Gilman (1993, pp. 21–22), "Do we really believe that a year of preschool can shape the course of human life? To do so is to ignore the many, many factors ranging from the quality of schooling to socialization influences from the family and community."

The second major theme is cost effectiveness. Given the greater use of cost-benefit analysis in social and educational research, knowledge about the level of cost effectiveness of early childhood programs across stages of development is needed more than ever. The chapters summarize the latest knowledge about the cost effectiveness of different intervention approaches as well as identify the potential for cost effectiveness among newer programs and approaches. Although model programs and those with longer histories are more likely to have completed long-term cost-benefit analyses, the evidence from the programs presented in this volume provides valuable information about the possible benefits of high-quality and well-implemented interventions. The common elements of effectiveness across studies also can be derived.

The third theme is program focus, which includes the intervention goals, content, and services, ranging from prenatal nutrition and parenting education to school readiness and achievement. ECD programs may include family services, parenting classes, curriculum-based educational enrichment for children, health services, and outreach services in the community. The programs and approaches covered include the full range of these foci and content. Although programs that are relatively narrow in scope can be effective and cost effective in achieving their goals, those providing a broader array of services over longer periods of time have the potential for larger and more enduring effects.

The fourth theme is scale. Programs vary dramatically in size and scope, target populations, funding, and level of monitoring. They range from one-site intensive interventions to federal- or state-funded programs serving thousands of families at different levels of service. There are three levels of scale. Efficacy trials are the initial pilot projects implemented in a single setting with relatively small samples. They assess whether interventions are effective under ideal conditions. Effectiveness trials are replication projects implemented within existing service systems, usually with larger samples in different locations. Sustained programs and practices are upscaled and established services that are routinely implemented within existing service systems over longer periods of time. Most early childhood research emphasizes model programs (efficacy and effectiveness trials) over larger scale (sustained) programs, even though the latter have greater generalizability and relevance for current practice. This book includes the full continuum of scale, from model programs such as Perry Preschool and Abecedarian Project, to state-funded programs, as well as historical and more recent federally funded programs such as Head Start, WIC, and Early Head Start. It also covers school policies and practices such as full-day kindergarten, small classes, and teacher practices.

Together, these four themes provide a unique and comprehensive framework to better understand the complex effects of ECD programs, their contributions to society, and future opportunities for research.

TRENDS IN EARLY CHILDHOOD PROGRAMS AND INVESTMENTS

The acceleration of human capital research in early childhood development should be interpreted within the larger context of changes in public policies at the state and national level. Several trends in early childhood policy reflect the high priority given to the investments in young children that are examined in this volume. They include (1) increased investments in early childhood programs, (2) increased access and participation, and (3) advances in effectiveness and cost-effectiveness research.

Increased Investments in Early Childhood Development Programs

In the past decade, all levels of government have increased resource investments in early childhood programs and services, ranging from prenatal nutrition and child care to early intervention and preschool programs. The broad aim of these investments is to promote child health and well-being with a particular focus on children's school readiness. Although the National Educational Goals Panel (1995) first proclaimed the goal that all children should begin school ready to learn, the resource investments needed to meet this goal have accelerated within the past decade.

As shown in Figure 1.1, total public investment in programs and services for children aged birth to 5 (before kindergarten entry) in 2007–2008 was approximately $33 billion (Barnett et al., 2009; Child Care Bureau, 2009).[1] These annual expenditures were more than double that of a decade ago (U.S. General Accounting Office, 1999). Of this total, 56% ($18.5 billion) was federal expenditures. The major categories of federal funding were Head Start (including Early Head Start; $6.8 billion); Special Supplemental Nutrition Program for Women, Infants, and Children (WIC; $4.7 billion); Child Care and Development Funds (CCDF; $2.7 billion); block grants to the states for Temporary Assistance for Needy Families (TANF; $1.6 billion); special education and early intervention services in the Individuals with Disabilities Education Act (IDEA, Parts B and C; $810 million); and preschool funding from Title I of the Elementary and Secondary Education Act (ESEA; $400 million). Notably, Title I funding to school districts for preschool education represented 3% of the

[1] Our estimates are inclusive of these sources. This estimate does not include expenditures from the Earned Income Tax Credit or the Dependent Care Credit. Also, expenditures from CCDF and TANF are exclusive to children from birth to age 5. Nationally, 55% of all children and youth served are in this age group; 75% of WIC participants are children from birth to age 5.

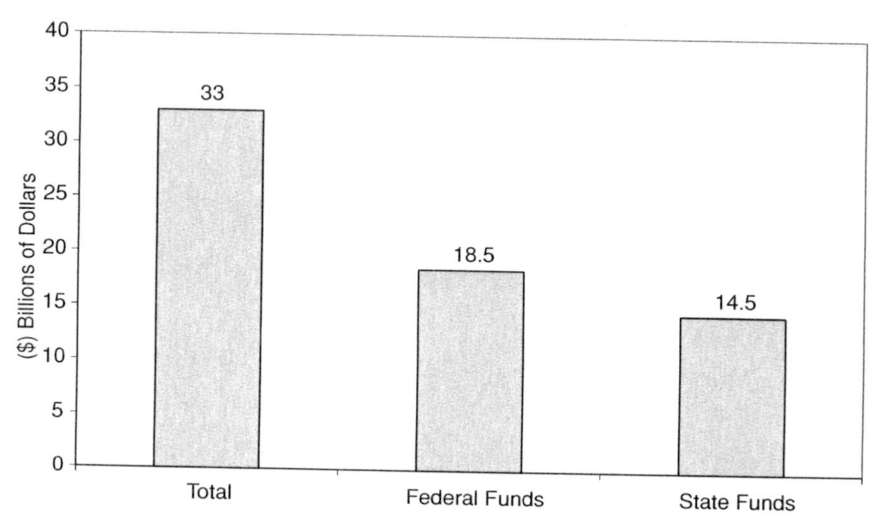

Figure 1.1. Public Investments in Early Childhood Programs, 2007–2008 (Authors' estimates from several sources; see text).

$14 billion total annual Title I expenditure. Among the largest increases in total funding since 1999 were for Head Start ($4.7 to $6.8 billion, or nearly a 45% increase) and CCDF ($1.5 billion to $2.7 billion, or nearly a 75% increase).

State and local government expenditures comprised the remaining 44% ($14.5 billion). The major categories were state and school district expenditures for preschool special education under IDEA, Part B ($5 billion); state-financed preschool programs for 3- and 4-year-olds ($4.6 billion); state and school district expenditures for early intervention services (IDEA, Part C; $2.3 billion); CCDF matching state funding ($1.2 billion); and state and local Head Start matching funding ($1.4 billion). Funding for state-financed preschool programs has nearly tripled since 1999 ($1.7 billion to $4.6 billion). In 2007–2008, 1 million preschool children were served in 38 states at an annual state expenditure per child of $4,061 (Barnett et al., 2009).

Increased Participation in Early Childhood Programs

Increased investment in early education has led to corresponding increases in the number of children served in ECD programs. Figure 1.2 shows the pattern of participation of 3-, 4-, and 5-year-olds from 1983 to 2007, using data from the National Center for Educational Statistics (U.S. Department of Education, 2003, 2009). Participation is defined as enrollment in center-based care and education programs for at least part of the day. The programs for 5-year-olds are kindergarten.

Although rates of participation have increased substantially over the past two decades, they vary by age group. In 2007, there were 12.3 million 3- to 5-year

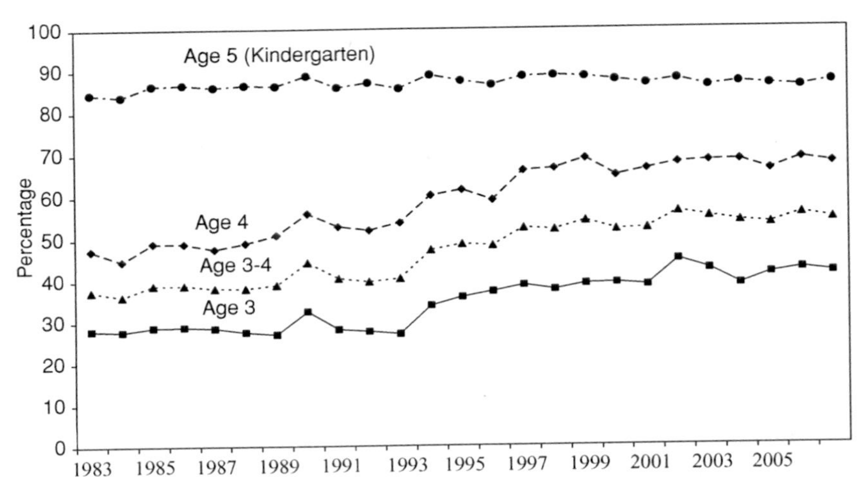

Figure 1.2. Percentage of U.S. Children in Early Childhood Programs (U.S. Department of Education, 2003, 2009).

olds, with 4.1 million in each of the three age groups (U.S. Department of Education, 2009). In that year, 67.8% of 4-year-olds were enrolled in center-based programs, an increase of 43% since 1983 (from 47.4%; Table 43, U.S. Department of Education, 2009). In the same year, 41.5% of 3-year-olds were enrolled in a center-based early education program, an increase of 48% since 1983 (from 28.1%). In 2007, considering all 3- and 4-year-olds, 54.5% were enrolled in center-based programs, an increase of 45% since 1983 (from 37.5%).

As expected, rates of participation vary by family income, education, and race/ethnicity. Based on data from National Household Education Surveys from 2005 (Table 44, U.S. Department of Education, 2009), children residing in families with annual earnings between $15,000 and $25,000 per year had a 29% rate of participation in center-based early education programs compared to 43% for those residing in families with annual earnings exceeding $50,000. This is a 48% higher rate of participation for higher income families. Parent education followed a similar pattern, with those in families with greater educational attainment having higher rates of center-based early education. Children of high school graduates, for example, had a 30% rate of participation compared to 45% for children of bachelor's-degree recipients. Finally, Hispanic children had a substantially lower rate of participation in center-based programs (25.2%) than Black (43.8%) and White children (37.8%). The higher rate of participation for Blacks is entirely due to their greater enrollment in Head Start (13.3%) compared to Whites (2.8%) and Hispanics (6.2%).

Although rates of participation in ECD programs have increased substantially, barriers to access remain and relate to affordability, availability of high-quality and full-day programs, and service fragmentation. For example, early childhood systems in most states and nationally are fragmented. The different funding mechanisms and administrative structures make coordination difficult, and continuity across ages is low. The most typical publicly funded center-based arrangement in prekindergarten, for example, is a part-day program for one year with little opportunity for transition support in the early grades. Moreover, the quality of programs is variable at best and generally mediocre. The average yearly expenditure per child for state-financed programs of $4,061 (Barnett et al., 2009) is based on minimum standards for class sizes and services. Expenditures exceed $5,000 per child for programs showing long-term effects and cost effectiveness (Reynolds & Temple, 2008).

One gap is the lack of comprehensive services. Although more than 70% of center-based providers offer education programs, less than 10% provide medical services and referrals, parental supports, and social services (U.S. General Accounting Office, 1999). The discrepancy is even larger for family-based programs and is little changed in the past decade (Karoly et al., 2005; Reynolds, Mathieson, & Topitzes, 2009; Zigler et al., 2006).

The quality of child care is generally low and very uneven, primarily because of low staff compensation, a lack of educational credentials, and high staff turnover (Bowman, Donovan, & Burns, 2000). Subsidized child care via CCDF provides fewer services than many center-based preschool programs and often lacks a broad educational mission. The cost of full-day and high-quality programs is high, which is another barrier to access for low- and middle-income families. Because the effectiveness and cost effectiveness of programs are dependent on the quality, structure, length, and breadth of services, these elements need to be examined closely to achieve optimal health and well-being.

Advances in Understanding Effectiveness

Knowledge about the effects of ECD programs has provided a strong foundation for both increased participation and investments. In recent years, several advances have strengthened the policy and social significance of ECD programs. First, a large body of research shows that ECD programs from birth to age 5 promote well-being in many domains from school entry to adulthood (Karoly et al. 2005; Nelson, Westhaus, & MacLoed, 2003; Reynolds & Temple, 2008). Long-term effects on remedial education, delinquency, educational attainment, and socioeconomic status are especially significant (Campbell et al., 2002; Consortium for Longitudinal Studies, 1983; Reynolds, Temple, Robertson, & Mann, 2002; Schweinhart et al., 2005). These findings are consistent with the length, intensity, and ecological focus of intervention. More recent larger scale state and federal programs also have demonstrated positive effects on short-term cognitive and social skills (Barnett et al., 2009; Reynolds & Temple, 2008). These findings predict later benefits and cost effectiveness.

A second advance is that both the timing and duration of intervention matter. In the past decade, empirical support for the importance of these attributes has grown substantially (McCall, Larsen, & Ingram, 2003; Reynolds et al., 2009; Reynolds & Temple, 2008). The most effective childhood prevention programs spanning home visitation to center-based preschool education have been those that began no later than age 3, continue for multiple years, and provide support to families (McCall et al., 2003; Reynolds et al., 2009; Zigler & Berman, 1983; Zigler et al., 2006). That the duration of intervention can matter at least as much as timing is supported by human capital (Becker, 1964; Heckman, 2000) and ecological (Bronfenbrenner & Morris, 1998) theories, whereby large initial impacts accumulate over time.

The third advance is that generative mechanisms of effects are being identified and understood. One major mechanism is the cognitive advantage hypothesis, which is supported by studies of model (Campbell, Pungello, Miller-Johnson, Burchinal, & Ramey, 2001; Consortium for Longitudinal Studies, 1983; Schweinhart et al., 1993) and larger scale programs (Reynolds, 2000; Reynolds et al., 2004). Although the enhancement of cognitive and scholastic skills has been found to initiate longer term effects on school success and educational attainment, generalizability to social and health outcomes has been underinvestigated. In addition, the contributions of socio-emotional development, family-support behavior, and school context and quality, although sizable for some outcomes, are just beginning to be investigated comprehensively and into adulthood (Cunha & Heckman, 2008; Heckman et al., 2006; Reynolds, Ou, & Topitzes, 2004; Reynolds & Temple, 2008).

As shown in Figure 1.3, ECD programs can affect life-course outcomes through one or more of five pathways: cognitive advantage, family support, motivational advantage, social adjustment, and school support. These pathways are consistent with theories of early enrichment, intervention theories, and the accumulated research on intervention effects (Reynolds, 2000; Reynolds & Temple, 2008). To the extent that programs have a meaningful impact on more than one of the paths, long-term effects and cost effectiveness would be more likely to occur, although the paths of influence would be expected to be a chain of links among the five hypotheses. In the absence of direct effects of intervention on any of the paths, long-term effects would be unlikely.

Although early childhood research and policy have advanced rapidly, many challenges remain. What are the longer term effects of sustained large-scale programs? Do the mechanisms of intervention effects vary by outcome? What is the optimal combination of timing and duration of services? What are key principles of effectiveness? What are the gaps in knowledge?

OVERVIEW OF THE VOLUME

The goal of the volume is to enhance knowledge about the cost effectiveness of ECD intervention. The chapters are updated versions of the papers presented at the national invitational conference (see the Appendix for discussion and

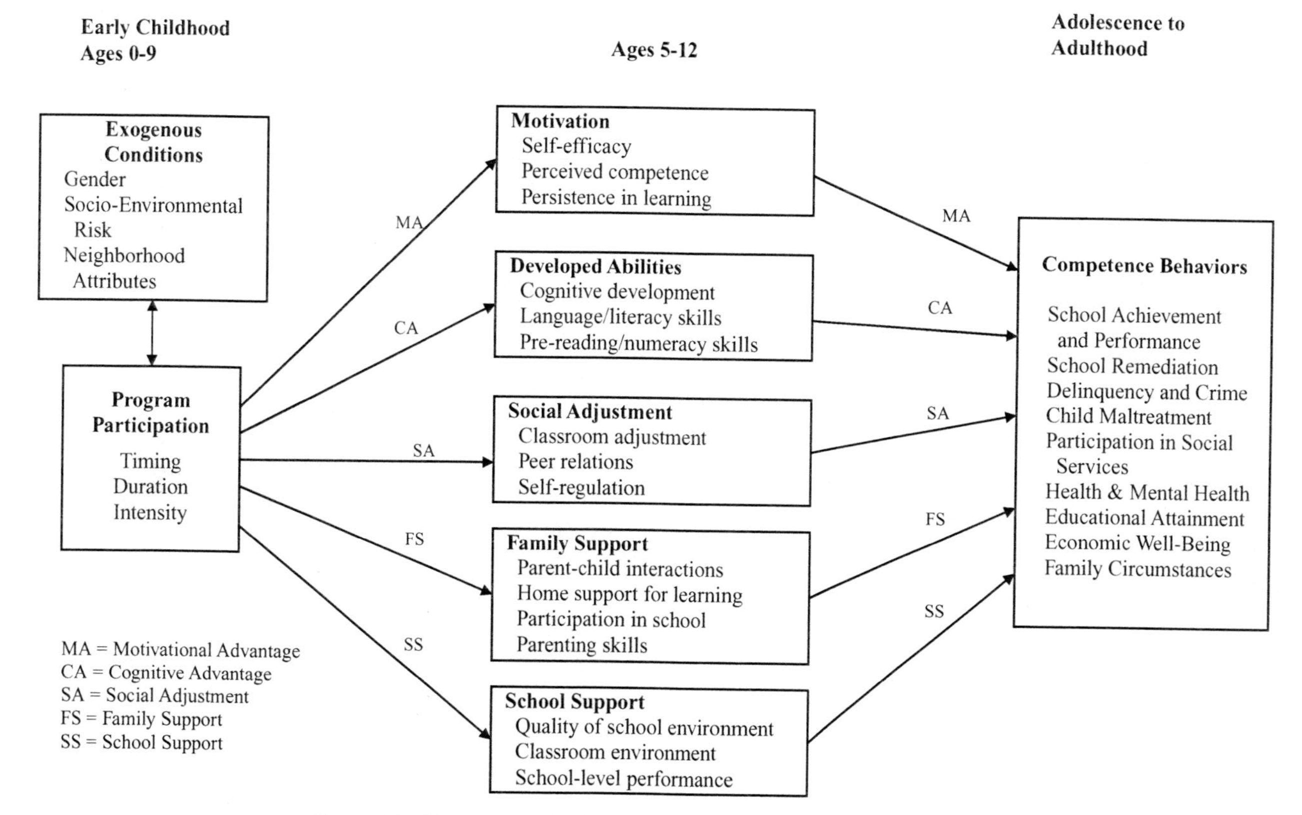

Figure 1.3. Common Paths from Early Childhood to Later Well-Being.

commentaries on these papers). In synthesizing the research on programs and practices and making recommendations for policy development, dissemination, and research, the contributors addressed these questions:

- What social conditions and needs led to the intervention strategy or practice?
- What are the conceptual foundations of the intervention approach?
- What are the essential services provided and at what levels of dosage and quality?
- How strong is the accumulated evidence of effectiveness on child well-being in the short and long term?
- Is there evidence of cost effectiveness for the program and intervention strategies?
- What are the limitations of the evidence base, and how are they being addressed?
- What recommendations and implications for policy follow from the evidence?

Part I: Prenatal and Infant Programs

In the first-decade perspective of ECD, prenatal and infant programs are critical to health and well-being and yet often have been disconnected from preschool and school-age services. This section has four chapters on the earliest family and child intervention services. In "WIC Turns 35: Program Effectiveness and Future Directions," Barbara Devaney reviews the literature on this well-known federal program and offers several recommendations for policy and program development. As noted, many low-income individuals are at risk of poor nutrition and health outcomes because of insufficient nutrition during pregnancy, infancy, and early childhood. The Special Supplemental Nutrition Program for Women, Infants, and Children (WIC) was established in 1972 to help meet the special needs of low-income women, infants, and children by providing three main benefits: (a) supplemental foods, (b) nutrition education, and (c) referrals to health care and social service providers. With annual funding of nearly $5 billion, WIC, as Devaney indicates, is a generally successful and popular program, largely because it serves a vulnerable population and because of its comprehensive research record over the past 35 years. She concludes, however, that in addition to significant and necessary changes to WIC food packages, the future research agenda of analyzing the effectiveness of the WIC program must advance well beyond the current state of affairs.

In "The Nurse-Family Partnership: From Trials to Practice," David L. Olds summarizes a 30-year program of research that has sought to improve early maternal and child health and future well-being through prenatal and infancy home visiting by nurses. The program is designed for low-income mothers who have had no previous live births. As described by Dr. Olds, the home-visiting nurses have three major goals: (a) to improve the outcomes of pregnancy by helping women improve their prenatal health; (b) to improve the child's health and development by helping parents provide more sensitive and competent care of the child; and (c) to improve the parental life-course by helping parents plan future pregnancies, complete their education, and find work. Extensive evidence from three large-scale randomized trials in Elmira (New York), Memphis, and Denver has indicated that the program has been successful in achieving two of its most important goals: the improvement of parental care of the child reflected in the advancement of several measures of child development and the improvement of maternal life-course outcomes reflected in reduced subsequent pregnancies, greater workforce participation, and reduced dependence on public assistance and food stamps. The impact of the program was greater on those segments of the population who were more susceptible to the problems under examination. Olds also discusses the importance of fidelity to the model in promoting well-being.

In the 1960s, cross-sectional examinations of the cognitive development of children from poor families indicated that their cognitive test scores tended to be within the average range in infancy, but disproportionate declines occurred after that period. Many scientists believed that early "environmental deprivation" was largely responsible for these declines. In the chapter entitled "Carolina Abecedarian Project," Frances A. Campbell and Craig T. Ramey review the history and findings of this storied intervention designed to prevent the observed cognitive decline through center-based educational enrichment beginning in infancy. Based on a sample of 111 children born into poverty in the early 1970s and experimentally assigned to 5 years of year-round early education, the study found persuasive evidence that the language-focused intervention strongly increased not only the cognitive skills of children up to age 21 but also enhanced their school performance, educational attainment, and economic well-being. The authors also found that intervention participants had lower levels of marijuana use by age 21, lower rates of smoking, and fewer depressive symptoms and were less likely to be parents as teenagers. Parents of participants also enhanced their own educational and economic development. Cost-benefit analysis at age 21 indicated a return of $2.50 per dollar invested. In support of a life-course perspective, the authors conclude that early education is most relevant "as a way to improve the chance that children from poor families will achieve in school and go on to higher education."

Poverty and associated risk factors exert their influence in the earliest years of child development. Yet, historically, most interventions are implemented after age 3, which may be too late for children and families at the highest risk for school failure and health-compromising behavior. In 1995, the federally initiated and financed Early Head Start program was established within the U.S. Department of Health and Human Services. The focus was birth to age 3 services including home visitation, center-based education, and combined programs that now reach more than 60,000 children annually. In "Early Head

Start Impacts at Age 3 and a Description of the Age 5 Follow-Up Study," Helen H. Raikes and colleagues summarize the findings and significance of the congressionally mandated national impact study. Based on an experimentally assigned sample of 3,001 low-income children and families in 17 sites studied beginning in 1997, impact findings at the end of the program at 36 months of age revealed statistically significant but relatively small effects on cognitive, language, and socio-emotional outcomes. However, the positive effects were broad and also included greater parenting skills, higher rates of immunization, lower rates of accident-related hospitalization, and improved parental well-being. Impacts varied by program model. As noted by the authors, "the broadest pattern of impacts was seen in mixed approach programs in which families were offered a mixture of center-based and home-based services." The authors also identified differences by race and ethnicity. The effects for Black children in mixed-service programs, for example, were more than double that for other racial and ethnic groups. Although follow-up of the sample to age 5 and beyond will be most informative, these initial findings provide valuable lessons about the benefits and challenges of large-scale implementation of early interventions.

Part II: Preschool Education

Preschool programs for 3- and 4-year-olds are widely considered to be one of the most effective ways to enhance children's well-being. Their unique attraction is the documented evidence that programs high in quality have enduring effects that can lead to high economic returns. This section has six chapters spanning the Great Society era to three current state-financed prekindergarten programs. A commentary also is provided by Edward Zigler, a Yale University professor and a founder of the Head Start program.

Project Head Start, the grandfather of preschool programs for the economically disadvantaged, opened in 1965 and today serves more than 900,000 families. Not surprisingly, a vast literature on the program is available. In "Project Head Start: Quality and Links to Child Outcomes," Gary Resnick reviews the history of research on this landmark program. The primary foci are the effects on participating children and families and the impact of program quality on children's outcomes. After describing the progression of research on the program since the 1970s, Dr. Resnick reviews in depth the two most comprehensive assessments of the Head Start program: the Head Start Family and Child Experiences Survey (FACES) in 2003 and the Head Start Impact Study (HSIS) begun in the fall of 2002. As described in the chapter, findings from FACES, a nationally representative sample of nearly 400 Head Start centers, address the issue of classroom quality and children's outcomes from fall to spring of their Head Start year and into the spring of kindergarten. As noted by Resnick, overall quality in classrooms is good, teachers increasingly have CDAs or BA degrees (although only 38% have at least a BA), and teacher qualifications predict quality through their beliefs and attitudes about early childhood education practices. As expected, children were found to experience gains from fall to spring and more substantial gains at the spring of kindergarten. Early results from the HSIS, in which more than 4,600 3- and 4-year-olds in 378 centers across the United States were randomly assigned to Head Start or no-Head Start services, show significant improvements in children's school readiness skills by the end of their Head Start year, compared to the control group. The largest effects were on pre-reading skills, primarily letter-word identification and letter naming. Many of these improvements were found to be reduced by the end of first grade. After noting the quality of research has advanced considerably in recent years, Resnick discusses several implications of findings for Head Start policy and practice. These include greater use of evidence-based curriculum models, emphasis on parent involvement in children's learning, and greater attention to the organization and distribution of program resources at the local level.

In "The Challenge of the HighScope Perry Preschool Study," Lawrence J. Schweinhart describes the history of the program and its impacts on participants. The Perry study examined the lives of 123 young African American children living in poverty who were randomly assigned to a program group that received a high-quality preschool program at ages 3 and 4 or to a no-program group. Since the initial entry of children in 1962, data have been collected on their well-being up to age 40. The study has the longest follow-up of any preschool or education program. As Dr. Schweinhart describes, the program group significantly surpassed the no-program group in school success, adult employment rates, and earnings and had half as many lifetime arrests and convictions for crime. At age 40, the economic return to society was found to be $16.14 per dollar invested. This study has enjoyed great attention and, along with similar studies, motivated public officials, practitioners, and many others to advocate for greater preschool investments for low-income children. Schweinhart also notes that few if any of those other program investments have achieved the structural and process characteristics of the original Perry Preschool program. Most of the chapter is focused on defining the characteristics of the program that led to its phenomenal success and considers what policies would be required to duplicate its success today. Four key characteristics are serving low-income 3- and 4-year-olds, using certified teachers with class sizes limited to 16, using a validated curriculum, and including parent outreach services such as home visits.

In "Impacts and Implications of the Child-Parent Center Preschool Program," Arthur J. Reynolds, Judy A. Temple, and Suh-Ruu Ou report findings from the Chicago Longitudinal Study of the Child-Parent Center (CPC) preschool program that address emerging research questions and illustrate advances in the field for enhancing effectiveness. In the ongoing study, a complete cohort of 989 CPC participants who attended 1 or 2 years of preschool from 1983–1985 and a matched comparison group of 550 who attended other early childhood programs have been followed prospectively up to age 26. The CPC program is especially relevant to early childhood policy. As the second oldest federally funded preschool program (after Head Start), CPC has been implemented successfully in the Chicago public schools for four decades. Beginning in 1967, the Chicago schools were the first district to use Title I funds for preschool education. The program is also innovative in its approach to education, blending an instructional philosophy of literacy and school readiness with intensive services for parents to strengthen the family–school relationship. The findings of the study have consistently shown enduring effects on life-course outcomes not only in education but also in general well-being, including school readiness, school performance and achievement, child maltreatment, juvenile delinquency, and educational attainment. Adult benefits also have been found relating to crime prevention, health insurance, depressive symptoms, and economic well-being. Benefits for parents such as greater parental involvement and greater educational attainment have also been demonstrated. Cost-benefit analysis at age 21 indicates a $10.15 return per dollar invested in the preschool program. School-age and extended intervention from preschool to third grade also have shown positive economic returns. The authors discuss five principles of effectiveness for improving early childhood programs, with a major one being establishment of a coordinated system of services from preschool to the third grade.

Parents and public officials are increasingly concerned about the school readiness of young children. In recent years, state governments have boosted their support for prekindergarten programs. In "Small Miracles in Tulsa: The Effects of Universal Pre-K on Cognitive Development," William T. Gormley Jr. asks these questions: Can a large-scale universal pre-K program also produce substantial benefits by enhancing the school readiness of young children? Do all children benefit from such a program? How large are the impacts? Tulsa, Oklahoma, is home to the largest school district in the state. In addition to its size, Tulsa has the advantage of a racially and ethnically diverse school population, which facilitates estimates of subgroup impact. The Oklahoma pre-K program enrolls 70% of all 4-year-olds, the highest level of participation of any state-financed program. As described by Gormley, participation in the universal program is associated with large increases in language, literacy, and math skills in kindergarten. Children from middle-class families also have been found to benefit substantially from the program. Because all teachers are certified and the program is run through the public schools, the Oklahoma model demonstrates an approach that other states can follow in strengthening their preschool investments.

Marijata Daniel-Echols, Elena V. Malofeeva, and Lawrence J. Schweinhart in their chapter, "Lessons From the Evaluation of the Great Start Readiness Program (GSRP): A Longitudinal Evaluation," summarize the findings from six major evaluation studies of Michigan's state-funded preschool program. Given the lack of evidence on long-term effects of state-funded programs, the Michigan studies are important to the field. The authors begin with a description of the preschool program and its history. They then report both short- and long-term outcomes of program participation. Highlighted are findings focused on grade retention, cognitive skills, and course enrollment. For example, from early elementary school through the eighth grade, studies have consistently found that the GSRP group had a significantly lower rate of grade retention compared to the non-GSRP group. Daniel-Echols and colleagues point out that, in middle school, this result was especially evident for children of color compared to White children and for boys compared to girls. The authors also indicate that, in addition to the impact on grade retention, all of the studies reviewed found that children in the GSRP group had more developed language, literacy, and math skills as well as school-readiness skills compared to the non-GSRP children. Daniel-Echols and colleagues conclude with implications for future research.

Although state-financed preschool programs have grown dramatically in the past decade, evaluations of their effects have only recently received special attention. Ellen Frede, W. Steven Barnett, and colleagues in their chapter, "Abbott Preschool Program Longitudinal Effects Study (APPLES) Year One Findings," describe early effects of this court-mandated and state-funded program. The Abbott program was established by the landmark New Jersey Supreme Court school-funding case, *Abbott v. Burke*. Beginning in the 1999–2000 school year, 3- and 4-year-old children in the highest poverty districts in the state were able to receive a high-quality preschool education that would prepare them to enter school with the knowledge and skills necessary to meet the state's quality and curriculum content standards. This study investigates the educational effects of state-funded prekindergarten education for children at ages 3 and 4 that came about as a result of this court order. Findings show the beneficial effects of the program in promoting children's early school success. The finding that full-day preschool programs are associated with greater school readiness and progress during kindergarten is particularly relevant for strengthening the impact of pre-K programs in other states.

Part III: Kindergarten and Early School-Age Services and Practices

Long-term effects of programs in the first 5 years of life are more likely to be realized if children have enriching kindergarten and early school-age experiences. Effective teaching and teaching practices are instrumental, but programs, practices, and services in kindergarten and beyond are influential on their own as well. This section includes three chapters.

In "Opportunity in Early Education: Improving Teacher–Child Interactions and Child Outcomes," Andrew J. Mashburn and Robert C. Pianta argue that not all features of preschool and related early childhood programs that are currently considered "preschool quality" directly affect children's development. In an alternative perspective, they propose that the quality of interactions that children have with adults, peers, and learning materials is the important mechanism responsible for positive outcomes. This interaction principle generalizes to school-age as well as infant and preschool programs. Mashburn and Pianta apply this perspective to the improvement of programs using Bronfenbrenner's bioecological model of development. They then discuss the design of MyTeachingPartner (MTP), an in-service teacher professional development and teacher education program, and present an initial evaluation of the effects of MTP on teachers' growth trajectories in each of seven Classroom Assessment Scoring System (CLASS) dimensions of teacher–child interactions over the course of a school year.

In "School Readiness and the Reading Achievement Gap: Can Full-Day Kindergarten Level the Playing Field?," Vi-Nhuan Le, Sheila Nataraj Kirby, and colleagues describe the increased push for implementation of full-day kindergarten and the development of school-readiness skills, broadly defined to include cognitive skills, socio-emotional development, and physical health. Although research on kindergarten programs has grown, the amount of evidence is relatively small compared to that on preschool programs. Using data from the Early Childhood Longitudinal Study – Kindergarten Class of 1998, a national probability sample of 20,000 children, the authors link full-day kindergarten attendance and school readiness at kindergarten entry to reading achievement trajectories through the fifth grade. Although participation in full-day kindergarten programs relative to half-day programs was associated with significant gains in kindergarten reading achievement, it was not associated with future reading performance. In contrast, cognitive, emotional, and physical readiness skills were predictive of later reading achievement. Recommendations are made for research to help policy makers improve the effectiveness of kindergarten programs.

In "Small Classes in the Early Grades: One Policy, Multiple Outcomes," Jeremy D. Finn, Allison E. Suriani, and Charles M. Achilles review the history of the Tennessee STAR (Student Teacher Achievement Ratio) class-size reduction experiment and the extensive research that has been conducted on the program. They also review research on effects of small classes in other projects and explanations for how and why small classes, in contrast to reduced pupil–teacher ratios, improve achievement. Beginning in 1985, students in 79 elementary schools throughout Tennessee were randomly assigned to small (13–17 students) classes or larger classes with or without a teacher's aide. Once students completed third grade, the experiment ended but data collection continued. The review by Finn and colleagues of both STAR research and other nonexperimental interventions indicates that small-class processes differ from those of larger classes and that small class sizes in the early grades improved test scores. The greatest gains were experienced by those who had more years of participation in small classes. Minority students or students attending inner-city schools experienced greater improvements in test scores than White or nonurban students. As the Tennessee students approached adulthood, more recent research has analyzed the effects of small class sizes on the decision to enroll in advanced courses while in high school, take college admission tests, and complete high school. Enrollment in small class sizes was associated with these long-term outcomes, and evidence of greater effects of small class sizes for students from lower income families was found for high school completion and the taking of college admissions tests. This chapter also summarizes the cost-benefit analyses that have been performed with Project STAR data, indicating that small classes demonstrate returns of up to 3 dollars per dollar invested. Finally, recognizing the importance of this randomized study for education researchers, the authors explain how others may obtain the STAR data and supporting documentation.

Part IV: Economic Syntheses of Early Childhood Investments

Although there exists a vast literature on the effects of ECD programs over the past four decades, the translation of these effects into economic benefits to society has advanced dramatically in the past decade. From a human capital perspective, not only does the efficiency of programs – the size of effects relative to the costs – need to be documented but so does their comparative value. This knowledge is important for prioritizing investments. Understanding the mechanisms through which these benefits are achieved is also critical to increasing the economic returns of programs and replicating their effects. This section includes five chapters, as well as a commentary by Gary H. Stern, past president of the Federal Reserve Bank of Minneapolis.

One approach to estimating economic benefits of future policy changes in early childhood programs is to conduct cost-benefit simulations, in which benefits of high-quality but routinely implemented programs are modified to account for the dissemination of services across population groups and the degradation of effect sizes that result when moving from smaller to larger scale or national implementation. In "The Cost Effectiveness of Public Investment in High-Quality Prekindergarten: A State-Level Synthesis," Robert G. Lynch provides estimates of the costs and benefits of establishing preschool programs in each state and across the nation. Estimates are primarily based on the findings of the large-scale and well-established CPC program, whereby the effects of broad-scale implementation of high-quality preschool were assumed to provide from 30% to 90% of the benefits demonstrated in the cost-benefit analysis of CPC. He estimates that by 2050, a high-quality targeted preschool program for 4-year-olds would cost $5,700 (2002 dollars) per child and return $3.18 per tax dollar invested (range of $2.83 to $3.51) in government budget savings alone. A universal program is estimated to return $2.00 per tax dollar invested (range of $1.50 to $2.51). These returns increase to $8 to $12 per tax dollar invested when crime, child welfare, and remedial education savings are added. These simulations find annual budgetary surpluses of $45 billion to $68 billion for a targeted program and $45 billion to $156 billion for a universal program for 4-year-olds. After showing robustness of estimates, Lynch concludes that a national program "either funded jointly by federal and state governments or financed largely by states, will have significant positive effects on the long-term budget outlooks of both federal and state governments. Thus a national pre-K initiative should be seen as a sound investment on the part of government that generates substantial long-term benefits."

In "The Fiscal Returns to Public Educational Investments in African American Males," Clive Belfield and Henry Levin assess the expected public returns gained by improving the educational attainments of Black males. Whether measured in terms of test scores, high school graduation, postsecondary attendance, or college graduation, educational outcomes of Black males lag substantially behind those of other groups. Black males, for example, have a rate of high school dropout that is 50% higher than White males (22% vs. 14%). This differential is predicted by parallel gaps in K-12 school achievement and performance. Individuals with low attainment and poor-quality education face inferior employment prospects, low wages, poor health, and greater involvement in the criminal justice system. After documenting the extent of educational inequality between Blacks and Whites, Belfield and Levin identify five educational interventions that would increase the rate of high school graduation for Black males, and they calculate their public costs. These cost effective interventions are the HighScope Perry Preschool, Chicago Child-Parent Center program, First Things First (school reform model), class-size reduction in the early grades, and teacher salary increases. Belfield and Levin also summarize the fiscal and social benefits of increasing the numbers of Black male high school graduates in terms of higher tax revenues, reduced public costs for health services, and reduced costs of criminal-justice services. At a median intervention cost of $91,000, total lifetime public benefits (net present value) for each additional Black male high school graduate was found to be $257,000. The benefit-cost ratio is $2.83 per each additional high school graduate. The authors conclude that investing more in the education of these individuals is in the economic interest of both the taxpayer and society.

As findings from the Perry Preschool program are widely cited to support the expansion of public investments in early education, researchers continue to assess and reassess the significance of the economic benefits of that program to society. In "A New Cost-Benefit and Rate of Return Analysis for the Perry Preschool Program: A Summary," James J. Heckman, Seong Hyeok Moon, Rodrigo Pinto, and colleagues provide an overview of their current research that refines the existing estimates of the societal rate of return on the program. Their research makes a number of important contributions, including new imputations of missing data on adult outcomes, new projections of lifetime earnings, and a more detailed analysis of the relationship between observed arrests and predicted crime. Some of the new estimates make use of the fact that the National Longitudinal Survey of Youth (NLSY79) contains a relevant group of African Americans who were born in the same year as the Perry participants. As noted, the authors reestimate only the largest categories of program benefits – higher earnings, lower crime, and reduced welfare participation. After obtaining new estimates of these major benefits, the researchers make two additional contributions. First, they incorporate estimates of the deadweight loss (or welfare cost) from taxation. For public programs that are funded from new tax revenues, it is important to include this excess burden of taxation, which takes into account the adverse consequences for society of taxes that distort incentives to work and invest. Second, although earlier work by economists has reported rates of return, Heckman and colleagues provide estimates of the rate of return accompanied by their associated standard errors. The results of the analysis indicate that the Perry program still produces significant benefits for both male and female participants and that the overall rate of return to society (inflation adjusted) is 7% to 10%.

Understanding the development and maintenance of human capital skills over the life-course has become a major focus of research in several disciplines. In "Investing in Our Young People," Flavio Cunha and James J. Heckman describe their economic perspective on trends in human capital research and policy. They review six key principles from the literature. Among the most notable are that skill gaps are evident in the early years of life for both cognitive and noncognitive domains, the economic returns to investments in young disadvantaged children are higher than for older children, and early investments in disadvantaged children are more effective if they are followed up with later investments. To better explain these empirical findings, the authors describe a model of skill formation that defines the nature and differential impacts on adult outcomes of cognitive and noncognitive skills at different ages and how much they can be changed by investment. The multistage technology model considers not only the effects of different types of skills and the extent to which investments in early, middle, and later stages of development make a difference but also how these skills and investments are influenced by parental inputs, children's levels of disadvantage, self-productivity, and complementarity. Special consideration is given to the direct and indirect effects of self-productivity, the early skills that lead to later learning, and dynamic complementarity, which is the synergism between early and later investments that is necessary for optimal effects. Although the authors report that the impact of cognitive and noncognitive skills differs across ages and by outcome, they further note that research is still in the early stages of identifying the optimal ratio of early to later investments in young people to promote enduring behavioral changes. For example, the precise mechanisms through which cognitive and noncognitive skills account for long-term effects of early childhood investments are not well documented across studies. This question is the focus of the final chapter.

Although there is now a critical mass of evidence in support of long-term effects of high-quality preschool programs, the causal mechanisms that account for these effects are not well understood. In "Paths of Effects of Preschool Participation to Educational Attainment at Age 21: A Three-Study Analysis," Arthur J. Reynolds, Michelle M. Englund, Suh-Ruu Ou, Lawrence J. Schweinhart, and Frances A. Campbell assess the shared and distinct paths of effectiveness of the Abecedarian Project, Chicago Child-Parent Centers, and Perry Preschool Program. They examine paths associated with five hypotheses: cognitive advantage, family support, social adjustment, motivational advantage, and school support. These five paths of influence from preschool to years of education were consistently significant and of relatively large size across all three studies: (a) the immediate effect of preschool on cognitive skills at age 5, (b) early cognitive skills to parent involvement, (c) early cognitive skills to academic motivation, (d) motivation to retention/special education, and (e) retention/special education to reading achievement at age 14/15. These findings indicate that the process of long-term effects begins with the enhancement of cognitive skills but continues to later attainment and performance through social adjustment and motivational changes. These intervening skills and experiences can be an intervention focus in their own right. Study findings support the value of the five-hypothesis model in accounting for long-term effects into adulthood. Given the substantial differences among the programs in services, context, and time period, that the sources of effects are traceable to children's personal resources and social contexts are encouraging for the applicability of the model to Head Start, state prekindergarten, and other early interventions.

CONCLUSION

The programs and practices discussed in this volume substantially affect multiple domains of well-being that contribute to cost effectiveness. These and many other factors and experiences need to be taken into account in designing, modifying, and disseminating early childhood programs. The authors provide many examples and recommendations for policy and research. As noted by human capital and developmental researchers (Bronfenbrenner, 1989; Heckman & Krueger, 2003; Zigler & Styfco, 1993), good well-being is the product of personal resources and experiences in relation to the total environment of the person over the life-course. In these perspectives, a key principle for promoting well-being is continuity or complementarity of services, in which program investments at different ages are mutually reinforcing and together strengthen learning and the potential for enduring effects. Bronfenbrenner (1989, p. 241) described continuity as "the degree of stability, consistency, and predictability over time" that is necessary to encourage optimal human development. To the extent that the enrichment is reinforced and strengthened from prenatal care and continuing through the school-age years, learning can be optimized.

It is this principle of continuity that provides the foundation for interpreting and understanding the contributions of the child, family, school, and broader factors on well-being. It is the fundamental perspective of the volume.

The importance of continuity and complementarity for children's programs has been recognized dating to the Head Start program in the mid-1960s, as is clear from this vision of the Head Start founders:

> It is clear that successful programs of this type must be comprehensive, involving activities associated with the fields of health, social services, and education. Similarly, it is clear that the program must focus on the problems of the child and parent and that these activities need to be carefully integrated with programs for the school years (Richmond, 1997, p. 122).

The perspective of the volume is that this vision is not only achievable but that, based on the accumulated knowledge to date, its realization can become commonplace and contribute to positive and enduring benefits on human capital.

REFERENCES

Barnett, W. S., Epstein, D. J., Friedman, A. H., Sansanelli, R. A., & Hustedt, J. T. (2009). *The 2008 state preschool yearbook.* New Brunswick, NJ: National Institute of Early Education Research.

Becker, G. S. (1964). *Human capital.* New York: Columbia University Press.

Bogard, K., & Takanishi, R. (2005). PK–3: An aligned and coordinated approach to education for children 3 to 8 years old. *Social Policy Report, XIX, No. III.* Washington, DC: Society for Research in Child Development.

Bourdieu, P. (1977). *Outline of a theory of practice.* Cambridge: Cambridge University Press.

Bowman, B., Donovan, M. S., & Burns, M. S. (Eds.). (2000). *Eager to learn: Educating our preschoolers.* Washington, DC: National Academy Press.

Bronfenbrenner, U. (1989). Ecological systems theory. *Annals of Child Development, 6,* 187–249.

Bronfenbrenner, U., & Morris, P. (1998). Ecological processes of development. In W. Damon (Ed.), *Handbook of child psychology: Theoretical issues* (Vol. 1, pp. 993–1028). New York: Wiley.

Burr, J., & Grunewald, R. (2006, April). *Lessons learned: A review of early child development studies.* Minneapolis: Federal Reserve Bank. Retrieved from http://www.minneapolisfed.org/publications_papers/studies/earlychild/lessonslearned.pdf.

Camilli, G., Vargas, S., Ryan, S., & Barnett, W. S. (2010). Meta-analysis of the effects of early education interventions on cognitive and social development. *Teachers College Record, 112*(3), 579–620.

Campbell, F. A., Pungello, E. P., Miller-Johnson, S., Burchinal, M., & Ramey, C. T. (2001). The development of cognitive and academic abilities: Growth curves from an early childhood educational experiment. *Developmental Psychology, 37*(2), 231–242.

Campbell, F. A., Ramey, C. T., Pungello, E., Sparling, J., & Miller-Johnson, S. (2002). Early childhood education: Young adult outcomes from the Abecedarian project. *Applied Developmental Science, 6*(1), 42–57.

Child Care Bureau. (2009). *Fiscal year 2008 federal child care and related appropriations.* Administration for Children and Families, U.S. Department of Health and Human Services. Retrieved from http://www.acf.hhs.gov/programs/ccb/ccdf/approp_2008.htm.

Coleman, J. S. (1988). Social capital in the creation of human capital. *American Journal of Sociology, 94*(Suppl.), S95–S120.

Consortium for Longitudinal Studies. (1983). *As the twig is bent... lasting effects of preschool programs.* Hillsdale, NJ: Erlbaum.

Cunha, F., & Heckman, J. J. (2008). Formulating, identifying, and estimating the technology of cognitive and noncognitive skill formation. *Journal of Human Resources, 43*(4), 738–782.

Currie, J. (2009). Healthy, wealthy, and wise: Socioeconomic status, poor health in childhood, and human capital development. *Journal of Economic Literature, 47*(1), 87–122.

Foss, D. J., & Spence, J. T. (1992, February). Human capital initiative: Report of the National Behavioral Science Research Agenda Committee [Special issue]. *APS Observer.* Washington, DC: American Psychological Society.

Gormley, W. T. (2007). Early childhood care and education: Lessons and puzzles. *Journal of Policy Analysis and Management, 26*(3), 633–671.

Grossman, M. (1972). On the concept of health capital and the demand for health. *Journal of Political Economy, 80*(2), 223–255.

Heckman, J. (2000). Policies to foster human capital. *Research in Economics, 54,* 3–56.

Heckman, J. (2003). Human capital policy. In J. Heckman & A. B. Krueger (Eds.), *Inequality in America: What role for human capital policy?* (pp. 23–55). Cambridge: MIT Press.

Heckman, J. J., & Krueger, A. B. (Eds.). (2003). *Inequality in America: What role for human capital policies?* Cambridge, MA: MIT Press.

Heckman, J. J., Stixrud, J., & Urzua, S. (2006). The effects of cognitive and noncognitive abilities on labor market outcomes and social behavior. *Journal of Labor Economics, 24,* 411–482.

Karoly, L. A., Kilburn, M. R., & Cannon, J. S. (2005). *Early childhood intervention: Proven results, future promise.* Santa Monica, CA: RAND.

Levin, H. M., & McEwan, P. J. (2001). *Cost-effectiveness analysis: Methods and applications* (2nd ed.). Thousand Oaks, CA: Sage.

McCall, R. B., Larsen, L., & Ingram, A. (2003). The science and policies of early childhood education and family services. In A. J. Reynolds, M. C. Wang, & H. J. Walberg (Eds.), *Early childhood programs for a new century* (pp. 255–298). Washington, DC: CWLA Press.

Mincer, J. (1958). Investments in human capital and personal income distribution. *Journal of Political Economy, 66*(4), 281–302.

National Educational Goals Panel. (1995). *National educational goals report: Building a nation of learners.* U.S. Department of Education. Washington, DC: U.S. Government Printing Office.

Nelson, G., Westhaus, A., & MacLeod, J. (2003). A meta-analysis of longitudinal research on preschool prevention programs for children. *Prevention and Treatment,* 6 (article 31).

O'Connell, M. E., Boat, T., & Warner, K. E. (Eds.). (2009). *Preventing mental, emotional and behavioral disorders among young people: Progress and possibilities.* Committee on the Prevention of Mental Disorders and Substance Abuse Among Children, Youth, and Young Adults. Washington, DC: National Academy Press.

Olds, D. L., Sadler, L., & Kitzman, H. (2007). Programs for parents of infants and toddlers: Recent evidence from randomized trials. *Journal of Child Psychology and Psychiatry, 48*, 355–391.

Reynolds, A. J. (2000). *Success in early intervention: The Chicago Child-Parent Centers.* Lincoln: University of Nebraska Press.

Reynolds, A. J. (2003). The added value of continuing early intervention into the primary grades. In A. J. Reynolds, M. C. Wang, & H. J. Walberg (Eds.), *Early childhood programs for a new century* (pp. 163–196). Washington, DC: CWLA Press.

Reynolds, A. J., Mathieson, L. C., & Topitzes, J. W. (2009). Do early childhood interventions prevent child maltreatment? A review of research. *Child Maltreatment, 14*, 182–206.

Reynolds, A. J., Ou, S., & Topitzes, J. W. (2004). Paths of effects of early childhood intervention on educational attainment and delinquency: A confirmatory analysis of the Chicago Child-Parent Centers. *Child Development, 75*(5), 1299–1328.

Reynolds, A. J., & Rolnick, A. J. (2009, December). *Human Capital Research Collaborative.* Minneapolis: University of Minnesota and Federal Reserve Bank of Minneapolis. Available at http://humancapitalrc.org.

Reynolds, A. J., & Temple, J. A. (2008). Cost-effective early childhood development programs from preschool to third grade. *Annual Review of Clinical Psychology, 4*, 109–139.

Reynolds, A. J., Temple, J. A., Ou, S., Robertson, D. L., Mersky, J. P., Topitzes, J. W., & Niles, M. D. (2007). Effects of a school-based, early childhood intervention on adult health and well-being: A 19-year follow-up of low-income families. *Archives of Pediatrics & Adolescent Medicine, 161*(8), 730–739.

Reynolds, A. J., Temple, J. A., Robertson, D. L., & Mann, E. A. (2002). Age 21 cost-benefit analysis of the Title I Chicago Child-Parent Centers. *Educational Evaluation and Policy Analysis, 24*, 267–303.

Reynolds, A. J., Wang, M. C., & Walberg, H. J. (Eds.). (2003). *Early childhood programs for a new century.* Washington, DC: CWLA Press.

Richmond, J. B. (1997). Head Start, a retrospective view: The founders; Section 3; The early administrators. In E. Zigler & J. Valentine (Eds.), *Project Head Start: The legacy of the war on poverty* (2nd ed., pp. 120–128). Alexandria, VA: National Head Start Association.

Rolnick, A., & Grunewald, R. (2003, December). Early childhood development: Economic development with a high public return. *The Region*, pp. 6–12. Minneapolis: Federal Reserve Bank of Minneapolis.

Rolnick, A. J., & Grunewald, R. (2007, Fall). The economics of early childhood development as seen by two Fed economists. *Community Investments*, pp. 13–14, 30.

Rutter, M., & Rutter, M. (1993). *Developing minds: Challenge and continuity across the life span.* New York: Basic Books.

Schultz, T. W. (1961). Investment in human capital. *American Economic Review, 51*(1), 1–17.

Schweinhart, L. J., Barnes, H. V., & Weikart, D. P. (1993). Significant benefits: The High/Scope Perry Preschool study through age 27. *Monographs for the High/Scope Educational Research Foundation, No. 10.* Ypsilanti, MI: High/Scope Educational Research Foundation.

Schweinhart, L. J., Montie, J., Xiang, Z., Barnett, W. S., Belfield, C. R., & Nores, M. (2005). *Lifetime effects: The HighScope Perry Preschool study through age 40.* Monographs for the HighScope Educational Research Foundation, No. 14. Ypsilanti, MI: HighScope Educational Research Foundation.

Smith, A. (1904). *An inquiry into the nature and causes of the wealth of nation: Vol. 2* (5th ed.). London: Methuen & Co. (Original work published 1776.)
Sweet, M. A., & Applebaum, M. I. (2004). Is home visiting an effective strategy? A meta-analysis review of home visiting programs for families with young children. *Child Development, 75*(5), 1435–1456.
Takanishi, R., & Kauerz, K. (2008, March). PK inclusion: Getting serious about a P–16 education system. *Phi Delta Kappan, 89*(7), 480–487.
Temple, J. A., & Reynolds, A. J. (2007). Benefits and costs of investments in preschool education: Evidence from the Child-Parent Centers and related programs. *Economics of Education Review, 26*(1), 126–144.
Todd, P. E., & Wolpin, K. I. (2007). The production of cognitive achievement in children: Home, school, and racial test score gaps. *Journal of Human Capital, 1*, 91–136.
U.S. Department of Education. (2003). *Digest of education statistics, 2002.* National Center for Education Statistics. Washington, DC: U.S. Government Printing Office.
U.S. Department of Education. (2009). *Digest of education statistics, 2008.* National Center for Education Statistics. Washington, DC: U.S. Government Printing Office.
U.S. General Accounting Office. (1999). *Education and care: Early childhood programs and services for low-income families* (Report no. GAO/HEHS-00–11). Washington, DC: Author.
Victora, C., Adair, L., Fall, C., Hallal, P., Martorell, R., Richter, L., et al. (2008). Maternal and child undernutrition: Consequences for adult health and human capital. *Lancet, 371*(9609), 340–357.
Weisbrod, B. A. (1962). Education and investment in human capital. *Journal of Political Economy, 70*(5), 106–123.
Zigler, E., & Berman, W. (1983). Discerning the future of early childhood intervention. *American Psychologist, 38*(8), 894-906. doi: 10.1037/0003-066X.38.8.894.
Zigler, E., Gilliam, W. S., & Jones, S. M. (2006). *A vision for universal preschool education.* New York: Cambridge University Press.
Zigler, E. F., & Styfco, S. J. (Eds.). (1993). *Head Start and beyond: A national plan for extended early childhood intervention.* New Haven, CT: Yale University Press.
Zigler, E. F., Styfco, S. J., & Gilman, E. (1993). The national Head Start Program for disadvantaged preschoolers. In E. F. Zigler & S. J. Styfco (Eds.), *Head Start and beyond: A national plan for extended early childhood intervention* (pp. 1–41). New Haven, CT: Yale University Press.

PART I

PRENATAL AND INFANT PROGRAMS

2

WIC Turns 35: Program Effectiveness and Future Directions

BARBARA DEVANEY

The Special Supplemental Nutrition Program for Women, Infants, and Children (WIC) provides supplemental foods, nutrition education, and social service and health care referrals to low-income pregnant, breastfeeding, and postpartum women; infants; and children up to age 5 who are at nutrition risk. The WIC program is based on the premise that many low-income individuals are at risk of poor nutrition and health outcomes because of insufficient nutrition during the critical growth and development periods of pregnancy, infancy, and early childhood. It is a supplemental food and nutrition program to help meet the special needs of low-income women, infants, and children during these periods. WIC provides three main benefits to participants: (a) supplemental foods; (b) nutrition education, including breastfeeding promotion; and (c) referrals to health care and social service providers.

WIC began as a pilot program in 1972 and was authorized permanently in 1974 (P.L. 94–105). Since then, WIC has become a key component of the nutrition safety net provided for low-income Americans. Today, WIC functions as a vital link in America's public health efforts to ensure that all of the nation's children have the resources they need to thrive. About half of *all* U.S. infants and a quarter of *all* U.S. children ages 1 to 5 receive WIC benefits.

The WIC program has been the focus of numerous and varied evaluations. In general, these studies show WIC to be effective, although several methodological issues have been raised about the existing research. Most of the evaluation evidence on WIC focuses on the relationship between prenatal WIC participation and birth outcomes. A major methodological issue in these studies is separating the effect of prenatal WIC participation from other factors that are related to both WIC participation and birth outcomes. Despite some controversy over the research evidence on WIC's effectiveness, the Program Assessment Rating Tool (PART) from the Office of Management and Budget rated WIC as "effective," based on a review of the literature showing positive effects on key health outcomes and the efficient use of program funds (www.whitehouse.gov/omb/expectmore/summary/10003027.2006.html).

This chapter reviews what we know from the first 35 years of WIC operations and describes the challenges as WIC moves forward. It first reviews the history of the WIC program and provides a detailed description of program eligibility and benefits. The chapter then describes major findings from evaluation studies of WIC, focusing on both the study findings and potential limitations of the research. The final sections focus on future program and research directions for WIC.

HISTORY OF THE WIC PROGRAM

The WIC program was an outgrowth of a 1969 White House Conference on Food, Nutrition, and Health, which recommended that special attention be given to the nutritional needs of low-income pregnant women and preschool children. Physicians had reported that increasing numbers of disadvantaged pregnant women and their newborns were visiting public health clinics and exhibiting symptoms associated with a lack of food (Leonard, 1994). In response, a group of community-based public health physicians and staff from both the U.S. Department of Agriculture and the U.S. Department of Health and Human Services met and developed a proposal to build food commissaries attached to neighborhood public health clinics. Food vouchers prescribed by clinic professionals would provide supplemental foods for low-income women, infants, and children. The first two food-commissary–clinic programs were demonstration programs that operated in Atlanta and Baltimore.

In September 1972, Congress expanded these demonstration projects and authorized a 2-year pilot program linking health care to food assistance for low-income pregnant and postpartum women, infants, and preschool children considered to be at health risk because of poor nutrition. Participants received specific foods, either by picking them up at WIC clinics or by using coupons or vouchers at local grocery stores. Initially, participants had to live in areas with a high proportion of pregnant and postpartum women at nutrition risk. The 1972 law also mandated an evaluation of the pilot program.

Since its inception as a pilot program in 1972 and then as a permanent program starting in 1974, the WIC program has grown dramatically (see Fig. 2.1). In fiscal year 1974, WIC served 88,000 women, infants, and children per month at an annual cost of $20.6 million. By fiscal year 1980, the program was serving 1.9 million women, infants, and children per month at a cost of $725 million. By fiscal year 2008, WIC was serving 8.7 million participants monthly at an annual cost of $6.2 billion.

WIC PROGRAM BENEFITS, ELIGIBILITY, AND PROGRAM ADMINISTRATION

As mentioned earlier, WIC provides three main benefits to program participants: (a) supplemental foods, (b) nutrition education (including

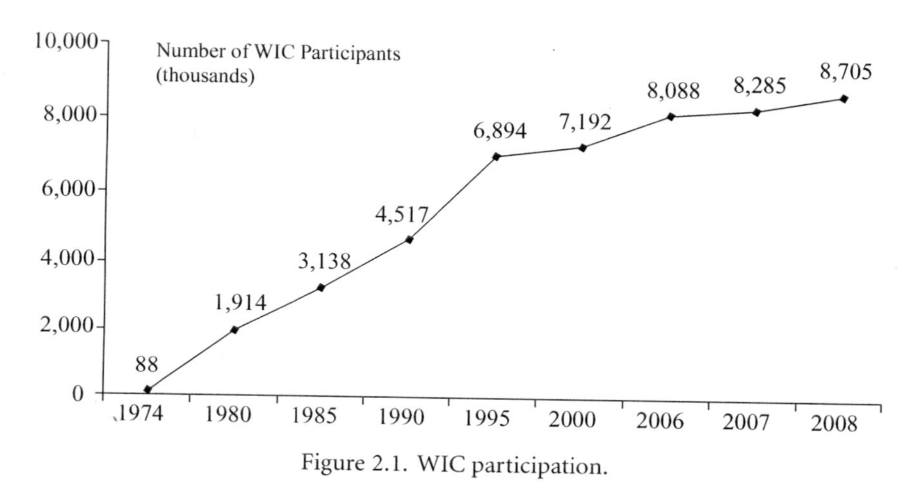

Figure 2.1. WIC participation.

breastfeeding promotion), and (c) referrals to health care and social service providers. Participants receive supplemental foods through food instruments – in the form of a voucher, check, or electronic benefit – that list the quantities of specific foods, as well as brand names, that can be purchased. The food packages are designed to provide specific nutrients that are thought to be lacking in the diets of eligible WIC participants. Initially and throughout much of WIC's history, these nutrients were protein, vitamins A and C, calcium, and iron; WIC food packages therefore included iron-fortified formula, milk and cheese, eggs, iron-fortified ready-to-eat cereals, fruit and vegetable juices, dried peas or beans, and peanut butter. These food packages were designed for seven categories of participants: (a) pregnant and breastfeeding women (basic); (b) postpartum, non-breastfeeding women; (c) breastfeeding women (enhanced); (d) infants from birth through 3 months of age; (e) infants 4 through 12 months of age; (f) children 1 through 4 years of age; and (g) women, infants, and children with special dietary needs.

Although the supplemental food packages are the cornerstone of the WIC program, WIC also provides nutrition education and health care and social service referrals to program participants. WIC nutrition education has two broad goals: (a) to emphasize the relationship between nutrition and good health, focusing on the needs of pregnant, postpartum, and breastfeeding women as well as the needs of infants and children under age 5; and (b) to help individuals achieve changes in their food habits and consume more healthy diets. As part of this effort, WIC provides support for and promotion of breastfeeding. Referrals to health care providers are expected to increase the women's use of prenatal and postpartum care and access to and use of routine preventive care for infants and children. Finally, social service referrals to programs such as housing assistance, Medicaid, Temporary Assistance for Needy Families (TANF), Supplemental Nutrition Assistance Program (SNAP) benefits (formerly food stamps), and mental-health and substance-abuse programs are expected to address the broad range of needs that low-income women, infants, and children face.

WIC eligibility is based on categorical criteria, income, and evidence of nutritional risk. To be *categorically eligible*, an individual must be in one of the following five groups: (a) a pregnant woman, (b) a breastfeeding woman less than 1 year postpartum, (c) a postpartum (non-breastfeeding) woman less than 6 months postpartum, (d) an infant up to 1 year of age, or (e) a child younger than 5 years of age. As of April 2004, 50% of all WIC participants were children; 26% were infants; and the remaining were pregnant (11%), breastfeeding (6%), or postpartum women (7%) (Bartlett et al., 2006).

States have the option of setting *income eligibility* at between 100% and 185% of the federal poverty level; since April 2004, all state agencies have used 185% of the poverty level as the income eligibility threshold. In addition, applicants may be adjunctively income eligible for WIC if they can document participation in Medicaid, TANF, or SNAP.

Finally, each participant must be determined to be at *nutritional risk* based on a medical or nutritional assessment by a "competent professional," such as a physician, nutritionist, nurse, or other health professional. For participants older than 6 months of age, assessment of nutritional risk includes, at a minimum, measures of height, weight, and a blood test for iron-deficiency anemia. Nutritional risk conditions include abnormal nutritional conditions detected by biochemical or physical measurements, other documented nutritionally related medical conditions, dietary deficiencies that may impair health, and conditions that predispose individuals to inadequate nutritional patterns or conditions.

The WIC program is federally funded by the Food and Nutrition Service (FNS) of the U.S. Department of Agriculture (USDA) and administered by state and local agencies. The four tiers of WIC administration are the following:

1. Federal: FNS issues regulations for the WIC program and, with its seven regional offices, monitors compliance with the regulations. Congress determines the funding amount annually, and FNS provides cash grants to state agencies.
2. State agencies: The state agencies include agencies in the 50 states, Puerto Rico, Guam, America Samoa, the American Virgin Islands, the District of Columbia, and 35 Indian Tribal Organizations. State agencies select, train, and monitor local agencies and food vendors. They also develop and manage benefit certification, issuance, reconciliation, and reporting systems.
3. Local WIC agencies: The local agencies provide services to WIC participants, including screening applicants for eligibility, certifying eligibility, and issuing benefits. In some states, the local agencies are arms of the state agency, whereas in other states they are autonomous agencies under

contract with the state agencies. Local agencies may be public health departments, community health care centers, community action agencies, public hospitals, or migrant worker health care centers.
4. Food vendors: Approximately 40,000 retail food stores and pharmacies have entered into agreements with state WIC agencies and redeem WIC food instruments for the specified WIC foods.

WIC is not an entitlement program; participation in the program is limited by the authorized funding level. If a local WIC agency reaches its maximum level of participation, it places all subsequent applicants on a waiting list. Participants are certified as eligible for a specified period of time. Pregnant women are certified for the duration of pregnancy and up to 6 weeks postpartum; postpartum women are certified for up to 6 months; and breastfeeding women are certified at 6-month intervals up to the infant's first birthday. Infants are certified up to their first birthday, and children are certified at 6-month intervals up to the end of the month in which they reach their fifth birthday.

MAJOR FINDINGS ON WIC PROGRAM EFFECTIVENESS

Conceptually, all aspects of the WIC intervention and benefits – supplemental food assistance, nutrition education, and health and social service referrals – are expected to improve the nutritional status of program participants by addressing the risk factors for poor outcomes (see Fig. 2.2). Supplemental foods offered through WIC are high in key nutrients needed during and after pregnancy, including protein, iron, calcium, and vitamins A and C. In conjunction with these supplemental foods, nutrition education can improve dietary quality and nutritional status both in the short term during pregnancy and in the long term by teaching key concepts of good nutrition and food-preparation techniques. Finally, with its emphasis on risk assessment and referrals, WIC serves as a gateway to the health care and social service systems. In particular, access to health care is enhanced through a referral process that includes advising clients about the types of health care available, accessible location of health care facilities, and how to receive health care and why it is useful.

Based on the conceptual framework in Figure 2.2, evaluation studies of WIC have asked the following key research questions:

- Is prenatal WIC participation associated with improved birth outcomes and use of prenatal care?
- Is WIC participation associated with better iron status of infants and children and a reduced incidence of iron-deficiency anemia?
- Does WIC participation lead to better diets for women, infants, and children?

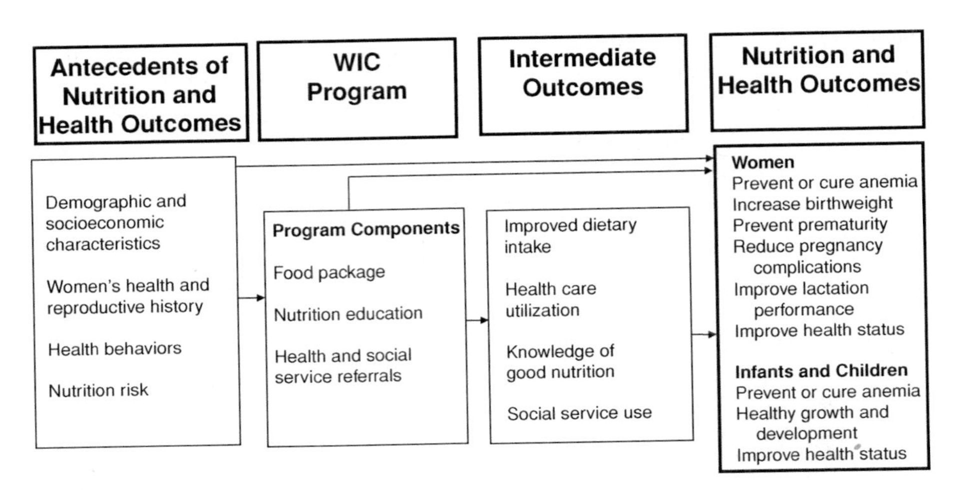

Figure 2.2. Conceptual framework for the effects of the WIC program.

- Do infant and child WIC participants comply with the recommended use of preventive health care?
- Does WIC participation affect children's physical growth and emotional and cognitive development?

Given available data sources and ongoing surveys, some of these research questions are easier to answer than others. Specifically, information on dietary outcomes and use of health care is available from surveys of low-income women and can be used to address research questions related to dietary status and the use of health care. Data from the standard U.S. birth certificate files can be used to analyze the relationship between prenatal WIC participation and birth outcomes. Surveillance data collected by the U.S. Centers for Disease Control and Prevention are useful for assessing trends in iron-deficiency anemia and WIC participation. However, because of the long-term nature and expense of collecting data on children's growth and development, only limited information is available on the relationship between WIC participation and the physical growth and emotional and cognitive development of children.

Prenatal WIC Participation and Birth Outcomes

Numerous studies document positive effects of WIC participation on birth outcomes, although variation in the magnitude of these effects exists because of differences in methodological approaches. By far, the most common birth outcome examined in the literature is newborn birthweight, and many studies find a significant effect of prenatal WIC participation on birthweight (Bitler & Currie, 2005; Buescher & Horton, 2000; Devaney, Bilheimer, & Schore, 1992; Gordon & Nelson, 1995; Kennedy, Gershoff, Reed, & Austin, 1982; Kotelchuck,

Schwartz, Anderka, & Finison, 1984; Metcoff et al., 1985). Easily more than 50 studies over the past 35 years, using different data sets and study designs, have examined the relationship between prenatal WIC participation and birthweight, arriving at widely varying estimates of the increase in birthweight associated with prenatal WIC participation:

- A five-state study of birth outcomes among Medicaid mothers found increases in birthweight ranging from 51 g in Minnesota to 117 g in North Carolina (Devaney et al., 1992).
- A study using the 1988 National Maternal and Infant Health Survey estimated an increase in birthweight of 68 g for prenatal WIC participants compared with low-income nonparticipants (Gordon & Nelson, 1995).
- A more recent study using data from the Pregnancy Risk Assessment Monitoring System (PRAMS) from 19 states found an increase in birthweight of 64 g for prenatal WIC participants (Bitler & Currie, 2005).

Several of these studies also found that prenatal WIC participation is associated with reductions in the rate of preterm births (birth before 36 weeks gestation) and the rates of low and very low birthweight (infant birthweight less than 2,500 and 1,500 g, respectively). For example, the study using PRAMS data from 19 states found a 29% reduction in the rate of low birthweight and more than a 50% reduction in the rate of very low birthweight (Bitler & Currie, 2005).

Not surprisingly, these estimated increases in birthweight and reductions in both preterm birth and low birthweight translate into substantial cost savings associated with prenatal WIC participation. The five-state study of birth outcomes among Medicaid mothers reported that each dollar spent on WIC benefits for low-income pregnant women resulted in savings that ranged from $1.77 to $3.13 in Medicaid costs during the first 60 days after birth (Devaney et al., 1992). In a synthesis of 17 major studies, the General Accounting Office (GAO) estimated that prenatal WIC services cost the federal government $296 million (in 1990 dollars) but would save $1.036 billion (present value) in federal, state, local, and private funds over the following 18 years (U.S. General Accounting Office, 1992). The estimated cost savings were driven almost entirely by the estimated reductions in low birthweight and very low birthweight associated with prenatal WIC participation. These GAO estimates are the source of the frequently cited finding that "every dollar spent on WIC saves $3.50" ($1.036 billion/$296 million = $3.50).

In recent years, however, several researchers have questioned the WIC results, claiming that they are overstated because of the studies' methodological limitations. In particular, the large reductions in preterm birth and low birthweight appear inconsistent with the clinical literature on reproductive health outcomes, which shows little or no impact of dietary supplementation on preventing preterm birth (Joyce, Racine, & Yunzal-Butler, 2007). In fact, the clinical literature as a whole shows the lack of success of intensive medical and nutritional interventions in preventing preterm birth, the main reason for low birthweight. How, then, could prenatal WIC participation have such dramatic impacts on preterm delivery and low birthweight? Two main methodological issues are frequently cited: selection bias and gestational age bias.

Selection Bias

The most commonly cited limitation of the evidence on WIC effectiveness is selection bias. Almost all the studies of prenatal WIC participation used a comparison-group methodology in which prenatal WIC participants were compared with income-eligible nonparticipants. Comparison-group designs almost always have the potential of selection bias, which occurs when underlying and unobservable differences between program participants and a comparison group of nonparticipants create differences in outcomes that are incorrectly attributed to program participation. For example, if prenatal WIC participants are more motivated and concerned about health and nutrition than nonparticipants, birth outcomes of WIC participants may be better than those of nonparticipants even in the absence of the WIC program. Alternatively, if WIC is successful at targeting and enrolling the highest risk women, any differences in birth outcomes between WIC participants and nonparticipants are likely to be understated because of preexisting differences in risk.

Most studies of prenatal WIC participation have not been successful in estimating models that adequately control for selection-bias issues. In attempting to do so, the main problem encountered is the lack of a good instrument for prenatal WIC participation to use in instrumental variables estimation, and, as a result, estimates of "selection-bias adjusted effects" are all over the map, ranging from huge negative effects to similarly large positive effects (Gordon & Nelson, 1995). Consequently, researchers either have tried to include a rich set of control variables to mitigate the effects of selection bias (Bitler & Currie, 2005; Gordon & Nelson, 1995) or to create a comparison group that is as similar as possible to prenatal WIC participants (Joyce et al., 2007). In general, analyses using the richer set of controls or more narrowly defined comparison groups still found a relationship between prenatal WIC participation and birth outcomes. Part of the reason for this may be because comparisons of the observed characteristics of WIC participants and eligible nonparticipants typically find that program participants are negatively selected on a wide array of socioeconomic and demographic characteristics (Bitler & Currie, 2005; Gordon & Nelson, 1995).

Gestational Age Bias

A more serious limitation of the existing literature, and the limitation that explains the inconsistency between the clinical literature and WIC evaluations, has been called gestational age bias. Put simply, gestational age bias occurs because women whose pregnancies last longer have more time to become a prenatal WIC participant. Many of the existing studies that compared all prenatal participants and income-eligible nonparticipants did not control for or consider the timing of WIC enrollment. In particular, women who enter WIC late in pregnancy are likely to have good birth outcomes simply because the pregnancy lasted long enough, not because of WIC. In the extreme, women who enter WIC after 36 weeks gestation could not possibly have lower rates of preterm delivery (defined as delivery before 36 weeks) due to WIC, yet some studies considered them as prenatal WIC participants.

Two approaches are used to control for gestational age bias. The first is simply to include a control for gestational age in the birthweight and low birthweight equation. With this approach, the estimated effects of prenatal WIC participation decline but are often still statistically significant. For example, the five-state WIC–Medicaid study found that gestation-adjusted savings in Medicaid costs during the first 60 days after birth associated with prenatal WIC participation were about half of the nonadjusted estimated savings, but estimates for four of the five states were still statistically significant (Devaney et al., 1992). A recent study using data from the Pregnancy Nutrition Surveillance System (PNSS) in nine states found that increases in birthweight associated with prenatal WIC participation fell from 63 to 40 g when a control for gestational age was included in the birthweight models (both results were statistically significant; Joyce et al., 2007).

A second way to control for gestational age bias is to restrict the sample to full-term births. This approach was used in at least two state studies of prenatal WIC participation. Both found significant effects of prenatal WIC participation on birthweight (Ahluwalia, Hogan, Grummer-Strawn, Colville, & Peterson, 1998; Lazariu-Bauer, Stratton, Pruzek, & Woelfel, 2004). However, the recent study using the PNSS data from nine states found a statistically significant, but quite small, reduction in the rate of low birthweight for WIC participants with full-term births as compared with nonparticipants with full-term births (Joyce et al., 2007).

In summary, reviews of the WIC evaluation studies often lead with "WIC Works." In recent years, however, the evidence on WIC's effectiveness has been scrutinized more carefully. Methodological issues – in particular, gestational age bias – are important to consider in interpreting the empirical evidence on WIC's effectiveness. When these limitations are considered, WIC's effects persist, but they are substantially more modest than the previously estimated savings of $3.50 for each $1.00 spent on WIC.

WIC Participation and Breastfeeding

Throughout its history, WIC has struggled with the competing priorities of promoting breastfeeding and providing iron-fortified formula to infants whose mothers cannot breastfeed or choose not to do so. Some question whether WIC's current practice of making substantial amounts of free formula available to women who choose not to breastfeed may discourage breastfeeding. However, *not* to make formula available in WIC would discourage program participation, thereby denying important nutritional benefits to vulnerable infants, and it might lead to even less desirable alternatives, such as feeding cow's milk to infants.

Most of the literature on the relationship between WIC participation and breastfeeding finds that participants are less likely to initiate breastfeeding and had shorter durations of breastfeeding than income-eligible nonparticipants (Chatterji, Bonuck, Dhawan, & Deb, 2002; Fox, Hamilton, & Lin, 2004; Schwartz, Guilkey, Akin, & Popkin, 1992). However, one study found that the impact of WIC participation on breastfeeding is mediated by the nutrition education and advice provided by the WIC clinic staff: Women who reported that they received encouragement from WIC staff to breastfeed were more likely to breastfeed than other WIC participants (Chatterji et al., 2002).

In general, the potential for selection bias in the estimates of the relationship between WIC participation and breastfeeding has never been adequately resolved. The estimated negative effect of WIC participation could well reflect underlying differences in the propensity to breastfeed that would persist even without WIC. Even the findings of the mediating analysis showing the positive effect of "receiving advice to breastfeed from WIC staff" could be the result of selection. One study estimated a selection-adjusted model and rejected the nonsignificant (but negative) findings in favor of the basic model that reported a negative effect of WIC on breastfeeding, based on a Hausman test suggesting that WIC participation was not endogenous (Chatterji et al., 2002).

In response to concerns associated with the lower prevalence and shorter duration of breastfeeding among WIC participants, the USDA has adopted standards and policies to promote and support breastfeeding. Legislation in 1989 provided $8 million in breastfeeding-support programs; 1992 legislation mandated a national breastfeeding-promotion program and instituted an enhanced food package for women who exclusively breastfeed. Funding has been available through WIC to support breastfeeding peer counselors at many local WIC agencies. As described in more detail later, the WIC food package has recently been revised to include incentives to increase breastfeeding among WIC participants.

WIC Participation by Infants and Children

In contrast to the large body of literature examining the effects of prenatal WIC participation, many fewer studies focus on the effects of WIC participation by infants and children. Nevertheless, several studies report generally positive effects of WIC participation. Outcomes examined include anemia and iron status, growth, dietary status, and access to and use of health care.

Anemia and Iron Status

Iron-deficiency anemia has long been one of the primary public health problems facing infants and children in the United States, especially low-income infants and children. Not only is iron-deficiency anemia a severe health problem, it also leads to long-term deficits in cognitive development. Data from the PNSS indicate that the prevalence of anemia among low-income children decreased from 7.8% in 1975, when WIC first started, to 2.9% in 1985, a finding largely attributed to improvements in childhood iron nutrition status and to positive effects of public health programs, especially supplemental foods offered through the WIC program (Yip, Binkin, Fleshood, & Trowbridge, 1987). In addition, a comparison of hematological tests of low-income children at enrollment in public health programs (primarily WIC) with tests at follow-up visits indicated declines in the prevalence of iron-deficiency anemia, suggesting positive impacts of participation in the public health programs, especially the WIC program (Yip et al., 1992). The literature suggests that WIC has had both a direct effect (as discussed earlier) and an indirect effect on reducing the prevalence of childhood anemia. The indirect effect comes from the mandate that all infant formula and all cereal provided in the WIC food packages be fortified with iron. Because WIC provides more than half of all formula sold in the United States and substantial proportions of infant and child/adult cereals, food companies now routinely produce primarily iron-fortified formulas and cereals. Consequently, WIC has contributed to an improvement in the iron status of all U.S. children, regardless of whether they participate in WIC.

Growth

Most studies examining the effect of WIC on growth have used measures of children's weight and height. An early evaluation by Edozien and his colleagues used data from a nationally representative sample of more than 6,000 infants and children ages 0 to 3 years in 1973–1976; it compared outcomes of clinical examinations for infants and children who had participated in WIC for 6 months with clinical data on newly enrolled infants and children. Their results indicated that WIC had a statistically significant impact on children's growth in weight and height (Edozien, Boyd, Switzer, & Bryan, 1979). However, because low weight and height are used as criteria for WIC eligibility, the increase in weight and height after WIC participation may be due to regression to the mean. Results from the National WIC Evaluation, conducted early in WIC's 35-year history, showed that WIC had no significant impact on weight but had a positive effect on weight and height for infants and children who had participated either prenatally or within 3 months after birth (Rush, Leighton, Sloan, Alvir, & Garbowski, 1986).

A crucial feature of these evaluations of the effects of WIC participation by infants and children is that they are based on data that are very old, and significant changes have since occurred in the WIC program. In addition, evaluating the effects of WIC participation on the physical growth and development of children is problematic; impacts of WIC may not be evident until several years after a child has enrolled in WIC, and longitudinal studies of children participating in WIC are difficult to design and expensive to conduct.

A more recent study using data from the Children's Sentinel Nutrition Assessment Project found that WIC infants were significantly longer and significantly less underweight than low-income non-WIC infants (Black et al., 2004). However, despite attempts by the authors to create comparison groups of nonparticipants that mitigated the issue of selection bias, the empirical results could still reflect underlying differences between WIC participants and nonparticipants.

Dietary Status

Numerous studies have examined the relationship between WIC participation by children and nutrient and food intakes. Overall, despite the potential for selection bias, the overarching conclusion is that WIC participation is associated with higher intakes of key nutrients and more consumption of WIC foods (Fox et al., 2004). Moreover, the evidence suggests that caloric intakes of WIC participants are not significantly different from the intakes of similar non-WIC children. Given the increasing prevalence of childhood overweight and adult obesity, the lack of a significant relationship between WIC participation and caloric intake is a positive program finding.

Utilization of Health Care

Finally, some studies have examined the impact of WIC participation on utilization of health care services. Data from the National WIC Evaluation showed that children receiving WIC benefits were significantly more likely to have a regular source of health care than non-WIC children and that WIC participation was associated with immunizations for some subgroups of infants and children (Rush et al., 1986). A study conducted using administrative data from the state of North Carolina found that low-income children participating in the WIC program were higher users of all types of health care services than low-income nonparticipants (Buescher et al., 2003). Compared with income-eligible WIC nonparticipants, child WIC participants used more preventive care services, more dental health services, and more emergency room and inpatient care. Moreover, children in WIC were more likely to be diagnosed and treated with common childhood illnesses – such as otitis media, gastroenteritis, upper and lower respiratory infections, and asthma. These results suggest that low-income children enrolled in WIC are linked to the health care system and are much more likely to be receiving preventive and curative care.

In summary, studies of infant and child WIC participation have examined a wide range of outcomes, especially in contrast to evaluation studies of prenatal WIC participation that have focused primarily on birth outcomes. Despite the persistent concern about potential selection bias, the findings suggest that WIC participation by infants and children is associated with improved iron status of infants, lower rates and duration of breastfeeding, positive effects on child growth, improved dietary status, and greater access to and use of health care.

LOOKING AHEAD: POLICY AND RESEARCH

Since WIC began in 1975, significant changes have occurred in the demographic characteristics and public health concerns of the population served by WIC, in the U.S. food supply and dietary patterns, in knowledge of nutrient requirements, and in dietary guidance, yet the WIC food packages have changed very little during its first 35 years. Initially, the WIC food package solely addressed concerns about the nutrient adequacy of participants' diets: It targeted specific nutrients that, at the time WIC was first authorized, were lacking in the diets of low-income women, infants, and children – namely, protein, vitamins A and C, calcium, and iron. Foods in the WIC packages, including iron-fortified formula, milk and cheese, eggs, iron-fortified infant cereals and ready-to-eat cereals, and 100% juices rich in vitamin C, were selected for their contributions to these targeted nutrients. In 1980, because of concerns about the adequacy of zinc intakes, dried peas or beans and peanut butter were added to the WIC food package.

In recent years, many policy makers, stakeholder groups, and researchers have highlighted the need to review the WIC food packages and consider whether revisions should be made in response to the following changes:

- *The characteristics of WIC participants have changed considerably since WIC's inception.* The number of monthly WIC participants has increased from 88,000 women, infants, and children in fiscal year 1974 to 8.7 million in 2008. During this time period, the racial and ethnic distribution of WIC participants also has shifted considerably, with Hispanics and Asian and Pacific Islanders now accounting for a significantly larger share of the total WIC population. Today, more low-income women are working than when WIC first started.
- *The health risks of the WIC population have shifted dramatically over time.* Concerns about diet and health have shifted from concerns about dietary adequacy to those about excessive intakes of calories and saturated fat;

inadequate consumption of fruits, vegetables, and whole grains; and the problems of obesity and chronic disease that are associated with these dietary patterns.

- *The food supply and dietary practices of the WIC population have changed.* The food supply has increased dramatically, and a greater variety of foods and food establishments are now available. More foods are fortified, and food labeling has been greatly improved. In addition, more Americans of all income levels now eat outside the home.
- *Knowledge of nutrient requirements and dietary guidance has improved.* Improved knowledge of nutrient requirements has resulted in a new set of nutrient reference standards, and regular updates of the *Dietary Guidelines for Americans* have led to improved tools and guidance on how to eat a healthy diet.

In response to these substantial changes in the context in which the WIC program operates, the FNS contracted with the Institute of Medicine in 2003 to provide scientifically based recommendations for updating the WIC food packages. Based on the resulting report, the FNS published an interim final rule in 2007 to change the WIC food packages. The revisions to the food packages are designed to be consistent with dietary guidance for infants and young children and to achieve these objectives: to promote and support breastfeeding; to encourage the consumption of fruit, vegetables, and whole grains; to discourage the consumption of saturated fat; and to appeal to a diverse population (Federal Register, 2007; Institute of Medicine, 2006).

The new food packages, if consumed as intended, should improve the diets and health of program participants. Nonetheless, much can happen when design is put into practice. The WIC program can control only the foods offered through the WIC food packages, not what participants actually consume. With the new food packages, food consumption patterns may change in unintended ways, leading to changes in food choices and nutrient intake. Additionally, the new food packages could increase or decrease the incentives for different groups to participate in the WIC program, and they could increase or decrease breastfeeding rates.

Thus, in thinking about the future policy and research agenda for WIC, a critical goal is to examine how the new food packages are implemented and whether they achieve the desired goal of more healthy diets and improved health of WIC participants. Given the reach of the WIC program in serving the target population – almost 50% of *all* infants receive WIC benefits, for example – the changes in the food package, especially if accompanied by effective nutrition education, have the potential to improve the diets of WIC participants and contribute to approaches to reduce childhood and adult obesity. To better understand the changes resulting from the revised food packages, the following research questions should be answered.

Will More Mothers Breastfeed Their Infants?

The WIC food-package changes include several recommendations designed to encourage more breastfeeding and increase the duration of breastfeeding among WIC mothers. The first recommendation is that during the first month after birth (called the "birth month"), partially breastfeeding infants should receive only a small amount of iron-fortified formula – the equivalent of 104 fluid ounces of reconstituted formula (about one can), at most. In addition, for *partially* breastfed infants after the first month, the revised food packages include a substantial reduction in the amount of formula provided, from the previous maximum of 806 fluid ounces for partially breastfed infants ages 1 to 3 months to a maximum of 364 fluid ounces. Other enhancements to the food packages for breastfeeding mothers and infants – namely, increased amounts of baby foods (including baby food meats) for fully breastfed older infants and the more generous food package for fully breastfeeding women – are also expected to make breastfeeding a more attractive option.

However, the revised WIC food packages could have unintended negative effects on breastfeeding decisions. Mothers may be reluctant to give up access to larger quantities of formula, even if they intend to initiate breastfeeding, and, as a result, may decide to certify as fully formula feeding and even choose to formula feed rather than try to partially breastfeed. In addition, WIC mothers may be concerned about the reduced quantity of formula provided for their older infants if they choose to partially breastfeed. Again, this characteristic of the proposed food packages could have the unintended consequence of causing more WIC mothers to certify as fully formula feeding or even to switch to fully formula feeding to ensure they have adequate formula to feed their infants.

Will WIC Participants Eat More Fruit and Vegetables?

The most fundamental change to the WIC food packages is the increase in the amount and variety of fruits and vegetables for all WIC participants 6 months of age and older. Previously, the WIC food packages provided 2 pounds of fresh carrots to fully breastfeeding mothers and significant quantities of vitamin-C-rich juice for infants, children, and women. The new food packages have a dramatically different content. Vitamin-C-rich juice is not provided at all for infants and is provided at substantially reduced quantities for children and all categories of women. The revised packages include baby food fruits and vegetables for infants 6 to 11 months of age; a $6 cash voucher for children 1 to 5 years of age; an $8 cash voucher for prenatal, partial breastfeeding, and postpartum women; and a $10 cash voucher for fully breastfeeding women. The cash vouchers can be used to purchase a wide variety of fresh fruits and vegetables, except for white potatoes; white potatoes are already prevalent in the diets of WIC participants and are often consumed in forms that are high in calories and saturated fat (e.g., French fries). If fresh fruits and vegetables are of limited availability, state WIC agencies allow participants to purchase canned, dried, or frozen fruits and vegetables instead.

Will the Delay in Providing Complementary Foods Lead to Improved Diets?

With the previous food package, WIC infants could start receiving iron-fortified infant cereal and vitamin-C-rich juice as early as 4 months of age. To be consistent with current recommendations of the American Academy of Pediatrics (2004) and other expert groups, the revised food packages require that infant cereal not be provided until 6 months of age and that no vitamin-C-rich juice be provided to infants at all. These recommendations are designed to increase the reliance on breast milk or formula as the main source of energy in the diets of infants up to 6 months of age.

However, research shows that 70% of infants consume complementary foods before 6 months of age, suggesting that despite the advice of most professionals, parents introduce complementary foods earlier than 6 months (Briefel, Reidy, Karwe, & Devaney, 2004). Moreover, some experts argue that complementary foods should be introduced when professionals and parents feel the child is developmentally ready, which is usually between 4 and 6 months of age. So, if WIC withholds nutritious complementary foods until 6 months of age, the empirical question is whether parents also will withhold complementary foods. If not, will the delay in providing appropriate complementary foods through WIC from 4 to 6 months lead some parents to introduce inappropriate foods?

What Will Be the Effects of the Changes to Whole Grains and Reduced-Fat Milk?

To increase the nutrient content of WIC participants' diets, as well as to address the increasing prevalence of overweight and obesity, the new food packages emphasize the consumption of whole-grain cereals and breads and limit milk to reduced-fat forms for children older than 2 years of age and for prenatal, breastfeeding, and postpartum women. However, if these foods are less appealing to WIC participants, the changes could lead to reduced participation among eligible women and children or reduced consumption of grain products and milk.

Research Steps

The changes to the WIC food packages are substantial and should be studied systematically to ensure that WIC continues to be effective in meeting the changing needs of its participants. Because of the magnitude of the changes, it is important to examine how WIC state and local agencies implement the proposed food packages, the effects of the proposed food packages on participation rates, and the extent to which the food and nutrient goals of the proposed revisions are achieved.

The first step in preparing to assess the effects of the food-package changes is to document all the changes to the WIC food packages, provide the rationale for them, and identify the possible modifications in behavior that could result from those key changes. For example, limiting milk to reduced-fat forms could have at least four different effects: (a) reduced fat and saturated fat intakes (if WIC participants simply substitute reduced-fat for whole milk); (b) reduced calcium (and saturated fat) intakes (if WIC participants consume less milk); (c) increased consumption of nonmilk beverages and potentially increased sugar intakes (if participants substitute other beverages for milk); and/or (d) reduced WIC participation (if WIC participants find the proposed food packages to be less desirable).

After the possible changes in behavior are identified, the next step is to consider data sets and research designs that could be used to determine what actually happened after the changes to the WIC food packages were implemented.

To examine changes in food consumption and nutrient intake, the most likely data set is the National Health and Nutrition Examination Survey (NHANES). The current NHANES began in 1999 and is an ongoing annual survey conducted by the National Center for Health Statistics that includes 24-hour dietary recalls administered to a nationally representative sample of individuals of all ages. Each year, approximately 7,000 randomly selected residents across the United States are asked to participate in the survey. Although in a given year the number of WIC participants (by WIC category of pregnant and postpartum women, infants, and children) is likely to be small, pooling data across years could provide sufficient sample sizes for analytic research needs.

One feasible research design using NHANES data is to estimate two models of food consumption and nutrient intake, one using the pre-implementation years of NHANES data and the other using post-implementation years. These models would estimate relationships between WIC participation and the consumption of the foods in the old and new food packages.[1] If the goals of the proposed food packages are achieved, we would expect to see a stronger relationship between WIC participation and consumption of foods in the new WIC food package in the post-implementation model than in the pre-implementation model.

[1] The proposed analysis is similar to that conducted by Oliveira and Chandran for their report, *Children's Consumption of WIC-Approved Foods* (Oliveira, Racine, Olmsted, & Ghelfi, 2002).

In addition to NHANES data on food consumption and nutrient intake, WIC administrative data might also be a feasible data source for research on the effects of the changes in the WIC food packages on participation and on food-instrument redemption. In particular, there could be food-item-specific analyses (for example, the amounts of milk and breakfast cereals "purchased" with WIC vouchers).

After considering potential data sets and research designs, feasible approaches for conducting research on the changes to the WIC food packages need to be identified. Studying some aspects of the food-package changes using extant data sources may not be feasible. For example, limited sample sizes of adult WIC participants in NHANES make it unsuitable for examining effects of changes in the WIC food package for fully breastfeeding women. Sample sizes in the full NHANES 1999–2004 may be adequate, however, to support analyses that used all women – pregnant, breastfeeding, and non-breastfeeding, postpartum women – in an NHANES analysis.

SUMMARY

In summary, WIC is generally a successful and popular program, largely because it serves a vulnerable population and because of a comprehensive research record over its history. Given the scope and magnitude of the changes to the WIC food packages, the future research agenda analyzing the effectiveness of the WIC program needs to change as well.

REFERENCES

Ahluwalia, I. B., Hogan, V. K., Grummer-Strawn, L., Colville, W. R., & Peterson, A. (1998). The effect of WIC participation on small-for-gestational-age births: Michigan, 1992. *American Journal of Public Health, 88*(9), 1374–1377.

American Academy of Pediatrics, Committee on Nutrition (2004). *Pediatric nutrition handbook* (5th ed.). Elk Grove, IL: Author.

Bartlett, S., Bobronnikov, E., Pacheco, N., et al. (2006, March). *WIC participant and program characteristics 2004.* Alexandria, VA: U.S. Department of Agriculture, Food and Nutrition Service, Office of Analysis, Nutrition and Evaluation.

Bitler, M., & Currie, J. (2005). Does WIC work? The effects of WIC on pregnancy and birth outcomes. *Journal of Policy Analysis and Management, 24*(1), 73–91.

Black, M. M., Cutts, D. B., Frank, D. A., Geppert, J., Skalicky, A., Levenson, S., et al. (2004). Special Supplemental Nutrition Program for Women, Infants, and Children participation and infants' growth and health: A multisite surveillance study. *Pediatrics, 114*, 169–176.

Briefel, R., Reidy, K., Karwe, V., & Devaney, B. (2004). Feeding infants and toddlers study: Improvements needed in meeting infant feeding recommendations. *Journal of the American Dietetic Association, 104*(Suppl. 1), S31–S37.

Buescher, P., & Horton, S. (2000). *Prenatal WIC participation in relation to low birth weight and Medicaid infant costs in North Carolina – a 1997 update.* Raleigh, NC: Center for Health Information and Statistics, North Carolina Department of Health and Human Services.

Buescher, P. A., Horton, S. J., Devaney, B., Roholt, S. J., Lenihan, A. J., Whitmire, T. J., & Kotch, J. B. (2003). Child participation in WIC: Medicaid costs and use of health care services. *American Journal of Public Health, 93*(1), 145–150.

Chatterji, P., Bonuck, K., Dhawan, S., & Deb, N. (2002). *WIC participation and the initiation and duration of breast-feeding* (Discussion Paper No. 1246-02). Madison, WI: Institute for Research on Poverty.

Devaney, B., Bilheimer, L., & Schore, J. (1992). Medicaid costs and birth outcomes: The effects of prenatal WIC participation and the use of prenatal care. *Journal of Policy Analysis and Management, 11*(4), 573–592.

Edozien, J., Boyd, M. D., Switzer, B., & Bryan, R. (1979). Medical evaluation of the Special Supplemental Food Program for Women, Infants, and Children. *American Journal of Clinical Nutrition, 32*, 677–692.

ExpectMore.gov. (n.d.). Retrieved from http://www.whitehouse.gov/omb/expectmore/summary/10003027.2006.html.

Federal Register. (2007, December 6). *Special Supplemental Nutrition Program for Women, Infants, and Children (WIC): Revisions in the WIC food packages*; Interim Rule, vol. *72*, No. 234, 68966–69032.

Fox, M. K., Hamilton, W., & Lin, B. (2004). *Effects of food assistance and nutrition programs on nutrition and health: Vol. 3. Literature review* (Food Assistance and Nutrition Research Report No. 19-3). Washington, DC: Economic Research Service, U.S. Department of Agriculture.

Gordon, A., & Nelson, L. (1995). *Characteristics and outcomes of WIC participants and nonparticipants: Analysis of the 1988 National Maternal and Infant Health Survey.* Princeton, NJ: Mathematica Policy Research.

Institute of Medicine. (2006). *WIC food packages: Time for a change.* Washington, DC: National Academy Press.

Joyce, T., Racine, A., & Yunzal-Butler, C. (2007). *Re-assessing the WIC effect: Evidence from the Pregnancy Nutrition Surveillance System.* Paper presented at the Annual Meetings of the Association for Public Policy and Management, Washington, DC.

Kennedy, E., Gershoff, S., Reed, R., & Austin, J. (1982). Evaluation of the effect of WIC supplemental feeding on birthweight. *Journal of the American Dietetic Association, 80*(3), 220–227.

Kotelchuck, M., Schwartz, J., Anderka, M., & Finison, K. (1984). WIC participation and pregnancy outcomes: Massachusetts statewide evaluation project. *American Journal of Public Health, 74*(10), 1086–1092.

Lazariu-Bauer, V., Stratton, H., Pruzek, R., & Woelfel, M. L. (2004). A comparative analysis of effects of early versus late prenatal WIC participation on birth weight: NYS, 1994. *Maternal and Child Health Journal, 8*(2), 77–86.

Leonard, R. (1994). Recalling WIC program's humble beginnings. *CNI Weekly Report, 24*(15), 4–7.

Metcoff, J., Costiloe, P., Crosby, W., Dutta, S., Sandstead, H., Milne, D., et al. (1985). Effect of food supplementation (WIC) during pregnancy on birth weight. *American Journal of Clinical Nutrition, 42*(May), 933–947.

Oliveira, V., Racine, E., Olmsted, J., & Ghelfi, L. M. (2002, September). *The WIC program: Background, trends, and issues* (Food Assistance and Nutrition Report No. 27). Washington, DC: Food and Rural Economic Division, Economic Research Service, U.S. Department of Agriculture.

Rush, D., Leighton, J., Sloan, N. K., Alvir, J. M., & Garbowski, G. C. (1986). *The National WIC Evaluation: An evaluation of the Special Supplemental Food Program for Women, Infants, and Children* (Vols. 1–3). Alexandria, VA: U.S. Department of Agriculture, Food and Nutrition Service.

Schwartz, J. B., Guilkey, D. K., Akin, J. S., & Popkin, B. (1992). *The WIC breastfeeding report: The relationship of WIC program participation to the initiation and duration of breastfeeding.* Alexandria, VA: U.S. Department of Agriculture, Food and Nutrition Service.

U.S. General Accounting Office. (1992, April). *Early intervention: Federal investments like WIC can produce savings* (GAO/HRD-92-18). Washington, DC: Author.

Yip, R., Binkin, N. J., Fleshood, L., & Trowbridge, F. L. (1987). Declining prevalence of anemia among low-income children in the United States. *Journal of the American Medical Association, 258*(12), 1610–1623.

Yip, R., Parvana, I., Scanlon, K., Borland, E., Russell, C., & Trowbridge, F. (1992). Pediatric Surveillance System – United States 1980–1991. *Morbidity and Mortality Weekly Report: CDC Surveillance Summaries, 41*(SS-7), 1–23.

3

The Nurse-Family Partnership: From Trials to Practice

DAVID L. OLDS

INTRODUCTION

Many of the most intractable problems that young children and parents face in our society today are uniquely associated with adverse maternal health-related behaviors during pregnancy, dysfunctional infant caregiving, and stressful environmental conditions that interfere with parental and family functioning. These problems include infant mortality, preterm delivery, low birthweight, and neurodevelopmental impairments in young children resulting from poor conditions for pregnancy, child abuse and neglect, accidental childhood injuries, youth violence, closely spaced pregnancy, and thwarted economic self-sufficiency of parents. In a series of randomized trials conducted in (a) Elmira, New York, begun in 1977 in a semirural area with a primarily White

---

The work reported here was made possible by support from many different sources. These include the Administration for Children and Families (90PD0215/01 and 90PJ0003); Biomedical Research Support (PHS S7RR05403–25); Bureau of Community Health Services, Maternal and Child Health Research Grants Division (MCR-360403–07-0); Carnegie Corporation (B-5492); Colorado Trust (93059); Commonwealth Fund (10443); David and Lucile Packard Foundation (95–1842); Ford Foundation (840–0545, 845–0031, and 875–0559); Maternal and Child Health, Department of Health and Human Services (MCJ-363378–01-0); National Center for Nursing Research (NR01–01691-05); National Institute of Mental Health (K05-MH01382, R01-MH49381, and R01MH061428); Pew Charitable Trusts (88–0211-000); Robert Wood Johnson Foundation (179–34, 5263, 6729, 9677, and 35369); U.S. Department of Justice (95-DD-BX-0181); and the W. T. Grant Foundation (80072380, 84072380, 86108086, and 88124688).

I thank John Shannon for his support of the program and data gathering through Comprehensive Interdisciplinary Developmental Services, Elmira, New York; Robert Chamberlin and Robert Tatelbaum for their contributions to the early phases of this research; Jackie Roberts, Liz Chilson, Lyn Scazafabo, Georgie McGrady, and Diane Farr for their home-visitation work with the Elmira families; Geraldine Smith for her supervision of the nurses in Memphis; Jann Belton and Carol Ballard for integrating the program into the Memphis/Shelby County Health Department; Harriet Kitzman, Robert Cole, John Eckenrode, Charlie Izzo, Charles Henderson, Beth Anson, Kim Sidora, and Jane Powers for their work on the Elmira and Memphis trials; Pilar Baca, Ruth O'Brien, JoAnn Robinson, John Holmberg, and Susan Hiatt for their work on the Denver trial; the many home-visiting nurses in Memphis and Denver; and the participating families who have made this program of research possible.

sample; (b) Memphis, Tennessee, begun in 1987 with a primarily Black sample; and (c) Denver, Colorado, begun in 1994 with a sample that included a large portion of Hispanics, our team has been examining the impact of a program of prenatal and early childhood home visitation by nurses on improving parental behaviors and environmental conditions early in the life cycle in an effort to prevent these maternal and child health problems. These trials have enabled us to examine the extent to which the effects of the program are consistent across these different populations, settings, and time periods. The Denver trial was designed to determine the extent to which lay community health visitors might be able to produce the same beneficial effects as nurses when trained in the same program model.

Both epidemiology and developmental theory guided the program of research reported in this chapter. Many early preventive interventions fail because they are not based on a thorough understanding of the following factors: (a) the risk and protective characteristics in the targeted population as they relate to the outcomes of interest; (b) the likely developmental pathways leading to the negative outcomes the interventions intend to prevent and the positive outcomes they intend to promote; and (c) the mechanisms, based on sound theory and evidence, through which their designers expect the programs to produce behavioral change (Olds & Kitzman, 1993). This chapter describes the empirical and theoretical foundations of this program of research; the design of the program itself; and the research designs, methods, and findings from the Elmira and Memphis trials. The final section of this chapter examines the policy implications of the findings and describes our current initiative to replicate the program model outside of research contexts while maintaining fidelity to the model tested in the trials.

A RESEARCH-BASED AND THEORY-DRIVEN MODEL

Research-Based Model

Research has guided decisions about the families to be served and the content of the program. All of the trials have examined program impact with women who have had no previous live births, and each has focused recruitment on low-income, unmarried, and adolescent women. Women with these characteristics were recruited because the problems that the program was designed to address (e.g., poor birth outcomes, child abuse and neglect, and diminished economic self-sufficiency of parents) are concentrated in those populations (Elster & McAnarney, 1980; Furstenberg, Brooks-Gunn, & Morgan, 1987; Overpeck, Brenner, Trumble, Trifiletti, & Berendes, 1998). The primary difference among the studies is that in the Elmira trial, any woman bearing a first child was allowed to register. In addition, program effects in Elmira were greater for the higher risk families, so the subsequent Memphis and Denver trials focused

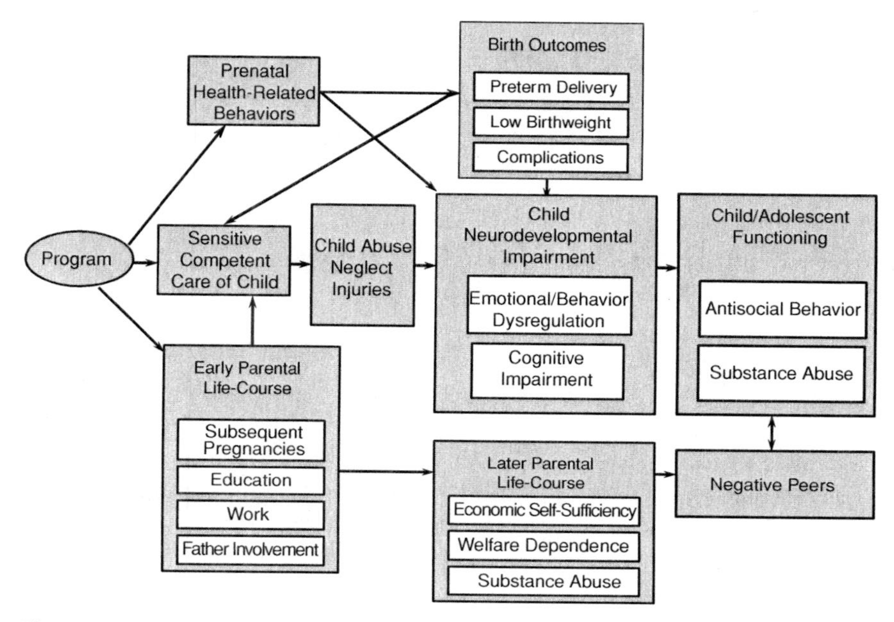

Figure 3.1. Conceptual model of program influences on maternal and child health and development.

recruitment more exclusively on those with overlapping risks (i.e., being both unmarried and from a low-income family).

All three trials focused on women who had no previous live births because it was hypothesized that such women would be more receptive to home-visitation services relating to pregnancy and child rearing than would women who had already given birth. Moreover, as parents learn parenting and other skills through the program, they should be better able to care for subsequent children, and the program should have an even greater positive effect. Finally, if the program helped parents plan subsequent births, then it would be easier for parents to finish their education and find work because they would experience fewer problems with child care (Furstenberg et al., 1987), and the children would benefit from more focused parental nurturance and guidance (Tygart, 1991).

The content of the program is also research based. The program seeks to modify specific risks that are associated with the negative outcomes of concern: poor birth outcomes, child abuse and neglect, injuries, and compromised parental life-course.

Figure 3.1 summarizes how these outcomes are thought to reinforce one another over time. On the far left side of this figure, we note the three broad domains of proximal risks and protective factors that the program was designed to affect: prenatal health-related behaviors; sensitive, competent care of the child; and early parental life-course (pregnancy planning, parents' completion of their education, finding work, and fathers' involvement in the lives of their children). The middle set of outcomes reflects corresponding child and parental outcomes that the program was originally designed to influence: birth outcomes (obstetric complications, preterm delivery, and low birthweight); child abuse, neglect, and unintentional injuries; child neurodevelopmental impairment (perturbations in emotional, behavioral, and cognitive development); and later parental life-course (family economic self-sufficiency, welfare dependence, maternal substance abuse). On the far right of Figure 3.1, we show child and adolescent outcomes that the program might affect years after children at age 2 complete the program, including school failure, antisocial behavior, and substance abuse. Part of the program effect on adolescent functioning was thought to be achieved by reducing children's exposure and susceptibility to negative peer influences.

When our team began this program of research in 1977, we did not allow ourselves to imagine that the changes the nurses attempted to make during pregnancy and the first 2 years of the child's life might really have an impact on adolescent outcomes. Nevertheless, results of the Elmira trial summarized later in the chapter indicate that the program has indeed affected adolescent behavior. Each of these sets of influences is discussed in greater depth later.

Prenatal Health Behaviors

MODIFIABLE RISKS FOR POOR BIRTH OUTCOMES AND CHILD NEURODEVELOPMENTAL IMPAIRMENT. Prenatal exposure to tobacco, alcohol, and illegal drugs are established risks for poor fetal growth (Kramer, 1987) and, to a lesser extent, preterm birth (Kramer, 1987) and neurodevelopmental impairment (e.g., attention deficit disorder or poor cognitive and language development) (Fried, Watkinson, Dillon, & Dulberg, 1987; Mayes, 1994; Milberger, Biederman, Faraone, Chen, & Jones, 1996; Olds, 1997; Olds, Henderson, & Tatelbaum, 1994a, 1994b; Streissguth, Sampson, Barr, Bookstein, & Olson, 1994). In all three trials (Elmira, Memphis, and Denver), the home visitors therefore sought to reduce mothers' use of these substances. The prenatal protocols also address other behavioral factors that increase the risk for low birthweight, preterm delivery, and poor child development: inadequate weight gain (Institute of Medicine, 1990), inadequate diet (Institute of Medicine, 1990), inadequate use of office-based prenatal care (Klein & Goldenberg, 1990), and failure to identify and treat in a timely manner obstetric complications, such as genitourinary tract infections and hypertensive disorders (e.g., high blood pressure) (Klein & Goldenberg, 1990).

Sensitive, Competent Care of the Child

MODIFIABLE RISKS FOR CHILD ABUSE AND NEGLECT AND INJURIES TO CHILDREN. Parents who empathize with their infants and sensitively read and respond to their babies' communicative signals are less likely to abuse or neglect them, and they are more likely to read their children's developmental competencies accurately, leading to fewer unintentional injuries (Peterson & Gable, 1998). Competent early parenting is associated with better child behavioral regulation, language, and cognition (Hart & Risley, 1995). As children enter early elementary school, responsive and positive parenting can provide some protection from the damaging effects of stressful environments and negative peers (Bremner, 1999) on externalizing symptoms and substance use (Baumrind, 1987; Grant et al., 2000). In general, poor parenting is correlated with low child serotonin levels (Pine, 2001, 2003), which, in turn, are implicated in stress-induced delays in neurodevelopment (Bremner & Vermetten, 2004).

Although it makes sense to target these proximal behaviors, it is also helpful to understand and address the general sets of influences that affect parents' abilities to care for their children. We have hypothesized that these influences on parenting skills can be moderated by targeted intervention strategies.

Ontogenetic and contextual factors affect parents' caregiving skills. Parents who grew up in households with punitive, rejecting, abusive, or neglectful caregiving are more likely to abuse or neglect their own children (Egeland, Jacobvitz, & Sroufe, 1988; Quinton & Rutter, 1984; Rutter, 1989). Parents' psychological immaturity and mental health problems can reduce their ability to care for their infants (Newberger & White, 1989; Sameroff, 1983). Although it is impossible to change parents' personal histories and very difficult to reduce personal immaturity and mental illness, as indicated later, the program has sought to mitigate the effect of these influences on parents' caregiving. In addition, unemployment (Gil, 1970), poor housing and household conditions (Gil, 1970), marital discord (Belsky, 1981), and isolation from supportive family members and friends (Garbarino, 1981) are all associated with higher rates of abuse and neglect, perhaps because they create stressful conditions in the household that interfere with parents' ability to care for their children (Bakan, 1971; Kempe, 1973). As noted later, the Nurse-Family Partnership is designed to increase parents' economic self-sufficiency, help parents find safe housing, improve partner communication and commitment, and reduce social isolation.

Moreover, recent evidence suggests that children's characteristics may affect the degree to which their parents care for them competently. Children born with subtle neurological perturbations resulting from prenatal exposure to substances such as tobacco and alcohol and to maternal stress and anxiety during pregnancy are more likely to be irritable and inconsolable and to have difficulty habituating to auditory stimuli in the first few weeks of life (Clark, Soto, & Bergholz, 1996; Saxon, 1978; Streissguth et al., 1994), making it more difficult for parents to find enjoyment in their care. Children with attention deficit hyperactivity disorder are at increased risk for becoming seriously injured (DiScala, Lescohier, Barthel, & Li, 1998), a link that may be explained in part by the difficulties parents may have with regulating and guiding their children's behavior. Thus, these child characteristics (which are affected to some degree by the quality of the uterine environment) may contribute to parents' abilities to become competent parents. Parents who are mature, married to supportive spouses, and have adequate incomes and few external stressors are more likely to manage the care of difficult newborns better than those parents without these resources. Unfortunately, children with subtle neurological vulnerabilities are more likely to be born into households where these salutary conditions are not present, multiplying the likelihood that caregiving will be compromised.

Early Parental Life-Course (Subsequent Pregnancies, Education, Work, and Fathers' Involvement)

MODIFIABLE RISKS FOR COMPROMISED MATERNAL LIFE-COURSE DEVELOPMENT. One of the major risks for compromised maternal educational achievement and workforce participation is rapid, successive pregnancy, particularly among unmarried women (Furstenberg et al., 1987). Such pregnancies often occur when women have limited visions for their futures in the areas of education and work (Musick, 1993), as well as a belief that they have limited control over their life circumstances and over their contraceptive practices in particular (Brafford & Beck, 1991; Heinrich, 1993; Levinson, 1986).

One of the more significant questions that young mothers must address is the role that the child's father will play in their lives. As indicated later, the program actively promotes fathers' involvement with their partners and children. In most cases, fathers are eager to be supportive partners and providers for their children. In some cases, they are ambivalent, unprepared, abusive, and involved in criminal activities. Couples who are married are more likely to achieve economic self-sufficiency, and their children are at lower risk for a host of problems (McLanahan & Carlson, 2002). However, it would be a mistake to conclude that simply promoting marriage for unmarried pregnant women is the right approach, without considering the quality of the possible relationship and the risk for domestic violence. The decision to marry is complex and requires careful consideration of whether the father (or other prospective partner) can be a good spouse and positive caregiver.

To the extent that families improve their economic conditions over time, they are less likely to live in unsafe, crime-ridden neighborhoods where children are exposed to negative peer influences. Even if children are exposed to negative peers, nurse-visited children are less likely to be susceptible to those negative influences because they will have stronger relationships with their parents, which will have helped them develop a stronger moral core (Emde & Buchsbaum, 1990).

The nurses are trained to guide young women as they make these significant life-shaping decisions. In this process, the nurses help women envision a future consistent with their deepest values and aspirations; they help women evaluate different contraceptive methods, child care options, and career choices; and they help women develop concrete plans for achieving their goals.

Early Life-Course Modifiable Risks for Early-Onset Antisocial Behavior

Many of the factors listed earlier are risk factors for early-onset antisocial behavior (Olds, 1997; Olds, Eckenrode, et al., 1997; Olds, Henderson, et al., 1998; Olds, Pettitt, et al., 1998), a type of disruptive behavior that frequently characterizes children who grow up to become violent adolescents and, sometimes, chronic offenders (Moffitt, 1993; Raine, Brennan, & Mednick, 1994). For example, children who develop early-onset disorder are more likely to have subtle neurodevelopmental deficits (sometimes due to poor prenatal health) (Milberger et al., 1996; Olds, 1997; Streissguth et al., 1994; Wakschlag et al., 1997) combined with abusive and rejecting care early in life (Moffitt, 1993; Raine et al., 1994). Recent evidence indicates that prenatal tobacco exposure is a unique risk for conduct disorder and youth crime (Brennan, Grekin, & Mednick, 1999; Moffitt, 1993; Wakschlag et al., 1997).

As mentioned earlier, adverse prenatal influences on fetal neurological development are sometimes exacerbated by adverse postnatal experiences. Children who have been abused are more likely to develop negative attribution biases that make them more likely to interpret ambiguous behaviors on the part of others as threatening (Dodge, Bates, & Pettit, 1990) and to have internal representations of interpersonal relationships characterized by dysregulated aggression and violence (Buchsbaum, Toth, Clyman, Cicchetti, & Emde, 1992), both of which probably reflect an adaptive neurological response to a threatening world (Teicher, 2000). They are more likely to come from large families, with closely spaced children (Tygart, 1991), in which parents themselves are involved in substance abuse and criminal behavior (Moffitt, 1993).

A similar configuration of risks is associated with early-onset major depressive disorder (MDD). Children who develop MDD in childhood, compared with those who develop MDD as adults, are more likely to have perinatal insults, motor-skill deficits, and behavioral and emotional problems (Jaffee et al., 2002) – especially impulsivity, risky decision making, and problems with verbal recognition memory and inattention (Aytaclar, Tarter, Kirisci, & Lu, 1999) – as well as caregiver instability, criminality, and psychopathology in their family of origin.

Both conduct disorder and early substance use increase the risk for later substance use disorders (SUDs) and chronic antisocial behavior (Boyle et al., 1992; Clark & Cornelius, 2004; Clark, Cornelius, Kirisci, & Tarter, 2005; Clark et al., 1997; Lynskey et al., 2003; Moffitt, 1993; Raine et al., 1994). Children who begin using cannabis in adolescence (<17 years) are at greater risk for developing SUDs (Lynskey et al., 2003). Adolescent substance use is also implicated in the development of adult antisocial behavior (Ridenour et al., 2002) and depression. The reduction in prenatal risks and dysfunctional care of the infant and the improvement in family context are thus likely to have long-term effects on youth antisocial behavior that has its roots in early experience.

Theory-Driven Model

The Nurse-Family Partnership (NFP) program is grounded in theories of human ecology (Bronfenbrenner, 1979, 1995), self-efficacy (Bandura, 1977), and human attachment (Bowlby, 1969). Together, these theories emphasize the importance of families' social context and individuals' beliefs, motivations, emotions, and internal representations of their experience in explaining the development of behavior. The integration of these theories has influenced the design of this program.

For example, human ecology theory emphasizes that children's development is influenced by how their parents care for them, which, in turn, is influenced by characteristics of their families, social networks, neighborhoods, communities, and the interrelations among them (Bronfenbrenner, 1979). Drawing from this theory, nurses attempt to enhance the material and social environment of the family by involving other family members, especially fathers, in the home visits and by linking families with needed health and human services.

Parents help select and shape the settings in which they find themselves, however (Plomin, 1986). Self-efficacy theory provides a useful framework for understanding how women make decisions about their health-related behaviors during pregnancy, about their care of their children, and about their own personal development. This theory suggests that individuals choose those behaviors that they believe (a) will lead to a given outcome, and (b) they themselves can successfully carry out (Bandura, 1977). In other words, individuals' perceptions of self-efficacy can influence their choices and can determine how much effort they put forth in the face of obstacles.

The NFP curriculum therefore is designed first to help women understand what is known about the influence of particular behaviors on their own health and on the health and development of their babies. The program guidelines are periodically updated to reflect the most recent evidence regarding influence on family and child health. Second, the home visitors help parents establish realistic goals and small achievable objectives that, once accomplished, increase parents' reservoir of successful experiences. These successes, in turn, increase women's confidence in taking on larger challenges.

Finally, the program is based on attachment theory, which posits that infants are biologically predisposed to seek proximity to specific caregivers in times of stress, illness, or fatigue to promote survival (Bowlby, 1969).

Attachment theory hypothesizes that children's trust in the world and their later capacity for empathy and responsiveness to their own children once they become parents are influenced by the degree to which they formed an attachment with a caring, responsive, and sensitive adult when they were growing up, which affects their internal representations of themselves and their relationships with others (Main, Kaplan, & Cassidy, 1985).

The NFP program therefore explicitly promotes sensitive, responsive, and engaged caregiving in the early years of the child's life (Barnard, 1990; Dolezol & Butterfield, 1994). In addition, home visitors try to help mothers and other caregivers review their own child-rearing histories and make decisions about how they wish to care for their children in light of the way they were cared for as children. Finally, the visitors seek to develop an empathic and trusting relationship with the mother and other family members because experience being in such a relationship is expected to help women eventually trust others and to promote more sensitive, empathic care of their children.

PROGRAM DESIGN

The same basic program design has been used in Elmira, Memphis, and Denver.

Frequency of Visitation

Mothers were enrolled in the NFP trials through the end of the second trimester of pregnancy and followed through the child's second birthday. The recommended frequency of home visits changed with the stages of pregnancy and was adapted to the parents' needs. When parents were experiencing crises, the nurses were allowed to visit more frequently than the protocol specified and, in some cases, mothers did not show up or dropped from the program. All estimates of program impact were conducted with all families originally randomized irrespective of the actual number of visits completed. In Elmira, Memphis, and Denver, the nurses completed an average of 9 (range 0–16), 7 (range 0–18), and 6.5 (range 0–17) visits during pregnancy and 23 (range 0–59), 26 (range 0–71), and 21 (range 0–71) visits from birth to the child's second birthday, respectively. Paraprofessionals in Denver completed an average of 6 (range 0–21) prenatal visits and 16 (range 0–78) during infancy. Each visit lasted approximately 75–90 minutes.

Nurses as Home Visitors

Nurses were selected to be the home visitors because of their formal training in women's and children's health and their competence in managing the complex clinical situations often presented by at-risk families. Nurses' abilities to competently address mothers' and family members' concerns about the complications of pregnancy, labor, and delivery and the physical health of the infant are thought to provide them with increased credibility and persuasive power in the eyes of family members.

Program Content

During the home visits, the nurses carried out three major activities: (a) they promoted improvements in women's (and other family members') behavior thought to affect pregnancy outcomes, the health and development of the child, and the parents' life-course; (b) they helped women build supportive relationships with family members and friends; and (c) they linked women and their family members to other needed health and human services.

The nurses followed detailed visit-by-visit guidelines whose content reflected the challenges that parents are likely to confront during specific stages of pregnancy and the first 2 years of the child's life. Nurses made specific assessments of maternal, child, and family functioning that corresponded to those stages and recommended specific activities to address problems and strengths identified through the assessments.

During pregnancy, the nurses helped women complete 24-hour diet histories on a regular basis and plot weight gains at every visit; they assessed the women's cigarette smoking and use of alcohol and illegal drugs and facilitated a reduction in the use of these substances through behavioral change strategies. They taught women to identify the signs and symptoms of pregnancy complications, encouraged women to inform the office-based staff about those conditions, and facilitated compliance with treatment. They gave particular attention to urinary tract infections, sexually transmitted diseases, and hypertensive disorders of pregnancy (conditions associated with poor birth outcomes). They coordinated care with physicians and nurses in the office and measured blood pressure when needed.

After delivery, the nurses helped mothers and other caregivers improve the physical and emotional care of their children. They taught parents to observe the signs of illness, to take temperatures, and to communicate with office staff about their children's illnesses before taking the child to the doctor's office or emergency department. Curricula promoted parent–child interaction by increasing parents' understanding of their infants' and toddlers' communicative signals, enhancing parents' interest in playing with their children in ways that promoted emotional and cognitive development, and helping parents create households that were safer for children.

The nurses also helped women clarify their goals and solve problems that might interfere with pursuing their education, finding work, and planning future pregnancies.

OVERVIEW OF RESEARCH DESIGNS, METHODS, AND FINDINGS

In each of the three studies, women were randomized to receive either home-visitation services or comparison services. Although the nature of the home-visitation services was essentially the same in each of the trials as described earlier, the comparison services were slightly different. All three studies employed a variety of data sources. The Elmira sample ($N = 400$) was primarily White. The Memphis sample ($N = 1{,}138$ for pregnancy and 743 for the infancy phase) was primarily Black. The Denver trial ($n = 735$) consisted of a large sample of Hispanics and systematically examined the impact of the program when delivered by paraprofessionals (individuals who shared many of the social characteristics of the families they served) versus nurses. We looked for consistency in program effect across those sources before assigning much importance to any one finding. Unless otherwise indicated, all findings reported next have significance levels at least $p < .05$, with 2-tailed tests, otherwise specified.

Elmira Results

Prenatal Health Behaviors

During pregnancy, compared to their counterparts in the control group, nurse-visited women improved the quality of their diets to a greater extent, and those identified as smokers smoked 25% fewer cigarettes by the 34th week of pregnancy (Olds, Henderson, Tatelbaum, & Chamberlin, 1986). By the end of pregnancy, nurse-visited women experienced greater informal social support and made better use of formal community services.

Pregnancy and Birth Outcomes

By the end of pregnancy, nurse-visited women had fewer kidney infections; among women who smoked, those who were visited by nurses had 75% fewer preterm deliveries; and among very young adolescents (aged 14–16), those who were nurse visited had babies who were 395 g heavier than their counterparts assigned to the comparison group (Olds et al., 1986).

Sensitive, Competent Care of the Child

At 10 and 22 months of the child's life, nurse-visited poor, unmarried teens exhibited less punishment and restriction of their infants and provided more appropriate play materials than did their counterparts in the control group (Olds, Henderson, Chamberlin, & Tatelbaum, 1986). At 34 and 46 months of life, nurse-visited mothers provided home environments that were more conducive to their children's emotional and cognitive development as rated by the Home Observation for Measurement of the Environment (HOME) inventory and that were safer, based on observations of safety hazards (Olds, Henderson, & Kitzman, 1994).

Child Abuse, Neglect, and Injuries

During the first 2 years of the child's life, nurse-visited children born to low-income, unmarried teens had 80% fewer verified cases of child abuse and neglect than did their counterparts in the control group (1 case or 4% of the nurse-visited teens versus 8 cases or 19% of the control group, $p = .07$). During the second year of life, nurse-visited children were seen in the emergency department 32% fewer times (0.74 versus 1.09 visits), a difference that was explained in part by a 56% reduction in visits for injuries and ingestions (0.15 versus 0.34 visits).

The effect of the program on child abuse and neglect in the first 2 years of life and on emergency-department encounters in the second year of life was greatest among children whose mothers had little belief in their control over their lives when they first registered for the program.

During the 2 years after the program ended, its impact on health-care encounters for injuries endured. Irrespective of risk, children of nurse-visited women made 35% fewer emergency-department visits (1.00 versus 1.53 visits) and visited a physician 40% fewer times for injuries and ingestions (0.34 versus 0.57 visits) (Olds et al., 1994). The impact of the program on state-verified cases of child abuse and neglect, in contrast, disappeared during that 2-year period (Olds et al., 1994), probably because of increased detection of child abuse and neglect in nurse-visited families and the nurses' linkage of families to needed services (including child protective services) at the end of the program at the child's second birthday (Olds, Henderson, Kitzman, & Cole, 1995).

Results from a 15-year follow-up of the Elmira sample (Olds et al., 1997) indicated that the Group 4-comparison differences in rates of state-verified reports of child abuse and neglect grew between the children's 4th and 15th birthdays. During the 15-year period after delivery of their first child, in contrast to women in the comparison group, those visited by nurses during pregnancy and infancy were identified as perpetrators of child abuse and neglect an average of 0.29 versus 0.54 verified reports per program participant, an effect that was greater for women who were poor and unmarried at registration (Olds et al., 1997).

Child Neurodevelopmental Impairment

At 6 months of age, nurse-visited poor, unmarried teens reported that their infants were less irritable and fussy than did their counterparts in the comparison group (Olds & Henderson, 1989). Subsequent analyses of these data indicated that these differences were concentrated among infants born to nurse-visited women who smoked 10 or more cigarettes per day during pregnancy in contrast to babies born to women who smoked 10 or more cigarettes per day in the comparison group (Olds, Pettitt, et al., 1998). Over the first 4 years of the child's life, children born to comparison-group women who smoked 10 or more cigarettes per day during pregnancy experienced a 4- to 5-point decline in intellectual functioning in contrast to comparison-group children whose mothers smoked 0–9 cigarettes per day during pregnancy (Olds et al., 1994a). In the nurse-visited condition, children whose mothers smoked 0–9 cigarettes per day at registration did not experience this decline in intellectual functioning, so that at ages 3 and 4, their IQ scores on the Stanford-Binet test were about 4–5 points higher than their counterparts in the comparison group whose mothers smoked 10+ cigarettes per day at registration (Olds et al., 1994b).

Early Parental Life-Course

By the time their first child was 4 years of age, nurse-visited low-income, unmarried women had fewer subsequent pregnancies, longer intervals between the birth of the first and second child, and greater participation in the workforce than did their counterparts in the comparison group (Olds, Henderson, Tatelbaum, & Chamberlin, 1988).

Later Parental Life-Course

At the 15-year follow-up, no differences were reported for the full sample on measures of maternal life-course, such as subsequent pregnancies or subsequent births, the number of months between first and second births, receipt of welfare, or months of employment. However, nurse-visited poor, unmarried women showed a number of enduring benefits. In contrast to their counterparts in the comparison condition, those visited by nurses both during pregnancy and infancy averaged 32% fewer subsequent pregnancies (1.5 versus 2.2 pregnancies), 31% fewer subsequent births (1.1 versus 1.6), intervals between the birth of their first and second children that were over 30 months longer (64.8 versus 37.3 months), about 30 fewer months on welfare (60.4 versus 90.3), about 37 fewer months receiving food stamps (46.7 versus 83.5), and 69% fewer arrests (0.18 versus 0.58) (Olds et al., 1997).

Child/Adolescent Functioning

The follow-up study also assessed children of the original participants when the children were 15 years of age (Olds, Henderson, et al., 1998). Recent reanalyses of the data from the 15-year follow-up (Nurse-Family Partnership, 2006) indicated that among the 15-year-old children of study participants, those visited by nurses had fewer arrests and adjudications as persons in need of supervision (PINS). These effects were greater for children born to mothers who were poor and unmarried at registration. Nurse-visited children reported fewer sexual partners and fewer convictions and violations of probation.

Cost Analysis
The RAND Corporation has conducted an economic evaluation of the program that extrapolates the results of the 15-year follow-up study to estimate cost savings generated by the program (Karoly, et al., 1998). While there were no net savings to government or society for serving families in which mothers were married and of higher social class, the savings to government and society for serving families in which the mother was low-income and unmarried at registration exceeded the cost of the program by a factor of four over the life of the child.

Memphis Results

Prenatal Health Behaviors
There were no program effects on women's use of standard prenatal care or obstetric emergency services after registration in the study. However, by the 36th week of pregnancy, nurse-visited women were more likely to use other community services than were women in the control group. There were no program effects on women's cigarette smoking, probably because the rate of cigarette use was only 9% in this sample, and women smoked fewer cigarettes per day than did women smokers in the Elmira trial.

Pregnancy and Birth Outcomes
In contrast to women in the comparison group, nurse-visited women had fewer instances of pregnancy-induced hypertension, and among those with the diagnosis, nurse-visited cases were less serious (Kitzman et al., 1997).

Sensitive, Competent Care of the Child
Nurse-visited mothers reported that they attempted breastfeeding more frequently than did women in the comparison group, although there were no differences in duration of breastfeeding. By the 24th month of the child's life, in contrast to their comparison-group counterparts, nurse-visited women held fewer beliefs about child rearing associated with child abuse and neglect (e.g., endorsement of the physical punishment of infants for misbehavior, unrealistic expectations for infants' knowledge and behavior). Moreover, the homes of nurse-visited women were rated on the HOME scale as more conducive to children's development. Although there was no program effect on observed maternal teaching behavior, children born to nurse-visited mothers with low levels of psychological resources were observed to be more communicative and responsive toward their mothers than were their comparison-group counterparts (Kitzman et al., 1997).

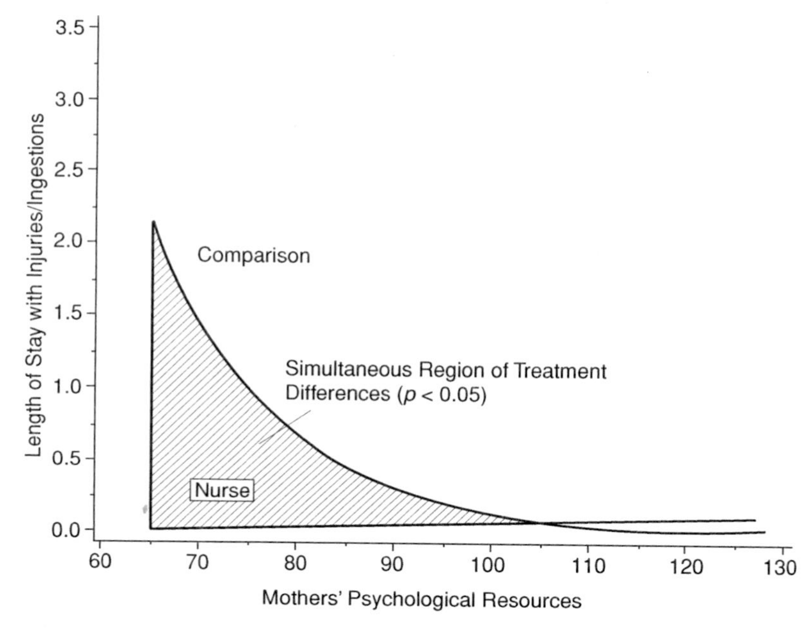

Figure 3.2. Program impact on days hospitalized with injuries intensified among children born to mothers with limited psychological resources (Memphis).

Child Abuse, Neglect, and Injuries

The rate of substantiated child abuse and neglect in the population of 2-year-old, low-income children in Memphis was too low (3–4%) to serve as a valid indicator of child maltreatment in this study. We therefore hypothesized that we would see a pattern of program effects on childhood injuries that would be similar to that observed in Elmira, reflecting a reduction in dysfunctional care of children.

During their first 2 years, nurse-visited children overall had 23% fewer health care encounters in which injuries and ingestions were detected than did children in the comparison group (0.43 versus 0.56), an effect that was accounted for primarily by a 45% reduction in outpatient clinic encounters (0.11 versus 0.20). Nurse-visited children also were hospitalized for 79% fewer days with injuries and/or ingestions than were children in the comparison group (0.04 versus 0.18 day). As illustrated in Figure 3.2, the effect of the program on injuries and ingestions was greater for children born to women with few psychological resources.

An examination of the children's hospital records provides insight into reasons why nurse-visited children were hospitalized for fewer days than children in the comparison group (see Table 3.1). Nurse-visited children tended to be older when hospitalized and to have less severe conditions. The conditions that characterized the hospitalizations suggest that many of the hospitalized

Table 3.1. *Diagnoses, child age, sex, and length of stay for children's hospitalizations for injuries or ingestions, birth through child age 2 (Memphis)*

Diagnosis	Age (in months)	Sex	Length of hospital stay (in days)
Nurse-visited (n = 206)			
First- and second-degree burns to face	12.0	M	2
Coin ingestion	12.1	M	1
Ingestion of iron medication	20.4	F	4
Comparison group (n = 465)			
Head trauma	2.4	M	1
Fractured fibula/congenital syphilis	2.4	M	12
Strangulated hernia with delay in seeking care/first-degree burn to lips	3.5	M	12
Bilateral subdural hematoma[a]	4.9	F	19
Fractured skull	5.2	F	5
Bilateral subdural hematoma (unresolved)/ aseptic meningitis – second hospitalization[a]	5.3	F	4
Fractured skull	7.8	F	3
Coin ingestion	10.9	M	2
Child abuse/neglect suspected	14.6	M	2
Fractured tibia	14.8	M	2
Second-degree burns to face/neck	15.1	M	5
Second- and third-degree burns to leg[b]	19.6	M	4
Gastroenteritis/head trauma	20.0	F	3
Burns – second hospitalization[b]	20.1	M	6
Finger injury/osteomyelitis	23.0	M	6

[a] One child was hospitalized twice with a single bilateral subdural hematoma.
[b] One child was hospitalized twice for burns resulting from a single incident.
Source: From "Effect of Prenatal and Infancy Home Visitation by Nurses on Pregnancy Outcomes, Childhood Injuries, and Repeated Childbearing: A Randomized Controlled Trial," by H. Kitzman, D. L. Olds, C. R. Henderson, Jr., C. Hanks, R. Cole, R. Tatelbaum, et al., 1997, *Journal of the American Medical Association, 278*(8), pp. 644–652. Reprinted with permission from the publisher.

comparison-group children suffered from more seriously deficient care than children visited by nurses.

Overall, nurse-visited children as a trend were less likely to die from birth through age 9 (4.50 versus 20.08 per thousand, OR = .22, p = .080), an effect accounted for by deaths due to potentially preventable causes (see Table 3.2) (Olds et al., 2007).

Child Neurodevelopmental Impairment

By child age 6, compared to their counterparts in the control group, children visited by nurses had higher intellectual functioning (92.34 versus 90.24 points, ES = 0.18) and receptive vocabulary scores (84.32 versus 82.13 points, ES = 0.17) and fewer behavior problems in the borderline or clinical range (1.8% versus 5.4%, OR = 0.55). Nurse-visited children born to mothers with

Table 3.2. *Causes of infant and child deaths (ICD-9) among first-born children through age 9*

Cause of death (ICD-9 Code)	Age at death, in days
Comparison group ($n = 498$)	
Extreme prematurity (7650)	3
SIDS (7980)	20
SIDS (7980)	35
Ill-defined intestinal infections (90)	36
SIDS (7980)	49
Multiple congenital anomalies (7597)	152
Chronic respiratory disease arising in perinatal period (7707)	549
Homicide assault by firearm (9654)	1569
Motor vehicle accident (8129)	2100
Accident caused by firearm (9229)	2114
Nurse-visited group ($n = 222$)	
Chromosomal abnormalities (7589)	24

Note: ICD-9, *International Classification of Diseases, Ninth Revision*; SIDS, sudden infant death syndrome.

Source: From "Effects of Nurse Home Visiting on Maternal and Child Functioning: Age-9 Follow-Up of a Randomized Trial," by D. L. Olds, H. Kitzman, C. Hanks, R. Cole, E. Anson, K. Sidora-Arcoleo, et al., 2007, *Pediatrics, 120*(4), pp. e832–845.

low psychological resources had higher arithmetic achievement test scores (88.61 versus 85.42 points, ES = 0.25) and expressed less aggression and incoherence in response to story stems (98.58 versus 101.10 standard score points, ES = −0.25) (Olds, Kitzman, et al., 2004). By age 9, nurse-visited children born to mothers with low psychological resources, compared to their control group counterparts, had higher grade-point averages and achievement test scores (averaging across math and reading) in Grades 1–3 (2.68 vs. 2.44, ES = 0.22, and 44.89 vs. 35.72, ES = 0.33, respectively) (Olds et al., 2007).

Early Parental Life-Course

At the 24th month of their first child's life, nurse-visited women reported fewer second pregnancies (36% versus 47%, OR = 0.60) and fewer subsequent live births (22% versus 31%, OR = 0.60) than did women in the comparison group. Nurse-visited women and their firstborn children relied on welfare for slightly fewer months during the second year of the child's life than did comparison-group women and their children (7.8 versus 8.4 months; Kitzman et al., 1997).

Later Parental Life-Course

During the 4.5-year period after the birth of their first child, in contrast to counterparts assigned to the comparison condition, women visited by nurses had fewer subsequent pregnancies (1.15 versus 1.34) and longer durations between the births of first and second children (30.25 versus 26.60 months); higher rates of living with a partner (43% versus 32%, OR = 1.64) and living with the biological father of the child (19% versus 13%, OR = 1.68); and with their children used fewer total person-months (based on administrative data) of Aid to Families with Dependent Children (AFDC) (32.55 versus 36.19 months) and food stamps (41.57 versus 45.04 months). By the time the first child reached age 6, women visited by nurses continued to have fewer subsequent pregnancies (1.16 versus 1.38, ES = −0.22) and births (1.08 versus 1.28, ES = −0.22); longer intervals between the births of their first and second children (34.38 versus 30.23, ES = 0.26); longer relationships with current partners (54.36 versus 45.00 months, ES = 0.24); and since the last follow-up at 4.5 years, fewer months of using welfare (7.21 versus 8.96 months, ES = −0.22) and food stamps (9.67 versus 11.50 months, ES = −0.24) (Olds et al., 2004). They also were more likely to register their children in formal out-of-home care between age 2 and 4.5 years of age (82.0% versus 74.9%, OR = 1.53; (Kitzman et al., 2000).

By the time the first-born child was 9 years of age, nurse-visited women had longer intervals between the births of their first and second children (40.73 vs. 34.09 months, ES = 0.29), fewer cumulative subsequent births per year (0.81 vs. 0.93, ES = −.14), and longer relationships with their current partners (51.89 vs. 44.48 months, ES = 0.23). From birth through child age 9, nurse-visited women used welfare and food stamps for fewer months (5.21 vs. 5.92 months per year, ES = −0.14; and 6.98 vs. 7.80 months per year, ES = −0.17, respectively) (Olds et al., 2007).

Denver Results

In the Denver trial, we were unable to use the women's or children's medical records to assess their health because the health care delivery system was too complex to enable us to reliably abstract all of their health care encounters as we had done in Elmira and Memphis. This limited the number of health outcomes we could examine in this trial. Moreover, as in Memphis, the rate of state-verified reports of child abuse and neglect was too low in this population (3–4% for low-income children 0 to 2 years of age) to allow us to use child protective service records to assess the impact of the program on child maltreatment. We therefore focused more of our measurement resources on the early emotional development of the infants and toddlers.

Denver Results for Paraprofessionals

There were no paraprofessional effects on women's prenatal health behavior (e.g., use of tobacco), maternal life-course, or child development, although at

24 months, paraprofessional-visited mother–child pairs in which the mother had low psychological resources interacted more responsively than did control group counterparts. By the time the child reached age 4, mothers and children visited by paraprofessionals, compared to controls, displayed greater sensitivity and responsiveness toward one another and, in those cases in which the mothers had low psychological resources at registration, had home environments that were more supportive of children's early learning (Olds, Robinson, et al., 2004). Children of low-resource women visited by paraprofessionals had better behavioral adaptation during testing than their control group counterparts (99.51 versus 96.66 standardized points, ES = 0.38). Although paraprofessional-visited women did not have statistically significant reductions in the rates of subsequent pregnancy, the reductions observed were clinically significant.

Denver Results for Nurses

The nurses produced effects consistent with those achieved in earlier trials of the program.

Prenatal Health Behaviors

In contrast to their control group counterparts, nurse-visited smokers had greater reductions in urine cotinine (i.e., the major nicotine metabolite) from intake to the end of pregnancy.

Sensitive, Competent Care of Child

During the first 24 months of the child's life, nurse-visited mother–infant dyads interacted more responsively than did control pairs, an effect concentrated in the low-resource group.

Child Neurodevelopmental Impairment

At 6 months of age, nurse-visited infants, in contrast to control group counterparts, were less likely to exhibit emotional vulnerability in response to fear stimuli, and those born to women with low psychological resources were less likely to display low emotional vitality in response to joy and anger stimuli. At 21 months, nurse-visited children were less likely to exhibit language delays than were children in the control group (6% versus 12%, OR = 0.48), an effect again concentrated among children born to mothers with low psychological resources (7% versus 18%, OR = 0.32). Nurse-visited 24-month-olds born to women with low psychological resources also had superior language and mental development in contrast to control group counterparts (101.52 versus 96.85 and 90.18 versus 86.20, respectively). At age 4, nurse-visited children whose mothers had low psychological resources at registration, compared to control group counterparts, had more advanced language skills (91.39 versus 86.72 points, ES = 0.31), superior executive functioning (100.16 versus

95.48 standard score points, ES = 0.47), and better behavioral adaptation during testing (100.41 versus 96.66 standard score points, ES = 0.38) (Olds, Robinson, et al., 2004).

Early Maternal Life-Course

By 24 months after delivery, nurse-visited women, compared to controls, were less likely to have had a subsequent pregnancy (29% versus 41%, OR = 0.60) and birth (12% versus 19%, OR = 0.58) and had longer intervals until the next conception. Women visited by nurses were employed longer during the second year following the birth of their first child than were controls (6.87 versus 5.73 months). By the time their first child reached age 4, nurse-visited women continued to have greater intervals between the birth of their first and second children (24.51 versus 20.39 months, ES = 0.32) and less domestic violence (6.9% versus 13.6%, OR = 0.47), and they enrolled their children less frequently in either preschool, Head Start, or licensed day care than did controls (54.4% versus 65.9%, OR = 0.62) (Olds, Robinson, et al., 2004).

Estimates of Nurse Versus Paraprofessional Effects

While the program was in operation, for most outcomes on which there was an effect, paraprofessionals produced effects for children that were approximately half the size of those produced by nurses.

SUMMARY OF RESULTS, POLICY IMPLICATIONS, AND PROGRAM REPLICATION

Policy Implications

One of the clearest messages that has emerged from this program of research is that the functional and economic benefits of the nurse home-visitation program are greatest for families at greater risk. In the Elmira study, it was evident that most married women and those from higher socioeconomic households managed the care of their children without serious problems and that they were able to avoid lives of welfare dependence, substance abuse, and crime without the assistance of the nurse home visitors. Similarly, their children on average avoided encounters with the criminal justice system. In contrast, low-income, unmarried women and their children in the comparison group were at much greater risk for these problems, and the program was able to avert many of these untoward outcomes for this at-risk population. Cost analyses suggested that the program's cost savings for government are primarily attributable to benefits accruing to this higher risk group. Among families at lower risk, the financial investment in the program was a loss. This pattern of results challenges the position that these kinds of intensive programs for targeted at-risk groups ought to be made available on a universal basis. Not only is the practice likely to be wasteful from an economic standpoint, it may also lead to a dilution of services for those families who need them the most, because of insufficient resources to serve everyone well.

During the past decade, new studies have been reported that have led us to doubt the effectiveness of home-visitation programs that do not adhere to the elements of the model studied in these trials (Gomby, Culross, & Behrman, 1999; Olds, Hill, Robinson, Song, & Little, 2000), including especially the hiring of nurses and the use of carefully constructed program protocols designed to promote adaptive behavior (Olds, Hill, O'Brien, Racine, & Moritz, 2003). These results should give policy makers and practitioners pause as they consider investments in home-visitation programs without careful consideration of program structure, content, methods, and likelihood of success.

Recent cost-benefit analyses of preventive interventions conducted by the Washington State Institute for Public Policy (WSIPP) have extended earlier cost analyses of the Nurse-Family Partnership conducted by the RAND Corporation, which had relied exclusively on the Elmira data to estimate cost savings (Aos, Lieb, Mayfield, Miller, & Pennucci, 2004). The WSIPP analyses, which relied on data from all three trials of the Nurse-Family Partnership, estimated that on a per-family basis, government and society realize a $17,000 return on investment over the life of the child. It is important to note that many of the early childhood interventions examined in the WSIPP analysis failed to realize a return on investment – despite their beginning early in life and, in some cases, despite huge per-child investments in preventive services. Although early interventions have the potential to produce cost savings, policy makers must choose wisely.

Julia Isaacs, formerly with the Congressional Budget Office and now with the Brookings Institution, has recently examined the literature on childhood interventions (Isaacs, 2007). Concluding that America's future economic well-being will benefit from targeted investments designed to ensure that children will have the skills to be productive members of society, she recommended a package of investments over a 5-year period totaling about $133 billion:

- $94 billion for high-quality early childhood education for 3- and 4-year-olds
- $14 billion for nurse home visiting to promote prenatal care and healthy child development
- $17 billion for school reform for programs in high-poverty elementary schools that improve students' basic skills
- $8 billion for programs that reduce the incidence of teenage pregnancy

This kind of bold investment in programs that have strong evidentiary foundations holds the promise to improve the lives of vulnerable children and families and the future life prospects of all of us. Isaacs recommended that a portion of the $14 billion devoted to nurse home visiting be used to conduct research on improving other home-visiting programs that do not yet have the evidentiary foundations that would warrant large public investments.

Replication and Scale-Up of the Nurse-Family Partnership

Even when communities choose to develop programs based on models with good scientific evidence, such programs run the risk of being watered down in the process of being scaled up. So, it is with some apprehension that our team has been working to make the program available for public investment in new communities (Olds et al., 2003). Since 1997, the Nurse-Family Partnership national office has helped new communities develop the program outside of traditional research contexts so that today, the program is operating in 280 counties nationally from 190 local operating sites. State and local governments are securing financial support for the Nurse-Family Partnership (about $4,500 per family per year in 2007 dollars) from existing funding sources, such as Temporary Assistance to Needy Families, Medicaid, the Maternal and Child Health Block Grant, and child-abuse and crime-prevention dollars. Sharing the costs among several government agencies reduces the strain on any one agency's budget but dilutes individual agencies' responsibility for supporting the program, a challenge that exists for many prevention programs (Graycar, 2006).

Each site choosing to implement the Nurse-Family Partnership needs certain capacities to operate and sustain the program with high quality, ideally expanding it gradually to reach a significant portion of the target population. These capacities include having an organization and community that are fully knowledgeable and supportive of the program, a staff that is well trained and supported in the conduct of the program model, and real-time information on implementation of the program and its achievement of benchmarks to guide efforts in continuous quality improvement. Staff members at the NFP national office are organized to help build these state and local capacities. Information on implementation of the program in community settings is used to improve its performance and the method of replicating it throughout the country.

Yet, it is not sufficient to have evidence that a program model has the potential to improve the lives of children and families. We must invest a corresponding effort in rigorous methods of program replication so we can have assurance that evidence-based models are well implemented in community practice. Doing so will help ensure that the promise of investing in early childhood interventions is realized.

REFERENCES

Aos, S., Lieb, R., Mayfield, J., Miller, M., & Pennucci, A. (2004). *Benefits and costs of prevention and early intervention programs for youth.* Olympia, WA: Washington State Institute for Public Policy.

Aytaclar, S., Tarter, R. E., Kirisci, L., & Lu, S. (1999). Association between hyperactivity and executive cognitive functioning in childhood and substance use in early adolescence. *Journal of the American Academy of Child and Adolescent Psychiatry, 38*(2), 172–178.

Bakan, D. (1971). *Slaughter of the innocents: A study of the battered child phenomenon.* San Francisco: Jossey-Bass.

Bandura, A. (1977). Self-efficacy: Toward a unifying theory of behavioral change. *Psychological Review, 84*(2), 191–215.

Barnard, K. E. (1990). *Keys to caregiving.* Seattle: University of Washington Press.

Baumrind, D. (1987). *Familial antecedents of adolescent drug use: A developmental perspective* (National Institute of Drug Abuse Monograph 56, DHHS Publication No. ADM 87–1335). Washington, DC: U.S. Government Printing Office.

Belsky, J. (1981). Early human experience: A family perspective. *Developmental Psychology, 17,* 3–23.

Bowlby, J. (1969). *Attachment and loss: Vol. 1. Attachment.* New York: Basic Books.

Boyle, M. H., Offord, D. R., Racine, Y. A., Szatmari, P., Fleming, J. E., & Links, P. S. (1992). Predicting substance use in late adolescence: Results from the Ontario Child Health Study follow-up. *American Journal of Psychiatry, 149*(6), 761–767.

Brafford, L. J., & Beck, K. H. (1991). Development and validation of a condom self-efficacy scale for college students. *Journal of American Collage Health, 39*(5), 219–225.

Bremner, J. D. (1999). Does stress damage the brain? *Biological Psychiatry, 45*(7), 797–805.

Bremner, J. D., & Vermetten, E. (2004). Neuroanatomical changes associated with pharmacotherapy in posttraumatic stress disorder. *Annals of the New York Academy of Sciences, 1032,* 154–157.

Brennan, P. A., Grekin, E. R., & Mednick, S. A. (1999). Maternal smoking during pregnancy and adult male criminal outcomes. *Archives of General Psychiatry, 56*(3), 215–219.

Bronfenbrenner, U. (1979). *The ecology of human development: Experiments by nature and design.* Cambridge, MA: Harvard University Press.

Bronfenbrenner, U. (1995). Developmental ecology through space and time: A future perspective. In P. Moen, G. H. J. Elder, & K. Luscher (Eds.), *Examining lives in context* (pp. 619–647). Washington, DC: American Psychological Association.

Buchsbaum, H. K., Toth, S. L., Clyman, R. B., Cicchetti, D., & Emde, R. N. (1992). The use of a narrative story stem technique with maltreated children: Implications for theory and practice. *Development and Psychopathology, 4,* 603–625.

Clark, A. S., Soto, S., & Bergholz, T. S. M. (1996). Maternal gestational stress alters adaptive and social behavior in adolescent rhesus monkey offspring. *Infant Behavior and Development, 19,* 453–463.

Clark, D. B., & Cornelius, J. (2004). Childhood psychopathology and adolescent cigarette smoking: A prospective survival analysis in children at high risk for substance use disorders. *Addictive Behaviors, 29*(4), 837–841.

Clark, D. B., Cornelius, J. R., Kirisci, L., & Tarter, R. E. (2005). Childhood risk categories for adolescent substance involvement: A general liability typology. *Drug and Alcohol Dependence, 77*(1), 13–21.

Clark, D. B., Pollock, N., Bukstein, O. G., Mezzich, A. C., Bromberger, J. T., & Donovan, J. E. (1997). Gender and comorbid psychopathology in adolescents with alcohol dependence. *Journal of the American Academy of Child and Adolescent Psychiatry, 36*(9), 1195–1203.

DiScala, C., Lescohier, I., Barthel, M., & Li, G. (1998). Injuries to children with attention deficit hyperactivity disorder. *Pediatrics, 102*(6), 1415–1421.

Dodge, K. A., Bates, J. E., & Pettit, G. S. (1990). Mechanisms in the cycle of violence. *Science, 250*(4988), 1678–1683.

Dolezol, S., & Butterfield, P. M. (1994). *Partners in parenting education.* Denver, CO: How to Read Your Baby.

Egeland, B., Jacobvitz, D., & Sroufe, L. A. (1988). Breaking the cycle of abuse. *Child Development, 59*(4), 1080–1088.

Elster, A. B., & McAnarney, E. R. (1980). Medical and psychosocial risks of pregnancy and childbearing during adolescence. *Pediatric Annals, 9*(3), 89–94.

Emde, R. N., & Buchsbaum, H. K. (1990). "Didn't you hear my mommy?": Autonomy with connectedness in moral self-emergence. In D. Cicchetti & M. Beeghley (Eds.), *The self in transition: Infancy to childhood* (pp. 35–60). Chicago: University of Chicago Press.

Fried, P. A., Watkinson, B., Dillon, R. F., & Dulberg, C. S. (1987). Neonatal neurological status in a low-risk population after prenatal exposure to cigarettes, marijuana, and alcohol. *Journal of Developmental and Behavioral Pediatrics, 8*(6), 318–326.

Furstenberg, F. F., Brooks-Gunn, J., & Morgan, S. P. (1987). *Adolescent mothers in later life.* Cambridge: Cambridge University Press.

Garbarino, J. (1981). An ecological perspective on child maltreatment. In L. Pelton (Ed.), *The social context of child abuse and neglect* (pp. 228–267). New York: Human Sciences Press.

Gil, D. (1970). *Violence against children: Physical child abuse in the United States.* Cambridge, MA: Harvard University Press.

Gomby, D. S., Culross, P. L., & Behrman, R. E. (1999). Home visiting: Recent program evaluations – analysis and recommendations. *Future Child, 9*(1), 4–26, 195–223.

Grant, K. E., O'Koon, J. H., Davis, T. H., Roache, N. A., Poindexter, L. M., Armstrong, M. L., et al. (2000). Protective factors affecting low-income urban African American youth exposed to stress. *Journal of Early Adolescence, 20*, 388–417.

Graycar, A. (2006, July–September). Public policy: Core business and by-products. *Public Administration Today*, 6–10.

Hart, B., & Risley, T. R. (1995). *Meaningful differences in the everyday experience of young American children.* Baltimore, MD: Brookes.

Heinrich, L. B. (1993). Contraceptive self-efficacy in college women. *Journal of Adolescent Health, 14*(4), 269–276.

Institute of Medicine. (1990). *Nutrition during pregnancy.* Washington, DC: National Academy Press.

Isaacs, J. B. (2007). *Cost-effective investments in children.* Washington, DC: Brookings Institution.

Jaffee, S. R., Moffitt, T. E., Caspi, A., Fombonne, E., Poulton, R., & Martin, J. (2002). Differences in early childhood risk factors for juvenile-onset and adult-onset depression. *Archives of General Psychiatry, 59*(3), 215–222.

Karoly, L. A., Greenwood, P. W., Everingham, S. S., Hoube, J., Kilburn, M. R., Rydell, C. P., et al. (1998). *Investing in our children: What we know and don't know about the costs and benefits of early childhood interventions.* Santa Monica, CA: RAND.

Kempe, C. H. (1973). A practical approach to the protection of the abused child and rehabilitation of the abusing parent. *Pediatrics, 51*(Suppl. 4), 804–812.

Kitzman, H., Olds, D. L., Henderson, C. R., Jr., Hanks, C., Cole, R., Tatelbaum, R., et al. (1997). Effect of prenatal and infancy home visitation by nurses on pregnancy outcomes, childhood injuries, and repeated childbearing: A randomized controlled trial. *Journal of the American Medical Association, 278*(8), 644–652.

Kitzman, H., Olds, D. L., Sidora, K., Henderson, C. R., Jr., Hanks, C., Cole, R., et al. (2000). Enduring effects of nurse home visitation on maternal life course: A 3-year follow-up of a randomized trial. *Journal of the American Medical Association, 283*, 1983–1989. PMID10789666.

Klein, L., & Goldenberg, R. L. (1990). Prenatal care and its effect on preterm birth and low birthweight. In I. R. Merkatz & J. E. Thompson (Eds.), *New perspectives on prenatal care* (pp. 501–529). New York: Elsevier.

Kramer, M. S. (1987). Intrauterine growth and gestational duration determinants. *Pediatrics, 80*(4), 502–511.

Levinson, R. A. (1986). Contraceptive self-efficacy: A perspective on teenage girls' contraceptive behavior. *Journal of Sex Research, 22*, 347–369.

Lynskey, M. T., Heath, A. C., Bucholz, K. K., Slutske, W. S., Madden, P. A., Nelson, E. C., et al. (2003). Escalation of drug use in early-onset cannabis users vs. co-twin controls. *Journal of the American Medical Association, 289*(4), 427–433.

Main, M., Kaplan, N., & Cassidy, J. (1985). Security in infancy, childhood, and adulthood: A move to the level of representation. *Monographs of the Society for Research in Child Development, 50*(1–2, Serial No. 209), 66–104.

Mayes, L. C. (1994). Neurobiology of prenatal cocaine exposure: Effect on developing monoamine systems. *Infant Mental Health Journal, 15*, 121–133.

McLanahan, S. S., & Carlson, M. J. (2002). Welfare reform, fertility, and father involvement. *Future Child, 12*(1), 146–165.

Milberger, S., Biederman, J., Faraone, S. V., Chen, L., & Jones, J. (1996). Is maternal smoking during pregnancy a risk factor for attention deficit hyperactivity disorder in children? *American Journal of Psychiatry, 153*(9), 1138–1142.

Moffitt, T. E. (1993). Adolescence-limited and life-course-persistent antisocial behavior: A developmental taxonomy. *Psychological Review, 100*(4), 674–701.

Musick, J. S. (1993). *Young, poor, and pregnant.* New Haven, CT: Yale University Press.

Newberger, C. M., & White, K. M. (1989). Cognitive foundations for parental care. In D. Cicchetti & V. Carlson (Eds.), *Child maltreatment: Theory and research on the causes and consequences of child abuse and neglect* (pp. 302–316). Cambridge: Cambridge University Press.

Nurse-Family Partnership. (2006). *Interview with Dr. David Olds.* Retrieved from http://www.nursefamilypartnership.org/resources/files/PDF/DavidOldsinterview1–24-06.pdf.

Olds, D. L. (1997). Tobacco exposure and impaired development: A review of the evidence. *Mental Retardation and Developmental Disabilities Research Reviews, 3*, 257–269.

Olds, D. L., Eckenrode, J., Henderson, C. R., Jr., Kitzman, H., Powers, J., Cole, R., et al. (1997). Long-term effects of home visitation on maternal life-course and child abuse and neglect: Fifteen-year follow-up of a randomized trial. *Journal of the American Medical Association, 278*(8), 637–643.

Olds, D. L., & Henderson, C. R. J. (1989). The prevention of maltreatment. In D. Cicchetti & V. Carlson, (Eds.), *Child maltreatment: Theory and research on the causes and consequences of child abuse and neglect* (pp. 722–763). Cambridge: Cambridge University Press.

Olds, D. L., Henderson, C. R., Jr., Chamberlin, R., & Tatelbaum, R. (1986). Preventing child abuse and neglect: A randomized trial of nurse home visitation. *Pediatrics, 78*(1), 65–78.

Olds, D. L., Henderson, C. R., Jr., Cole, R., Eckenrode, J., Kitzman, H., Luckey, D., et al. (1998). Long-term effects of nurse home visitation on children's criminal and antisocial behavior: 15-year follow-up of a randomized controlled trial. *Journal of the American Medical Association, 280*(14), 1238–1244.

Olds, D. L., Henderson, C. R., Jr., & Kitzman, H. (1994). Does prenatal and infancy nurse home visitation have enduring effects on qualities of parental caregiving and child health at 25 to 50 months of life? *Pediatrics, 93*(1), 89–98.

Olds, D., Henderson, C. R., Jr., Kitzman, H., & Cole, R. (1995). Effects of prenatal and infancy nurse home visitation on surveillance of child maltreatment. *Pediatrics, 95*(3), 365–372.

Olds, D. L., Henderson, C. R., Jr., & Tatelbaum, R. (1994a). Intellectual impairment in children of women who smoke cigarettes during pregnancy. *Pediatrics, 93*(2), 221–227.

Olds, D. L., Henderson, C. R., Jr., & Tatelbaum, R. (1994b). Prevention of intellectual impairment in children of women who smoke cigarettes during pregnancy. *Pediatrics, 93*(2), 228–233.

Olds, D. L., Henderson, C. R., Jr., Tatelbaum, R., & Chamberlin, R. (1986). Improving the delivery of prenatal care and outcomes of pregnancy: A randomized trial of nurse home visitation. *Pediatrics, 77*(1), 16–28.

Olds, D. L., Henderson, C. R., Jr., Tatelbaum, R., & Chamberlin, R. (1988). Improving the life-course development of socially disadvantaged mothers: A randomized trial of nurse home visitation. *American Journal of Public Health, 78*(11), 1436–1445.

Olds, D. L., Hill, P. L., O'Brien, R., Racine, D., & Moritz, P. (2003). Taking preventive intervention to scale: The Nurse-Family Partnership. *Cognitive and Behavioral Practice, 10*(4), 278–290.

Olds, D. L., Hill, P., Robinson, J., Song, N., & Little, C. (2000). Update on home visiting for pregnant women and parents of young children. *Current Problems in Pediatrics, 30*(4), 107–141.

Olds, D. L., & Kitzman, H. (1993). Review of research on home visiting for pregnant women and parents of young children. *Future of Children, 3*(3), 53–92.

Olds, D. L., Kitzman, H., Cole, R., Robinson, J., Sidora, K., Luckey, D., et al. (2004). Effects of nurse home visiting on maternal life-course and child development: Age-six follow-up of a randomized trial. *Pediatrics, 114*, 1550–1559.

Olds, D. L., Kitzman, H., Hanks, C., Cole, R., Anson, E., Sidora-Arcoleo, K., et al. (2007). Effects of nurse home visiting on maternal and child functioning: Age-9 follow-up of a randomized trial. *Pediatrics, 120*(4), e832–845.

Olds, D., Pettitt, L., Robinson, J., Eckenrode, J., Kitzman, H., Cole, R., et al. (1998). Reducing risks for antisocial behavior with a program of prenatal and early childhood home visitation. *Journal of Community Psychology, 26*, 65–83.

Olds, D. L., Robinson, J., Pettitt, L., Luckey, D. W., Holmberg, J., Ng, R. K., et al. (2004). Effects of home visits by paraprofessionals and by nurses: Age-four follow-up of a randomized trial. *Pediatrics, 114*, 1560–1568.

Overpeck, M. D., Brenner, R. A., Trumble, A. C., Trifiletti, L. B., & Berendes, H. W. (1998). Risk factors for infant homicide in the United States. *New England Journal of Medicine, 339*(17), 1211–1216.

Peterson, L., & Gable, S. (1998). Holistic injury prevention. In J. R. Lutzker (Ed.), *Handbook of child abuse research and treatment* (pp. 291–318). New York: Plenum.

Pine, D. S. (2001). Affective neuroscience and the development of social anxiety disorder. *Psychiatric Clinics of North America, 24*(4), 689–705.

Pine, D. S. (2003). Developmental psychobiology and response to threats: Relevance to trauma in children and adolescents. *Biological Psychiatry, 53*(9), 796–808.

Plomin, R. (1986). *Development, genetics, and psychology*. Hillsdale, NJ: Erlbaum.

Quinton, D., & Rutter, M. (1984). Parents with children in care – II. Intergenerational continuities. *Journal of Child Psychology and Psychiatry, 25*(2), 231–250.

Raine, A., Brennan, P., & Mednick, S. A. (1994). Birth complications combined with early maternal rejection at age 1 year predispose to violent crime at age 18 years. *Archives of General Psychiatry, 51*(12), 984–988.

Ridenour, T. A., Cottler, L. B., Robins, L. N., Compton, W. M., Spitznagel, E. L., & Cunningham-Williams, R. M. (2002). Test of the plausibility of adolescent substance use playing a causal role in developing adulthood antisocial behavior. *Journal of Abnormal Psychology, 111*(1), 144–155.

Rutter, M. (1989). Intergenerational continuities and discontinuities in serious parenting difficulties. In D. Cicchetti & V. Carlson (Eds.), *Child maltreatment: Theory and research on the causes and consequences of child abuse and neglect* (pp. 315–348). Cambridge: Cambridge University Press.

Sameroff, A. J. (1983). Parental views of child development. In R. A. Hoekelman (Ed.), *A round-table on minimizing high-risk parenting* (pp. 31–45). Media, PA: Harwal.

Saxon, D. W. (1978). The behavior of infants whose mothers smoke in pregnancy. *Early Human Development, 2*, 363–369.

Streissguth, A. P., Sampson, P. D., Barr, H. M., Bookstein, F. L., & Olson, H. C. (1994). The effects of prenatal exposure to alcohol and tobacco: Contributions from the Seattle longitudinal prospective study and implications for public policy. In H. L. Needleman & D. Bellinger (Eds.), *Prenatal exposure to toxicants: Developmental consequences* (pp. 148–183). Baltimore, MD: Johns Hopkins University Press.

Teicher, M. H. (2000). Wounds that time won't heal: The neurobiology of child abuse. *Cerebrum, 2*(4), 50–67.

Tygart, C. E. (1991). Juvenile delinquency and number of children in a family: Some empirical and theoretical updates. *Youth and Society, 22*, 525–536.

Wakschlag, L. S., Lahey, B. B., Loeber, R., Green, S. M., Gordon, R. A., & Leventhal, B. L. (1997). Maternal smoking during pregnancy and the risk of conduct disorder in boys. *Archives of General Psychiatry, 54*(7), 670–676.

4

Carolina Abecedarian Project

FRANCES A. CAMPBELL AND CRAIG T. RAMEY

HISTORY OF THE PROGRAM/POLICY

The Abecedarian study was designed to learn the extent to which an early childhood intervention program might prevent progressive developmental retardation among children born into poverty. Forty years ago, cross-sectional examinations of the cognitive development of children from poor families indicated that their cognitive test scores tended to be within the average range in infancy, but that disproportionate declines occurred after that period (Ramey, 1971). A particularly striking cross-sectional graph charted this kind of progressive decline in intellectual test performance among children born to mothers who themselves had low IQs (Heber, Dever, & Conry, 1968). Because at that time no biologically based etiology for most cases of mild retardation had been identified, many scientists believed that early "social deprivation or environmental deprivation" was implicated in the development of this condition. It followed that intervening to improve the intellectual stimulus value of the environment might prevent or ameliorate the disorder.

Largely based on animal research, evidence mounted that early experience supported development in ways that were critical for later functioning (e.g., Hunt, 1961). More to the point, this line of reasoning was supported by human-subject research conducted by Skeels and his colleagues (1938) in which one group of infants reared within institutions showed dramatic gains in developmental abilities when they were given the kinds of affectionate attention and handling not experienced by others from the same orphanage. Gray, Ramsey, and Klaus (1982) described how this groundbreaking research was dismissed at the time because of the strong belief that intelligence was a fixed, inborn capacity and not malleable. Starkly contradicting that belief and supporting what Skeels and his colleagues had found was the dramatic boost in intellectual test performance reported by the investigators of the Milwaukee Project (Garber, 1988). This program enrolled children born to mothers with IQs of 75 or lower. One group of infants had intensive early childhood intervention from infancy through their kindergarten year. Contrasted with a comparison group of children born to similar mothers, the treated children displayed approximately a 20-point IQ advantage during the preschool years. Hence, there was good reason to believe that intensive early childhood intervention that began very early in the life span might make a dramatic difference in the intellectual development of children at risk.

Finally, a crucial impetus for beginning intervention early in the life span was the first experience with Head Start, initially designed as a short-term program to prepare 4-year-olds from poor families for school success. Many perceived this program to be a failure when an early evaluation found that no lasting benefits were detectable after 3 years in school (Cicirelli, 1969). The scientific community therefore needed more well-controlled research to learn what kinds of intellectual gains could be achieved if intervention began in early infancy. The Abecedarian study provided a randomized controlled trial designed to address this question.

Two major theoretical positions underlay the study: Ramey, MacPhee, and Yeates (1982) suggested that "a variation" on general systems theory (Bertalanffy, 1975) helps explain how a child's development is the product of a system of units that interact with one another, are linked across time, differ in complexity and in stability, and mutually regulate one another. The young child is an "active organism" that continually adapts in the face of changing demands, and the child herself or himself constitutes some of those demands. Rather than a "true" theory that can predict with precision, this system is a "perspective or paradigm in which the many components of the system interact to produce strong, synergistic effects" (Ramey et al., 1982, p. 353). Bronfenbrenner's ecological theories (Bronfenbrenner, 1986) have also influenced the thinking of the Abecedarian investigators in their effort to understand how the particular segment of the population that they undertook to study – children born into poverty – might develop within the various contexts of their families, their child care settings, their schools, and their communities.

DESCRIPTION OF THE PROGRAM

The Abecedarian study was funded through a federal grant from the Mental Retardation and Developmental Disabilities Branch of the National Institutes of Health. Based on the argument that convincing proof was lacking that "environmental deprivation" was a major cause of developmental delays or even mild mental retardation, Craig Ramey and Joe Sparling convinced the agency to fund a trial of what could be achieved through intentional education that began in early infancy. Over the years, in addition to major program project grants from the National Institute of Child Health and Human Development (NICHD), funding from the State of North Carolina, the Spencer and Carnegie foundations, and the Department of Education helped support the work. Rather than a dramatic manipulation of the early environment, the experimental treatment was designed to be carried out within a natural setting then (and now) being experienced by an increasing number of infants, namely full-time out-of-home child care. Situated within North Carolina, where the 1970 Census indicated that 20% of the population had incomes below the federal poverty line and where the poverty percentage for minority individuals was higher still, the study was designed to take advantage of the critical shortage of full-time child care for infants while at the same time providing a well-controlled scientific study of the degree to which children's development might be enhanced through early intervention. (The other three investigators on the original grant were all pediatricians. Important research on the health of young children in group care settings was also done within the same child care setting.) The actual cost of mounting the intervention program was significantly subsidized because it was housed within a University of North Carolina research building. Having the use of this facility plus the grant funds that covered the cost of program staff and research personnel meant that the program was essentially free to participants.

The design called for four cohorts of infants to enter the study, each to consist of 28 children, for a total of 112. Half were to be given the full-time child care program, and the other half were untreated controls. The child care program was housed within the Frank Porter Graham Child Development Center (now Institute); its nursery could accommodate 14 infants. The other 14 of a given cohort thus served as untreated controls. The children were admitted in four cohorts between the fall of 1972 and the late summer of 1977.

Prospective families were identified by local agencies serving pregnant women and young children, primarily prenatal clinics or the Department of Social Services. Professionals at these sites acquainted women with the possibility of enrolling in the study; those who expressed interest were then identified to study personnel, who set up home visits to screen for eligibility. Screening was based on the study's High-Risk Index that contained such socio-demographic factors as parental education, family income, use of welfare funds, evidence of academic failure in other family members, and other indications of problems within the family (Ramey & Smith, 1977). Those who appeared qualified then came into the Center for further interviewing and a full-scale IQ test, following which a final determination of eligibility was made.

In all, 123 families were invited to enroll; 89% eventually did so. More families declined the early child care program than declined the control group; not every family sought full-time child care for its infant. Table 4.1 describes the families who enrolled in the program and whose child, if in the treated group, attended for any length of time.

Parents were invited to enroll in the study with the understanding that they had a 50:50 chance of being in the treatment group or an untreated control group. Ultimately, 109 families, to whom 111 children were born, accepted their

Table 4.1. *Entry demographic characteristics for families in Abecedarian Study by preschool group*

	Preschool Group		
	Treated	Control	Total
Demographic measure	(*N*=55)	(*N*=54)	(*N*=109)
Maternal age (years)			
M	19.6	20.3	19.9
SD	3.9	5.8	4.9
Maternal education (years)			
M	10.4	10.0	10.2
SD	1.8	1.9	1.8
Maternal Full Scale IQ (WAIS)			
M	85.5	84.2	84.8
SD	12.4	10.8	11.6
Percent two-parent family	23	26	24
Percent African American family	96	100	98
Percent male child	51	43	47

random assignments (one set of identical twins, one sibling pair). This group comprised the base sample for the study, with 57 of the children randomly assigned to the treated group and 54 in the control group. All families were low income, most were female-headed households, and 98% of the sample was African American. Approximately half the mothers were teenagers (defined as younger than 20 years old, range of 13 to 44 years). Children could begin attending the Center as young as 6 weeks of age; the mean age at entry was 4.4 months, with a range of 6 weeks to 6 months at entry age.

The Center operated full days, 5 days per week, year-round except for vacation and holiday closings. The children were provided a warm, secure, and contingently stimulating environment in which each had an individualized program of learning activities. The children had breakfast, lunch, and a snack during the day as well.

The curriculum, developed by Joseph Sparling and Isabel Lewis, was individually implemented for each baby. In describing the development of this curriculum, an early grant application noted that its underlying assumption was not that "sensory deprivation (was) the major cause of developmental retardation . . . but rather that the child received vague or competing sensory messages which (were) useless to him at the moment." Thus, the developers saw their task as "(1) designing an organized resource bank of unambiguous experiences or activities and (2) making each activity available to the child at a time and in a way that she can successfully use and master it." These activities were designed to enhance perceptual-motor, cognitive, language, and social development. They involved simple, age-appropriate, adult–child interactions such as talking to an infant, showing him or her toys or pictures, and offering infants a chance to react to sights or sounds in the environment. As children grew, the educational content became more conceptual and skill based. Language development was emphasized. However, children always had freedom to choose activities, and the focus on individual development was paramount throughout. The educational materials were given the name Learningames and were eventually published in two volumes: one covered games for children up to 36 months of age (Sparling & Lewis, 1979), and the second contained games for 3- and 4-year-old children (Sparling & Lewis, 1984). Updated versions of this curriculum are now available (e.g., Sparling & Lewis, 2007). Other preschool curricula for pre-reading and mathematics skills were utilized as children were old enough. Teachers were also extensively trained in ways to enhance sociolinguistic skills (Ramey, McGinness, Cross, Collier & Barrie-Blackley, 1982).

In addition to providing children with an intentional curriculum that was applied throughout the day as the infants were receptive, the Center had other noteworthy features. Coincidentally with the psychological and educational stimulation that was offered, the health of the children in the group care was carefully monitored, and a large body of research, especially on communicable upper respiratory disease, grew out of the study. The children had primary pediatric care on-site, with a full-time nurse practitioner and a medical aide based at the center. Several pediatricians were also involved. A second feature of the treatment program was its proactive nature; station wagons equipped with child safety seats went throughout the neighborhoods to collect the treated infants, toddlers, and preschoolers and to take them home again in the evenings.

To control for the possibility that any developmental gains seen in the treated children were actually because they had better nutrition at the Center, children in the control group were offered free iron-fortified formula for the first 15 months of life, the period of most rapid brain growth. An additional (and very popular) incentive for families in the control group was a supply of free disposable diapers until the child was trained.

A standard protocol of individual assessments was used for the children in both groups, administered by a person independent of the design or provision of the treatment program. To ensure that the child care staff did not teach children how to do the tasks from the standardized instruments, parents were required to be present on all testing occasions. Caregivers were not allowed to accompany children. Appointments and transportation, if necessary for these assessments, were made by the evaluators, not the child care providers. They assessed infants using the Bayley Scales (Bayley, 1969) at 3, 6, 9, 12, and 18 months of age; the Stanford Binet Form LM (1962 version; Terman & Merrill, 1972) at 24, 36, and 48 months; the McCarthy Scales (McCarthy, 1972) at 30, 42, and 54 months; and the age-appropriate version of the Wechsler Preschool and Primary Scale of Intelligence (Wechsler, 1967) at 60 months. In addition, studies of mother–infant interaction were carried out on a regular basis in an effort to learn if this kind of full-time treatment had discernible effects of how

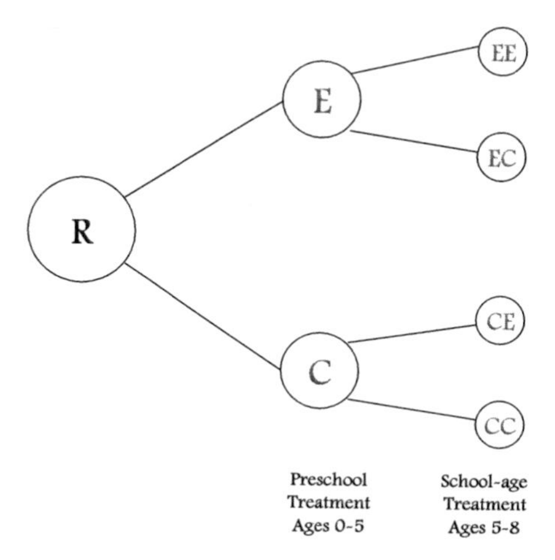

Figure 4.1. Preschool and school-age program. EE = experimental/experimental (treatment in preschool and school-age); EC = experimental/control (treatment in preschool phase only); CE = control/experimental (treatment in school-age phase only); CC = control/control (no treatment in either phase).

the children related to their mothers. Researchers also carried out basic studies on the ways that infants reacted to stimuli.

School-Age Treatment Phase

When children were old enough to enter public school (kindergarten at age 5), the children within the preschool treatment and control groups were re-randomized by matching pairs within groups as closely as possible on their 48-month Stanford-Binet score and then randomly assigning one of each pair to a school-age treatment or control group. Figure 4.1 depicts the study model for the preschool and school-age phases of the work.

Those assigned to treatment during the school-age phase had the services of a home school resource teacher (HST) for the first 3 years they attended public school (kindergarten to Grade 2, unless retained at some point). The HSTs made alternating visits to each child's classroom and home. At school, they consulted with the teacher to learn which concepts were being taught and to identify areas where the child might need extra help. They then designed customized learning activities for parents to use at home to help the child grasp the concept. These activities were designed to be fun, so that children and parents would enjoy the time devoted to their use, but they also taught basic concepts underlying reading and mathematics. Activity packets were delivered to the home on alternating weeks. HSTs were also expected to function as advocates for families within the community to help them secure any services they might need such as help with housing, child care, and health care. The variety of activities they carried out was impressive, ranging from securing emergency food to setting up play dates and accompanying a socially isolated child and his custodial grandmother to the playground, where he could spend extra time with children his own age.

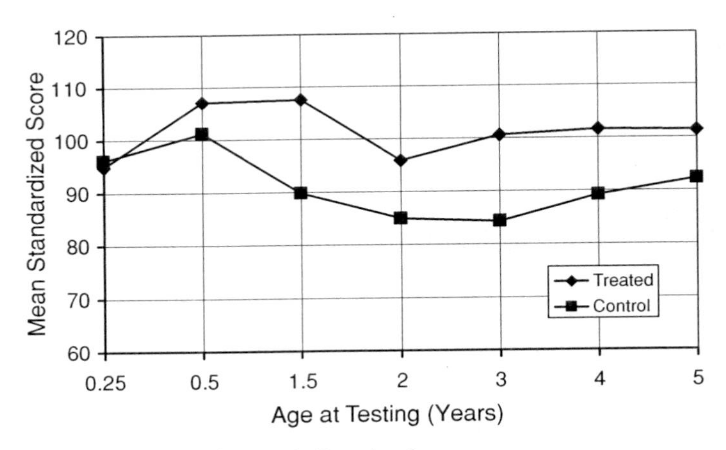

Figure 4.2. Preschool test scores.

MAJOR FINDINGS

Short-Term Effects

Figure 4.2 depicts preschool cognitive growth trajectories for children from infancy through age 5. The infants in the treated and control groups appeared to be at the same developmental level in early infancy but began to diverge by 6 months of age. By 18 months of age, those in the treatment group scored significantly higher on tests of infant–toddler development. Thereafter, during the remaining preschool years, the treated group maintained a significant advantage over the control group in standardized intellectual test scores (Ramey & Campbell, 1984). As Figure 4.2 shows, however, the control group showed a gradual rise in scores after the age of 3 years, a trend likely related to the fact that the children in this group were beginning to attend other preschool programs in the area (Burchinal, Lee, & Ramey, 1989).

Six children were lost to early attrition because of death (4), an undiscovered biological condition that rendered the child ineligible (1), or permanent withdrawal from the program (1). Nine children moved away from the area prior to age 4, and another withdrew from participation; thus, they had no 48-month IQ and could not be given a school-age assignment. In all, 96 children were given school-age assignments and could potentially contribute data for an analysis of school-age findings. However, further mobility among participants resulted in there being only 90 who contributed IQ data and 88 with academic test scores at the treatment endpoint (age 8).

After the children entered public school, standardized tests of reading and mathematics achievement were administered in the fall and spring of each of the first 3 years. Children were also administered the Wechsler Intelligence Scale for Children-Revised (Wechsler, 1978) at age 6½ and 8 years. At this point,

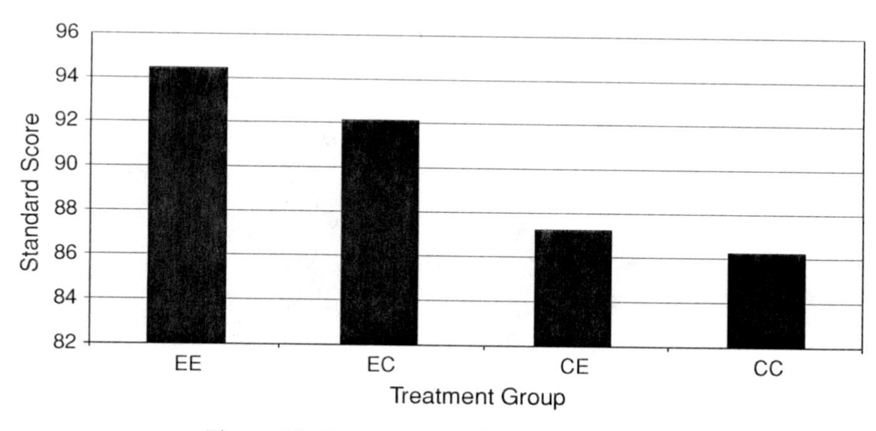

Figure 4.3. Four-group reading scores at age 8.

data were analyzed according to the four-group assignment of the children. The school-age phase of treatment seemed to have no effect on intellectual test score performance. A multivariate analysis of variance for repeated measures tested the effect of preschool and school-age intervention on the three Wechsler IQ data points (age 5, 6½, and 8 years), plus the interaction between the two phases. The results showed a significant difference for preschool treatment across this time period, but no effect for the school-age phase and no interaction. A linear trend downward (approximately a 2-point IQ drop from age 5 to age 8) was seen in both groups. Because this trend was consistent across the groups, it does not represent a fade-out of the preschool treatment effect (Ramey & Campbell, 1991).

For the first 2 years, the fall and spring achievement tests were the Peabody Individual Achievement Tests (Dunn & Markwardt, 1970); for the third year, the Woodcock-Johnson Psycho-Educational Battery, Part 2, Tests of Academic Achievement was substituted (WJ; Woodcock & Johnson, 1977). These tests were individually administered to the children within their respective schools but by project staff. During the primary years, the local schools also administered standardized tests of reading and mathematics, and these scores were released by parents to the study. Figures 4.3 and 4.4 show the "endpoint" results for the four school-age groups – that is, how they scored on the WJ reading and mathematics subtests at the end of 3 years in school. These scores are age referenced rather than grade referenced because not all children had completed second grade after 3 years in school. As can be seen in the figures, there is a linear trend for the reading scores such that the scores increase perfectly as a function of the number of years of intervention; that is, those with 8 years of intervention outscore those with 5 years only, whereas those with 5 years outscore those with 3 years only, who in turn outscore those with no intervention at all. The same linear trend is apparent for mathematics but, as Figure 4.4 shows, it is not as striking as the trend for reading.

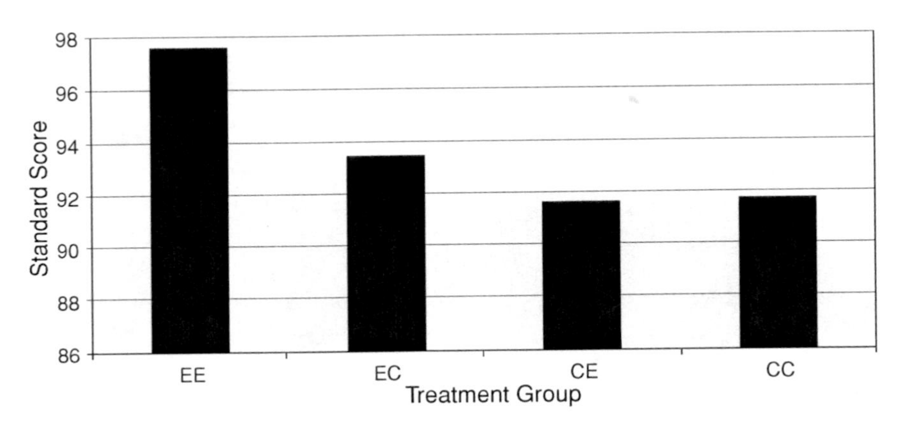

Figure 4.4. Four-group math scores at age 8.

Adaptation to school was assessed through teacher ratings on the Classroom Behavior Inventory (Schaefer, Edgerton, & Aaronson, 1977). These data were somewhat ambiguous with respect to the children's behavior and adjustment within their classrooms. Based on the ratings obtained from teachers in the spring of the child's third year in school, no strong trends were seen. Ratings of Verbal Intelligence tended to increase as a function of years of treatment; that is, children with more years of treatment tended to be rated by teachers as appearing to be brighter. No such trend was seen for ratings of positive social behavior (Considerateness minus Hostility). Data based on the first three cohorts of children who entered primary school indicated that teachers perceived students who had been in the preschool treatment group (disregarding school-age assignments) to be more physically and verbally aggressive than students who had been preschool controls (Haskins, 1985). This trend did not replicate when subsequent cohorts of children from the Abecedarian and its related study, CARE, entered school (Burchinal, Campbell, & Bryant, 1995).

Longer-Term Effects

Early and middle adolescent follow-up studies were conducted after students had attended public school for 7 years (age 12) and, again, after 10 years (age 15). The first of these studies occurred after children should have completed elementary school at sixth grade (this study occurred before the shift to a middle school system). The second took place after they should have finished ninth grade, what was then the transition point to the senior high school. For both of these follow-up studies, the analyses were based on the four-group assignment model, comparing outcomes as a function of preschool treatment, school-age treatment, and the interaction between the two.

For the age-12 follow-up, data were available for 90 children who had received a school-age assignment. In addition, all available children earlier lost to attrition were invited to take part, and 11 of 12 did so.

Intellectual test data were analyzed longitudinally for all available cases with complete data ($n = 83$) using multivariate analysis of variance for repeated measures, with the factors being preschool treatment, school-age treatment, age at testing, and age by treatment interactions. Separate intellectual growth curves were estimated for the four treatment groups. When averaged across ages, preschool treatment, but not school-age treatment, had a significant effect on intellectual test scores. All groups showed linear change across time, with a decline from infancy scores to those at age 12. The preschool treated group maintained its advantage at all points but showed more linear change than the preschool control group, whereas the preschool control group had a more variable pattern of change over time with an upward inflection after age 4 and the same overall decline after age 8.

Academic scores in reading, written language, and knowledge showed linear trends to increase as the number of years of intervention increased, and significant preschool treatment effects, but no significant effect for school-age and no preschool by school-age interactions. In this round of analyses, mother's IQ was entered as a covariate to learn if it affected age-12 intellectual and academic outcomes independently of treatment. Although holding this powerful predictor of child outcomes constant slightly strengthened the preschool treatment effect, essentially it seemed to have affected child outcomes in the same way across treatment groups.

The age-15 follow-up took place after the participants had completed 10 years in school (after ninth grade if they were never retained). For this round of data collection, 92 of the 93 who had some form of school-age treatment took part, plus 12 of the individuals in the early attrition group who lacked a school-age group assignment. The intellectual and academic outcomes at age 15 were essentially the same as at age 12. Higher IQ scores over time were related to preschool treatment (those with either 8 or 5 years of treatment always outscored those with only 3 years or none – $F(1, 80) = 8.92$, $p < .004$). The linear decline that was already detected persisted at the same rate in both early childhood groups. Academic age-referenced test scores for both WJ Reading and Mathematics Clusters showed significant linear trends and significant preschool treatment effects.

Preschool treatment was associated with fewer grade retentions up through age 15. Overall, 31.2% of those with preschool treatment had been retained at some point compared with 54.5% of those in the preschool control group, a statistically significant difference [$\chi^2(1, N = 93) = 5.10$, $p = .02$]. Likewise, those with preschool treatment were less likely to be identified as needing some form of special services (i.e., special help for speech and language delays, learning disabilities, or behavior problems). Of those in the preschool treated group, 24.5% were identified as needing such services compared with 47% of those in the preschool control group, a significant difference [$\chi^2(1, N = 93) = 5.47, p = .02$]. The group least likely to be seen as needing special services was the EC group, which had 5 years of preschool intervention (12%). Being in the most intensely treated group (EE; 8 years in all) made it more, not less, likely that a student would be given special services (36%). Evidently, the HST advocated for the student to be given extra help. However, for those who were in the preschool control group, having a HST neither increased nor decreased the likelihood of their being given special services. The rate of assignment for services was virtually identical (48%) in the CE and CC groups (Campbell & Ramey, 1995).

At age 12 and age 15, students were asked to complete Harter's scholastic competence rating scales (Harter, 1982, 1988). A longitudinal analysis of these scores showed a significant preschool by school-age interaction such that the group that had 3 years of treatment in the primary grades scored highest on this measure and, paradoxically, the group having the full 8 years of treatment scored lower than the group with 5 years only, despite actually having the highest standardized scores on academic measures. Speculatively, the characteristics of the local public schools may have contributed to this outcome: Being located in a university town, local public schools were highly competitive, and "average" performance on standardized tests was generally well above national averages. Thus, the students with most intensive intervention may have expected more of themselves and, in this context, tended to down-rate themselves (Campbell, Pungello, & Miller-Johnson, 2002).

Young Adult Findings

The most recent Abecedarian data were those collected from study participants as young adults, age 21. At this stage of young adulthood, data were available on high school graduation, postsecondary education, job histories, marital status, parenthood, and evidences of social maladjustment such as breaking the law and drug use. These data were collected as close to the 21st birthday as possible, the goal being to assess participants within plus or minus 30 days of their birth date.

At age 21, 105 of the original 111 infants were still living and eligible for follow-up. Of these, all were located and 104 took part (1 declined), giving an overall retention rate of 93.7% of the original infant participants and 99% of those living and eligible at this age. The decision was made at this point to adopt an "intent-to-treat" model in which each participant was classified according to his or her original preschool group assignment rather than the four-group model that took preschool and school-age treatment status into account. This model had two advantages: It increased the number of cases that could contribute data, and it also constituted the most stringent test of the treatment by including as treated all cases so assigned regardless of early attrition.

Data collection at this point consisted of standardized tests: the Wechsler Adult Intelligence Scale-Revised (WAIS-R; Wechsler, 1981) and the Woodcock-Johnson Broad Reading and Broad Math scores (WJ; Woodcock & Johnson, 1989). An interview covered life history to this point, and a battery of self-report psychological scales measured other constructs. These included the Youth Risk Behavior Survey (Centers for Disease Control, 1992), which covers a variety of behaviors associated with injury or illness in young adults (i.e., violence, tobacco use, alcohol, and other controlled-substance use and abuse). Another measure used was the Brief Symptom Inventory (BSI; Derogatis, 1993), a 53-item version of the Symptom Checklist 90 (Derogatis, 1975), a screening measure of mental health.

Long-Term Intellectual Test Score Findings

Intellectual and academic findings from the Abecedarian young adult follow-up are most fully explained in Campbell, Pungello, Miller-Johnson, Burchinal, and Ramey (2001). Tested in isolation, intellectual test scores for Abecedarian participants showed that those with preschool treatment scored significantly higher on Full Scale IQ, $F(1, 100) = 5.71$, $p < .05$, and Verbal IQ, $F(1, 100) = 5.21$, $p < .05$. There was no treatment effect for Performance IQ. Main effects for gender were not found, but the preschool group by gender interaction approached significance for the Verbal IQ score ($p < .10$). Treated females scored about 8 points higher than untreated females, whereas scores for males differed by less than 1 point across treatment and control conditions. Given that most other early-intervention programs in which long-term comparisons were possible have found that significant treatment/control differences in intellectual test performance were not seen beyond a few years in primary school (Lazar, Darlington, Murray, Royce, & Snipper, 1982), the persistence of a treatment effect on IQ scores into young adulthood was not expected.

Figure 4.5 shows the longitudinal function for intellectual test scores from ages 3 to 21 years. These data were analyzed using hierarchical linear modeling (HLM). The polynomial regression model included a term for treatment as a between-subject predictor, a term representing which childhood cognitive test was administered (i.e., the Stanford-Binet administered when the children were 3 and 4 years of age or the Wechsler scales thereafter), linear and quadratic age terms to examine patterns and rates of change over time, another term that represented time of assessment (i.e., younger than age 6 versus older than age 6), and this term's interactions with linear and quadratic age to allow the rate of change to differ between the time period in which children received early treatment and the posttreatment period. The full analysis model included all main effects and all two- and three-way interactions among treatment group,

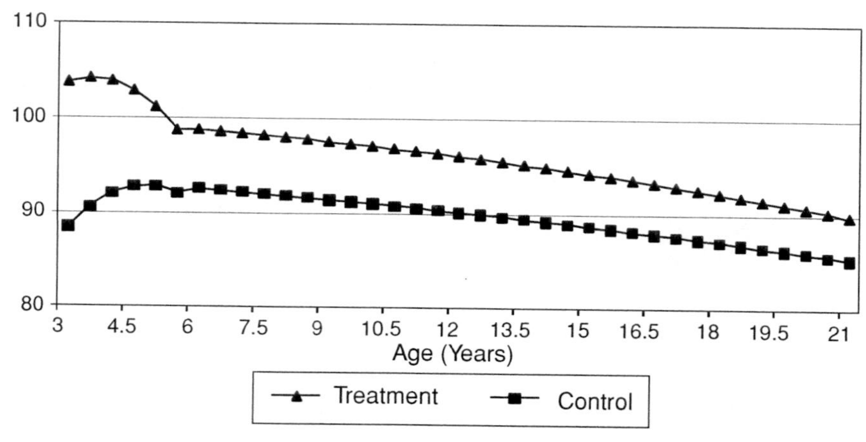

Figure 4.5. Cognitive growth curves as a function of preschool treatment. Copyright © 2001 by the American Psychological Association. Reproduced with permission.

instrument used, timing of assessment, and the linear and quadratic age terms. The model was simplified when higher order interactions were not significant.

Children who received the early educational treatment achieved higher overall IQ scores than children in the control group. Across all subjects, IQ scores showed a linear decline over time. Finally, a significant main effect was found for the test administered, indicating that children tended to score higher on the Stanford-Binet than on the Wechsler scales.

These main effects were qualified by significant higher order interactions. The magnitude of the difference between the treatment and control groups varied as a function of time of assessment (i.e., during treatment versus after treatment). Although the magnitude was greater while treated children were still receiving the intervention, the treatment difference was significant both during the preschool period and in the follow-up period. A significant two-way interaction indicated that across all subjects, more curvature existed during the preschool period than in the post-preschool period. Finally, these two-way interactions were qualified by a significant three-way interaction found for treatment group by time of assessment by linear age. The difference between treated and control groups in linear decline was greater during the preschool period than during the follow-up period, but the groups demonstrated a parallel linear decline in IQ scores in the period after treatment.

Adjusted means and treatment/control effect sizes for cognitive test scores are given in Table 4.2. Two effect sizes were calculated. The first used the pooled sample standard deviation ($SD = 6.30$), given the truncated nature of the sample (compared to the population on which the Wechsler scales were standardized). A more conservative estimate of the effect size was also calculated using the standard deviation of the Wechsler IQ tests ($SD = 15$). According to Cohen (1988, p. 40), an effect size of .20 is considered "small"

Table 4.2. *Cognitive test scores over time as a function of treatment and age: Adjusted means and estimated effect sizes*

	Adjusted means			Effect size	
Phase	Treated	Control	Difference[a]	Pooled sample d^b	Test d^c
Treatment	103.0	92.0	11.0	1.75	.74
Follow-up	94.1	88.6	5.71	.87	.37

Note: The adjusted means given for the treatment phase are those at age 4 (the midpoint of that phase), and the adjusted means given for the follow-up phase are those at age 15 (close to the midpoint of that phase).

[a] Difference refers to the difference between the treatment and control group.

[b] Pooled sample d = the effect sizes calculated using the pooled standard deviation ($SD = 6.30$).

[c] Test d = the effect sizes calculated using the standard deviation of the Wechsler IQ test ($SD = 15$).

but may be meaningful, an effect size of .50 is "medium," and one of .80 is "large." As Table 4.2 shows, even the more conservative estimates are in the range considered educationally meaningful, and both estimates for the early childhood treatment period are considered large.

Academic Achievement Scores

Analyzed across the four test points, individuals who received the early educational treatment achieved higher reading scores than those in the control group, $F(1, 187) = 8.34$, $p = .004$. Across all subjects, from age 8 to 21 years, reading scores were characterized by generally flat levels of change over time (see Fig. 4.6). The treatment and control groups maintained their positions relative to national norms across time, making progress at roughly the same rate.

With respect to math achievement, a significant main effect was found for the treatment group, $F(1, 187) = 6.02$, $p = .015$, indicating that children who received the early educational treatment achieved higher math scores than those in the control group. In addition, significant linear ($F\,[1, 104] = 79.15$, $p = .0001$) and quadratic ($F[1, 187] = 9.39$, $p = .0025$) main effects were found (Fig. 4.7). Across both groups, math scores from age 8 to age 21 were characterized by linear and quadratic change, but the rate and pattern of change were equivalent for both. Both experienced a relatively steeper decline in standardized math scores from age 8 to age 12, compared to a more gradual decline in standardized math scores from age 12 to age 21.

Based on the age 15 test results, treatment effect sizes were calculated for reading and math. As with the intellectual test scores, two effect sizes were calculated, one using the pooled sample standard deviation (reading $SD = 4.85$; math $SD = 6.41$) and a more conservative estimate calculated using the standard deviation of the Woodcock-Johnson (reading and math $SD = 15$).

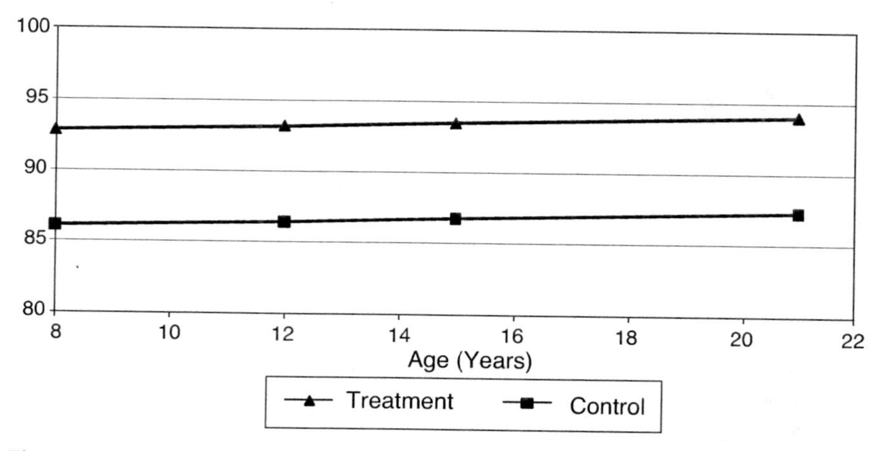

Figure 4.6. Longitudinal scores for reading, ages 8–21. Copyright © 2001 by the American Psychological Association. Reproduced with permission.

Educators consider effect sizes of .25 or greater to have practical significance (Cohen, 1988). Using the pooled standard deviation of the sample, the effect sizes were large for both reading (1.40) and math (.86). Those based on the test standard deviation were within the range considered moderate (.45 for reading and .37 for math).

Four-Group Differences in Young Adult Academic Scores

To learn if school-age treatment effects persisted over time, academic achievement was examined reverting to the four-group analysis model used during the school-age phase and adolescent follow-up studies (testing for preschool

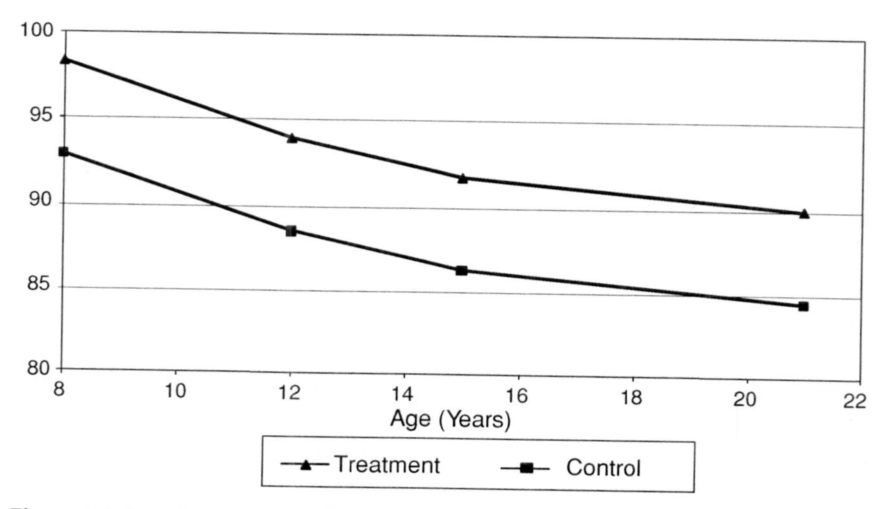

Figure 4.7. Longitudinal scores for math, ages 8–21. Copyright © 2001 by the American Psychological Association. Reproduced with permission.

effects, school-age effects, and the interaction of preschool by school age). Using this model means a loss of power because only data from those individuals who were randomly assigned to one of the four school-age groups can be included, meaning that 95 instead of the full 104 individuals contributed data (the intent-to-treat rule was again applied; hence, the models included three cases who were assigned but not actually treated in the school-age phase). Using the four-group model, at age 21 neither of the aggregate WJ scores, Broad Reading or Broad Mathematics, showed statistically significant preschool effects, school-age effects, or preschool by school-age treatment interactions. However, disaggregating the WJ scores into their component subtests revealed trends toward preschool, treatment effects for Letter-Word Identification, $F(1, 91) = 2.88$, $p < .10$; and Calculation, $F(1, 91) = 3.58$, $p < .10$. Effect sizes were calculated by subtracting the mean of the CC group from that of each of the other groups and dividing the remainder in each instance by the standard deviation of the CC group. Judging by the effect sizes thus obtained, the Abecedarian treatment influenced reading achievement more strongly than mathematics achievement. Through age 21, large to medium effect sizes for the full 8 years of treatment were found for reading (ranging from 1.04 at age 8 to .79 at age 21). The effect size for preschool treatment alone varied from .75 at age 8 to .28 at age 21. In contrast, effect sizes for school-age treatment alone (CE group) ranged from .28 at age 8 to .11 at age 21, all in the small range or less. For mathematics, effect sizes for the full 8 years of treatment ranged from .64 to .42, whereas those for preschool treatment alone ranged from .27 at age 8 to .73 at age 21. Effect sizes for school-age treatment alone ranged from .11 at age 8 to .26 at age 21 (Campbell, Ramey, Pungello, Sparling, & Miller-Johnson, 2002).

Educational Attainment

The most important outcome insofar as education was concerned was that young adults with preschool treatment were almost three times as likely to attend a 4-year college or university than the preschool control group (35.9% for treated compared to 13.7% for the control group [χ^2 $(1, N = 104) = 6.78$, $p < .01$]. Irrespective of college attendance, those treated in preschool completed significantly more years of education by age 21 than did preschool controls, $F(1, 99) = 5.00$, $p < .05$. Although there was not a significant main effect for gender, the interaction of treatment by gender was significant, $F(1, 99) = 4.19$, $p < .05$. Females with preschool treatment earned 1.2 more years of education than females without. In contrast, treated and untreated males earned almost identical amounts of education, differing only by 0.1 years.

Skilled Employment

Individuals in the preschool treated and control groups did not differ significantly in the percentage employed but did differ significantly in the level of employment they reported. Based on Hollingshead (n.d.) scores of 4 or higher, young adults with preschool treatment were more likely to be engaged in skilled jobs: 47% of treated individuals compared with 27% of the controls, $[\chi^2(1, N = 100) = 4.50, p < .05]$. Electrician is one example of a job rated 4 on the Hollingshead scale.

Parenthood

Few of the individuals in the study sample were married by age 21; five females and two males had married, one of whom was, by then, separated. However, 46 had become parents by that age, 4 of whom were among the 7 who had married. Within this sample, females tended to have more children than males, $F(1, 103) = 3.09, p < .10$. In all, 40 children had been born to females compared to 24 reported by males. Among those who did have children by age 21, preschool treatment was associated with a significant delay in the average age at first birth. The mean age at the birth of a first child was 19.1 years, $SD = 2.1$ years, for the preschool treatment group compared with 17.7 years, $SD = 1.5$ years, for preschool controls, $F(1, 41) = 5.26, p < .05$. However, the youngest parent in both groups was 15 years old when she or he reported having a child. Defining a teen parent as one aged 19 or younger when a first child was born, preschool treatment was associated with a significant reduction in teen parenthood (26% of those treated compared with 45% of controls had children as teens), $\chi^2(1, N = 104) = 3.96, p < .05$.

Social Adjustment

Indices of social adjustment included self-reported use of legal and illegal substances, substance abuse, violence, and crime. Marijuana use within the past 30 days was significantly less among the treated individuals. Eighteen percent cited some level of usage during that period compared to 39% of controls, $\chi^2(1, N = 102) = 5.83, p < .05$. Use of any other kind of recreational drug was rarely acknowledged within this sample (cocaine use was denied by 99 of the 102 individuals who completed the Risk Survey). Moderate alcohol use was commonly acknowledged but was comparable among those with and without preschool treatment. Of more importance, a tendency existed for those with preschool treatment to be less likely to describe themselves as regular smokers – 39% of the treated group compared with 55% of the controls.

Unlike the Perry Preschool study, which has consistently reported preschool-treatment-related reductions in criminal involvement for its study sample, no such reduction was found in the Abecedarian study. When responding to the questions on the young adult interview about convictions for misdemeanors or felonies, few admitted such experiences. One female from the treatment group reported a misdemeanor conviction compared to four in the control group. No female in either group reported a felony conviction. For males, the number reporting misdemeanor convictions was the same for both groups ($n = 5$), whereas six control-group males and four treated-group males reported felony convictions. These differences were not statistically significant.

Mental Health

Because research indicates a higher incidence of depressive symptoms among the poor (Gilman, Kawachi, Fitzmaurice, & Buka, 2003), Abecedarian investigators examined the extent to which having early childhood educational intervention might be associated with a reduced incidence of depressive symptoms. Using early intervention and the intellectual stimulus quality of the early childhood home environment as predictors, multiple regressions with missing data imputed were estimated to see if these factors predicted falling above the clinical cut score for Depressive Symptoms on the Brief Symptom Inventory (BSI). For this dichotomous outcome, neither predicted falling within that range. However, when the full range of scores on the depression scale was the outcome, having had early childhood treatment led to endorsement of fewer depression items. In addition, early treatment seemed to moderate the effect of the early home environment such that for those who had early treatment, endorsement of depressive symptoms did not increase as the quality of the early home environment decreased. In contrast, those in the preschool control group did show an increase in depressive symptoms as the quality of the early home decreased. Thus, treated individuals seem to have been buffered to some extent against the effects of the early home environment on later depressive symptoms (McLaughlin, Campbell, Pungello, & Skinner, 2007).

Cost-Benefit Analysis

Economists external to the program have calculated cost-benefit ratios for the Abecedarian program. A complete explanation of the method they used is given in Masse and Barnett (2002). In brief, costs were estimated on the basis of records kept by the university and the program operators; benefits were estimated in seven categories: (1) earnings and fringe benefits of participants, (2) earnings and fringe benefits of future generations, (3) maternal earnings, (4) elementary and secondary education cost savings, (5) improved health, (6) higher education costs, and (7) welfare use.

Total cost of the program (in 2002 dollars) was estimated at $67,000 per child.[1] Given that treated children were more likely to attend college, an increased cost of higher education was estimated at $8,128. However,

[1] In these analyses, discount rates of 3%, 5%, and 7% were used. In each case, the project demonstrated benefits; analyses from the 3% rate are presented here.

because of increased educational attainment, the benefits of increased lifetime income were estimated to be $37,522. In addition, the program was estimated to increase the earnings of future generations (i.e., children of the participants) by $5,700 because of such factors as enhanced cognitive functioning and achievement, greater educational attainment, and timing and spacing of when the children were born. An estimated benefit of $68,278 was found due to increased earning of the mothers of the program participants. Having their children receive free, high-quality care from infancy through age 5 allowed the mothers to make greater progress in terms of educational and occupational success. Cost savings were also found for K–12 schooling in the forms of reduced special-education placements and fewer grade retentions, resulting in an estimated benefit of $8,836. An estimated benefit of $17,781 resulted from reduced smoking rates. Finally, an estimated benefit of $196 was found for reduced costs from welfare administration. All totaled, the estimated benefits per child were calculated at $158,278, giving an estimated benefit-cost ratio of 2.5:1 (Barnett & Masse, 2007).

FUTURE RESEARCH DIRECTIONS

Collection of data from the Abecedarian study participants when they attained age 30 was recently completed (2009), and analyses are now underway. At this stage, the study is focusing on the educational attainments and economic circumstances of the participants to learn if the better educational attainment and increased likelihood of going to college seen at age 21 have translated into better, more self-sufficient lives. The primary method of data collection at this age was an extensive interview covering the life experiences of the individuals to this point. Data were also collected on children aged 3 and older born to the study participants to learn if intergenerational effects could be detected. Children were given age-appropriate measures of readiness of skills in reading and math, and parents described their social adjustment. Parenting efficacy was also measured among those of the sample who were parents.

We also collected limited young-adult data on participants in a second, closely related randomized trial of early childhood educational intervention, the Carolina Approach to Response Education (Project CARE). This study was begun immediately after the youngest Abecedarian participants graduated from the infant program. CARE offered one group of participants 5 full years of educational intervention within a child care setting except that in this case, the infant's caregiver made regular visits to the home to demonstrate the curriculum to parents and to encourage them to use the Learningames at home. In addition, CARE had a second treatment model that consisted of home visits only, such that those children did not have center-based educational intervention but rather home-based, parent-provided exposure to the same kinds of stimulating early childhood experiences that the children who attended the center-based program had. Standardized tests of cognitive functioning and academic achievement were not collected for the CARE sample as young adults, but educational, vocational, and family status were examined. We tested outcomes for the CARE sample alone as well as determining if results were consistent across the two studies. The CARE sample replicated the Abecedarian findings with respect to early childhood benefits on young-adult educational and vocational outcomes. Those treated attained more years of education, had a greater likelihood of going to college, and had, on average, better jobs when examined in the CARE sample alone and when the two studies were combined. The reduction in early childbearing was not replicated in CARE. An outcome likely to have a positive impact on health (i.e., having those with early treatment report a more active lifestyle as young adults) was found within both studies singly and in combination (Campbell, Wasik, Pungello, Burchinal, Barbarin, Kainz, et al., 2008).

IMPLICATIONS FOR POLICY

The findings from the Abecedarian study speak most directly to the importance of early childhood education as a way to improve the chance that children from poor families will achieve in school and go on to higher education. That significantly more of those with early childhood treatment did go to a 4-year college or university indicates that development of their learning potential was enhanced. Moreover, data collected from the parents of the Abecedarian participant when the adolescent was 15 years of age indicated that those mothers who had the benefit of the 5 years of stable, quality child care made more gains in their own lives, as reflected in attaining more years of education themselves and also in having higher level jobs at that point. The data at that point suggested that the worst-case scenario was to be a teen mother who did not have the benefit of the child care program. This group of mothers was least likely to have made gains on their own.

Specific recommendations would be, first, to recognize that money used to fund early childhood programs for poor children is money well spent in that it increases the likelihood that children born into poverty may make more educational gains and, it is hoped, enhance their own economic capital.

Second, Abecedarian data clearly suggest that the more powerful and enduring effects from its two phases of intervention were due to the 5 years of educational intervention from infancy to kindergarten entry. Effects of the school-age learning supports, although evident in the short term, were never as strong as those from the preschool program alone and were not discernible in young adulthood in the absence of the preschool program having come before.

Third, data from Abecedarian parent outcomes suggest that having reliable child care during the preschool years makes a difference in the lives of very young mothers, giving them a better chance to enhance their own development in terms of getting more education and better jobs.

REFERENCES

Barnett, W. S., & Masse, L. M. (2007). Comparative benefit-cost analysis of the Abecedarian program and its policy implications. *Economics of Education Review, 26*(1), 113–125.

Bayley, N. (1969). *Bayley scales of infant development.* New York: Psychological Corporation.

Bertalanffy, L. V. (1975). *Perspectives on general system theory.* New York: George Braziller.

Bronfenbrenner, U. (1986). Ecology of the family as a context for human development: Research perspectives. *Developmental Psychology, 22,* 723–742.

Burchinal, M., Campbell, F. A., & Bryant, D. M. (1995). *Early child care and public school aggressiveness: An attempted replication study.* Unpublished manuscript.

Burchinal, M., Lee, M., & Ramey, C. T. (1989). Type of day care and preschool intellectual development in disadvantaged children. *Child Development, 60,* 128–137.

Campbell, F. A., Pungello, E. P., & Miller-Johnson, S. (2002). The development of perceived scholastic competence and global self-worth in African American adolescents from low-income families: The roles of family factors, early educational intervention, and academic experience. *Journal of Adolescent Research, 17,* 277–302.

Campbell, F. A., Pungello, E. P., Miller-Johnson, S., Burchinal, M., & Ramey, C. T. (2001). The development of cognitive and academic abilities: Growth curves from an early childhood educational experiment. *Developmental Psychology, 37,* 231–242.

Campbell, F. A., & Ramey, C. T. (1995) Cognitive and school outcomes for high-risk African American students at middle adolescence: Positive effects of early intervention. *American Educational Research Journal, 32*(4), 743–772.

Campbell, F. A., Ramey, C. T., Pungello, E. P., Sparling, J. J., & Miller-Johnson, S. (2002). Early childhood education: Young adult outcomes from the Abecedarian Project. *Applied Developmental Science, 6,* 42–57.

Campbell, F. A., Wasik, B. H., Pungello, E. P., Burchinal, M. R., Barbarin, O., Kainz, K., et al. (2008). Young adult outcomes from the Abecedarian and CARE early childhood educational interventions. *Early Childhood Research Quarterly, 23,* 452–466.

Centers for Disease Control. (1992). *Chronic disease and health promotion reprints from the MMWR.* Washington, DC: U.S. Government Printing Office.

Cicirelli, V. G. (1969). *The impact of Head Start: An evaluation of the effects of Head Start on children's cognitive and affective development* (Vol. 1). Athens, OH: Westinghouse Learning Corporation, Ohio University.

Cohen, J. (1988). *Statistical power analysis* (2nd ed.) Hillsdale, NJ: Erlbaum.

Derogatis, L. R. (1975). *SCL-90-R; Symptom Checklist-90-R.* Minneapolis, MN: National Computer Systems.

Derogatis, L. R. (1993). *Brief Symptom Inventory: Administration, scoring and procedures manual.* Minneapolis, MN: National Computer Systems.

Dunn, L. M., & Markwardt, F. C., Jr. (1970). *Peabody Individual Achievement Test.* Circle Pines, MN: American Guidance Service.

Garber, H. L. (1988). *The Milwaukee Project: Prevention of mental retardation in children at risk.* Washington, DC: American Association on Mental Retardation.

Gilman, S. E., Kawachi, I., Fitzmaurice, G. M., & Buka, S. L. (2003). Family disruption in childhood and risk of adult depression. *American Journal of Psychiatry, 160,* 939–946.

Gray, S. W., Ramsey, B. K., & Klaus, R. A. (1982). *From 3 to 20: The early training project.* Baltimore, MD: University Park Press.

Harter, S. (1982). The perceived competence scale for children. *Child Development, 53,* 87–97.

Harter, S. (1988). *Manual for the self-perception profile for adolescents.* Denver, CO: University of Denver.

Haskins, R. (1985). Public school aggression among children with varying day-care experience. *Child Development, 56,* 689–703.

Heber, R., Dever, R., & Conry, J. (1968). The influence of environmental and genetic variables on intellectual development. In H. J. Prehm, L. A. Hamerlynck, & J. E. Crosson (Eds.), *Behavioral research in mental retardation* (pp. 1–23). Eugene: University of Oregon Press.

Hollingshead, A. B. (n.d.). *Four factor index of social status* (Working paper, photocopied). New Haven, CT: Yale University, Department of Sociology.

Hunt, J. McV. (1961). *Intelligence and experience.* New York: Ronald Press.

Lazar, I., Darlington, R., Murray, H., Royce, J., & Snipper, A. (1982). Lasting effects of early education: A report from the Consortium for Longitudinal Studies. *Monographs of the Society for Research in Child Development, 47*(2–3, Serial No. 195).

Masse, L. N., & Barnett, W. S. (2002). A benefit-cost analysis of the Abecedarian early childhood intervention. In H. Levin & P. McEwan (Eds.), *Cost-effectiveness and educational policy: 2002 Yearbook of the American Educational Finance Association* (pp. 157–176). Larchmont, NY: Eye on Education.

McCarthy, D. (1972). *McCarthy scales of children's abilities.* New York: Psychological Corporation.

McLaughlin, A. E., Campbell, F. C., Pungello, E. P., & Skinner, M. (2007). Depressive symptoms in young adults: The influences of the early home environment and early educational childcare. *Child Development, 78,* 746–756.

Pungello, E. P., Campbell, F. A., & Barnett, S. W. (2006). *Poverty and early childhood education. Center for Poverty, Work and Opportunity: Policy Brief Series.* Retrieved from http://www.law.unc.edu/povertycenter.

Ramey, C. T. (1971). *Carolina Abecedarian Project.* Unpublished manuscript, Frank Porter Graham Child Development Center, University of North Carolina, Chapel Hill.

Ramey, C. T., & Campbell, F. A. (1984). Preventive education for high-risk children: Cognitive consequences of the Carolina ABC [Special issue]. *American Journal of Mental Deficiency, 88*(5), 515–523.

Ramey, C. T., & Campbell, F. A. (1991). Poverty, early childhood education, and academic competence: The Abecedarian experiment. In A. C. Huston (Ed.), *Children in poverty: Child development and public policy* (pp. 190–221). Cambridge: Cambridge University Press.

Ramey, C. T., MacPhee, D., & Yeates, K. O. (1982). Preventing developmental retardation: A general systems model. In J. M. Joffee & L. A. Bond (Eds.), *Facilitating infant and early childhood development* (pp. 343–401). Hanover, NH: University Press of New England.

Ramey, C. T., McGinness, G. D., Cross, L., Collier, A. M. & Barrie-Blackley, S. (1982). The Abecedarian approach to social competence: Cognitive and linguistic intervention for disadvantaged preschoolers. In K. Borman (Ed.). The social life of children in a changing society. Hillsdale, NC: Erlbaum Associates.

Ramey, C. T., & Smith, B. (1977). Assessing the intellectual consequences of early intervention with high-risk infants. *American Journal of Mental Deficiency, 81,* 318–324.

Schaefer, E., Edgerton, M., & Aaronson, M. (1977). *Classroom Behavior Inventory.* Unpublished manuscript. Available from Earl Schaefer, Department of Maternal and Child Health, University of North Carolina at Chapel Hill, Chapel Hill, NC, 27599.

Skeels, H. M., Updegraff, R., Wellman, B. I., & Williams, H. M. (1938). A study of environmental stimulation: An orphanage preschool project. *University of Iowa Studies in Child Welfare, 15,* 7–19.

Sparling, J. J., & Lewis, I. (1979). *Learningames for the first three years: A guide to parent–child play.* New York: Walker.

Sparling, J. J., & Lewis, I. (1984). *Learningames for threes and fours: A guide to adult and child play.* New York: Walker.

Sparling, J., & Lewis, I. (2007). *LearningGames.* Hillsborough, NC: MindNurture.

Terman, L. M., & Merrill, N. Q. (1972). *Stanford-Binet intelligence scale: 1972 norms editions.* Boston: Houghton Mifflin.

Wechsler, D. (1967). *Wechsler preschool and primary scale of intelligence.* New York: Psychological Corporation.

Wechsler, D. (1978). *Wechsler intelligence scale for children – revised.* New York: Psychological Corporation.

Wechsler, D. (1981). *Wechsler adult intelligence test – revised.* Allen, TX: Psychological Corporation.

Woodcock, R. W., & Johnson, M. B. (1977). *Woodcock-Johnson psycho-educational battery: Part 2: Tests of academic achievement.* Boston: Teaching Resources Corporation.

Woodcock, R. W., & Johnson, M. B. (1989). *Woodcock-Johnson psycho-educational battery – revised.* Allen, TX: DLM.

5

Early Head Start Impacts at Age 3 and a Description of the Age 5 Follow-Up Study

HELEN H. RAIKES, RACHEL CHAZAN-COHEN, JOHN M. LOVE, AND JEANNE BROOKS-GUNN

Early Head Start is a federal, two-generation child development program for low-income children under the age of 3 and their families; as of 2007, it was serving approximately 63,000 children in some 700 communities. After its rapid expansion during the 1990s and a period marked by little expansion from 2001 through 2008, Early Head Start received $1.1 billion under the American Recovery and Reinvestment Act of 2009, which enabled it to serve an additional 55,000 children.

In 1995, the Early Head Start program, in accordance with congressional mandate, began a rigorous, random-assignment evaluation in 17 of the first sites funded. Here, we describe (a) features of the Early Head Start program, (b) methods of the Early Head Start program evaluation, (c) findings when children were 3 and when this cohort of children ended the program, and (d) methods of the follow-up study conducted when children were 5 (findings from the follow-up study have recently been released in another venue).

CHARACTERISTICS OF EARLY HEAD START PROGRAMS

Early Head Start had its beginnings in 1994 when Congress passed legislation reauthorizing Head Start and mandating that up to 3% of the Head Start budget for 1995 be used to establish a new program of comprehensive services for families with infants and toddlers below preschool age. That same year, then-Secretary of Health and Human Services Donna Shalala convened a committee of experts in the field of early education and infant development to lay out the principles and operating features for the new program. That committee's work was published as the *Statement of the Advisory Committee on Services to Families with Infants and Toddlers* (Administration on Children, Youth, and Families [ACYF], 1994) and became the initial operating guidelines for Early Head Start. The first 68 programs were funded in 1995. Expansion of the program accelerated with the Coats Human Services Amendments of 1998 that incrementally increased Early Head Start appropriations annually to 10%

of the total Head Start budget, the level before implementation of the Recovery and Reinvestment Act in 2009. Prior to the recent expansion, Early Head Start served about 3% of the infants and toddlers who are eligible for its services.

Early Head Start belongs to the Head Start family of programs that provide preschool services for children ages 3 to 5, including migrant families, Native Americans, and Alaskan natives. As is true for all of these programs, quality in Early Head Start is ensured by adherence to the Head Start Performance Standards (Administration for Children and Families [ACF], 1996), which are followed by all Head Start programs and formally monitored every 3 years.

Early Head Start offers discrete service models that may be home-based (weekly home visits with bimonthly group meetings for parents and children), center-based (high-quality center care combined with regular parenting support), or a mixture of these services. Early Head Start also provides family support and referrals to community agencies that address special needs of families. Local programs have been encouraged to find ways to adapt their services to family needs, leading to rapid expansion of more complicated "mixed approaches" to serving families with combinations of center-based and home-based services. For example, some families may receive home-based services, others may use center-based services, and many more may receive the benefits of both program models, perhaps at different times in the children's development. When the home-based model is selected, in accordance with the Performance Standards, the families are intended to receive weekly home visits for 90 minutes and are strongly encouraged to attend monthly group meetings; family support services are also provided. When the center-based model is selected, children attend high-quality center-based care, and families receive a minimum of two home visits a year together with comprehensive support services. Other models provide for a combination of center-based and home-based services and are referred to as comprehensive or locally designed. For purposes of the research, these programs were characterized as "mixed-approach" models.

Early Head Start programs are directed to serve those with the greatest needs within their community. Most of the families served have incomes at or below the poverty level, but other criteria may also be employed to target underserved families locally (e.g., teen parents and non-English-speaking families). At least 10% of the enrollments must be offered to children with disabilities, and up to 10% of children can be from families with incomes above the poverty line, especially if admitting higher income families assists programs in meeting the disability requirement. Program Information Report (PIR) data for 2007–8 (Administration for Children and Families, 2009) indicated that about 26% of families then enrolled in Early Head Start did not speak English as their primary language. The majority of the non-English-speaking families spoke Spanish (84%), and the most common other languages spoken were East Asian, African, European, Slavic, and Central or South American languages other than Spanish (with 3% or fewer in each of those groups). In that same year, about one-third of the enrollees in Early Head Start were of Hispanic origin (32%). About 41% were White, 25% were African American, 6% were Native Americans or Alaskan Natives, and the remaining were from other racial or mixed racial groups. Some states and private funders have added support for Early Head Start to the federal funding so that in some localities, Early Head Start funds are blended with state and other funds while retaining the core features of the Head Start Performance Standards.

RESEARCH AND EVALUATION METHODS

Evaluation was mandated by the original congressional legislation, and impact reports were further mandated in subsequent authorizing legislation. The 1998 authorization specified that expansion of the program would be contingent on demonstration of benefits from the evaluation reports. The Advisory Committee for Services to Families with Infants and Toddlers (ACYF, 1994) also recommended rigorous and multifaceted research.

Seventeen of the sites from the first two cohorts were purposively selected to participate in the program evaluation. These sites reflected the racial and ethnic mix of program participants nationally, had a relatively equal breakdown of program models (about one-third were home-based, a third were center-based, and a third combined these features), and were balanced in terms of rural and urban localities. The research employed an experimental design in which 3,001 families were randomly and approximately equally assigned to program and control groups at the 17 sites, with approximately 150 children and families from each site participating. Programs recruited families using typical procedures, and families assigned randomly to the control group were invited to use all of the services available in their communities *except for Early Head Start.* The programs that participated in the research were located throughout the United States: Washington State (2), California, Utah, Colorado (2), Kansas, Missouri, Iowa, Arkansas, Tennessee, Michigan, Pennsylvania, New York, Vermont, South Carolina, and Virginia. Analyses of the research samples documented that they reflected the demographic characteristics of program families served by all Early Head Start programs funded in 1996 and 1997 (ACF, 2002).

The Administration for Children and Families selected Mathematica Policy Research (MPR) in Princeton, New Jersey, as lead evaluator for the project, together with Columbia University and the National Center for Children and Families. A unique feature of the evaluation was the inclusion of local evaluation partners. Each site partnered with a local university; in all, 15 university partners were selected. Together, the national contractor and the 15 university partners conducted the research, with MPR and Columbia providing the oversight and local research partners collecting cross-site and local data. All collaborated through a consortium that met twice annually.

Data Collection

The data-collection protocol included child and parent measures collected when children were 14, 24, and 36 months of age and service-use interviews that took place at 7, 16, and 28 months after random assignment. Child assessments included measures of cognitive development (Bayley Mental Development Index for Scales of Infant Development [Bayley, 1993]); language development (Communicative Development Inventories [CDI] at 14 and 24 months [Fenson et al., 1994] and the Peabody Picture Vocabulary Test-III (PPVT-III) at 36 months [Dunn & Dunn, 1997]); and socio-emotional development (videotape assessments of child engagement, attention, and negativity using the 3-Bag Test, a variation [Brady-Smith, 2004] of the 3-Box Test from the National Institute of Child Health and Human Development Study of Early Child Care [NICHD, 2005; Vandell, 1979] at all three ages, as well as parent ratings of aggression [Achenbach & Rescorla, 2000] at 24 and 36 months of age). Parent assessments included the Home Observation for Measurement of the Environment (HOME) resulting in full and factor subscores (Caldwell & Bradley, 1984); measures of parental supportiveness, detachment, intrusiveness, warmth, and negativity from the 3-Bag Test mentioned earlier; self-reports of parenting; and parent stressors including the Parenting Stress Index Distress Scale and Parent–Child Dysfunctional Interaction Scale (Abidin, 1995), the Center for Epidemiological Studies-Depression Scale (Radloff, 1977), and others (see ACF, 2007a).

RESULTS: AGE 3 IMPACTS

Detailed reports of the overall program impacts when children were 24 and 36 months of age are available in government reports (see http://www.acf.hhs.gov/programs/opre/ehs/ehs_resrch/index.html; ACF, 2002; Love et al., 2005). Here, we provide findings for the sample overall at the time this cohort of children ended the program and for selected subgroups based on the types of program models in which the children and families were enrolled and the race/ethnicity of the families. Response rates were comparable for the program and control groups and varied to some extent by the type of measure (see Tables 5.1–5.3). Further discussion of response rates is available in the study's final technical report (ACF, 2002) and at the website mentioned earlier.

Impacts on Services

Analyses when children were 36 months of age demonstrated that program families received significantly more services than control-group families, a

Table 5.1. *Selected Early Head Start overall impacts on children and parents*

Outcome	Program-group participants[a]	Control group[b]	Estimated impact per participant[c]	Effect size[d]
Child cognitive and language development				
Average Bayley MDI	91.4	89.9	1.6*	0.12
Percentage with MDI < 85	27.3	32.0	−4.7+	−0.10
PPVT-III standard score	83.3	81.1	2.1*	0.13
Percentage with PPVT-III < 85	51.1	57.1	−6.0*	−0.12
Child socio-emotional development				
CBCL aggressive behavior	10.6	11.3	−0.7*	−0.11
Sustained attention with objects during play	5.0	4.8	0.2**	0.16
Engagement of parent during play	4.8	4.6	0.2**	0.20
Negativity toward parent during play	1.2	1.3	−0.1*	
Child health				
Child's health status	4.0	4.0	−0.0	−0.02
Immunizations (%)	99.0	97.7	1.2+	0.09
Parenting				
HOME support of language and learning	10.6	10.4	0.2*	0.10
HOME warmth	2.6	2.5	0.1*	0.09
Supportiveness in play	4.0	3.9	0.1**	0.15
Detachment in play	1.2	1.3	−0.1+	−0.09
Parent reads to child daily (%)	56.8	52.0	4.9*	0.10
Spanked child last week (%)	46.7	53.8	−7.1**	−0.14
Parent–child play	4.4	4.3	0.1*	0.09
Parent well-being and self-sufficiency				
CES-Depression Scale	7.4	7.7	−0.03	−3.7
Percentage of parents ever employed or in an education program in first 26 months	93.9	90.5	3.4*	11.1
Sample size				
Parent interview	**1,083**	**989**	**2,072**	
Parent services interview	**1,075**	**1,008**	**2,083**	
Parent–child interactions	**875**	**784**	**1,659**	
Bayley MDI	**879**	**779**	**1,658**	
PPVT-III	**738**	**665**	**1,403**	

Note: Parent interviews, interviewer observations, and assessments of semi-structured parent–child interactions conducted when children were approximately 37 months old. Immunization data from parent services interviews conducted an average of 7, 16, and 28 months after random assignment. MDI = Mental Development Index; PPVT-III = Peabody Picture Vocabulary Test-III; CBCL = Child Behavior Checklist; HOME = Home Observation for Measurement of the Environment. All impact estimates were calculated using regression models, in which each site was weighted equally.

[a] A participant is defined as a program-group member who received more than one Early Head Start home visit, met with an Early Head Start case manager more than once, received at least 2 weeks of Early Head Start center-based care, and/or participated in Early Head Start group parent–child activities.

[b] The control-group mean is the mean for the control-group members who would have participated in Early Head Start if they had been assigned to the program group instead. This unobserved mean was estimated as the difference between the program-group mean for participants and the impact per participant.

[c] The estimated impact per participant is measured as the estimated impact per eligible applicant divided by the proportion of program-group members who participated in Early Head Start services (which varied by site). The estimated impact per eligible applicant is measured as the difference between the regression-adjusted means for all program- and control-group members.

[d] The effect size was calculated by dividing the estimated impact per participant by the standard deviation of the outcome measure for the control group.

+ $p < .10$; * $p < .05$; ** $p < .01$

Table 5.2. *Impacts on selected child and family outcomes by program model*

	Program–control differences											
	Center-based programs				Mixed-approach programs				Home-based programs			
Outcome	Program-group participants[a]	Control group[b]	Impact estimate[c]	Effect size[d]	Program-group participants[a]	Control group[b]	Impact estimate[c]	Effect size[d]	Program-group participants[a]	Control group[b]	Impact estimate[c]	Effect size[d]
Child cognitive and language development												
Average Bayley MDI	89.8	88.9	**0.9**	**0.07**	89.3	87.9	1.4	0.10	94.1	92.8	1.2	0.10
Percentage with MDI <85	26.5	36.1	**−9.7**	**−0.21**	36.1	38.4	−2.2	−0.05	20.5	22.0	−1.4	−0.03
PPVT-III standard score	83.2	81.8	1.5	0.09	82.2	78.5	3.7**	0.23	84.6	83.1	1.5	0.09
Percentage with PPVT-III <85	52.4	54.7	**−2.3**	**−0.05**	56.0	67.7	−11.6**	−0.23	45.6	48.6	−3.0	−0.06
Child socio-emotional development												
CBCL aggressive behavior	9.6	10.8	**−1.2**	**−0.18**	10.7	11.3	−0.6	−0.09	11.2	11.7	−0.5	−0.08
Sustained attention with objects	5.0	5.0	0.0	0.5	5.0	4.7	0.3***	0.31	5.0	4.9	0.1	0.11
Engagement of parent	4.9	4.7	0.2	0.17	4.7	4.4	0.3***	0.31	4.8	4.6	0.2**	0.19
Negativity toward parent	1.2	1.4	**−0.2****	**−0.27**	1.3	1.3	−0.1	−0.15	1.3	1.3	−0.0	−0.07
Child health												
Child's health status	3.9	4.1	**−0.2**	**−0.17**	4.1	4.1	0.0	0.02	4.0	4.0	−0.0	−0.04
Immunizations (%)	NA	NA	**NA**	**NA**	NA	NA	**NA**	**NA**	NA	NA	N[a]	NA
Parenting												
HOME support of language and learning	10.7	10.5	**0.3**	**0.13**	10.3	10.1	0.2	0.09	10.9	10.7	0.2	7.0
HOME warmth	2.6	2.4	0.1	0.15	2.4	2.3	0.1	0.09	2.7	2.7	−0.0	−0.01

Supportiveness in play	4.1	4.0	0.1	0.09	4.0	3.8	0.2**	0.21	4.0	3.9	0.1**	0.16
Detachment in play	1.2	1.1	0.1	0.16	1.2	1.4	−0.2**	0.24	1.2	1.3	−0.1	0.09
Parent reads to child daily (%)	57.9	50.8	7.0	14.1	59.0	45.0	14***	0.28	54.5	55.7	−1.2	−2.4
Spanked child last week (%)	51.4	61.0	−9.6	−0.19	46.6	57.6	−10.9**	−0.22	44.1	49.6	−5.5	−0.11
Parent–child play	4.6	4.3	0.2*	0.26	4.4	4.2	0.2*	0.18	4.4	4.4	−0.1	−0.06
Parent well-being and self-sufficiency												
CES-Depression Scale	7.3	7.1	**0.2**	**0.03**	**7.2**	**7.8**	**−0.6**	**−0.08**	7.7	7.9	−0.1	−0.02
Percentage of parents ever employed or in an education program in first 26 months	97.7	94.6	**3.1**	**0.10**	**95.6**	**90.1**	**5.5****	**0.18**	90.5	88.9	1.6	0.05
Sample size												
Parent interview	254	211			351	344			502	448		
Parent services interview	230	204			358	354			488	453		
Parent–child interactions	227	181			251	255			396	348		
Bayley MDI	217	172			266	257			**396**	**350**		

Note: Parent interviews, interviewer observations, and assessments of semi-structured parent–child interactions conducted when children were approximately 37 months old. Immunization data from parent services interviews conducted an average of 7, 16, and 28 months after random assignment. MDI = Mental Development Index; PPVT-III = Peabody Picture Vocabulary Test-III; CBCL = Child Behavior Checklist; HOME = Home Observation for Measurement of the Environment. All impact estimates were calculated using regression models, in which each site was weighted equally.

[a] A participant is defined as a program-group member who received more than one Early Head Start home visit, met with an Early Head Start case manager more than once, received at least 2 weeks of Early Head Start center-based care, and/or participated in Early Head Start group parent–child activities.

[b] The control-group mean is the mean for the control-group members who would have participated in Early Head Start if they had been assigned to the program group instead. This unobserved mean was estimated as the difference between the program-group mean for participants and the impact per participant.

[c] The estimated impact per participant is measured as the estimated impact per eligible applicant divided by the proportion of program-group members who participated in Early Head Start services (which varied by site). The estimated impact per eligible applicant is measured as the difference between the regression-adjusted means for all program- and control-group members.

[d] The effect size was calculated by dividing the estimated impact per participant by the standard deviation of the outcome measure for the control group.

+ $p < .10$; * $p < .05$; ** $p < .01$

Table 5.3. *Impacts on selected child and family outcomes by race/ethnicity*

Outcome	Program–control differences											
	White non-Hispanic				African American				Hispanic			
	Program-group participants[a]	Control group[b]	Impact estimate[c]	Effect size[d]	Program-group participants[a]	Control group[b]	Impact estimate[c]	Effect size[d]	Program-group participants[a]	Control group[b]	Impact estimate[c]	Effect size[d]
Child cognitive and language development												
Average Bayley MDI	94.8	93.3	1.5	0.12	88.5	86.9	1.6	0.13	94.1	92.8	1.2	0.10
Percentage with MDI <85	21.1	23.2	−2.3	−0.05	36.0	37.5	−1.4	−0.03	20.5	22.0	−1.4	−0.03
PPVT-III Standard Score	87.7	86.9	0.8	0.05	82.6	78.8	3.8**	0.23	84.6	83.1	1.5	0.09
Percentage with PPVT-III <85	37.0	42.5	−5.5	−0.11	55.9	64.2	−8.3	−0.17	45.6	48.6	−3.0	−0.06
Child socio-emotional development												
CBCL aggressive behavior	11.9	12.2	−0.4	−0.07	9.1	11.4	−2.2***	−0.35	11.2	11.7	−0.5	−0.08
Sustained attention with objects	5.1	5.0	0.2	0.10	5.1	4.6	0.5***	0.48	4.8	4.8	−0.0	−0.4
Engagement of parent	4.8	4.8	0.1	0.09	4.8	4.3	0.5***	0.48	4.7	4.7	−0.0	−1.4
Negativity toward parent	1.3	1.3	0.0	0.03	1.2	1.4	−0.2***	−0.37	1.2	1.3	−0.1	−8.3
Child health												
Child's health status	4.0	4.0	−0.0	−0.02	4.1	4.1	−0.0	−0.04	4.0	3.9	0.1	10.3
Immunizations (%)	99.4	98.1	1.3		99.3	98.5	−0.4		99.4	99.1	0.3	
Parenting												
HOME support of language and learning	11.1	11.2	−0.1	0.04	10.6	10.1	0.5**	0.23	10.3	9.8	0.5*	21.2
HOME warmth	2.6	2.6	0.0	0.04	2.5	2.3	0.2**	0.25	2.5	2.6	−0.1	0.10

Supportiveness in play	4.1	4.1	0.1	0.08	4.0	3.6	0.4***	0.47	3.8	3.8	0.0	0.04
Detachment in play	1.2	1.2	0.0	0.05	1.3	1.4	−0.1	−0.18	1.2	1.3	−0.0	−0.05
Parent reads to child daily (%)	66.6	62.7	3.9	0.08	54.5	49.7	4.7	0.10	45.1	30.9	14.2**	0.29
Spanked child last week (%)	43.6	49.8	−6.3	−0.13	60.7	65.5	−4.8	−0.10	42.5	43.9	−1.4	−0.03
Parent–child play	4.5	4.5	−0.0	−0.02	4.4	4.3	0.1	0.09	4.2	4.1	0.1	0.13
Parent well-being and self-sufficiency												
18 CES-Depression Scale	8.6	8.9	−0.03	−0.05	7.5	8.1	−0.5	−0.07	6.1	5.4	0.7	0.10
Percentage of parents ever employed or in an education program in first 26 months	94.6	91.1	3.5	11.5	96.0	86.8	9.2***	0.30	91.8	85.5	6.3	0.21
Sample size												
Parent interview	431	3,900	821		354	**332**	**686**		259	211	470	
Parent services interview	393	3,766	769		373	**336**	**709**		250	225	475	
Parent–child interactions	334	3,055	639		271	**243**	**514**		224	181	405	
Bayley MDI	326	3,077	633		287	**241**	**528**		**220**	**177**	**397**	

Note: Parent interviews, interviewer observations, and assessments of semi-structured parent–child interactions conducted when children were approximately 37 months old. Immunization data from parent services interviews conducted an average of 7, 16, and 28 months after random assignment. MDI = Mental Development Index; PPVT-III = Peabody Picture Vocabulary Test-III; CBCL = Child Behavior Checklist; HOME = Home Observation for Measurement of the Environment. All impact estimates were calculated using regression models, in which each site was weighted equally.

[a] A participant is defined as a program-group member who received more than one Early Head Start home visit, met with an Early Head Start case manager more than once, received at least 2 weeks of Early Head Start center-based care, and/or participated in Early Head Start group parent–child activities.

[b] The control-group mean is the mean for the control-group members who would have participated in Early Head Start if they had been assigned to the program group instead. This unobserved mean was estimated as the difference between the program-group mean for participants and the impact per participant.

[c] The estimated impact per participant is measured as the estimated impact per eligible applicant divided by the proportion of program-group members who participated in Early Head Start services (which varied by site). The estimated impact per eligible applicant is measured as the difference between the regression-adjusted means for all program- and control-group members.

[d] The effect size was calculated by dividing the estimated impact per participant by the standard deviation of the outcome measure for the control group.

+ $p < .10$; * $p < .05$; ** $p < .01$

pattern particularly true for home visits and parent education and less pronounced, although still detectable, in regard to child care services.

Impacts on Children

Early Head Start had impacts on children's development when children were 36 months of age (see Table 5.1). Early Head Start children had significantly higher scores in cognitive, language, and socio-emotional development (including fewer reported aggressive behaviors and better attention and engagement of adults) than control-group children. Differences were found in both higher mean scores for the program group and lower proportions of program-group children scoring in the low ranges of functioning. Overall impacts were modest, with effect sizes from .10 to .20. Early Head Start also had modest impacts on some of children's health outcomes, notably by lowering rates of hospitalization for accidents and injuries (not shown) and by producing significantly higher rates of immunizations (even though both program and control groups had relatively high rates of preventive health services).

Impacts on Parenting

Because Early Head Start has a two-generation emphasis, the programs also aimed to influence parenting behaviors, self-sufficiency, and healthy family functioning. Home-based programs in particular, but all programs to some extent, subscribed to a theory of change by which support for parenting was intended to lead to long-term effects for children. At the 36-month assessment, Early Head Start parents had more stimulating and supportive home environments; were observed to be more supportive, less detached, and less negative in interaction with their children; played and read with their children more; and were less punitive than the control-group parents. As we found for child impacts, there were many favorable impacts on parents across many domains, usually of modest magnitude but with considerably larger impacts for some subgroups, as we report later.

Many of the programs aimed to help parents attain greater self-sufficiency. A fairly large proportion of parents had not graduated from high school when the program began. Additionally, the program was launched just as welfare reform was being implemented through the Temporary Assistance for Needy Families (TANF) legislation. In this context, Early Head Start parents were significantly more likely to be in school or training than control-group parents at multiple measurement intervals and were more likely to be employed when the program ended (not shown). There was no impact on cash assistance (not shown); both program- and control-group families appreciably reduced their reliance on cash assistance.

Subgroups: Impacts by Program Model and Race/Ethnicity

Program Model

As noted, Early Head Start programs may offer families services through a home-based or center-based option or a combination of both. The evaluation examined program impacts for the 17 program sites according to the predominant program model offered to families in each site. Seven sites offered predominantly home-based services to families, four carried out Early Head Start services under a center-based model, and the remaining six sites in the study offered a combination of services and were characterized as "mixed-approach" programs. In the mixed-approach programs, some families may have received home-based services and some had center-based services. In one of the mixed-approach programs, the families received home-based services during the first year and switched to center-based services during the second year, much like the services of the Infant Health and Development Program (Brooks-Gunn, Klebanov, Liaw, & Spiker, 1993). In other Early Head Start mixed-approach programs, the children received center-based services, but families also received home visits on a more regular basis than seen in typical center-based programs. All of the programs followed the Head Start Program Performance Standards (ACF, 1996). Some of the standards are specific to program models (e.g., if families are enrolled in home-based services, weekly home visits are required), and a number of the standards pertain irrespective of program model (e.g., health services).

Regression-adjusted impact analyses were conducted for each of the subgroups, comparing children and families who received program services to the control group in those sites. The broadest pattern of impacts was found in the mixed-approach programs (see Table 5.2). Children in these programs demonstrated significantly better language and socio-emotional development (engagement of parent and sustained attention during play). Parents in these programs were observed to be more supportive and less detached during play, played with their children more, read more, and spanked less frequently than control group parents. Effect sizes ranged from .18 to .31. Children and parents in center-based programs also fared better than control-group children on a number of outcomes with similar effect sizes. Center-based children were less frequently in the lowest cognitive functioning group and had better socio-emotional functioning (less negativity toward the parent and fewer aggressive behaviors). Parents played with their children more frequently than control-group parents and spanked them less. Fewer of the impacts in center-based sites achieved statistical significance because of the smaller sample size; however, significant impacts were found for reduced child negativity and parent spanking and increased parent play relative to the control group. For home-based sites, children in the program group more frequently engaged parents during play, and parents were observed to be more supportive during play.

Subgroups: Impacts by Race/Ethnicity

Early Head Start serves a diverse group of low-income families. The Early Head Start Research and Evaluation Study created a number of family subgroups (e.g., parents who were teens at the time of the child's birth versus parents who were older; parents who spoke English as a first language versus those who did not). Here, we provide findings according to family race/ethnicity for Whites, African Americans, and Hispanics. We do not provide results for "Other" because this group was small and diverse. Results from other subgroup analyses are available at http://www.acf.hhs.gov/programs/opre/ehs/ehs_resrch/index.html.

Results in Table 5.3 show that African American children consistently displayed the most favorable impacts from the program. African American children who received Early Head Start program services had higher PPVT-III scores (effect size = .23), fewer parent-reported aggressive behaviors (effect size = .35), less observed negativity toward parents (effect size = .37), more observed engagement during play (effect size = .48), and greater observed attention with objects (effect size = .48).

African American parents were observed to be more supportive during play (effect size = .47) than was true for control-group parents. These program parents also provided more support for learning in the home environment (effect size = .47), as did Hispanic program parents relative to the control group (effect size = .21). Hispanic families more often read daily to their children (effect size = .29). African American program parents were more often employed or in training than African American control-group parents.

FOLLOWING UP: CONTINUITY OF SERVICES BEYOND EARLY HEAD START

The Advisory Committee on Services to Families with Infants and Toddlers (ACYF, 1994) recommended that Early Head Start services begin early, during pregnancy if possible, and that children be transitioned to high-quality early childhood education programs after Early Head Start, which ends at age 3; this transition provides for continuity of services from before birth through the preschool years, consistent with principles advanced by Ramey and Ramey (1998) and findings about the need for follow-up services to maintain early-intervention effects (Heckman & Masterov, 2004).

At the end of the program, service providers are charged with ensuring that children receive transition support, which includes finding Head Start or quality early childhood programs in their communities or home-based services.

The 2004 Head Start Program Information Report (ACF, 2005) stated that, nationally, between one-quarter and one-half of 2-year-old children in Early Head Start enroll in Head Start the next year as 3-year-olds. A smaller percentage enroll in other early childhood programs, often drawing on partnerships already established with community child care providers.

To learn whether the early gains achieved by children and parents in the Early Head Start program were maintained, we conducted a follow-up study. We contacted families at intervals after Early Head Start ended and assessed children and interviewed families the spring before children entered kindergarten. When children were enrolled in a form of formal early child care and education (defined as center-based child care, Head Start, or a prekindergarten program), we observed the quality in these programs and interviewed teachers.

Achieving the purposes of the follow-up study required conducting both experimental and nonexperimental analyses, which addressed the following study questions:

- Were there impacts of Early Head Start 2 years after the program ended, immediately prior to kindergarten entry?
- Where did the children go after Early Head Start, and was the program effective in helping families find quality care and center-based education programs for their children during the prekindergarten years, ages 3–5?
- What were the effects of prekindergarten care and education programs?
- What were the cumulative effects of Early Head Start and preschool care and education?

Measures

Measures for the follow-up study were designed to provide continuity with the earlier study; several measures were selected to facilitate longitudinal analyses. When new or substitute measures were selected, we prioritized measures that had been employed in the Head Start Family and Child Experiences Survey (FACES; ACF, 2003b, 2007b) or other national surveys (e.g., Early Childhood Longitudinal Survey). We conducted tracking interviews within the first and second years after Early Head Start ended and completed child assessments in the spring or summer before children entered kindergarten. As was true for the earlier data collection, children were assessed in their homes, a videotaped semi-structured parent–child interaction task was completed, and parents were interviewed. Trained observers conducted quality assessments of the classrooms in which the prekindergarten children were enrolled.

Child assessments included measures of cognitive development (Woodcock Johnson Letter-Word Identification and Applied Problems Scales [Woodcock & Johnson, 1990]); language development (the PPVT-III [Dunn & Dunn, 1997] and the TVIP [*Test de Vocabulario en Imágenes Peabody*] for Spanish-speaking children [Dunn, Padilla, Lugo, & Dunn, 1986]); child positive approaches to learning (FACES Social Skills and Positive Approaches to Learning Scale [Administration for Children and Families, 2007b] and the Leiter International Performance Scale-Revised [Leiter-R; Roid & Miller, 1997]); socio-emotional development (videotaped assessments of child engagement, attention, and negativity using a Play-Doh task based on 54-Month Parent–Child Structured Interaction Qualitative Rating Scales [Fauth, Brady-Smith, & Brooks-Gunn, 2003; Owen, Barfoot, Vaughn, Domingue, & Ware, 1996]; and parent ratings of aggression [Achenbach & Rescorla, 2000]. Parent assessments included the Home Observation for Measurement of the Environment (HOME), resulting in overall and factor subscores (Caldwell & Bradley, 1984); measures of parent supportiveness, detachment, intrusiveness, warmth, and negativity from the Play-Doh task just mentioned; the Center for Epidemiological Studies–Depression Scale (Radloff, 1977); and many survey questions on parents' participation in children's lives and other questions about parent well-being. Early education and care quality was measured using the Arnett Caregiver Interaction Scale (Arnett, 1989) and the Early Childhood Environment Rating Scale-Revised (ECERS-R; Harms, Clifford, & Cryer, 1998).

Data Collection

Similar data-collection procedures were used in the prekindergarten follow-up as for earlier phases and, in many cases, the same data collectors visited children and families in their homes. Across tracking and the prekindergarten follow-up interviews, 77.6% of the original sample of 3,001 was contacted at least once. Prekindergarten child data were collected on 2,142 children (71.4% of the sample). This response rate is similar to that found in the 3-year data collection period 2 years earlier (ACF, 2002). Contact response rates were somewhat higher for the Early Head Start program group than for the control group (80.4% versus 74.7% overall and across all data-collection periods). Response rates were slightly higher for the parent interviews than for child assessments and videotaped parent–child interactions. Research conducted with children prior to their kindergarten entry in our evaluation sample will enable more detailed descriptions of the early childhood experiences of former Early Head Start and control-group children during the preschool years.

DISCUSSION

Early Head Start is a relatively new program, now a decade and a half old, but much has been learned during its early history, in part because of the decision to implement a randomized control study soon after its inception. Because there are fewer studies of program impacts focused on infants and toddlers than of prekindergarten interventions, each early-intervention study is particularly important for creating a developmental approach to understanding intervention effects.

In this section, we draw a number of conclusions about the contributions this study makes to the literature on interventions for infants and toddlers living in poverty. We identify salient program features of Early Head Start, summarize the findings from the Early Head Start study when children were 3, and then attempt to place these results in the context of other findings for children in intervention programs, ages 0–3.

Program Features of Early Head Start

As we have stressed, Early Head Start programs follow alternative program models, whether home-based or center-based, as well as the increasingly more common mixed-approach models, which may have enabled programs to improve fit between family service needs and program services and notably to provide two-generation services (child and parent) intensively to both. The design and guidelines for Early Head Start had been influenced by lessons learned from the Comprehensive Child Development Program (CCDP), which did not find widespread favorable impacts from a predominantly case-management demonstration program delivered to a similar population as in Early Head Start (Goodson, Layzer, St. Pierre, Bernstein, & Lopez, 2000). Drawing on the CCDP findings, Early Head Start programs were directed to include a greater emphasis on direct and intensive child development services, while maintaining parenting education and family support. Thus, more center-based and the mixed-approach programs were seen in Early Head Start than had been true for the CCDP programs, which had been primarily home-based, and Early Head Start home-based programs also placed more emphasis on child development (ACF, 2003a). Furthermore, more mixed-approach programs appeared in Early Head Start over time: As programs sought to find the best models for focusing on both children and parents, they increasingly offered parents both center-based and home-based services (ACF, 2003a).

Moreover, although Early Head Start programs are Head Start programs for pregnant women and infants and toddlers and follow the same Performance Standards that guide Head Start program features, the diversity of Early Head Start program models and their potentially greater emphasis on parenting education through home-based services contrast somewhat with Head Start programs for 3- to 5- year-olds, which are primarily center-based, whether part-day/part-year or full-day/full-year. In Head Start programs serving 3- to 5-year-olds, 95% of children receive the center-based option, 3% receive the home-based option, and 2% receive a variety of other services (e.g., combination of center and home options, family child care, or a locally designed option). In contrast, 51% of children served by Early Head Start receive the center-based option, 41% the home-based option, 4% the combination of the center- and home-based option, and 4% family child care or a locally designed option. These percentages include those children and families receiving more than one option (or the mixed-approach design).

Impacts

The Early Head Start program had a wide pattern of modest impacts across all areas of child development and parenting. That the impacts ranged across multiple domains (child socio-emotional, health, cognitive, and language development, as well as across parenting variables assessed by natural observation, semi-structured observations, and self-report of parenting practices and self-sufficiency outcomes) suggests that the impacts are not likely to be spurious. The findings are also notable in that the programs were newly implemented and the study tested a program that was implemented at scale in the field under typical circumstances for large-scale federal programs at a time when many control-group children were also receiving some services. As would be expected under at-scale circumstances, Early Head Start served a heterogeneous population. We now elaborate on these last two points and thereby attempt to place Early Head Start findings in the context of intervention programs for infants and toddlers, showing how the Early Head Start programs and findings are similar to and different from other age 0–3 programs in the United States that have been studied under rigorous conditions.

First, the structure of Early Head Start contrasts with demonstration programs for infants and toddlers such as the Abecedarian program (see Chapter 4; Ramey & Campbell, 1984) and Nurse-Family Partnership (see Chapter 3; e.g., Olds, Sadler, & Kitzman, 2007) or the Parent-Child Development Centers (e.g., Johnson & Walker, 1991), in which single-site interventions were carefully controlled. Both types of experiments (demonstration and at-scale) are valuable, but they represent programs at different stages in the dissemination process. Indeed, the Early Head Start at-scale programs included some sites that were not fully implemented; however, as expected, impacts were larger for the sites that were fully implemented (ACF, 2002). In addition, variability in families' actual receipt of services, or dosage, has been reported (ACF, 2002).

The context in which Early Head Start has operated contrasts with that of some of the best-known early age 0–3 studies, which were carried out at a time when fewer mothers of infants were in the labor force and control-group children were less likely to be in group care or to receive other services. Infant Health and Development Program babies (Brooks-Gunn et al., 1993) were born in 1985 when more mothers were in the labor force than had been true for the Abecedarian program on which it was modeled, but fewer than in 1996–1998 when Early Head Start study babies were born, a time when mothers receiving cash assistance in program and control groups were also expected to be employed under the recently passed welfare-reform measures of 1996.

Next, and somewhat related, Early Head Start program services were offered to a varied or heterogeneous population, whereas demonstration programs studied earlier generally delivered services to homogeneous populations. For example, the Abecedarian study's sample was 96% African Americans, whereas the Nurse-Family Partnership's randomized control studies examined three separate population groups in separate trials and found different patterns of impacts in these different population groups. Thus, it may be helpful to contrast comparable population groups across demonstration and at-scale studies, such as results for African American parents. The Early Head Start effect sizes in the overall impact analyses are smaller than those seen in the Abecedarian study, which found effect sizes of about 1 standard deviation for cognitive outcomes at age 3. When Early Head Start results for African Americans are compared to those of the Abecedarian study, we see that the largest Early Head Start effect sizes (about .48) are about half of those of the largest effect sizes for Abecedarian. However, their effect sizes still represent a sizable impact in the contemporary "real world" where programs are at-scale and control-group families have access to infant–toddler services in their communities. There are fewer clear referents for 0–3 programs that have been rigorously studied for Whites and Hispanics than for African Americans. With the exception of the Nurse-Family Partnership study in Denver (Olds et al., 2004), the Houston Parent-Child Development Center (Johnson & Walker, 1991), and some Infant Health and Development Program sites (Brooks-Gunn et al., 1993), studies of services for Hispanics during the 0–3 years are less prevalent than those focused on African Americans, and it is likely that programs may be able to improve their effectiveness in providing 0–3 services to Hispanic families. Regarding White families, the Elmira Nurse-Family Partnership (NFP) program findings (Olds, Henderson, Tatelbaum, & Chamberlin, 1986) would suggest that more impacts are possible than were seen in Early Head Start. However, Elmira NFP White parents were first-time parents, whereas Early Head Start parents were both prima and multiparas. Additionally, the higher functioning among the Early Head Start White control-group children, compared to other race/ethnicity control groups, may suggest the need to develop special strategies for this group.

In addition to African Americans, some other child and family subgroups in this heterogeneous population in Early Head Start demonstrated substantially larger impacts than the sample overall, as reported elsewhere (e.g., families who entered during pregnancy). It would be reasonable for the reader to deduce that if some groups experienced larger impacts, there would be others that experienced fewer or smaller impacts than the overall sample. However, it was notable that positive impacts (more than would be expected by chance) were found in nearly every subgroup, although consistent with the heterogeneity of the sample, there were different patterns of impacts for different subgroups, which may have contributed to an overall flattening of effects.

A final major finding of the study was that effects varied by program model, and the broadest pattern of impacts was seen in mixed-approach programs in which families were offered a mixture of center-based and home-based services. The results are consistent with those from the Infant Health and Development Program, which also offered a pattern of home visits and center-based care (Brooks-Gunn et al., 1993). The theories of change at work within Early Head Start revealed that home-based programs tended to aim at parent outcomes with the intention that changes in parenting would translate into child outcomes and that center-based programs aimed directly at children's cognitive development (ACF, 2002). Thus, it is not surprising that programs offering a combination of parent and child services yielded the broadest pattern of impacts on both parenting and child outcomes, consistent with conclusions by Benasich and Brooks-Gunn (1996) and Gomby (2005). This mixed-approach model offers intensive child services through center-based programming and parent-focused home visiting that may optimize the potential of age 0–3 programs. This model is in contrast to more child-focused, center-based services that are offered more commonly in age 3–5 programs, whether Head Start or state prekindergarten programs.

Although impacts of the newly formed Early Head Start programs that were studied in the randomized control trial (RCT) were significant and widespread, overall effect sizes were modest, which indicates that more needs to be learned and accomplished to provide fully adequate, at-scale early intervention for diverse populations of infants and toddlers living in circumstances of extreme poverty and stress. The research we have described provides support for local and national efforts aimed at the "earliest" childhood intervention, and there is new information about children that will help programs more effectively target the mechanisms of development and intervention services needed for the future. It is also important that research from the Early Head Start experiment continue to inform the field through follow-up studies, ongoing analyses, and the development of systems that make the data widely available for further study.

REFERENCES

Abidin, R., (1995). *Parenting Stress Index: Professional manual* (3rd ed.). Lutz, FL: Psychological Assessment Resources.

Achenbach, T. M., & Rescorla, L. A. (2000). *Manual for ASEBA preschool forms and profiles.* Burlington: University of Vermont, Research Center for Children, Youth, and Families.

Administration for Children and Families (ACF; 1996, November 5). Head Start program: Final rule (61–215). *Federal Register*, 57186–57227.

Administration for Children and Families (ACF; 2002). *Making a difference in the lives of infants and toddlers and their families: The impacts of Early Head Start.* Washington, DC: U.S. Department of Health and Human Services.

Administration for Children and Families (ACF; 2003a). *Pathways to quality and full implementation of Early Head Start programs.* Washington, DC: U.S. Department of Health and Human Services.

Administration for Children and Families. (ACF; 2003b). *Head Start FACES 2000: A whole-child perspective on program performance.* Washington, DC: U.S. Department of Health and Human Services.

Administration for Children and Families (ACF; 2005). *Head Start program information report 2004–2005.* Washington, DC: U.S. Department of Health and Human Services.

Administration for Children and Families (ACF; 2007a). *Early Head Start Research and Evaluation Project (EHSRE) 1996–current, instruments.* Retrieved from http://www.acf.hhs.gov/programs/opre/ehs/ehs_resrch/index.html#instru.

Administration for Children and Families. (ACF; 2007b). *Head Start Family and Child Experiences Survey (FACES), 1997–2010, instruments.* Retrieved from http://www.acf.hhs.gov/programs/opre/hs/faces/index.html#instru.

Administration for Children and Families (ACF; 2009). *Head Start program information report, 2007–2008.* Washington, DC: U.S. Department of Health and Human Services.

Administration on Children, Youth, and Families. (ACYF; 1994). *The statement of the Advisory Committee on Services for Families with Infants and Toddlers.* Washington, DC: U.S. Department of Health and Human Services.

Arnett, J. (1989). Caregivers in day-care centers: Does training matter? *Journal of Applied Developmental Psychology, 10,* 541–552.

Bayley, N. (1993). *Bayley scales of infant development* (2nd ed.). San Antonio, TX: Psychological Corporation.

Benasich, A. A., & Brooks-Gunn, J. (1996). Maternal attitudes and knowledge of child-rearing: Associations with family and child outcomes. *Child Development, 67,* 1186–1205.

Brady-Smith, C. (2004). Three-bag task. In *Baby steps: Creating measures for the Early Head Start Research and Evaluation Project* (Part II) [Early Head Start Research and Evaluation Project DVD]. Washington, DC: Xtria, LLC.

Brooks-Gunn, J., Klebanov, P., Liaw, F., & Spiker, D. (1993). Enhancing the development of low-birthweight premature infants: Changes in cognition and behavior over the first three years. *Child Development, 64,* 736–753.

Caldwell, B. M., & Bradley, R. H. (1984). *Administration manual: Home Observation for Measurement of the Environment.* Little Rock: University of Arkansas at Little Rock.

Dunn, L. M., & Dunn, L. M. (1997). *Peabody Picture Vocabulary Test* (3rd ed.). Circle Pines, MN: American Guidance Service.

Dunn, L. M., Padilla, E. R., Lugo, D. E., & Dunn, L. M. (1986). *Examiner's manual for the Test de Vocabulario en Imagenes Peabody (Peabody Picture Vocabulary Test) Adaptacion Hispanoamericana (Hispanic-American adaptation).* Circle Pines, MN: American Guidance Service.

Fauth, R. C., Brady-Smith, C., & Brooks-Gunn, J. (2003). *Early Head Start follow-up: Transition from preschool to kindergarten (TPK): Parent–child interaction rating scales for the Play-Doh task.* Unpublished documentation, National Center for Children and Families, Columbia University.

Fenson, L., Dale, P., Reznick, J., Bates, E., Thal, D., & Pethick, J. (1994). Variability in early communication development. *Monographs of the Society for Research in Child Development, 59*(5, No. 242).

Gomby, D. S. (2005). *Home visitation in 2005: Outcomes for children and parents.* Washington, DC: Committee for Economic Development: Invest in Kids Working Group.

Goodson, B., Layzer, J., St. Pierre, R., Bernstein, L., & Lopez, M. (2000). Effectiveness of a five-year family support program for low-income children and their families: Findings from the Comprehensive Child Development Program. *Early Childhood Research Quarterly, 15,* 5–39.

Harms, T., Clifford, R. M., & Cryer, D. (1998). *Early Childhood Environment Rating Scale* (rev. ed.). New York: Teachers College Press.

Heckman, J. J., & Masterov, D. V. (2004). *The productivity argument for investing in young children* (Working Paper No. 5). Washington, DC: Invest in Kids Working Group, Committee for Economic Development.

Johnson, D. L., & Walker, T. (1991). A follow-up evaluation of the Houston Parent-Child Development Center: School performance. *Journal of Early Intervention, 15*(3), 226–236.

Love, J., Kisker, E. E., Ross, C., Raikes, H., Constantine, J., Boller, K., et al. (2005). The effectiveness of Early Head Start for 3-year-old children and their parents. *Developmental Psychology, 41,* 885–901.

National Institute of Child Health and Human Development (NICHD) Early Child Care Research Network (2005). *Child care and child development.* New York: Guilford Press.

Olds, D., Henderson, C. R., Tatelbaum, R., & Chamberlin, R. (1986). Improving the delivery of prenatal care and outcomes of pregnancy: A randomized trial of Nurse Home Visitation, *Pediatrics, 77*(1), 16–28.

Olds, D., Robinson, J., Pettitt, L., Luckey, D., Holmberg, J., Ng, R., et al. (2004). Effects of home visits by paraprofessionals and by nurses: Age-four follow-up of a randomized trial. *Pediatrics, 115,* 1560–1568.

Olds, D. L., Sadler, L., & Kitzman, H. (2007). Programs for parents of infants and toddlers: Recent evidence from randomized trials. *Journal of Child Psychology and Psychiatry, 48*(3/4), 355–391.

Owen, M. T., Barfoot, B., Vaughn, A., Domingue, G., & Ware, A. M. (1996). *54-Month Parent–Child Structured Interaction Qualitative Rating Scales.* Washington, DC: NICHD Study of Early Child Care Research Consortium.

Radloff, L. S. (1977). The CES-D Scale: A self-report depression scale for research in the general population. *Applied Psychological Measurement, 1,* 385–401.

Ramey, C. T., & Campbell, F. A. (1984). Preventative education for high-risk children: Cognitive consequences of the Carolina ABC [Special issue]. *American Journal of Mental Deficiency, 88*(5), 515–523.

Ramey, C. T., & Ramey, S. L. (1998). Early intervention and early experience. *American Psychologist, 53*(2), 109–120.

Roid, G. H., & Miller, L. J. (1997). *Leiter International Performance Scale–revised.* Wood Dale, IL: Stoelting.

Vandell, D. (1979). Effects of a playgroup experience on mother–son and father–son interaction. *Developmental Psychology, 15,* 379–385.

Woodcock, R. W., & Johnson, M. B. (1990). *Woodcock-Johnson Revised Tests of Achievement.* Itasca, IL: Riverside.

PART II

PRESCHOOL EDUCATION

6

Project Head Start: Quality and Links to Child Outcomes

GARY RESNICK

INTRODUCTION

Head Start began in 1965 as part of the Johnson administration's War on Poverty efforts to help reduce the gap in achievement between children from low-income families and their more advantaged peers. When Head Start began in 1965, publicly funded early childhood education programs for children 3–5 years of age were not widely available, especially not for families living in poverty. Head Start became one of the most widely recognized and popular federal programs. Today, it consists of two programs: Head Start and Early Head Start, which was established during the 1994 Head Start reauthorization

---

The FACES research project was sponsored by the Administration for Children and Families, U.S. Department of Health and Human Services (DHHS), under contract #HHHS-105–96–1912, Head Start Quality Research Consortium's Performance Measurement Center. The Head Start Impact Study project was sponsored by the Office of Planning, Research and Evaluation, Administration for Children and Families, U.S. DHHS, under contract #HHS282–00–0022, Head Start Impact Study. I am grateful to the Child Outcomes Research and Evaluation, Office of Planning, Research and Evaluation, Administration for Children and Families, U.S. DHHS, Washington, DC, for their support of both the FACES and Head Start Impact Study projects.

I also acknowledge the hard work of key members of both the FACES and HSIS project teams. The FACES project team for the 1997, 2000, and 2003 cohorts was led by Nicholas Zill (Westat), project director, and included Peggy Hunker, Kwang Kim, and Alberto Sorongon (Westat); Ruth Hubbell-McKey (co-project director), Shefali Pai-Samant, and Cheryl Clark (Xtria); and Robert O'Brien and Mary Ann D'Elio (the CDM Group). The HSIS project team responsible for the first-year report was led by Ronna Cook, project director (Westat), and included Michael Puma (Chesapeake Associates), Stephen Bell (ABT Associates), Camilla Heid, Nicholas Zill, Gary Shapiro, Pam Broene, Liz Quinn, Janet Friedman, and Haidee Bernstein (Westat); Gina Adams; Monica Rohacek; and Debra Mekos (Urban Institute). As well, I wish to thank the statistical programming assistance provided by members of Westat's programming group, including John Brown (manager), Ban Cheah, and Kristen Madden. Finally, I am grateful to Ronna Cook and Camilla Heid for their review of the draft manuscript and ensuring accuracy in presenting the HSIS results. Correspondence should be addressed to Gary Resnick, Director of Research, Harder+Company Community Research, 299 Kansas Street, San Francisco, CA 94103.

(see Chapter 5). In fiscal year 2008, Head Start was allocated approximately $6.9 billion, of which $6.2 billion funded 1,905 programs providing services to 976,150 children and their families, according to the latest Program Information Record (PIR) data from the 2006–2007 fiscal year. Head Start is funded through a combination of federal funds given directly to local grantees (80%) plus a local match or in-kind contributions (the remaining 20%). In-kind contributions may be in the form of monetary contributions, donations of goods or services, or volunteer hours. Grantees receiving funds to operate Head Start programs tend to be community action agencies (32%), public/private school systems (17%), or private/public nonprofits, such as churches and nonprofit hospitals (37%).[1]

Whether Head Start is able to reduce the achievement gap and indeed whether it "works" has been a hotly debated topic since its inception, and legislative pressures to demonstrate program performance and accountability are increasing. Evaluation of its effectiveness has had a somewhat checkered past, partly because of changes in program philosophy, debates about the most appropriate and expectable outcomes from the program, and the evaluation methods that can best demonstrate these effects. In particular, several key questions have emerged, broadly stated as follows:

1. What is the quality of Head Start classrooms as early learning environments, how does it compare to other early childhood education settings, and what factors predict variations in quality?
2. Do children make significant gains in their school-readiness skills during the Head Start year and into kindergarten, and are these gains due to their exposure to Head Start?
3. Is program quality related to children's gains during Head Start and into kindergarten?
4. What difference does participation in Head Start make to key school-readiness outcomes and parental practices for children and parents from low-income families?
5. Under what circumstances does Head Start achieve the greatest impact? What works for which children? Which Head Start services are most related to impact?

To answer these key questions, this chapter reviews the state of the national Head Start program, with emphasis on the findings from the Head Start Child and Family Experiences Survey (FACES) and the Head Start Impact Study (HSIS).

[1] Source: National Head Start Association Issue Brief: Head Start Basics. Retrieved July, 2009, from http://www.nhsa.org/files/static_page_files/A97D606C-1D09–3519-AD7E2646D5EA7CDB/08FactSheetHSBasics.pdf.

HEAD START EFFECTIVENESS STUDIES

To understand the current context of research in Head Start, one must understand its origins and development. Since its inception, Head Start provided early learning experiences primarily based in early childhood education centers for families and children living within a given income range of the national poverty guidelines. Initially a brief summer program, it gradually expanded to half-day and finally full-day sessions that coincided with the school year. Rather than being a single program, it is best considered as a "family of programs" (Edelman, 1978, cited in Valentine & Zigler, 1983) that provide a host of ancillary support and health services to children and parents, including parenting classes, assistance with GED or English as a second language (ESL) classes, social services, and preventive health services including nutritious meals, health check-ups, immunizations, and dental care. Many of these services were revolutionary in their focus on providing support to the family unit rather than to just the individual child. Most families living at or below the poverty level were often not able to obtain such services for their children.

Demonstration efforts over the year expanded the original program to include Parent-Child Centers, the Child and Family Resource Program, the Home Start demonstration, the National Transition Study, and, finally, Early Head Start. Later programmatic changes created different versions of the Head Start program for migrant and seasonal workers (the Migrant and Seasonal Head Start program) and Native Americans (the American Indian and Alaska Native program). These expansions reflect an important strength of Head Start over the years: Its ability to adapt to the changing goals and needs of families living in poverty.

Over the course of its long and storied history, Head Start has undergone pendulum-like shifts in philosophy. Teaching children letters and numbers was in fashion early on but then evolved toward less didactic and more discovery-learning approaches. With increasing congressional questioning of the benefits of Head Start during its periodic reauthorization debates, Head Start came under criticism for an over-emphasis on socialization, whole language, and discovery-learning approaches. As part of the Head Start reauthorization legislation in 1998, Congress mandated an explicit set of preliteracy skills that were modeled on the "Developmental Accomplishments of Literacy Acquisition" for 3- to 4-year-olds from the report of the National Academy of Sciences Committee on the Prevention of Reading Difficulties in Young Children (Snow, Burns, & Griffin, 1998, Table 2–1, p. 61); one such skill was the ability to identify 10 letters of the alphabet. The congressional mandate also included a broad definition of "social competence" to include language, cognitive, physical, and social domains. Later Head Start reauthorizations placed even greater importance on children's emergent literacy skills, including prereading, numeracy, and phonemic awareness. There were also unsuccessful attempts to remove outcomes such as children's social competence, emotional development, and cultural diversity (Schumacher, Greenberg, & Mezey, 2003, cited in Raver & Zigler, 2004).

Evaluation research is most effective when the program outcomes are clear and are derived from a fully realized theory of change. Shifts over the years in philosophical emphasis and performance measurement of Head Start programs are reflected in the many attempts to evaluate program performance and, ultimately, its effectiveness. Head Start began as "policy proposals based on scientific advances" (Pizzo & Tufankjian, 2004), but was not based on an extensive body of research. Rather, a small set of intervention studies largely focused on educational enrichment for mentally retarded children served as the basis for the program design (Valentine & Zigler, 1983). As the intervention target shifted from mental retardation to social disadvantage, expected outcomes from Head Start focused on intellectual performance. However, even in the early days of the program, there was concern about variations in the quality of local Head Start programs and the possible linkage between these variations and child and family outcomes (Valentine & Zigler, 1983). By the mid-1980s, the goals of the program evolved to focus on family outcomes and the provision of multiple services for children and families. Children's socio-emotional development, in addition to cognitive and literacy outcomes, became an additional indicator of program success (Valentine & Zigler, 1983).

Since Head Start's early days, questions have arisen about the quality of the programs at the local level. However, early studies such as the well-known Westinghouse study did not take into account the differing levels of quality found in local Head Start programs, although some early evaluation efforts did attempt to identify the effects of different Head Start curricula on children's outcomes. The Planned Variation Head Start study (Rivlin & Timpane, 1975), which examined multiple curricula that were implemented in Head Start programs throughout the country, produced inconclusive results about differential effects. In 1985, the Head Start Evaluation, Synthesis, and Utilization Project (McKey et al., 1985), reporting the results of a meta-analysis of more than 75 Head Start research studies, found that Head Start produced immediate, meaningful gains in all areas of cognitive development, as well as in social behavior, achievement motivation, and health status, but the methodological rigor of the constituent studies used in this meta-analysis was highly variable and overall was weak, throwing these conclusions into question. In later analyses of contrasting curricular approaches used in Project Follow-Through, children who scored lowest on pretest measures showed greater gains from the cognitive curriculum, but the effects were sufficiently small to raise questions about their practical significance (Bereiter & Kurland, 1981; Watkins, 1996).

Even early evaluation studies of Head Start reported that initial cognitive and socio-emotional gains of Head Start children appeared to fade over time

(Datta, 1979; Lee et al., 1990, cited in Barnett, 1998). The so-called fade-out effect has been linked to the lack of supportive school experiences and home environments when children leave Head Start and enter public education (Lee et al., 1990, cited in Barnett, 1998). Where there were attempts to use large-scale data to assess the efficacy of Head Start, methodological issues weakened the conclusions. The Educational Testing Services (ETS) Head Start study eliminated from testing children who had been retained in their grade or placed in special-education classes, so that test scores for these children were lost as the cohorts aged over time, thereby reducing the chances of finding significant differences between control and program groups (Barnett, 1998). More recent research has provided evidence on the effectiveness of newer curricula, such as those studied by members of the Head Start Quality Research Centers Consortia, but the impact of these interventions on preschoolers' literacy outcomes appears to be relatively short-lived. Other early evaluations of Head Start also demonstrated immediate positive gains in social behavior and achievement motivation but not necessarily long-term effects (Love, Ryer, & Faddis, 1992; McKey et al., 1985).

Some studies attempted to take advantage of existing large-scale data sets, such as Currie and Thomas's analysis of the National Longitudinal Survey of Youth (NLSY), which reported large and significant gains in receptive vocabulary for both the White and African American children attending Head Start over their siblings, as well as gains for Hispanic children (Currie & Thomas, 1995, 1999). However, a critique of the study concluded that the NLSY data set was limited in its ability to estimate Head Start effects (Barnett & Camilli, 1997).

Head Start has also played an important role as a national laboratory for studying best practices in early childhood education and family support services in low-income communities. Contributions to evidence-based early childhood education practice have been made by Head Start University Partnership Grants, Head Start Young Scholars programs, and the National Head Start Transition Study, as well as the more recent Head Start Quality Research Centers Consortia, all of which have influenced current national evaluations of Head Start, notably the development of the Head Start Child and Family Experiences Survey (FACES).

HEAD START FAMILY AND CHILD EXPERIENCES SURVEY (FACES)

FACES was launched in the fall of 1997 as part of the Head Start Program Performance Measures Initiative, in accordance with the Government Performance and Results Act (GPRA) of 1993 under Public Law 103–62, and the 1994 reauthorization of Head Start (Head Start Act, as amended May 18, 1994, Section 649-d). FACES was the first national longitudinal evaluation of Head Start's program performance describing the characteristics and experiences of children and families served by Head Start, the quality of Head Start classrooms, and the accomplishments of Head Start children in cognitive, language, and social domains including their readiness for school.

FACES does not use a counterfactual such as a nonpoor control group or a comparison group of children from low-income families who do not attend Head Start. This makes it difficult to provide rigorous evidence linking changes in children and families to the presence (or absence) of Head Start while controlling for selection effects and other threats to validity. However, FACES was not meant to demonstrate this linkage; rather, it was designed to provide national longitudinal data on a periodic basis to assist in program improvement and accountability (Zill, Sorongon, Kim, Clark, & Woolverton, 2006). The strength of the FACES design lies in its use of a large, nationally representative sample of Head Start programs, classrooms, and children and the direct assessment of children's emerging literacy skills employing norm-referenced, standardized measures. By making standard score comparisons with the published test norms, controlling for age, FACES is able to identify the "achievement gap" between children attending Head Start and their more economically privileged peers and the degree to which this gap was reduced at the end of Head Start, through kindergarten, and into first grade. These data provide circumstantial but not conclusive evidence that any gains are related to exposure to Head Start and not to other factors. As well, FACES uses complex statistical modeling to rule out other confounding factors or statistical artifacts, such as regression to the mean or maturation effects, and the large sample size provides a high level of precision.

Analyses of the FACES data have been guided by a conceptual framework specifying the role of Head Start in reducing the achievement gap of children from disadvantaged families (Zill & Resnick, 2006a). This chapter focuses on the following key issues that FACES data are designed to address:

- quality in Head Start classrooms and predictions of quality (influences of teacher backgrounds and qualifications and program factors)
- children's cognitive, language, and social skills and the gains made in these skills during the Head Start year and into kindergarten
- relationship between classroom quality and children's gains in cognitive, language, and social skills
- trends across cohorts in program quality and children's skills and gains over time

Other areas of investigation by the FACES team have been detailed in a variety of reports, particularly the *FACES 2000 Technical Report* (Zill, Resnick, Kim, O'Donnell, Sorongon, et al., 2006), the *FACES 2003 Research Brief* (Zill, Sorongon, et al., 2006), and in a host of conference presentations by the FACES team available at the Administration for Children and Families website[2] (Resnick, 2004, 2006; Zill & Resnick; 2005). Finally, data sets from the first three cohorts of FACES are now publicly available and are housed at the Inter-University Consortium for Political and Social Research at the University of Michigan.[3] Thus, researchers can explore additional themes and content in FACES that have not hitherto been studied.

Design Overview

The first cohort of FACES began in the fall of 1997, following a spring 1997 national field test, with a second national cohort, FACES 2000, starting in the fall of 2000. A third national cohort, FACES 2003, began in the fall of 2003, and a fourth national cohort, FACES 2006, was launched in the fall of 2006. Detailed accounts of the research designs and methods, as well as the findings, are available elsewhere, such as in the *FACES 2003 Research Brief* (Zill, Sorongon, et al., 2006), *FACES 2000 Technical Report* (Zill, Resnick, et al., 2006), as well as in published book chapters (cf. Zill & Resnick, 2006a, 2006b). The Office of Planning, Research, and Evaluation (OPRE) within the Administration for Children and Families maintains a website that includes many reports and presentations coming out of both FACES and the HSIS.[4] This chapter summarizes the findings from the second and third FACES cohorts: FACES 2000 and 2003.

FACES Classroom Quality and Factors Predicting Quality

FACES broke new ground by describing the quality of Head Start classrooms in a nationally representative sample. Creating benchmarks for quality is important both for continuous quality-improvement efforts and in understanding the relationship between quality and children's outcomes. The average ECERS-R scores across FACES 2000 and 2003, collected in the fall of each data-collection period, were highly consistent and indicated that the quality in Head Start is good. Comparisons of ECERS-R scores with those from other large-scale early childhood education studies revealed that the quality of Head Start classrooms is higher than in many other early childhood education settings, including community-based, school-based, nonprofit, and for-profit organizations (Zill & Resnick, 2006a; Zill, Sorongon, et al., 2006). Additionally, the variation in scores was lower than that found for these other programs. There were relatively few Head Start classrooms with low quality, supporting the influence of the Head Start Program Performance Standards.

[2] http://www.acf.hhs.gov/programs/opre/hs/faces/index.html.
[3] Persistent URL: http://dx.doi.org/10.3886/ICPSR22580.
[4] http://www.acf.hhs.gov/programs/opre/hs/faces/index.html.

The qualifications and experience of teachers are important contributors to quality in the classroom. From FACES 2000 to FACES 2003, there were no significant differences in the length of time teachers in Head Start classrooms had been teaching in Head Start or in all educational settings. In general, most of the trends from the first to the second cohort of FACES in teaching experience remained or increased in magnitude by the third cohort (Table 6.1).

Increasingly, the national trend is to raise teacher qualifications, with an emphasis on college degrees in early childhood education (ECE), child development (CD), or a related field (Whitebook, 2003). The most recent Head Start reauthorization bill, the Improving Head Start for School Readiness Act of 2007, requires that by 2013, at least 50% of Head Start teachers nationwide in center-based programs have either a baccalaureate or an advanced degree in early childhood education, or a baccalaureate or an advanced degree and coursework equivalent to a major relating to early childhood education, with experience teaching preschool-age children. Furthermore, assistant teachers in center-based programs must have at least a child development associate credential or be enrolled in a program leading to an associate or a baccalaureate degree or in a child development associate credential program that will be completed within 2 years (P.L. 110–134, 42 U.S.C. 9843a(2), 2007). The educational-research literature suggests the importance of teachers with higher education degrees, particularly the bachelor's degree (Whitebook, 2003), but some later studies have found that the relationship between higher teacher education and classroom quality is either null or contradictory (Early et al., 2007). As Whitebook (2003) has pointed out, it is not clear what we gain from the bachelor's over the associate's degree or what value is added with an advanced degree.

The percentages of Head Start teachers with a bachelor's degree or higher in the first three FACES cohorts were lower than those of teachers in public elementary schools. In a survey of prekindergarten classrooms in U.S. public schools in 2000–2001, 86% of prekindergarten teachers had a bachelor's or higher degree (Smith, Kleiner, Parsad, & Farris, 2002), compared with 37.8% having a bachelor's degree or higher in FACES 2003. However, it found that 72.1% had an associate's degree or higher and 68% of all teachers reported having the Child Development Associate (CDA) credential or a state-awarded preschool certificate, with 54.5% having the Child Development Associate only.

The proportion of teachers with a bachelor's degree or higher increased significantly from fall 1997 to fall 2000 and then stabilized from fall 2000 to fall 2003. The increase over the first two cohorts was primarily due to an increase in the proportion of teachers with graduate-level degrees, defined as a master's degree, its equivalent, or higher. From fall 2000 to fall 2003, there was a large, statistically significant increase in the proportion of teachers with

Table 6.1. *Comparison of lead teacher backgrounds, FACES 1997, 2000, and 2003 (fall only), weighted data*

Teacher Variable	Categories	Fall 1997 (N = 437)	Fall 2000 (N = 257)	Fall 2003 (N = 326)
Years teaching Head Start	1–2 yrs	14.2	20.0	18.7
	3–4 yrs	22.7	22.6	20.1
	5–9 yrs	34.1	29.0	24.8
	10+ yrs	29.0	28.3	36.4
	Total	100.0	100.0	100.0
Highest level of education achieved	High school or equivalent	10.8	9.0	4.9
	Some college	31.4	34.1	23.0
	Associate's diploma	29.8	18.3	34.3
	Bachelor's degree or equivalent	24.9	27.1	31.4
	Graduate or professional degree	3.2	11.4	6.4
	Total	100.0	100.0	100.0
Teacher age category	18–29	14.7	15.1	12.1
	30–39	33.3	33.7	29.1
	40–49	31.8	28.3	34.3
	50–59	15.9	15.7	20.5
	60 or older	4.3	7.1	4.0
	Total	100.0	100.0	100.0
Membership in ECE association	No	38.5	38.0	52.6
	Yes	61.5	62.0	47.4
	Total	100.0	100.0	100.0
Child Development Associate certificate or equivalent	No	23.9	25.5	32.3
	Yes	76.1	74.5	67.7
	Total	100.0	100.0	100.0
Teacher ethnicity	Caucasian, non-Hispanic	41.1	49.7	51.3
	African American, non-Hispanic	34.2	31.6	26.6
	Hispanic[a]	22.4	16.1	16.8
	Asian	2.3	1.2	2.8
	Multiple race/other	na	1.3	2.6
	Total	100.0	100.0	100.0

[a] Puerto Rico was represented in FACES 1997 but not in the FACES 2000 and 2003 samples, explaining the lower percentage of Hispanic teachers in these later cohorts.

associate's degrees or higher, and the percentage of teachers with a bachelor's or an associate's degree or higher increased significantly from 39.9% in fall 2000 to 60.9% in fall 2003. Compared to previous cohorts, in fall 2003 there was a trend toward Head Start teachers having achieved at least their associate's diploma and to be Caucasian, younger, new to teaching Head Start, and, continuing a trend from fall 2000, entering with higher educational levels and training in early childhood education. Overall, the data reveal that Head Start teachers are experienced and qualified to teach early childhood education, but the percentage with bachelor's degrees or higher is lower than what is found in school-based early childhood education settings.

An important area of study beginning with the first FACES cohort is the analysis of variations in quality in order to identify those factors that are most predictive of quality. This analysis is designed to provide guidance for ways to improve quality in Head Start and to help policy makers, researchers, and program designers understand the mechanisms linking quality to children's outcomes. This examination of quality attempts to build a model that essentially "unpacks" the critical ingredients of quality in Head Start by accounting for explainable variation according to factors at the classroom, center, and program levels. If we know that variations in quality at the program level contribute significantly to classroom quality, we can then look for those factors that seem to make the difference. Factors "beyond the classroom door" might include program management styles, resources, and demographics of the community, which may directly influence decisions about quality made by center directors (e.g., the quality of teachers who can be recruited) and, indirectly, influence teachers in individual classrooms (Blau, 1997; Hofferth & Chaplin, 1998, cited in Phillips, Mekos, Scarr, McCartney, & Abbott-Shim, 2000).

Initial analyses of the FACES data set showed that there was indeed a relatively larger amount of variation in quality between programs (under which centers and classrooms are nested) compared to the variation within programs, supporting the notion that factors at the level of the program's organization may make significant contributions to predictions of quality. In FACES 2000,[5] additional analyses of factors that explained variations in quality were conducted using a series of multilevel models. This approach was designed to predict the average quality scores of Head Start classrooms from factors at both the classroom and program levels.

The analytic method has been described previously (Zill & Resnick, 2006b). In all of these models, the initially significant linear regressions predicting classroom quality from teacher and classroom factors disappeared when program-level characteristics were entered. The results of these analyses

[5] As of this writing, the following analyses using the FACES 2003 classroom data have not yet been done. With the availability of the FACES 2003 public use data set, investigators are encouraged to conduct these analyses to determine whether the models from FACES 2000 fit the FACES 2003 classroom data.

are presented in detail in the *FACES 2000 Technical Report* (Zill, Resnick, et al., 2006) and are only briefly summarized here to highlight selected quality indicators.

Predicting ECERS-R Total Scores

The final two-level model accounted for 5.5% of the total variation and 28.3% of the between-program variation in ECERS-R total scores. The findings suggested that high-quality classrooms are likely to be those where programs have a higher percentage of nonminority students and of language-minority students (e.g., Spanish speakers) and of teachers who have more positive attitudes and knowledge about early childhood education practices. Additionally, a similar set of analyses was conducted using the ECERS-R Language Subscale, and the findings revealed that teachers with higher scores for attitudes and knowledge about early childhood education practice were likely to be in classrooms with higher quality of language activities and materials.

Predicting Arnett Caregiver Interaction Scale (CIS) scores

The final two-level model accounted for 20.4% of the total variation and 59.7% of the between-program variation in Arnett CIS scores. Classrooms with sensitive and responsive teachers were likely to be those that use the Creative Curriculum by Teaching Strategies Inc.,[6] in which the teachers have more years of teaching experience and they hold more positive attitudes and knowledge about practices in early childhood education.

Predicting Quality Factor Scores

The final two-level model accounted for 19.2% of the total variation and 55.9% of the between-program variation in quality factor scores. Classrooms with higher scores for quality on this indicator (comprising the ECERS-R Language Scale and the Assessment Profile Scheduling and Learning Environment Scales in FACES 2000) were those from Head Start programs with a higher percentage of language-minority students and whose teachers had more positive attitudes and knowledge of early childhood education practice.

Predicting Child:Adult Ratio

The final two-level model accounted for 5.5% of the total variation and 28.3% of the between-program variation in child:adult ratios, which are relatively small effects when compared to the earlier models using more process-oriented measures of quality. These findings suggest that variation in child:adult ratios is not strongly explained by program- and classroom-level factors. Classrooms with lower child:adult ratios, indicating higher quality, are those in which teachers are better paid.

[6] http://www.creativecurriculum.net/.

In all of these models, teacher education, indicated by whether or not teachers had an associate's or bachelor's degree, was not significantly predictive of quality, even though in some cases (e.g., the Arnett), it was related in earlier analyses that did not include program-level factors. In fact, the direct relationships occurred most consistently and strongly for attitudes and knowledge about early childhood education practice and to a lesser extent for teacher experience, rather than with teacher education. When these other factors were not included, there was a significant relationship between teacher education and classroom quality, suggesting that the role of teacher education in influencing classroom quality is an indirect one. Teachers with higher levels of education had more positive attitudes and knowledge about early childhood education practice, and they were more likely to be in classrooms rated higher in quality. Teacher attitudes and knowledge toward early childhood education practice, as measured by a modified version of the Teacher Beliefs Scale, appears to mediate the role of teacher education in explaining classroom quality. In the case of the predictions to the Arnett Caregiver Interaction Scale, teacher beliefs combined with type of curriculum used and the teacher's level of experience were strongly predictive of teacher sensitivity and responsiveness.

These findings are consistent with other studies in which the relationship between teachers' education and classroom quality was found mainly when zero-order correlations were conducted and tended to weaken or disappear when more complex models were used (Whitebook, 2003). Although a meditational argument has been used to explain these results (Whitebook, 2003), others have suggested that perhaps more highly educated teachers are selected into higher quality settings (Hamre & Bridges, 2004, cited in Whitebook, 2003), and this also may be the case for Head Start. Head Start programs that provide for a common integrative curriculum across classrooms, such as the Creative Curriculum, and that pay their teachers better have sufficient resources available to positively influence classroom quality through the quality of teachers hired and teacher experience and attitudes.

FACES Children's Outcomes and Relationships to Quality

The question of whether quality in early childhood education settings such as those provided by Head Start is related to children's cognitive, language, and social development is a central theme in FACES. By testing this relationship in Head Start programs, we can provide guidance to policy makers and developers of programs in their quality-improvement efforts. The direct relationship between classroom quality, including teacher qualifications and experience, and improved children's school-readiness outcomes has gained some support in the research literature, but that relationship is relatively modest (Peisner-Feinberg & Burchinal, 1997). Although some studies of community child care settings have supported this relationship (Bryant, Burchinal, Lau,

& Sparling, 1994; NICHD Early Child Care Research Network, 2000; Phillips, McCartney, & Scarr, 1987; Whitebook, Howes, & Phillips, 1989), not all studies have found such a link.

To assess the contribution of quality in early childhood education settings on children's cognitive and language skills, a series of multifactor, multilevel models were employed. The analytic approach and details about the findings have been explained elsewhere (cf. Zill & Resnick, 2006b), and here only the key findings are summarized. In general, multilevel modeling identified the degree to which program quality indicators contribute significantly to children's achievement levels and gains. Most analyses used the more recent FACES 2003 data sets whenever possible and, in some cases, both FACES 2000 and FACES 2003 data sets were used to identify the degree to which the findings were comparable across cohorts. Analyses of gains through kindergarten relied on the FACES 2000 data set, with children's gain scores from fall to spring of their Head Start year and then from the spring of Head Start to the spring of kindergarten. Some of these findings are also reported in the *FACES 2003 Research Brief* (Zill, Sorongon, et al., 2006). It should be noted that FACES also conducted extensive measures of children's social competence using rating scales from teachers and parents, but space in this chapter does not allow explication of these findings (see Zill, Resnick, et al., 2006; and Zill, Sorongon, et al., 2006). This section describes changes in skill levels of Head Start children from fall to spring of their Head Start year and into kindergarten, and the relationships to variations in classroom quality.

The majority of children who entered Head Start in fall 2003 came into the program with early literacy and numeracy skills that were less developed than those of most children of the same age (Zill & Resnick, 2006a). The literacy and number skills of the average Head Start child entering the program varied from a half standard deviation to a full standard deviation below national averages, which was consistent with earlier studies of low-income children without preschool experience (Haskins, 1989; McKey et al., 1985; White, 1986). For vocabulary (PPVT-III) and early math (Woodcock-Johnson III Applied Problems), the average scores were almost a full standard deviation below national averages, whereas the average scores for early writing (Woodcock-Johnson III Spelling) were closer to national norms, and letter-naming scores (Woodcock-Johnson III Letter-Word Identification) were almost at national norms.

From the beginning to the end of the program year, Head Start children showed significant advances in vocabulary, early math, early writing, and letter-word identification, but continued to lag behind national norms (Zill & Resnick, 2006a). There was a 3.3 standard-score point gain in vocabulary, a 1.8 point gain in early math, a 0.8 point gain in early writing, and a 4.2 point gain in early reading (i.e., Letter-Word Identification measure). The sizes of the gains were comparable to earlier studies on the immediate effects of Head

Start on children's intellectual performance (Haskins, 1989, p. 277; McKey et al., 1985). All of these gains were statistically significant and, particularly for vocabulary and letter-word identification, the gains were large enough to have meaningful programmatic and policy implications. Still, they were less than half the size of standard-score gains in IQ and achievement reported in earlier studies in which gains of one-half of a standard deviation or approximately 8 standard-score points had been reported in evaluations of more intensive interventions with children from disadvantaged families (Barnett, 1998).

Across the three cohorts of FACES, the size of the gains in vocabulary remained the same, whereas for early reading (Letter-Word Identification) there was a significant increase in fall to spring gains in FACES 2003 – from 0.71 and 0.73 IRT scale score gains in FACES 1997 and FACES 2000, respectively – to 0.84 scale score gains in FACES 2003.[7] In fact, FACES 2003 early reading scores on the Letter-Word Identification measure reduced the gap with national norms compared with the gap in earlier FACES cohorts (Zill, Sorongon, et al., 2006). This finding supports one of the key goals of Head Start, which is to provide disadvantaged children with compensatory learning experiences that will reduce the gap between their skills and the skills of more advantaged peers before entry into kindergarten.

These analyses were based on children who were assessed in English in both the fall and spring of the Head Start year. Based on the results of the language screener used in FACES 2003, 60% of Hispanic children had sufficient English skills to be assessed in English in both fall 2003 and spring 2004. By the spring, these children showed gains of 4.9 standard-score points in English vocabulary, which were larger than those shown by African American (+2.1 standard-score points) and White (+2.3 standard score point) children (Zill, Sorongon, et al., 2006). Those Spanish-speaking children who primarily spoke Spanish at home and were assessed in Spanish[8] also had significant gains in Spanish vocabulary from fall 2003 to spring 2004 (Zill, Sorongon, et al., 2006).

When looking at the gains from the end of Head Start to the spring of their kindergarten year, focusing only on those children assessed in English at all time periods, the average Head Start graduate came close to national norms in early reading and early writing, with average standard scores of 99.3 and 98, respectively (Zill & Resnick, 2006b). However, these children continued to score significantly below national norms in vocabulary, early math, and general knowledge (using a norm-referenced measure from the Early Childhood Longitudinal Study Kindergarten cohort, ECLS-K). Additionally, the gains had varying effect sizes. For gains made during the Head Start year,

[7] These data are based on the fall-to-spring gains expressed as percentages of the fall standard deviations, after having equated the scale scores of the measures using IRT methods.

[8] These children lacked sufficient English skills to be assessed in English, based on the results of the English screener.

the largest effect size was for vocabulary (0.25), but effect sizes were much lower for the other skill areas (0.13 for prewriting, 0.07 for early math, and 0.03 for prereading). Gains made by spring of their kindergarten year were much larger on the basis of effect size; the highest gains were made for prewriting (0.81) and prereading (0.43), followed by early math (0.39) and, finally, vocabulary (0.26). It is important to note that the gains made by Head Start graduates in kindergarten for vocabulary were much less than those in the other skills areas and were more comparable to the gains made while in Head Start.

Taking into account the initial gap between Head Start children's skill levels in the fall of their Head Start year compared with national norms, by the spring of children's kindergarten year, the gap was significantly reduced for the prereading and prewriting skill measures (i.e., Letter-Word Identification and Spelling subtests of the Woodcock-Johnson Achievement Scales). Given the earlier reported finding that for the FACES 2003, the gap was already reduced by the spring of their Head Start year, we can develop a picture suggesting that smaller gains made from fall to spring contributed somewhat to the reduction in the gap between children's scores and national norms, but that one year later, in the spring of kindergarten, a considerable portion of the remaining gap was further "made up" in early reading and early writing skills. As Zill and Resnick (2006b) noted, approximately 90% and 86% of the gap between the children's initial skills and national norms in early reading and early writing, respectively, were bridged. The fact that less of the gap was bridged for early math (52%) and vocabulary (41%) suggested the need for greater intervention to improve these skills in Head Start.

To determine the linkage between variations in classroom quality and children's emergent literacy, a series of multilevel models using the FACES 2003 national sample from 60 programs was performed. The analytic approach has been described previously (Zill & Resnick, 2006b), and only the main findings are described here.

The results indicated that variation in skill levels among children by the end of their Head Start year may be explained more by socioeconomic and family characteristics of the population served than by differences in teacher qualifications or program quality. If such family-background factors were not included as controls, spring 2004 scores would vary most among children within the same classrooms. Looking at the sources of variation in the fall-to-spring gains in scores, much less variation was explained by either between-program or between-classroom sources; that is, sources of variation attributable to characteristics of the programs or classrooms. Fall-to-spring gains in scores for vocabulary were explained mainly by within-classroom sources (88% of the variation), with very little explained by either between-program (6%) or between-classroom (6%) sources. Similarly, fall-to-spring gains in scores for early reading were explained mainly by within-classroom sources (89% of

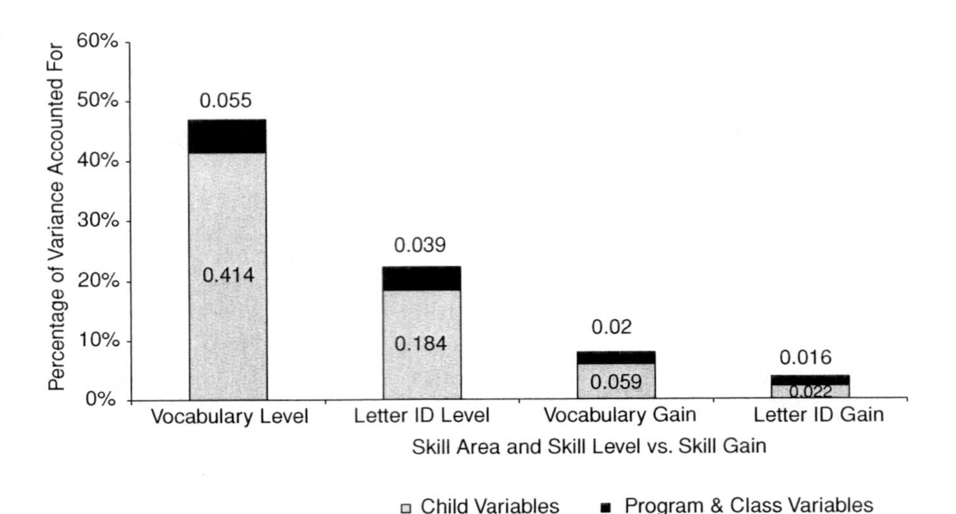

Figure 6.1. Percentage of variance in assessment scores accounted for by child-level, program-level, and class-level variables (from Zill & Resnick, 2006).

the variation), with very little explained by either between-program (6%) or between-classroom (5%) sources.

To determine the relative contribution to explained variation of child and family factors (e.g., socio-demographic, family structure, or ethnic composition) compared with program and classroom factors (e.g., program quality and curriculum and teacher experience, credentials, and knowledge or belief), two additional models were tested. One model predicted the child's skills on graduation from Head Start (spring of the Head Start year), whereas the second model predicted the gains in skills made by the children from fall to spring of their Head Start year. As in the previous findings, much less overall variation in gain scores was explained by either program or classroom factors; the same general pattern held, in which most of the variation was due to child/family factors (Fig. 6.1).

The models were also able to identify which of the program and classroom factors appeared to contribute significantly to the explained variation (Zill & Resnick, 2006b). The average annual lead teacher salary was associated with higher spring scores in vocabulary, letter-word identification, and early math and with greater gains in letter recognition. Higher Caregiver Interaction Scale scores, indicating greater teacher sensitivity and responsiveness, were associated with children's spring vocabulary and early math scores and higher positive scores on teacher-reported approaches to learning (as measured by the Preschool Learning Behaviors Scale). Classrooms with teachers having a 4-year college degree or an associate's degree in education or a closely related field tended to have children with higher early writing scores in the spring of their Head Start year. Finally, children whose parents reported reading to their children "every day" had significantly higher mean vocabulary scores in the spring of their Head Start year than did children whose parents reported reading "three to six" times. Further, children whose parents reported reading to their children "once or twice per day" had significantly lower mean scores for approaches to learning than children whose parents reported reading "three to six" times. Significant effects of parental reading were obtained even after controlling for parent education level, the mother's score on a measure of adult literacy (the K-FAST), and an indicator of the presence of books in the home.

Overall, these results emphasize the importance of family background, particularly education levels and related characteristics, as the most important influences on children's scores leaving Head Start. The results of the multilevel models provide only mixed support for the linkage between classroom quality and children's school-readiness skills, particularly when it comes to the process measures of quality, which assess the frequency and quality of Head Start classroom learning activities, materials, and staff–child interactions. Supporting the initial hypotheses, CIS scores were associated with higher vocabulary and early math skills and positive approaches to learning. Additionally, ECERS-R Language Scale scores were associated with higher fall-to-spring gains in positive approaches to learning, but there were no associations with any of the other process measures of quality. However, it is important to interpret these findings with some caution because these factors as a group accounted overall for only 5.5% of the total variation in children's school-readiness scores on their graduation from Head Start (spring 2004). Thus, relatively small amounts of total variation in children's school readiness skills are explained by classroom and program quality, even if the predictions are significant.

We also have to consider the strong and consistent findings predictive of classroom quality and compare these trends to those found linking quality to outcomes. In earlier models, we were able to explain a great deal of the variation in classroom quality through such factors as teacher beliefs and attitudes, curriculum, and the population served by the program. It seems that we can do a pretty good job of explaining variations in quality, but these significant relationships do not help explain children's school-readiness skills when they leave Head Start and enter kindergarten.

FACES has produced much important and new information to assist programs in making improvements and that describes more accurately how children fare by the time they leave Head Start. Overall, although the results indicate that children in Head Start make gains, the lack of a counterfactual in the FACES design has limited the degree to which the gains can be ascribed to Head Start as opposed to other factors, particularly the self-selection into Head Start; this limitation makes it difficult to distinguish the effects of the program from the effects of family characteristics that influence families' enrollment decisions (Barnett, 1998). The FACES results clearly showed the strong influence of family characteristics on explaining variation in children's outcomes and thus raise the issue of selection bias. Other studies have reported the same results and that the effects of preschool tend to be less consistent and diminish when controls for parental selection are included in the estimation models (Fuller, Holloway, & Liang, 1996). Findings from the Feasibility Study of Head Start Recruitment and Enrollment reported that recruitment efforts by Head Start staff were not always successful in targeting the "neediest of the needy" (Administration on Children, Youth, and Families, 2001). To counteract the effects of selection bias on interpreting the results of evaluation studies, a more rigorous design is required – one that randomly assigns children to intervention (Head Start) or no-intervention (no–Head Start) groups. This became the critical rationale for the initiation of the Head Start Impact Study.

HEAD START IMPACT STUDY (HSIS)

In the 1998 reauthorization of Head Start, Congress mandated that the U.S. Department of Health and Human Services determine, on a national level, the impact of Head Start on the children it serves. The legislative mandate required assessing the impact of Head Start on children's school readiness and parental practices that support children's development and identifying under which circumstances Head Start achieves its greatest impact, for which children, and with which Head Start services. With this legislative mandate, the Head Start Impact Study (HSIS) was born. A final report was published early in 2010 presenting the results of analyses following the children from their Head Start year through kindergarten and first grade (Administration for Children and Families, 2010a). This chapter presents some of the key findings focused primarily on program quality and children's school-readiness outcomes.

The difficulty of designing and carrying out randomized controlled trial (RCT) studies of a program such as Head Start cannot be underestimated. It is difficult to find a suitable control group and to implement random assignment protocols, which often run against the enrollment procedures typically followed by Head Start programs. In fact, these were very real concerns for the HSIS research team and stakeholders, who were worried that random assignment and subsequent data-collection efforts would be difficult, if not impossible, to execute (Administration for Children and Families [ACF], 2005). Making this task even more difficult were the requirements that the sample of programs had to be nationally representative, so that results could be generalized to the national program.

To address these issues, the study design was based on selecting only those Head Start programs that had more children eligible for Head Start than could be served with the existing number of funded slots. Doing so avoided the ethical issue inherent in RCT designs in which service is denied to those most in need of it. Information about the full recruitment and assignment procedures is available from the *Head Start Impact Study Technical Report* available on the OPRE website (Administration for Children and Families, 2010b) and is briefly summarized here.

The study used a multistage sampling process to select a representative group of Head Start programs and centers. Where necessary, stratification of programs and centers was used, such as in situations where the degree of saturation varied by program option (e.g., part-day versus full day). Then, random assignment to groups at each center was conducted separately for newly entering 3-year-olds and newly entering 4-year-olds. Children were randomly assigned either to a treatment group that had access to Head Start services or to a control group that could receive any other non-Head Start services available in the community, chosen by their parents. Under this randomized design, a simple comparison of outcomes for the two groups would yield an unbiased estimate of the impact of access to Head Start on children's school readiness. The study assessed the difference between the outcomes observed for Head Start participants and what would have been observed for these same individuals had they not participated in Head Start. This answers the key policy question of how well Head Start performs compared to alternatives if Head Start was not available, such as parental care, center-based, or family child care programs.

Staff from the participating agencies implemented their existing enrollment procedures based on locally established admission criteria. For programs participating in the HSIS, the list of newly entering children who would ordinarily have been enrolled was "extended" to add a specified number of children needed for the non–Head Start control group. The children added were those who would normally be "next in line" for admission if the initially targeted children could not be enrolled (ACF, 2010b). Children were then randomly assigned across the entire expanded list. Within the final set of 84 programs (i.e., the grantees or delegate agencies that administered the program locally), random assignment was attempted at a total of 383 randomly selected Head Start centers; it could not be completed in only 5 centers (or 1.3%), resulting in a final sample of 378 centers with successful random assignment. The goal was to randomly select, on average, 27 children from the expanded list at each of the sampled centers: 16 to be assigned to the Head Start group and 11 to be assigned to the non–Head Start group. In approximately one–half of the centers, the desired sample could not be obtained (i.e., because lower application rates resulted in smaller sample sizes and higher rates resulted in larger sample sizes). To compensate for these differences in expected enrollment rates, some center sample sizes were adjusted upward or downward (ACF, 2010b).

The study was designed to achieve a slightly lower sample size for the non–Head Start group than the Head Start group, with a roughly 60/40 split in sample size between the two groups. Although this imbalance reduced the precision of the impact estimates, the reduction was relatively trivial (less than

2% compared to a balanced 50:50 design). In addition, this design had several key advantages, including significantly increasing the ability to recruit Head Start grantees and centers by decreasing the number of children assigned to the control group, decreasing the loss of sites due to saturation, and saving considerably on data collection costs because it requires less effort to track and interview Head Start group members over time than children in the non–Head Start control group. The final sample came from programs in 23 different states and consisted of 84 randomly selected Head Start grantees/delegate agencies, 378 randomly selected Head Start centers, and a total of 4,667 newly entering children, including 2,559 in the 3-year-old group and 2,108 in the 4-year-old group.

Data collection began in the fall of 2002 and continued through the spring of 2006, following children from the age of entry into Head Start through the end of first grade. It included direct child assessments, interviews with parents, surveys of teachers (Head Start and non–Head Start), interviews with center directors and other care providers (for both groups of children), and observations of quality in both Head Start and non–Head Start care settings.

An important consideration in this study involved tracking the kinds of services in which the non–Head Start control parents and children were involved. As intended by the research design, the non–Head Start (control) group was not a "no service" group. Parents of children in the control group were not precluded from enrolling their children in other types of preschool or child-care arrangements ranging from parent care at home to non–Head Start center-based programs. In some cases, these alternatives looked very much like Head Start, whereas others looked very different. Evaluating Head Start against the current mixture of alternative arrangements isolated the contribution that the federal program was making relative to the array of other settings in which preschool-aged children from low-income families are cared for prior to their entry into kindergarten.

Another important feature of the intended design was that the 3-year-old cohort of children who had one more year before kindergarten could not be denied access to Head Start for a second year. In fact, as the 2010 final report shows, many of the children in the 3-year-old cohort did enter Head Start in the second year of the study (Administration for Children and Families, 2010a). Thus, the impacts represent the effects of an earlier year of Head Start, which answers the policy question about whether earlier age at entry makes a difference but does not answer the question of one versus two years of Head Start. Essentially, the design focused on the effects of one year of Head Start compared with alternative early childhood experiences prior to children's entry into kindergarten.

The findings summarized here primarily present estimates of the average impacts of access to Head Start for the sample of children randomly assigned to either Head Start or to the non-Head Start group, labeled the Intent To Treat (ITT) impacts. These estimates show the effect of Head Start on the average child given access to the program (Administration for Children and Families, 2010b). However, as is usually the case in randomized designs, there are deviations from random assignment in the form of "crossovers" and "no shows." The "crossovers" occurred when some of the children (13.8 percent of the 4-year-olds and 17.8 percent of the 3-year-olds) in the control group "found their way into Head Start" (Administration for Children and Families, 2010a). As well, during the first study year, 15 percent of the 3-year-old cohort and 20 percent for the 4-year-old cohort assigned to Head Start did not enroll and receive any amount of the Head Start program. Thus, a second set of results were presented in the final report estimating the impact of Head Start taking into account the effects of "crossovers" and "no shows," referred to as the Impact on the Treated (IOT). These estimates were developed by reinterpreting the overall difference in mean outcomes between the entire treatment group and the entire control group that constituted the initial ITT estimate, using Head Start's average impact on participants and on no-shows, separately (Administration for Children and Families, 2010b). This chapter presents only the ITT estimates, showing the impact of access to Head Start, while the HSIS final report provides both ITT and IOT estimates (Administration for Children and Families, 2010a). The *Head Start Impact Study Technical Report* describes the methods used for the IOT calculations (Administration for Children and Families, 2010b).

When considering impacts, we must first consider the children's variety of experiences in early childhood or child care programs in each year of the study. During the first year of the study, fall 2002 and spring 2003, children in the Head Start group were twice as likely as those in the non–Head Start group to use center-based early childhood education programs, whereas a greater proportion of the control-group children received primarily parental care (defined as less than 5 hours per week in any other nonparental care setting). Still, this means that most of the control-group children, approximately 60 percent, participated in child care (nonparental) or early childhood education programs during the first year of the study. A surprising finding was that the use of center-based settings did not vary by the child's age, despite considerable research indicating that older children are more likely to be in center-based arrangements.

In terms of the quality of these arrangements, during the first year of the study, children in the Head Start group were in environments that were significantly higher on all measures of quality compared to the non–Head Start children (Administration for Children and Families, 2010a). Head Start classrooms had lower teacher-child ratios, positive teacher-child interactions, teachers with higher qualifications, spent more time in early literacy and numeracy activities, and had higher global measures of quality (e.g., scores of five or higher on the seven-point ECERS-R scales).

However, by the second year of the study, when the control-group children (mainly the 3-year-olds) had access to Head Start, comparable and high percentages of children from both Head Start and control groups were participating in center-based early childhood education programs, and about half of the control-group children were enrolled in Head Start. As a result, many of the first-year differences in the quality of early childhood program experiences of control versus Head Start children disappeared, with the exception of three key differences. Head Start children in the second study year were less likely to be in a school-based program, were more likely to be in classrooms in which a teacher has a CDA (Child Development Associate) degree, and were more likely to receive vision and hearing screening and referral services.

Following the study children into kindergarten and first grade revealed that access to Head Start did not have any relationship to the types of schools they attended at these time periods. On the vast majority of school quality measures, there were no differences between the control and Head Start groups, for either the 3-year-old or 4-year-old cohorts. In general, most study children from both groups attended schools with higher levels of poverty compared to schools nationwide and with higher proportions of minority students (Administration for Children and Families, 2010a).

Children's school-readiness skills were measured using a direct child assessment battery and the results focused on three key domains: language and literacy (including receptive vocabulary, oral comprehension, and phonological awareness), prewriting, and early math skills. Although there was some overlap in the tests used in FACES, there were also a number of additional norm-referenced tests employed in the Head Start Impact Study, including tests that captured additional literacy, language, and cognitive outcomes as children aged into kindergarten and first grade. As well, parents were asked to provide their perceptions of their child's emerging literacy and language skills, social skills, and positive approaches to learning, problem behavior, and health status. Similar ratings were also administered to Head Start and non–Head Start teachers. Parents also reported on home educational activities, discipline strategies, and child safety practices.

The cognitive and socio-emotional impacts of Head Start from the end of the Head Start year into kindergarten and first grade, separately for the 3-year-old and 4-year-old children, are summarized in Table 6.2. Additional impacts regarding health status, health access, safety, and parenting practices, as well as subgroup analyses by home language, race, depression, urbanicity, special needs, child's pre-academic skills, and household risk, were detailed in the 2010 final report and are not discussed in this chapter.

Table 6.2. *Head Start Impact Study main findings*[a]

	Effect sizes[b,c]						
	3-year-olds				4-year-olds		
Domains, constructs, and measures	Head Start year	Age 4	K	Grade 1	Head Start year	K	Grade 1
	Cognitive Domain						
Language, Literacy, and Prewriting							
Color Identification					0.16		
McCarthy Draw A Design	0.14						
Emergent Literacy Scale (parent-reported)	0.35	0.16			0.31		
Letter-Naming	0.24				0.25		
Test of Phonological Processing (CTOPPP-Elision)	0.10	0.15					
PPVT-III Adapted	0.18				0.09		0.09
Woodcock-Johnson III Letter-Word Identification	0.26				0.22		
Woodcock-Johnson III Spelling					0.15		
Oral Comprehension (WJ-III)				0.08			
Pre-Academic Skills (WJ-III)	0.22				0.19		
Phonetic Skills – Word Attack (WJ-III)							
Basic Reading (WJ-III)							
Academic Applications (WJ-III)							
Academic Skills (WJ-III)							
Passage Comprehension (WJ-III)							
Writing Sample (WJ-III)							
Spanish Language							
Receptive Vocabulary (TVIP)							
Batería WM Identificación de letras y palabras			0.26				
Math Skills							
One-to-One Counting (Counting Bears)							
Applied Problems (WJ-III)	0.15						
Quantitative Concepts (WJ-III)							
Math Reasoning (WJ-III)							
Calculation (WJ-III)							
School Performance							
School Accomplishments							
Promotion (Parent Report)							
Language and Literacy Activity							
Math Ability (School Performance Records)			−0.19				
Social Studies and Science Ability (School Performance Records)							

(*continued*)

Table 6.2 *(continued)*

	Effect sizes[b,c]						
	3-year-olds				4-year-olds		
Domains, constructs, and measures	Head Start year	Age 4	K	Grade 1	Head Start year	K	Grade 1
	Social-Emotional Domain						
Parent-Reported Measures							
Aggressive Behavior[d]							
Hyperactive Behavior[d]	−0.21		−0.12				
Withdrawn Behavior[d]							−0.13
Total Behavior Problems[d]	−0.14						
Social Skills and Positive Approaches to Learning		0.11	0.14				
Closeness				0.10			
Conflict							
Positive Relationships				0.10			
Teacher-Reported Measures[e]							
Aggressive (ASPI)							
Interactive/Hyperactive (ASPI)							
Oppositional (ASPI)							
Problems with Peer Interaction (ASPI)							
Shy/Socially Reticent (ASPI)							0.19
Problems with Structured Learning (ASPI)							
Problems with Teacher Interaction (ASPI)							0.13
Closeness							
Conflict							
Positive Relationships							

[a] Shaded areas show where specific measures were not administered. Blank areas identify where no statistically significant effects were found.

[b] All effect sizes are based on statistically significant treatment and control differences of at least $p \leq 0.05$.

[c] Effect sizes relate the magnitude of impacts to the variation of the outcome as measured by the estimated treatment and control differences relative to the magnitude of the standard deviation on the measure of interest (i.e., as a fraction of one standard deviation).

[d] Negative effect sizes mean reduction in total problem behaviors, hyperactive behavior, and spanking. Positive effect sizes indicate negative impacts for these behaviors (e.g., shy/socially reticent and problems with teacher interaction).

[e] Although the ASPI was administered to teachers of 3-year-olds prior to kindergarten (first two time periods on the table), there were too few teachers for children in the control group to provide an adequate comparison between groups.

Source: Administration for Children and Families (2010a).

At the end of the Head Start year, there were strong impacts of Head Start among both 3- and 4-year-old children. Among the 3-year-old children at the end of the Head Start year, the strongest effects of Head Start were reported for letter-naming skills, letter-word identification, pre-academic skills (Woodcock-Johnson III pre-academic skills subtest) and receptive vocabulary (PPVT-III), with the strongest effects found for the parent-reported emergent literacy-skills measure. There were also significant but smaller effects for psychomotor skills (McCarthy Draw A Design), phonological processing, and early math skills. There were no effects for color identification, prewriting (Woodcock-Johnson III Spelling), one-to-one counting (FACES Bears task), and oral comprehension skills. Among Spanish-speaking 3-year-olds, there were also no differences between the Head Start and control groups on Spanish language skills. As well, there were Head Start impacts on parent-reported emergent literacy and phonological processing skills in the second study year (prior to their entry into kindergarten).

For the 4-year-old cohort, the largest impacts of Head Start were found for letter-identification skills (Woodcock-Johnson III Letter-Word Identification and a letter-naming task), prewriting (Woodcock-Johnson III Spelling), the Woodcock-Johnson III Pre-Academic Skills subtest, and color identification, with the strongest effects found for parent-reported emergent literacy skills. Smaller impacts were reported for receptive vocabulary (Peabody Picture Vocabulary Test III). There were no impacts of Head Start among the 4-year-olds on psychomotor skills (McCarthy Draw A Design), oral comprehension, phonological processing skills, or any of the math skills measures. Further, among those children tested in Spanish, there were no impacts on Spanish receptive vocabulary (using the TVIP) or the Spanish version of the Woodcock-Johnson Letter-Word Identification task.

The impacts of Head Start on children's social and emotional skills, including behavioral problems and positive social skills, as reported by parents and teachers, appear to accrue largely among the 3-year-olds rather than the 4-year-olds (see Table 6.2). At the end of the Head Start year, 3-year-olds in the Head Start group showed reduced hyperactive and total problem behaviors as reported by parents, but there were no impacts among the 4-year-olds. There was no overall impact of Head Start for parent-reported social skills or positive approaches to learning for children in either age group.

Across time, as the children entered kindergarten and first grade, the impacts of Head Start were not as strong or as persistent as they were at the end of the Head Start year. At kindergarten, Spanish-speaking 3-year-olds in the Head Start group showed higher scores on Spanish letter-word identification. However, at kindergarten, 3-year-olds in the Head Start group revealed lower teacher assessment of Head Start children's math ability compared with children in the non–Head Start group, which may have been related to a greater percentage of students at or above the proficient level in math in the schools attended by control-group children compared with the schools attended by the Head Start children. Also, at kindergarten, 3-year-olds in the Head Start group showed lower scores for hyperactive behavior and higher scores on positive approaches to learning (both parent-reported), compared with children in the control group. In first grade, 3-year-olds in the Head Start group showed higher oral comprehension scores as well as higher parent-reported closeness and positive relationships, compared with children in the control group.

Four-year-olds in the Head Start group at kindergarten showed no significant differences in cognitive or social skills compared to the control-group children. At first grade, the 4-year-olds in Head Start had higher receptive vocabulary scores and lower scores on withdrawn behavior, compared to children in the control group, but there was also an unfavorable impact on shyness and reticence (teacher-reported) and teacher–child interaction problems (also teacher-reported) for 4-year-olds in the Head Start group.

Overall, in the short term, the results are impressive in terms of the variety of significant impacts reported across a number of domains related to school readiness, including cognitive, language, and social skills. Although some effect sizes are relatively modest, the impacts of Head Start were consistently positive across a wide variety of outcomes for both 3- and 4-year-old children, but primarily in the Head Start year. The number of statistically significant effects found exceeded what one would expect by chance. It would appear that Head Start produced impacts in prereading, letter recognition, and some prewriting skills, as well as reduced levels of hyperactivity, and fewer behavior problems at the end of their Head Start year.

The final report concluded that the benefits of access to Head Start are largely absent by first grade for the program population as a whole (Administration for Children and Families, 2010a).

So, what do we make of these findings? It is important to recognize that many of the control-group children did, in fact, receive child care or early childhood education, and spent more time in these care arrangements. Essentially, the impacts of Head Start were measured against the impacts from a wide range of alternative care settings rather than against a "no service" or "parental care only" condition (Administration for Children and Families, 2010a). Head Start children had to outperform what children received from these alternative settings and, as the report notes, improved child care and pre-K standards nationally may have reduced the differences found between the Head Start and control-group children.

It could be argued that the combined effects of the "crossovers" during the first year of the study as well as the 49.6 percent of the control-group children who were allowed, by design, to enter Head Start at age 4 may have muted some of the impacts. According to this argument, the 3-year-olds in the control group, after the second year of the study, probably looked much more like the 3-year-old Head Start group after having received one year of Head

Start. However, the final report shows that the Impact on the Treated (IOT) estimates were larger than the Intent to Treat (ITT) estimates (Administration for Children and Families, 2010a) suggesting that once crossovers and no-shows were taken into account, the impact of Head Start on those actually exposed to the program was larger compared with those given access.

IMPLICATIONS FOR HEAD START RESEARCH AND POLICY

Evaluation of Head Start has come a long way since the early days, with its more rigorous design using nationally representative samples and with examination of outcomes for children and parents across a wide variety of dimensions. The key results from FACES seem to indicate that although quality in Head Start is good and better than most early childhood education programs, higher levels of classroom quality do not appear to explain a great deal of variation in children's school-readiness skills by the end of the Head Start year and into the spring of their kindergarten year. At the same time, the results regarding the potential compensatory effect of Head Start are promising, with findings revealing that in some areas of school readiness, the gap between Head Start children and their more advantaged peers is narrowing by the time they enter formal education. This compensatory effect was also found in the more rigorous Head Start Impact Study, which showed promising results confirming the modest but significant influence of Head Start on children's outcomes. However, we still do not know what may be considered to be the "active ingredients" of Head Start that contribute most to child and parent outcomes, although some evidence may be available in future reports from this study.

Findings from FACES suggest that having a well-developed standard curriculum such as High/Scope or Creative Curriculum is predictive of greater quality, and FACES has gone a long way toward identifying those aspects of teacher qualifications and training that produce higher levels of quality, but we still do not know whether quality influences children's outcomes. Compared to other studies in which quality played a modest but significant role in explaining children's outcomes, the FACES findings stand out as somewhat discrepant. One reason that has been offered previously (Zill & Resnick, 2006b) is that Head Start classrooms generally are of good quality but with a much limited range of variation in quality, relative to other early childhood education settings. The limited variation in quality places constraints on the magnitude of any potential relationship between quality and children's outcomes. Although this is a potential source of the discrepancy, FACES cannot fully explain significant features of classroom quality that might play a stronger role in predicting children's outcomes. Here, FACES is consistent with the literature in which various factors at the classroom level and beyond have been implicated.

The lack of a strong relationship between quality and children's outcomes may also be due to our limited methods of measuring quality because relatively little of the variation in the current measures can actually explain variations in children's outcomes. Within the past few years, several new measures, such as the Classroom Assessment Scoring System (CLASS) developed by La Paro, Pianta, and Stuhlman (2004) and the Early Childhood Environment Rating Scales Extended edition (ECERS-E) (Sylva, Sammons, Melhuish, Siraj-Blatchford, & Taggart, 2005), may further explain variations in classroom quality. It may well be the case that we have only begun to tap the surface of measuring classroom quality and that if we can predict more of the variation in quality, we might better explicate the link between quality and children's outcomes. An alternative view is that we have already reached the limits of our ability to measure quality and that, put simply, quality may only explain at best modest amounts of variation in children's gains, suggesting that it may be a necessary but not sufficient condition.

With the Head Start population changing over time and with renewed political debate regarding the benefits of this large-expenditure public program, it is important for Head Start to continue to monitor programs via the FACES study and at the same time to continue to mine the large amount of data from the HSIS. In 2006, DHHS continued to follow the HSIS children and their families through the spring of their third-grade year (i.e., spring 2007 and spring 2008). Thus, a great wealth of data on the impacts of Head Start and promising practices in Head Start linked to outcomes should be emerging in the next few years. Further, the data are expected to be made available to outside researchers through a public use data set that could well expand the utility of the HSIS for years to come.

Both FACES and HSIS have identified programmatic implications, particularly in the domains of children's school-readiness skills that showed improvement, and there is a high degree of congruency in their findings. Interestingly, not all domains show the same degree of gains over time (FACES) or differences between Head Start versus no Head Start (HSIS). The impacts of Head Start were higher for prereading and early writing skills but were lower for vocabulary and early math skills. Although these children made significant progress toward national norms in prereading and prewriting skills, they remained below national norms in vocabulary and early math skills at the end of kindergarten.

It has been suggested that Head Start should focus its program improvement efforts on helping children make gains in the "outside-in" skills such as vocabulary and general knowledge. However, doing that may be more challenging than strengthening "inside-out" skills such as letter knowledge and early writing because programs are working against children's home educational experiences, which appear to serve as powerful influences either for holding children back or for enhancing learning (Zill & Resnick, 2006b). In both FACES and HSIS, parental reading to children played a crucial role but in different ways. In FACES, parental reading predicted children's gains in emergent literacy skills, whereas in HSIS, the Head Start group revealed improved rates of parental reading. Taken together, the results suggest that parental reading plays an important role by either enabling or constraining the effects of exposure to Head Start for both parents and their children. Parents improve their frequency of reading (HSIS), and children show gains in language and emergent literacy (FACES). To date, HSIS has not looked at this sequence of relationships, but it is an important question for future analyses. These effects may be a function of the distance between the quality of the learning environment provided by Head Start and the quality of the learning environment in the child's home and community (Barnett, 1998), and it would appear that this distance can be closed through exposure to Head Start.

However, FACES also revealed that much of what goes on in Head Start classrooms is related to the level of resources that programs overseeing individual centers and classrooms have with which to make improvements. Indeed, Head Start classroom quality may be affected by factors that are more program related, particularly the characteristics of the program, than classroom related because federal funds go directly to local organizations to implement a Head Start program in a number of centers within the community catchment area, often with several classrooms within each center. In fact, one might speculate that choices made by the program, such as the amount of resources (e.g., funding, staffing) and where these resources are placed (e.g., buying an integrative curriculum versus saving money by designing their own), may influence quality in the classrooms. Many of these choices might well be dictated by the community in which the programs are located and the needs of the families they serve. The location of the programs as well as their ability to pay teachers will affect the quality of the teachers hired and, in many cases, Head Start programs are limited both in terms of the size of the teacher pool and the resources available to pay teachers or to pay for expensive curricula. For example, programs located in far-flung and relatively isolated areas might have a significantly reduced pool of teachers from which to draw, thereby limiting the kinds of teachers they can hire. These analyses also imply that in future FACES cohorts, additional factors at the program level might well be worth exploring, such as management styles. From a policy perspective, system-wide changes for Head Start may be required, in which well-educated teachers are hired and paid well and local policies are in place to improve the existing early childhood education workforce in isolated and outlying areas, where the Head Start program is the "biggest game in town." Many of these issues are currently being investigated in the early childhood education field, and Head Start as a national laboratory can do much to lead the way toward policy-specific solutions to workforce development and strategic planning with local Head Start programs.

Yet, there is a larger policy-based issue that serves as a backdrop to any discussion about how to improve Head Start. Given what we know about the achievement gap between children from disadvantaged families and their more advantaged peers, the question we should be asking is this: What is reasonable to expect of early childhood education programs generally and Head Start specifically? Is it realistic to expect Head Start to completely erase this achievement gap in the face of the strong and compelling evidence that family factors are more important than program factors in explaining children's readiness for school? Public programs in general are trying their best but are swimming against a strong current of persistent poverty and poor environments for raising healthy children. Without addressing the underlying systemic causes more broadly than what Head Start can do, we may not realize the largest effects of a program such as Head Start. Certainly, Head Start is only one element pitted against these challenges.

A related question is: What should we expect for children's outcomes from improvements in quality, given its relatively small role thus far? It is unlikely to expect that an increase in the average ECERS-R score by one point (a full standard deviation) would correspond to a full standard deviation increase in children's vocabulary skills. The evidence from Head Start and from evaluations of other early childhood education programs (not to mention the national Early Head Start evaluation) simply does not support this hypothesis.

Because of the inherent complexity of the question, asking what is realistic for Head Start to achieve is sometimes answered by the conclusion that the glass is either half-full or half-empty, often depending on which side of the legislative debate one is situated. Overall, Head Start has lived up to its reputation as a national laboratory for the study of early childhood education practices and for evaluation of these programs. FACES and HSIS form a formidable, complementary research program within the Administration for Children and Families, making the future of evaluation research in Head Start very promising.

REFERENCES

Administration for Children and Families. (2005). *Head Start Impact Study: First year findings.* Washington, DC: U.S. Department of Health and Human Services, Administration for Children and Families. Retrieved from http://www.acf.hhs.gov/programs/opre/hs/impact_study/reports/first_yr_finds/firstyr_finds_title.html.

Administration for Children and Families (2010a). *Head Start Impact Study: Final Report.* Washington, DC: U.S. Department of Health and Human Services, Administration for Children and Families. Retrieved from http://www.acf.hhs.gov/programs/opre/hs/impact_study/reports/impact_study/hs_impact_study_final.pdf.

Administration for Children and Families (January 2010b). *Head Start Impact Study. Technical Report.* Washington, DC: U.S. Department of Health and Human Services, Administration for Children and Families. Retrieved from http://www.acf.hhs.gov/programs/opre/hs/impact_study/reports/impact_study/hs_impact_study_tech_rpt.pdf.

Administration on Children, Youth, and Families. (2001). *Reaching out to families: Head Start recruitment and enrollment practices.* Washington, DC: U.S. Department of Health and Human Services. Retrieved from http://www.acf.hhs.

gov/programs/core/ongoing_research/faces/reaching_out_families/reaching_title.html.

Barnett, W. S. (1998). Long-term effects on cognitive development and school success. In W. S. Barnett & S. S. Babcock (Eds.), *Early care and education for children in poverty* (pp. 11–44). Albany: State University of New York Press.

Barnett, W. S., & Camilli, G. (1997). *Definite results from loose data: A response to "Does Head Start make a difference?"* Updated version of paper presented at the Seminar on Labor and Industrial Relations, Princeton University. Mimeo. New Brunswick, NJ: Rutgers University, Graduate School of Education.

Bereiter, C., & Kurland, M. (1981, Winter). A constructive look at follow-through results. *Interchange, 12.*

Blau, D. (1997). The production of quality in child care centers. *Journal of Human Resources, 32*(2), 354–387.

Bryant, D., Burchinal, M., Lau, L., & Sparling, J. (1994). Family and classroom correlates of Head Start children's developmental outcomes. *Early Childhood Research Quarterly, 9*(3–4), 289–309.

Currie, J., & Thomas, D. (1995). Does Head Start make a difference? *American Economic Review, 85*(3), 341–364.

Currie, J., & Thomas, D. (1999). Does Head Start help Hispanic children? *Journal of Public Economics, 74*(2), 235–262.

Early, D. M., Maxwell, K. L., Burchinal, M., Alva, S., Bender, R. H., Bryant, D., et al. (2007, March–April). Teachers' education, classroom quality, and young children's academic skills: Results from seven studies of preschool programs. *Child Development, 78*(2), 558–580.

Fuller, B., Holloway, S. D., & Liang, X. (1996). Family selection of child-care centers: The influence of household support, ethnicity, and parental practices. *Child Development, 67*, 3320–3337.

Haskins, R. (1989). Beyond metaphor: The efficacy of early childhood education. *American Psychologist, 44*(2), 274–282.

Hofferth, S. I., & Chaplin, D. D. (1998). State regulations and child care choice. *Population Research and Policy Review, 17*(2), 111–140.

La Paro, K. M., Pianta, R. C., & Stuhlman, M. (2004). The Classroom Assessment Scoring System: Findings from the pre-kindergarten year. *The Elementary School Journal, 104*(5), 409–426.

Love, J., Ryer, P., and Faddis, B. (1992). *Caring environments: Program quality in California's publicly funded child development programs.* Report on the legislatively mandated 1990–91 staff–child ratio study. Portsmouth, NH: RMC Research Corporation.

McKey, R. H., Condelli, L., Ganson, H., Barrett, B. J., McConkey, C., & Plantz, M. C. (1985). *The impact of Head Start on children, families, and communities* (DHHS Publication No. OHDS 85–31193). Washington, DC: U.S. Government Printing Office.

NICHD Early Child Care Research Network (ECCRN). (2000). The relation of child care to cognitive and language development. *Child Development, 71*, 823–839.

Peisner-Feinberg, E. S., & Burchinal, M. R. (1997). Relations between preschool children's child-care experiences and concurrent development: The Cost, Quality and Outcomes Study. *Merrill-Palmer Quarterly, 43*(3), 451–477.

Peisner-Feinberg, E. S., Burchinal, M. R., Clifford, R. M., Culkin, M. L, Howes, C., Kagan, S. L., et al. (2001). The relation of preschool child-care quality to children's cognitive and social developmental trajectories through second grade. *Child Development, 72*(5), 1534–1553.

Phillips, D., McCartney, K., & Scarr, S. (1987). Childcare quality and children's social development. *Developmental Psychology, 23*(4), 537–543.
Pizzo, P. D., & Tufankjian, E. E. (2004). A persistent pattern of progress: Parent outcomes in longitudinal studies of Head Start children. In E. Zigler & S. J. Styfco (Eds.), *The Head Start debates* (pp. 379–396). Baltimore, MD: Brookes.
Raver, C. C., & Zigler, E. F. (2004). Public policy viewpoint: Another step back? Sole reliance on cognitively oriented assessments may hurt rather than help preschoolers in Head Start. *Young Children, 59*(1), 58–63.
Resnick, G. (2004, June). "The play's the thing": Links between classroom quality and children's play in Head Start. In R. H. McKey (Chair), *Longitudinal perspectives on Head Start Performance: Findings from FACES 2000 and its kindergarten follow-ups.* Symposium conducted at Head Start's Seventh National Head Start Research Conference, Washington, DC.
Resnick, G. (2006, June). Program quality findings from the 2003 Family and Child Experiences Survey (FACES 2003). In M. Woolverton (Chair), *Program quality and services findings from the Head Start Impact Study and Family and Child Experiences Survey.* Symposium conducted at Head Start's Eighth National Head Start Research Conference, Washington, DC.
Rivlin, A. M., & Timpane, P. M. (1975). *Ethical and legal issues of social experimentation.* Washington, DC: Brookings Institution.
Smith, T., Kleiner, A., Parsad, B., & Farris, E. (2002). *Prekindergarten in U.S. public schools: 2000–2001* (NCES 2003–019). Washington, DC: U.S. Department of Education, National Center for Education Statistics.
Snow, C. E., Burns, M. S., & Griffin, P. (Eds.) (1998). *Preventing reading difficulties in young children.* Washington, DC: National Academy Press.
Sylva, S., Sammons, P. M., Melhuish, E., Siraj-Blatchford, I., & Taggart, B. (2005). The effects of early education on children's development: Evidence from England. In M. R. Burchinal (Chair), *Early care and children's development in the primary grades: Follow-up results from four national studies.* Symposium conducted at the biennial meeting of the Society for Research on Child Development, Atlanta, GA.
Valentine, J., & Zigler, E. F. (1983). Head Start: A case study in development of social policy for children and families. In E. F. Zigler, S. L. Kagan, & E. Klugman (Eds.), *Children, families, and government: Perspectives on American social policy* (pp. 266–280). Cambridge: Cambridge University Press.
Watkins, C. L. (1996, Winter). Follow through: Why didn't we? *Effective School Practices, 15,* 1. Retrieved from http://darkwing.uoregon.edu/~adiep/ft/watkins.htm.
White, K. R. (1986). Efficacy of early intervention. *Journal of Special Education, 19*(4), 401–416.
Whitebook, M. (2003). *Early education quality: Higher teacher qualifications for better learning environments – A review of the literature.* Berkeley: Institute of Industrial Relations, University of California.
Whitebook, M., Howes, C., & Phillips, D. (1989). *Who cares? Childcare teachers and the quality of care in America* (Final Report of the National Child Care Staffing Study). Oakland, CA: Child Care Employee Project.
Zill, N., & Resnick, G. (2005, April). Child care quality and school readiness outcomes in Head Start: Findings from FACES. In M. R. Burchinal (Chair), *Early care and children's development in the primary grades: Follow-up results from four national studies.* Symposium conducted at the biennial meeting of the Society for Research on Child Development, Atlanta, GA.

Zill, N., & Resnick, G. (2006a). Emergent literacy of low-income children in Head Start: Relationships with child and family characteristics, program factors and classroom quality. In D. Dickinson & S. Neumann (Eds.), *Handbook of early literacy research*: Vol. 2, pp. 347–371. New York: Guilford.

Zill, N., & Resnick, G. (2006b). Low-income children in Head Start and beyond: Findings from FACES. In N. F. Watt, C. Ayoub, R. H. Bradley, J. E. Puma, & W. A. Lebeouf (Eds.), *Early intervention programs and policies: Vol. 4. The crisis in youth mental health: Critical issues and effective programs* (Praeger Series in Child Psychology and Mental Health), pp. 253–289. Portsmouth, NH: Greenwood.

Zill, N., Resnick, G., Kim, K., O'Donnell, K., Sorongon, A., McKey, R. H., et al. (2003). *Head Start FACES 2000: A whole-child perspective on program performance, fourth progress report.* Washington, DC: Administration for Children and Families, U.S. Department of Health and Human Services. Retrieved from http://www.acf.hhs.gov/programs/opre/hs/faces/reports/faces00_4thprogress/faces00_title.html.

Zill, N., Resnick, G., Kim, K., O'Donnell, K., Sorongon, A., Ziv, Y., et al. (2006). *Head Start performance measures center, Family and Child Experiences Survey (FACES 2000) technical report.* Washington, DC: Administration for Children and Families, Department of Health and Human Services. Retrieved from http://www.acf.hhs.gov/programs/opre/hs/faces/reports/technical_2000_rpt/tech2k_title.html.

Zill, N., Sorongon, A., Kim, K., Clark, C., & Woolverton, M. (2006). *Children's outcomes and program quality in Head Start* (FACES 2003 Research Brief). Washington, DC: Administration for Children and Families, Department of Health and Human Services. Retrieved from http://www.acf.hhs.gov/programs/opre/hs/faces/reports/research_2003/research_2003_title.html.

FURTHER READING

Administration on Children, Youth, and Families. (2001). *Head Start FACES: Longitudinal findings on program performance. Third progress report.* Washington, DC: U.S. Department of Health and Human Services. Retrieved from http://www.acf.dhhs.gov/programs/core/pubs_reports/faces/meas_99_intro.html.

Administration on Children, Youth, and Families. (2003). *Head Start FACES 2000: A whole child perspective on program performance: Fourth progress report.* Washington, DC: U.S. Department of Health and Human Services. Retrieved from http://www.acf.dhhs.gov/programs/core/ongoing_research/faces/faces00_4thprogress/faces00_title.html.

Bradley, R. H., Caldwell, B. M., Rock, S. L., Ramey, C.T., Barnard, K. E., Gray, C., Hammond, M. A., et al. (1989). Home environment and cognitive development in the first 3 years of life: A collaborative study involving six sites and three ethnic groups in North America. *Developmental Psychology, 25*(2), 217–235.

Bredekamp, S. (1986). The reliability and validity of the early childhood classroom observation scale for accrediting early childhood programs. *Early Childhood Research Quarterly, 1*(2), 103–118.

Brick, J. M., & Morganstein, D. (1997). Computing sampling errors from clustered unequally weighted data using replication: WesVarPC. *Bulletin of the International Statistical Institute, Proceedings, 1*, 479–482.

Bryk, A. S., & Raudenbush, S. W. (1992). *Hierarchical linear models: Applications and data analysis methods.* Newbury Park, CA: Sage.

Burts, D. C., Hart, C. H., Charlesworth, R., & Kirk L. (1990). A comparison of frequencies of stress behaviors observed in kindergarten children in classrooms with

developmentally appropriate versus developmentally inappropriate practices. *Early Childhood Research Quarterly, 5*(3), 407–423.
Consortium for Longitudinal Studies. (1983). *As the twig is bent. Lasting effects of preschool programs.* Hillsdale, NJ: Erlbaum.
Cost, Quality & Child Outcomes Study Team. (1999). *The children of the Cost, Quality, and Outcomes Study go to school: Executive summary.* Chapel Hill, NC: Frank Porter Graham Child Development Center.
Currie, J., & Thomas, D. (1998). *School quality and the longer-term effects of Head Start.* Washington, DC: National Bureau of Economic Research.
Dickinson, D. K., & Tabors, P. O. (Eds.). (2001). *Beginning literacy with language.* Baltimore, MD: Brookes.
Dunn, L. M., Padilla, E. R., Lugo, D. E., & Dunn, L. M. (1986). *Test de Vocabulario en Imagenes Peabody.* Circle Pines, MN: American Guidance Service.
Fischel, J. E., Storch, S. A., Spira, E. G., & Stolz, B. M. (2003). *Enhancing emergent literacy skills in Head Start: First year curriculum evaluation results.* Paper presented at the Biennial Meeting of the Society for Research in Child Development, Tampa, FL.
Hart, B., & Risley, T. R. (1995). *Meaningful differences in the everyday experience of young American children.* Baltimore, MD: Brookes.
Hayes, C., Palmer, J., & Zaslow, M. (1990). *Who cares for America's children? Childcare policy for the 1990s.* Report of the Panel on Child Care Policy, Committee on Child Development Research and Public Policy, National Research Council. Washington, DC: National Academy Press.
Horn, W. F., & Packard, T. (1985). Early identification of learning problems: A meta-analysis. *Journal of Educational Psychology, 77*(5), 597–607.
Kontos, S., & Fiene, R. (1987). Childcare quality, compliance with regulations, and children's development: The Pennsylvania Study. In D. Phillips (Ed.), *Quality in child care: What does the research tell us?* (pp. 57–79). Washington, DC: National Association for the Education of Young Children.
Lambert, M. C., Mayfield, W. A., Thornburg, K. R., Hestenes, L., & Cassidy, D. J. (2009, April). Using IRT to evaluate the psychometric properties of the ECERS-R. In D. J. Cassidy (Chair), *Accountability in early childhood classrooms: The role of the ECERS-R.* Symposium conducted at the biennial meeting of the Society for Research on Child Development, Denver, CO.
Layzer, J., Goodson., B., & Moss, M. (1993). *Final report volume 1: Life in preschool.* Cambridge, MA: ABT Associates.
Lazar, I., Darlington, R., Murray, H., Royce, J., & Snipper, A. (1982). Lasting effects of early education: A report from the Consortium for Longitudinal Studies. *Monographs of the Society for Research in Child Development, 47*(2–3, Series No. 195).
Phillips, D., & Howes, C. (1987). Indicators of quality in child care: Review of the research. In D. A. Phillips (Ed.), *Quality in child care: What does research tell us?* (pp. 1–19). Washington, DC: National Association for the Education of Young Children.
Phillips, D., Howes, C., & Whitebook, M. (1992). The social policy context of childcare: Effects on quality. *American Journal of Community Psychology, 20*(1), 25–51.
Phillips, D., Mekos, D., Scarr, S., McCartney, K., & Abbott-Shim, M. (2000). Within and beyond the classroom door: Assessing quality in child care centers. *Early Childhood Research Quarterly, 15*(4), 475–496.
Phillips, M., Brooks-Gunn, J., Duncan, G. J., Klebanov, P., & Crane, J. (1998). Family background, parenting practices, and the black-white test score gap. In C. Jencks & M. Phillips (Eds.), *The black-white test score gap* (pp. 103–145). Washington, DC: Brookings Institution.

Pianta, R. C., & Cox, M. J. (Eds.) (1999). *The transition to kindergarten.* Baltimore, MD: Brookes.

Pianta, R. C., & McCoy, S. J. (1997). The first day of school: The predictive validity of early school screening. *Journal of Applied Developmental Psychology, 18*(1), 1–22.

Pikulski, J. J., & Tobin, A. W. (1989). Factors associated with long-term reading achievement of early readers. In S. McCormick, J. Zutell, P. Scharer, & P. O'Keefe (Eds.), *Cognitive and social perspectives for literacy research and instruction.* Chicago: National Reading Conference.

Resnick, G., McKey, R. H., & Klayman, D. (2001). *The evaluation of early childhood education programming in the 30 Abbott school districts: First-year report on program implementation and descriptions of children and families* (Contract No. A43078). Trenton, NJ: New Jersey Department of Human Services and New Jersey Department of Education.

Resnick, G., & Zill, N. (2001, April). "Unpacking" quality in Head Start classrooms: Relationships among dimensions of quality at different levels of analysis. In R. H. McKey & L. B. Tarullo (Co-Chairs), *Longitudinal findings from the Head Start FACES study: Family, neighborhood and preschool quality factors in school readiness.* Symposium conducted at the biennial meeting of the Society for Research in Child Development, Minneapolis, MN.

Resnick, G., & Zill, N. (2002, June). Relationships of teacher beliefs and qualifications to classroom quality in Head Start. In L. B. Tarullo (Chair), *Improving the performance of the Head Start program: Findings from FACES 2000.* Symposium conducted at Head Start's Sixth National Head Start Research Conference, Washington, DC.

Resnick, G., & Zill, N. (2003). Understanding quality in Head Start classrooms: The role of teacher and program-level factors. In L. B. Tarullo & R. H. McKey (Co-Chairs), *A whole-child perspective on Head Start reform: Findings on children's cognitive and socio-emotional development from FACES 2000.* Symposium conducted at the Biennial Meeting of the Society for Research on Child Development, Tampa, FL.

Reynolds, A. T. (1995). One year of preschool intervention or two: Does it matter? *Early Childhood Research Quarterly, 10*(1), 1–31.

Sakai, L. M., Whitebook, M., Wishard, A., & Howes, C. (2003). Evaluating the Early Childhood Environment Rating Scale (ECERS): Assessing differences between the first and revised edition. *Early Childhood Research Quarterly, 18*(4), 427–445.

Snow, C. E., Barnes, W., Chandler, J., Goodman, L., & Hemphill, L. (1991). *Unfulfilled expectations: Home and school influences on literacy.* Cambridge, MA: Harvard University Press.

Snow, C. E., Tabors, P. O., Nicholson, P. A., & Kurland, B. F. (1995). SHELL: Oral language and early literacy skills in kindergarten and first-grade children. *Journal of Research in Early Childhood Education, 10*(1), 37–48.

Sprigle, J. E., & Schaefer, L. (1985). Longitudinal evaluation of the effects of two compensatory preschool programs on fourth- through sixth-grade students. *Developmental Psychology, 21*(4), 702–708.

Tarullo, L., West, J., Aikens, N., & Hulsey, L. (2008). *Beginning Head Start: Children, families and programs in fall 2006.* Washington, DC: Administration for Children and Families, Department of Health and Human Services. Retrieved from http://www.acf.hhs.gov/programs/opre/hs/faces/reports/beginning_hs/beginning_hs.pdf.

Whitehurst, G. J., & Lonigan, C. J. (1989). Child development and emergent literacy. *Child Development, 69*(3), 848–872.

Zigler, E., & Berman, W. (1983). Discerning the future of early childhood intervention. *American Psychologist, 38*(8), 894–906.

Zigler, E., & Styfco, S. J. (2006). Epilogue. In N. F. Watt, C. Ayoub, R. H. Bradley, J. E. Puma, & W. A. Lebeouf (Eds.), *Early intervention programs and policies: Vol. 4. The crisis in youth mental health: Critical issues and effective programs* (Praeger Series in Child Psychology and Mental Health), pp. 347–371. Westport, CT: Praeger.

Zill, N., & Resnick, G. (2002, June). Relationships of type of curriculum and teacher-directed activities to children's progress in Head Start. In L. B. Tarullo (Chair), *Improving the performance of the Head Start program: Findings from FACES 2000.* Symposium conducted at Head Start's Sixth National Head Start Research Conference, Washington, DC.

Zill, N., & Resnick, G. (2003, April). Cognitive gains in Head Start and achievement in kindergarten: Comparison of children in FACES 2000 and 1997. In L. B. Tarullo & R. H. McKey (Co-Chairs), *A whole-child perspective on Head Start reform: Findings on children's cognitive and socio-emotional development from FACES 2000.* Symposium conducted at the Biennial Meeting of the Society for Research on Child Development, Tampa, FL.

Zill, N., Resnick, G., & Hubbell-McKey, R. (2002, June). Constancy and change in Head Start classroom quality and school-readiness gains. In L. B. Tarullo (Chair), *Improving the performance of the Head Start program: Findings from FACES 2000.* Symposium conducted at Head Start's Sixth National Head Start Research Conference, Washington, DC.

Zill, N., Resnick, G., Kim, K., McKey, R. H., Clark, C., Pai-Samant, S., et al. (2001). *Head Start FACES: Longitudinal findings on program performance, third progress report.* Washington, DC: Research, Demonstration, and Evaluation Branch and the Head Start Bureau, Administration on Children, Youth, and Families, U.S. Department of Health and Human Services. Retrieved from http://www.acf.hhs.gov/programs/opre/hs/faces/reports/perform_3rd_rpt/meas_99_title.html.

7

The Challenge of the HighScope Perry Preschool Study

LAWRENCE J. SCHWEINHART

HIGHSCOPE PERRY PRESCHOOL STUDY METHODOLOGY

The HighScope Perry Preschool Study is a scientific experiment that has identified the short- and long-term effects of a high-quality preschool education program for young children living in poverty (Schweinhart et al., 2005). From 1962 through 1967, David Weikart and his colleagues in the Ypsilanti, Michigan, school district operated the preschool program for young children to help them avoid school failure and related problems. They identified a sample of 123 African American children living in poverty who were assessed to be at high risk of school failure. They randomly assigned 58 of them to a group that received a high-quality preschool program at ages 3 and 4 and 65 to a group that received no preschool program. Because of the random-assignment strategy, children's preschool experience is the best explanation for subsequent group differences in their performance over the years. Project staff collected data annually on both groups from ages 3 through 11 and again at ages 14, 15, 19, 27, and 40, with a missing data rate of only 6% across all measures.

This study has followed the lives of 123 persons who originally lived in the attendance area of the Ypsilanti school district's Perry Elementary School, a predominantly African American neighborhood in a low-income part of town. Project staff identified a pool of children for the study sample from a census of the families of students then attending the school, referrals from neighborhood groups, and door-to-door canvassing. They selected families of low socioeconomic status and children with low intellectual performance at study entry who showed no evidence of organic handicap. Only three families with children identified for the study refused to participate in it.

Project staff identified families of low socioeconomic status, defined by their low scores for parents' years of schooling, parents' occupational levels, and rooms per person in their households. Because of these selection criteria, families whose children participated in the study were considerably worse off in most ways than the U.S. population at the time and slightly worse off in most ways than the African American population at the time (Schweinhart & Weikart, 1980). For example, half of the mothers in the study had left school by the end of ninth grade, and half of the fathers had left school by the end of eighth grade; these educational levels were just a few months below the median of U.S. African Americans but several years below the median of the U.S. population. A family survey of Head Start parents in 1997 (O'Brien et al., 2002) permits the following comparisons: 73% of Head Start parents graduated from high school, as compared to only 17% of the Perry study parents, and 42% of Head Start children lived with two parents, as compared to 53% of the Perry study children.

Project staff used the Stanford-Binet Intelligence Test (Terman & Merrill, 1960) to assess the intellectual performance of the young children of families of low socioeconomic status. They selected for the study those children whose intellectual performance scores (IQs) at this initial testing qualified them as "borderline educable mentally impaired."

Although 128 children were originally selected for the study, 4 children did not complete the preschool program because they moved away, and 1 child died shortly after the study began, so that the longitudinal study had 123 participants. Children entered the study in five successive classes annually from the fall of 1962 to the fall of 1965. Program-group children attended the preschool program at ages 3 and 4, except for the first class of children, who attended only at age 4. All study participants were African American, as was almost everyone in the Perry School neighborhood at the time they attended.

The study has an experimental design in which study participants were *randomly assigned* either to a "program group" enrolled in the preschool program or to a "no-program group" not enrolled in any preschool program. The research staff followed these steps. They identified pairs of study participants matched on initial Stanford-Binet intellectual performance scores (IQ; Terman & Merrill, 1960) and assigned pair members to either of two undesignated groups. As part of the initial assignment procedure, they exchanged one or two pair members per class to ensure that the groups were matched on mean socioeconomic status, mean intellectual performance, and percentages of boys and girls. By flipping a coin, they randomly assigned one group to the program condition and the other to the no-program condition. In addition, as part of the initial assignment procedure in later classes, they exchanged one or two pair members per class to reduce the number of children of employed mothers in the program group, because arranging home visits with them was found to be difficult. In addition, they assigned younger siblings to the same group as their older siblings to prevent the preschool program from affecting siblings in the no-program group. Statistical analyses indicated that these exchanges did not appreciably affect the findings of this study.

These assignment procedures made it highly probable that group comparisons reflected the effects of the preschool program. Comparisons indicating that groups were not significantly different on various background characteristics made it even more likely. The two groups did not differ significantly (with a two-tailed probability of less than .05) at study entry on Stanford-Binet IQ (Terman & Merrill, 1960), family socioeconomic status, mother's or father's highest year of schooling, number of children in the family, number of siblings older or younger than the study participant, child's age, mother's or father's age, rooms in home or persons per rooms in home, participants' gender, family configuration (i.e., single-parent vs. two-parent, nuclear vs. extended), father's employment level, family welfare status, family in public housing, mother born in the South or elsewhere, population of mother's birthplace, or family religion. However, the program-group members had significantly fewer employed mothers than the no-program–group members (9% vs. 31%), mostly because of the exchanges that moved them from the program group to the no-program group.

Seven background variables were selected as covariates for the outcome analyses: participants' gender, Stanford-Binet IQ at study entry, mother's schooling, father's occupational status, household rooms per person, father at home, and mother's employment. One of the study's special strengths is that attrition in the study sample has been very low. Across the 48 measures of 123 cases, a median 7 cases (5.7%) were missing. At the age 40 interview, of the 123 original study participants, 112 were interviewed, 4 living ones were not, and 7 were deceased. Criminal justice and social services records were considered to have no missing cases because the names of all the study participants were included in these searches, and the lack of a record indicated no arrests or no social services. School records were found for all but 11 cases (8.9%). The low rates of missing data mean that attrition usually had a negligible effect on either sample representativeness or group comparisons.

HighScope Perry Preschool Program teachers conducted daily 2½-hour classes for children on weekday mornings and made weekly 1½-hour home visits to each mother and child on weekday afternoons. The 30-week school year began in mid-October and ended in May. Of the 58 children in the program group, the 13 in the first class participated in the program for one school year at age 4, and the 45 in subsequent classes participated in the program for two school years at ages 3 and 4. Successive program group classes – first and second, second and third, third and fourth, and fourth and fifth – attended the program together, the older class at age 4 and the younger at age 3. In 1966–1967, the final year of the program, a sixth class of 11 3-year-olds who were not included in the longitudinal sample joined the 12 4-year-olds in the fifth class. Thus, the four teachers in the program served 20 to 25 children each school year, forming a child:teacher ratio varying from 5.00 to 6.25 children per teacher. This ratio was set to accommodate the demands of the weekly home visits – that is, only one or two families could be visited per weekday afternoon. Friday afternoons were generally used for staff training and project meetings.

The HighScope early childhood educational model, used in the Perry Preschool classroom and home visits, was and is an open framework of educational ideas and practices based on the natural development of young children. Drawing on the child development ideas of Jean Piaget, it emphasizes the idea that children are *intentional learners*, who learn best from activities that they themselves plan, carry out, and review afterward. Adults introduce new ideas to children through adult-initiated small- and large-group activities. Adults observe, support, and extend the children's play as appropriate. They arrange interest areas in the learning environment; maintain a daily routine that permits children to plan, carry out, and review their own activities; and join in children's activities, asking appropriate questions that extend their plans and help them think about their activities. They add complex language to the discussion to expand children's vocabulary. Using key developmental indicators derived from child-development theory as a framework, adults encourage children to make choices, solve problems, and engage in activities that contribute to their intellectual, social, and physical development.

HIGHSCOPE PERRY PRESCHOOL STUDY RESULTS

As shown in Table 7.1, the program group outperformed the no-program group on various intellectual and language tests from their preschool years up to age 7 (e.g., Terman & Merrill, 1960); school achievement tests at ages 9, 10, and 14 (Tiegs & Clark, 1963, 1971); and literacy tests at ages 19 and 27. Fewer of the program group than the no-program group were diagnosed and treated for mental impairment (15% vs. 35%). More of the program group than the no-program group graduated from regular high school (65% vs. 45%), specifically, more program females than no-program females (84% vs. 32%). At ages 15 and 19, the program group had better attitudes toward school than the no-program group, and program-group parents had better attitudes toward their 15-year-old children's schooling than did no-program-group parents. More of the program group than the no-program group were employed at ages 27 (69% vs. 56%) and 40 (76% vs. 62%). The program group had higher median annual earnings than the no-program group at ages 27 ($12,000 vs. $10,000) and 40 ($20,800 vs. $15,300). More of the program group than the no-program group owned their own homes at ages 27 (27% vs. 5%) and 40 (37% vs. 28%). More program than no-program males raised their own children (57% vs. 30%). By age 40, fewer of the program group than the no-program group were arrested five or more times (36% vs. 55%); fewer were arrested for violent crimes (32% vs. 48%), property crimes (36% vs. 58%), and drug crimes (14% vs. 34%); and fewer were sentenced to prison or jail (28% vs. 52%).

Cost-benefit analysis indicates that, in constant 2000 dollars discounted at 3%, the economic return to society for the program was $244,812 per participant on an investment of $15,166 per participant ($8,540 per child per year) – $16.14 per dollar invested. Of that return, 80% went to the general public, and 20% went to each participant in the form of increased lifetime earnings. Of the public return, 88% came from crime savings, and 1% to 7%

Table 7.1. *Statistically significant differences in group outcomes*

Characteristic	Ages	Program group	No-program group
Intellectual performance (Stanford-Binet)	4–7		
Nonverbal and language test performance	4–5		
School achievement	9, 10, 14		
Literacy	19, 27		
Ever diagnosed as mentally impaired		15%	35%
Graduated from regular high school		65%	45%
Females graduated from regular high school		84%	32%
Attitudes toward school	15, 19		
Parents' attitudes toward school	15		
Employed	27	27%	5%
	40	37%	28%
Mean annual earnings	27	$12,000	$10,000
	40	$20,800	$15,300
Home ownership	27	27%	5%
	40	37%	28%
Males raised own child	40	57%	30%
Five or more arrests by	40	36%	55%
Arrested for violent crime by	40	32%	48%
Arrested for property crime by	40	36%	58%
Arrested for drug crime by	40	14%	34%
Convicted and sentenced by	40	28%	52%
Cost-benefit analysis through age 40			
Program cost		$15,166	
Program cost per year		$8,540	
Public return, total		$195,621	
Public return, per dollar invested		$12.90	
Societal return, total		$244,812	
Societal return, per dollar invested		$16.14	

came from each of three sources: education savings, increased taxes due to higher lifetime earnings, and welfare savings. Remarkably, 93% of the public return through age 40 was attributable to males because of the program's large reduction of male crime, and only 7% was due to females.

THE CHANGING CONTEXT OF POVERTY

U.S. poverty today resembles U.S. poverty in 1962 in some ways and differs from it in others. It is still defined as the lack of money and material possessions. The federal poverty threshold has existed with modest modifications since 1965, increasing primarily with inflation. The welfare reforms of recent years have transformed programs such as Aid to Families with Dependent Children into the streamlined Temporary Assistance to Needy Families.

The cycle of poverty is the idea that the connection from schooling to poverty within an individual's lifetime becomes an intergenerational connection from families' poverty to children's schooling (Solon, 1992). Children born in poverty perform more poorly in school, a smaller percentage of them graduate from high school, and then schooling affects economic success. For example, in 1997, U.S. poverty rates were 22% for high school dropouts, 9% for high school graduates, and 2% for college graduates (U.S. Census Bureau, 2003).

The U.S. crime rate in general has doubled from the time of the HighScope Perry Preschool program to now, even though it has dropped in the last two decades. According to the Federal Bureau of Investigation's Uniform Crime Reports of arrests throughout the United States, the crime index rate per 100,000 inhabitants was 2,020 in 1962, peaked at 5,950 in 1980, and was 4,124 in 2000 (Disaster Center, 2004). The violent crime rate was 162 in 1962, peaked at 758 in 1991, and was 506 in 2000. The much higher crime rate has changed our society in general and poor neighborhoods in particular.

PRESCHOOL PROGRAM RESEARCH

Preschool research flourished through the 1960s and 1970s, with many studies of preschool and parent education programs, compared to no program, and analyses that compared various types of programs. In the late 1970s, the principal investigators brought a dozen of the best studies together to form the Consortium for Longitudinal Studies (1983). Collaborating in data collection and analysis, the consortium found robust evidence of preschool program effects on children's intellectual performance at school entry, reduced need for placements in special education, and reduced need for retention in grade. The longest lasting of the studies found that a greater percentage of preschool program graduates than those without preschool became high school graduates.

In addition to the study reported here, two preschool program follow-up studies stand out for their duration and methodological quality: the Carolina Abecedarian Project study (see Chapter 4) and the Chicago Child-Parent Centers study (see Chapter 8). These three studies offer the best recent evidence of the long-term effects of good preschool programs. The Carolina Abecedarian Project (Campbell, Ramey, Pungello, Sparling, & Miller-Johnson, 2002) randomly assigned 57 infants from poor families to a special program group and 54 to a typical child care group that used the child care arrangements in homes and centers that were prevalent in the 1970s. This was the first study to find preschool program benefits on participants' intellectual performance and academic achievement *throughout* their schooling. Achievement scores at age 15 were higher. Fewer of the program group than the no-program group had been retained in grade or received special services. More of the program group graduated from high school or received a GED certificate, and more attended a 4-year college. Fewer in the program group became teen parents. However, the program and no-program groups did not differ significantly in arrests by age 19 (Clarke & Campbell, 1998). Cost-benefit analysis indicated that in 2000 dollars discounted at 3% annually (converted from the 2002 dollars reported), the program cost $34,476 per child ($13,362 per child per year) and yielded benefits to society of $130,300 – $3.78 return per dollar invested (Masse & Barnett, 2002).

Beginning in 1985, the Chicago Longitudinal Study, conducted by Arthur Reynolds and his colleagues, examined the effects of the Chicago Child-Parent Centers (CPC) program offered by the nation's third largest public school district (Reynolds, Temple, Robertson, & Mann, 2001). This program was city-wide – much larger in scale than the research programs of the Perry Preschool and Abecedarian studies. Hence, the study sample was larger, with 1,539 low-income children – 989 who had been in the CPC program and 550 who had not. Families in this study went to their neighborhood schools, and children were not randomly assigned to groups. Preschool-program group members attended a part-day preschool program when they were 3 and 4 years old, whereas the no-preschool-program group did not. The preschool-program group did significantly better than the no-preschool-program group in educational performance and social behavior, with lower rates of grade retention and special education placement, followed by a higher rate of high school completion and lower rates of school dropout and juvenile arrests. Analysis of the costs and benefits of the program indicated that in 2000 dollars discounted at 3% annually (converted from the 1998 dollars reported), the program cost $6,956 per child and yielded benefits of $49,564 per participant – $7.10 return per dollar invested (Reynolds, Temple, Robertson, & Mann, 2002).

Recent short-term early childhood program studies have examined the effects of typical and enhanced Head Start programs (e.g., Administration for Children and Families, 2005; Goodson, Layzer, St. Pierre, Bernstein, & Lopez, 2000), state preschool programs (Barnett, Lamy, & Jung, 2005; Gilliam & Zigler, 2001), and typical child care centers (e.g., NICHD Early Child Care Research Network, 2005). The consensus finding of these studies is that most typical and even special publicly funded early childhood programs have no more than modest effects on children's literacy and social skills and parents' behavior, clearly not as large as the effects found for model programs. The lesser magnitude of recent effects casts doubt on whether these short-term studies, if extended in time, would identify long-term effects and return on investment.

DISCUSSION

Because of the random assignment to groups and the low attrition of participants, the HighScope Perry Preschool Study has strong internal validity.

The external validity or generalizability of the study findings extends to those programs that are reasonably similar to the HighScope Perry Preschool program. A reasonably similar program is a preschool education program run by teachers with bachelor's degrees and certification in education, each serving up to eight children living in low-income families. The program runs two school years at 3 and 4 years of age, uses the HighScope educational model, with daily classes of 2½ hours or longer, and teachers visit families at least every 2 weeks. The HighScope Preschool Curriculum Comparison Study (Schweinhart & Weikart, 1997a, 1997b), which immediately followed the HighScope Perry Preschool Study, suggested that curriculum had a lot to do with its impact. This study found that young people born in poverty experience fewer emotional problems and felony arrests if they attended a preschool program that used HighScope rather than scripted direct instruction.

Programs inspired by the HighScope Perry Preschool program have seldom if ever fully replicated it. Inadequate funding and varying conceptions of early childhood programs have conspired to prevent its full replication by Head Start and state preschool programs. In contrast to the Perry program, Head Start splits public school teacher salaries between teachers and family service workers, requires only two home visits a year rather than weekly ones, and uses the HighScope curriculum in only 10% of its programs. A few state preschool programs require state-certified lead teachers, but none requires regular home visiting or use of only validated curriculum models. Recent research on Head Start and similar programs, such as the National Head Start Impact Study, has found that they have only modest initial effects. It seems reasonable that preschool programs that did replicate the Perry Preschool program on a wider scale would have large initial effects, long-term effects, and a sizable return on investment.

The tension between replication and application is due to changing social conditions as well as political compromises. Critical applications include whether typical practices in Head Start, various state preschool programs, and child care centers have the same impact and whether the Perry program would have the same effectiveness for a general population of children not limited to those in poverty. Nonetheless, the closer the replication to the Perry program, the greater the probability of success.

Replicating the program means focusing a program on children whose parents lack schooling and skilled jobs. The program itself must meet four qualifications. Some leeway might be permitted as long as these criteria are substantially in place:

1. It serves children 3 and 4 years old living in poverty.
2. It employs state-certified early childhood teachers so that each class has a certified teacher, an assistant teacher, and no more than 16 children.

3. Teachers and assistant teachers have taken a substantial preschool curriculum course or the equivalent and use the HighScope curriculum or another validated curriculum model in their programs. Their implementation of the curriculum and children's progress are checked regularly.
4. Teachers and assistant teachers engage in extensive parent outreach, including weekly visits to children in their homes or elsewhere.

The simple implication of this study is that all young children living in low-income families should have access to preschool programs that have features reasonably similar to the HighScope Perry Preschool program. This study and others reviewed here have motivated policy makers to invest in preschool programs. Yet, because policy makers practice the art of compromise and must address a variety of contexts, these programs have seldom met the reasonable similarity standard. This study is a symbol of what government programs can achieve; it inspires the passionate belief of those who want to believe in what government can accomplish and the passionate disbelief of those who want to believe that government cannot accomplish much of anything. Yet, ultimately, the public is not served by beliefs that are either too optimistic or too pessimistic. Although the study can serve as grounds for debate, it is better to see it as a challenge. It shows what can be done, and the challenge is to do it. The HighScope Perry, Abecedarian, and Chicago studies and other such studies lay down the same challenge: to do what we know how to do to prevent poverty from being a malevolent birthright handed down from generation to generation by the very schooling established to stop it. The challenge is to provide high-quality preschool programs that include low-income children so that these children get a fair chance to achieve their potential to contribute to society.

REFERENCES

Administration for Children and Families. (2005). *Head Start Impact Study: First year findings.* Washington, DC: U.S. Department of Health and Human Services. Retrieved from http://www.acf.hhs.gov/programs/opre/hs/impact_study/index.html.

Barnett, W. S., Lamy, C., & Jung, K. (2005). *The effects of state prekindergarten programs on young children's school readiness in five states.* New Brunswick, NJ: National Institute for Early Education Research, Rutgers University. Retrieved from http://nieer.org/docs/index.php?DocID=129.

Campbell, F. A., Ramey, C. T., Pungello, E. P., Sparling, J., & Miller-Johnson, S. (2002). Early childhood education: Young adult outcomes from the Abecedarian project. *Applied Developmental Science, 6,* 42–57.

Clarke, S. H., & Campbell, F. A. (1998). Can intervention early prevent crime later? The Abecedarian Project compared with other programs. *Early Childhood Research Quarterly, 13,* 319–343.

Consortium for Longitudinal Studies. (1983). *As the twig is bent... lasting effects of preschool programs.* Hillsdale, NJ: Erlbaum.

Disaster Center. (2004). *United States crime index rates per 100,000 inhabitants.* Retrieved from http://www.disastercenter.com/crime/uscrime.htm.

Gilliam, W. S., & Zigler, E. F. (2001). A critical meta-analysis of all evaluations of state-funded preschool from 1977 to 1998: Implications for policy, service delivery, and program implementation. *Early Childhood Research Quarterly, 15,* 441–473.

Goodson, B. D., Layzer, J. I., St. Pierre, R. G., Bernstein, L. S., & Lopez, M. (2000). Effectiveness of a comprehensive, five-year family support program for low-income families: Findings from the Comprehensive Child Development Program. *Early Childhood Research Quarterly, 15,* 5–39.

Masse, L. N., & Barnett, W. S. (2002). A benefit-cost analysis of the Abecedarian early childhood intervention. In H. Levin & P. McEwan (Eds.), *Cost effectiveness analysis in education: Methods, findings and potential. 2002 Yearbook of the American Education Finance Association.* Retrieved from http://nieer.org/resources/research/AbecedarianStudy.pdf.

NICHD Early Child Care Research Network. (2005). Early child care and children's development in the primary grades: Follow-up results from the NICHD Study of Early Child Care. *American Educational Research Journal, 42*(3). Related material retrieved from http://secc.rti.org.

O'Brien, R. W., D'Elio, M. A., Vaden-Kiernan, M., Magee, C., Younoszai, T., Keane, M. J., et al. (2002, January). *A descriptive study of Head Start families: FACES technical report I.* Washington, DC: Administration on Children, Youth, and Families, U.S. Department of Health and Human Services. Retrieved from http://www.acf.hhs.gov/programs/opre/hs/faces/reports/technical_report/technical_report.pdf.

Reynolds, A. J., Temple, J. A., Robertson, D. L., & Mann, E. A. (2001). Long-term effects of an early childhood intervention on educational achievement and juvenile arrest: A 15-year follow-up of low-income children in public schools. *Journal of the American Medical Association, 285,* 2339–2346.

Reynolds, A. J., Temple, J. A., Robertson, D. L., & Mann, E. A. (2002). Age 21 cost-benefit analysis of the Title I Chicago child-parent centers. *Educational Evaluation and Policy Analysis, 4,* 267–303. Retrieved from http://www.waisman.wisc.edu/cls/cbaexecsum4.html.

Schweinhart, L. J., Montie, J., Xiang, Z., Barnett, W. S., Belfield, C. R., & Nores, M. (2005). *Lifetime effects: The HighScope Perry Preschool Study through age 40.* Ypsilanti, MI: HighScope Press.

Schweinhart, L. J., & Weikart, D. P. (1980). *Young children grow up: The effects of the Perry Preschool program on youths through age 15* (Monographs of the HighScope Educational Research Foundation, 7). Ypsilanti, MI: HighScope Press.

Schweinhart, L. J., & Weikart, D. P. (1997a). *Lasting differences: The High/Scope Preschool Curriculum Comparison Study through age 23* (Monographs of the HighScope Educational Research Foundation, 12). Ypsilanti, MI: HighScope Press.

Schweinhart, L. J., & Weikart, D. P. (1997b). The High/Scope Preschool Curriculum Comparison Study through age 23. *Early Childhood Research Quarterly, 12,* 117–143.

Solon, G. (1992, June). Intergenerational income mobility in the United States. *American Economic Review, 82,* 393–408.

Terman, L. M., & Merrill, M. A. (1960). *Stanford-Binet Intelligence Scale Form L-M: Manual for the third revision.* Boston: Houghton-Mifflin.

Tiegs, E. W., & Clark, W. W. (1963). *California Achievement Tests: Complete battery, 1957 ed.* Monterey Park, CA: California Test Bureau (McGraw-Hill).

Tiegs, E. W., & Clark, W. W. (1971). *California Achievement Tests* (1970 ed.). Monterey Park, CA: California Test Bureau (McGraw-Hill).

U.S. Census Bureau, Housing and Household Economic Statistics Division. (2003). *Transitions into and out of poverty, by selected characteristics: 1996–1997* (Table 5). Retrieved from http://www.census.gov/hhes/www/poverty/sipp96/table05.html.

8

Impacts and Implications of the Child-Parent Center Preschool Program

ARTHUR J. REYNOLDS, JUDY A. TEMPLE, AND SUH-RUU OU

INTRODUCTION

Preschool programs are widely considered to be one of the most effective ways to enhance children's well-being (Reynolds, Wang, & Walberg, 2003). Their unique attraction is the documented evidence that programs high in quality have enduring effects and high economic returns. The prominent status of the early education field provides an opportunity to highlight recent findings and emerging research directions. Four questions have received renewed attention:

1. Do the effects of large-scale public programs endure? Can these programs have an impact on broader health and well-being?
2. What are the causal mechanisms that promote long-term effects?
3. What is the evidence in support of cost effectiveness?
4. What are the key principles for enhancing program effectiveness?

In this chapter, we report findings from the Chicago Longitudinal Study of the Child-Parent Center (CPC) preschool program to address these questions and illustrate advances in the field for enhancing effectiveness. The CPC program is especially relevant to early childhood policy. As the second oldest federally funded preschool program, CPC has been implemented successfully in the Chicago public schools for four decades. In contrast to many others, the CPC program is a sustained intervention funded and administered through public schools. Funded by Title I of the Elementary and Secondary Education Act (now the No Child Left Behind Act), the program is also innovative in its approach to education. It blends an instructional philosophy of literacy and school readiness with intensive services for parents to strengthen the family–school relationship.

In addition to small classes of 17 children and 2 staff, including a certified teacher, each center has a head teacher who functions as a principal, a parent-resource teacher who runs the parent program in the parent-resource room, a school-community representative, and school nurses and other auxiliary staff who provide health-related services. Kindergarten and school-age components have also been implemented as part of the larger CPC extended intervention model.

The CPC program has demonstrated high economic returns to the public and society at large through promoting school achievement, higher educational attainment, and economic well-being and reducing rates of remedial education, child maltreatment, and juvenile and adult crime. Given the program's history of successful implementation within existing services systems, these findings have special relevance for policy.

CHILD-PARENT CENTER PROGRAM

The CPC program began in 1967 through funding from Title I of the Elementary and Secondary Education Act of 1965, which provided grants to local public school districts serving high concentrations of low-income children. The CPC program includes three components: a child-centered focus on the development of reading/language skills, parental involvement, and comprehensive services (Reynolds, 2000). Figure 8.1 shows the program components. CPC includes a half-day preschool program for 3- and 4-year-olds, a half-day or an all-day kindergarten program, and 2 or 3 years of school-age intervention in co-located elementary schools. It operates on the 9-month school-year calendar, although it also provides an 8-week summer program.

Each site is under the direction of a head teacher and is located adjacent to the elementary school or as a wing of the school. Major features of the program are as follows:

- a structured but diverse set of language-based instructional activities designed to promote academic and social success; an activity-based curriculum called the Chicago EARLY (Chicago Board of Education, 1988) has been frequently used and field trips are common
- a multifaceted parent program that includes participating in parent room activities, volunteering in the classroom, attending school events, and enrolling in educational courses for personal development, all under the supervision of the parent-resource teacher
- outreach activities coordinated by the school-community representative, which include resource mobilization, home visitation, and enrollment of children most in need
- a comprehensive school-age program from first to third grade that supports children's transition to elementary school through reduced class sizes (up to 25 children); the addition of teacher aides in each class, extra instructional supplies, and coordination of instructional activities; staff development; and parent-program activities organized by the curriculum parent-resource teacher

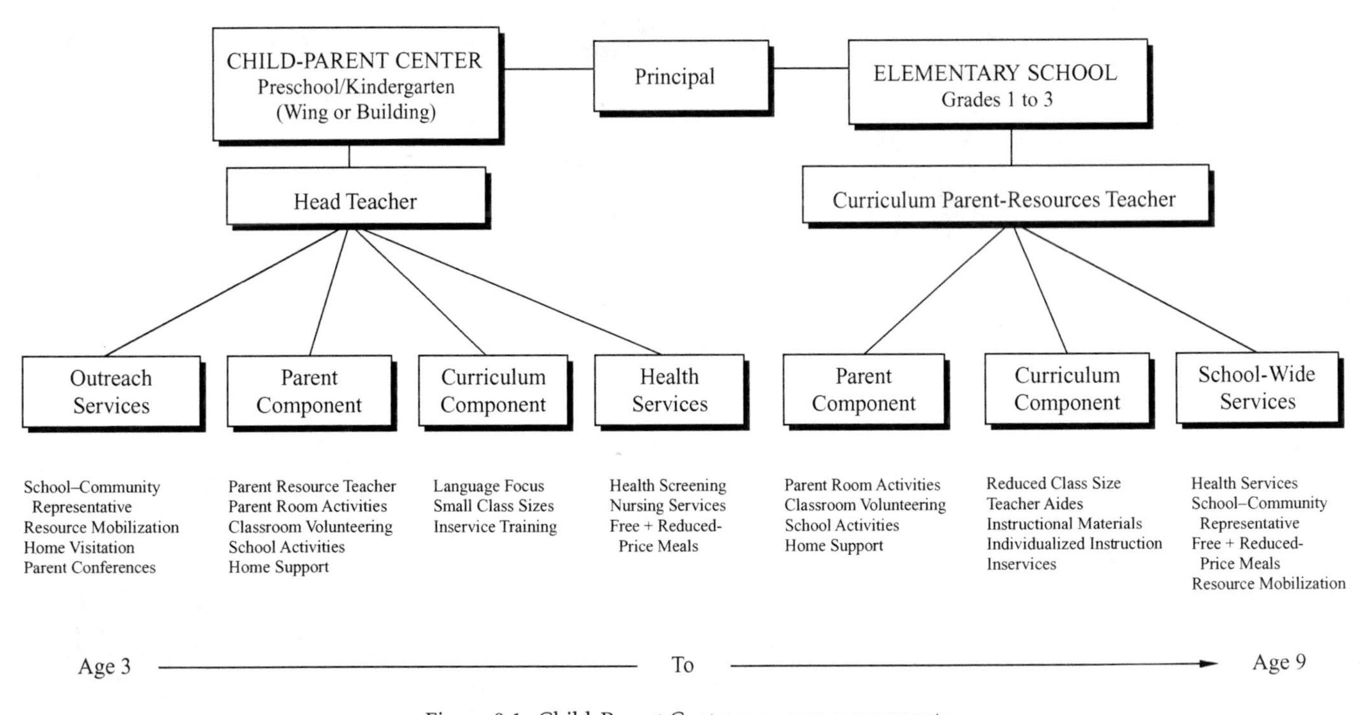

Figure 8.1. Child-Parent Center program components.

The program theory underlying the intervention is that children's scholastic readiness for school will be facilitated through the provision of (a) systematic language-learning activities in center-based early intervention, and (b) opportunities for family-support experiences through direct parent participation in the program with and on behalf of their children (Reynolds, 2000; Sullivan, 1971). This goal statement embodies the central program theory: "[CPC is] designed to reach the child and parent early, develop language skills and self-confidence, and to demonstrate that these children, if given a chance, can meet successfully all the demands of today's technological, urban society" (cf. Naisbitt, 1968).

CHICAGO LONGITUDINAL STUDY

Now in its 22nd year, the Chicago Longitudinal Study (CLS; 2005) investigates the life-course development of 1,539 children, 93% of whom are African American, who attended government-funded early childhood programs in preschool or kindergarten in high-poverty neighborhoods in the Chicago public schools. The three major goals of the CLS are to (a) evaluate the effects of the Child-Parent Center preschool program over time, (b) identify the mechanisms through which the effects of participation are manifested, and (c) investigate the influence of a variety of family and school factors on children's adjustment. During the 20+ years of the study, extensive information on parent involvement as measured by teachers and parents has been collected along with data on other child and family experiences and on children's school success.

The sample includes a complete cohort of 989 children born in 1979–1980 who participated in the Child-Parent Center preschool program between 1983 and 1985 in the poorest neighborhoods in Chicago. The comparison group consists of 550 children of the same age from randomly selected schools that were implementing full-day kindergarten and other intervention strategies for at-risk children in low-income communities. In addition to full-day kindergarten, 15% of the "treatment as usual" comparison group attended Head Start preschools.

Program and comparison groups were well matched on eligibility for intervention, family socioeconomic status, gender, and race/ethnicity. For example, program and comparison groups experienced an average of four out of six family risk factors (e.g., low education, poverty status, single-parent status). At age 24, roughly 1,400 participants (91% of the original sample) were still active in the study. Table 8.1 summarizes the characteristics of the groups and their intervention experiences.

CONFIRMATORY RESEARCH APPROACH

To investigate the effects of the CPC program and other influences, we have used a confirmatory research approach called confirmatory program

Table 8.1. *Characteristics of study groups*

	CPC intervention	Comparison
Sample	Complete cohort	Random sample of K sites
Recovery, by age 24	902 of 989 (91%)	487 of 550 (89%)
Key attributes	Reside in highest poverty areas More than 80% of children enroll	Reside in high-poverty areas Had school-based enrichment
	Mean no. of risks = 4.5; 73% with 4 or more risks	Mean no. of risks = 4.5; 71% with 4 or more risks
	Parent ed > than in c-group	Area poverty < than in p-group
Intervention levels		
Preschool	100% 1 or 2 years	15% in Head Start
Kindergarten	60% full day	100% full day
School age	69% 1 year 56% 2–3 years	30% 1 year 0% 2–3 years

evaluation (CPE) (Reynolds, 1998). CPE is a theory-driven methodology for investigating the effects of social and educational programs. A theory-driven impact evaluation highlights the explicit theory of the program to establish an a priori model of how the program is expected to exert its influence (Chen, 1990). Causal uncertainty is reduced through an examination of the empirical pattern of findings against the expectations inherent in the program. CPE addresses three key questions: (1) Is program participation independently and consistently associated with key outcomes?; (2) What are the processes or pathways through which participation leads to children's outcomes?; and (3) Are the estimated effects conditional on child and family attributes or on particular program components? Given their emphasis on multivariate prediction, theory-driven evaluations are more confirmatory than other evaluation approaches.

CPE is aided by the use of six empirically verifiable criteria that strengthen the validity of research findings and their applicability to research findings: temporality, size, gradient (dosage response), specificity, consistency, and coherence. For example, specificity refers to the situation in which the program-outcome relationship is limited, based on a priori theory, to certain domains of behavior or to particular subgroups such as individuals at high risk of problems. Causal inference is more straightforward in such cases. Consistency indicates whether the estimated effect is similar across sample populations, at different times and places, and under different types of analyses and model specifications. At the highest level of causal interpretation is coherence – the extent to which the evaluation findings show a clear pattern of effects relative to the causes of behaviors that the program is attempting to affect, the target population, the program theory, and the program implementation. These criteria and others were used to determine that smoking causes lung cancer (Susser, 1973; U.S. Department Health, Education and Welfare, 1964).

Figure 8.2 shows five hypothesized pathways through which preschool and other early education programs may affect later child competence. Because the major purpose of early intervention concerns educational enrichment, many outcomes assess school performance. Indeed, enhancing school performance and enhancing success are the most frequently reported findings in the literature.

Derived from the 40-year literature on the effects of preschool, the hypotheses associated with these pathways provide a foundation for understanding how early childhood programs lead to longer term effects, as well as the environmental conditions that promote or limit success. As shown, the effects of preschool are transmitted through (a) developed cognitive and scholastic abilities (cognitive advantage hypothesis), (b) social development and adjustment (social adjustment hypothesis), (c) parents' behavior with or on behalf of children (family support hypothesis), (d) children's motivation or self-efficacy (motivational advantage hypothesis), and (e) quality of the school environments that children experience postprogram (school support hypotheses). Most previous studies have addressed, at most, one or two of these hypotheses and never through formal empirical tests. These hypotheses are described later (see Reynolds, 2000; Reynolds, Ou, & Topitzes, 2004; Reynolds & Robertson, 2003).

RESEARCH EXAMPLES IN THE CLS

We summarize findings on the effects of the CPC preschool program in three areas: impacts on adult health and well-being, economic benefits, and pathways of change leading to greater adult well-being.

CPC Preschool and Well-Being at Age 24

Given that the immediate and longer term effects through adolescence are well documented in prior studies for both preschool and school-age participation (Reynolds, 2000; Reynolds, Temple, Robertson, & Mann, 2001), we summarize impacts of the CPC preschool program into adulthood. In the age-24 follow-up study for 1,400 study participants, Reynolds and colleagues (2007) found that after adjusting for many family-background factors, CPC preschool participants had greater well-being in health and social behavior and higher educational attainment and occupational status. Table 8.2 shows the major findings, which are summarized in this section.

Educational Attainment

Preschool participants had significantly higher rates of high school completion at age 24 than the comparison group (79.4% vs. 70.7%), and they had more years of education (11.97 vs. 11.65). Rates of attendance in 4-year colleges were similar but slightly favored the preschool group (13.6% vs. 10.4%). Effects on

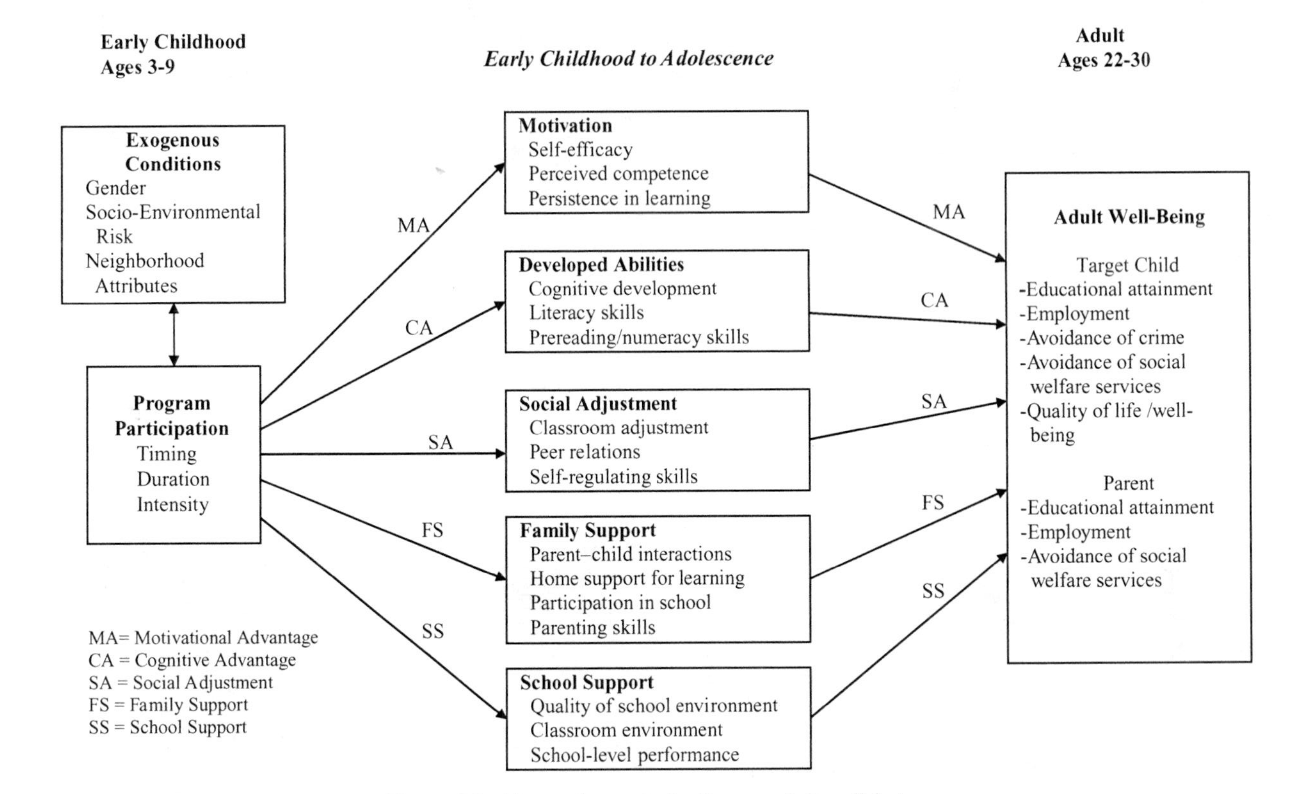

Figure 8.2. Alternative paths leading to adult well-being.

Table 8.2. *Adjusted means and rates for ages 22–24 well-being in the CPC study*

Outcome	Preschool group	Control group	Difference
Education by age 24			
High school completion, %	79.4	70.7	8.7*
Years of education	11.97	11.65	0.32*
4-Year college attendance, %	13.6	10.4	3.1
Occupation and work			
Occupational prestige, % (semiskilled or >)	28.2	21.5	6.7*
Full-time employment	39.4	37.4	2.0
Crime			
Arrest, %			
Felony arrest	16.5	21.1	−4.6*
Conviction	15.3	19.7	−4.4*
Incarceration			
Health			
Out-of-home placement	4.5	8.4	−3.9*
Health insurance coverage	71.9	61.0	10.9*
Daily smoking	17.9	22.1	−4.2
Substance misuse	14.0	17.0	−3.0
Mental health			
Depressive symptoms, %	12.8	17.4	−4.6*

Note: Control variables were measured from birth to age 3 as follows: sex of child, race/ethnicity, parent a high school graduate, single-parent family, parent employment, four or more children in family, parent a teen at child's birth, eligible for fully subsidized school lunches, AFDC participation, and involvement in child welfare system. CPC school age was also a covariate. Occupational prestige was a Hollingshead score of 4 or higher on an 8-point scale.

* $p < .10$. Except for depressive symptoms ($p = .06$), all significant differences were $p < .05$.

educational attainment were consistent across different model specifications and assumptions, including sample attrition. As shown in the Appendix to this chapter, group differences were robust after accounting for children's propensity to be included in the educational attainment sample.

Occupational Prestige

CPC preschool graduates were more likely than their comparison counterparts to have higher skilled jobs. Whereas 28.2% of the preschool group had jobs defined as semiskilled or higher (4 or more on the 8-point Hollingshead scale), this was the case for only 21.5% of the comparison group.

Crime

The preschool group had lower rates of criminal behavior, ranging from lower felony arrests and incarceration. Whereas 16.5% of the preschool group had a felony arrest by age 24, 21.1% of the comparison group did – a reduction in arrests of 21%. For rates of incarceration or jail, the reduction associated with program participation was 20% (20.6% vs. 25.6%). No program-group differences were found for nonfelony arrests. Corrections for sample attrition yielded similar effects (see the Appendix).

Health

Most important, preschool participants had higher rates of health insurance coverage (71.9% vs. 61.0%) and lower rates of out-of-home placement in the child welfare system (4.5% vs. 8.4%). Most of the differences in health insurance came from the higher percentage of preschool participants with private health insurance than the comparison group (see the Appendix). Although rates of daily smoking and substance misuse were lower for the preschool group, they were not significantly different.

Mental Health

The main finding regarding mental health was that preschool participants had a significantly lower rate of one or more depressive symptoms (12.8% vs. 17.4%), which was a 26% reduction over the comparison group. The adult survey assessed depressive symptoms at ages 22–24. Having frequent feelings of depression, sadness, and loneliness in the past month was the key criterion.

Participation in the school-age program and in the extended CPC intervention also was linked to better health and well-being on some indicators. Some program effects were stronger for males, 2-year preschool participants, and children in centers rated high in child-initiated activities (see Reynolds et al., 2001, 2007). For example, among males, program participants had much higher rates of high school completion than the comparison group. Generally, males benefited more from the program than did females (Reynolds et al., 2007).

Pathways of Change From Preschool to Lower Felony Arrest at Age 24

We investigated the causal mechanisms and processes from preschool participation to the adult outcome of felony arrest based on the five-hypothesis model in Figure 8.2. Because preschool participation was associated with reductions in felony arrest, the processes that led to this reduction should be able to be identified by the confirmatory research approach described earlier. Figure 8.3 shows the full estimated model, and Figure 8.4 shows select influential paths that help explain the process of change. The model was estimated in LISREL (Jöreskog & Sörbom, 1996) structural equation modeling. It included indicators of all five hypotheses and fit the data reasonably well, $\chi^2 = 300.63$ (29), RMSEA = .08, AGFI = .88. It accounted for 80% of the variance in any felony arrest by age 24.

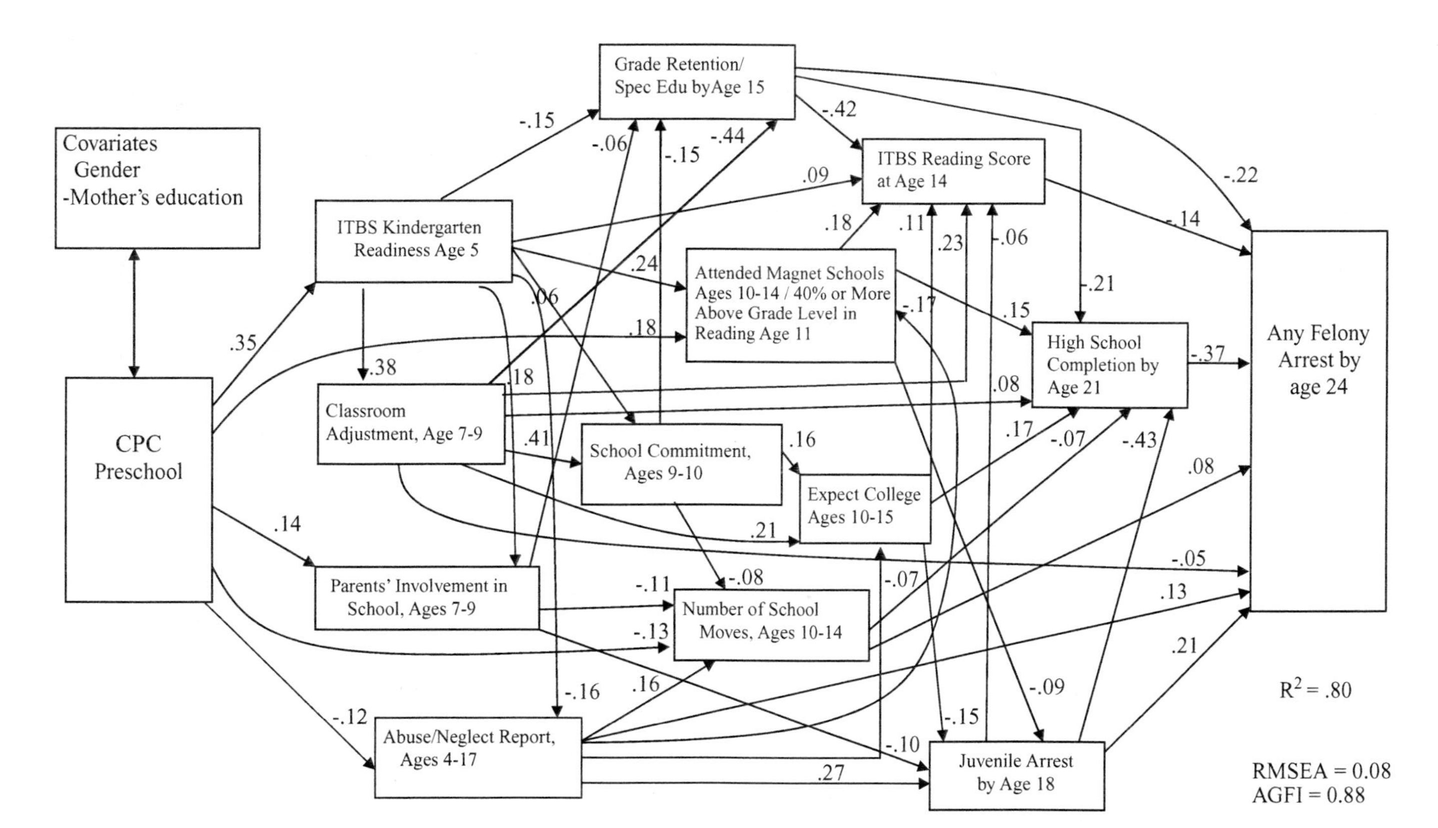

Figure 8.3. LISREL mediation model for any felony arrest by age 24; coefficients standardized and adjusted for measurement errors.

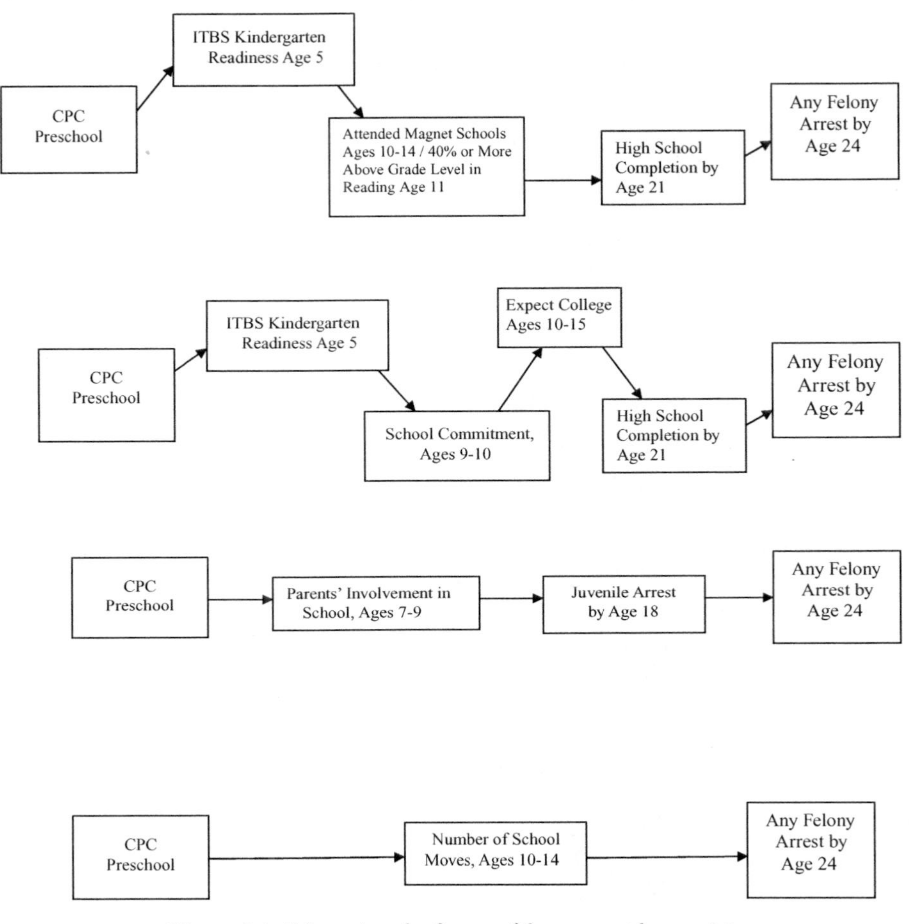

Figure 8.4. Selected paths for any felony arrest by age 24.

Figure 8.3 shows the significant, standardized coefficients of the model. The paths leading from preschool participation to felony arrest were diverse, although two intervening factors directly mediated the main effect of preschool participation: number of school moves (ages 10–14) and abuse/neglect report (ages 4–17). Preschool participation was associated with a lower incidence of child abuse and neglect ($b = -.12$), which was in turn associated with felony arrest by age 24 in the expected direction ($b = .13$). Preschool participation was associated with a lower rate of school mobility ($b = -.13$), which in turn was associated with lower felony arrest ($b = .08$).

The cognitive-advantage hypothesis contributed to the preschool effect directly, and its impact was widespread through other intervening factors as well. Program participation was associated with an immediate boost in kindergarten readiness ($b = .35$), which led to a lower rate of grade retention or special-education placement by age 15 ($b = -.15$) and then to a lower rate of felony arrest ($b = -.22$). Kindergarten readiness also was associated with higher academic achievement at age 14 ($b = .09$) and to a lower rate of felony arrest ($b = -.14$).

In addition to abuse/neglect, another indicator of family support – parents' involvement in the school – mediated the effect of preschool participation through juvenile arrest. Program participation was associated with higher parental involvement ($b = .14$), which in turn was associated with a lower rate of juvenile arrest ($b = -.10$) and of felony arrest ($b = .21$). Similar to the family-support hypothesis, another indicator of school support – magnet school attendance or 40% or more above grade level in reading at age 11 – mediated the effect of preschool through high school completion and juvenile arrest. Preschool participation was associated with a higher rate of attending magnet schools ($b = .18$); attending a magnet school then was associated with both a higher rate of high school completion ($b = .15$) and a lower rate of juvenile arrest ($b = -.09$). High school completion and juvenile arrest were associated with felony arrest ($b = -.37$ and .21, respectively), such that both higher rates of high school completion and lower rates of juvenile arrest led to lower rates of felony arrest.

Some additional findings from the CLS are notable. Using the five-hypothesis model, Reynolds and colleagues (2007) investigated pathways through which participation in the CPC preschool program affects broader health and well-being, including socioeconomic status, educational attainment, health insurance coverage, criminal behavior, and depressive symptoms. Measures of cognitive advantage (e.g., school-readiness scores), family support (e.g., parent involvement), school support (e.g., school quality), social adjustment (e.g., juvenile crime), and motivational advantage (e.g., achievement motivation) were mediators and were measured from ages 5 to the end of adolescence. Hierarchical regression analysis indicated that when considered together, the five sets of mediators accounted for 48% of the preschool effect on years of education, 70% on occupational prestige, 47% on health insurance coverage, 100% on depressive symptoms, 48% on incarceration, and 84% on felony arrest. For most outcomes, the cognitive-advantage, social-adjustment, and school-support hypotheses made the largest contributions to the program effect.

Estimation of the model for court-reported juvenile arrest by age 18, which is significantly associated with preschool participation (Reynolds et al., 2001), indicated that the school-support hypothesis, mainly magnet-school attendance, accounted for 48% of the indirect effect of the program. This finding is interpreted as the combined effect of peers and school quality. The cognitive-advantage hypothesis accounted for 19% of the indirect effect on juvenile arrest and the family-support hypothesis for 21%. For the latter, parental involvement contributed positively to the maintenance of effects, and child abuse and neglect contributed negatively.

Table 8.3. *Itemized benefits per participant in 2006 dollars for the CPC preschool program*

Costs and benefits	Benefit per participant	Percent of total benefit
Program cost	8,277	–
Program benefits		
Child care	2,049	2.4%
K–12 education savings	6,026	7.2%
Child welfare savings	976	1.2%
College	−689	–
Participant earnings	25,376	30.2%
Taxes	8,958	10.7%
Crime savings		
Criminal justice system	8,819	10.5%
Victimization	32,517	38.7%
Tangible	7,578	9.0%
Intangible	24,939	29.7%
Total benefits	84,032	100.0%
Public and crime victims	56,837	67.6%
Participants	27,195	32.4%

Note: See the CBA report for the estimation procedures. The negative benefits of college attendance reflect the fact that taxpayers fund two thirds of the cost of college. This cost slightly offsets the earnings increases to participants as well as the increased tax revenues. Earnings are estimates of total compensation before taxes.

Economic Returns Relative to Costs

Cost-benefit analysis (CBA) is ready-made for translating evaluation findings into language relevant to the policy-making process. It assesses both effectiveness and efficiency, the latter indicating the largest return at the lowest cost. At a minimum, the economic benefit should equal the amount invested in the program – a return of at least one dollar per dollar invested.

Chicago study investigators conducted the first cost-benefit analysis of a large-scale public early childhood program (Reynolds et al., 2002). They estimated program benefits in 2006 dollars for five categories: reductions in expenditures for remedial education, reductions in criminal justice system expenditures for both juvenile and adult arrest and treatment, reductions in child welfare system expenditures, averted tangible expenditures to crime victims as a result of lower rates of arrest and to victims of child maltreatment, and increases in projected earnings of program participants and tax revenues as a result of higher levels of educational attainment (Reynolds et al., 2002).

At a cost of roughly $8,000 per child for 1.5 years of half-day preschool, the program generated a societal return per participant of more than $84,000 (see Table 8.3). This translated into a return per dollar invested of $10.15. Exclusive of intangible crime victim savings, the return per dollar invested was $7.14.

Total benefits to the general public (taxpayers and crime victims) were about $57,000 per child. The largest benefit was in crime savings: 49% of the total benefits were in reduced criminal justice system costs and averted crime victim savings. The second and third largest benefit categories were program participants' increased earnings capacity (30.2% of total) and resulting tax revenues projected from higher educational attainment (10.7% of total). K–12 savings in remedial education (2.4% of total benefits) and child welfare savings (1.2% of total benefits) also provided significant benefits to the public. Savings in the child welfare system associated with lower maltreatment also contributed. Table 8.3 shows the categorical breakdown of economic benefits and costs per program participant.

Because the Child-Parent Center study is the first cost-benefit analysis of a large-scale public preschool program, the findings increase the generalizability of results to publicly funded programs, including emerging universal access programs. The findings also indicate that school-based prevention programs during early childhood can lead to reduced child maltreatment and delinquency. These findings are of special significance given the paucity of evidence that treatment programs prevent maltreatment and delinquency.

Comparing the evidence on economic returns of preschool programs such as CPC to other intervention programs and policies is instructive. Small class sizes are associated with increased school achievement, but impacts are not large or enduring. The benefits of remedial education such as tutoring and summer school are, at best, inconsistent and short-lived. The track record of child welfare treatment, delinquency, and dropout prevention programs is weak and, given their treatment focus, even the best have low cost effectiveness. Many of these programs have an important role to play, but preventive investments in high-quality preschool have demonstrated the largest and most enduring benefits.

Figure 8.5 shows the returns per dollar invested for several types of programs with available cost-benefit analyses over the first 9 years of life by the age of entry into intervention. These include family-centered home-visiting programs, preschool and prekindergarten programs, full-day kindergarten, and class-size reduction programs. Age 0 refers to intervention begun prenatally (i.e., WIC and Nurse-Family Partnerships). Although programs at all ages show evidence of positive economic returns exceeding $1 per dollar invested, preschool programs for 3- and 4-year-olds generally show the highest returns. For comparability, we limited the studies in Figure 8.5 to assessments of benefits into early adulthood. Returns for the Perry Preschool Program assessed at age 40 were estimated at more than $16 per dollar invested (Schweinhart et al., 2005).

PRINCIPLES OF EFFECTIVENESS

Findings from the CPC study and other projects show the need for larger investments in high-quality programs that provide child education and intensive resources for parental involvement. Because the availability and quality of

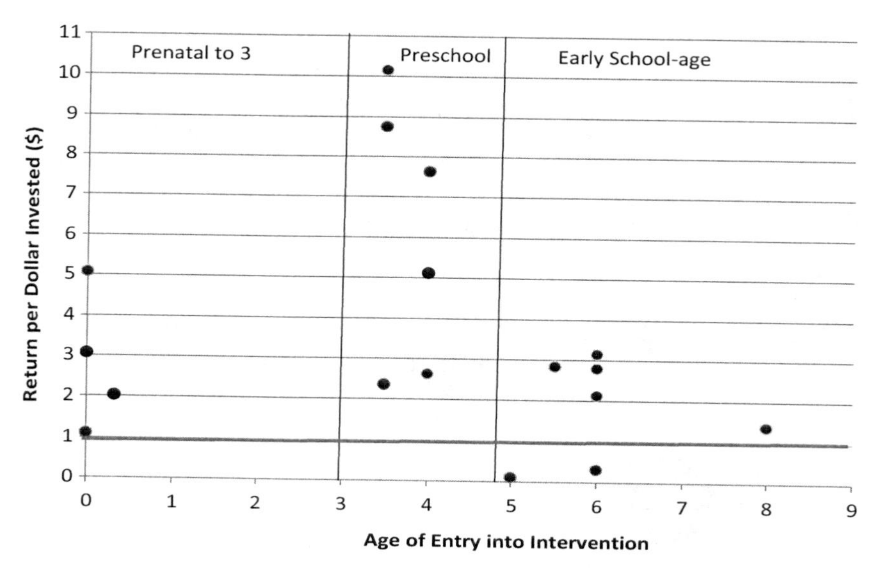

Figure 8.5. Return per dollar invested by age of entry into intervention.

most preschool services are not high, programs with demonstrated effectiveness such as CPC warrant emulation. Research on the CPC program suggests that six main principles of effectiveness are key to preschool programs' long-term effects and cost effectiveness.

First, a coordinated system is in place beginning at age 3 and continues to the early school grades. Program implementation within a single administrative system in partnership with communities can promote stability in the child's learning environment, which can provide smooth transitions from preschool to kindergarten and from kindergarten to the early grades. Today, most preschool programs are not integrated within public schools, and children usually change schools more than once by the early grades. In the movement to universal access to early education, schools can take a leadership role in partnering with community agencies. Programs that provide coordinated or "wrap-around" services may be more effective under a centralized leadership structure rather than under a case-management framework. For example, the CPC program is an established program in the third largest school system in the nation. Findings from the CPC cost-benefit analysis give a good indication of the size of effects that could be possible in public schools, the largest administrative system of any universal program.

The second principle of effectiveness is that *program length strengthens learning gains.* The CPC program was offered beginning at age 3 so that children could participate for 2 years before entering kindergarten. Preschool length was positively associated with school-readiness skills (Reynolds, 1995), lower rates of remedial education in the early grades, and lower rates of later child maltreatment. Moreover, the total number of years of CPC preschool and school-age intervention linked to higher school achievement and well-being into adulthood (Reynolds et al., 2007).

A third principle of CPC effectiveness is that *teaching staff should be trained and compensated well*, preferably with bachelor's degrees and certification in early childhood, and they should earn competitive salaries. These characteristics are much more likely to be realized under a public-school model of universal access, notwithstanding the need for established partnerships with community child care agencies. It is no coincidence that programs showing the highest economic returns – the CPC and Perry preschools – were implemented in public schools by teachers with at least bachelor's degrees and appropriate certification in early childhood. Staff turnover in school-based programs is also much lower than in other early education settings.

Fourth, educational content should be responsive to all of children's learning needs, but *special emphasis should be given to cognitive and school readiness skills through a structured but diverse set of learning activities.* The CPC and other cost-effective programs have a strong emphasis on cognitive and language skills within a responsive learning environment. Child:staff ratios of less than 9:1 in preschool help as well. The curriculum itself appears to be less important, because the programs ranged from Perry's child-initiated approach to Chicago's blended, teacher-directed approach. Extrapolating these findings, we find that preschool and other social programs are more likely to have enduring effects if they provide services that are intensive and are dedicated to the enhancement of educational and social skills.

A fifth principle of CPC effectiveness is that *comprehensive family services are provided to meet the different needs of children.* As child-development programs, preschools must be tailored to family circumstances and thus provide opportunities for positive learning experiences in school and at home. Those with special needs or who are most at risk benefit from intensive and comprehensive services. In the CPC program, parental involvement is very intensive, as each center has a parent-resource room run by a certified teacher and provides school-community outreach. Facilitating parents' own educational and personal development is an important program goal. Other programs, such as the Perry Preschool and Abecedarian Project, also provided family services. Abecedarian provided medical and nutritional services, and the Perry Preschool had weekly home visits by teachers.

Finally, *commitment to ongoing evaluations of effectiveness and cost effectiveness is paramount.* From its inception, the CPC program has been assessed on a regular basis using different methods and approaches. There have been frequent investigations of longer term effects. Even today, longitudinal studies of effectiveness are rare in other early childhood education programs. Such studies are essential for conducting cost-benefit analysis of alternative programs, and they are more likely to accurately assess the total impact of program participation. Nevertheless, greater attention to differential effects is needed across a range of child, family, and program attributes. The identification of the processes of effects or "active ingredients" that promote enduring effects also remains a high priority.

SUMMARY

Although significant progress continues to be made in understanding the effects of preschool programs, questions remain about the reliability of long-term impacts for large-scale programs, the programs' cost effectiveness, and the causal mechanisms of change. In this chapter, we describe recent findings on the impact of the CPC preschool program into adulthood and the processes that led to these effects. Given that the program has been run by the Chicago public schools for 40 years, its consistent evidence of positive effects and high economic returns has significant implications for policy development and modification. The findings also show how a confirmatory, theory-driven approach can help advance knowledge in enhancing children's well-being. Key principles of effectiveness are described for promoting enduring effects.

REFERENCES

Chen, H. T. (1990). *Theory-driven evaluations.* Newbury Park, CA: Sage Publications.

Chicago Board of Education. (1988). *Chicago EARLY: Instructional activities for ages 3 to 6.* Vernon Hills, IL: ETA.

Chicago Longitudinal Study. (2005). *Chicago Longitudinal Study: User's guide* (Version 7). Madison: Waisman Center, University of Wisconsin.

Consortium for Longitudinal Studies. (1983). *As the twig is bent . . . lasting effects of preschool programs.* Hillsdale, NJ: Erlbaum.

Jöreskog, K., & Sörbom, D. (1996). *LISREL 8: User's reference guide.* Chicago: Scientific Software.

Naisbitt, N. (1968). *Child-Parent Education Centers, ESEA Title I, Activity I.* Unpublished manuscript.

Reynolds, A. J. (1995). One year of preschool or two: Does it matter? *Early Childhood Research Quarterly, 10,* 1–31.

Reynolds, A. J. (1998). Confirmatory program evaluation: A method for strengthening causal inference. *American Journal of Evaluation, 17,* 21–35.

Reynolds, A. J. (2000). *Success in early intervention: The Chicago Child-Parent Centers.* Lincoln: University of Nebraska Press.

Reynolds, A. J. (Chair). (2007). *Paths of influence from preschool intervention to adult well-being: Age 24 findings from the Chicago Longitudinal Study.* A symposium presented at the Biennial meeting of the Society for Prevention Research in Boston, MA, March 31, 2007.

Reynolds, A. J., Ou, S., & Topitzes, J. D. (2004). Confirmatory program evaluation: Pathways of long-term effects of early childhood intervention on educational attainment and juvenile arrest. *Child Development, 75*(5), 1299–1328.

Reynolds, A. J., & Robertson, D. L. (2003). School-based early children intervention and later maltreatment in the Chicago Longitudinal Study. *Child Development, 74,* 3–26.

Reynolds, A. J., Temple, J. A., Ou, S., Robertson, D. L., Mersky, J. P., Topitzes, J. W., et al. (2007). Effects of a school-based, early childhood intervention on adult health and well-being: A 19-year follow-up of low-income families. *Archives of Pediatrics and Adolescent Medicine, 161*, 730–739.

Reynolds, A. J., Temple, J. A., Robertson, D. L., & Mann, E. A. (2001). Long-term effects of an early childhood intervention on educational achievement and juvenile arrest: A 15-year follow-up of low-income children in public schools. *Journal of the American Medical Association, 285*(18), 2339–2346.

Reynolds, A. J., Temple, J. A., Robertson, D. L., & Mann, E. A. (2002). Age 21 cost-benefit analysis of the Title I Chicago Child-Parent Centers. *Educational Evaluation and Policy Analysis, 24*, 267–303.

Reynolds, A. J., Wang, M. C., & Walberg, H. J. (Eds.). (2003). *Early childhood programs for a new century.* Washington, DC: CWLA Press.

Schweinhart, L. J., Montie, J., et al. (2005). *Lifetime effects: The HighScope Perry Preschool Study through age 40.* Ypsilanti, MI: High/Scope Educational Research Foundation.

Sullivan, L. M. (1971). *Let us not underestimate the children.* Glenview, IL: Scott, Foresman.

Susser, M. (1973). *Causal thinking in the health sciences: Concepts and strategies of epidemology.* New York: Oxford University Press.

U.S. Department of Health, Education, and Welfare. (1964). *Smoking and health: Report of the advisory committee to the surgeon-general of the Public Health Service* (Public Health Service Publication No. 1103). Washington, DC: U.S. Government Printing Office.

Appendix

Outcomes Regressions – With and Without Attrition Correction

	High school completion							
	No attrition correction		Attrit. Correct. model 1		Attrit. Correct. model 2		Attrit. Correct. model 3	
	dF/dx	P>z	dF/dx	P>z	dF/dx	P>z	dF/dx	P>z
Gender	0.148	0.00	0.129	0.00	0.117	0.00	0.133	0.00
Race	−0.137	0.00	−0.154	0.00	−0.143	0.00	−0.150	0.00
Any preschool	0.087	0.00	0.085	0.00	0.091	0.00	0.086	0.00
Any school-age intervention	0.024	0.34	0.017	0.50	0.014	0.58	0.019	0.45
Single parent 0–3	0.014	0.64	0.023	0.46	−0.008	0.79	0.021	0.52
Mother is less than 18 years old, 0–3	−0.005	0.87	−0.026	0.44	−0.036	0.29	−0.023	0.51
Mother completed hs, 0–3	0.094	0.00	0.079	0.00	0.059	0.04	0.083	0.01
Mother had some college, 0–3	0.066	0.12	0.067	0.11	0.079	0.06	0.065	0.13
TANF/AFDC, age 0–3	−0.109	0.00	−0.098	0.01	−0.095	0.01	−0.097	0.01
Mother full/part-time employment	0.004	0.91	0.009	0.80	−0.006	0.87	0.008	0.82
Child welfare, age 0–3	−0.059	0.36	−0.029	0.64	−0.008	0.90	−0.034	0.59
Free lunch 0–3	−0.056	0.12	−0.073	0.04	−0.083	0.02	−0.068	0.06
Missing values-risk factors (dummy)	0.044	0.19	0.080	0.02	0.084	0.01	0.065	0.07
Propensity score			0.497	0.00				
attrition sample* quartile ranking					0.058	0.00		
q2 dummy							0.143	0.00
q3 dummy							0.170	0.00
q4 dummy							0.146	0.00
Predict %	76.47		76.87		76.72		76.89	
Number of obs	1,372		1,372		1,372		1,372	
LR chi2(12)	132.94		165.94		153.29		166.81	
Prob > chi2	0		0		0		0	
Pseudo R2	0.085		0.106		0.098		0.107	
Log likelihood=	−715.85		−699.35		−705.67		−698.91	

	Any felony arrest							
	No attrition correction		Attrit. Correct. model 1		Attrit. Correct. model 2		Attrit. Correct. model 3	
	dF/dx	P>z	dF/dx	P>z	dF/dx	P>z	dF/dx	P>z
Gender	−0.334	0.00	−0.330	0.00	−0.336	0.00	−0.335	0.00
Race	0.033	0.31	0.035	0.28	0.033	0.31	0.033	0.29
Any preschool	−0.047	0.02	−0.047	0.02	−0.047	0.02	−0.046	0.02
Any school-age intervention	0.009	0.63	0.011	0.57	0.009	0.64	0.009	0.64
Single parent 0–3	−0.031	0.19	−0.029	0.20	−0.030	0.19	−0.028	0.23
Mother is less than 18 years old, 0–3	−0.010	0.68	−0.007	0.76	−0.011	0.66	−0.004	0.88
Mother completed hs, 0–3	−0.036	0.07	−0.035	0.08	−0.036	0.07	−0.033	0.10
Mother had some college, 0–3	−0.061	0.02	−0.061	0.03	−0.061	0.02	−0.059	0.03
TANF/AFDC, age 0–3	0.072	0.01	0.072	0.01	0.072	0.01	0.071	0.01
Mother full/part-time employment	0.052	0.06	0.052	0.06	0.051	0.07	0.052	0.06
Child welfare, age 0–3	0.173	0.00	0.175	0.00	0.172	0.00	0.164	0.00
Free lunch 0–3	0.027	0.26	0.029	0.24	0.027	0.27	0.028	0.24
Missing values-risk factors (dummy)	0.011	0.67	−0.005	0.87	0.013	0.65	0.006	0.83
Propensity score			−0.113	0.33				
attrition sample* quartile ranking					0.002	0.85		
q2 dummy							−0.002	0.93
q3 dummy							−0.029	0.31
q4 dummy							0.015	0.65
Predict %	11.26		11.27		11.25		11.11	
Number of obs	1,413		1,413		1,413		1,413	
LR chi2(12)	342.24		343.19		342.27		345.1	
Prob > chi2	0		0		0		0	
Pseudo R2	0.249		0.250		0.249		0.251	
Log likelihood=	−516.68		−516.2		−516.66		−515.25	

	Private health insurance							
	No attrition correction		Attrit. Correct. model 1		Attrit. Correct. model 2		Attrit. Correct. model 3	
	dF/dx	P>z	dF/dx	P>z	dF/dx	P>z	dF/dx	P>z
Gender	−0.030	0.28	−0.055	0.13	−0.048	0.34	−0.059	0.26
Race	−0.051	0.37	−0.049	0.39	−0.050	0.38	−0.048	0.40
Any preschool	0.065	0.04	0.062	0.05	0.063	0.05	0.064	0.05
Any school-age intervention	0.012	0.69	0.014	0.64	0.015	0.64	0.014	0.65
Single parent 0–3	−0.096	0.01	−0.093	0.01	−0.092	0.01	−0.094	0.01
Mother is less than 18 years old, 0–3	0.095	0.02	0.085	0.04	0.088	0.04	0.093	0.03
Mother completed hs, 0–3	0.094	0.00	0.092	0.01	0.093	0.00	0.095	0.00
Mother had some college, 0–3	0.047	0.31	0.044	0.34	0.045	0.34	0.045	0.34
TANF/AFDC, age 0–3	−0.179	0.00	−0.169	0.00	−0.171	0.00	−0.172	0.00
Mother full/part-time employment	−0.013	0.74	−0.008	0.84	−0.010	0.80	−0.013	0.74
Child welfare, age 0–3	−0.113	0.12	−0.110	0.13	−0.110	0.13	−0.110	0.13
Free lunch 0–3	0.039	0.34	0.026	0.53	0.030	0.50	0.029	0.51
Missing values-risk factors (dummy)	−0.010	0.81	0.030	0.60	0.005	0.93	0.007	0.91
Propensity score			0.239	0.28				
attrition sample* quartile ranking					0.012	0.66		
q2 dummy							−0.015	0.74
q3 dummy							0.032	0.62
q4 dummy							0.034	0.68
Predict %	38.04		38.04		38.04		38.04	
Number of obs	1,303		1,303		1,303		1,303	
LR chi2(12)	88.52		89.69		88.71		89.46	
Prob > chi2	0.000		0.000		0.000		0.000	
Pseudo R2	0.051		0.052		0.051		0.052	
Log likelihood=	−824.76		−824.18		−824.67		−824.30	

Prediction of Propensity Scores by Outcomes

	Education Attainment sample n = 1,372		Crime sample n = 1,413		Health insurance sample n = 1,303	
	dF/dX	p-value	dF/dX	*p* value	dF/dX	*P* value
Gender	0.0086	0.305	0.02587	0.035	0.111	0.000
Race	−0.0029	0.837	−0.00444	0.845	−0.017	0.627
Any preschool	−0.0001	0.994	−0.00058	0.965	0.012	0.553
Any school-age intervention	0.0027	0.756	0.00131	0.919	−0.020	0.283
Single parent 0–3	0.0118	0.311	0.00624	0.690	−0.022	0.315
Mother is less than 18 years old, 0–3	0.0089	0.453	0.02473	0.133	0.044	0.069
Mother completed hs, 0–3	0.0129	0.184	0.00465	0.743	0.013	0.539
Mother had some college, 0–3	−0.0060	0.702	0.00883	0.655	0.021	0.478
TANF/AFDC, age 0–3	−0.0037	0.787	−0.00917	0.628	−0.051	0.059
Number of children in the household age 0–3	0.0028	0.800	0.04326	0.006	0.028	0.244
Mother full-time/part-time employment	0.0066	0.625	0.01377	0.463	−0.016	0.558
Child welfare, age 0–3	−0.0321	0.184	0.00190	0.955	−0.016	0.734
Free lunch 0–3	0.0111	0.410	0.01369	0.479	0.060	0.033
Low birthweight	0.0102	0.388	0.03549	0.044	0.032	0.233
Missing values for risk factors (dummy)	−0.0255	0.052	−0.06165	0.001	−0.122	0.000
Income (inc60)	−0.0108	0.226	−0.00014	0.992	0.026	0.201
Word test, kindergarten (sswordk)	−0.0001	0.669	0.00056	0.233	0.000	0.774
Home environment problems (continuous)	dropped		dropped		dropped	
Have at least one health problem 0–5	0.0134	0.627	dropped		dropped	
Missing values for home environment probl.	−0.3023	0.000	dropped		dropped	
Have SSN	0.1180	0.000	0.31466	0.000	0.339	0.000
n=	1539		1539		1539	
Predicted value	89.15%		91.79%		84.64%	

9

Small Miracles in Tulsa: The Effects of Universal Pre-K on Cognitive Development

WILLIAM T. GORMLEY JR.

Parents and public officials are increasingly concerned about the school readiness of young children. In response, in recent years, state governments have boosted their support for pre-K programs. Several states, including Oklahoma, have opted for universal pre-K, making it available, on a voluntary basis, to all 4-year-olds. At the same time, the federal government, through the No Child Left Behind Act, has imposed new testing requirements on public schools to determine whether students as a whole and particular subgroups of students are making good academic progress. These trends have heightened interest in the effectiveness of pre-K programs.

The Oklahoma pre-K program is of special interest because it enrolls a higher percentage of 4-year-olds than any pre-K program in the United States (Barnett, Epstein, Friedman, Sansanelli, & Hustedt, 2009). It is also of particular interest because it is based in the public schools and because it places strong emphasis on high quality: All lead teachers must have a college degree and be early-childhood certified; to facilitate the recruitment and retention of outstanding individuals, lead teachers are paid at the same rate as other public school teachers.

Many studies have demonstrated that considerable benefits flow from a high-quality targeted pre-K program. But can a large-scale universal pre-K program also produce substantial benefits by enhancing the school readiness of young children? Do all children benefit from such a program? Do some children benefit more? And how large are the impacts of such a program, in absolute or relative terms?

We set out to answer these questions in Tulsa, Oklahoma, the largest school district in Oklahoma. In addition to its size, Tulsa has the advantage of having

The research reported here, from 2003 test score data, was funded by the Foundation for Child Development, the National Institute for Early Education Research (NIEER), and the Pew Charitable Trusts. I thank them for their generous support. I also thank my collaborators, Ted Gayer and Deborah Phillips, and my wonderful research assistants at the Center for Research on Children in the U.S. (CROCUS). I alone am responsible for the contents of this chapter.

a racially and ethnically diverse school population, which facilitates estimates of subgroup impact.[1] With the cooperation of the Tulsa Public Schools (TPS), we were able to test students in August 2003 using a nationally normed test. This study, the results of which have been reported elsewhere (Gormley, Gayer, Phillips, & Dawson, 2005), built on an earlier study in which we used a home-grown testing instrument (Gormley & Gayer, 2005).

KEY FEATURES OF THE OKLAHOMA PRE-K PROGRAM

Oklahoma opted for a universal pre-K program in 1998, when its state legislature decided that state-funded pre-K should be an option for all 4-year-olds. The state legislature funded the program through general appropriations and specified that the funds would flow to participating school districts, which could offer pre-K services themselves or contract out to other service-delivery organizations. The program is voluntary for both school districts and parents. The overwhelming majority of school districts have chosen to participate, as have approximately 70% of parents with age-eligible children.

Under Oklahoma law, participating school districts are required to meet a number of standards aimed at ensuring a high-quality program. Every lead teacher must have a bachelor's degree and be early-childhood certified. Child:staff ratios of 10:1 must be maintained. Lead teachers who work for public schools are compensated at the same rate as other public-school teachers, a practice that facilitates recruitment and retention. Contractors, such as Head Start programs, are required to meet the same regulatory standards, although they are responsible for setting salaries. In practice, some contractors, such as the Community Action Project of Tulsa County, have chosen to compensate their lead teachers at the same wage rates as public-school teachers in their jurisdiction.

Each participating school district is free to offer full-day programs, half-day programs, or a mixture of both. Under the state funding formula, compensation for full-day programs is understandably higher than compensation for half-day programs. In practice, participating school districts have often provided full-day programs in more disadvantaged neighborhoods and half-day programs in more advantaged neighborhoods. In disadvantaged neighborhoods, school districts can use Title I funding from the federal government to help defray the costs of additional hours of service.

METHODOLOGY

Unlike previous researchers, who often used cross-sectional data or a pretest–posttest research design, we decided early on that a better research strategy was

[1] In the fall of 2003, the pre-K cohort in TPS was 36% White, 36% Black, 18% Hispanic, 9% Native American, and 1% Asian.

to use a regression–discontinuity design that takes advantage of a September 1 birthday requirement for enrollment in pre-K. If a student turned 4 years old on or before September 1, 2002, then he or she was eligible to enroll in Oklahoma's pre-K program in 2002–2003. If a student turned 4 years old any time between September 2, 2002, and August 31, 2003, then he or she had to wait until the 2003–2004 school year to enroll.

By taking advantage of this cutoff policy, which was strictly enforced, we were able to construct a comparison group that closely resembles our treatment group: TPS kindergarten students who participated in the TPS pre-K program in 2002–2003. Our comparison group consists of TPS pre-K program entrants in 2003–2004. The principal strength of this research design is that both sets of students have parents who affirmatively chose to place them in the TPS pre-K program. This helps ensure that the students are alike in their talent and motivation – intangibles that are extremely difficult to measure.

Of course, the two groups do differ in one key respect: Students in the treatment group are, on average, exactly 1 year older than students in the control group. However, this discrepancy is easy to deal with through the use of a statistical control for the child's age (as measured by the date of birth). We have also found it useful to control for other demographic variables (i.e., gender, race/ethnicity, school-lunch status, and mother's education), even though these controls (other than age) should, in theory, be unnecessary if the regression–discontinuity design works properly.

DATA

In August 2003, we administered three subtests of the Woodcock-Johnson Achievement Test. The testers were TPS kindergarten and pre-K teachers, who administered the tests just before the commencement of classes (i.e., a genuine pretest). We trained them to administer these tests, with help from Barbara Wendling, an independent consultant from Dallas, Texas, who is an expert on the Woodcock-Johnson test. All tests were administered one-on-one while the child's parent (or guardian) sat in a nearby room. While waiting, the parent (or guardian) completed a survey that provided valuable information to us, including the mother's educational level.

The three subtests selected were the Letter-Word Identification Test, which measures prereading skills; the Spelling Test, which measures prewriting skills; and the Applied Problems Test, which measures premath skills. We selected particular subtests that are thought to be especially appropriate for relatively young children.

Our aim was to test as many kindergarten students and pre-K students as possible, at the same point in time. Ultimately, we were successful in testing 85.0% of all kindergarten students (3,149/3,727) and 84.5% of all pre-K

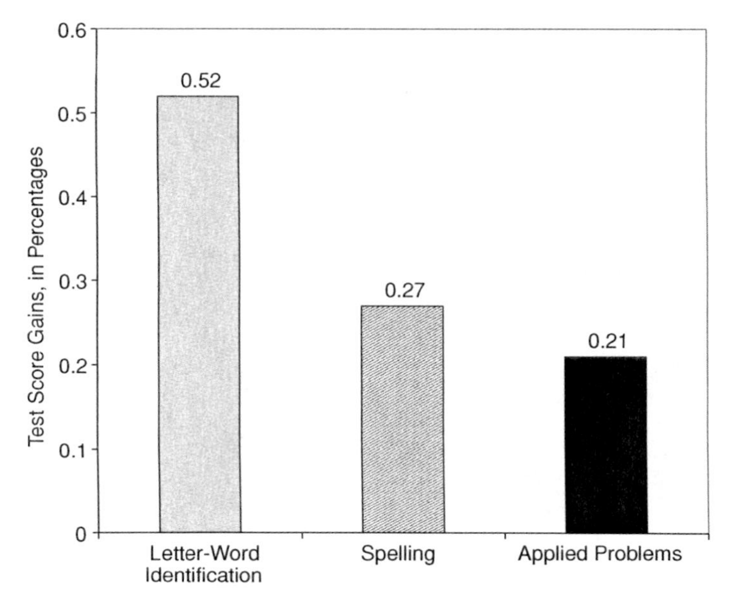

Figure 9.1. Overall effects of the Tulsa pre-K program.

students (1,567/8,843). In general, the tested children closely resembled the universe of children from which they were drawn, although there were some discrepancies.[2]

Once the testing and coding were completed, we compared those kindergarten students who were in TPS pre-K the previous year (our treatment group) with those students who were about to begin TPS pre-K (our control group). With only two exceptions, the treatment-group students closely resembled the control-group students in their demographic characteristics.[3]

FINDINGS

As Figure 9.1 indicates, the overall effects of the TPS pre-K program are substantial. For children as a whole, we saw a 52% gain in the Letter-Word Identification test score, a 27% gain in the Spelling test score, and a 21% gain in the Applied Problems test score. That is the average change in each test score attributable to the TPS pre-K program, above and beyond the gains that

[2] The tested pre-K children were somewhat more likely to be Black than the universe of pre-K children, and the tested kindergarten children were somewhat less likely to be Hispanic than the universe of kindergarten children. The tested kindergarten children also differed somewhat from the universe of kindergarten children in their eligibility for free lunch (Gormley et al., 2005, p. 874).

[3] Students in the comparison group were somewhat less likely to be Hispanic and to have a mother with no high school degree than students in the treatment group (Gormley et al., 2005, p. 877).

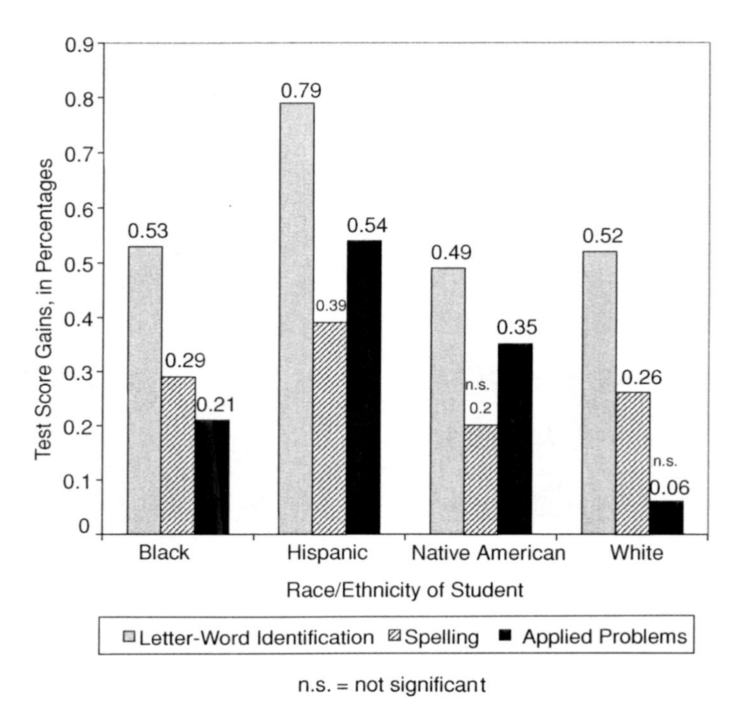

Figure 9.2. Effects of the Tulsa pre-K program by race/ethnicity of the student.

naturally occur as the child ages one year and after controlling for various demographic variables, including age.

Because TPS has a diverse student population, we were able to break these findings down by race and ethnicity. As Figure 9.2 indicates, all racial and ethnic groups benefited from the TPS pre-K program. Hispanic students and Black students experienced statistically significant gains for all three tests. Native American and White students experienced statistically significant gains for two of three tests. Gains for Hispanic students were especially impressive: a 79% gain in Letter-Word ID, a 39% gain in Spelling, and a 54% gain in Applied Problems, above and beyond the gains that occur as the child ages 1 year and after controlling for demographic differences.

Because Oklahoma's 4-year-old students are eligible for pre-K irrespective of income, we were also able to break down our results by socioeconomic status, as measured by eligibility for a free or reduced-price lunch. As Figure 9.3 indicates, all socioeconomic groups benefited from the TPS pre-K program. Students eligible for a free lunch (the poorest students) experienced statistically significant gains for all three tests, whereas students eligible for a reduced-price lunch and students who must pay for a full-price lunch experienced statistically significant gains for two of three tests. In general, more

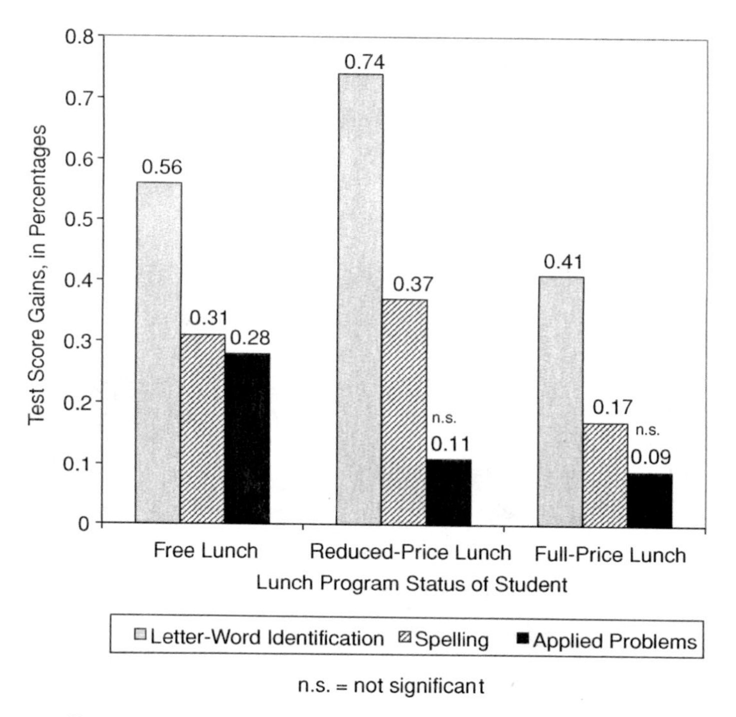

Figure 9.3. Effects of the Tulsa pre-K program by free-lunch program status of the student.

disadvantaged students (free and reduced-price lunch) benefited more from TPS pre-K than did more advantaged students (full-price lunch).

Evaluators sometimes measure effect sizes by comparing the test score gain coefficient to the standard deviation for the control group. Doing so helps facilitate comparisons across studies by creating a common metric. As Figure 9.4 indicates, effect sizes for the Tulsa pre-K program were quite substantial: 0.79 of a standard deviation for Letter-Word Identification, 0.64 of a standard deviation for Spelling, and 0.38 of a standard deviation for Applied Problems. By way of comparison, these effect sizes exceed those reported for other pre-K programs (Magnuson, Ruhm, & Waldfogel, 2007) and for high-quality child care programs (NICHD & Duncan, 2003; Peisner-Feinberg et al., 2001). They come close to the effect sizes reported for such legendary early childhood demonstration programs as the Perry Preschool Project (Ramey, Bryant, & Suarez, 1985) and the Abecedarian Project (Ramey et al., 2000).

For a hypothetical child who just made the pre-K eligibility cutoff by one day (born on September 1, 1998) and another hypothetical child who just missed the pre-K eligibility cutoff by one day (born on September 2, 1998), it is possible to convert raw test scores into age-equivalent test scores. As

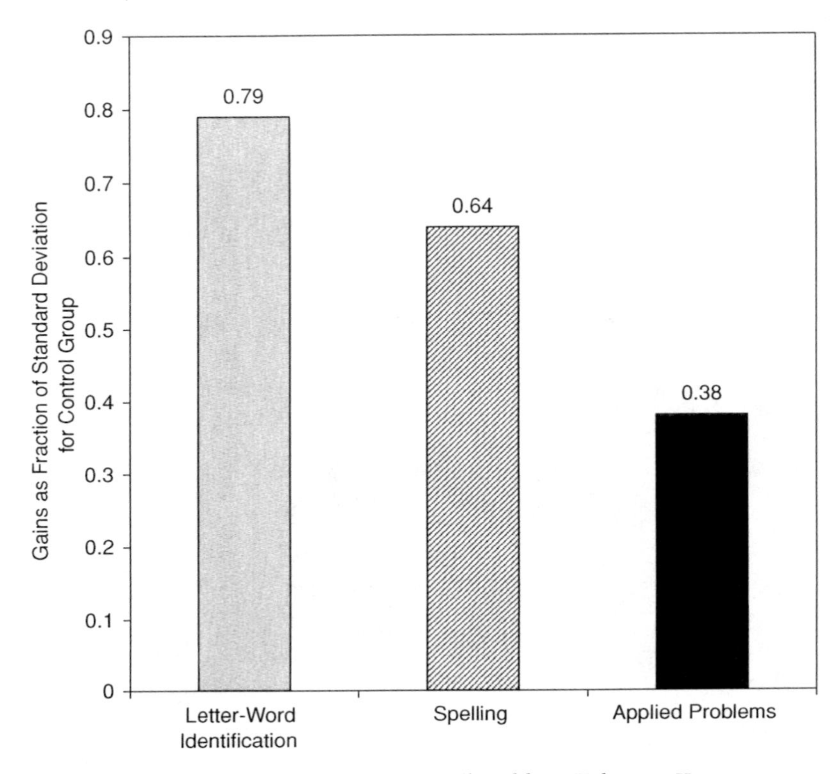

Figure 9.4. Test score gains attributable to Tulsa pre-K.

Figure 9.5 reveals, the child exposed to TPS pre-K would be substantially better off. Whereas the child not yet exposed to TPS pre-K falls below national norms for a 5-year-old (more precisely, a child who is exactly 5 years old) for all three tests, the child exposed to TPS pre-K would exceed national norms in Letter-Word Identification and equal national norms in Spelling. Expressed a bit differently, TPS pre-K yields test score gains of approximately 7 months for Letter-Word ID, 6 months for Spelling, and 4 months for Applied Problems.

DISCUSSION

In the past few years, Tulsa has become a showcase for early childhood education. Oklahoma is the nation's leader in providing state-funded pre-K, serving approximately 70% of all 4-year-olds, and it is unique in offering universal pre-K through the public schools, as opposed to a mixed-services delivery system. The Tulsa Public Schools pre-K program has attracted attention in part because of the results reported here but also because we do not normally think of a relatively poor, relatively conservative state as leading the nation in an important social-policy realm. When Appalachian State beats

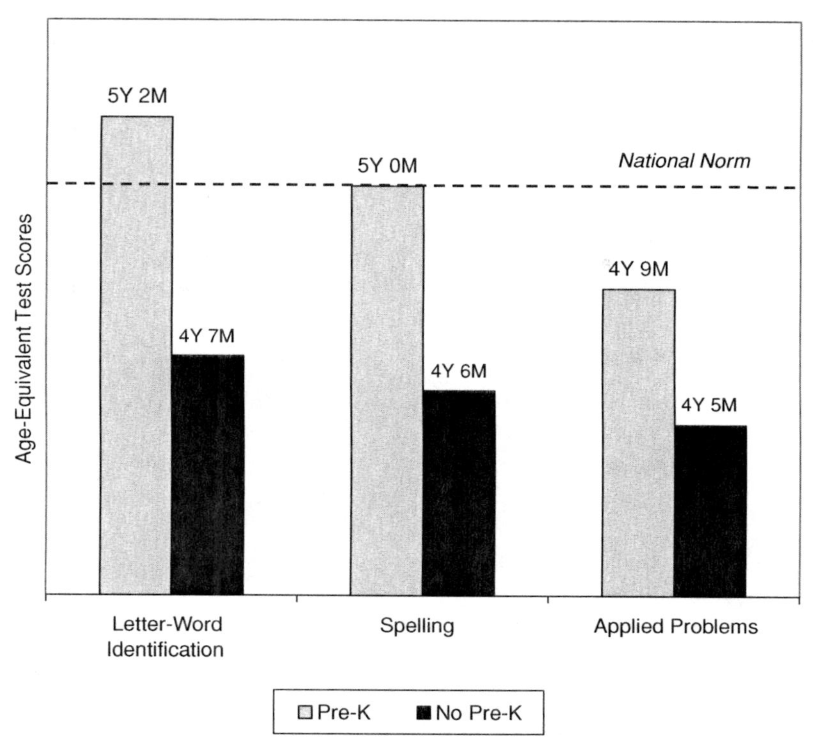

Figure 9.5. Age-equivalent test scores for children exposed to Tulsa pre-K.

the University of Michigan, that is news. When Tulsa outshines the rest of the nation in early childhood education, that is also news.

But what exactly can we learn from these results? And what remains to be investigated? First, a well-designed universal pre-K program can produce impressive improvements in school readiness. Thanks to the TPS pre-K program, most incoming kindergarten students in the Tulsa Public Schools have better prereading skills, better prewriting skills, and better premath skills. They are more ready to learn than they otherwise would be. In short, the pre-K program has given Tulsa children a valuable boost in cognitive development as they begin their school years.

Second, a well-designed universal pre-K program can benefit children from diverse racial and ethnic backgrounds and from diverse social strata. The TPS pre-K program benefits White, Black, Hispanic, and Native American children. It benefits poor children (eligible for a free lunch), near-poor children (eligible for a reduced-price lunch), and nonpoor children (ineligible for any school lunch subsidy). Although some critics have contended that only working-poor children benefit from a universal pre-K program (Fuller, 2007), there is no basis for that allegation. As we have seen, children ineligible for a school-lunch subsidy benefited greatly from the Tulsa pre-K program. In 2003, the reduced-price lunch income cutoff point (as specified by the U.S. Department of Agriculture) was approximately $35,000, just short of the median income of families with children in Oklahoma – which was approximately $39,000. Thus, children who were ineligible for a school lunch subsidy came from families with incomes above or close to the state's median income for families with children. By any reasonable definition, these children are middle class.

Third, a well-designed universal pre-K program produces benefits that compare quite favorably to those produced by other human investment initiatives, including class-size-reduction programs and job-training programs. Overall, students benefit about 0.15 standard deviations from assignment to a smaller class (Schanzenbach, 2006) – a much smaller benefit than those reported here. Job-training programs also seem to be less efficacious than well-designed early childhood education programs (Heckman, 2000).

Fourth, a well-designed universal pre-K program need not impose major burdens on taxpayers. In Oklahoma, the state's contribution to the TPS pre-K program is approximately $4,000 for a full-day slot, even less for a half-day slot. To be sure, other resources augment these expenditures, including in-kind contributions from the local school system (e.g., physical plant, maintenance) and Title I contributions from the federal government (used to help fund full-day programs that serve disadvantaged children). Nevertheless, the overall costs to taxpayers are relatively modest.

Several questions remain that this study does not answer. It says nothing about the long-term effectiveness of the TPS pre-K program, and there are reasons to be concerned about this limitation. A number of studies have shown that "fade-out" can occur over time if public schools do not work vigorously to sustain short-term gains experienced by students who have attended a Head Start program (Currie & Thomas, 1995; Lee & Loeb, 1995; McKey et al., 1985: III-20). In contrast, other studies have shown that fade-out is not inevitable (Currie & Thomas, 1999; Garces, Thomas, & Currie, 2002; Ludwig & Miller, 2007). The key question, in Tulsa and elsewhere, is whether public schools (and, for that matter, other schools) make adjustments in their curriculum (especially K–3) that take into account the dramatic changes in school readiness that are taking place. If schools adjust their teaching styles and tempos accordingly, then short-term cognitive gains may persist over time. If they do not, then short-term cognitive gains are likely to evaporate.

Our study also cannot directly answer this question: How have the Tulsa Public Schools managed to produce such wonderful short-term results? Is it because all the teachers have a bachelor's degree and are early-childhood certified? That question is hotly disputed. Is it because all the pre-K programs (except for authorized collaboratives) are located within the public schools? That is also unclear.

However, based on recent data gathered in the spring of 2006, we can report that TPS pre-K classrooms differ significantly from other school-based pre-K programs in 11 states (Phillips, Gormley, & Lowenstein, 2009). Specifically, TPS pre-K programs offer higher levels of "instructional support" (as measured by the Classroom Assessment Scoring System) than other school-based programs. They also devote considerably more time to prereading, prewriting, and premath skills than other school-based programs. Some critics have charged that this focus comes at the expense of attention to socio-emotional development or to higher order critical-thinking skills (Fuller, 2007), but that allegation appears to be unfounded. If we look at attention to higher order critical-thinking skills, as measured by a "concept development" score, the score is higher in TPS pre-K programs than in other school-based pre-K programs. If we look at levels of emotional support in the classroom, they are neither higher nor lower in TPS pre-K programs than they are in other school-based pre-K programs.[4] In short, Tulsa teachers seem to be educating 4-year-olds in a developmentally appropriate way.

CONCLUSION

The TPS pre-K program, which became universal in 1998 as a result of state legislation, has been remarkably effective in enhancing the school-readiness skills of young children. Kindergarten children who participated in the state-funded pre-K program have stronger prereading skills, stronger prewriting skills, and stronger premath skills than would otherwise be the case. Children from diverse racial and ethnic backgrounds and from diverse socioeconomic backgrounds benefit from the program. Although Hispanics benefit the most from the program, Blacks, Whites, and Native Americans also benefit considerably. Although disadvantaged children benefit the most from the program, middle-class children also benefit considerably.

Now that the Oklahoma pre-K program is firmly established, the challenge for the TPS and other school districts will be to build on the gains of 4-year-olds by adapting elementary-education teaching practices to the new skills that most kindergarten students now possess. The challenge for other states that seek to realize similar gains through a universal pre-K program will be to determine which elements of the Tulsa pre-K experience need to be replicated to achieve similar learning gains.

REFERENCES

Barnett, W. S., Epstein, D., Friedman, A., Sansanelli, R., & Hustedt, J. (2009). *The state of preschool 2006*. New Brunswick, NJ: National Institute for Early Education Research, Rutgers University.

Currie, J., & Thomas, D. (1995, June). Does Head Start make a difference? *American Economic Review, 85*, 341–364.

[4] Of four emotional-support dimensions in the Classroom Assessment Scoring System, TPS pre-K classrooms score higher than other school-based pre-K classrooms in one and lower in another. There are no statistically significant differences for the other two.

Currie, J., & Thomas, D. (1999, November). Does Head Start help Hispanic children? *Journal of Public Economics, 74*, 235–262.

Fuller, B. (2007). *Standardized childhood: The political and cultural struggle over early education.* Stanford, CA: Stanford University Press.

Garces, E., Thomas, D., & Currie, J. (2002, September). Longer term effects of Head Start. *American Economic Review, 92*, 999–1012.

Gormley, W., & Gayer, T. (2005, Summer). Promoting school readiness in Oklahoma: An evaluation of Tulsa's pre-K program. *Journal of Human Resources, 40*, 533–559.

Gormley, W., Gayer, T., Phillips, D., & Dawson, B. (2005, November). The effects of universal pre-K on cognitive development. *Developmental Psychology, 41*, 872–884.

Heckman, J. (2000). Policies to foster human capital. *Research in Economics, 54*, 3–56.

Lee, V., & Loeb, S. (1995, Spring). Where do Head Start attendees end up? One reason why preschool effects fade out. *Educational Evaluation and Policy Analysis, 17*, 62–82.

Ludwig, J., & Miller, D. (2007). Does Head Start improve children's life chances? Evidence from a regression discontinuity design. *Quarterly Journal of Economics, 122*, 159–208.

Magnuson, K., Ruhm, C., & Waldfogel, J. (2007). Does pre-kindergarten improve school preparation and performance? *Economics of Education Review, 78*, 115–157.

McKey, R., Condelli, L., Ganson, H., Barrett, B., McConkey, C., & Plantz, M. (1985, June). *The impact of Head Start on children, families and communities* (Final Report of the Head Start Evaluation, Synthesis and Utilization Project). Washington, DC: CSR.

National Institute of Child Health and Human Development & Duncan, G. (2003). Modeling the impacts of child care quality on children's preschool cognitive development. *Child Development, 74*, 1454–1475.

Peisner-Feinberg, E., Burchinal, M., Clifford, R., Culkin, M., Howes, C., Kagan, S. L., et al. (2001, September/October). The relation of preschool child-care quality to children's cognitive and social developmental trajectories through second grade. *Child Development, 72*, 1534–1553.

Phillips, D., Gormley, W., & Lowenstein, A. (2009). Inside the pre-kindergarten door: Classroom climate and instructional time allocation in Tulsa's pre-k programs. *Early Childhood Research Quarterly, 24*(3), 213–228.

Ramey, C., Bryant, D., & Suarez, T. (1985). Preschool compensatory education and the modifiability of intelligence: A critical review. In D. K. Detterman (Ed.), *Current topics in human intelligence: Vol. 1. Research methodology* (pp. 247–296). Norwood, NJ: Ablex.

Ramey, C., Campbell, F., Burchinal, M., Skinner, M., Gardner, D., & Ramey, S. (2000). Persistent effects of early childhood education on high-risk children and their mothers. *Applied Developmental Science, 4*, 2–14.

Schanzenbach, D. W. (2006, August). *What have researchers learned from Project Star?* (Harris School Working Paper Series 06.06). Chicago: Harris School of Public Policy.

10

Lessons From the Evaluation of the Great Start Readiness Program (GSRP): A Longitudinal Evaluation

MARIJATA DANIEL-ECHOLS, ELENA V. MALOFEEVA, AND LAWRENCE J. SCHWEINHART

INTRODUCTION

The Great Start Readiness Program (GSRP) has existed as a state-funded preschool initiative for more than 20 years.[1] Since 1995, GSRP has been evaluated by the HighScope Educational Research Foundation. This chapter starts by describing the program and its history. It then provides an overview of GSRP child outcome findings from six studies that were reported between 1997 and 2007. This summary focuses both on short-term and longitudinal outcomes and concludes with implications for future research.

HISTORY OF THE PROGRAM

The GSRP, an initiative of the Michigan Department of Education (MDE), provides services to 4-year-olds at risk of school failure. It began as a pilot project in 1985, when 53 programs were funded with the goal of identifying effective early childhood education models that could be taken to scale across the state. During the past 23 years, GSRP has grown from serving 8,208 children in its pilot year to 23,060 children in fiscal year 2008 (FY08).

The definition of "at risk for school failure" was established early on in the implementation of GSRP. In 1988, 25 factors were identified as placing children at risk for low educational achievement. To be eligible for the program, a child must have at least two risk factors and be 4 years old by December 1 in the year he or she is enrolled.[2] Additionally, at least half of the children

[1] When GSRP began, it was known as the Michigan School Readiness Program (MSRP). In 2008, the name of the program was changed to the Great Start Readiness Program (GSRP).

[2] During the 2008–2009 program year, a new structure for determining eligibility was approved by the Michigan State Board of Education. It groups types of risk into eight categories and prioritizes extremely low income over the presence of multiple risk factors. After legislative approval, the new criteria was instituted statewide in the 2009–2010 program year.

in a program must be considered low income.[3] The 25 risk factors are as follows:

1. Low birthweight
2. Developmentally immature
3. Physical and/or sexual abuse and neglect
4. Nutritionally deficient
5. Long-term or chronic illness
6. Diagnosed handicapping condition (mainstreamed)
7. Lack of a stable support system or residence
8. Destructive or violent temperament
9. Substance abuse or addiction
10. Language deficiency or immaturity
11. Non-English or limited-English-speaking household
12. Family history of low school achievement or dropout
13. Family history of delinquency
14. Family history of diagnosed family problems
15. Low parent/sibling educational attainment or illiteracy
16. Single parent
17. Unemployed parent/parents
18. Low family income
19. Family density
20. Parental/sibling loss by death or parental loss by divorce
21. Teenage parent
22. Chronically ill parent/sibling (physical, mental, or emotional)
23. Incarcerated parent
24. Housing in rural or segregated area
25. Other (can only apply to 10% of the enrolled children)

Table 10.1 shows the six most common risk factors experienced by GSRP children from 1996 to 2007. In any given year, at least 20% of the children had each of those six factors, and in some cases 67% of the children had them. Between 1996 and 2007, nearly 80% of GSRP children were eligible for the program because they met between two and five of the qualifying risk factors.

DESCRIPTION OF THE PROGRAM

Administration

The Michigan Department of Education's Office of Early Childhood Education and Family Services administers the GSRP. Within that office, early childhood

[3] Before the 2008–2009 program year, low income was defined as a household income that is less than or equal to 250% of the federal poverty level. In 2008–2009, the standard was changed to 300% of the federal poverty level.

Table 10.1. *Risk factor trends 1996–2007 (% of children enrolled in GSRP)*

# Risk factors	1996 $n = 19{,}435$	1998 $n = 18{,}831$	1999 $n = 19{,}937$	2000 $n = 24{,}016$	2001 $n = 25{,}198$	2002 $n = 24{,}737$	2003 $n = 25{,}046$	2004 $n = 25{,}087$	2005 $n = 24{,}355$	2006 $n = 23{,}704$	2007 $n = 23{,}060$	Avg %
Low family income	67.6	67.2	64.4	62.6	59.1	57.2	58.3	58.2	58.0	64.1	66.9	62.1
Single parent	41.0	41.6	40.1	38.1	36.7	37.3	37.0	35.7	34.9	33.8	33.8	37.3
Housing in rural or segregated area	28.6	25.2	30.4	29.4	27.8	30.3	30.0	30.9	29.1	30.2	30.2	29.3
Family history of low school achievement or dropout	25.1	31.4	29.8	30.2	27.6	27.2	26.7	27.1	27.5	25.8	25.7	27.6
Unemployed parent(s)	24.2	24.6	21.1	20.1	20.0	22.9	24.5	23.7	23.8	23.5	24.2	23.0
Teenage parent	20.2	21.4	21.0	22.1	22.5	22.7	23.7	23.5	23.5	22.1	21.5	22.2

consultants provide training and technical assistance as well as implementation oversight to a mix of public-school and nonprofit community-based providers. Each consultant is assigned a region of the state for which he or she is responsible. Those consultants report to a supervisor who reports to the department's director. Every GSRP grantee is required to have an early childhood specialist on staff who serves as a professional development resource to teachers and sometimes functions as the program's director as well.

GSRP grantees are expected to use three primary documents to guide the administration of their grant and implementation of the program: the state's *Quality Program Standards for Preschools and Prekindergarten Programs* and companion *Early Learning Expectations for Three- and Four-Year-Old Children*, which are both contained in the *Early Childhood Standards of Quality for Prekindergarten* (Michigan Department of Education, 2005), and the *Great Start Readiness Program Implementation Manual* (Michigan Department of Education, 2008).

Funding

When it began, GSRP was funded through the Department of Education Appropriation Act. Since 1987, it has received its funding through the State School Aid Act as well. Local public school districts, public school academies (PSAs), intermediate school districts (ISDs), and public and private nonprofit agencies are all eligible to apply for GSRP funding. School districts and PSAs are considered state school aid grantees, whereas ISDs, nonprofit agencies, and public school districts and PSAs that are also Head Start grantees are designated as competitive grantees.

To obtain funds, applicants must demonstrate that they exist within a community that has a concentration of at-risk children who are currently not receiving school-readiness services. To ensure that GSRP funds supplement but do not supplant existing services, applicants are required to submit to the state a community needs assessment with their funding application. Additionally, grantees are required to work in collaboration with Head Start to recruit eligible children. Children who meet Head Start's income requirement must first be referred to Head Start before they can be considered for enrollment in GSRP.

Once awarded a GSRP grant, a school district or organization remains a grantee for 3 years. The number of children for whom a state school aid grantee will receive GSRP funding is based on a poverty ranking, which is calculated using a formula that takes into consideration rates of children receiving free or reduced lunch from Grades 1–5 in the district and kindergarten enrollment. Competitive grantees request a specific number of slots in their applications, but that number cannot exceed 144.

Grantees are permitted to run classrooms that enroll both GSRP- and non-GSRP-funded children. Several types of blended-funding classrooms exist

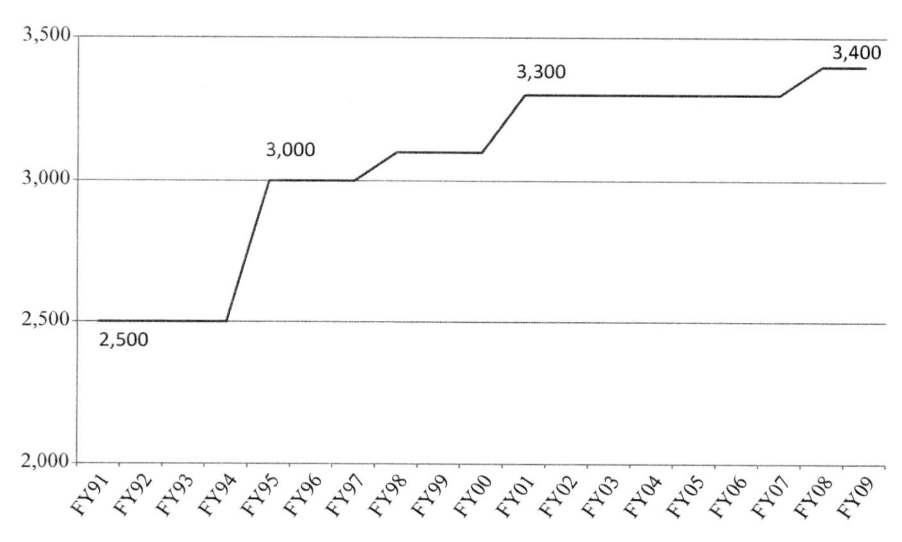

Figure 10.1. State spending per child by fiscal year.

across the state; for example, GSRP–Head Start combinations and GSRP–tuition-based combinations. GSRP grantees running blended-funding classrooms are required to meet the requirements of whichever funding source has the highest standards for any given aspect of program quality and implementation.

Figure 10.1 shows the level of spending per enrolled child that the state has provided grantees to help subsidize service delivery over the history of the GSRP program. In 18 years, state funding per child has slowly risen by less than $1,000 to $3,300 per child.

Structure

GSRP grantees have the option to implement three different types of services: center-based, home-based, and parental involvement and education programs. Center-based options include half-day, full-day, all-day/alternate-day, and migrant services. Of the 1,129 classrooms operating in 2007–2008, 81.7% were run by school districts/PSAs, 98.1% were center-based, and 62.4% of center-based programs were half-day (HighScope Educational Research Foundation, 2008). Table 10.2 provides an overview of the minimum requirements for each of these program options.

With regard to staffing requirements, early childhood specialists must have at least a master's degree in early childhood education or child development. In center-based programs, lead teachers must have a valid Michigan teaching certificate with an early childhood specialist endorsement, a valid Michigan teaching certificate with a child development associate (CDA) or a bachelor's

Table 10.2. *Minimum requirements by GSRP program option*

Program option	Minimum requirements
Center-based: half-day	2.5 hours/day, 4 days/week 20–30 weeks/year 8:1 adult:child ratio Maximum class size = 18
Center-based: full-day	Same length of day as local district's first-grade program for at least 4–5 days/week for 30 weeks/year 8:1 adult:child ratio Maximum class size = 18
Center-based: all-day/ alternate-day	2 full days per week 8:1 adult:child ratio Maximum class size = 18
Center-based: migrant	2.5 hours/day, 4 days/week minimum 6 weeks/year 8:1 adult:child ratio Maximum class size = 18
Home-based	60 minutes/visit, 30 visits/year, 10–15 group activities/year 16:1 family:visitor ratio
Parent involvement and education	Minimum 2 home visits and 2 parent-teacher conferences 18:1 parent:child ratio, minimum 2 parents/guardians

Source: Data from Michigan Department of Education (2008).

degree in child development with a focus on preschool. Associate teachers must have either a CDA or an associate's degree in early childhood/preschool education or 120 clock hours of training from a MDE-approved training organization. Home visitors must have a bachelor's degree or an associate's degree in child or human development, early childhood education, family life education, parenting, or social work, or a CDA (Michigan Department of Education, 2008).

A consistent trend among lead and associate teachers in center-based programs is that those employed by state school aid grantees make more money than their competitive agency counterparts. For example, during the 2007–2008 program year, state school aid grantee lead teachers reported earning an hourly rate that was $4.71 higher per hour ($20.46 versus $15.75) and an average annual salary that was $18,936 more per year than that of lead teachers in competitive grantee agencies ($49,507 versus $30,571; HighScope Educational Research Foundation, 2008).

Curriculum

Although the Michigan Department of Education does not endorse any particular curriculum, it does encourage grantees to use research-based, developmentally appropriate curricula. Grantees are also encouraged to select a curriculum that has scope and sequence, develops all domains of a child's knowledge and skills, has learning objectives that align with state standards, uses appropriate materials, includes an instructional approach that has a balance of teacher- and child-initiated activities and supports child observation as a form of assessment, and includes professional development opportunities. The *GSRP Implementation Manual* lists the following center-based curricula as examples for grantees to consider: Bank Street, Creative Curriculum, HighScope, Montessori, The Project Approach, Reggio Emilia, and Tools of the Mind.

In keeping with the state's preference for developmentally appropriate curriculum and practice, grantees are required to collect child-development data. The observation-based assessment tools offered for grantees' consideration include HighScope's Child Observation Record; Creative Curriculum's Developmental Continuum; the Work Sampling System; and the Assessment, Evaluation, and Programming System.

Quality of Implementation

GSRP has a process in place for on-site reviews of grantees to assess program quality, in which an early childhood consultant conducts document reviews, classroom observations, and staff interviews. The Michigan Department of Education also relies on grantees' self-reported data. In particular, grantees use the second edition of the *Preschool Program Quality Assessment* (PQA) (HighScope Educational Research Foundation, 2003b) as a part of their midyear reporting. The PQA measures both structural (parental involvement, family services, staff qualifications and development, and program management) and process (learning environment, daily routine, adult–child interaction, curriculum planning, and assessment) quality and was originally developed to align with GSRP program standards. Other self-reported data include yearly narrative summaries and child risk-factor reports.[4]

The state uses all of the self-reported program quality data to plan for statewide professional-development activities. Consultants also provide guidance on how grantees can use program and child assessment data to set local staff-development goals and inform instruction.

MAJOR FINDINGS

GSRP grantees are required to conduct local evaluations of their programs and to follow the progress of their graduates through first grade. The reality is that these local evaluations are of mixed quality and, until recently, there was no way for early childhood programs to enter and retrieve data from the state's

[4] A significant challenge to using self-reported data is that they are consistently very positive and potentially inflated. For example, in the three most recent midyear PQA reports (05–06, 06–07, and 07–08), grantees gave themselves, on average, a score of 4.40, 4.47, and 4.48 out of 5 on the PQA.

district-wide database. As a result, those local evaluation efforts have been of limited use in determining the effectiveness of GSRP.

Since 1995, the HighScope Educational Research Foundation has served as an independent evaluator of GSRP. In that time, it has conducted a mix of process and outcome evaluations, which the Michigan Department of Education has used to understand and improve GSRP implementation and to demonstrate the program's ability to influence child outcomes. Groups of GSRP classrooms have been followed over time to help answer questions about differential quality, teacher compensation, and staff professional development. For example, a multiyear study of full-day versus half-day GSRP classrooms found that although full-day classrooms were, on average, of higher quality than half-day classrooms, there were no differences in the impact of full- and half-day GSRP classes on child outcomes (see Jurkiewicz, Xiang, & Schweinhart, 2004).

This chapter focuses on child outcomes first enumerated in six evaluation reports to the state of Michigan between 1997 and 2007. They included cohorts of GSRP children followed from preschool through the eighth grade. Four reports (*Early Returns 1997, Points of Light 2000, Effects Five Years Later 2002,* and the *6–8th Grade Follow Up Study 2007*) analyzed data collected over time from an original cohort of 596 children (338 GSRP graduates and 258 matched non-GSRP children) from six districts across the state. The comparison-group children were selected based on two criteria: They did not have a preschool experience and they were low income. Selection of both the GSRP and comparison group took place during the children's kindergarten year. The fifth project was a collaboration between HighScope and the National Institute for Early Education Research (NIEER). The sixth project, the GSRP Variation Study, recently completed data collection through first grade.

The evaluations of GSRP summarized here were similar to most other evaluations of state-funded preschool initiatives. That is, they depended primarily on quasi-experimental designs, although the more recent ones included newer techniques like regression–discontinuity designs, and they found evidence that attending preschool has short-term positive outcomes for children. Specifically, the GRSP evaluations focused on whether preschool graduates were ready to enter kindergarten or how preschool attendees versus nonattendees fared in kindergarten and first grade. A unique feature of the GSRP evaluation work is its longitudinal examination of a state-funded pre-K program. Effects of GSRP through middle school have been reported (Malofeeva, Daniel-Echols, & Xiang, 2007).

Findings are presented by grade level to help make clear the short- and long-term program influences that have been found. Many of the studies found a strong effect on grade retention. As shown in Figure 10.2, starting in early elementary school and persisting through middle school, the GSRP group has had a significantly lower rate of grade retention than the

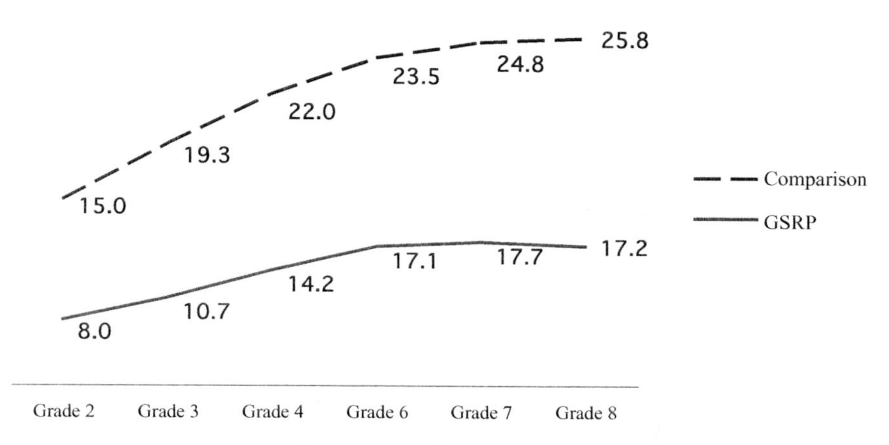

Figure 10.2. Group differences in percentage of grade retention over time.

non-GSRP comparison group. Another consistent finding across all of the studies is that GSRP children have been found through teacher reports, independent observations, and direct assessments to be more ready for school and to possess more developed language, literacy, and math skills.

Kindergarten

During their kindergarten year, data on children's knowledge and skills were collected from a cohort of 596 children through observation and kindergarten teacher reports. As reported by Florian, Schweinhart, and Epstein (1997), during their kindergarten year, GSRP children were observed and rated by teachers as being more developed than the comparison group. That is, GSRP children had higher average scores in all domains – social relations, initiative, language and literacy, music and movement, creative representation, and logic and mathematics – of the *Child Observation Record for 2 ½ to 6 Year Olds* (COR) (High/Scope Educational Research Foundation, 1992). Kindergarten teachers, who did not know to which group – GSRP or comparison – children belonged, consistently rated GSRP graduates as being more advanced in being imaginative and creative, showing initiative, retaining learning, completing assignments, and school attendance.

In 2005, HighScope worked with the NIEER to include Michigan in a multistate evaluation of state-funded preschool programs. Using a regression-discontinuity design, data were collected from a statewide sample of 865 children (384 in the preschool group and 481 in the no-preschool group). The child assessment tools used included the Peabody Picture Vocabulary Test–III (Dunn & Dunn, 1997), the Applied Problems Subtest from the Woodcock-Johnson Tests of Achievement–III (Woodcock, McGrew & Mather, 2001), and the Blending subtest from the Preschool Comprehensive Test of Phonological and Print Processing (Lonigan, Wagner, Torgeson, & Rashotte, 2002). It was found that at kindergarten entry, GSRP attendance produced statistically significant positive effects on early math and print awareness scores (Barnett, Jung, Wong, Cook, & Lamy, 2007).

Second Grade

In 2000, Xiang and colleagues used additional student background information not available when HighScope investigated kindergarten differences in its sample of 596 children to reconfirm those initial kindergarten findings and investigate potential group differences at second grade. This reanalysis of the data did in fact confirm the kindergarten findings. It also showed that second-grade teachers rated GSRP graduates higher on being ready to learn, able to retain learning, maintaining good attendance, and having an interest in school. It is at second grade that the first findings related to grade retention and GSRP attendance were discovered. Specifically, in second grade, the GSRP group had a significantly lower rate of retention (8%) than the comparison group (15%).

Fourth Grade

Before passage of the No Child Left Behind Act, the State of Michigan did not give its statewide standardized test, the Michigan Educational Assessment Program (MEAP), to students until they reached the fourth grade. In 2002, HighScope produced a report based on following those original 596 children into fourth grade and looking at MEAP performance and rates of grade retention. Figure 10.3 summarizes those findings. Specifically, GSRP attendees had higher rates of passing the MEAP and lower rates of retention (Xiang & Schweinhart, 2002).

Middle School

In 2007, Malofeeva and colleagues completed a longitudinal follow-up that studied the original cohort of 596 children and looked at their performance in middle school; they were able to retrieve data for 93% (556 children) of the sample. Their study focused on five outcomes of interest: seventh-grade MEAP scores, grade retention measured at the end of Grades 6–8, school attendance measured at the end of Grades 6–8, course enrollment for math and science courses (Grades 7 and 8), and special-education services received measured at the end of Grades 6–8. Analyses and findings presented in that report were based on nine waves of data (fall, spring, and end of the year) for each of the three grades (Grades 6, 7, and 8). The primary methodological approach used in that report was hierarchical linear modeling.

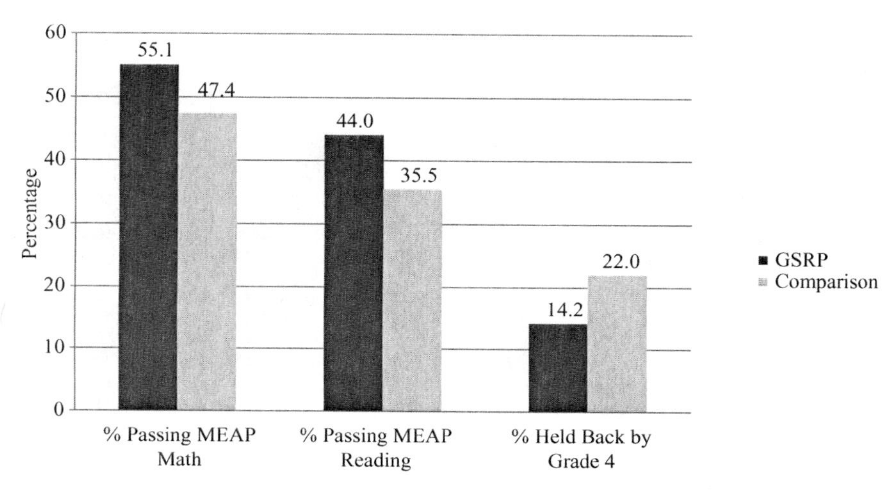

Figure 10.3. Fourth-grade MEAP and grade-retention findings.

No group differences were found for seventh-grade MEAP scores, attendance, science-course enrollment, or receipt of Title I or at-risk services.[5] However, Malofeeva et al. (2007) found that GSRP attendance was associated with a decreased likelihood of GSRP graduates being retained in Grades 6, 7, and 8. The odds of GSRP children being retained in Grade 6 were 36.1% less than the odds of retention for the comparison group. In both seventh and eighth grade, an interaction between race and GSRP was found such that GSRP significantly reduced the likelihood of being retained for children of color (by 18.7% in seventh grade and 21% in eighth grade) while having no similar effect among White GSRP graduates. In addition to the interaction of program and race, it was found that in eighth grade, attending GSRP reduced the likelihood of being retained for boys as compared to comparison-group boys, but there was no similar effect among girls.

Findings related to math- and science-course enrollment were mixed. For example, in seventh grade, boys who went to GSRP took more courses than comparison-group boys, whereas attending GSRP seemed to decrease the number of math courses taken by girls. Similarly, whereas non-White GSRP students took more math courses than non-Whites in the comparison group, GSRP attendance seemed to decrease math-course enrollment for White students.

[5] Although there were no group differences in seventh-grade MEAP scores, there were differences in whether a student took the MEAP test on time or 1 year later. Among the GSRP group, 84.7% of children took the MEAP test on time as compared to 77.7% of the comparison group. Taking the test on time is related to the differential grade-retention rates for the GSRP and comparison groups. Analyses of seventh-grade MEAP data used all available test scores, some of which came from students who took the test on time and some of which came from students who had been held back a grade.

Analyses revealed that GSRP attendees had higher rates of special-education services in both seventh and eighth grade. Having a diagnosed handicapping condition is one of the 25 risk factors that make a child eligible for GSRP. When the sample was originally drawn, information was not collected on the prevalence of risk factors for the comparison group. Without that information, it is unclear whether increased receipt of special-education services represents a success or failure of the GSRP in achieving its goal to serve that population.

Ongoing Analysis (Preschool, Kindergarten, and First Grade)

In 2004, HighScope began the Preschool Variation Study, which drew a new sample of children from a mix of programs across the state. Data collection, which ended in the spring of 2007, gathered child, parent, teacher, classroom, program, principal, and school data for 407 children through their preschool, kindergarten, and first-grade years. The original intent of the study was to fully describe the policies, practices, and resources related to child outcomes across multiple settings: private child care, Head Start, and GSRP centers. However, the blended-funding nature of programs across the state has essentially made these program type distinctions nonexistent. The clearest contrast is between GSRP and private child-care programs because most blending of funds occurs between GSRP and Head Start programs.

Nevertheless, preschool-level data have already provided a rich description of aspects of program quality, such as curriculum use and literacy-rich environments. For example, Early Language and Literacy Classroom Observation (ELLCO) (Smith, Dickinson, Sangeorge, & Anastasopoulos, 2002) data revealed that GSRP classrooms had a statistically significantly higher score than private childcare (3.45 vs. 2.37 on a scale from 0–5) on writing activities (e.g., children writing during play, teachers modeling writing). GSRP classrooms also had, on average, statistically significantly higher scores than Head Start (5.86 vs. 4.80 on a scale of 1–8) on book-reading activities (e.g., full-group book reading, one-on-one teacher–child reading). GSRP programs used a wider variety of curricula compared to private child care. GSRP programs reported using HighScope (27%), Creative Curriculum (9%), state-developed curriculum (9%), Montessori (5%), "child-centered classroom" (5%), and other (typically a homegrown or an eclectic approach, 40%). In contrast, 25% of private child-care programs reported using Creative Curriculum, 13% used High Reach, and 62% used Other.

In addition to the Variation study, in 2008 HighScope began a mixed approach – using both a regression discontinuity design and a comparison group design – study of GSRP. Analysis of that data through first grade including longitudinal analyses, using growth models, of children's literacy, math, and social skill development over time are ongoing.

FUTURE RESEARCH DIRECTIONS

At least three critical issues must inform how policy makers judge the evidence on the effectiveness of these early childhood investments. First, quasi-experimental designs enable evaluations to produce evidence of a relationship between GSRP attendance and child outcomes, but cannot definitely establish a causal relationship.

Second, evaluations of state-funded preschool programs must consider child outcomes in context. It is important to assess children and program characteristics that might enhance or hinder program effects. In Michigan, the regression–discontinuity design study, although a methodologically stronger design than matched comparison designs, had no measure of preschool or kindergarten classroom quality.

The third critical issue is closely related to the importance of considering context. Early childhood researchers are continuing to explore the relative importance of different aspects of program quality. Program quality consists of both structural factors (e.g., teacher qualifications, adult–child ratios, hours of instruction) and process factors (e.g., adult–child interaction). Recent studies have found that structural variables such as years of teacher experience and teacher credentials are less related to child outcomes than the nature of the interactions between teachers and children (e.g., Early et al., 2006). At the same time, others have suggested that teacher qualifications do matter – it is just that we have not yet clearly defined which types of qualifications matter more than others and which professional development supports are needed (e.g., Bogard, Traylor, & Takanishi, 2007). It is in response to this debate that HighScope is working with the Michigan Department of Education to answer this question: What are the aspects of quality that GSRP should emphasize?

The middle-school findings discussed in this chapter present a mixed bag of outcomes, some of which imply that GSRP produces more long-term benefits for non-White children. A recent evaluation of South Carolina's state-funded preschool initiative found a similar trend for short-term impacts of that program (Browning, Daniel-Echols, & Xiang, 2006). The question posed by Malofeeva et al. (2007) is worth repeating here: "What is it about these populations of children, the GSRP program, and the social and educational contexts they share that lead to better outcomes for some and poorer ones for others?" To answer this question, future evaluations of GSRP must employ more rigorous designs; for example, regression–discontinuity designs that include program contextual variables, comparison-group designs that use propensity score analysis, and, if possible, random-assignment designs.

IMPLICATIONS FOR POLICY

The GSRP has a 24-year history of providing high-quality preschool experiences to 4-year-old children at risk of school failure. Data over time have consistently found both short- and long-term positive outcomes for GSRP attendees. The ongoing partnership between the Michigan Department of Education and HighScope's team of researchers has nurtured a strong, direct connection among research, policy, and practice.

GSRP has succeeded on these fronts despite expanding its services with relatively little increases in funding: only an additional $900 per child over its original 1985 funding level. For GSRP to continue to respond to changing community needs (e.g., increased numbers and diversity in non-English-speaking homes, increased numbers of income-eligible children as a result of economic decline in the state), it will need new strategies and additional support. Resources are needed at both the per-child level and the funds available for program administration. In recent years, the grantee:MDE consultant ratio has produced large caseloads (i.e., more than one hundred grantees per consultant). It is difficult to enforce quality accountability under such circumstances.

An encouraging development in the state is the Early Childhood Investment Corporation (ECIC). The ECIC is a public–private venture designed to help local collaboratives assess and respond to the early childhood care and education needs within their communities. ECIC collaboratives bring together a mix of stakeholders: early childhood professionals, business leaders, politicians, parents, and social service agencies. Despite many years of state budgetary declines and crisis, Michigan Governor Jennifer Granholm remains committed to the ECIC and to early childhood issues. The GSRP is perfectly situated to inform and benefit from this initiative.

REFERENCES

Barnett, W. S., Jung, K., Wong, V., Cook, T., & Lamy, C. (2007, October). *Effects of five state prekindergarten programs on early learning.* New Brunswick, NJ: National Institute for Early Education Research, Rutgers University, Northwestern University, and the Robin Hood Foundation.

Bogard, K., Traylor, F., & Takanishi, R. (2007, September). *Teacher education and PK outcomes: Are we asking the right questions?* New York: Foundation for Child Development.

Browning, K. G., Daniel-Echols, M., & Xiang, Z. (2006). *From implementation to impact: An evaluation of the South Carolina First Steps to School Readiness Program.* Ypsilanti, MI: HighScope Educational Research Foundation.

Dunn, L. M., & Dunn, L. M. (1997). *Peabody Picture Vocabulary Test* (3rd ed.). Circle Pines, MN: American Guidance Services.

Early, D. M., Bryant, D. M., Pianta, R. C., Clifford, R. M., Burchinal, M. R., Ritchie, S., et al. (2006). Are teachers' education, major, and credentials related to classroom quality and children's academic gains in pre-kindergarten? *Early Childhood Research Quarterly, 1*(2), 174.

Florian, J. E., Schweinhart, L. J., & Epstein, A. S. (1997). *Early returns: First-year report of the Michigan School Readiness Program evaluation.* Ypsilanti, MI: High/Scope Educational Research Foundation.

HighScope Educational Research Foundation (1992). *Preschool child observation record for 2 ½ to 6 year olds.* Ypsilanti, MI: HighScope Press.

HighScope Educational Research Foundation (2003a). *Preschool child observation record* (2nd ed.). Ypsilanti, MI: HighScope Press.

HighScope Educational Research Foundation. (2003b). *Preschool program quality assessment* (2nd ed.). Ypsilanti, MI: HighScope Press.

HighScope Educational Research Foundation (2008, August). *2007–2008 Great Start Readiness Program quality assessment statewide data report.* Ypsilanti, MI: HighScope Press.

Jurkiewicz, T. C., Xiang, Z., & Schweinhart, L. (2004). *The Michigan full-day preschool comparison study.* Ypsilanti, MI: HighScope Educational Research Foundation.

Lamy, C., Barnett, W. S., & Jung, K. (2005). *The effects of the Michigan School Readiness Program on young children's abilities at kindergarten entry.* New Brunswick, NJ: National Institute for Early Education Research, Rutgers University.

Lonigan, C., Wagner, R., Torgeson, J., & Rashotte, C. (2002). *Preschool comprehensive test of phonological and print processing* (Pre-CTOPPP). Gainesville: Department of Psychology, University of Florida.

Malofeeva, E. V., Daniel-Echols, M., & Xiang, Z. (2007). *Findings from the Michigan School Readiness Program 6 to 8 follow up study.* Ypsilanti, MI: HighScope Educational Research Foundation.

Michigan Department of Education (2008, August). *Great Start Readiness Program implementation manual (draft).* Lansing: Michigan Department of Education, Office of Early Childhood Educational and Family Services.

Michigan State Board of Education (2005, March 8). *Early childhood standards of quality for prekindergarten.* Lansing: Michigan Department of Education, Office of Early Childhood Educational and Family Services.

Smith, M. W., Dickinson, D., Sangeorge, A., & Anastasopoulos, L. (2002) *Early language and literacy classroom observation (ELLCO) toolkit, research edition.* Baltimore, MD: Brookes.

Woodcock, R. W., McGrew, K. S., & Mather, N. (2001). *Woodcock-Johnson tests of achievement.* Itasca, IL: Riverside.

Xiang, Z., & Schweinhart, L. J. (2002). *Effects five years later: The Michigan School Readiness Program evaluation through age 10.* Ypsilanti, MI: HighScope Educational Research Foundation.

Xiang, Z., Schweinhart, L. J., Hohmann, C., Smith, C., Storer, E., & Oden, S. (2000). *Points of light: Third year report of the Michigan School Readiness evaluation.* Ypsilanti, MI: HighScope Educational Research Foundation.

11

Abbott Preschool Program Longitudinal Effects Study Year One Findings

ELLEN FREDE, W. STEVEN BARNETT, KWANGHEE JUNG, CYNTHIA ESPOSITO LAMY, AND ALEXANDRA FIGUERAS

INTRODUCTION

This study investigates the educational effects of a state-funded prekindergarten education program for children at ages 3 and 4 that came about as a result of a court order. As part of the landmark New Jersey Supreme Court school-funding case, *Abbott v. Burke*, the court established the Abbott Preschool Program. Beginning in the 1999–2000 school year, 3- and 4-year-old children in the highest poverty districts in the state were able to receive a high-quality preschool education that would prepare them to enter school with the knowledge and skills necessary to meet the *New Jersey Preschool Teaching and Learning Expectations: Standards of Quality* (New Jersey Department of Education [NJDOE], 2004b) and the *New Jersey Kindergarten Core Curriculum Content Standards* (NJDOE, 2004a). Through a New Jersey Department of Education (DOE) and Department of Human Services (DHS) partnership, Abbott preschool classrooms combine a DOE-funded 6-hour, 180-day component with a DHS-funded wrap-around program that provides daily before- and after-care and summer programs. In total, the full-day, full-year program is available 10 hours per day, 245 days a year.

Enrollment in the Abbott Preschool Program has increased dramatically since its inception in 1999 (see Fig. 11.1). During the 2005–2006 school year, its seventh year, the 31 Abbott districts served more than 40,500 3- and 4-year-old

The research reported in this chapter was conducted under a Memorandum of Agreement as part of the Early Learning Improvement Consortium (ELIC) with the New Jersey Department of Education (NJDOE) and with partial funding from the Pew Charitable Trusts. The conclusions are those of the authors and do not necessarily represent the views of the funding agencies.

We wish to acknowledge the support and assistance of the other members of the Early Learning Improvement Consortium: Ellen Wolock, New Jersey Department of Education; and Holly Seplocha and Janis Strasser, William Paterson State University. We are grateful to Jacqueline Jones, former Assistant Commissioner, Division of Early Childhood Education, NJDOE, for comments on an earlier draft. We wish to express our appreciation to Thomas Cook and Vivien Wong for advice on analysis of the regression-discontinuity data.

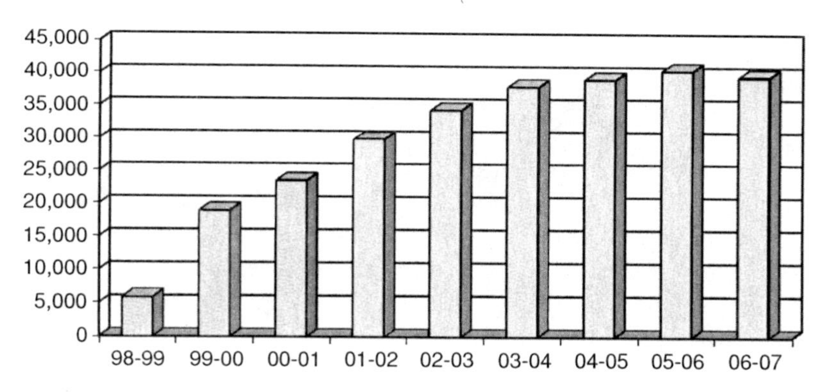

Figure 11.1. Abbott Preschool Program enrollment, 1998–2007.

children in preschool – 78% of a possible 52,160 children. The enrollment for the 2006–2007 school year was 39,678 children with a DOE budget of almost $500 million. Through contracts with the school districts, private child care providers and Head Start agencies, in addition to public schools, offer Abbott Preschool: 37% of children are served in district-run classrooms, 7% are served in Head Start classrooms, and 56% are in private-provider classrooms.

In mandating the Abbott Preschool Program, the court established some basic program standards: a maximum class size of 15, certified teachers with early childhood expertise, assistant teachers in every classroom, comprehensive services, and a developmentally appropriate curriculum designed to meet learning standards. To ensure high quality and consistency for children across auspice and district and to assist administrators and staff who may have been inadequately prepared in early childhood education, in 2005 the Office of Early Childhood Education in the DOE developed more detailed operational standards (*Abbott Preschool Program Implementation Guidelines*) (NJDOE, 2005). These standards were also necessary because the court made clear that funding through an across-the-state per-pupil formula would not be adequate and that budget decisions must be based on district contexts.

Since 2002, the New Jersey DOE has implemented an assessment system for the Abbott Preschool Program (see Frede, 2005, for details on this system). To measure and assess progress statewide, the DOE formed the Early Learning Improvement Consortium (ELIC), a group of the state's top early childhood education faculty. Drawing on research previously conducted by the Center for Early Education Research (Barnett, Tarr, Esposito Lamy, & Frede, 2002), ELIC is responsible for collecting and reporting on data on children and classrooms. Every fall from 2002 through 2005, it conducted assessments of kindergartners' skills to measure progress toward preparing children to succeed in school. In addition, members of ELIC conducted classroom observations on a random sample of Abbott preschool classrooms to measure progress in program quality.

Findings have been reported yearly (Frede et al., 2004; Lamy, Frede, & ELIC, 2005).

In the 2004–2005 school year, ELIC reported that classroom quality scores had reached acceptable levels and that children were entering kindergarten with language and literacy skills closer to the national average than in prior years (Frede et al., 2004; Lamy et al., 2005). Given these trends, an evaluation seemed warranted to more precisely estimate the learning gains from the Abbott prekindergarten program and the extent to which gains persist into elementary school. This chapter presents the methods and results of that evaluation through the end of the kindergarten year.

The evaluation was conducted in such a way as to build on the previous annual descriptive studies and to provide continuity with respect to measures and the sample. However, it moved beyond the previous Abbott Preschool studies by using multiple approaches to the evaluation of the preschool programs and their impacts on children. These mixed methods assessed classroom quality in terms of children's experiences and teacher practices and estimated the immediate impact of the program at age 4 using a regression–discontinuity design (RDD). The RDD approach explicitly addresses the problem of selection bias and is applicable even if all of the children in a district attend the preschool program (Cook & Campbell, 1979; Trochim, 1984). However, the RDD approach cannot be used to estimate the effects of the program beyond kindergarten entry, neither could it provide estimates of the effects of 1 versus 2 years of the program. Thus, we employed a second approach in which we compared three groups of children: those who had not attended the Abbott Preschool Program, those who had 1 year of Abbott preschool education, and those who had 2 years of Abbott preschool education. These children could be followed and compared from kindergarten through elementary school. This second approach to estimating program effects is more likely to suffer from selection bias. However, we can measure the direction and size of such bias by comparing the second set of estimates to those from the RDD approach.

ABBOTT PRESCHOOL PROGRAM QUALITY

Structured classroom observations have been conducted from the inception of the Abbott program in 1999 through 2006. The Center for Early Education Research at Rutgers University (the predecessor of the National Institute for Early Education Research [NIEER]) measured classroom quality in a subsample of 19 Abbott districts from 1999 through 2001. Thus, change in aspects of classroom quality since before 2002 was measured across this subsample. Beginning in 2003, ELIC administered observations annually in all Abbott districts. In randomly selected preschool classrooms, trained data collectors used structured classroom observation instruments to assess educational materials, the environment, and teacher–child interactions. Observers typically were advanced undergraduates, graduate students, or former teachers, usually with experience teaching at the preschool level. Each observer was shadow scored and had to reach an 80% inter-rater reliability rate before qualifying to conduct observations for the study. Shadow scoring was repeated every 6 weeks to ensure that observer reliability did not drift over time. Each classroom was observed once during the winter or spring of the year for 3 to 4 hours. In 2005–2006, the sample consisted of 316 classrooms that proportionately represented the population with respect to auspices (104 public school, 176 private, and 25 Head Start programs). Each of the three measures is described next.

Measures

Early Childhood Environment Rating Scale–Revised (ECERS-R)

The ECERS-R (Harms, Clifford, & Cryer, 2005) was used to assess overall quality. This measure has been used extensively in the field and has well-established validity and reliability. Internal consistency as measured by Cronbach's alpha was reported by the authors of the instrument to be .81 to .91, which is adequate, and we found it to be .90 in this study. The seven ECERS-R subscales are Space and Furnishings, Personal Care Routines, Language-Reasoning, Activities, Interaction, Program Structure, and Parents and Staff. Classroom quality was rated on a 7-point Likert scale ranging from 1 (*inadequate*) to 7 (*excellent*). Average subscale scores were calculated, as well as a total scale score averaged across all 43 items in the scale.

Supports for Early Literacy Assessment (SELA)

The SELA measures the extent to which the classroom environment supports children's literacy development (Smith, Davidson, & Weisenfeld, 2001). This measure was revised for this study by the deletion of four items that overlapped with the ECERS-R. The revised measure included 16 items that were each rated on a scale from 1 (*low support*) to 5 (*high support*). Six subscales are the Literate Environment, Language Development, Knowledge of Print/Book Concepts, Phonological Awareness, Letters and Words, and Parent Involvement. Internal consistency as measured by Cronbach's alpha on the current sample was good at .87.

Preschool Classroom Mathematics Inventory (PCMI)

The PCMI measures classroom support for the development of children's early mathematical skills (Frede, Weber, Hornbeck, Stevenson-Boyd, & Colon, 2005). It assesses the materials and strategies used in the classroom to support children's early mathematical concept development, including counting, comparing, estimating, recognizing number symbols, classifying, seriating, manipulating geometric shapes, and understanding spatial relations. The standards of the National Council of Teachers of Mathematics and the National Association for the Education of Young Children (2002) inform the measure, which comprises 11 items on a 5-point scale, from 1 (*low support*) to 5 (*high support*). It has two subscales: Materials and Numeracy, and Other Mathematical Concepts. Internal consistency among the test items as measured by Cronbach's alpha was good at .86. The PCMI has been found to predict child progress on a standardized math assessment (Frede, Lamy, & Boyd, 2005).

Preliminary Results

To evaluate the extent to which the Abbott Preschool Program might be expected to produce substantial gains in children's learning and development, we examined means and the distribution of scores across classrooms in 2005–2006. In addition, we compared these results to those obtained in 1999–2000 when quality was essentially what it had been before implementation of the court order. Taken as a whole, the advances in classroom quality are notable. In 2006, the average score on the ECERS-R was 4.81, compared to 3.86 in 2000 (a gain of 1.3 standard deviations). In 2006, almost 90% of the classrooms scored above the mean for 2000. The 2006 average score was similar to that found in other studies of publicly funded preschool in this country (Early et al., 2007). In those areas most likely to be directly related to child learning – Language and Reasoning, Activities, Interactions, and Program Structure – classrooms on average scored in the good to excellent range.

An average score in 2006 of 3.46 on the SELA also reflects practices that are likely to lead to more learning, with the highest scores in supplying materials that support language and literacy development and in teaching practices that enhance oral language development. Fully 75% scored a 3 or higher. However, in the special case of language and literacy, the lower scoring items were mostly related to specific language and literacy skill development, including introducing new vocabulary, assisting children in developing print awareness and letter recognition, supporting phonological development (children's ability to hear the sounds in words), and promoting interest in writing. Assisting parents in supporting their children's language and literacy development and supporting bilingual language development also scored lower.

Results on the PCMI, however, were not so heartening. The only scores higher than a 3, on a scale of 1 to 5, were on items that reflected the materials in the classroom. Given that the Abbott classrooms are well funded, even these scores seem low and likely represent the same lack of understanding of mathematical learning and teaching shown by the very low scores for teaching support. Six of the seven items that measure whether the teachers actively plan for and support mathematical learning had scores between 1 and 2. Thirty to 50% of the classrooms scored a 1 on these items, meaning that none of the desired teaching practices was observed on these items. Clearly, math learning is enhanced when math is incorporated throughout the classroom activities (Arnold, Fischer, Doctoroff, & Dobbs, 2002). However, a great deal of math reasoning is also done by the child while using math-related materials (Ginsburg, Inoue, & Seo, 1999). Thus, the slightly better scores on mathematics materials are meaningful, but overall questions remain about whether the program provides enough support for children's learning in this domain to produce large gains.

For some of the low-scoring items on SELA and PCMI that measure fairly specific teaching strategies, it is difficult to judge how much teachers should be expected to use these techniques regularly during the 3.5–4.0-hour observation period. However, in the 4 years that these measures have been used in Abbott classrooms, there has always been a small percentage of classrooms that have scored higher than a 4 on the items, and all classrooms have improved over time. This indicates that it is possible to meet the criteria needed to score well on these items and suggests that professional development should continue to focus on these areas.

Of particular interest in these findings is the fact that public school and private child care center classrooms scored the same across almost all measures of quality teaching practices in 2006. In contrast, in 2000, the private centers scored much more poorly across most measures of quality. This increase in scores in a private program within a public system is evidence that standards, funding, and professional development are the conduits to quality and that specific auspices are irrelevant within a public system. Although there is clearly room for improvement, the observational measures indicate that the Abbott Preschool Program is providing good- to high-quality education to most children. Additional detail is provided by Frede and colleagues (2007).

EFFECTS ON CHILDREN'S LEARNING AND DEVELOPMENT

Beginning in the fall of 2005, NIEER and its ELIC partners designed and implemented a two-step research process to estimate the long-term effects of attendance in an Abbott preschool classroom. The first step was to employ an RDD approach to estimate the effects of the program on children's abilities at kindergarten entry. To define the study groups, this approach took advantage of each district's strict enrollment policy, which determines enrollment by the child's date of birth. By relying on this assignment rule, one that is unlikely to be related to child and family characteristics, the RDD seeks to reduce the likelihood of selection bias. Thus, rather than compare children who attended and did not attend the program (raising concerns that the family factors that led to this difference might also contribute to differences in learning and development), the RDD approach compares two groups of children who enroll in the Abbott Preschool Program. One group has been in the program and the other is just entering it.

One way to interpret the RDD approach is to view it as similar to a randomized trial for children near the age cutoff. The RDD creates groups that *at the margin* differ only in that some were born a few days before the age cutoff and others a few days after the cutoff. When these children are about to turn 5 years old, the slightly younger children will enter the preschool program and the slightly older children will enter kindergarten having already attended the preschool program. If all of the children are tested at that time, the difference in their scores can provide an unbiased estimate of the preschool program's effect under reasonable circumstances. Of course, if only children with birthdays a few days on either side of the age cutoff were included in a study, the sample size would be unreasonably small. Alternatively, the RDD can be viewed as modeling the relationship between an assignment variable (age) and measures of children's learning and development. The pre-cutoff sample is used to model the relationship before treatment. The post-cutoff sample is used to model the relationship after the treatment. This approach can be applied to wider age ranges around the cutoff. However, its validity depends on correctly modeling the relationship. Under either approach, it is important that there is minimal misallocation (exceptions to the rule) around the cutoff.

Unfortunately, the RDD approach cannot provide an estimate of effects beyond kindergarten entry. If it were to be employed a year later, it would provide an estimate of the added effects of kindergarten. Thus, to obtain estimates beyond kindergarten entry, we used a conventional no-treatment comparison group but employed it at kindergarten entry as well so we could compare its estimates to the RDD estimates. If the initial estimates from both analyses were similar, then we would have greater confidence in the longitudinal results. If not, then at least we would have an indication of the likely direction and magnitude of the bias in the longitudinal estimates.

Thus, in addition to the two samples drawn for the RDD study, we drew an additional comparison sample of kindergarten children who did not attend the Abbott Preschool Program. We intend to follow both samples of kindergarten children through Grade 3 to assess their performance on measures of academic abilities and the extent to which they are retained in grade or placed in special education. Because some children attended preschool for 1 year at age 4 and others attended preschool for 2 years at ages 3 and 4, we are able to separately estimate the effects of 1 year and 2 years of preschool attendance using this second design. In a later follow-up, we will obtain measures of family characteristics, such as mother's education level, language spoken in the home, and family income. However, the present analyses draw on only two family background characteristics: ethnicity and free- or reduced-lunch status. This design is less of a problem than it might be because the communities in our study are fairly homogeneous – all are larger, low-income urban school districts in a single state. In addition, we ensured that the treatment and comparison samples are balanced with respect to district, and we controlled for district in the analyses.

Sampling Strategy

To limit the logistical costs of data collection, we limited the study to children in the 15 largest Abbott school districts. These districts enroll the vast majority of children in the Abbott Preschool Program so that distortion introduced is small. However, this strategy likely underestimates the program effect on all children in the state. Previous analyses have shown that classroom quality and children's scores at kindergarten entry are somewhat higher in the 16 smaller districts omitted from the study than in the 15 largest districts.

At the beginning of the school year, we randomly sampled individual preschool classrooms from a list of all preschool classrooms in the 15 districts. From each of the randomly sampled classrooms, we selected four children, providing the no-treatment control sample ($n = 778$) for the RDD because these children had just enrolled in preschool and thus had not yet received the treatment. In addition, using a similar procedure, we randomly selected a kindergarten sample in these districts and then randomly selected four children who were first-time entrants to kindergarten from each classroom. Because this selection was done without consideration of preschool participation, the sample included a representative proportion of children who did and did not attend Abbott preschool. From this sample of new kindergarten entrants, we constructed the treatment group ($n = 766$) for the RDD study and the 1-year ($n = 461$), 2-year ($n = 305$), and no-treatment comparison ($n = 305$) groups for the longitudinal study. The longitudinal study no-treatment comparison included a small number of children ($n = 59$) who attended a preschool program not part of the Abbott Preschool Program. Overall, the sample was 49% female, and the ethnic breakdown was 51% Hispanic, 40% African American, and 8% Other. There were no statistically significant differences between the treatment and comparison groups on either gender or ethnicity.

Measurement

Trained research staff from NIEER, William Paterson University, and the College of New Jersey visited each sampled program site, selected children into the sample using a procedure to ensure randomness, and conducted the child assessments as early as possible in the school year. A liaison at each kindergarten site gathered information on the children's preschool status, usually from existing school records but occasionally from parent report, and was reimbursed $5 per sample child. Identical measures were administered to preschoolers and kindergartners in the first year of the study. The battery of child assessments took an average of approximately 25 minutes per child and were administered at the child's school program, in a room or quiet area appropriate for assessment.

Receptive Vocabulary

Children's receptive vocabulary was measured using the Peabody Picture Vocabulary Test (3rd ed.) (PPVT-III) (Dunn & Dunn, 1997); for Spanish speakers, the Test de Vocabulario en Imágenes Peabody (TVIP) (Dunn, Padilla, Lugo, & Dunn, 1986) was used. The PPVT is predictive of general cognitive abilities and is a direct measure of vocabulary size. The rank order of item difficulties is highly correlated with the frequency with which words are used in spoken and written language. The test is adaptive (to avoid floor and ceiling problems), establishing a floor below which the child is assumed to know all the answers and a ceiling above which the child is assumed to know none of the answers. Reliability is good as judged by either split-half reliabilities or test–retest reliabilities. The TVIP is appropriate for measuring growth in Spanish vocabulary for bilingual students and for monolingual Spanish speakers.

All children in our sample were administered the PPVT, regardless of home language, to get some sense of their receptive vocabulary ability in English. All children who spoke some Spanish were also subsequently administered the TVIP. The testing session was then continued, with the additional measures administered in either English or Spanish, depending on what the child's teacher designated as the child's best testing language.

Mathematical Skills

Children's early mathematical skills were measured with the Woodcock-Johnson Tests of Achievement (3rd ed.) (Woodcock, McGrew, & Mather, 2001) Subtest 10 Applied Problems. For Spanish speakers, the *Bateria Woodcock-Munoz Pruebas de Aprovechamiento – Revisado* (Woodcock & Munoz, 1990) *Prueba 25 Problemas Aplicados* was used. Subtests of the Woodcock-Johnson are reported to have good reliability.

Print Awareness

Children's print awareness was measured using the Print Awareness subtest of the Preschool Comprehensive Test of Phonological and Print Processing (Pre-CTOPPP) (Lonigan, Wagner, Torgeson, & Rashotte, 2002). The Pre-CTOPPP was designed as a downward extension of the Comprehensive Test of Phonological Processing (CTOPP) (Wagner, Torgeson, & Rashotte, 1999), which measures phonological sensitivity in elementary school–age children. Although not yet published, the Pre-CTOPPP has been used with middle-class and low-income samples and includes a Spanish version. Because the Pre-CTOPPP was developed only recently, relatively little technical information is available about its performance and psychometric properties. Print Awareness items measure whether children recognize individual letters and letter-sound correspondences and whether they differentiate words in print from pictures and other symbols. The percentage of items answered correctly out of the 36 total subtest items is reported and analyzed.

The skills and knowledge measured by the Pre-CTOPPP (which are predictive of later literacy ability) are expected to be present by the end of the preschool year. Thus, it is not an appropriate test for the end of kindergarten, and results are not reported past kindergarten entry. In later years, additional literacy assessments will be administered.

Results

Regression-Discontinuity Design

To estimate program effects on children's test scores, we conducted a series of RDD analyses to guard against model misspecification. The model accounted for the number of days between birth dates and enrollment cutoff dates for each sample child, as well as gender, ethnicity (classified as African American, Hispanic, or Other), and age. We allowed slope to differ pre- and post-treatment. Analyses were conducted using raw scores. All standard errors were clustered by classroom, and we used STATA (StataCorp, 2005) to conduct the regressions.

In these models, the effect of attending the preschool program was estimated at the birth-date cutoff for enrollment. We defined a "treatment" variable by assigning all children with birth dates after the cutoff date with a value of 1 (treatment) and all other children a value of 0 (comparison). We then rescaled the selection variable (the age difference between birth date and cutoff date) so that the zero-point corresponded to the cut point. Thus, children in the treatment group had positive values and children in the comparison group had negative values. We constructed an interaction term by multiplying the cutoff dummy variable by the rescaled selection variable.

The RDD relies on several assumptions that can be tested. One is that programs must adhere to the fairly strict use of a birth-date cutoff date for program enrollment. Each school district employed a birth-date cutoff date for program enrollment, which varied by district from September 30 through December 31. Fortunately, departures from the selection rule were extremely rare. Thus, we conducted "sharp" regression–discontinuity models that dropped the handful of children in our sample whose birth-date information seemed to be inconsistent with the birth-date cutoff requirement for their programs.

Another key assumption is that the unmeasured population characteristics do not change with birth date. We could not directly test this assumption. However, we did assess the extent to which results might be changed as we move away from the birth-date cutoff. Thus, we repeated our analyses on two subgroups, one limited to children with birth dates within 60 days of the birth-date cutoff and the other limited to children with birth dates within 30 days of the birth-date cutoff. Analyses of these subgroups produced highly similar estimates of program effects.

The RDD approach also requires that we correctly model functional form. Because there is no a priori expectation that the estimated relationship should be linear, we estimated higher order polynomial forms of the equation, including squared and cubic transformations of the selection variable (i.e., the difference between the birth date and the cutoff date and its interaction with the cutoff dummy variable). We began analyzing third-order (cubic) polynomial regression models and found that the coefficients for the cubic term and its interaction with the cutoff dummy variable were not statistically significant. These terms were dropped. When we estimated the second-order polynomial, the coefficients for the quadratic terms and quadratic interaction terms were not significant. Thus, we dropped the quadratic term and its interaction term for the analyses.

Finally, when interpreting the RDD results, it is important to note that when the response functions are parallel and linear, one can generalize treatment effects across the entire distribution of the assignment variable. When these assumptions do not hold, only the local average treatment effect at the point of discontinuity can be estimated. In that case, treatment effects would be estimated only for the sample of children with birthdays near the cutoff. In the present study, the response functions seemed to be linear and reasonably parallel. Moreover, as birth-date cutoffs varied by district, the cutoff in our data set occurred over a range, with interpolated points and not a single point. Thus, the estimated effects generalized over a broader range of children than would be the case with a single cutoff, even if the assumptions of parallel and linear functions did not hold.

The estimated effects of the Abbott Preschool Program were significant for all three measures. Attending the Abbott program at age 4 was estimated to increase PPVT scores by 4.57 raw score points, which represents an improvement of about 28% of the standard deviation for the control (*No Preschool*) group (es = .28). Using the control group to calculate expected growth in PPVT scores over 12 months, we can interpret the estimated program effect as 35% more growth over the year in children's average vocabulary scores. The estimated effect on children's early math skills as measured by the Woodcock-Johnson-III Applied Problems subtest scores was 1.36 raw score points (es = .36), which is equal to a 41% increase in growth over the year. The estimated effect on Print Awareness was 14% more items answered correctly (es = .56), which is equal to 96% more growth over the year in print awareness.

Longitudinal Study

We conducted regression analyses estimating program effects on the longitudinal sample, with independent variables for student ethnicity, gender, age, and school district, as well as dummy variables indicating 1 or 2 years attendance in an Abbott Preschool Program. We conducted analyses on raw scores and standard scores (which are more easily interpreted) for the PPVT, raw scores for the Applied Problems test, and percentage correct for Print Awareness.

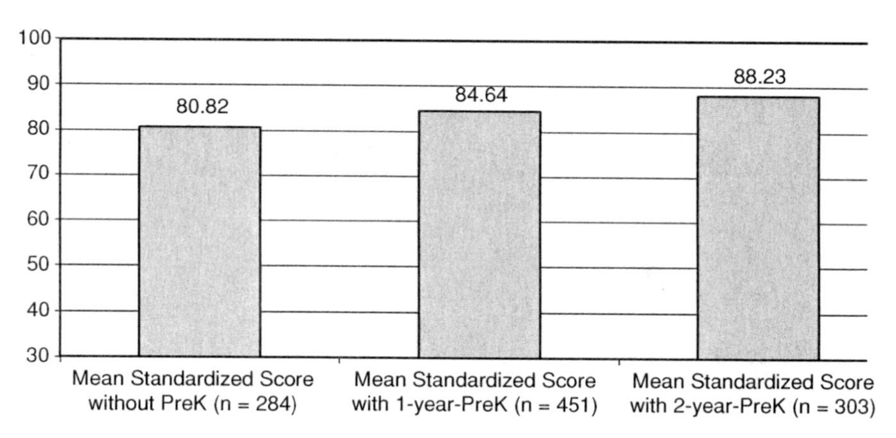

Figure 11.2. Longitudinal study receptive vocabulary at kindergarten entry by years of attendance ($N = 1{,}038$).

Again, we used the STATA, and we took intra-cluster correlation into account through the estimation of cluster-robust standard errors. The estimated effects at kindergarten entry and the end of kindergarten are reported later in the text and in figures that report scores for each group: no preschool, 1 year of preschool at age 4, and 2 years of preschool at ages 3 and 4.

The estimated effects of Abbott preschool on the PPVT were statistically significant at both kindergarten entry and exit. Figure 11.2 portrays estimated gains in receptive vocabulary at the beginning of kindergarten. One year of the Abbott Preschool Program at age 4 was estimated to increase PPVT scores by 3.82 standard score points at kindergarten entry (es = .21). Two years of Abbott preschool at ages 3 and 4 were estimated to increase PPVT scores by 7.41 standardized score points (es = .42). Figure 11.3 portrays gains on the PPVT at kindergarten exit, when the estimated effect was 3.39 standard score

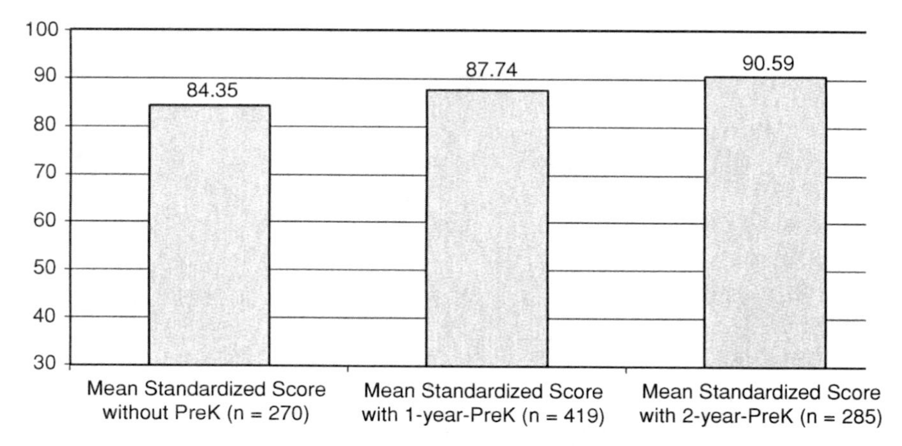

Figure 11.3. Longitudinal study receptive vocabulary at the end of kindergarten by years of attendance ($N = 974$).

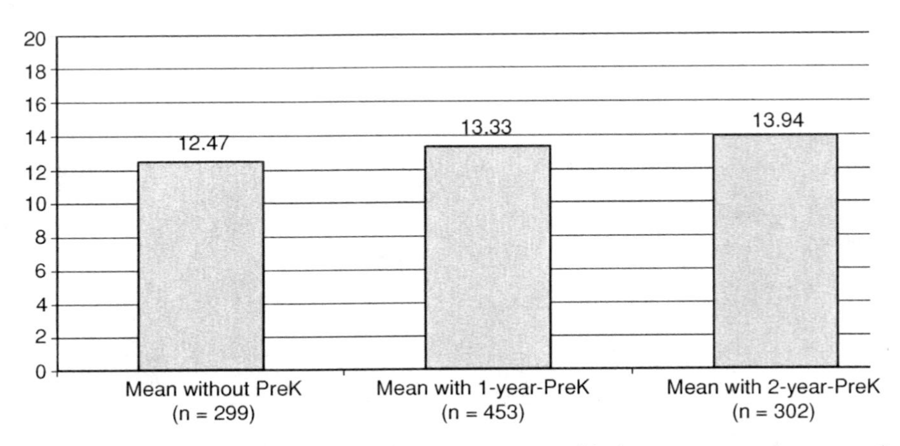

Figure 11.4. Longitudinal study mathematics scores at kindergarten entry by years of attendance ($N = 1{,}054$).

points (es = .22) for 1 year and 6.24 standard score points (es = .41) for 2 years.

Estimated effects on children's early math skills as measured by the Woodcock-Johnson-III Applied problems subtest were statistically significant at the start and end of kindergarten (see Figs. 11.4 and 11.5). At the start of kindergarten, the estimated increases in raw score were .86 (es = .20) from 1 year and 1.47 (es = .34) from 2 years of Abbott preschool participation. At the end of kindergarten, the estimated effects were .61 raw score points (es = .13) from 1 year and 1.38 raw score points (es = .29) from 2 years.

Even though the Print Awareness measure is no longer appropriate at the end of kindergarten, we estimated effects to see what we might find then as well

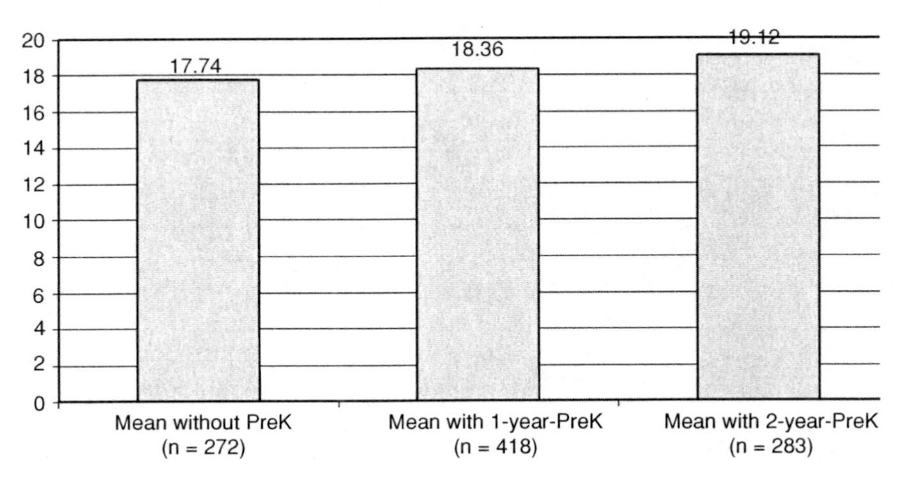

Figure 11.5. Longitudinal study mathematics scores at the end of kindergarten by years of attendance ($N = 973$).

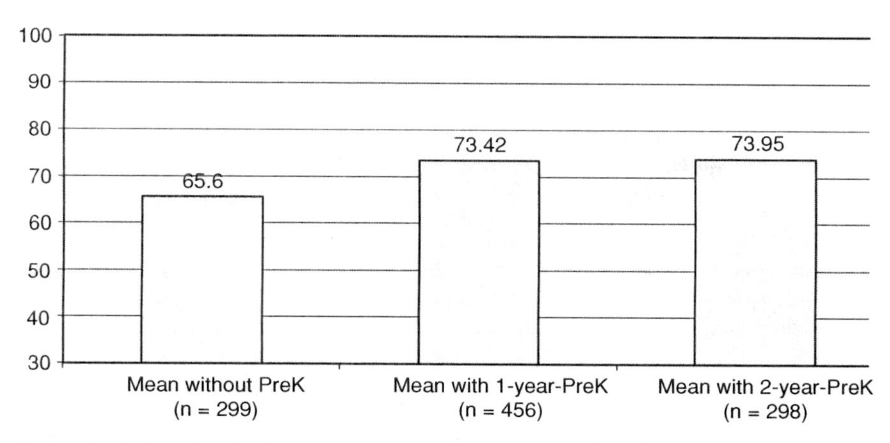

Figure 11.6. Longitudinal study print awareness scores at kindergarten entry by years of attendance (% correct) ($N = 1{,}053$).

as at kindergarten entry. At kindergarten entry (see Fig. 11.6), the estimated effects of Abbott preschool education were statistically significant and equaled 7.8% more items correct (es = .29) for 1 year and 8.4% more items correct (es = .31) for 2 years. By the end of kindergarten, only the estimated effect of 2 years (1.9%, es = .14) remained significant, but it is apparent that many children topped out on the measure. Even the no-treatment group scored on average 91% correct by the end of kindergarten, compared to about 93% for the 1- and 2-year groups. Although one can interpret these results as reflecting a measurement problem, they can also be viewed as evidence that most children master this skill by the end of kindergarten regardless of previous experiences.

To compare the RDD and longitudinal results, we reestimated the effects of Abbott preschool education on the PPVT at kindergarten entry using raw scores. In the raw-score analyses, 1 year of preschool education at age 4 was estimated to increase PPVT scores by 4.06 raw-score points. This effect was slightly smaller (11%) than the estimated 4.57-point gain found using the RDD approach. However, using the longitudinal-study comparison group, the immediate estimated effects of 1 year of preschool were reduced by 37% for math (.86 versus 1.36 RDD) and 44% for print awareness (7.8% versus 14% RDD). These findings suggest that sample selection bias may be leading to substantial underestimation of program effects in the longitudinal study.

DISCUSSION

Considerable attention and resources have been invested in the Abbott Preschool Program. Its relatively high per-pupil cost of around $11,000 reflects not only New Jersey's high cost of living (K–12 costs $14,000 per child) but also high program standards. The program operates for a full school day, employs licensed teachers paid on the same scale as public school teachers, has a maximum class size of 15 with an assistant teacher assigned to each classroom, and has dedicated staff to work with parents (Barnett, Hustedt, Hawkinson, & Robin, 2006). It is also notable that most classrooms are operated by private providers under contract to the public schools. The population served by the Abbott districts is made up primarily of low-income families of Hispanic and African American origins. Thus, there is a great deal of interest in how effective Abbott classrooms are in helping to improve the knowledge, skills, and dispositions of these children as they enter kindergarten and proceed through school. This chapter brings together evidence from several different types of analyses to address this question.

The effectiveness of any program depends on how well it is implemented, but quality of implementation is not always analyzed in program evaluations. In this study, we assessed program quality using multiple instruments. These assessments indicated that program quality was generally good and that it was considerably higher for the cohort of children in our study than it was several years earlier before full implementation of Abbott preschool standards. However, the quality assessments were not so high as to preclude further improvements. The level of quality observed led us to expect moderate gains for children. Somewhat smaller gains might be expected in math given the relatively poor performance of teachers on the math observation. However, it also may be the case that the children had fewer supports for math learning (compared to language and literacy) outside the classroom. The scores on the most commonly used assessment of classroom quality were similar to those found for many other public preschool education programs, which supports some generalization of the results from this study.

Earlier studies – including analyses employing RDD on a somewhat broader sample of Abbott districts (Barnett, Jung, Lamy, Wong, & Cook, 2007; Wong, Cook, Barnett, & Jung, 2008) – had indicated that the Abbott Preschool Program had beneficial effects on children's skills at kindergarten entry (Frede et al., 2004; Lamy et al., 2005). We found positive effects on children's learning in the areas of oral language, literacy, and math skills, with effect sizes that ranged from .20 to .56 depending on the measure and research design. The effects of 2 years were significantly and substantially larger for language and math but not for print awareness. Despite evidence of downward bias in the longitudinal-study estimates, we found that substantial gains in language and math persisted through the end of kindergarten. By the end of kindergarten, the test of print awareness was no longer age appropriate, and most children had mastered the print-awareness skills tested. Thus, conclusions regarding the persistence of program effects on literacy other than oral language cannot really be drawn.

Children's early print-awareness and receptive-vocabulary skills have been found to predict reading abilities in the early elementary grades (Snow,

Burns, & Griffin, 1998). Thus, the effects found in this study are the first link in a chain that can produce the long-term school success and economic benefits found in other preschool education studies that have followed children into adulthood (Campbell, Ramey, Pungello, Sparling, & Miller-Johnson, 2002; Ou & Reynolds, 2006; Schweinhart et al., 2005).

We conducted two separate studies of program effects at kindergarten entry to address concerns that the simple comparison of children who attended and those who did not attend Abbott Preschool Programs might be biased by unmeasured differences between the groups. This does seem to have been the case. The RDD, which attempts to control for these unmeasured differences, provided estimates for the effects of 1 year of preschool education that were higher by 11% for language (PPVT), 37% for math, and 44% for print awareness. These findings indicate that the estimated effects in our longitudinal study underestimate the effects of preschool by meaningful amounts.

Thus, even though the longitudinal study addresses the question of the extent to which effects may fade out over time, it must be understood that this study somewhat underestimated the effects of the Abbott Preschool Program. At least for PPVT, the underestimation seemed to be fairly modest. Results of the study indicated that there were persistent effects on children's learning through the end of kindergarten, with only modest declines in the advantages from attending Abbott Preschool Programs for language and math. (Curiously, the largest decline was for the effect of 1 year of preschool education on math scores, and the smallest decline for the effect of 2 years of preschool education on math scores.) Tests at the end of first grade will include measures of literacy more broadly.

Very little research exists that compares the effects of 1 year versus 2 years of preschool attendance. Children who attended the Abbott Preschool Program for 2 years at ages 3 and 4 outperformed children who attended for only 1 year at age 4 and those who did not attend on all of the outcome measures, with one exception. The gains in language and math from 2 years were quite large, nearly double for language and 70% larger for math. In contrast, children who had 2 years of preschool did not score significantly differently from those who had 1 year on the Print Awareness test. This is not a great surprise because this test is designed to assess preschool children's preschool literacy skills, and the majority of the children score well on it by the end of kindergarten.

Caution must be used in interpreting these results. We cannot control for possible selection bias across the groups. Parents who know about and choose to send their children to preschool at age 3 may be different in immeasurable ways from those who only send them at age 4. For this comparison, we do not have the estimates from the more rigorous RDD to verify our results. Yet, because this is a large-scale study and it is fairly safe to assume that the quality of the program was similar for both years, one can have confidence in the findings.

FUTURE RESEARCH DIRECTIONS

We plan to continue the present study until the children in the study sample complete third grade. In future analyses, it will be important to add literacy skills measures that are age appropriate and to expand data collection to include information on grade retention and special-education placement, as well as achievement-test results. In addition, it would be useful to add a measure of social and emotional development because recent studies have shown that well-designed preschool education programs can produce positive gains in self-regulation and other areas of development that are at least as important for later life success as the domains measured by achievement tests (Diamond, Barnett, Thomas, & Munro, 2007).

One aspect of the Abbott Preschool Program that is unusual is that rather than targeting individuals who are from low-income families, it serves entire communities with high percentages of children from low-income families. This approach may have resulted in differences in who participates that go beyond permitting the participation of children from higher income families. These differences may obtain only to universal programs and not those serving only low-income families. The inclusion of children from a broader range of backgrounds could have improved the preschool learning experiences for children from low-income families, as well as their kindergarten learning experiences; for example, by improving the classroom climate, allowing teachers to spend less time on remediation, or even raising the overall level of classroom interactions. Future studies that could shed light on these questions would undoubtedly be useful.

Studies that focus on the contributions of quality and quantity to program effectiveness would seem to be desirable. This program seems to have larger effects than typical early education and child care programs but smaller effects than found for some others. In this current study, we did not have sufficient resources to tie the classroom quality scores in preschool to the child outcome data. Future research designed to do this would help determine the relationship between level of implementation and program effectiveness. Randomized trials that study both program standards and observed program quality (perhaps using coaching or other approaches to professional development to induce changes in quality) would be especially useful. A better understanding of the dosage of specific math and literacy classroom practices that is necessary to produce large gains in children's learning might be obtained from such studies. Prospective studies comparing the effects of 1 year of preschool education at age 4 versus 2 years of preschool education starting at age 3 also appear to be warranted.

Our study suggests that selection bias can be a problem in the commonly used nonequivalent comparison-group studies. However, selection bias might be less of a problem in studies with many good statistical controls for family background and home learning experiences, and a pretest measure of children's abilities. Of course, preschool program evaluations often lack pretest measures because of the difficulties of identifying children who do not attend a preschool education program prior to kindergarten entry. Additional studies comparing results of randomized trials, RDD, and more typical quasi-experimental designs using overlapping data for the same program and population would be extremely useful.

IMPLICATIONS FOR POLICY

The results of this study add to the considerable body of evidence indicating that quality preschool education can make significant contributions to children's learning and development (Frede, 1998). It also adds to the evidence that substantial benefits persist at least through the end of kindergarten. Moreover, this study confirms that such effects can be produced with today's children on a large scale by a public program administered through the public schools, reinforcing recent findings from Tulsa, Oklahoma (see Chapter 9) (Gormley, Gayer, Phillips, & Dawson, 2005). The population in this study was largely minority, heavily Hispanic, and mostly low income. However, the program was not targeted to individuals but rather to communities with large percentages of children from low-income families. This may or may not have contributed to its success, but it appears to be one effective strategy. The Abbott Preschool Program had high program standards, and the contrast between its estimated impacts and those of more typical child care and other programs should give policy makers one more reason to be circumspect about the potential for programs with lower standards to produce similarly strong results (Magnuson, Ruhm, & Waldfogel, 2007; NICHD Early Child Care Research Network, 2006).

This study establishes that public programs can produce reasonably strong results using private providers. States and localities that find it difficult to expand the public school system to provide preschool education because of space limitations and other constraints should consider a mixed-delivery system using public schools, private schools and child care centers, and Head Start agencies. Private programs can provide equally effective preschool education as long as they are held to the same high standards as public schools and receive public funds adequate to meet those standards. In the Abbott program, oversight from the state and local schools provides financial and educational accountability (Frede, 2005). Whether other approaches that grant private programs more autonomy and depend on parent choice in the market for educational accountability would produce similar results is unknown.

Two of the studies most widely cited in support of public investments in preschool education are the Perry Preschool (see Chapter 7) and Chicago Child-Parent Center studies (see Chapter 8) (Reynolds et al., 2007; Schweinhart et al., 2005). In both of these studies, the preschool programs provided most children with 2 years of education beginning at age 3. Our study suggests that it would be unwise to expect similar results from 1 year of preschool education, even if other characteristics of the program were equivalent. Policy makers who are seeking to enhance the effectiveness of their investments in preschool education, including those focused on decreasing the achievement gap between advantaged and disadvantaged children, should consider serving children for at least 2 years beginning at age 3. Other studies suggest that this is not the only quantity issue relating to effectiveness and that length of the day and of the school year are also deserving of scrutiny by policy makers seeking better educational outcomes (Robin, Frede, & Barnett, 2006).

One final lesson for policy makers from this study is that it can be important to avoid rushing to evaluate the effectiveness of a new program. Programs take time to develop and to be implemented as intended. Initial program evaluations might best focus on determining whether the program is implemented as designed and how well it is actually delivering education. Such studies provide valuable information to those responsible for developing the program. Once an acceptable quality level is attained, including quality of classroom practice, then evaluation of the effects on children's learning and development can reveal the extent to which implementing the program as planned achieves desired goals. Premature evaluation of outcomes without attention to implementation could easily find only that an inadequately developed, partially, or even poorly implemented program was not very effective.

REFERENCES

Arnold, D. H., Fischer, P. H., Doctoroff, G. L., & Dobbs, J. (2002). Accelerating math development in Head Start classrooms. *Journal of Educational Psychology, 94*, 762–770.

Barnett, W. S., Hustedt, J. T., Hawkinson, L. E., & Robin, K. B. (2006). *The state of preschool 2006: State preschool yearbook.* New Brunswick, NJ: National Institute for Early Education Research.

Barnett, W. S., Jung, K., Lamy, C., Wong, V., & Cook, T. (2007, March). *Effects of five state prekindergarten programs on early learning.* Paper presented at the biannual Society for Research in Child Development, Boston.

Barnett, W. S., Tarr, J., Esposito Lamy, C., & Frede, E. (2002). *Fragile lives, shattered dreams: A report on implementation of preschool education in New Jersey's Abbott districts.* Rutgers University, New Brunswick, NJ: CEER.

Campbell, F. A., Ramey, C. T., Pungello, E. P., Sparling, J., & Miller-Johnson, S. (2002). Early childhood education: Young adult outcomes from the Abecedarian Project. *Applied Developmental Science, 6*, 42–57.

Cook, T. D., & Campbell, D. T. (1979). *Quasi experimentation: Design and analysis issues for field settings.* Boston: Houghton Mifflin.

Diamond, A., Barnett, W. S., Thomas, J., & Munro, S. (2007). Preschool program improves cognitive control. *Science, 318*, 1387–1388.

Dunn, L. M., & Dunn, L. M. (1997). *Peabody Picture Vocabulary Test* (3rd ed.) (PPVT-3). Circle Pines, MN: American Guidance Service.

Dunn, L. M., Padilla, E. R., Lugo, D. E., & Dunn, L. M. (1986). *Test de Vocabulario En Imágenes Peabody (TVIP).* Circle Pines, MN: American Guidance Service.

Early, D. M., et al. (2007). Teachers' education, classroom quality, and young children's academic skills: Results from seven studies of preschool programs. *Child Development, 78*(2), 558–580.

Frede, E. (1998). A sociocultural analysis of the long-term benefits of preschool for children in poverty. In W. S. Barnett & S. S. Boocock (Eds.), *Early care and education: Lasting effects for children in poverty* (pp. 77–98). Buffalo, NY: SUNY Press.

Frede, E. (2005). *Assessment in a continuous improvement cycle: New Jersey's Abbott preschool program.* Invited paper for the National Early Childhood Accountability Task Force with support from the Pew Charitable Trusts, the Foundation for Child Development, and the Joyce Foundation.

Frede, E., Jung, K., Barnett, W. S., Lamy, C. E., & Figueras, A. (2007) *The Abbott Preschool Program Longitudinal Effects Study (APPLES).* National Institute for Early Education Research Online Report. Retrieved from http://www.nieer.org/docs/index.php?DocID=173.

Frede, E., Lamy, C. E., & Boyd, J. S. (2005). *Not just calendars and counting blocks: Using the NAEYC/NCTM joint position statement "Early childhood mathematics: Promoting good beginnings" as a basis for measuring classroom teaching practices and their relationship to child outcome.* Paper presented at the annual conference of the National Association for the Education of Young Children, Washington, DC.

Frede, E., Lamy, C. E., with Seplocha, H., Strasser, J., Jambunathan, S., Juncker, J., & Wolock, E. (2004). *A rising tide: Classroom quality and language skills in the Abbott Preschool Program: Year two preliminary update of the early learning improvement consortium.* Trenton, NJ: New Jersey Department of Education. Retrieved from http://www.nj.gov/njded/ece.

Frede, E., Weber, M., Hornbeck, A., Stevenson-Boyd, J., & Colon, A. (2005). *Preschool classroom mathematics inventory.* Available from the first author at http://www.efrede@nieer.org.

Ginsburg, H. P., Inoue, N., & Seo, K. H. (1999). Young children doing mathematics: Observations of everyday activities. In J. Copley (Ed.), *Mathematics in the early years* (pp. 88–100). Washington, DC: NAEYC.

Gormley, W. T., Gayer, T., Phillips, D., & Dawson, B. (2005). The effects of universal pre-K on cognitive development. *Developmental Psychology, 41*(6), 872–884.

Harms, T., Clifford, R., & Cryer, D. (2005). *Early childhood environment rating scale (ECERS-R)* (rev. ed.). New York: Teachers College Press.

Lamy, C., Frede, E., & ELIC. (2005). *Giant steps for the littlest children: Progress in the sixth year of the Abbott Preschool Program.* Trenton, NJ: New Jersey Department of Education. Retrieved from http://www.nj.gov/njded/ece.

Lonigan, C., Wagner, R., Torgeson, J., & Rashotte, C. (2002). *Preschool comprehensive test of phonological and print processing (Pre-CTOPPP).* Tallahassee: Florida State University, Department of Psychology.

Magnuson, K., Ruhm, C., & Waldfogel, J. (2007). Does prekindergarten improve school preparation and performance? *Economics of Education Review, 26*, 33–51.

National Council of Teachers of Mathematics & National Association for the Education of Young Children [NCTM & NAEYC]. (2002). *Early childhood mathematics: Promoting good beginnings. A joint position statement of the National Association for the*

Education of Young Children (NAEYC) and the National Council for Teachers of Mathematics (NCTM). Retrieved from http://www.naeyc.org/about.positions/psmath.asp or http://www.nctm.org/about/content.aspx?id=6352.

NICHD Early Child Care Research Network (2006). Child care effect sizes for the NICHD Study of Early Child Care and Youth Development. *American Psychologist, 61*, 99–116.

New Jersey Department of Education (2004a). *New Jersey kindergarten core curriculum content standards.* Trenton: Author.

New Jersey Department of Education (2004b). *New Jersey preschool teaching and learning expectations: Standards of quality.* Trenton: Author.

New Jersey Department of Education. (2005). *Abbott Preschool Program implementation guidelines* (rev. ed.). Trenton: Author.

Ou, S., & Reynolds, A. J. (2006). Early childhood intervention and educational attainment: Age 22 findings from the Chicago Longitudinal Study. *Journal of Education for Students Placed at Risk, 11*(2), 175–198.

Reynolds, A. J., Temple, J. A., Ou, S., Robertson, D. L., Mersky, J. P., Topitzes, J. W., et al. (2007). Effects of a school-based, early childhood intervention on adult health and well-being: A 19-year follow-up of low-income families. *Archives of Pediatrics and Adolescent Medicine, 161*(8), 730–739.

Robin, K., Frede, E., & Barnett, W. S. (2006). *Is more better? The effects of full-day vs. half-day preschool on early school achievement.* Retrieved from http://www.nieer.org/docs/index.php?DocID=144.

Schweinhart, L. J., Montie, J., Xiang, Z., Barnett, W. S., Belfield, C. R., & Nores, M. (2005). *Lifetime effects: The HighScope Perry Preschool study through age 40* (Monographs of the HighScope Educational Research Foundation, 14). Ypsilanti, MI: HighScope Educational Research Foundation.

Smith, S., Davidson, S., & Weisenfeld, G. (2001). *Supports for early literacy assessment for early childhood programs serving preschool-age children.* New York: New York University.

Snow, C., Burns, M. S., & Griffin, P. (Eds.). (1998). *Preventing reading difficulties in young children.* Washington, DC: National Academy Press.

StataCorp. 2005. *Stata Statistical Software: Release 9.* College Station, TX: StataCorp LP.

Trochim, W. M. K. (1984). *Research design for program evaluation: The regression-discontinuity approach.* Beverly Hills, CA: Sage Publications.

Wagner, R., Torgeson, J., & Rashotte, C. (1999). *Comprehensive test of phonological processing (CTOPP).* Austin, TX: Pro-Ed.

Wong, V. C., Cook, T. D., Barnett, W. S., & Jung, K. (2008). An effectiveness-based evaluation of five state prekindergarten programs. *Journal of Policy Analysis and Management, 27*(1), 122–154.

Woodcock, R. W., McGrew, K. S., & Mather, N. (2001). *Woodcock-Johnson tests of achievement.* Itasca, IL: Riverside.

Woodcock, R. W., & Munoz, A. F. (1990). *Bateria Woodcock-Munoz pruebas de aprovechamiento – Revisados.* Itasca, IL: Riverside.

Commentary: Are We Promising Too Much for Preschool Education Programs?

EDWARD ZIGLER

I have been closely involved with our nation's Head Start program since the 1960s. I was on the project's planning committee, served for 2 years as the federal official responsible for administering it, and have since advised every presidential administration – both Democrat and Republican – on Head Start issues. I have been witness to the advances and retreats, the positives and negatives, in how early intervention has been perceived by decision makers, scientists, and the public over the years. Certain facts in the history of early intervention have been lost in the mist of time, and you know what they say about those who do not know history being destined to repeat it. The primary purpose of this brief paper is to remind readers of these facts so they can recognize the patterns before they again bedevil our efforts on behalf of young children.

Shortly after the birth of Head Start, both Bettye Caldwell and I feared that the program was being oversold and could not possibly fulfill the expectations that policy makers such as President Johnson and his War on Poverty czar, Sargent Shriver, had raised. The president confidently promised Americans that Head Start would soon put an end to poverty and enable the preschool graduates to avoid welfare dependency, crime, and imprisonment when they grew up. This was certainly a lot to expect from an untried program that enrolled poor children for a mere 6 to 8 weeks during the summer before they began elementary school, which is how the program started.

For his part, Shriver created Head Start for the practical reason of preparing poor children for school entry. When he became enamored with Susan Grey's experimental project that appeared to increase the IQ scores of children with mental retardation, he thought Head Start could do the same for poor children of average intelligence. Although he only used this card when it was politically expedient to do so, the notion that Head Start could make children smarter was impossible to uproot once it was planted. Scientists obliged and conducted study after study showing that children's IQ scores did go up after their brief Head Start experience. Once this advantage was found to be fleeting, the Head

Start program was put on the federal chopping block. In fact, one of my first assignments when I arrived in Washington was to phase the program out over the next 3 years. My superior, Elliot Richardson, saved Head Start by appealing directly to the White House.

We knew in the 1960s that growing up in poverty was detrimental to a child's development. In the years since, we have learned a great deal about the extent to which specific mechanisms of poverty can compromise a child's potential. However, even before this evidence was in, Head Start's planners never believed that a brief summer program would have much effect on a poor child's life-course. We just didn't do a good job convincing policy makers and the public. Once the momentum built, we could not extinguish their hopes that this one little program could eradicate the centuries-old problem of poverty and make poor children smarter to boot.

The story was repeated in the 1990s when studies using neurological imaging revealed that brain development in the earliest years of life could be tracked and potentially linked to environmental events. Suddenly, there was a revival of the belief that enriched early experiences can accelerate cognitive development. No wonder Head Start didn't boost intelligence; it was offered too late in the cycle of the developing brain. Efforts to extend Head Start to younger children had begun shortly after the program did, but the early brain research gave advocates the ammunition they needed to validate an expansion of Head Start services to infants and toddlers. Although I believe with all my heart in the wisdom and value of Early Head Start, I fear it was advertised for the wrong reasons. Neurological science only shows us how brain development works, not how to make it work faster or better. If Early Head Start is eventually shown to have no demonstrable effect on synaptic development or, for that matter, if the Family and Medical Leave Act cannot be shown to change the brain's architecture, support for these worthy efforts will inevitably decline.

Although after 45 years we should know better, the tendency to imbue Head Start with unreal expectations of what the program can achieve persists. In a recent example, former president George W. Bush criticized Head Start on the grounds that the at-risk children who attend do not attain the same degree of school readiness as more affluent children. Of course they don't. Head Start cannot single-handedly fix broken families, raise incomes, quell neighborhood violence, improve health care and nutrition, and provide the multitude of enriching experiences middle-class children have before they set foot in preschool. In response to Bush's comments, Jeanne Brooks-Gunn (2003) wrote a report she titled, "Do You Believe in Magic?" It is magical thinking indeed to expect a year or two of preschool to eliminate the persistent achievement gap between poor and wealthier children.

There has never been an inoculation against the injurious effects of poverty, even if it is several years of a model intervention program. I have argued that to overcome the ravages of poverty on human development, we must mount three dovetailed efforts: a home-visiting program from pregnancy to 3 years of age, followed by 2 years of high-quality preschool and then coordinated programming from kindergarten through the third grade. I believe this is the intensity of programming required to offset the harmful developmental effects of poverty.

Today's most vocal preschool-education advocates are economists, and they strike me as a mixed blessing. Their approach is to quantify early intervention's monetary benefits. Their cost-benefit analyses support their argument that early childhood programs are a good investment for taxpayers and will eventually raise the quality of the American workforce and ensure our nation's productivity and competitiveness in global markets. The literature and the media are filled with their varying estimates that every dollar spent on early childhood programs saves $7, or $41, or provides an 18% return on investment, or some other tantalizing figure. It seems to me the economists have brought the field full circle to Head Start's beginnings when the program was hurt by promises that this little preschool gesture would end poverty in America. If the savings to society the economists are promising do not materialize or cannot be precisely quantified, the concept of early intervention will again disappoint. State preschool programs, many of which were mounted on the hope of economic returns, will be threatened or deemed failures.

The economists make their predictions and build their cost-benefit analyses mainly based on three model programs – the HighScope Perry Preschool Program, Abecedarian Project, and Chicago Child-Parent Centers. Allow me to be clear. I believe the HighScope and Abecedarian projects are theoretically of great importance. However, I think it is unwise to make predictions about future benefits based on these two quite small interventions, each done in only one location many years ago. What has been ignored is that the poor children selected for these two programs are not representative of the poor population, so we cannot generalize from these findings to poor children in general. In the early days of intervention, there were close ties between intervention efforts and the desire to reduce the prevalence of mental retardation. Thus, both HighScope and Abecedarian recruited children who were lower in intelligence than most children who live in poverty, many of whom have superior intelligence.

Another problem is that these programs were mounted decades ago, and the results might not be replicable today. The face of poverty has certainly changed, especially with the surge of single-parent, fatherless households. Further, when these studies were done, it was possible to compare the experimental group with controls who had no alternative program. The differences between the groups reflected the poor performance of the controls as well as the enhanced performance of the children who experienced the intervention. Such controls no longer exist. Modern comparisons of experimentals and controls are essentially value-added studies attributed to the intervention. Today, the HighScope control children would probably be attending Head Start or

Michigan's state preschool program. The North Carolina children would be in Head Start or the state's Smart Start Centers.

Another issue is that in absolute terms, the performance of the experimentals in both programs was pretty poor compared to more affluent populations. Although we invariably find that intervention children do better than comparison children, they still are held back in grade and get arrested more frequently than their middle-class peers. Again, let us not oversell how much preschool intervention can accomplish in closing the achievement gap between poor and more advantaged children.

Another problem is that rolling out interventions in the real world where sound implementation and quality have been hard to come by should not be justified on the basis of efficacy studies. The question is: How well will the intervention travel and how will it fare when run by people who are not its inventors? We have no effectiveness evidence on either the HighScope or the Abecedarian projects. As a scholar, I admire the theoretical contribution of these studies, but as a one-time decision maker and an advisor to decision makers, I would ignore them in setting policy. Not only did the creators conceptualize and implement their models, they also evaluated them. One would like arm's-length tests across many sites utilizing the model, which is what we have in the Head Start National Impact Study as well as the evaluation of Early Head Start.

I find myself in agreement with Greg Duncan, who told me the only program among the three famous models worthy of decision makers' attention is the Chicago Child-Parent Centers. The intervention has been conducted with representative poor children across many sites for many years. I also think we should pay much more attention to the Oklahoma universal preschool program, a program of high quality that is being externally evaluated by Bill Gormley and his colleagues. The results to date have certainly been impressive. The NIEER (National Institute for Early Education Research) center and many others are currently providing us with other evidence we need to make a solid case for the benefits of early intervention.

Nonetheless, at this point in time, I do not believe we have the evidentiary base to support the promises we are making to decision makers and the public. I therefore advise caution and restraint. Much more evidence is needed. Thus, we should rely less on programs mounted decades ago and conduct the research on contemporary programs and populations that will give us current data for predictions and cost-benefit analyses. I am not saying that the legacy programs are no longer relevant. They alerted us to the potential of early-intervention programs to have an impact on a wide range of desirable outcomes. I just do not think they should be used as the sole basis for advancing the cause of early childhood intervention or universal preschool, which is what I see being done.

I am not here to depress anyone. The point I am trying to convey is that there is no need to take undue risks by riding the coattails of the latest popular, scientific, or political fads to promote our agenda. When we promise higher IQ scores, an end of poverty, invigorated brain development, or tempting savings from investments in early childhood programming, we promise too much, or at least more than our science can support. Although I approach the evidence skeptically, I remain a champion of the value of both high-quality preschool intervention programs and the concept of home visiting. If we use the evidence we have judiciously and conservatively, I remain optimistic that we will eventually produce the sound empirical base adequate to the task of informing policy makers about the best course of action to take to improve the life chances of children who live in poverty.

REFERENCE

Brooks-Gunn, J. (2003). Do you believe in magic? What we can expect from early childhood intervention programs. *SRCD Social Policy Report, 17*, 3–14.

PART III

KINDERGARTEN AND EARLY SCHOOL-AGE SERVICES AND PRACTICES

12

Opportunity in Early Education: Improving Teacher–Child Interactions and Child Outcomes

ANDREW J. MASHBURN AND ROBERT C. PIANTA

INTRODUCTION

Attending preschool produces short-term and long-term benefits for children and benefits to communities that outweigh the costs of providing those programs (e.g., Barnett & Masse, 2007; FPG Child Development Institute, 2005; Lamb & Ahnert, 2006; Lazar, Darlington, Murray, Royce, & Snipper, 1982; Reynolds, 2000; Reynolds, Temple, Robertson, & Mann, 2001; Schweinhart, Barnes, & Weikart, 1993). The ability to realize these benefits for children and communities depends in part on whether preschool programs are designed and structured in ways that maximize opportunities for children to learn and develop within these settings. Policy makers are currently debating decisions to invest in specific program features intended to optimize outcomes for children, such as requiring teachers to have a bachelor's degree or specialized training in early childhood education, mandating small class sizes, adopting intensive professional development programs, and instituting systems of program quality monitoring. These decisions have implications for both the costs of providing preschool programs and the benefits for children who attend.

To help inform decision making about the optimal design of preschool settings, a generation of experimental and natural-history studies about preschool quality clearly demonstrates that variations in how programs are structured have consequences for children's physical and psychological well-being and

Support for writing this chapter came from the Institute of Education Sciences, U.S. Department of Education, through Grant R305A060021 to the University of Virginia. The research reported in this chapter was funded by (a) the U.S. Department of Education's Institute of Education Sciences, which supports the work conducted by the National Center for Research in Early Childhood Education; and (b) the National Institute of Child Health and Human Development and the Interagency Consortium on School Readiness, which support the work conducted by the MyTeachingPartner Study team. However, the contents of this chapter do not necessarily represent the positions or policies of the funding agencies, and endorsement by these agencies should not be assumed.

development of social and academic competencies (e.g., Howes, 1990; NICHD-Early Child Care Research Network (ECCRN), 1999, 2002; Peisner-Feinberg & Burchinal, 1997; Peisner-Feinberg et al., 2001). However, across these numerous studies, there is mixed evidence concerning which program features have the strongest impacts on which developmental outcomes and for whom, triggering debates about which, if any, of these features should be the focus of policy or program development initiatives.

This inconsistency across the literature in results, conclusions, and interpretations of evidence about the associations between preschool quality and children's development is the focus of the present chapter. We argue that one reason for these inconsistent findings has been an improper assumption, evident in both theory and analytic approach, that all features of preschool programs that are collapsed under the category of preschool quality *directly* affect children's development. We further posit that one specific component of preschool quality – the quality of interactions that children directly experience with adults, peers, and learning materials – is the mechanism responsible for the positive effects of early education on child outcomes. We then discuss implications of this perspective for improving preschool programs in ways that most effectively support children's development of school-readiness skills. The remainder of this chapter has two primary aims: (a) to describe a theoretical framework based on the bioecological model of development (Bronfenbrenner & Morris, 2006) that clarifies how different features of the preschool ecology are proposed to affect children's development, and (b) to discuss the implications of this framework for designing in-service teacher professional development programs and teacher education programs that lead to positive impacts on children's school readiness.

PRESCHOOL ECOLOGY AND CHILDREN'S DEVELOPMENT

Nearly every regulation pertaining to public preschool programs emphasizes the importance of creating a high-quality preschool environment that maximizes children's opportunities to learn. However, despite all of the attention directed toward high-quality preschool, there is no singular approach for conceptualizing, defining, or measuring preschool quality. For example, teachers may define high-quality preschool in terms of the type of curriculum used and the quality of the space, furnishings, and learning materials that support their implementation of this curriculum. Parents' definitions may concern whether the program is open for extended hours, is located near their home or work, has flexible scheduling; whether teachers appear emotionally supportive of their children's needs; or whether children are learning letters and numbers. Professional organizations concerned with the well-being of young children (e.g., the American Public Health Association and the American Academy of Pediatrics [APHA & AAP, 1992], the National Association for the Education of

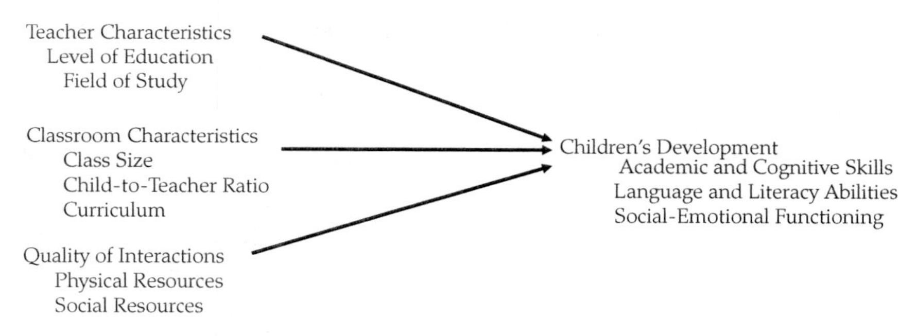

Figure 12.1. Direct effects of ecological features of preschool on children's development.

Young Children [NAEYC, 2005], and the National Institute for Early Education Research [NIEER] (Barnett, Hustedt, Robin, & Schulman, 2007) typically define preschool quality as whether teachers, classrooms, and programs meet recommended minimum standards regulated through program policies.

A long history of research on effective preschool programs has included numerous definitions and measures of preschool quality to examine the impacts of specific features of preschool quality on children's school readiness, and a simplified version of Bronfenbrenner's (1979) ecological systems theory of development has served as the predominant organizing framework that has guided much of this research. This theory generally posits that individuals are embedded within multiple ecological settings that affect development. The most proximal influences on development are the multiple *microsystems* within which the individual spends time, most notably the family and school/classroom environment. Development is also affected by *mesosystems* that comprise interactions among microsystems (e.g., connections between the family and school/classroom); the *exosystem*, which includes distal forces such as the school system, the community, and the mass media; and the *macrosystem*, which involves even more distal inputs such as societal conditions, economic patterns, and national customs and values. Guided by this theory, much of the research related to effective preschool programs has examined the extent to which children's development is directly influenced by variable features of the preschool ecology, including characteristics of teachers and the classroom and the nature of children's experiences within the preschool milieu.

Figure 12.1 depicts this ecological systems framework that has served as the implicit model guiding much of the research about the effects of preschool quality on children's outcomes. Not surprisingly, results from these studies have provided a convoluted story about which features of preschool programs influence which developmental outcomes and for whom. In general, results have supported a positive association between higher preschool quality (defined heterogeneously) and children's development of school-related competencies (Bryant, Burchinal, Lau, & Sparling, 1994; Dunn, 1993; Hestenes,

Kontos, & Bryant, 1993; Howes, Phillips & Whitebook, 1992; Howes & Smith, 1995; Lamb & Ahnert, 2006; NICHD-ECCRN, 1999; NICHD-ECCRN, 2002; Peisner-Feinberg & Burchinal, 1997; Peisner-Feinberg et al., 2001; Schliecker, White, & Jacobs, 1991; Vandell, Henderson & Wilson, 1988). However, relations between preschool quality and development tend to be small (NICHD-ECCRN & Duncan, 2003); significant associations are not evident across all studies (e.g., Chin-Quee & Scarr, 1994; Deater-Deckard, Pinkerton, & Scarr, 1996; Goelman & Pence, 1987; Kontos, 1991; Kontos & Feine, 1987); results may depend in part on child characteristics such as gender (Baydar & Brooks-Gunn, 1991; Bryant et al., 1994), race/ethnicity (Bryant, Peisner-Feinberg, & Clifford, 1993; Burchinal, Ramey, Reid, & Jaccard, 1995; Peisner-Feinberg & Burchinal, 1997), and home and family risk factors (Baydar & Brooks-Gunn, 1991; Bryant et al., 1994; Caughy, DiPietro, & Strobino, 1994; Hagekull & Bohlin, 1995; Peisner-Feinberg & Burchinal, 1997); and results depend on which features of program quality and which developmental outcomes are included in studies and how they are measured. Thus, the general conclusion that higher quality preschool has a positive impact on children's school readiness is modified almost immediately when looking across the literature, with the proviso that it appears that *different features of preschool programs have different impacts on different developmental outcomes for different children.*

These mixed findings leave policy makers, program administrators, and early childhood educators who are responsible for the design of effective preschool programs with little guidance about how to structure programs in ways that are most beneficial for children who attend. As a result, current preschool program improvement efforts and policies have become organized around a wide range of quality metrics, each of which exerts effects on child outcomes in different ways; program development, professional development, and policy efforts have begun to target resources and delivery mechanisms to any or all of these various quality measures. The risk to the field of this lack of clarity is confusion about inputs, outcomes, and the links that connect them, which in the end can erode our capacity to understand effects of early childhood programming, strengthen those effects, and communicate clearly about those effects to the public.

We argue that the lack of cogent understanding of the effects that features of preschool programs have on children's development is due in part to an improper theoretical specification about how ecological features of preschool programs such as teacher and classroom characteristics act to affect children. The original ecological systems theory (Bronfenbrenner, 1979) identifies the importance of interactions across the multiple levels of this ecology by positing that distal conditions and forces influence development at least in part as a consequence of how they shape proximal processes and opportunities that individuals directly experience within microsystems. Thus, from a conceptual standpoint, this theory indicates that understanding the ecology of early childhood education and its effects on child development would require careful attention to ways in which features of the ecology interact with one another – moderating and mediating effects and influences over time – in relation to child outcomes; this is a fairly complex framework that would shape equally complex research designs and understandings of policy and program development. However, the framework as it has been most often applied to the study of preschool quality and children's development is based on an incomplete and overly simplistic presumption derived from ecological systems theory that all variable features of preschool programs are *directly* associated with development (see Fig. 12.1).

To elevate this nuanced explanation for how ecological settings affect individual development, Bronfenbrenner and Morris (2006) refined the ecological systems theory with the bioecological model of development, which encompasses two propositions that implicate direct, mediating, and moderating effects of the ecology on development. Put simply, the first proposition states that human development takes place through interactions between the individual and the persons, objects, or symbols in the individual's immediate external environment that occur on a fairly regular basis over extended periods of time. The second proposition states that the impacts of these interactions on individual development vary systematically as a function of the environment, person, and time (Bronfenbrenner & Morris, 2006). When applied to preschool settings, these two propositions articulate a more sophisticated and complete specification about how the preschool ecology affects children's development.

In this revised framework, learning within preschool settings is viewed as the direct result of a child's sustained interactions with both physical and social resources in preschool settings. Interactions with physical resources must be appropriate for the ability level of the child, become increasingly complex to meet the growing demands as the child develops, be used regularly and for extended periods to offer continual challenges that promote growth, and can occur in the absence of other individuals. The nature of social interactions between a child and his or her teachers and peers is another direct mechanism through which children develop school-readiness skills, as substantiated numerous times in the literature. For example, classrooms characterized by emotionally supportive interactions between teachers and children are positively associated with children's social development during preschool, and classrooms characterized by rich language and instructional techniques that develop concepts are positively associated with children's development of academic, language, and literacy skills (e.g., Mashburn et al., 2008). Peers have also been shown to make a positive contribution to children's development during preschool (Henry & Rickman, 2007; Mashburn, Justice, Downer, & Pianta, 2009), particularly in classrooms characterized by affectively positive social interactions between teachers and children (Mashburn et al., 2009). Thus, the first proposition about effective preschools that is derived from the

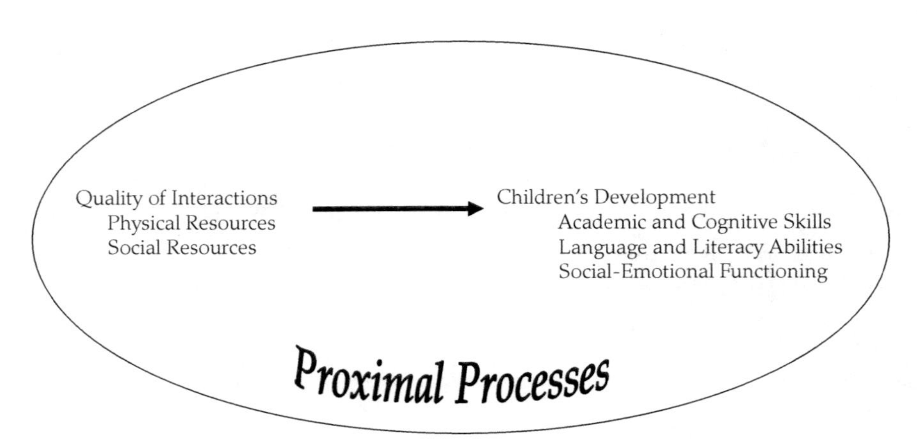

Figure 12.2. Children's interactions with physical and social resources are the proximal processes that promote development.

bioecological model of development posits that *children's frequent and sustained exposure to high-quality physical and social resources is the direct mechanism, or proximal process, through which learning and development occur within preschool settings.* This proposition is depicted in Figure 12.2.

The second proposition of the bioecological model of development applied to preschool programs indicates that the extent to which children's interactions with physical and social resources affect their development depends on characteristics of the individual and of the classroom environment.[1] This statistical interaction between child characteristics and quality of classroom interactions has been supported in numerous studies by results that suggest that children who experience greater social and economic risks benefit more from higher quality social and physical environments than their more advantaged peers (Baydar & Brooks-Gunn, 1991; Bryant et al., 1993, 1994; Burchinal et al., 1995; Caughy et al., 1994; Hagekull & Bohlin, 1995; Mashburn, 2008; Peisner-Feinberg & Burchinal, 1997).

The bioecological model of development also posits that classroom characteristics (e.g., class size, child:teacher ratio, type of curriculum) may affect children's development in two ways. First, as stated in the second proposition, the associations between the quality of children's interactions with physical and social resources in preschool and children's school readiness may be moderated by these features of classroom settings. No studies to date have tested the extent to which the impacts of high-quality classroom processes on children's development are conditioned on features of the classroom such as the number

[1] The impacts of interactions on children's development also depend on time, such that the impacts may be more or less effective for children of different ages or at different developmental stages. Because preschool programs serve children with rather homogeneous ages and developmental stages, the impacts of time on the associations between physical and social interactions on children's development may be less pronounced than in contexts that include children with more variability in age, such as elementary schools.

of children enrolled, the child:teacher ratio, or the type of curriculum used. However, a number of plausible and testable examples follow. Positive social interactions between teachers and children may have a stronger influence on children's development of social competencies in classrooms with lower child:teacher ratios, so that individual children may have more opportunities to engage in supportive interactions directly with a teacher. Classrooms with stimulating and developmentally appropriate physical resources may have a stronger influence on children's development of academic competencies in classrooms that use a curriculum that structures activities in ways that better support children's use of these materials in appropriate ways. Teachers' use of organizational strategies that effectively manage children's behavior may have a stronger influence on children's development of self-regulatory skills within classrooms with fewer students compared to classrooms with many students.

Thus, classroom characteristics such as class size, child:teacher ratio, and curriculum, which have been central to research and policy regarding high-quality preschool, are not proposed to have direct impacts on children's development, as is depicted in Figure 12.1. Instead, the effects of high-quality interactions with social and physical resources on children's development may depend on these features of the classroom environment. In other words, class size, child:teacher ratio, and curriculum type are features of preschool classrooms that may magnify or reduce the direct effects that classroom interactions have on children's development.

In addition to potential moderating effects of classroom characteristics on children's development, classroom characteristics may affect children's development through a mediated process. Specifically, a small class size, low child:teacher ratio, and comprehensive curriculum may directly influence the quality of interactions that children experience in classrooms, which in turn affects children's development. The first step in this mediated pathway has been confirmed in a study of first-grade classrooms that found classrooms with smaller class sizes and lower child:teacher ratios had higher quality instructional and emotional interactions (NICHD-ECCRN, 2004). A mediated process also was tested within preschool classes, and results indicated that the positive effects of small class sizes on children's development of cognitive and social competence were partially mediated by the quality of caregiving that children experienced in classrooms (NICHD-ECCRN, 2002).

Teacher characteristics such as level of education, type of training, and amount of professional development in which teachers participate are also very often the focus of policy and program development efforts. The bioecological model of development posits that these program features may have an impact on children's development; however, the effects are not direct. Instead, higher levels of teacher education, specialized training in early childhood education, and participation in intensive and coherent professional development programs are proposed to affect children's school readiness to the extent that these teacher characteristics improve the quality of emotional, instructional, and organizational interactions that teachers facilitate within their classrooms and the ways that classrooms are structured to provide children with opportunities for sustained engagement with appropriate physical materials. Despite the proposed mediated process in which teacher characteristics affect children's development, nearly all of the preschool-quality research has examined direct associations between teacher characteristics and children's development, with one notable exception. From the NICHD Study of Early Child Care, the positive associations between teachers' levels of education and children's cognitive and social competence were found to be explained, in part, by a higher quality relationship between the caregiver and the child (NICHD-ECCRN, 2002).

Figure 12.3 presents a theoretical model derived from the bioecological model of development (Bronfenbrenner & Morris, 2006) that depicts the proposed moderating and mediating mechanisms through which classroom and teacher characteristics in preschool programs influence children's learning and development. In sum, this ecological framework indicates that features of preschool programs affect development in the following three ways:

1. Children's interactions with physical and social resources in classrooms are the direct mechanisms through which preschool programs transmit benefits to children.
2. Classroom characteristics (e.g., class size, child:teacher ratio, and curriculum) and teacher characteristics (e.g., level of education and field of study) may have indirect effects on children's development to the extent that they have direct impacts on the quality of interactions with physical and social resources that children experience within classrooms.
3. Classroom characteristics are also classroom conditions that may, in part, determine the extent to which high-quality interactions with physical and social resources affect children's development.

IMPLICATIONS OF ECOLOGICAL THEORY FOR IMPROVING SCHOOL READINESS

As discussed in the previous section, the features of preschool settings that matter most for development are the quality of the social and physical resources in classrooms with which children directly and frequently engage. As such, we argue that definitions of preschool quality should primarily focus on these features of preschool programs and that teacher characteristics and classroom conditions should be defined as part of the program design and infrastructure that help support this linkage between the quality of interactions and children's development. This repositioning or reframing is not just a semantic activity – it explicitly defines quality in a more narrow way in terms of interactions that produce developmental change, which has important implications for understanding how preschool affects school readiness. In this section, we discuss

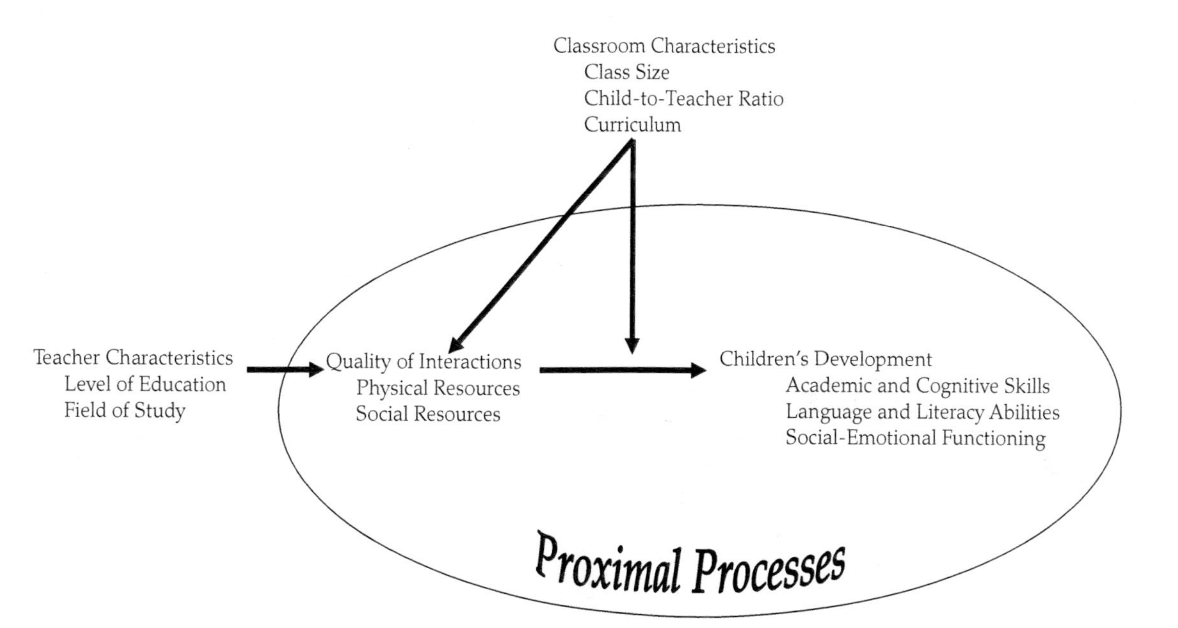

Figure 12.3. Mediated effects of teacher and classroom characteristics and moderated effects of classroom characteristics on children's development.

how this framework also serves as a useful guide for understanding the logic behind how program improvement efforts have an impact on school readiness.

Efforts to improve preschool occur via two common approaches – in-service teacher professional development programs and teacher education programs. As derived from the bioecological model of development, for these program improvement efforts to benefit children's school readiness, they must improve the quality of social interactions between children and teachers and the quality of children's experiences with physical learning materials; failure of these approaches to improve children's experiences will yield no benefits for children's school readiness. Figure 12.4 presents the logic model that identifies this proposed process through which teacher professional development programs and teacher education programs affect children's school readiness. In the next two subsections, we consider examples of a teacher professional development program and a teacher education program that use this logic model as the basis for providing resources and supports to improve the quality of social interactions in preschool classrooms and, in turn, support children's development of school-readiness competencies.

Effective Teacher Professional Development Programs

There is currently widespread agreement that the training and professional development of the early education workforce are key components for ensuring that early childhood education programs make good on the hopes of policy makers, parents, and educators for improving children's success in school (Bogard & Takanishi, 2005; Zaslow & Martinez-Beck, 2005). Consequently, it is of paramount importance to identify effective, relevant, and scalable approaches to training the early education workforce. However, traditional teacher professional development approaches have fallen short in a number of ways. Short-term training programs, many of which are knowledge or technique based, are the most common forms of teacher professional development, but there is virtually no evidence of their effectiveness (Birman, Desimone, Porter, & Garet, 2000; Garet, Porter, Desimone, Birman, & Yoon, 2001), presumably because they tend to place teachers in a passive learner role; content is vague, irrelevant, or disconnected from classroom context; and there is limited follow-up (Haymore-Sandholtz, 2002). Despite the lack of evidence of the effectiveness of commonly used professional development approaches, contemporary estimates of annual spending on professional development range from $2,000 to $7,900 per teacher, which in a city such as Chicago totaled $193 million in 2002 (Odden, Archibald, Fermanich, & Gallagher, 2002).

Drawing from the literature on adult learning (Abdal-Haqq, 1995; Darling-Hammond & McLaughlin, 1995; Putnam & Borko, 1997; Richardson & Anders, 2005), educators have started to reconceptualize professional development as a pursuit of knowledge and skill that is active, collaborative, linked to classroom

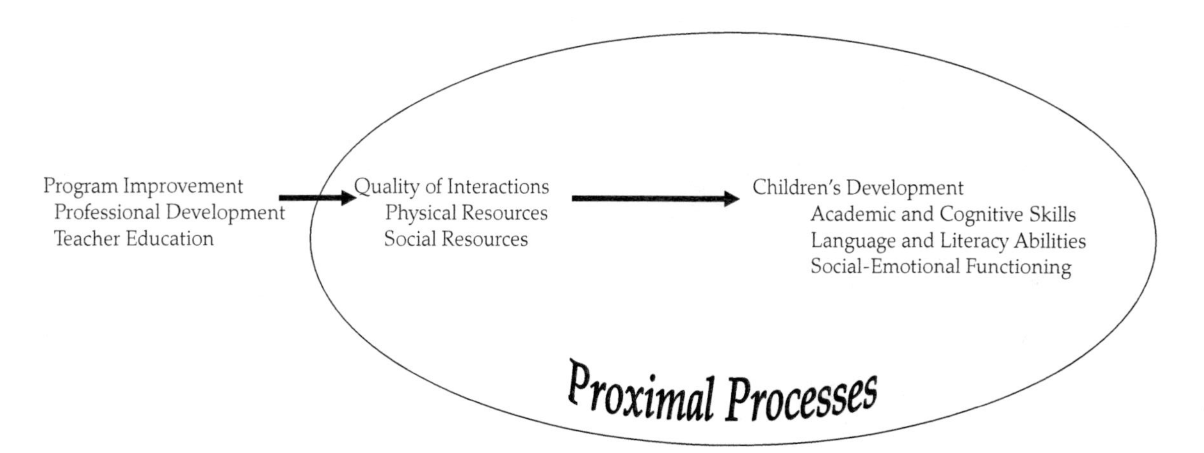

Figure 12.4. Logic model for the impacts of program improvement efforts on children's development.

context, and embedded in school culture (Darling-Hammond & McLaughlin, 1995; Lieberman, 1995). The No Child Left Behind legislation (U.S. Department of Education, 2002) describes high-quality professional development for teachers as intensive, sustained, and classroom focused. Emerging from this reconceptualization of teacher professional development is a shift from a static, knowledge-based focus of training to the use of coaching, mentoring, and consultation approaches that provide more continuous, practice-focused support and guidance to teachers (Ingersoll & Kralik, 2004; Pianta, 2005). Given that consultation approaches are identified by teachers both as relevant and as reducing isolation (a particular problem for pre-K teachers), it is not surprising that new forms of teaching consultation now dominate the teacher-training landscape. The implications of the bioecological model of development suggest that for in-service professional development consultation to improve children's school readiness, it must have an explicit focus and measurable effect on the quality of interactions that children experience within preschool classrooms.

An example of a program that involves professional development consultation designed to improve the quality of classroom interactions is MyTeachingPartner (MTP). MTP is designed to support effective teacher–child interactions in preschool classrooms using a collaborative, web-mediated consultation process and web-based video exemplars of effective practices. Its conceptual basis is that effective professional development for pre-K teachers (and for those in K–12) requires extensive opportunities for (a) *observation* of effective instructional, language, and social interactions between teachers and children, through analysis and viewing of multiple video examples based on validated observation tools; and (b) repeated *opportunities for individualized feedback* and *effectiveness-enhancing support* related to a teacher's own interactions with children (e.g., Hadden & Pianta; 2006; Landry, Swank, Smith, Assel, & Gunnewig, 2006; Pianta, Belsky, Houts, Morrison, & NICHD ECCRN, 2007; Wasik, Bond, & Hindman, 2006). Central to the MTP approach is that *all* observations of classroom interactions, as well as feedback and support to teachers, are based on a shared, standardized framework for defining and observing high-quality social interactions in classrooms – the Classroom Assessment Scoring System (CLASS) (Pianta, La Paro, & Hamre, 2008) – which has been validated via links to growth in child outcomes within large-scale studies, many of which even isolate classroom effects from family influences (Hamre & Pianta, 2007; Mashburn et al., 2008; Pianta et al., 2007).

An initial, experimental study of the effects of MTP tested whether it was both feasible and effective to provide teaching consultation that improves preschool teachers' interactions with children and enhances children's development of literacy, language, and social skills. This study included two types of professional development resources designed to support teachers' implementation of instructional activities: (a) access to video exemplars of high-quality teacher–child interactions tied to specific dimensions of CLASS, and (b) a consultation process that provides regular, multimodal, ongoing, targeted feedback to pre-K teachers through a standardized protocol that focuses on specific dimensions of teachers' emotional, organizational, and instructional interactions with students, using CLASS as the basis for a common, validated understanding of teacher behavior.

To test the feasibility and effectiveness of MTP, teachers were randomly assigned to one of three study conditions: (1) Materials, in which teachers received only language/literacy and social/emotional materials and activities; (2) Web Only, in which teachers received workshop training in the curriculum and had access to the video exemplars; and (3) Consultancy, in which teachers received workshop training and access to the video exemplars and participated in the web-mediated consultation. Teachers in the Web Only and Consultancy conditions videotaped their implementation of an instructional activity and shared this footage with the research team every 2 weeks. In the Consultancy condition, consultation between a teacher and consultant occurred every 2 weeks, which proceeded with the following cycle of events. The teaching consultant edited each tape submitted by the teacher into a series of 1- to 2-minute segments that focused on a specific aspect of social interactions. Those edited segments were posted on a private website so the teacher could view them and respond to specific prompts about the interactions. Teachers and consultants then met online in a video chat to discuss the prompts and feedback and to determine future goals.

The evaluation of MTP indicated that it is feasible to deliver video-based professional development resources to a large number of teachers statewide using the Internet as the medium for access. Specifically, teachers with access to the MTP web resources spent an average of more than 21 minutes on the website per week; teachers who participated in the consultation engaged in an average of more than 12 cycles of observation and feedback with their consultant each year; and, according to their questionnaire responses, teachers were overwhelmingly positive about the helpfulness of the MTP website and consultation process (Downer, Kraft-Sayre, & Pianta, 2009).

This experimental study of the impacts of MTP also found positive effects of the consultation on the quality of classroom interactions. Specifically, differences in the rates of change in the observed quality of teachers' interactions with children were compared for teachers in the Web Only and Consultation conditions (Pianta et al., 2008). Hierarchical linear modeling (HLM) estimated teachers' growth trajectories for each of seven CLASS dimensions of teacher–child interactions over the course of the school year. Teachers assigned to the Consultation condition had more positive growth on each of the seven dimensions of teacher–child interactions than those assigned to the Web Only condition. For three dimensions of interaction quality – Teacher Sensitivity ($d = .82$), Instructional Learning Formats ($d = .77$), and Language Modeling ($d = .97$) – the rates of change were significantly different between the two groups, and the magnitude of the effects on the quality of classroom interactions at the end of the year was large.

In a series of follow-up analyses (Pianta et al., 2008), the effects of the MTP Consultation on improving the quality of classroom interactions were found to be more positive in classrooms with higher proportions of children living in poverty. Specifically, in classrooms with 50% of children classified as poor, there were no differences in the rates of change between teachers in the Consultancy and Web Only conditions. However, in classrooms with 100% of children classified as poor, the differences in rates of changes in Teacher Sensitivity ($d = 2.29$) and Instructional Learning Formats ($d = 2.13$) between teachers randomly assigned to the Consultation and Web Only groups were large.

In addition to these positive effects of the MTP Consultation on the quality of teacher–child interactions in preschool classrooms, particularly in classrooms serving higher proportions of children who experience economic risk, a series of studies provided estimates of the impacts of teachers' participation in MTP on children's development of language, literacy, and social skills. For example, in a series of quasi-experimental, treatment-on-treated analyses, developmental outcomes of children whose teachers were in the Consultation and Web Only conditions were compared to estimate the value-added of the MTP Consultation, while factoring in teachers' compliance to the components of the MTP Consultation (Mashburn, Hamre, Downer, Justice, & Pianta, 2009). A compliance threshold was set for teachers in the Consultation condition – teachers participated cumulatively in consultation activities for 20 hours over the course of 2 years – and child outcomes were compared for teachers in three groups: high-compliant Consultation (more than 20 hours), low-compliant Consultation (less than 20 hours), and Web Only (zero hours). Controlling for relevant covariates (pretest scores and child, teacher, and classroom characteristics), results indicated that children showed higher gains in (a) directly assessed receptive language when their teachers received more than 20 hours of Consultation support, compared to those who were in classrooms with teachers who received less than 20 hours ($d = .42$) or no such support ($d = .57$); and in (b) directly assessed emergent literacy when their teachers received more than 20 hours of Consultation support, compared to those who were in classrooms with teachers who received less than 20 hours ($d = .32$) or no such support ($d = .29$).

Multilevel modeling was also used to estimate mean differences in teachers' ratings of children's end-of-the-year social skills (controlling for beginning-of-the-year social skills, gender, maternal education, and language spoken in the home) among classrooms with teachers participating in the Materials, Web Only, and Consultation conditions (Hamre, Hamagami, Downer, Mashburn, &

Pianta, 2009). There were no differences across study conditions related to children's development of problem behaviors during pre-K. However, there were significant differences related to the children's development of task-oriented competence and one aspect of social skills: assertiveness. Specifically, compared to children whose teachers were assigned to the Materials condition, children whose teachers were assigned to the Web Only and Consultation conditions demonstrated higher levels of task orientation (Consultation vs. Materials: $d = .25$; Web Only vs. Materials: $d = .23$) and assertiveness (Consultation vs. Materials: $d = .36$; Web Only vs. Materials: $d = .29$).

In sum, results from the experimental evaluation of MTP indicate that a web-based, professional development program with consultation that is explicitly focused on improving the quality of emotional, instructional, and organizational interactions in preschool classrooms is feasible, effective in promoting high-quality classroom interactions, and associated with children's development of language, literacy skills, and socio-emotional skills. These findings support the logic model derived from the bioecological model of development that effective teacher professional development programs focused on improving classroom interactions can improve children's school readiness. They also encourage new directions for consultation-based teacher professional development programs that are ongoing, collaborative, and classroom focused and have an explicit goal of improving the quality of teacher–child interactions.

Effective Teacher Education Programs

Enrollment of 3- and 4-year-olds in early education programs now approaches 70% of the population, and the numbers are growing annually (National Institute for Early Education Research [NIEER], Barnett et al., 2007; West, Denton, & Germino-Hausken, 2000). The rapid expansion of public preschool programs has placed heavy demands on the supply chain for early childhood educators, with estimates that 50,000 new teachers will be needed by 2020 (Clifford & Maxwell, 2002). States currently rely on a variety of strategies to meet these needs: Teachers with elementary-grade certifications and teachers with 2-year degrees may be grandfathered into certification (Clifford, Early, & Hills, 1999); many teachers take required courses while already employed and use work sites for student teaching (Howes, James, & Ritchie, 2003); several states address the staffing and qualification crisis by improving salaries and benefits; other states encourage child care and preschool providers to seek additional training; and the early childhood education system becomes more formal and programmatic (see Peters & Bristow, 2005; Pianta, 2005).

These efforts to meet the demand for "trained" teachers are moving ahead rapidly without any systematic evaluation of their impact on the nature and quality of instruction in classrooms and on child outcomes (Clifford et al., 1999; Hart, Stroot, Yinger, & Smith, 2005; Ramey & Ramey, 2005); this is a recipe for continued mediocrity and inequity that will ultimately undermine the promise of early education in closing the achievement gap. Leveraging the value of public investments in preschool education requires that research and development efforts focus on identifying effective and replicable approaches to teacher training that produce positive and even accelerated gains in children's academic performance (Brandon & Martinez-Beck, 2005; Ramey & Ramey, 2005). As described in the bioecological model of development, for teacher training programs to improve children's school readiness, they must produce demonstrable changes in the quality of interactions that children experience within preschool classrooms.

The National Center for Research in Early Childhood Education (NCRECE) has recently begun a large-scale study to develop and test the impacts of a teacher-training program that provides a sequence of focused coursework specifically designed to support high-quality teacher–child interactions in preschool settings. The 14-unit course, titled *Support of Language and Literacy Development in Preschool Classrooms Through Effective Teacher–Child Interactions and Relationships*, teaches teachers to (a) identify specific effective behaviors and interactions in the practice of other teachers and in their own teaching; (b) understand and state clear and explicit intentions for what and how they are teaching and interacting with children; (c) identify how to make use of interactions as instructional opportunities; (d) learn to explicitly target opportunities related to children's language and literacy skills; and (e) learn the language of CLASS, so that they can identify and describe observed interactions using a common language.

A multisite experimental study of the impacts of the course on classroom interactions and children's school readiness is currently underway. In the study, approximately 400 teachers will be randomly assigned to participate in the course or to a control group, and the study will evaluate the impacts of the course on teachers' knowledge about high-quality interactions, observation skills to detect high-quality interactions, quality of classroom interactions, and quality of implementation of language and literacy activities. In addition, six children (three boys and three girls) will be randomly selected from each classroom to determine impacts of teachers' participation in the course on children's development of literacy, language, social, and academic skills.

Further, after the course phase of the study, teachers will be randomized again to participate in either the MTP Consultation or be assigned to a control group. As a result, there will be four groups of teachers (Course/Consultancy, Course/No Consultancy, No Course/Consultancy, No Course/No Consultancy), and analyses will determine the impacts of the course, the Consultation, and the combination of these two programs in producing changes in classroom interactions and children's school readiness. The result of this work will be an organized, manualized training approach for improving teacher–child interactions that may be administered within any of several sectors of the workforce supply chain, including in 2- and 4-year colleges and universities as a part of teachers' preservice training or as an in-service professional development intervention for current teachers.

CONCLUSIONS

Because of the recent creation and expansion of public preschool programs, a majority of children now begin education at age 4. To realize the benefits of preschool programs in closing achievement gaps for children who experience social and economic risks and in reducing the incidence of difficulties among all children in their adjustment to school, preschool settings must be designed and structured in ways that support opportunities for children to learn and develop. Previous research falls short in identifying the mechanisms through which preschool transmits benefits to children who attend. Applying the bioecological model of development (Bronfenbrenner & Morris, 2006) to preschool settings helps advance the understanding about the ecological inputs to children's development. Specifically, the theory proposes that the proximal process through which attending preschool affects children's school readiness is the quality of children's interactions with physical and social resources; classroom characteristics and teacher characteristics may have indirect effects on children's development to the extent that they improve the quality of interactions with physical and social resources that children experience within classrooms; and classroom characteristics are conditions that may, in part, determine the extent to which high-quality interactions affect children's development. The primary implication of this framework is that for any program improvement initiative to benefit children's school readiness, it must improve the quality of children's interactions in preschool classrooms. The MTP professional development approach and the NCRECE course are two promising examples of program improvement efforts to improve children's school readiness by targeting resources and supports for teachers that promote high-quality social interactions in classrooms.

One can also readily see the implications of this bioecological model of development for policy making and policy debates taking place about the best ways to invest program resources to promote school readiness. Policies that require teachers to have a bachelor's degree or specialized training in early childhood education or to participate in professional development programs and those that mandate classrooms to have small class sizes and participate in systems of program quality monitoring all come with costs, and the bioecological model of development provides a framework for estimating the expected benefits of each policy initiative. To the extent that "benefits" are defined in terms of children's development of school-readiness skills, then the effectiveness of any policy initiative depends on its capacity to improve interactive processes in preschool settings. For example, mandating that preschool teachers have a minimum of a bachelor's degree in early childhood education will affect children's school readiness only if the coursework and training in which teachers participate to earn these credentials translate into higher quality experiences for children in preschool classrooms. The failure to recognize this reality and adhere to its implications is likely to result in continued arguments about the importance of this or that structural feature and of investments at that level, which may or may not penetrate to the actual processes that are responsible for learning and development (Hamre & Pianta, 2007).

Finally, the bioecological model of development has implications for the next generation of research on preschool quality and children's outcomes. The general conclusion from previous research – different features of preschool programs have different impacts on different developmental outcomes for different children – provides almost no constructive guidance about how best to structure programs that are most beneficial for children. Future research that is grounded in the bioecological model of development (see Fig. 12.3) involves a fairly complex framework that must examine the hypothesized direct, moderating, and mediating impacts of various features of the preschool ecology on school readiness.

We propose the following agenda for research on effective preschool programs that addresses questions about how and under what conditions ecological features of the preschool programs promote school readiness: Do teachers with bachelor's degrees and/or specialized training in early childhood education provide higher quality emotional, instructional, and organizational interactions in preschool classrooms than teachers with lower levels of education or no specialized training? Do any positive effects on the quality of interactions related to higher teacher education or type of training result in indirect benefits on children's development? Does the quality of classroom interactions depend on the number of children enrolled in the classroom, the child:teacher ratio, or the type of curriculum used? Do any positive effects on the quality of interactions related to a specific class size, child:teacher ratio, or type of curriculum result in indirect benefits on children's development? Which specific dimensions of high-quality social interactions – emotional support, instructional support, and organizational support – have positive impacts on specific dimensions of school readiness (e.g., literacy, language, mathematics, physical, social, and personal)? Are the impacts of high-quality social interactions on children's school readiness stronger when class sizes are smaller, child:teacher ratios are lower, or when a specific curriculum is used? Which specific dimensions of high-quality social interactions have the strongest impacts on school readiness for children who experience greater levels of social or economic risks? The answers to these questions not only will advance our understanding about effective preschool programs but also will lead to the development of policies and program improvement efforts that structure the preschool ecologies in ways that most efficiently and effectively support children's school readiness.

REFERENCES

Abdal-Haqq, I. (1995). *Making time for teacher professional development (Digest 95–4).* Washington, DC: ERIC Clearinghouse on Teaching and Teacher Education.

American Public Health Association and the American Academy of Pediatrics. (1992). *Caring for our children: National health and safety performance standards: Standards for out of home child care programs.* Ann Arbor, MI: Author.

Barnett, W. S., Hustedt, J. T., Robin, K. B., & Schulman, K. L. (2007). *The state of preschool: 2008 state preschool yearbook.* New Brunswick, NJ: National Institute for Early Education Research, Rutgers University.

Barnett, W. S., & Masse, L. N. (2007). Comparative benefit-cost analysis of the Abecedarian program and its policy implications. *Economics of Education Review, 26*(1), 113–125.

Baydar, N., & Brooks-Gunn, J. (1991). Effects of maternal employment and child-care arrangements on preschoolers' cognitive and behavioral outcomes: Evidence from the children of the National Longitudinal Survey of Youth. *Developmental Psychology, 27*(6), 932–945.

Birman, B. F., Desimone, L., Porter, A. C., & Garet, M. S. 2000. Designing professional development that works. *Educational Leadership, 57*(8), 28–33.

Bogard, K., & Takanishi, R. (2005). PK–3: An aligned and coordinated approach to education for children 3 to 8 years old. *SRCD Social Policy Reports, 19*(3), 1–23.

Brandon, R., & Martinez-Beck, I. (2005). Estimating the size and characteristics of the United States early care and education workforce. In M. Zaslow & I. Martinez-Beck (Eds.), *Critical issues in early childhood professional development* (pp. 49–76). Baltimore, MD: Brookes.

Bronfenbrenner, U. (1979). *The ecology of human development: Experiments by nature and design.* Cambridge, MA: Harvard University Press.

Bronfenbrenner, U., & Morris, P. A. (2006). The bioecological model of human development. In R. M. Lerner (Ed.), *Handbook of child psychology: Vol. 1. Theoretical models of human development* (6th ed., pp. 793–828). Hoboken, NJ: Wiley.

Bryant, D., Burchinal, M., Lau, L., & Sparling, J. (1994). Family and classroom correlates of Head Start children's developmental outcomes. *Early Childhood Research Quarterly, 9,* 289–309.

Bryant, D., Peisner-Feinberg, E., & Clifford, R. M. (1993). *Evaluation of public preschool programs in North Carolina: Final report.* Chapel Hill, NC: Frank Porter Graham Child Development Center.

Burchinal, M., Ramey, S., Reid, M., & Jaccard, J. (1995). Early child care experiences and their association with family and child characteristics during middle childhood. *Early Childhood Research Quarterly, 10,* 33–61.

Caughy, M., DiPietro, J., & Strobino, D. (1994). Day-care participation as a protective factor in the cognitive development of low-income children. *Child Development, 65,* 457–471.

Chin-Quee, D., & Scarr, S. (1994). Lack of early child care effects on school-age children's social competence and academic achievement. *Early Development and Parenting, 3*(2),103–112.

Clifford, R. M., Early, D. M., & Hills, T. (1999). Almost a million children in school before kindergarten: Who is responsible for early childhood services? *Young Children, 54*(5), 48–51.

Clifford, R. M., & Maxwell, K. (2002, April). *The need for highly qualified prekindergarten teachers.* Chapel Hill: Frank Porter Graham Child Development Institute, University of North Carolina.

Darling-Hammond, L., & McLaughlin, M. W. (1995). Policies that support professional development in an era of reform. *Phi Delta Kappan, 76*(8), 597–604.

Deater-Deckard, K., Pinkerton, R., & Scarr, S. (1996). Child care quality and children's behavioral adjustment: A four-year longitudinal study. *Journal of Child Psychology and Psychiatry, 37*(8), 937–948.

Downer, J. T., Kraft-Sayre, M., & Pianta, R. C. (2009). On-going, web-mediated professional development focused on teacher-child interactions: Early childhood educators' usage rates and self-reported satisfaction. *Early Education & Development, 20*(2), 321–345.

Dunn, L. (1993). Ratio and group size in day care programs. *Child Youth Care Forum, 22*(3), 193–226.

FPG Child Development Institute. (2005). *The Carolina Abecedarian Project.* Retrieved from http://www.fpg.unc.edu/~abc/.

Garet, M., Porter, A., Desimone, L., Birman, B., & Yoon, S. (2001). What makes professional development effective? Results from a national sample of teachers. *American Educational Research Journal, 38*(1), 915–945.

Goelman, H., & Pence, A. (1987). Effects of child care, family and individual characteristics on children's language development: The Victoria day care research project. In D. A. Phillips (Ed.), *Quality in child care: What does research tell us?* (pp. 89–104). Washington, DC: National Association for the Education of Young Children.

Hadden, D. S., & Pianta, R. C. (2006). MyTeachingPartner: An innovative model of professional development. *Young Children 61*(2): 42–43.

Hagekull, B., & Bohlin, G. (1995). Day care quality, family, and child characteristics and socio-emotional development. *Early Childhood Research Quarterly, 10,* 505–526.

Hamre, B. K., Hamagami, F., Downer, J., Mashburn, A., & Pianta, R. C. (2009). *Effects of web-mediated teacher professional development on children's social skills.* Unpublished manuscript.

Hamre, B. K., & Pianta, R. C. (2007). Learning opportunities in preschool and early elementary classrooms. In R. C. Pianta, M. J. Cox, & K. Snow (Eds.), *School readiness, early learning and the transition to kindergarten* (pp. 49–83). Baltimore, MD: Brookes.

Hart, P., Stroot, S., Yinger, R., & Smith, S. (2005). *Meeting the teacher education accountability challenge: A focus on novice and experienced teacher studies.* Mount Vernon, OH: Teacher Quality Partnership.

Haymore-Sandholtz, J. (2002). Inservice training or professional development: Contrasting opportunities in a school/university partnership. *Teaching and Teacher Education, 18*(7), 815–830.

Henry, G. T., & Rickman, D. K. (2007). Do peers influence children's skill development in preschool? *Economics of Education Review, 26,* 100–112.

Hestenes, L., Kontos, S., & Bryant, D. (1993). Children's emotional expression in child care centers varying in quality. *Early Childhood Research Quarterly, 8,* 295–307.

Howes, C. (1990). Can the age of entry into child care and the quality of child care predict adjustment in kindergarten? *Developmental Psychology, 26,* 292–303.

Howes, C., James, J., & Ritchie, S. (2003). Pathways to effective teaching. *Early Childhood Research Quarterly, 18,* 104–120.

Howes, C., Phillips, D. A., & Whitebook, M. (1992). Thresholds of quality: Implications for child care and children's social development. *Child Development, 63,* 449–460.

Howes, C., & Smith, E. W. (1995). Relations among child care quality, teacher behavior, children's play activities, emotional security, and cognitive activity in child care. *Early Childhood Research Quarterly, 10,* 381–404.

Ingersoll, R. M., & Kralik, J. (2004). *The impact of mentoring on teacher retention: What the research says* (pp. 1–23). Denver, CO: Education Commission of the States.

Kontos, S. (1991). Child care quality, family background, and children's development. *Early Childhood Research Quarterly, 6,* 249–262.

Kontos, S., & Feine, R. (1987). Childcare quality: Compliance with regulation and children's development: The Pennsylvania study. In D. Phillips (Ed.), *Quality in childcare: What does research tell us?* (pp. 57–80).Washington DC: National Association for the Education of Young Children.

Lamb, M., & Ahnert, L. (2006). Nonparental child care: Context, concepts, correlates and consequences. In W. Damon, R. M. Lerner, K. A. Renninger, & I. E. Sigel (Vol. Eds.), *Handbook of child psychology: Vol. 4. Child psychology in practice* (6th ed., pp. 664–679). New York: Wiley.

Landry, S. H., Swank, P. R., Smith, K. E., Assel, M. A., & Gunnewig, S. B. (2006). Enhancing early literacy skills for preschool children: Bringing a professional development model to scale. *Journal of Learning Disabilities, 39*(4), 306–324.

Lazar, I., Darlington, R., Murray, H., Royce, J., & Snipper, A. (1982). Lasting effects of early education: A report from the consortium for longitudinal studies. *Monograph of the Society for Research in Child Development, 47*(2–3, Serial No. 195).

Lieberman, A. (1995). *The work of restructuring schools: Building from the ground up.* New York: Teachers College Press.

Mashburn, A. J. (2008). Quality of social and physical environments in preschools and children's development of academic, language, and literacy skills. *Applied Developmental Science 12*(3), 113–127.

Mashburn, A. J., Hamre, B. K., Downer, J. D., Justice, L. M., & Pianta, R. C. (2009). *Teachers' utilization of professional development resources and children's development of language and literacy skills during pre-kindergarten.* Unpublished manuscript.

Mashburn, A. J., Justice, L. J., Downer, J. T., & Pianta, R. C. (2009). Peer effects on children's language development during pre-kindergarten. *Child Development, 80*(3), 686–702.

Mashburn, A. J., Pianta, R. C., Hamre, B. K., Downer, J. T., Barbarin, O., Bryant, D., et al. (2008). Measures of pre-k quality and children's development of academic, language and social skills. *Child Development, 79*(3), 732–749.

National Association for the Education of Young Children. (2005). *Position statements of NAEYC.* Retrieved from http://www.naeyc.org/about/positions.asp.

NICHD Early Child Care Research Network. (1999). Child outcomes when child care center classes meet recommended standards for quality. *American Journal of Public Health, 89,* 1072–1077.

NICHD Early Child Care Research Network. (2002). Child-care structure-process-outcome: Direct and indirect effects of child-care quality on young children's development. *American Psychological Society, 13*(3), 199–206.

NICHD Early Child Care Research Network. (2004). Does class size in first grade relate to changes in child academic and social performance or observed classroom processes? *Developmental Psychology, 40,* 651–664.

NICHD Early Child Care Research Network, & Duncan, G. (2003). Modeling the impacts of child care quality on children's preschool cognitive development. *Child Development, 74*(5), 1454–1475.

Odden, A., Archibald, S., Fermanich, M., & Gallagher, H. A. (2002). A cost framework for professional development. *Journal of Education Finance, 28*(1), 51–74.

Peisner-Feinberg, E., & Burchinal, M. (1997). Relations between preschool children's child-care experiences and concurrent development: The cost, quality, and outcomes study. *Merrill-Palmer Quarterly, 43*(3), 451–477.

Peisner-Feinberg, E., Burchinal, M., Clifford, R., Culkin, M., Howes, C., Kagan, S., et al. (2001). The relation of preschool child-care quality to children's cognitive and social development trajectories through second grade. *Child Development, 72*(5), 1534–1553.

Peters, H. E., & Bristow, B. (2005). Early childhood professional development programs: Accounting for spillover effects and market interventions. In M. Zaslow & I. Martinez-Beck (Eds.), *Critical issues in early childhood professional development* (pp. 339–350). Baltimore, MD: Brookes.

Pianta, R. C. (2005). A new elementary school for American children. *SRCD Social Policy Report, 19*(3), 4–5.

Pianta, R. C., Belsky, J., Houts, R., Morrison, F., & NICHD Early Child Care Research Network. (2007). Opportunities to learn in America's elementary classrooms. *Science, 315*, 1795–1796.

Pianta, R. C., La Paro, K. M., & Hamre, B. K. (2008). *Classroom Assessment Scoring System (CLASS) – Pre-k* [CLASS]. Baltimore, MD: Brookes.

Pianta, R., Mashburn, A., Downer, J., Hamre, B., & Justice L. (2008). Effects of web-mediated professional development resources on teacher–child interactions in pre-kindergarten classes. *Early Childhood Research Quarterly, 23*, 431–451.

Putnam, R. T., & Borko, H. (1997). Teacher learning: Implications of new views of cognition. In B. J. Biddle, T. L. Good, & I. F. Goodson (Eds.), *The international handbook of teachers and teaching* (Vol. 2, pp. 1223–1296). Dordrecht, The Netherlands: Kluwer.

Ramey, S., & Ramey, C. (2005). Creating and sustaining a high-quality workforce in child care, early intervention, and school-readiness programs. In M. Zaslow & I. Martinez-Beck (Eds.), *Critical issues in early childhood professional development* (pp. 355–368). Baltimore, MD: Brookes.

Reynolds, A. J. (2000). *Success in early intervention: The Chicago Child-Parent Centers.* Lincoln: University of Nebraska Press.

Reynolds, A. J., Temple, J. A., Robertson, D. L., & Mann, E. A. (2001). Long-term effects of an early childhood intervention on educational achievement. *Journal of the American Medical Association, 285*, 2339–2346.

Richardson, V., & Anders, P. L. (2005). Professional preparation and development of teachers in literacy instruction for urban settings. In J. Flood & P. L. Anders (Eds.), *Literacy development of students in urban schools* (pp. 205–230). Newark, DE: International Reading Association.

Schliecker, E., White, D., & Jacobs, E. (1991). The role of day care quality in the predication of children's vocabulary. *Canadian Journal of Behavioural Science, 23*(1), 12–24.

Schweinhart, L. J., Barnes, H. V., & Weikart, D. P. (1993). Significant benefits: The High/Scope Perry Preschool study through age 27. *Monographs of the High/Scope Educational Research Foundation, 10.* Ypsilanti, MI: High/Scope Press.

U.S. Department of Education. (2002). *No Child Left Behind desktop reference.* Jessup, MD: Education Publishing Center.

Vandell, D., Henderson, V., & Wilson, K. (1988). A longitudinal study of children with day care experiences of varying quality. *Child Development, 59*, 1288–1292.

Wasik, B., Bond, M., & Hindman, A. (2006). The effects of a language and literacy intervention on Head Start children and teachers. *Journal of Educational Psychology, 98*(1), 63–74.

West, J., Denton, K., & Germino-Hausken, E. (2000). *America's kindergarteners* (NCES 2000–070). Washington, DC: National Center for Education Statistics.

Zaslow, M., & I. Martinez-Beck, I. (Eds.). (2005). *Critical issues in early childhood professional development.* Baltimore, MD: Brookes.

13

School Readiness and the Reading Achievement Gap: Can Full-Day Kindergarten Level the Playing Field?

VI-NHUAN LE, SHEILA NATARAJ KIRBY, HEATHER BARNEY, CLAUDE MESSAN SETODJI, AND DANIEL GERSHWIN

In light of the trend toward high-stakes testing and other accountability demands, policy makers are focusing on the early childhood years as a crucial step in developing the competencies that form the basis of future academic success (Russell, 2006). In particular, there has been increased attention paid to ensuring that children enter school "ready to learn."[1] Although there is little consensus on the specific skills and knowledge that comprise school readiness, many educators, researchers, and policy makers adopt a broad perspective that extends beyond literacy and cognitive skills. The standards put forth by the National Education Goals Panel, for example, define five dimensions of school readiness: (a) physical well-being and motor development; (b) social and emotional development; (c) approaches to learning (e.g., curiosity, persistence, and other dispositions toward learning); (d) language development; and (e) cognition and general knowledge (Kagan, Moore, & Bredekamp, 1995).

Although the significance of early cognitive skills to school readiness is self-evident, it is also important to understand the role that nonacademic skills, such as physical and socio-emotional development, play in preparing children for school. Young children learn through physical exploration of their environments (Cassidy & Shaver, 1999; Smith & Pederson, 1988), and lags in the development of age-appropriate gross and fine motor skills (e.g., being able to run and skip or hold a pencil) can hinder their learning opportunities (Brown, 1982; Poest, Williams, Witt, & Atwood, 1990; Seefeldt, 1980). Analogously, children who enter school with difficulties paying attention, controlling disruptive behaviors, or forming social relations with peers tend to be less engaged in the classroom and to exhibit more disciplinary problems

[1] In this study, we adopt a broad definition of school readiness that encompasses both "readiness to learn" and "readiness for school." According to the North Central Regional Educational Laboratory, readiness to learn "involves a level of development at which the child has the capacity to learn specific materials," and readiness for school "involves a specific set of cognitive, linguistic, social, and motor skills that enables a child to assimilate the school's curriculum" (see http://www.ncrel.org/sdrs/areas/issues/students/earlycld/ea700.htm).

(Arnold et al., 1999; McClelland, Morrison, & Holmes, 2000). The importance of nonacademic behaviors to school success may explain why a poll of public-school kindergarten teachers nationwide indicated that good physical health, sociability (e.g., taking turns and sharing), and enthusiasm for learning were more important readiness skills than knowledge of letters and numbers (Heaviside & Farris, 1993; Lewit & Baker, 1995).

Despite the attention on school readiness, recent research shows that large skill gaps exist even before children enter kindergarten, with minority students showing, on average, poorer school-readiness skills. Racial/ethnic differences in cognitive and literacy aspects of school readiness have been well documented (see, e.g., Alexander, Entwisle, & Dauber, 1993; Phillips, Crouse, & Ralph, 1998; Stipek & Ryan, 1997), but it is also important to recognize the racial/ethnic inequities in the nonacademic aspects of school readiness. Zill (1999) reported that one in six children has a difficult entry into school, showing problems following directions or working independently. Minority children made up a disproportionate percentage of this group. Similarly, Chase-Lansdale, Gordon, Brooks-Gunn, and Klebanov (1997) found that Whites were less likely than Blacks to exhibit internalizing (e.g., loneliness or anxiety) or externalizing (e.g., acting out or impulsivity) behaviors on school entry. In a survey of 3,500 kindergarten teachers nationwide, Rimm-Kaufman, Pianta, and Cox (2000) found that teachers rated Hispanic and Black students as having more difficulty working in groups than did White students. They also found that teachers teaching in schools with a high proportion of minority students were much more likely to report substantial behavioral and transition-to-school problems than did teachers in schools with low proportions of minorities.

Although much research has shown that racial/ethnic achievement differences in the academic skills of children when they start school can explain differences in test-score performance in later grades (Phillips et al., 1998), less attention has been paid to how differences in nonacademic skills in the early stages of schooling can play a role in explaining the minority–White achievement gap. However, there is some evidence that physical development, social skills, and problem behaviors are predictive of academic achievement, at least in the short term. Agostin and Bain (1997) reported that cooperation and self-control measured at the end of kindergarten predicted retention status and reading, mathematics, and language achievement at the end of first grade. They also found that a measure of fine motor skills could be used to effectively discriminate among children who were retained, promoted, or needed to be placed in an intensive-assistance classroom. These findings were similar to those reported by McClelland et al. (2000), who found that cooperation and self-control predicted variance in academic outcomes for kindergarten through second-grade students. Likewise, Ladd, Birch, and Buhs (1999) found that kindergartners' class participation (e.g., following classroom rules and complying with their teachers' requests) was associated with higher achievement at kindergarten, and Kwon (2005) reported socio-emotional competence to be a major protective factor moderating socio-demographic risk factors in kindergarten and first-grade students. Taken together, these findings suggest greater scrutiny should be paid to the relationship between nonacademic readiness skills and achievement.

THE CASE FOR FULL-DAY KINDERGARTEN

As noted earlier, despite the importance of school-readiness skills to later achievement, an increasing number of children are entering kindergarten without the cognitive or social maturity or maturation necessary for success in school (Pianta, 2002; West, Denton, & Reaney, 2001). As a result, some educators and policy makers are pushing for the implementation of full-day kindergarten programs as a way to help level the playing field for disadvantaged children with much lower levels of initial school readiness (National Association of Early Childhood Specialists in State Departments of Education, 2000). Advocates argue that half-day programs do not allow enough time to both prepare children for first grade and enable children to attain goals for kindergarten (Porch, 2002), and that the additional time available in full-day programs can be used to promote achievement.

Whether participation in a full-day program is associated with improved achievement has been the focus of intense inquiry, but reaching definitive conclusions has been stymied by studies with small sample sizes, lack of statistical controls, potential self-selection bias, a focus on short-term outcomes, and other methodological weaknesses (Ackerman, Barnett, & Robin, 2005; Cryan, Sheehan, Wiechel, & Bandy-Hadden, 1992; Lee, Burkam, Ready, Honigman, & Meisels, 2006; Long Beach Unified School District, 2000; Plucker et al., 2004). The existing literature on the associations between full-day kindergarten attendance and student achievement finds positive outcomes in the proximal years but little difference as children progress through school. For example, Cryan et al. (1992) analyzed data on 8,290 students in 27 Ohio school districts and found a positive relationship between participation in full-day kindergarten and school success through first grade, as measured by grade retention, special-education placements, standardized test scores, and teacher rankings. Using a nationally representative database of more than 21,000 children, Lee et al. (2006) reported a significant positive effect of full-day kindergarten on student achievement at the end of kindergarten. Similarly, Kaplan (2002) found significantly greater linear growth through the end of first grade for full-day kindergarten students, after controlling for age and socioeconomic status. However, Rathbun and West (2004) and Walston, West, and Rathbun (2005) examined subsequent waves from this database and concluded that these effects did not persist into the third grade.

Both sets of findings were supported by Cannon, Jacknowitz, and Painter (2006), who reported a positive achievement effect of full-day kindergarten through the end of kindergarten but also found that the effect was reduced by half at the end of first grade and eliminated by the end of third grade. The authors also reported no significant relationship between full-day kindergarten attendance and grade retention through third grade.

PURPOSE OF THIS STUDY

The evidence just reviewed suggests that early competencies lay the foundation for future academic success. Therefore, understanding the conditions and experiences of children as they enter school is critical to improving their outcomes in subsequent years. This study helps fill some of the information gap by examining how school readiness and attendance in full-day kindergarten contribute to longer term achievement outcomes. It addresses two main questions:

1. What is the relationship between children's school-readiness skills at kindergarten entry and reading achievement through the fifth grade?
2. Does attendance in full-day kindergarten attendance help narrow the reading achievement gap between minorities and Whites?

METHODS

Data Source

This study analyzes public-use data from the Early Childhood Longitudinal Study, Kindergarten Class of 1998–1999 (ECLS-K). The ECLS-K study, sponsored by the National Center for Education Statistics (NCES), provides extensive information on the social, cognitive, and health outcomes for children at the beginning of kindergarten, as well as at several points during their elementary school years. The study also collects information from students' parents, teachers, and school administrators about community resources, as well as family and school environments. To date, the study has collected information through the end of fifth grade. Using a complex design in which there are multiple levels of stratification and certain populations are oversampled (i.e., Asian/Pacific Islanders), the ECLS-K database provides nationally representative information derived from 21,260 incoming kindergarten students in 1998–1999.[2]

[2] More technical information about the ECLS-K, including information about its sampling design, can be found in the ECLS-K Base Year Public-Use Data Files and Electronic Codebook (NCES, 2001).

Sample Size

The targeted population for our study was first-time kindergartners in 1998–1999 whose English-language proficiency was sufficient to enable them to take the full battery of cognitive tests. We also limited the study to children who did not switch from a full-time kindergarten program to a part-time program (or vice versa) and whose parents participated at every wave of data collection (discussed in a later section). These criteria resulted in an unweighted sample of 7,897 children; White children ($n = 5{,}056$) comprised the majority of the population, followed by Hispanics ($n = 1{,}338$), Blacks ($n = 730$), Asian/Pacific Islanders ($n = 427$), and "other race" ($n = 346$) students. "Other race" students were Native American, Alaskan Native, or of multiple races. Across waves, between 2,500 and 3,500 teachers responded to the surveys, and between 900 and 1,500 schools participated.

Data Collection and Measures

The full sample of children, parents, teachers, and administrators was assessed during five waves of data collection: fall of kindergarten and the spring of kindergarten, first grade, third grade, and fifth grade. Information about children's development, early learning experiences, and learning contexts was collected through a variety of instruments, including direct assessment, parent interviews, and teacher and school-administrator surveys. More information about the measures derived from each data source is provided next.

Direct Assessment of Children

On entry to kindergarten, children completed a psychomotor assessment to evaluate their fine and gross motor skills. Fine motor skills require the coordination of small muscle movements, whereas gross motor skills require the coordination of large muscle movements. Measures of children's psychomotor skills were obtained only during the initial wave of data collection (i.e., fall kindergarten).

In contrast, children's cognitive outcomes were assessed at every wave of data collection. Children were assessed in mathematics, reading, and general knowledge during kindergarten and first grade, and in mathematics, reading, and science during third and fifth grades. The same set of achievement tests was used in kindergarten and first grade, but the tests were changed to reflect appropriate grade-level content in later years.[3] Item response theory (IRT) was used to create a scale score for each of the achievement tests in each grade. IRT facilitates a longitudinal scale score across grades, in which the scores reflect children's achievement gains as they progress through school.

[3] In kindergarten and first grade, children were provided with a routing test to determine which test form (i.e., low, medium, or high difficulty) they should take.

Parent Interviews
At each wave, parents were asked to provide information that was likely to be correlated with children's reading achievement. We included the following child-level variables in our models:

- *Extracurricular Activities* is a five-item scale that assesses the number of out-of-school activities in which the student participated. These include activities such as dance, music, or clubs.
- *Parental Involvement* is a six-item scale measuring parents' involvement with their child's school. Items asked about whether the parent attended school events, such as open house or parent–teacher conferences.
- *Income* is a measure of the family's annual income.[4]
- *Center Care* is a measure of whether the child received care from a center- or school-based preschool program before entering kindergarten.
- *Early Entry* and *Delayed Entry* are measures of whether the age at which the child entered kindergarten was earlier or later than the school guidelines for kindergarten enrollment, respectively.
- *Disability* indicates whether the child was diagnosed with a learning disability or had received therapy services for a disability before entering kindergarten.

The creation of the Parental Involvement and Extracurricular Activities scales posed a challenge because of the longitudinal nature of the study. Extracurricular activities or parental behaviors that are developmentally appropriate at kindergarten (e.g., reading to the child) may not be considered developmentally appropriate by fifth grade. In creating these scales, we chose items that were relevant across the different grade levels.

Teacher Surveys
SCHOOL READINESS MEASURES. Teachers' evaluation of children's literacy skills served as an indicator of children's cognitive readiness for school with respect to reading achievement. This measure, labeled *Literacy Skills*, is on a 5-point scale, where 1 = *not yet proficient*, 3 = *in progress*, and 5 = *proficient*. The other dimensions of school readiness encompass the nonacademic aspects of readiness, including social, emotional, and physical development of children. These scales, obtained from the ECLS-K database, include the following (NCES, 2001, pp. 2–16):

- The *Approaches to Learning* Scale measures behaviors that affect the ease with which children can benefit from the learning environment. It includes six items that rate the child's attentiveness, task persistence, eagerness to learn, learning independence, flexibility, and organization.

[4] Income was initially on a 13-point categorical scale, but we converted the variable from fixed categories to approximate yearly wages using the heading descriptors as a guide.

- The *Self-Control* Scale has four items that indicate the child's ability to control behavior by respecting the property rights of others, controlling temper, accepting peer ideas for group activities, and responding appropriately to pressure from peers.
- The five *Interpersonal Skills* items rate the child's skill in forming and maintaining friendships; getting along with people who are different; comforting or helping other children; expressing feelings, ideas, and opinions in positive ways; and showing sensitivity to the feelings of others.
- *Externalizing Problem Behaviors* include acting-out behaviors. Five items on this scale rate the frequency with which a child argues, fights, gets angry, acts impulsively, and disturbs ongoing activities.
- The *Internalizing Problem Behaviors* Scale asks about the apparent presence of anxiety, loneliness, low self-esteem, and sadness. This scale comprises four items.

Each of these nonacademic readiness dimensions was rated on a 4-point metric, where higher scores denote that children possess more of those skills or traits.

SCHOOL PROGRAM CHARACTERISTICS. We also included several school-level aggregates relating to teaching practices, class size, teaching experience, and adequacy of facilities. We chose these program factors because they have been shown to be related to student achievement (see, e.g., Stipek, Feiler, Daniels, & Millburn, 1995, for teaching practices; Ferguson, 1991, for class size; and Greenwald, Hedges, & Laine, 1996, for teaching experience).[5] We focused on the following teaching-practice variables:

- *Child-Selected* assesses the number of hours per day that children were allowed to select their own instructional activities.
- *Whole-Class* consists of teachers' reports of the hours per day that teacher-directed instruction takes place in a whole-class setting.
- *Individual Activities* measures the number of hours per day of teacher-directed individual activities.
- *Small-Group* measures the number of hours per day teachers report spending in teacher-directed small-group instruction.

These variables were originally on a 5-point scale, where 1 represented *no time*, 3 represented about *one hour*, and 5 represented *3 hours* or more. We converted these variables from fixed categories to hours per day using the

[5] We considered other program characteristics, such as teachers' education level and certification type. However, because the mechanism by which teachers' qualifications influence student achievement is through instruction, we focused on teachers' instructional practices.

heading descriptors as a guide. For instance, a teacher response of "5" for a particular instructional practice was converted to 3 hours.

In addition, we included the following program characteristics:

- *Class Size* represents the number of students in the class.
- *Experience at Grade* indicates the total number of years in which teachers taught at the grade level in question.
- *Activity Centers* indicates the number of interest areas or activity centers (e.g., art area or reading area with books) available at kindergarten.

Teachers also indicated whether children were enrolled in a part- or full-time kindergarten program. Because 6% of kindergartens have both full-day and part-time programs, we consider full-time attendance to be a child-level characteristic.[6]

CLASSROOM LEARNING CONTEXT FACTORS. As a measure of learning context, kindergarten teachers indicated the proportion of students in the class who could recognize letters, read words, and read sentences. They also rated the general behavior of the class. We created four separate variables to represent aggregate measures of peers' school-readiness behaviors and included them in the models to capture potential peer effects.

School-Administrator Survey

We used the school-administrator surveys to construct school-level demographic variables that provide a context for children's learning experiences. These included variables such as the proportion of the student population who were minorities or eligible for free or reduced-price lunch. At kindergarten, we measured whether the school was a public or private school and whether it was a regular type of kindergarten.[7] Furthermore, we obtained information about school urbanicity (i.e., suburban, rural, or city) as well as the geographic region from which the schools were drawn (i.e., Northeast, West, South, and Midwest). It is important to include information about geographic location because there is tremendous regional variability in the provision of full-day kindergarten. According to Ackerman et al. (2005), only nine states currently require districts to offer a full-day program, and eight of these nine states are in the South, where 80% of public schools provide full-day kindergarten. Only

[6] We do not make a distinction between morning and afternoon part-time programs because preliminary analyses did not show any differences between the two program types.

[7] A regular kindergarten is a 1-year program intended to serve 5-year-old children. Two-year programs, programs with multiple grades or that are ungraded, and transitional programs (i.e., intended for children who are not ready for first grade) are excluded from the regular kindergarten designation.

one third of schools in the West and Northeast provide full-day programs, and about 57% of Midwest schools do so (Ackerman et al., 2005).

ANALYTIC APPROACH

Multiple Imputation

Approximately 63% of the sample had test scores, demographic records, and teacher- and school-level information across the five waves of data collection. However, limiting the analysis to complete records does not capitalize on important information contained in partially complete records. Furthermore, there can be systematic differences between individuals with complete data and individuals with incomplete data. Indeed, there is evidence that the patterns of missing data are not random, as students who have nonmissing test score data perform significantly better on the observed achievement scores than do students who have missing test scores on two or more waves. Thus, we used a multiple-imputation technique to correct for missing data, in which each missing value was replaced with a random sample of plausible values.

For time-invariant child-level variables (e.g., gender), the imputation occurred at the level of the student. For time-varying variables (e.g., parental involvement), we imputed at the level of student by year using all observed data in a multivariate normal model as a basis for predicting missing values. We conducted analogous imputation processes for missing school-level variables. Dichotomous variables were treated as continuous in the imputation process and then rounded back to dichotomous variables for analysis. We imputed 10 sets of plausible values and then synthesized the results in a manner that accounted for the uncertainty due to the missing information (see Schafer, 1997).

Although data were collected during the fall and spring of kindergarten, some variables were measured only during the spring. For these variables (i.e., parental involvement, extracurricular activities, income, percent minority students, and percent of students eligible for free or reduced-price lunch), we did not impute missing values but instead used values collected during the spring of kindergarten. That is, we assumed that there would be little change in responses between the fall and spring on these particular variables. For the remainder of the waves, we collected information on these variables, thereby allowing us to model them as time varying.

Model Details

Because many students change schools over time as they progress from kindergarten to fifth grade, traditional hierarchical linear modeling (HLM) methods designed for nested data structures are not appropriate. Instead, we conducted a longitudinal, cross-classified analysis in which students' outcomes over the five time points were modeled in relation to their school-program characteristics, learning context factors, school-readiness skills at kindergarten entry, and other covariates. We also used weights provided by the ECLS-K database on the descriptive statistics for the child-level variables and on the regression analyses to allow us to make inferences to the national population.[8]

Our models included both time-varying and time-invariant variables. It was necessary to treat certain school-level factors (i.e., teaching practice, class size, teacher experience, and school-level demographics) as time varying because student achievement is likely to be influenced by past as well as contemporaneous school-program characteristics. For the same reason, we treated certain student-level covariates as time varying, including variables relating to income, participation in extracurricular activities, parental involvement, and disability status. We treated the remaining variables as time invariant.[9]

For the ith student in the jth school at time point t, we define X_{ijt} as the time-varying student-level predictor variables (e.g., home-background factors), W_{ij} as the time-invariant student-level predictors (e.g., gender), Z_j as the student's school-level predictor (e.g., percentage of minority students), and Y_{ijt} as the reading-achievement score. We included both random and fixed effects for school- and student-level variables in our models. We fit models of the form

$$Y_{ijt} = \alpha_{ij} + \delta X_{ijt} + \varepsilon_{ijt} \tag{13.1}$$

$$\alpha_{ij} = \mu_j + \lambda W_{ij} + \zeta_{ij} \tag{13.2}$$

$$\mu_j = \theta + \gamma Z_j + \omega_j, \tag{13.3}$$

where ε_{ijt}, ζ_{ij}, and ω_i are random errors assumed to be normally distributed with mean 0 and different standard deviations. Equation (13.1) estimates, for each ith student, the relationship between the time-varying student-level predictors and reading-achievement score. The effect of the time-varying student-level predictors, indicated by the parameter δ, is assumed to be the same across all students. However, the average reading score, represented by the intercept α_{ij} of the ith student in the jth school, is allowed to vary across students. The random error ε_{ijt} describes the variability within student outcomes across waves.

Equation (13.2) models the intercept α_{ij} as a function of the time-invariant student-level predictors W_{ij}. The parameter λ estimates the relationships between the time-invariant student-level predictors and reading-achievement score and is assumed to be constant from one school to the next. The term ζ_{ij} describes the variability of children's reading score within the same school.

[8] This is the C1_6FP0 weight, which is used for longitudinal analysis of the full sample of children up to fifth grade.

[9] Although students could change geographic region, we found that less than 1% of students actually did so. Thus, we treated geographic region as time invariant.

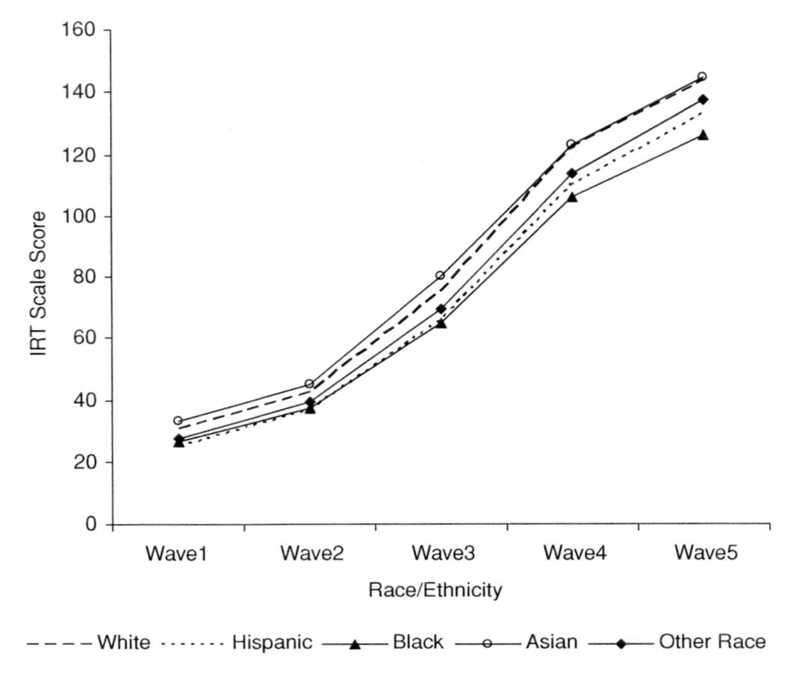

Figure 13.1. Distribution of reading achievement by race/ethnicity, fall of kindergarten to spring of fifth grade.

Because of the hierarchical structure of the data, we also assume that the average student-level intercept α_{ij} differs from one school to another. The parameter μ_j, indicated in Equation (13.3), captures this school-level variability and is assumed to be correlated with the school-level variables Z_j. In Equation (13.3), the parameter γ quantifies the relationships between the school-level variables and reading-achievement score; Y_{ijt} and θ estimate the overall average reading score.[10] The random errors ζ_{ij} and ω_i account for the variability between student and between schools, respectively.

RESULTS

Racial/Ethnic Differences in Reading Achievement

Figure 13.1 provides the average reading distributions for the different ethnic groups from one wave to the next wave. On average, White and Asian students entered kindergarten with the highest scores in reading, whereas Hispanic and Black students demonstrated the lowest scores. The achievement gaps became more pronounced over time, with White and Asian students scoring approximately three-fourths of a standard deviation higher than Hispanics

[10] Time and age at assessment were highly correlated ($r = .96$). Thus, we used age at assessment as a proxy for time in the models.

Table 13.1. *Average school-readiness scores at kindergarten entry by race/ethnicity*

Scale	White	Hispanic	Black	Asian	Other Race
Approaches to learning	3.05 (.64)	2.99 (.68)	2.80 (.87)	3.15 (.49)	2.95 (.70)
Self-control	3.15 (.59)	3.11 (.60)	2.90 (.82)	3.24 (.38)	3.04 (.67)
Interpersonal skills	3.04 (.60)	2.98 (.61)	2.82 (.81)	3.04 (.44)	3.00 (.64)
Externalizing behaviors	1.59 (.60)	1.54 (.60)	1.79 (.89)	1.52 (.44)	1.73 (.70)
Internalizing behaviors	1.52 (.48)	1.53 (.53)	1.50 (.63)	1.45 (.37)	1.58 (.47)
Fine motor	5.93 (1.88)	5.73 (2.08)	5.01 (2.82)	6.35 (1.58)	6.11 (1.69)
Gross motor	6.26 (1.82)	6.37 (1.95)	6.53 (2.21)	6.33 (1.40)	6.35 (1.78)
Literacy skills	2.62 (.66)	2.21 (.73)	2.42 (.88)	2.59 (.64)	2.46 (.74)

Note: Standard deviations given in parentheses. Includes imputed values.

and nearly one standard deviation higher than Blacks by the end of fifth grade. The finding that achievement differences between minorities and Whites on kindergarten entry cannot be overcome in later years has been well documented in the literature (Coley, 2002; Rouse, Brooks-Gunn, & McLanahan, 2005; West et al., 2001).

Racial/Ethnic Differences in School-Readiness Skills at Kindergarten Entry

Table 13.1 provides the distributions for the school-readiness indicators at kindergarten entry by race/ethnicity. An examination of these distributions indicates racial/ethnic differences among groups, although variation is much larger within groups than between groups.[11] Teachers evaluated White and Asian students as having, on average, the highest levels of socio-emotional readiness skills on kindergarten entry. On average, Whites and Asians received the highest scores on dispositions toward learning, self-control, and interpersonal skills. Asians were also more likely to exhibit low incidences of internalizing and externalizing behaviors. Teachers rated Black students as having, on average, the poorest interpersonal skills, approaches toward learning, and self-control. Black students also tended to rate most poorly on externalizing behaviors. That Blacks were less likely to be socially and emotionally prepared than Whites for school is consistent with other studies (Chase-Lansdale et al., 1997).

With respect to fine motor skills, Asians and Other-Race students tended to perform best, and Blacks tended to perform poorest. On tests of gross motor skills, Blacks, on average, performed best, and White students were most likely to score poorest. It is important to note that students of all ethnic groups tended to perform well on gross motor skills, with the average score being a 6.33 (out of a maximum score of 8).

[11] Statistical tests (either *t*-tests or ANOVA where applicable) indicated that average racial/ethnic differences were significant at the .01 level.

Table 13.2. *Descriptive statistics for learning context and home-background measures at kindergarten entry*

Scale	Mean	Standard Deviation	Minimum	Maximum
Learning Context				
Percent recognize letters	48.90	25.85	.00	100
Percent read words	10.38	11.64	.00	94.73
Percent read sentences	3.38	5.92	.00	57.04
Class behavior	3.46	.59	1.00	5.00
Percent minority[a]	40.37	31.14	.00	100
Percent reduced-price lunch[a]	8.51	6.49	.00	32.50
Percent free lunch[a]	35.95	28.57	.00	100
Home Background/Student Characteristics				
Income[a]	55,935	37,290	.00	150,000
Age at assessment (months)	68.30	4.11	54.00	79.00
Extracurricular activities[a]	1.03	1.01	.00	5.00
Parent involvement[a]	3.97	1.49	.00	6.00

Note: Includes imputed values.
[a] Indicates information was collected during spring kindergarten.

Descriptive Statistics for Learning Context, Home Background, and Student Demographic Variables

Table 13.2 presents the descriptive statistics for selected learning-context and home-background variables. The table provides the distributions measured at kindergarten entry; readers interested in the distributions for the other waves are referred to Le, Kirby, Barney, Setodji, and Gershwin (2006). Approximately 50% of children could recognize letters, but few could read words (10%), and even fewer could read sentences (3%). Teachers rated classroom behavior as average, meaning that children tended to misbehave occasionally.

With respect to school-context factors, approximately 9% of the children were eligible for reduced-price lunches, and another 36% were eligible for free lunches. Minority students comprised, on average, 40% of a school population. For the home-background variables, the average family income was approximately $56,000, and the average child was assessed when he or she was a little more than 5 years old. Children tended not to participate in extracurricular activities during kindergarten, and parents were moderately involved with the children's schools.

Table 13.3 presents descriptive statistics for the dichotomous variables – the percentages of schools or students with the selected characteristics. Nearly 95% of kindergarten programs were classified as a regular type. Geographically, kindergarten programs were most frequently located in cities and in the South. Approximately half the students were enrolled in a full-day kindergarten

Table 13.3. *Percentage of students or schools with selected characteristics at kindergarten entry*

Characteristics	Percent
Learning Context	
Regular kindergarten type	94
Public	78
West	25
South	31
Northeast	19
Midwest	25
Urban	37
Rural	21
Central city	42
Student Characteristics	
Disability	2
Attending a full-day kindergarten	53
Center care	78
Delayed entry	7
Early entry	1

Note: Includes imputed values.

program, and 78% received care in a center before entering kindergarten. Additionally, few children were classified with a learning disability, and few children started kindergarten earlier or later than the school guidelines for enrollment.

Table 13.4 provides the school-program factors, delineated by full-day and part-day kindergarten program. Consistent with the findings of Lee et al. (2006), instructional activities occurred more often in full-day programs, but they did not represent a "double dosage." The patterns of instructional practices were the same across full-day and part-day programs. In both types of programs, child-selected and teacher-directed individual activities were practiced less than 1 hour per day, whereas small-group activities and whole-class instruction took place more than 1 hour per day. The average kindergarten class size was about 20 students, and teachers had, on average, 8 to 9 years of teaching experience at kindergarten. Additionally, most kindergartens had numerous activity centers (e.g., reading area, sandboxes), with an average score of 9 (out of a maximum score of 11).

Relationships Between Reading Achievement and School-Readiness Skills

Table 13.5 provides the results for a regression that models the reading-achievement trajectory from kindergarten through fifth grade as a function of time-varying school-program factors, learning-context variables, and

Table 13.4. *Characteristics of school-program factors at kindergarten entry*

	Full-day kindergarten				Part-day kindergarten			
Scale	Mean	Std	Min	Max	Mean	Std	Min	Max
Child-selected	.98	.42	.00	3.00	.74	.34	.00	2.00
Whole-class	1.91	.66	.50	3.00	1.40	.55	.50	3.00
Individual activities	.77	.35	.00	3.00	.58	.256	.00	2.17
Small-group	1.22	.53	.25	3.00	.96	.45	.00	3.00
Class size	20.61	4.43	9.50	30.00	19.66	4.20	9.50	30.00
Experience at grade	8.26	4.91	1.00	30.00	9.02	5.50	1.00	30.00
Activity centers	9.16	1.58	1.00	11.00	9.19	1.49	3.00	11.00

Note: Includes imputed values.

home-background indicators. The table provides two sets of results: one in which nonacademic school-readiness skills are included in the models and one in which the nonacademic indicators are excluded. This allows us to explore whether and how the inclusion of nonacademic school-readiness skills affects interpretations.

The regression coefficient for the independent variable is the difference in IRT reading score for a one-unit change in the independent variable.[12] For a dichotomous independent variable such as race, the coefficient represents the average mean difference between minorities and Whites, holding all other variables constant. For example, a regression coefficient of −1.047 for Black students indicates that Black students score, on average, about one IRT scale point lower than White students, all else being equal. Similarly, the regression coefficient for the continuous independent variables represents the predicted difference in IRT scale score given a one-unit change in the independent variable. For instance, in the case of externalizing behaviors, a 1-point difference on this scale represents a difference of approximately 1.5 IRT scale points.

As expected, literacy proficiency at kindergarten entry is a strong predictor of reading achievement. However, nonacademic school-readiness skills are also important because they explain approximately 6% of the between-child variation in reading. Many of the included indicators of nonacademic school readiness were statistically significant, although not necessarily in the anticipated direction. Interpersonal skills, internalizing and externalizing behaviors, and gross motor skills were negatively related to reading performance, whereas fine motor skills were positively predictive of reading scores. At this point, we

[12] Because the nonacademic readiness skills were measured on a Likert scale, we present unstandardized regression coefficients to facilitate interpretation. Standardized regression coefficients can be computed by multiplying the unstandardized coefficient by the ratio of the standard deviation of the independent variable to the standard deviation of the dependent variable (Gardner, 2001).

Table 13.5. *Coefficients for reading-achievement trajectory from kindergarten through fifth grade*

Scale	Estimate	Std Error	Estimate	Std Error
Intercept	−194.970	6.128**	−199.198	3.738**
School-Program Characteristics				
Child-selected	−0.963	0.290**	−0.935	0.305**
Whole-class	3.479	0.201**	3.818	0.218**
Individual activities	1.457	0.275**	1.525	0.267**
Small-group	1.526	0.358**	1.535	0.299**
Class size	−0.019	0.028	−0.008	0.028
Experience at grade	−0.040	0.025	−0.009	0.038
Activity centers	0.275	0.232	0.325	0.222
Learning Context				
Percent recognize letters	0.040	0.017*	0.058	0.015**
Percent read words	−0.106	0.040**	−0.141	0.040**
Percent read sentences	0.256	0.070**	0.325	0.074**
Class behavior	0.622	0.603	0.792	0.592
Regular kindergarten	−1.593	1.626	−2.124	2.101
Public	−5.505	0.936**	−5.611	0.926**
West	2.237	0.974*	1.771	1.140
Northeast	1.057	0.981	0.426	1.050
Midwest	−2.331	0.881**	−3.169	0.918**
City	−0.870	0.711	−1.611	0.745*
Rural	−1.855	0.968	−3.831	1.010**
Percent minority	0.007	0.011	−0.003	0.015
Percent reduced-price lunch	−0.213	0.090*	−0.133	0.107
Percent free lunch	−0.024	0.014	−0.021	0.007**
School Readiness at Kindergarten Entry				
Approaches to learning	0.356	0.429		
Self-control	0.180	0.542		
Interpersonal skills	−1.480	0.456**		
Externalizing problem behaviors	−1.510	0.376**		
Internalizing problem behaviors	−0.225	0.346		
Fine motor	0.213	0.095*		
Gross motor	−0.344	0.099**		
Literacy skills	7.754	0.328**	7.917	0.257**
Home Background				
Income	0.000	0.000**	0.000	0.000**
Parental involvement	0.093	0.074	0.120	0.060*
Extracurricular activities	0.508	0.103**	0.449	0.083**
Student Characteristics				
Age at assessment	3.732	0.047**	3.633	0.034**
Age at assessment squared	−0.010	0.000**	−0.010	0.000**
Disability	−2.448	1.142*	−0.204	0.681
Hispanic	−1.098	0.592	−1.434	0.678
Asian	4.777	0.807**	5.031	0.793**
Black	−1.047	0.770	−1.587	0.673*
Other race	−0.748	0.873	−0.623	0.890
Male	−1.222	0.322**	−1.224	0.311**
Center care	0.046	0.431	−0.044	0.411
Delayed entry	−11.241	0.652**	−11.219	0.680**
Early entry	5.069	1.371**	4.835	1.324**
Full-day kindergarten attendance	−0.803	0.669	−0.757	0.722

* Indicates significance at $p < .05$. ** Indicates significance at $p < .01$.

can only speculate on some of the reasons why interpersonal skills are negatively related to performance (e.g., kindergarten teachers may not have accurately assessed children), but the findings merit further investigation and replication.

Consistent with the results of other studies that found that academic benefits dissipated after first grade, we found that attendance in a full-day kindergarten program was not related with reading performance at the end of fifth grade. Furthermore, additional sensitivity analyses designed to explore whether lower income students benefited more than nonpoor students from full-day kindergarten programs revealed no differential effects for poorer students. These results, however, should be interpreted cautiously because we have not controlled for potential self-selection biases that may be muting effects.

Of the school-program factors, class size and teaching experience were not significantly related with reading performance. However, all of the teaching-practice variables were significant, with whole-class instruction, teacher-directed individual activities, and small-group teaching showing positive relationships with reading scores, and child-selected activities showing negative associations with reading performance. It is possible that the latter finding is related to the developmental appropriateness of this practice. Namely, as students progressed through the years, there was a systematic decrease in the number of hours that teachers allowed students to choose their own activities. It may be the case that allowing children to choose their own instructional activities is an effective practice in kindergarten but becomes less effective as children grow older. Indeed, preliminary cross-sectional analyses suggest that this practice is positively signed with kindergarten achievement but negatively signed with achievement at older grades. Additional research about the potentially differential effectiveness of teaching practices at different grade levels would shed more insight on this finding.

The inclusion or exclusion of the nonacademic readiness skills in the models changed the significance of several variables, particularly those relating to parental involvement, disability status, and school-context variables. Most notably, controlling for nonacademic readiness indicators changed interpretations about the Black–White average reading-achievement differences. There were significant differences, on average, between Black and White students when nonacademic readiness skills were excluded from the model, but these differences were not significant once the nonacademic variables were included. This finding suggests that part of the differences between Black and White students is attributable to differences in their nonacademic readiness skills on kindergarten entry. However, the reading scores for Hispanics and Other-Race students were not significantly different from those of White students in either specification, and Asian students outperformed White students by nearly 5 points in both specifications.

DISCUSSION

Providing early learning and educational experiences is an overarching goal of social and educational policy in our country today (Committee for Economic Development, 2002). Our study suggests that policy initiatives that focus on the development of nonacademic school-readiness skills may prove promising because those skills at kindergarten entry were significantly associated with reading achievement from kindergarten through the fifth grade. Investments in the development of nonacademic school-readiness skills may not only raise overall reading achievement but also may narrow the achievement gap between minority and White students. Indeed, White students, on average, entered kindergarten with better fine motor skills than Blacks and Hispanics and were ranked higher on self-control, interpersonal skills, and approaches to learning than Blacks. We found the Black–White achievement gap in reading disappeared with the inclusion of nonacademic readiness skills in the regression model, which suggests that racial/ethnic differences in achievement might be narrowed if we could enhance the nonacademic readiness skills of minority students, particularly Black students.

In contrast to nonacademic readiness skills, attendance in a full-day kindergarten was not associated with reading achievement. This finding is consistent with other studies that show no achievement benefits beyond third grade (Cannon et al., 2006; Rathbun & West, 2004). However, because our study did not take into account potential self-selection bias and may not have fully accounted for the quality of the full-day program, it is possible that some of our findings are driven by unobserved characteristics.

The decision as to whether states and school districts should continue to push for a full-day kindergarten requirement or direct funds to other avenues (e.g., the promotion of nonacademic readiness skills) hinges on additional factors that are currently under-researched. For example, there is some evidence that the initial academic advantages held by students in full-day programs erode if the curriculum in the upper grades is not changed to reflect the progress made during kindergarten (VanFleet, 2002). This suggests that participation in full-day programs would have more enduring benefits if early education programs could be redesigned in a manner that would allow curricula to be better coordinated across grades (see, e.g., Bogard & Takanishi, 2005).

More research is also needed to understand the mechanism by which nonacademic readiness skills are related to student achievement. It is unclear whether those skills are an antecedent for learning or whether such skills are an indirect marker for learning opportunities. For example, having better nonacademic readiness skills (e.g., motivation toward learning) may directly facilitate learning and test performance. It also may be the case that individuals with better nonacademic readiness skills engage in more activities that provide greater opportunities to learn. A better understanding of how nonacademic skills relate to the improvement of achievement can help policy makers design more effective intervention programs.

Ultimately, the decision of where to direct funds needs to be guided by a cost-benefit analysis that compares investments in full-day kindergarten programs to investments in other types of interventions, such as those that promote nonacademic readiness skills. Although full-day kindergarten programs may have some initial positive effects on student achievement, it is unknown whether the lack of enduring benefits and the potentially negative impact on nonacademic skills merit the costs associated with their implementation. A program of research that works toward a better understanding of how full-day programs and nonacademic skills influence outcomes and the associated costs of each type of intervention would provide a strong foundation for future decisions about effective programs.

REFERENCES

Ackerman, D. J., Barnett, W. S., & Robin, K. B. (2005). *Making the most of kindergarten: Present trends and future issues in the provision of full-day programs.* National Institute for Early Education Research (NIEER). Retrieved from http://nieer.org/resources/policyreports/report4.pdf.

Agostin, T. M., & Bain, S. K. (1997). Predicting early school success with developmental and social skill screeners. *Psychology in the Schools, 34,* 219–228.

Alexander, K. L., Entwisle, D. R., & Dauber, S. L. (1993). First-grade classroom behavior: Its short and long-term consequences for school performance. *Child Development, 64,* 801–814.

Arnold, D. H., Ortiz, C., Curry, J. C., Stowe, R. M., Goldstein, N. E., Fisher, P. H., Zeljo, A., & Yershova, K. (1999). Promoting academic success and preventing disruptive behavior disorders through community partnership. *Journal of Community Psychology, 27*(5), 589–598.

Bogard, K., & Takanishi, R. (2005). PK-3: An aligned and coordinated approach to education for children 3 to 8 years old. *Social Policy Report, 19*(3).

Brown, R. (1982). Exercise and mental health in the pediatric population. *Clinics in Sports Medicine, 1,* 515–527.

Cannon, J. S., Jacknowitz, A., & Painter, G. (2006). Is full better than half? Examining the longitudinal effects of full-day kindergarten attendance. *Journal of Policy Analysis and Management, 25*(2), 299–321.

Cassidy, J., & Shaver, P. R. (1999). *Handbook of attachment: Theory, research, and clinical applications.* New York: Guilford.

Chase-Lansdale, P. L., Gordon, R. A., Brooks-Gunn, J., & Klebanov, P. K. (1997). Neighborhood and family influences on the intellectual and behavioral competence of preschool and early school-age children. In J. Brooks-Gunn, G. Duncan, & J. L. Aber (Eds.), *Neighborhood poverty: Context and consequences for children* (Vol. 1, pp. 119–145). New York: Russell Sage Press.

Coley, R. J. (2002). *An uneven start: Indicators of inequality in school readiness.* Princeton, NJ: Educational Testing Service Policy Center. Retrieved from http://www.ets.org/research/dload/Unevenstart.pdf.

Committee for Economic Development. (2002). *Preschool for all: Investing in a productive and just society*. New York: Author.

Cryan, J. R., Sheehan, R., Wiechel, J., & Bandy-Hadden, I. G. (1992). Success outcomes of full-day kindergarten: More positive behavior and increased achievement in the years after. *Early Childhood Research Quarterly, 7*, 187–203.

Ferguson, R. F. (1991). Paying for public education: New evidence on how and why money matters. *Harvard Journal on Legislation, 28*(2), 465–498.

Gardner, R. C. (2001). *Psychological statistics using SPSS for Windows*. New York: McGraw-Hill.

Greenwald, R., Hedges, L. V., & Laine, R. D. (1996). The effect of school resources on student achievement. *Review of Educational Research, 66*(3), 361–396.

Heaviside, S., & Farris, E. (1993). *Public school kindergarten teachers' views of children's readiness for schools* (NCES 1993–410). Washington, DC: Department of Education, National Center for Education Statistics.

Kagan, S. L., Moore, E., & Bredekamp, S. (Eds.). (1995). *Reconsidering children's early learning and development: Toward shared beliefs and vocabulary*. Washington, DC: National Education Goals Panel.

Kaplan, D. (2002). Methodological advances in the analysis of individual growth with relevance to education policy. *Peabody Journal of Education, 77*(4), 189–215.

Kwon, Y. A. (2005). Protective mechanisms that moderate academic risk levels in young children: HLM applications with the Early Childhood Longitudinal Study (ECLS-K) kindergarten–first grade data set. *Dissertation Abstracts International Section A: Humanities and Social Sciences, 66*(1-A), 87.

Ladd, G. W., Birch, S. H., & Buhs, E. S. (1999). Children's social and scholastic lives in kindergarten: Related spheres of influence? *Child Development, 70*(6), 373–400.

Le, V., Kirby, S. N., Barney, H., Setodji, C. M., & Gershwin, D. (2006). *School readiness, full-day kindergarten, and student achievement: An empirical investigation*. MG-558-RF/FF. Santa Monica, CA: RAND. Retrieved from http://www.rand.org/pubs/monographs/2006/RAND_MG558.pdf.

Lee, V. E., Burkam, D. T., Ready, D. D., Honigman, J., & Meisels, S. J. (2006). Full-day versus half-day kindergarten: In which program do children learn more? *American Journal of Education, 112*, 163–208.

Lewit, E. M., & Baker, L. S. (1995). School readiness. *Future of Children, 5*(2), 128–139.

Long Beach Unified School District Office of Research, Planning and Evaluation. (2000). *Research summary: Full day academic kindergarten*. Long Beach, CA: Long Beach Unified School District.

McClelland, M. M., Morrison, F. J., & Holmes, D. L. (2000). Children at risk for early academic problems: The role of learning-related social skills. *Early Childhood Research Quarterly, 15*(3), 307–329.

National Association of Early Childhood Specialists in State Departments of Education (2000). *Still unacceptable trends in kindergarten entry and placement: A position statement developed by National Association of Early Childhood Specialists in State Departments of Education*. Baton Rouge, LA: Author.

National Center for Education Statistics. (2001). *ECLS-K base year public-use data files and electronic codebook* (NCES Report No. 2001029 rev.). U.S. Department of Education. Washington, DC: U.S. Government Printing Office. Retrieved from http://nces.ed.gov/pubsearch/pubsinfo.asp?pubid=2001029rev.

Phillips, M., Crouse, J., & Ralph, J. 1998. Does the black-white test score gap widen after children enter school? In C. Jencks & M. Phillips (Eds.), *The black-white test score gap* (pp. 229–272). Washington DC: Brookings Institution.

Pianta, R. C. (2002). *School readiness: A focus on children, families, communities, and school.* Arlington, VA: Educational Research Service.

Plucker, J. A., Eaton, J. J., Rapp, K. E., Lim, W., Nowak, J., Hansen, J. A., et al. (2004). *The effects of full day versus half day kindergarten: Review and analysis of national and Indiana data.* Indianapolis: Center for Evaluation and Education Policy.

Poest, C. A., Williams, J. R., Witt, D. D., & Atwood, M. L. (1990). Challenge me to move: Large muscle development in young children. *Young Children, 45,* 4–10.

Porch, S. (2002). *Full-day kindergarten.* Arlington, VA: Educational Research Service.

Rathbun, A., & West, J. (2004). *From kindergarten through third grade: Children's beginning school experiences.* Washington, DC: National Center for Education Statistics.

Rimm-Kaufman, S. E., Pianta, R. C., & Cox, M. J. (2000). Teachers' judgments of problems in the transition to kindergarten. *Early Childhood Research Quarterly, 15,* 147–166.

Rouse, C. E., Brooks-Gunn, J., & McLanahan, S. (2005). Introducing the issue. *Future of Children, 1,* 5–14.

Russell, J. L. (2006). An enduring tension: Kindergarten education in an era of accountability. In C. Miskel & W. Hoy (Eds.), *Contemporary issues in educational policy and school outcomes (research and theory in educational administration)* (pp. 215–240). Greenwich, CT: Information Age.

Schafer, J. L. (1997). *Analysis of incomplete multivariate data.* New York: Chapman and Hall.

Seefeldt, V. (1980). Physical fitness guidelines for preschool children. *Proceedings of the National Conference on Physical Fitness and Sports for All* (pp. 5–19). Washington, DC: President's Council on Physical Fitness and Sports.

Smith, P., & Pederson, D. (1988). Maternal sensitivity and patterns of infant-mother attachment. *Child Development, 59,* 1097–1101.

Stipek, D., Feiler, R., Daniels, D., & Millburn, S. (1995). Effects of different instructional approaches on young children's achievement and motivation. *Child Development, 66*(1), 209–223.

Stipek, D. J., & Ryan, R. H. (1997). Economically disadvantaged preschoolers: Ready to learn but further to go. *Developmental Psychology, 33,* 711–723.

VanFleet, W. (2002). *All-day kindergarten report.* Muncie, IN: Muncie Public Schools, Office of the Director of Elementary Instruction.

Walston, J., West, J., & Rathbun, A. H. (2005). *Do the greater academic gains made by full-day kindergarten children persist through third grade?* Paper presented at the annual meeting of the American Educational Research Association, Montreal.

West, J., Denton, K., & Reaney, L. M. (2001). *The kindergarten year: Findings from the Early Childhood Longitudinal Study, kindergarten class of 1998–99.* Washington, DC: National Center for Education Statistics. Retrieved from http://www.nces.ed.gov/pubs2001/2001023.pdf.

Zill, N. (1999). Promoting educational equity and excellence in kindergarten. In R. C. Pianta & M. Cox (Eds.), *The transition to kindergarten* (pp. 67–105). Baltimore, MD: Brookes.

14

Small Classes in the Early Grades: One Policy, Multiple Outcomes

JEREMY D. FINN, ALLISON E. SURIANI, AND CHARLES M. ACHILLES

The idea that small classes are desirable for instruction is not new; indeed, it dates back at least to biblical times (Angrist & Lavy, 1996). In the 20th and 21st centuries, small classes, a distinguishing feature of American private schools and a fundamental component of all remedial programs, have been posited as a way to bolster student achievement in public schools generally.

Tennessee's Project STAR (Student Teacher Achievement Ratio) is not a "program" in the traditional sense. It was a large-scale experiment to test the effectiveness of this basic principle of school organization – that is, arranging classes in the early grades so they have a relatively small number of students in a classroom with a full-time teacher.

Because of the reported effectiveness of small classes in STAR, the experiment has been followed by class size reduction (CSR) initiatives across the country. According to one recent survey, 33 states had statewide CSR programs for the early grades, of which 13 were mandatory (McCabe, 2006). The number of districts with their own CSR programs is undocumented but probably quite large. President Clinton introduced a nationwide CSR program in 1998, which was discontinued by the Bush administration.

STAR has also been followed by additional research on small classes, by several analyses of CSR costs and benefits, and by some arguments that the research on CSR or the conclusions drawn from the research is faulty. This chapter summarizes these developments. Although Project STAR is emphasized, it is discussed in the context of class-size research and policy more broadly. The chapter has the following six sections:

1. a brief history of Project STAR
2. a description of the STAR experiment and its defining features
3. a summary of the short-term and long-term findings of STAR and of other evaluations that followed STAR
4. attempts to explain how small classes benefit student achievement and behavior (the dynamics of small classes)

5. attempts to evaluate the costs and benefits of CSR
6. a description of a new public-access database containing information on the STAR students from kindergarten through high school

BEWARE OF TERMINOLOGY: HEFFALUMPS ARE NOT ELEPHANTS

Class size (CS) is *the number of students regularly in a teacher's classroom for whom that teacher is responsible.* Assessing class size is easy – just count the students in the room or count the names on the teacher's roster.[1] A class with 15 students and one teacher has a class size of 15. A class with 28 students and one teacher has a class size of 28. A class with 28 students and two teachers and a full-time teacher aide also has a class size of 28.[2] Class size is important to parents, who want their children to attend a small class, and to teachers because it shapes their interactions with students. It is clearly related to the amount of material that can be learned – an observation supported by scientific data (see later discussion).

Seems simple, right? Guess again! A second "look-alike" construct, used primarily by economists, muddies the waters.

Pupil:teacher ratio (PTR) is *the ratio of the number of students in an educational unit to the number of full-time-equivalent professionals assigned to that unit.* The number of "teachers" may include teaching assistants, special education and Title I teachers, and specialty teachers who do not have their own classes (e.g., music or foreign-language teachers or librarians), as well as administrators.[3] Pupil:teacher ratios are usually computed for large educational units; for example, districts, states, or the entire nation. Many large urban districts have small PTRs (e.g., 13:1) because of the large number of ancillary staff members, *despite having overcrowded classrooms* (Boozer & Rouse, 2001; Lewit & Baker, 1997; Miles, 1995).

PTR does not describe the proximal setting in which teachers are teaching and students are learning. It does not play the same obvious role in any particular classroom – indeed, it may play no role at all. It is not surprising that the relationship of PTR with student achievement is weak at best (Ferguson & Ladd, 1996; Hanushek, 1989; Hedges & Greenwald, 1996; Hedges, Laine, & Greenwald, 1994).

PTRs and class size do not translate easily into one another for two reasons: PTRs are usually computed for schools, districts, and other larger units, obscuring variation from classroom to classroom, and PTRs include personnel who are not responsible for classes of students on a regular or full-time basis.

Why is this distinction important? The distinction between PTR and class size is important because PTR data have been used erroneously to "prove" that

[1] There may be some disagreement due to absenteeism.
[2] But a pupil:teacher ratio of about 9:1.
[3] A ratio is obtained by division, and the divisor is important.

class size is unrelated to student achievement – and these arguments have been echoed widely in the media. As a result, students for whom the benefits of CSR might be far-reaching may be denied the opportunities offered by small classes.

Consider these three examples: In 1998, Hanushek published a monograph entitled "The Evidence on Class Size." The monograph summarized studies of the relationship of PTRs to academic achievement, using data from the National Assessment of Educational Progress (NAEP) and other surveys that did not collect class-size information. Further, the main results in the monograph were based on 277 estimates from econometric studies that "consider teacher-pupil ratios" (p. 21) – a statement easily verified by examining the studies themselves. However, the monograph concluded that "the estimates are almost equally divided between those suggesting that *small classes* are better and those suggesting that they are worse" (pp. 21–22; emphasis added). The report has been cited and quoted by Hanushek and others,[4] including in testimony given to Congress, in the courts, and in the popular press.

Other high-profile publications also have confused the issue. A full issue of *Psychological Science in the Public Interest* was subtitled "Class Size and Student Achievement" (Ehrenberg, Brewer, Gamoran, & Willms, 2001a).[5] The monograph begins with the exhortation that "class size is not the same thing as the pupil/teacher ratio. Indeed it is quite different" (Ehrenberg et al., 2001a, p. 1) and notes that "class size is more closely linked to learning" (p. 2). Yet, much of the report summarized research on PTRs (including a review of Hanushek's findings). To its credit, the report also discussed Tennessee's STAR experiment and asked this fundamental question, "How can we explain the class size effects on achievement that have been reported?" (Ehrenberg et al., 2001a, p. 24). Contradicting the data on class size (and with very few data on salaries), the report concluded that funds might be better spent if used to increase teachers' salaries (pp. 25–26).

An overview of the correlates of human capital by Carneiro and Heckman (2003) was discussed in the *Wall Street Journal* (Heckman, 2006). The *Journal* article made reference to a "cost-benefit analysis of classroom-size [*sic*][6] reduction on adult earnings" and concluded, "While smaller classes raise the adult earnings of students, the earnings gains do not offset the costs"

[4] Table 6 of the monograph summarizes the results of 78 value-added studies of PTRs. The table is entitled "Percentage Distribution of Other Estimated Influences of Teacher-Pupil Ratio on Student Performance" (p. 24). The same table was published in a 1999 article in *Educational Evaluation and Policy Analysis* (Hanushek, 1999), but in that article the title was "Percentage Distribution of Effect of Class Size on Student Performance" (Table 2, p. 148, emphasis added).

[5] A similar article by the same authors entitled "Does Class Size Matter?" was published in *Scientific American* (Ehrenberg, Brewer, Gamoran, & Willms, 2001b).

[6] Class sizes are counted in numbers of persons. Classroom size is measured in square or cubic feet.

(p. A14). However, in the original Carneiro and Heckman article, the two and a half pages that discuss the issue alternate between "class size" and "pupil-teacher ratio" (pp. 44–47). It said explicitly that the cost-benefit analysis involved large-scale changes in PTRs but made no reference to teaching or learning processes in classes or whether decreasing the PTR would result in fewer students in classrooms.

The message is clear: Examine what you read about class size carefully. (The remainder of this chapter is about class size.) If small classes are needed in your school(s), make sure that each targeted class is small. Extra effort may be required to ensure that CSR initiatives reach the classroom level.[7]

A BRIEF HISTORY OF STAR

In May 1985, the Tennessee legislature passed House Bill (HB) 544, funding a policy study to determine the effects of class size on student achievement in the primary grades.[8] The legislation directed that the study address these three questions:

1. What are the effects of a reduced class size on the achievement (i.e., norm-referenced and criterion-referenced tests) and development (e.g., self-concept, attendance) of students in public elementary school grades (K–3)?
2. Is there a cumulative effect of being in a small class over an extended time (4 years) as compared with a 1-year effect for students in a small class for 1 year?
3. Does effective use of teacher aides improve student performance as compared with teachers who have no special preparation for their altered conditions?

To design and conduct the study, the Tennessee State Department of Education formed a consortium of researchers from the department, the state board of education, the state superintendents' association, and representatives from four Tennessee universities. Responsibility for direct contact with schools was delegated to the university representatives. The consortium reviewed prior class-size research as one basis for making these design decisions about the study: It would begin in the earliest grades, where small classes would be most likely to show positive effects; the small classes would have no fewer than 13 students and no more than 17 students; and it would allow disaggregation

[7] Some states affected by school-funding litigation are implementing PTR reductions or combinations of class size and PTR reductions, despite courts' judgments that class sizes should be reduced (e.g., New Jersey and New York).

[8] More complete histories are given in the STAR *Final Report* (Word et al., 1990), from which this section was adapted; in the STAR *Database User's Guide* (Finn, Boyd-Zaharias, Fish, & Gerber, 2007); and in Ritter and Boruch (1999). The *Final Report* and *User's Guide* are available on the website of HEROS, Inc.: http://www.heros-Inc.org.

of the data by school location (urbanicity), student race/ethnicity, gender, age, and socioeconomic status (SES).

Most important, the study was a randomized experiment in which causal connections between class size and student outcomes could be discerned. This design, often considered the gold standard of empirical research, would set STAR apart from prior (and, to date, all subsequent) research on class size, including observational studies and regression analyses of existing databases (e.g., production-function analyses).

The state paid the costs associated with the study, including the salaries of extra teachers required to reduce class sizes and of project teacher aides. The total cost of the 4-year project, plus data analysis and reporting in the fifth year, was approximately $13 million.

Selection of Schools

All Tennessee school systems were invited to participate. Schools were to plan to participate in the project for 4 years, beginning with kindergarten in 1985–1986. All participating teachers had to be certified for the grade level they were teaching. Schools had to agree to the random assignment of teachers and students to different class conditions (i.e., class sizes).

Initially, 180 schools expressed an interest in participating, of which about 100 schools had enough kindergarten students to be eligible to participate. A minimum of 57 students was necessary, providing enough students for one class for each of three conditions (with 13, 22, and 22 students, respectively). Ultimately, 79 schools across the state were selected to participate (17 inner-city, 16 suburban, 8 urban, and 38 rural schools).[9]

THE STAR EXPERIMENT

The STAR experiment followed for 4 years one cohort of students: those entering kindergarten in 1985 (or those who began schooling in first grade in 1986). Within each school, all students entering kindergarten were assigned at random to one of three conditions: a small class (S) with 13–17 students, a regular class (R) with 22–25 students, or a regular class with a full-time teacher aide (RA) and 22–25 students. Teachers were assigned at random to the classes.[10]

The randomization of students among conditions meant that each class comprised a cross-section of students from the school population. Class arrangements were maintained all day (including kindergarten classes), all year long. The only interventions in STAR were class size and teacher aides: No other curricular changes or school policies were imposed on the STAR classes

[9] Approximately 6,300 students from the 79 schools participated in STAR in the kindergarten year.

[10] The STAR consortium monitored the randomization regularly. One school could not maintain the randomized classes throughout and withdrew from STAR after kindergarten.

or teachers, and all other school services, including special education programs, functioned as usual.

In total, 128 small classes, 101 regular classes, and 99 regular-aide classes were formed in kindergarten. Because kindergarten attendance was not mandated in Tennessee at the time, a substantial number of students joined STAR when they entered first grade. They were assigned at random to the three conditions.

Once assigned to a class type, students remained in the assigned class type as long as they were in the experiment. A new teacher was assigned at random to the class in each subsequent grade. Students moving into STAR schools from non-STAR schools during the 4-year experiment were assigned at random to one of the class types, with the constraint that small classes could not exceed 17 students. Students moving from one STAR school to another were assigned to the same type of class as they had participated in previously.

Students with the longest duration participated from kindergarten (1985–1986) through Grade 3 (1988–1989). In all, 27% of the 11,601 STAR students participated for 4 consecutive years, and 42% remained in the experiment for 3 or more years.[11] Students who participated in STAR for 1, 2, or 3 years made it possible to study different patterns of small-class participation.

Measures

Academic achievement (norm-referenced and criterion-referenced) and self-concept/motivation were measured in the spring of each year (1986–1989). The norm-referenced tests were the Stanford Achievement tests (SATs); the criterion-referenced tests were the Basic Skills First (BSF) tests, developed by the Tennessee State Department of Education. Self-concept and motivation were assessed with the SCAMIN instrument (Milchus, Farrah, & Reitz, 1968). Additional data included logs of time use, interviews with teachers and aides, and responses to the Teacher Problem Checklist (Cruickshank, 1980).

The experiment ended in the spring of 1989, when most students had completed third grade. In fourth grade, all students returned to full-size classes. Researchers continued to collect data on the STAR students in subsequent grades. Five stages of additional data collection were undertaken:

1. Academic-achievement test scores were obtained annually in Grades 4–8; scores were provided by the state department of education on the Comprehensive Tests of Basic Skills (CTBS) and on later-grade versions of the state's BSF tests.
2. Teachers' ratings of students' classroom participation and behavior were obtained in Grades 4 and 8, using the Student Participation Questionnaire (SPQ) (Finn, Folger, & Cox, 1991).

[11] Students who were retained in their grade or who moved out of STAR schools participated for fewer years.

3. Students' identification with school was assessed in Grade 8, using the Identification with School Scale (Voelkl, 1996).
4. College-entrance examination scores were obtained for STAR students.[12]
5. Complete high school transcripts were obtained for approximately 5,300 STAR students, which included courses taken, grades, and whether students had graduated or dropped out of school.

The primary data analyses were conducted by the STAR consortium; other teams have conducted secondary analyses. A number of questions remain, and analyses using the STAR data continue today (see the "Continuing Research" section).

The Particular Strengths of Project STAR

The STAR experiment had several strengths: (a) The within-school randomized experiment permitted causal conclusions to be drawn and also controlled for differences among schools (e.g., populations served, resource availability, teacher morale, and school size); (b) it built on prior research findings about the timing of small classes and about recommended class sizes; (c) it was extensive, involving more than 6,000 students each year and almost 12,000 students in the 4-year span; and (d) the students were assessed regularly during the experimental years (K–3) and were followed through high school.

SHORT- AND LONG-TERM FINDINGS

The most in-depth analyses of academic achievement are given in the STAR *Final Report* (Word et al., 1990); in Finn and Achilles (1990) and Finn, Gerber, Achilles, and Boyd-Zaharias (2001); and in Krueger (1999).[13] Books and articles that review the STAR outcomes and other class-size research in nontechnical terms include Achilles (1999), Biddle and Berliner (2002), Finn (2002), Mosteller (1995), and Wang and Finn (2000).

Short-Term Outcomes

The short-term findings of STAR are as follows:

- STAR demonstrated that small classes yield academic benefits in every grade, K–3, and in every subject tested. Table 14.1 summarizes the magnitude of the benefits both as effect sizes and in months of schooling. Overall effect sizes were in the range of 0.20 to 0.30 standard deviations, which

[12] This work was spearheaded by Princeton economist Alan Krueger.

[13] Other publications, some listed in the following pages, address particular questions (e.g., the effects of teacher aides, the "whys" of small classes). The STAR *Database User's Guide* (Finn et al., 2007) includes a more complete bibliography.

Table 14.1. *Effect sizes for small classes in Grades K–3*

	SAT tests[a]			BSF tests[a]		SAT grade equivalents (months of schooling)		
Grade/contrast	Total reading	Word study skills	Total mathematics	Reading	Mathematics	Total reading	Word study skills	Total mathematics
Kindergarten	0.21***	0.20***	0.19***	–	–	0.5	0.5	1.6
Grade 1: All	0.30***	0.29***	0.31***	0.31***	0.21***	1.3	0.9	2.8
1 year – regular	0.16**	0.20***	0.23***	0.23***	0.17**	0.6	0.6	2.0
2 years – regular	0.40***	0.37***	0.38***	0.38***	0.25***	1.9	1.3	3.4
Grade 2: All	0.26***	0.25***	0.25***	0.21***	0.18***	3.9	4.8	3.5
1 year – regular	0.12*	0.08	0.16*	0.13*	0.13*	1.8	1.5	2.2
2 years – regular	0.24***	0.23***	0.24***	0.20***	0.18***	3.7	4.4	3.3
3 years – regular	0.36***	0.38***	0.32**	0.28***	0.22***	5.8	7.8	4.6
Grade 3: All	0.22***	0.21***	0.15**	0.14**	0.11*	4.5	5.5	2.6
1 year – regular	0.08	0.09	0.08	0.08	0.07	1.5	2.4	1.3
2 years – regular	0.16**	0.16*	0.12*	0.11*	0.09	3.3	4.3	2.1
3 years – regular	0.24***	0.23***	0.17**	0.15**	0.12**	5.2	6.2	2.9
4 years – regular	0.33***	0.30***	0.21***	0.19***	0.15**	7.1	8.2	3.7

[a] Difference between mean performance of small-class students and regular-class students, divided by the standard deviation of regular-class students.

*$p < .05$; **$p < .01$; ***$p < .001$.

Source: Table adapted from Finn, Gerber et al. (2001), Table 1 and Figure 1.

translated to benefits of ½ to 5½ months of schooling (see Finn, Gerber et al., 2001).

- Starting small classes early and continuing in small classes for multiple years are important. As shown in Table 14.1, students who entered small classes in kindergarten and remained in small classes for 2 or more years received the greatest benefits – in general, the more the better.[14]
- In each grade, there were significant interactions with race/ethnicity or with school urbanicity.[15] The benefits of small classes were greater for minority students or students attending inner-city schools than for White students in nonurban schools. In terms of effect sizes, the advantages for minorities were often two to three times as great, thus reducing the White–minority achievement gap. This finding has led to recommendations that small classes should be "targeted" to schools serving low-income and minority students.

These findings have been corroborated in nonexperimental research. Wisconsin's Project SAGE reported effect sizes similar to those in Table 14.1 (Molnar, Smith, & Zahorik, 1999; Molnar et al., 2000). California's statewide CSR, evaluated mainly in third grade, yielded effect sizes similar to those of STAR for Grade 3 students who had been in small classes for 1 or 2 years (see CSR Research Consortium, 2000). Evaluations in other high-poverty communities (Achilles, Harman, & Egelson, 1995; Achilles, Nye, & Zaharias, 1995) and analyses of several large-scale databases have documented benefits of CRS; for example, with first-grade students (NICHD Early Child Care Research Network, 2004) and in a national sample of kindergarten students (Walston, West, & Rathbun, 2002).

In addition to achievement gains, STAR researchers found the following:

- Fewer small-class students were recommended for in-grade retention (being "held back") in Grades 1, 2, and 3.[16] The differences were statistically significant in Grade 1, in which retentions are more common (7.5% compared to 11.9% in full-size classes), and in Grade 3 (3.1% compared to 4.6%).
- No academic benefits were found for teacher-aide classes in any subject matter in any grade, *no matter what functions the aides performed in the classroom* (Boyd-Zaharias & Pate-Bain, 1998; Finn, Gerber, & Achilles, 2000; Gerber, Finn, Achilles, & Boyd-Zaharias, 2001).[17]

[14] The analysis used a multitude of socioeconomic control variables to reduce the confounding with student mobility.

[15] Not shown in the table.

[16] Retention data were not collected at the end of kindergarten.

[17] Note that the addition of a teacher aide to a classroom decreases the PTR but does not alter the class size.

Table 14.2. *Small-class effect sizes for duration analysis*

Grade/contrast	CTBS tests: Total reading	CTBS tests: Total mathematics	CTBS tests: Science	CTBS tests: Social science	BSF tests: Reading	BSF tests: Mathematics
Grade 4						
1 year – regular	0.04	0.17	0.05	0.10	0.03	0.01
2 years – regular	0.12	0.22**	0.11	0.15*	0.12	0.11
3 years – regular	0.20**	0.27***	0.17**	0.21***	0.22***	0.21***
4 years – regular	0.28***	0.32***	0.24***	0.26***	0.31***	0.31***
Grade 6						
1 year – regular	0.04	0.06	0.00	0.05	0.30*	0.13
2 years – regular	0.09*	0.09*	0.02	0.11**	0.36**	0.18
3 years – regular	0.14**	0.13**	0.04	0.17***	0.42***	0.23*
4 years – regular	0.19***	0.17**	0.05	0.24***	0.48***	0.27*
Grade 8						
1 year – regular	−0.06	−0.02	−0.02	−0.03	−0.03	−0.04
2 years – regular	0.03	0.06	0.04	0.05	0.06	0.04
3 years – regular	0.12**	0.14**	0.10*	0.14***	0.16***	0.11*
4 years – regular	0.22***	0.21***	0.17**	0.23***	0.25***	0.19***

Note: $^{*}p < .05$; $^{**}p < .01$; $^{***}p < .001$.

Source: Table adapted from Finn, Gerber et al. (2001), Figure 2. Difference between mean performance of small-class students and regular-class students, divided by the standard deviation of regular-class students.

Long-Term Outcomes

After students returned to full-size classes, the academic benefits continued in all subsequent grades (see Table 14.2 for effect sizes). Analyses of test scores for Grades 4, 6, and 8 found the following:

- Students who had attended small classes in K–3 scored significantly better on all achievement tests in Grade 4, on all tests except science in Grade 6, and on four of six tests in Grade 8.[18]
- The strength and duration of carryover effects depended on the number of years that students had attended small classes. In any given grade (4, 6, or 8), the effects were mostly nonsignificant for students who had attended small classes for one year, marginally significant for students who had been in small classes for 2 years, and consistently significant for students who had been in small classes for 3 or 4 years.
- The interactions with socioeconomic status and race, found in the earlier grades, were no longer statistically significant. That is, the carryover effects were similar for students from all backgrounds.

[18] Unfortunately, standardized testing in Tennessee ended in Grade 8.

Three analyses examined other (nonachievement) high school outcomes. The first used data on college entrance examinations (SATs and ACTs) to see if students who attended small classes in K–3 were more likely to take the exams than were students who had attended full-size classes (Krueger & Whitmore, 2001). The authors argued that taking college-entrance examinations reflected aspirations to attend postsecondary schooling. The study found a significant increase in test-taking for students who attended small classes. The benefit for Black students was substantially greater than for White students, reducing the Black–White gap in college-entrance test-taking by 54%.

A second study examined enrollment in advanced coursework (Finn, Fox, McClellan, Achilles, & Boyd-Zaharias, 2006). Using high school transcripts of STAR participants, researchers quantified the number and level of courses taken in mathematics, science, and foreign languages. Small-class participation had a significant positive impact on the amount of foreign-language courses taken and the highest levels taken in foreign languages and mathematics. Although the effect sizes were small, the greatest course-taking benefits accrued to students who spent 3 or more years in small classes in Grades K–3. No differential effect by SES was found.

The third study examined graduation/dropout rates of students who had participated in STAR (Finn, Gerber, & Boyd-Zaharias, 2005). Graduation/dropout information was available for 4,948 STAR participants through high school or state education department records. The small-class effect on graduation rates was greater with each additional year of small-class participation. For all students combined, the effects of attending small classes for 4 years increased the odds of graduation by about 80%. For students from low-income homes, the effect of attending small classes for 3 years increased the odds of graduating by approximately 67%, and attending small classes for 4 years more than doubled the odds. The rates for low-income students with 3 or more years of small-class participation were as high as those of higher income students. These results, like those of Krueger and Whitmore (2001), support the recommendation that small classes be targeted to schools serving low-income or minority students.

Secondary Analyses of the Achievement Data

Other groups of researchers have reanalyzed the STAR achievement data using a variety of statistical approaches. Goldstein and Blatchford (1998); Hedges, Nye, and Konstantopoulos (2000); and Krueger (1999) reexamined short-term effects. Hedges, Nye, and Konstantopoulos (1999, 2004) and Krueger and Whitmore (2001) reported long-term effects. Both general and specific results of these analyses were similar to the original STAR findings.

THE DYNAMICS OF SMALL CLASSES

Two questions are asked often: Which "frame conditions" have to be present to realize the academic benefits of small classes? How do small classes affect student performance? Answers to the first question have come from the STAR design and findings. Answers to the second question have proven to be more elusive.

The Frame Conditions

The STAR experiment embodied two principles that characterize interventions with sustained effects (Ramey & Ramey, 1998):

1. *Start early and continue.* STAR students began in kindergarten and continued in small classes through successive grades. Students who entered small classes in kindergarten had the greatest immediate impact on performance. Those who entered small classes in kindergarten and continued for 3 or 4 years had the strongest carryover effects (Finn, Gerber, et al., 2001). CSR programs that begin in later grades or have shorter duration (e.g., 1 year) are less likely to have the same benefits.
2. *Program intensity.* STAR small classes were maintained throughout the day for the full school year. Kindergartens were full-day kindergartens.

The following conditions, if absent, could dilute the benefits of small classes:

- *Heterogeneous classes.* Through random assignment, each STAR class had a cross-section of students in a particular grade level in a school. Experience suggests that if the class comprises only students who are difficult to teach, the same benefits may not be realized. Strict randomization may not be necessary, but heterogeneity was an important feature of the STAR classes.
- *Cohort effects.* In the STAR experiment, the same class grouping was maintained across the years. Krueger and Whitmore's (2001) analysis suggested that this condition contributed to the impact of small classes.
- *Qualified teachers.* STAR demonstrated that certified teachers, in general, produced greater learning gains with small classes than with larger classes. We do not argue that small classes are the only factor that affects academic achievement, neither do we believe that small classes can compensate for poor teaching.

How Do Small Classes Affect Student Performance?

There are few data that show *how* small classes affect teaching and student achievement. The most common hypothesis is that teachers of small classes provide more individualized instruction. Although teachers often report that small classes help them do this, systematic interviews and classroom observations have not supported this perception (Evertson & Folger, 1989; Shapson, Eason, Wright, & Fitzgerald, 1980).

A broader argument has been made that "small classes let teachers use effectively what they already know . . . but large classes stifle or negate the effective use of good teaching methods" (Achilles, 1999, p. 112). That is, small classes permit teachers to be better teachers. In the report of the National Commission on Teaching and America's Future, Darling-Hammond (1998) argued that "school reform cannot succeed unless it focuses on creating the conditions in which teachers can teach and teach well" (p. 6). Many of the conditions listed in the report (pp. 6–11) characterize small classes.

Some evidence supports this argument. Studies have found that teachers of small classes spend more time on instruction and less on classroom management or matters of discipline (Achilles, Kiser-Kling, Aust, & Owen, 1995; Blatchford, 2003; Bourke, 1986; Molnar et al., 1999). Indeed, data show consistently that teachers of small classes have more time to "listen to children, to get to know their personal lives and concerns" (Johnston, 1990, p. 12; also Finn, Forden, Verdinelli, & Pannozzo, 2001; Kiser-Kling, 1995).

However, the most visible and obvious changes when class sizes are reduced are not in teachers' behavior but rather in *students' behavior.* The review by Finn, Pannozzo, and Achilles (2003) summarized theory and data to support this view. In the studies reviewed, 38 of 42 measures of learning behavior indicated that students in small classes were more engaged in learning, and 17 of 24 measures of pro- and anti-social behavior indicated that students in small classes were better behaved. With only one exception (in 66 measures), no significant difference favored large classes.

The authors discussed two principles that explain these effects. The first, visibility of the individual, is also termed the "firing-line hypothesis." In a small class, each student feels continuous pressure to participate; there are no "back corners" in which to hide. Moreover, the teacher cannot easily ignore any particular student. The second principle is termed "sense of belonging." Small classes are more cohesive groups than are large classes; there is a smaller proportion of nonparticipants, and splinter groups are rare. Further, in small classes, students tend to be more supportive of one another and develop a stronger sense of identification with their classmates and with the group as a whole; this phenomenon has been termed "psychological sense of community" (Sarason, 1974).

Only 19 studies (with 66 different measures) were found that examined these principles in small and large classes. The studies were very diverse and varied in quality but included several that were well designed and well conducted. In sum, observations show that student behavior changes, sometimes dramatically, when class sizes are reduced, but more research is needed on the mechanisms by which learning is affected.

THE ECONOMICS OF CLASS SIZE REDUCTION

Several approaches have been taken to evaluating the costs and benefits of small classes. Simplistic evaluations are entirely cost oriented; they assume that CSR can be accomplished only by increasing funding to enable the addition of teachers and facilities to the budget. For better or worse, California accomplished its statewide reduction of K–3 class sizes in a matter of months by the rapid expenditure of about $1 billion (Bohrnstedt & Stecher, 1999). From this perspective, it is little surprise that decision makers view CSR as expensive and off-putting. It has also been shown that CSR can be accomplished by reallocating existing resources within a district, with little or no additional cost per pupil (see Achilles, 2005).

Other evaluations have analyzed the benefit side of the equation. Some benefits accrue to the schools, and many are realized by the larger community; for example, the savings associated with reduced dropout rates or reduced health care or welfare expenditures or the increased earning power of higher achieving students. School administrators may have difficulty taking these factors into account, especially when the benefits occur in the years after students leave school.

Simplistic View of the Costs

In 1999, Brewer, Krop, Gill, and Reichardt estimated the operational costs, such as additional teachers, classrooms, and supplies, that would be needed for nationwide CSR programs under various program alternatives. Alternatives included the degree of CSR (20, 18, or 15 students), the grades involved, and whether all students would be part of the program or just "targeted" students. Using data from several national databases, Brewer et al. (1999) modeled possible CSR programs in Grades 1–3 for school years 1998–1999 through 2007–2008. At the high end, they estimated that the cost of reducing class size to 15 for all students in Grades 1–3 in the United States would be $11 billion. However, if only targeted students were included in the program, such as those with free and reduced-price lunches, the total cost dropped to approximately $2 billion. In either case, this analysis was based on the assumptions that operational costs were universal throughout the nation and that no existing resources could be reallocated to support CSR.

Yet, it has been demonstrated that CSR can be implemented at much lower costs. In Burke County, North Carolina, a successful CSR program was implemented in Grades 1–3 by creatively using funds, classroom space, and personnel (Achilles, Harman, & Egelson, 1995; Egelson, Harman, Hood, & Achilles, 2005). Classrooms that housed sixth graders (who were moved to the middle school) were converted to elementary rooms, mobile units were added, and, in some cases, older schools were reopened and remodeled. Through attrition, salaries of teaching assistants were used to fund teacher positions. The district's per-pupil expenditure remained nearly the same while achieving small classes and increased student achievement.

Although the reallocation of resources to reduce class sizes was effective in a mid-sized, highly committed school district, it remains to be seen whether such changes would encounter significant obstacles if attempted in other types of communities or on a larger scale. In any event, this work demonstrated that existing resources can be used to control the costs of CSR.

Academic Achievement, Dropping Out, and Grade Retention

More complete analyses have considered the cost savings produced by CSR. In an analysis of data from Project STAR, Krueger (2003) weighed the costs of CSR against the lifetime earnings of students. He estimated costs based on current per-pupil expenditures and the number of additional classes that would be required to reduce class size. Benefits were based on previous research showing a statistical relationship between academic achievement and wages (Neal & Johnson, 1996).[19] Krueger (2003) used this relationship to calculate the internal rate of return of reduced size classes under a variety of economic scenarios (e.g., different rates of economic growth during the work lives of the students).

The analysis showed that reducing class size from 22 to 15 for Grades K–3 would yield an internal rate of return of approximately 6% (Krueger, 2003). Assuming a 4% interest rate, the benefits of reducing class size to 15, in terms of lifetime earnings, would be *43% greater than the costs* and 100% greater than the costs if real wages grew by 1 percent per year.[20] More recent analyses have found similar results, with estimated rates of return from CSR ranging from 5% to 10% and with earnings exceeding the investment by $2,900 to $48,335 (Schanzenbach, 2006). In 14 of 15 economic scenarios shown by each author, the benefits in earnings were greater than the costs of CSR – even without considering other types of payoffs (e.g., reduced crime or welfare costs).

Based on the impact of small classes on high school graduation rates, Levin, Belfield, Muennig, and Rouse (2007) evaluated a broader range of outcomes (see Chapter 16). Potential savings were based on the fact that each adult cohort of 20-year-olds includes approximately 700,000 dropouts. Levin et al. (2007) estimated the fiscal consequence of these dropouts to be $148 billion in lost tax revenues and additional public expenses over a lifetime.

[19] Neal and Johnson (1996) estimated that a 1–standard deviation increase in test scores translates into a 0.2–standard deviation increase in wages, a value accepted by most economists. On this basis, Krueger (2003) used STAR data to estimate that the average effect of attending small classes would translate into an 8% increase in earnings.

[20] Assuming that people would be in the workforce from ages 18 to 65.

They estimated the cost of CSR in Grades K–3 to be $143,600 per expected high school graduate.[21] Using multiple data sources to estimate the benefits of increased graduation rates, they found that graduates have higher earnings than do dropouts, which translate into higher tax revenue; lower crime rates and lower judicial costs[22]; lower public assistance payments; and less Medicaid and Medicare expenses (Levin et al., 2007). Graduates also enjoy improved health and lower mortality. For example, Muennig and Woolf (2007) estimated that the health status of an average 45-year-old graduate is comparable to that of an average 25-year-old dropout.

Taking these factors into account, Levin et al. (2007) estimated that the average lifetime economic benefit per expected high school graduate is $209,100.[23] Even with a high estimate of the cost of CSR, this translates into a benefit to the community of $65,500 per dropout. Whether the estimates are precise or not, Levin et al. (2007), like Krueger (2003), concluded that CSR produces significant economic benefits.

One of the most consistent precursors of dropping out (together with poor academic achievement) is in-grade retention (Goldschmidt & Wang, 1999; Kaufman & Bradby, 1992; Rumberger, 1995). This practice has its own costs and also affects the costs associated with dropping out. Shepard and Smith (1990) estimated that U.S. school districts spent almost $10 billion on the costs of retaining students – these were dollars spent on extra materials, classroom space, and personnel. In 1988–1989 in California alone, the cost of retaining 34,000 students in Grades 1–6 was estimated at $212 million (Schwager, Mitchell, Mitchell, & Hecht, 1992). CSR has been shown to reduce rates of retention. To our knowledge, the savings that result from reducing in-grade retentions have not been factored into any cost-benefit analysis of CSR.

Small Classes as Incentives

Although not considered in any cost-benefit analysis to date, small classes may be an incentive to teachers because of improved working conditions and increased student outcomes. Several surveys have documented this point. In 1989, 234 STAR teachers were asked to choose among three possibilities: a small class, a full-size class with an aide, or a $2,500 bonus.[24] Of teachers who had been teaching small classes, 81% said they preferred a small class over a full-sized class with an aide, and 70% chose the small class over the salary increase. Of teachers in teacher-aide classes, 56% preferred a small class to a full-sized class with an aide, and 63% chose a small class over the salary increase (Word

[21] We believe this to be an overestimate, but the basic conclusions remain the same.
[22] Dropouts account for an estimated 50% of the state prison population (Bonczar, 2003).
[23] This amount varies by gender and race, with savings from $196,300 to $268,500 for males and from $143,000 to $174,600 for females.
[24] A substantial sum in 1989.

et al., 1990, Table X-5). More recently, Howell, West, and Peterson (2007) conducted the *2007 Education Next – PEPG Survey*, "What Americans Think About Their Schools." One question asked, "Which do you think is a better use of our education dollars, increasing teacher salaries or decreasing class size?" (p. 24). Of all respondents, 23% chose a salary increase, and 77% chose decreasing class size. Among teachers, 19% chose a salary increase, and 81% chose CSRs.

The economic and policy implications of such findings are considerable. Educators and economists have called for teacher incentives that promise to reduce teacher turnover and attract qualified candidates to the profession (Darling-Hammond, 1998; Ehrenberg et al., 2001a; Hanushek, 1998). Small classes may be one such incentive.

Summary

Economists have long been interested in resources provided to schools and how those resources are related to student achievement. The costs and benefits of educational policies such as class size reduction have sparked many debates in the education and economic communities. Any complete evaluation of large-scale interventions must consider a full range of benefits, whether in terms of increased achievement, higher graduation rates, or the potential for improved health and lower crime rates.

CONTINUING RESEARCH: A 13-YEAR PUBLIC ACCESS DATABASE

A host of questions about small classes remains unanswered. For example, we know of no research that addresses these questions:

- Can small-class benefits be increased if used in conjunction with other interventions (e.g., remedial reading programs or full-day kindergarten in place of half-day programs)?
- Will small classes in K–3 reduce or prevent the "fade-out effect" found in follow-up studies of effective preschool programs (including Head Start)?

To assist with continuing research, Project STAR has generated an extraordinary data set on almost 12,000 students. The data can be used to address policy issues and basic questions about child and adolescent development and to develop statistical methodology.

With support from the W. T. Grant Foundation, the data have been cleaned and compiled into SPSS files now available on a public-access website.[25] A *User's Guide* is available in electronic and hard-copy form[26] (Finn, Boyd-Zaharias,

[25] The data files and documentation are available at http://www.heros-inc.org/data.htm; additional information may be obtained from STARDATA@heros-inc.org or by contacting the authors of this chapter.

[26] At no cost.

Fish, & Gerber, 2007); it also includes a bibliography of studies conducted with the STAR data.

The files contain data on 11,601 students who participated in the experiment for at least one school year, their teachers, and schools. They include the following information:

- demographic variables
- school and class identifiers
- school and teacher background information
- experimental condition ("class type")
- norm-referenced and criterion-referenced achievement test scores administered annually
- motivation and self-concept scores

Data from follow-up studies include the following:

- achievement test scores for the students when they were in Grades 4–8, obtained from the Tennessee State Department of Education
- teachers' ratings of student behavior on the SPQ in Grades 4 and 8
- students' self-reports of school engagement and peer effects in Grade 8
- courses taken in mathematics, science, and foreign language in high school, obtained from student transcripts
- SAT/ACT participation and scores, obtained from ACT, Inc., and from the Educational Testing Service
- graduation/dropout information, obtained from high school transcripts and the Tennessee State Department of Education

Additional files include the following:

- student data on 1,780 students in Grades 1–3 in 21 comparison schools, matched with STAR schools but not participating in the experiment
- a school-level file with information about each of the 80 STAR elementary schools
- a school-level file with information about each high school attended by STAR students

The database has already been used for a number of ancillary studies. We hope that it will continue to be a valuable resource to the research community.

REFERENCES

Achilles, C. M. (1999). *Let's put kids first, finally: Getting class size right.* Thousand Oaks, CA: Corwin Press.

Achilles, C. M. (2005). *Financing class size reduction.* Greensboro, NC: University of North Carolina at Greensboro School of Education, Southeast Regional Educational Laboratory (SERVE).

Achilles, C. M., Harman, P., & Egelson, P. (1995). Using research results of class size to improve achievement outcomes. *Research in the Schools, 2,* 23–30.

Achilles, C. M., Kiser-Kling, K., Aust, A., & Owen, J. (1995). *A study of reduced class size in primary grades of a fully Chapter-I eligible school: Success starts small.* Paper presented at the annual meeting of the American Educational Research Association, San Francisco.

Achilles, C. M., Nye, B. A., & Zaharias, J. B. (1995). *Policy use of research results: Tennessee's Project Challenge.* Paper presented at the annual meeting of the American Educational Research Association, San Francisco.

Angrist, J. D., & Lavy, V. (1996). Using Maimonides' rule to estimate the effect of class size on children's academic achievement. *Quarterly Journal of Economics, 114,* 533–535.

Biddle, B. J., & Berliner, D. C. (2002). Small class size and its effects. *Educational Leadership, 59*(5), 12–23.

Blatchford, P. (2003). A systematic observational study of teachers' and pupils' behaviour in large and small classes. *Learning and Instruction, 13,* 569–595.

Bohrnstedt, G. W., & Stecher, B. M. (Eds.). (1999). *Class size reduction in California: Early evaluation findings, 1996–1998* (CSR Research Consortium, Year 1 Evaluation Report). Palo Alto, CA: American Institutes for Research.

Bonczar, T. P. (2003). *Prevalence of imprisonment in the U.S. population, 1974–2001* (Special Report, NCJ 197976). Washington, DC: U.S. Department of Justice, Bureau of Justice Statistics.

Boozer, M., & Rouse, C. (2001). Intra-school variation in class size: Patterns and implications. *Journal of Urban Economics, 50,* 163–189.

Bourke, S. (1986). How smaller is better: Some relationships between class size, teaching practices, and student achievement. *American Educational Research Journal, 23,* 558–571.

Boyd-Zaharias, J., & Pate-Bain, H. (1998). *Teacher aides and student learning: Lessons from Project STAR.* Arlington, VA: Educational Research Service.

Brewer, D., Krop, C., Gill, B. P., & Reichardt, R. (1999). Estimating the costs of national class-size reductions under different policy alternatives. *Educational Evaluation and Policy Analysis, 21,* 179–192.

Carneiro, P., & Heckman, J. J. (2003). *Human capital policy.* Cambridge, MA: National Bureau of Economic Research Working Paper 9495. Retrieved from http://papers.nber.org/papers/w9495.

Cruickshank, D. R. (1980). *Teaching is tough.* Englewood Cliffs, NJ: Prentice Hall.

CSR Research Consortium (2000). *Class size reduction in California: The 1998–1999 evaluation findings.* Sacramento: California Department of Education.

Darling-Hammond, L. (1998). Teachers and teaching: Testing policy hypotheses from a National Commission Report. *Educational Researcher, 27,* 5–15.

Egelson, P., Harmon, P., Hood, A., & Achilles, C. M. (2005). *How class size makes a difference.* Greensboro, NC: University of North Carolina at Greensboro School of Education, Southeast Regional Educational Laboratory (SERVE).

Ehrenberg, R. G., Brewer, D. J., Gamoran, A., & Willms, J. D. (2001a). Class size and student achievement. *Psychological Science in the Public Interest, 2,* 1–29.

Ehrenberg, R. G., Brewer, D. J., Gamoran, A., & Willms, J. D. (2001b). Does class size matter? *Scientific American, 385*(5), 32–40.

Evertson, C. M., & Folger, J. K. (1989). *Small class, large class: What do teachers do differently?* Paper presented at the annual meeting of the American Educational Research Association, San Francisco, CA.

Ferguson, R. F., & Ladd, H. F. (1996). How and why money matters: An analysis of Alabama schools. In H. F. Ladd (Ed.), *Holding schools accountable: Performance-based reform in education* (pp. 265–298). Washington, DC: Brookings Institution.

Finn, J. D. (2002). Small classes in American schools: Research, practice, and politics. *Phi Delta Kappan, 83*, 551–560.

Finn, J. D., & Achilles, C. A. (1990). Answers and questions about class size: A statewide experiment. *American Educational Research Journal, 27*, 557–577.

Finn, J. D., Boyd-Zaharias, J., Fish, R. M., & Gerber, S. B. (2007). *Project STAR and beyond: Database user's guide.* Lebanon, TN: HEROS, Inc. Retrieved from http://www.heros-inc.org/data.htm.

Finn, J. D., Folger, J., & Cox, D. (1991). Measuring participation among elementary grade students. *Educational and Psychological Measurement, 51*, 393–402.

Finn, J. D., Forden, M. A., Verdinelli, S., & Pannozzo, G. M. (2001). *Evaluation of the class size reduction initiative – Buffalo Public Schools.* Buffalo, NY: University at Buffalo, Graduate School of Education.

Finn, J. D., Fox, J. D., McClellan, M., Achilles, C. M., & Boyd-Zaharias, J. (2006). Small classes in the early grades and course taking in high school. *International Journal of Education Policy and Leadership, 1*, 1–13. Retrieved from http://www.ijepl.org.

Finn, J. D., Gerber, S. B., & Achilles, C. A. (2000). Teacher aides: An alternative to small classes? In M. C. Wang & J. D. Finn (Eds.), *How small classes help teachers do their best* (pp. 131–173). Philadelphia, PA: Temple University Center for Research on Human Development and Education and the U.S. Department of Education.

Finn, J. D., Gerber, S. B., Achilles, C. M., & Boyd-Zaharias, J. (2001). The enduring effects of small classes. *Teachers College Record, 103*, 145–183.

Finn, J. D., Gerber, S. B., & Boyd-Zaharias, J. (2005). Small classes in the early grades, academic achievement, and graduating from high school. *Journal of Educational Psychology, 97*, 214–223.

Finn, J. D., Pannozzo, G. M., & Achilles, C. M. (2003). The "why's" of class size: Student behavior in small classes. *Review of Educational Research, 73*, 321–368.

Gerber, S. B., Finn, J. D., Achilles, C. M., & Boyd-Zaharias, J. (2001). Teacher aides and students' academic achievement. *Educational Evaluation and Policy Analysis, 23*, 123–143.

Goldschmidt, P., & Wang, J. (1999). When can schools affect dropout behavior? A longitudinal multilevel analysis. *American Educational Research Journal, 36*, 715–738.

Goldstein, H., & Blatchford, P. (1998). Class size and educational achievement: A review of methodology with particular reference to study design. *British Educational Research Journal, 24*, 255–268.

Hanushek, E. A. (1989). The impact of differential expenditures on school performance. *Educational Researcher, 18*(4), 45–65.

Hanushek, E. A. (1998). *The evidence on class size.* Rochester, NY: University of Rochester, W. Allen Wallis Institute of Political Economy.

Hanushek, E. A. (1999). Some findings from an independent investigation of the Tennessee STAR experiment and from other investigations of class-size effects. *Educational Evaluation and Policy Analysis, 21*, 143–163.

Heckman, J. J. (2006, January 10). Catch 'em young. *Wall Street Journal*, p. A14.

Hedges, L. V., & Greenwald, R. (1996). Have times changed? The relationship between school resources and student performance. In G. Burtless (Ed.), *Does money matter? The effect of school resources on student achievement and adult success* (pp. 74–92). Washington, DC: Brookings Institution.

Hedges, L. V., Laine, R. D., & Greenwald, R. (1994). Does money matter? A meta-analysis of studies of the effects of differential school inputs on student outcomes. *Educational Researcher, 23*(3), 5–14.

Hedges, L. V., Nye, B., & Konstantopoulos, S. (1999). The long-term effects of small classes: A five-year follow-up of the Tennessee class-size experiment. *Educational Evaluation and Policy Analysis, 21*, 127–142.

Hedges, L. V., Nye, B., & Konstantopoulos, S. (2000). The effects of small classes on achievement: The results of the Tennessee class-size experiment. *American Educational Research Journal, 37*, 123–151.

Hedges, L. V., Nye, B., & Konstantopoulos, S. (2004). Do minorities experience greater lasting benefits from small classes? Evidence from a five-year follow up of the Tennessee class-size experiment. *Journal of Educational Research, 97*, 94–100.

Howell, W. C., West, M. R., & Peterson, P. (2007). What Americans think about their schools: The 2007 Education Next – PEPG survey. *Education Next, 7*(4), 13–26.

Johnston, J. M. (1990). *What are teachers' perceptions of teaching in different classroom contexts?* (ERIC Document Reproduction Service No. ED 320 867). Paper presented at the annual meeting of the American Educational Research Association, Boston.

Kaufman, P., & Bradby, D. (1992). *Characteristics of at-risk students in NELS:88* (National Center for Education Statistics Report No. 92–042). Washington, DC: U.S. Department of Education, National Center for Education Statistics.

Kiser-Kling, K. (1995). *A comparative study of life in first grade classrooms of 1:14 and 1:23 teacher-pupil ratios.* Unpublished doctoral dissertation, University of North Carolina at Greensboro.

Krueger, A. B. (1999). Experimental estimates of education production functions. *Quarterly Journal of Economics, 114*, 497–532.

Krueger, A. B. (2003). Economic considerations and class size. *Economic Journal, 113*, 34–63.

Krueger, A. B., & Whitmore, D. M. (2001). The effect of attending a small class in the early grades on college-test taking and middle-school test results: Evidence from project STAR. *Economic Journal, 111*, 1–28.

Levin, H., Belfield, C., Muennig, P., & Rouse, C. (2007). *The costs and benefits of an excellent education for all of America's children.* Retrieved from the Columbia University website: http://www.cbcse.org/media/download_gallery/.

Lewit, E. M., & Baker, L. S. (1997). Class size. *Future of Children, 7*, 112–121.

McCabe, M. (2006, January 4). State of the states. *Education Week, 26*(17), 72–76.

Milchus, N., Farrah, G., & Reitz, W. (1968). *The self-concept and motivation inventory: What face would you wear?* Dearborn Heights, MI: Person-0-Metrics.

Miles, K. H. (1995). Freeing resources for improving schools: A case study of teacher allocation in Boston Public Schools. *Educational Evaluation and Policy Analyses, 17*, 476–493.

Molnar, A., Smith, O., & Zahorik, J. (1999). *1998–99 evaluation results of the Student Achievement Guarantee in Education (SAGE) program.* Milwaukee: University of Wisconsin School of Education.

Molnar, A., Smith, O., Zahorik, J., Ehrle, K., Halback, A., & Kuehl, B. (2000). *1999–2000 evaluation results of the Student Achievement Guarantee in Education (SAGE) program.* Milwaukee: University of Wisconsin School of Education.

Mosteller, F. (1995). The Tennessee study of class size in the early school grades. *Future of Children, 5*, 113–127.

Muennig, P., & Woolf, S. H. (2007). Health and economic benefits of reducing the number of students per classroom in US primary schools. *American Journal of Public Health, 97*(11), 2020–2027.

Neal, D., & Johnson, J. (1996). The role of premarket factors in black-white wage differentials. *Journal of Political Economy, 104*, 869–895.

NICHD Early Child Care Research Network (2004). Does class size in first grade relate to children's academic and social performance or observed classroom processes? *Developmental Psychology, 40*, 651–664.

Ramey, C. T., & Ramey, S. L. (1998). Early intervention and early experience. *American Psychologist, 53*, 109–120.

Ritter, G. W., & Boruch, R. F. (1999). The political and institutional origins of a randomized controlled trial on elementary school class size: Tennessee Project STAR. *Educational Evaluation and Policy Analysis, 21*, 111–125.

Rumberger, R. W. (1995). Dropping out of middle school: A multilevel analysis of students and schools. *American Educational Research Journal, 32*, 583–625.

Sarason, S. B. (1974). *The psychological sense of community: Prospects for a community psychology*. San Francisco, CA: Jossey-Bass.

Schanzenbach, D. W. (2006). What have researchers learned from Project STAR? *Brookings Papers on Education Policy, 2006–2007*, 205–228.

Schwager, M. T., Mitchell, D. E., Mitchell, T. K., & Hecht, J. B. (1992). How school district policy influences grade-level retention in elementary schools. *Educational Evaluation and Policy Analysis, 14*, 421–438.

Shapson, S. M., Eason, G., Wright, E. N., & Fitzgerald, J. (1980). An experimental study of the effects of class size. *American Educational Research Journal, 17*, 141–152.

Shepard, L. A., & Smith, M. L. (1990). Synthesis of research on grade retention. *Educational Leadership, 47*(8), 84–88.

Voelkl, K. E. (1996). Measuring students' identification with school. *Educational and Psychological Measurement, 56*, 760–770.

Walston, J., West, J., & Rathbun, A. (2002). *Kindergarten program features and gains in reading and mathematics achievement of public school children: Class size, length of school day and classroom aides.* Paper presented at the annual meeting of the American Educational Research Association, New Orleans, LA.

Wang, M. C., & Finn, J. D. (Eds.). (2000). *How small classes help teachers do their best.* Philadelphia, PA: Temple University Center for Research on Human Development and Education and the U.S. Department of Education.

Word, E., Johnston, J., Bain, H. P., Fulton, D. B., Boyd-Zaharias, J., Lintz, M. N., et al. (1990). *Final report: Student/teacher achievement ratio (STAR): Tennessee's K–3 class-size study.* Nashville: Tennessee State Department of Education. Retrieved from http://www.heros-inc.org.

PART IV

ECONOMIC SYNTHESES OF EARLY CHILDHOOD INVESTMENTS

Commentary at the Human Capital Research Collaborative Conference

GARY H. STERN

Let me begin by welcoming you, once again, to the Federal Reserve Bank of Minneapolis and also by telling you what a pleasure it is to sponsor this conference with the University of Minnesota. I've had the privilege of leading this institution for a number of years now, and it has been a rewarding experience to observe and participate in the fruitful relationship that exists between the bank and the university.

Working together, the university's economics department and the bank's research department – and you would be forgiven if you think those are one and the same – have produced research that has sparked revolutions in economic theory and monetary policy making, and has even helped spawn a Nobel Prize or two along the way. In addition, this academic partnership – which is further realized by the bank's cooperation with the university's Humphrey Institute of Public Affairs, its journalism and law schools, and other departments – has generated educational programs and influenced public-policy initiatives, often in surprising ways. In that regard, perhaps none is more surprising than forming an Early Childhood Research Collaborative and holding research conferences on the subject of early childhood development.

I use the word "surprising" because when you think of the Federal Reserve and its research and policy responsibilities, the first topic that comes to mind is likely not early childhood development. Frankly, it is unlikely to be even the second or third topic that comes to mind. But that's changing. Increasingly, state and local governments are looking to their Federal Reserve banks for support on this emerging issue – and not just the Minneapolis Fed. Why is this happening? Let me begin to answer that question by citing some recent speeches by my colleagues in the Fed:

Sandy Pianalto said that when she became president of the Cleveland Fed, she asked her research department to put a sharper focus on the issues that are shaping her district. Education was at the top of the list. "We all should care about this issue," Sandy said, "and I am convinced that it begins with early childhood education."

Janet Yellen, president of the San Francisco Fed, has noted that "skill acquisition is a cumulative process that works most effectively when a solid foundation has been provided in early childhood. As such, programs to support early childhood development, such as preschool programs for disadvantaged children, not only appear to have substantial payoffs early but also are likely to continue paying off throughout the life cycle."

Finally, a few words from Jeff Lacker at Richmond: "On many issues, the economics of the question are not decisive, though economics does tend to spotlight the often-overlooked costs associated with many otherwise seemingly attractive ideas. On some questions, however, economic research sends a fairly clear message. I believe that early childhood development is such an issue."

So as you can see, other Federal Reserve banks have also been out front on this seemingly un-Fed-like topic. But let me step back and put these statements in a broader context that will further explain why the Federal Reserve has taken an active interest in early childhood development.

As all of you know, this country's central banking system includes 12 district banks and a Board of Governors in Washington, DC. While the role and purpose of those 12 district banks could be the subject of a separate speech, one clear function of those banks is to understand what makes their regional economies tick. This recalls Sandy Pianalto's charge to her research department: Tell me what issues matter most to our district's economy.

This charge is one shared by all Federal Reserve banks, and it is a responsibility that has attained a sharper focus in recent decades as Congress has passed a series of laws, beginning with the Community Reinvestment Act of 1977, to ensure equal access to financial services and equal opportunity for all citizens. More than just supervising banks to ensure that they are upholding the letter of the law, Federal Reserve banks are working with their local communities on issues ranging from housing to credit availability to education.

But it's not just our district economies and our legal mandates that have motivated us to take a hard look at education: This topic circles back to core economic research, the very kind that the bank and university have contributed to over the years. One such field of investigation is that which compares the economies of various countries and tries to answer one of the most vexing questions in economics: Why are some nations rich and others poor?

Bob Lucas has made important contributions to this line of research, especially on the issue of human capital. In a 2003 *Annual Report* essay for the Minneapolis Fed, Lucas made a key point that has relevance for the work done by many of you in this room: "It is a unique feature of human capital that it yields returns that cannot be captured entirely by its 'owner.' . . . These pervasive external effects introduce a kind of feedback into human capital theory: Something that increases the return on human capital will stimulate greater accumulation, in turn stimulating higher returns, stimulating still greater accumulation and so on." The key words there are "and so on." To all of you familiar with the benefit/cost ratio attributed to certain early childhood development programs, the "and so on" of these programs adds up to some serious positive external effects.

On the question of the comparative wealth of nations, Lucas famously said that once you start thinking about that question, it's hard to think of anything else. I would suggest that the same is true at a more micro level for the United States: When you start thinking about why some states and cities are richer than others, it's hard to think of anything else. It's a motivating question that, when you come right down to it, frames much of the economic and policy debate in this country. And if the answer to this question involves human capital, then the next question follows: Why are some states and cities better educated, or better at education, than others? These are the types of questions that perplex policy makers and economists, and also Federal Reserve banks, and that's why we keep asking them.

And, of course, there are no easy answers, which is why all of you made the questionable decision to travel to Minnesota in December. You would think that with all of that intellectual firepower that I referred to at the beginning of this speech, we would have picked a more temperate month for you to pay a visit. Or maybe this just reveals how serious we are about this topic, and how seriously all of you take this issue.

Before I close, I want to briefly describe the current efforts underway here at the Minneapolis Fed on this issue. As many of you know, Art Rolnick and Rob Grunewald, following on the work of some of you in this room, have been making the economic case for early childhood programs for at-risk children for a number of years. Over this time, they have been challenged by skeptics to bring their ideas to scale. It's one thing to cite focused studies with relatively small numbers of families and tout the high returns, these skeptics say, but it's quite another to actually implement those ideas in a broad way.

Art and Rob accepted that challenge and drafted a proposal that, in effect, puts the market to work to stimulate demand and create a supply of quality child care programs. I won't go into the details here, but I will add that Art and Rob's plan – as adopted by the Minnesota Early Learning Foundation, a unique nonprofit funded mostly by corporate donations – will get its first real test in St. Paul beginning in January, when 1,200 at-risk families will receive scholarships for high-quality child care. Additionally, other Twin Cities school districts, as well as those in rural Minnesota and other parts of the country, have begun programs that incorporate Art and Rob's market-based approach. Will the skeptics be proved wrong? Time will tell, but as an economist, I can say that I'm hopeful. Finally, I would like to end with a fitting quote from

Fed Chairman Ben Bernanke, who gave a talk earlier this year on this very subject:

> Although education and the acquisition of skills is a lifelong process, starting early in life is crucial. Recent research – some sponsored by the Federal Reserve Bank of Minneapolis in collaboration with the University of Minnesota – has documented the high returns that early childhood programs can pay in terms of subsequent educational attainment and in lower rates of social problems, such as teenage pregnancy and welfare dependency. The most successful early childhood programs appear to be those that cultivate both cognitive and noncognitive skills and that engage families in stimulating learning at home.

There's that partnership again. And in that quote, Bernanke also makes reference to the academic work underpinning this conference, for he cites research by Jim Heckman, who of course is in attendance. And speaking of Jim, I would be remiss not to acknowledge the huge debt that the profession owes him for almost single-handedly establishing the economic bona fides of this issue. His research was the foundation for the work produced at this bank and by the university and has influenced every serious economic and policy research project on this issue, which means he has also had a vicarious hand in many of the policy reforms taking place across the country – however nervous that makes him feel.

Thank you very much.

15

The Cost Effectiveness of Public Investment in High-Quality Prekindergarten: A State-Level Synthesis

ROBERT G. LYNCH

Numerous studies have calculated the cost effectiveness of public investment in high-quality prekindergarten (pre-K). The benefits and costs of investment in pre-K have typically been quantified in standard benefit-cost ratios expressed in net present value terms or in rate of return calculations. Long-term analyses of high-quality pre-K programs have found favorable benefit:cost ratios that varied from a minimum of 3.78 to 1 to a high of 17.07 to 1 (e.g., Barnett, 1993; Masse & Barnett, 2002; Reynolds, Temple, Robertson, & Mann, 2002; Schweinhart, Barnes, Weikart, Barnett, & Epstein, 1993; Schweinhart et al., 2005). Rate of return calculations have similarly illustrated cost effectiveness. For example, Rolnick and Grunewald (2003) estimated that annual real rates of return on public investments in the Perry Preschool pre-K program were 12% for the nonparticipating public and government and 4% for participants, so that total returns exceeded 16%.

One drawback of these methods of calculating the cost effectiveness of pre-K investment is that they are not well understood or routinely used by the legislators, typically at the state level, who actually formulate public policy with respect to pre-K. State legislators are more likely to examine the budgetary implications of policy proposals by analyzing their state-level year-by-year expenditure and revenue impacts. Thus, one potentially useful way of depicting the overall benefits and costs of pre-K investment is to translate net present value benefit:cost ratios and rate of return calculations into annual budget outlay and revenue consequences for each state. This is the approach adopted in this chapter and outlined in more detail in Lynch (2007).

Specifically, I analyze the costs and many, but not all, of the benefits of public investment in (a) a *targeted* voluntary, high-quality pre-K program that serves only 3- and 4-year-old children who live in families in the lowest quarter of the income distribution; and (b) a similar but *universal* voluntary pre-K program made available to all 3- and 4-year-old children. Both pre-K programs and their estimated costs and benefits are modeled on the Chicago

Child-Parent Center (CPC) program (see Reynolds, 2000, and Reynolds et al., 2002, for details). The governmental costs and benefits of both publicly funded pre-K programs, measured as year-by-year expenditure, budget savings, and revenue impacts, are estimated from hypothetical program implementation in 2007 through the year 2050, or over a period of 44 years. For illustration purposes, I assume that the programs were fully phased in by 2008. In addition to the government budgetary consequences, I calculate the earnings and crime implications for individuals and society for the same years. All these costs and benefits are broken down at the national and state-by-state level and are expressed in real 2006 dollars (see Lynch, 2007, for a full description of the methodology).

The next section describes the costs and benefits of each prospective pre-K program for every state to illustrate their potential cost effectiveness. This is followed by a discussion of omitted costs and benefits and an explanation of some of the difficulties in estimating the effects of prospective pre-K programs. A sensitivity analysis is performed to account for a wide range of estimates of the effects of current preschool participation and the impact of children from different economic backgrounds attending pre-K on the cost effectiveness of high-quality pre-K. Finally, I discuss the policy implications of this study.

COST EFFECTIVENESS OF HIGH-QUALITY PREKINDERGARTEN

My state-level estimates capture variation in costs and benefits across states due to factors such as population, income distribution, average annual pay, teacher salaries, crime rates, tax burdens, and current expenditures on all levels of education, child welfare, and criminal justice. States with greater current commitments to pre-K need less additional public expenditure to finance the proposed high-quality pre-K program. Given that pre-K costs are largely driven by teacher salaries, states with higher teacher pay experience greater pre-K costs. Because the proposed pre-K programs generate budget savings in special education, K–12 education, juvenile and adult criminal justice, and child welfare, states that are making larger financial commitments in these areas save more money than states that are making smaller financial commitments in these areas. Likewise, because the prospective pre-K programs increase the future earnings of participants and their guardians, states with higher average pay and tax burdens will experience greater earnings and tax revenues increases than will states with lower average pay and tax burdens. Differences in state-level savings to individuals from less crime are largely due to variations in state crime rates.

Although the costs and benefits from pre-K investment vary by state, the pattern of cost and benefit growth is similar across states. Initially, the costs of the program are relatively stable, growing only with inflation and increases in the child population served. Eventually, however, there will be additional increases in government expenditures due to the increased educational attainment of pre-K participants who complete more years of high school and attend college at higher rates. Increased public high school costs appear when the first cohort of participants turns 17, and increased public higher education costs appear when the first cohort turns 18.

Offsetting budget, earnings, and crime benefits are small initially but grow rapidly and eventually outstrip the costs. Budget savings in the first year of the program manifest as reductions in child welfare expenditures because pre-K participants are less likely to be the victims of child abuse and neglect. In addition, some parents take advantage of the fact that part of their child care needs are covered by the pre-K program by securing employment, earning income, and paying more in taxes. When the pre-K participants enter the K–12 public school system, additional budget savings appear because these children are less likely to repeat a grade or need expensive special education services. When the first cohort of children turns 10, additional budget and crime savings begin to be realized because pre-K participants have lower juvenile crime rates, generating savings in public expenditures on the juvenile justice system. As adults, the pre-K participants will be less engaged in crime, have higher educational attainment, and earn more income. Thus, there will eventually be savings to the adult criminal justice system and increased tax revenue derived from the labor earnings of pre-K participants.

COST EFFECTIVENESS OF A TARGETED PROGRAM

The annual budgetary, earnings, and crime benefits of a high-quality, publicly funded, *targeted* pre-K program that was hypothetically begun in 2007 would begin to exceed the annual costs of the program within 6 years and would do so by a growing margin every year thereafter. After 44 years, or by the year 2050, the annual benefits would total $315 billion ($83 billion in government budget benefits, $156 billion in increased compensation of workers, and $77 billion in reduced costs to individuals from less crime and child abuse) and would surpass the costs of the program in that year by a ratio of 12.1:1.[1] Broken down by state, in 2050, the annual benefits would outstrip the annual costs of the program by a minimum of 8.1 to 1 for residents of Alabama and by as much as 29.1 to 1 for the residents of Delaware (see Table 15.1).

A high-quality targeted pre-K program would cost nearly $6,300 per participant and could be expected to enroll just more than 2 million children in 2008 when fully phased in. With offsets for some current expenditure on state pre-K programs, special education, and Head Start services for children who will be attending the proposed high-quality pre-K program, the program

[1] These benefits of a targeted program are similar in magnitude to those estimated in Lynch (2004) for a targeted program modeled on the Perry Preschool program.

Table 15.1. *State-by-state costs and benefits of targeted program*

State	Government budget benefits in 2050 (millions of 2006 dollars)	Increased compensation in 2050 (millions of 2006 dollars)	Savings to individuals from reduced crime in 2050 (millions of 2006 dollars)	Total budget, compensation, and crime benefits in 2050 (millions of 2006 dollars)	Ratio of total annual benefits to program costs in 2050
National	82,659	155,519	76,969	315,147	12.1
Alabama	890	2,219	594	3,703	8.1
Alaska	197	452	217	865	13.1
Arizona	2,681	4,917	3,217	10,814	11.4
Arkansas	822	1,393	722	2,937	12.0
California	12,551	25,670	9,750	47,971	12.1
Colorado	1,052	2,090	1,455	4,596	16.7
Connecticut	667	1,347	489	2,504	23.8
Delaware	111	211	123	445	29.1
District of Columbia	387	656	367	1,410	10.3
Florida	5,897	8,995	5,580	20,472	9.9
Georgia	3,376	6,019	3,122	12,517	11.3
Hawaii	217	458	245	920	17.3
Idaho	395	763	573	1,731	13.1
Illinois	3,134	6,185	2,914	12,233	12.6
Indiana	1,327	2,982	1,549	5,858	9.8
Iowa	526	1,096	550	2,172	13.1
Kansas	654	1,230	618	2,502	14.1
Kentucky	1,205	1,961	1,220	4,386	17.5
Louisiana	1,086	2,058	1,248	4,392	11.9
Maine	177	347	190	714	16.2
Maryland	1,243	2,511	1,065	4,820	13.6
Massachusetts	874	1,998	537	3,409	13.6
Michigan	2,414	4,702	1,385	8,501	13.8

Minnesota	982	1,829	1,139	3,950	27.0
Mississippi	796	1,574	1,004	3,374	12.3
Missouri	1,283	2,580	1,124	4,987	12.6
Montana	177	328	210	716	13.2
Nebraska	359	719	413	1,491	13.9
Nevada	805	1,535	1,095	3,436	11.0
New Hampshire	149	352	124	626	15.2
New Jersey	1,175	2,520	896	4,591	16.3
New Mexico	549	1,019	599	2,168	12.1
New York	5,942	8,884	4,533	19,359	12.0
North Carolina	2,762	4,941	2,548	10,251	8.8
North Dakota	91	164	130	386	24.1
Ohio	2,477	4,652	2,442	9,571	16.7
Oklahoma	658	1,471	772	2,901	13.3
Oregon	949	1,826	1,202	3,978	15.3
Pennsylvania	2,634	4,740	2,530	9,903	12.4
Rhode Island	249	479	202	929	11.6
South Carolina	1,081	2,025	943	4,049	9.8
South Dakota	179	344	192	715	14.2
Tennessee	1,550	2,952	991	5,492	9.2
Texas	8,962	18,966	9,899	37,828	11.3
Utah	687	1,480	916	3,083	13.7
Vermont	77	154.4	34	266	20.4
Virginia	1,428	3,516	883	5,826	10.5
Washington	1,607	3,342	1,408	6,357	12.8
West Virginia	289	563	142	994	11.8
Wisconsin	1,385	2,559	1,161	5,104	13.6
Wyoming	83	154.1	125	362	19.7

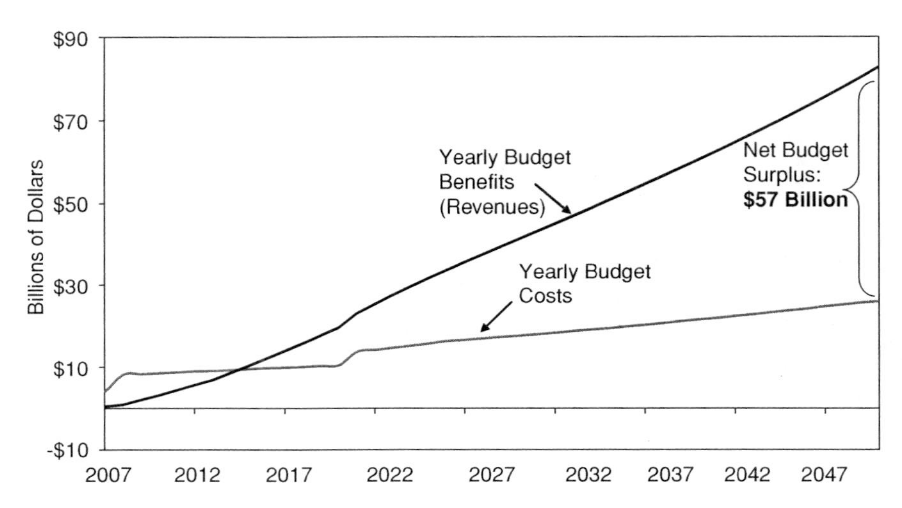

Figure 15.1. Total budget costs and benefits of a targeted pre-K program.

would require $8.2 billion in *additional* government outlays in 2008 once it is fully phased in.

It would take a while for offsetting budget benefits to outstrip the costs, but once they do, the gap becomes substantially favorable over time. For the first 8 years of a targeted program, costs exceed offsetting budget benefits, but by a declining margin. Thereafter, starting in the ninth year, offsetting budget benefits exceed costs by a growing margin each year, culminating in a net budgetary surplus of some $57 billion in 2050, the last year estimated. This pattern is illustrated in Figure 15.1, which shows annual government revenue impacts and costs in real terms.

By 2050, every dollar spent on the program by taxpayers is offset by $3.18 in budget savings, or $83 billion versus $26 billion in budget costs, in that year. Approximately 38% of the total budgetary benefits accrue to the federal government, and 62% go to state governments. If the costs of the pre-K program were divided between the federal and state governments in proportion to their shares of the budgetary benefits, the net budgetary benefit would be favorable in every state but would vary from state to state. For example, by 2050, every dollar spent on the program in Alabama would be offset by $1.95 in budget savings in that year, and every dollar spent in Delaware would be offset by $7.25 in budget savings. On average, states would experience net budget savings within 9 years, but this varies from as few as 4 years in Connecticut, Delaware, and Vermont to no more than 18 years in Alabama (see Table 15.2).

If the federal government refused to pay a share of the additional costs of the pre-K program and simply maintained its efforts in Head Start and special education (allowing states to move some federal Head Start and special education funds into the program, redistributing these federal commitments

Table 15.2. *Government budget effects of targeted program, by state*

State	Additional taxpayer costs in 2008 (millions of 2006 dollars)	Years before annual budget benefits exceed annual costs	Total government surplus in 2050 (millions of 2006 dollars)	Ratio of government budget benefits to program costs in 2050
National	8,197	9	56,677	3.18
Alabama	171	18	434	1.95
Alaska	15	8	130	2.97
Arizona	247	11	1,735	2.84
Arkansas	78	8	577	3.36
California	1,311	9	8,593	3.17
Colorado	79	10	776	3.81
Connecticut	22	4	562	6.34
Delaware	4	4	96	7.25
District of Columbia	44	8	250	2.82
Florida	591	9	3,836	2.86
Georgia	316	9	2,264	3.04
Hawaii	18	8	164	4.10
Idaho	42	11	263	3.00
Illinois	343	9	2,165	3.23
Indiana	211	17	731	2.22
Iowa	67	10	360	3.17
Kansas	65	8	476	3.67
Kentucky	72	5	955	4.82
Louisiana	139	10	717	2.94
Maine	14	7	133	4.01
Maryland	103	9	890	3.52
Massachusetts	79	8	622	3.48
Michigan	207	7	1,798	3.92
Minnesota	32	5	836	6.70
Mississippi	105	10	522	2.90
Missouri	144	9	888	3.25
Montana	19	7	123	3.28
Nebraska	40	9	252	3.35
Nevada	73	12	493	2.58
New Hampshire	13	9	108	3.62
New Jersey	74	7	894	4.18
New Mexico	68	10	369	3.05
New York	569	7	4,326	3.68
North Carolina	313	11	1,596	2.37
North Dakota	5	5	75	5.70
Ohio	190	7	1,904	4.32
Oklahoma	70	11	440	3.02
Oregon	66	8	688	3.64
Pennsylvania	298	9	1,833	3.29
Rhode Island	29	9	169	3.12
South Carolina	141	10	668	2.62
South Dakota	18	8	128	3.54
Tennessee	184	10	949	2.58
Texas	943	12	5,610	2.67
Utah	68	13	462	3.05
Vermont	2.5	4	64	5.92
Virginia	169	13	872	2.57
Washington	129	10	1,112	3.24
West Virginia	31	6	204	3.43
Wisconsin	126	8	1,010	3.69
Wyoming	7	7	65	4.51

equitably among states, and holding states harmless from potential losses of federal funds),[2] the program would still be a worthwhile investment from the perspective of state budgets. On average, states would experience net budget savings within 10 years, varying from as few as 4 years in Delaware to no more than 29 years in Alabama. By 2050, every state tax dollar spent on the program would be offset by an average of $2.15 in budgetary savings for state governments: by at least $1.17 in Alabama and by as much as $4.97 in Delaware. When compensation and crime benefits are added to the budget benefits, the ratio of total state benefits to program costs in 2050 would vary from a minimum of 7.9 to 1 in Alabama to 28.8 to 1 in Delaware (see Table 15.3).

Regardless of which level of government pays the costs of the pre-K program, the net budgetary benefits to all levels of government remain unchanged – only the cost burden shifts. In the case of a largely state-funded program, in 2050, the federal government would receive net budget benefits of more than $29 billion without incurring most of the costs of the program, and state governments would receive more than $27 billion in net budget benefits.

COST EFFECTIVENESS OF A UNIVERSAL PREKINDERGARTEN PROGRAM

The annual budgetary, earnings, and crime benefits of a voluntary, high-quality, publicly funded, *universal* pre-K program would begin to outstrip the annual costs of the program within 9 years and would do so by a growing margin every year thereafter. By the year 2050, the annual benefits would total $779 billion: $191 billion in government budget benefits, $432 billion in increased compensation of workers, and $156 billion in reduced costs to individuals from less crime and child abuse. These annual benefits in 2050 would exceed the costs of the program in that year by a ratio of 8.2 to 1. Broken down by state, in 2050, the total annual benefits would outstrip the annual costs of the program by a minimum of 6.1 to 1 for residents of Alabama and by as much as 11.4 to 1 for the residents of Wyoming (see Table 15.4).

A high-quality universal pre-K program would cost almost $6,300 per participant and could be expected to enroll nearly 7 million children in 2008 when fully phased in. With offsets for some of the current expenditures on state pre-K programs, special education, and Head Start services for children who would be attending the proposed universal pre-K program, the program would require approximately $33.3 billion in *additional* government outlays in 2008.

[2] This results in states paying 95% and the federal government picking up 5% of the net program costs.

Table 15.3. *State-by-state effects of a state-funded targeted program with federal maintenance of effort*

State	Years before annual budget benefits exceed annual costs	State government surplus in 2050 (millions of 2006 dollars)	Ratio of state government budget benefits to program costs in 2050	Ratio of total state benefits to state program costs in 2050	Federal government surplus in 2050 (millions of 2006 dollars)
National	10	27,456	2.15	11.9	29,221
Alabama	29	70	1.17	7.9	364
Alaska	10	46	1.77	12.9	84
Arizona	16	660	1.75	11.1	1,075
Arkansas	8	315	2.52	12.7	262
California	11	3,648	1.96	11.2	4,945
Colorado	11	383	2.47	16.1	392
Connecticut	5	331	4.27	22.4	231
Delaware	4	56	4.97	28.8	40
District of Columbia	11	108	1.81	9.5	142
Florida	10	2,029	2.14	10.3	1,807
Georgia	10	1,182	2.25	11.9	1,082
Hawaii	11	71	2.46	16.9	93
Idaho	16	106	1.83	12.3	158
Illinois	11	1,012	2.08	11.8	1,152
Indiana	21	203	1.36	9.3	528
Iowa	12	154	1.97	12.4	206
Kansas	10	217	2.26	13.0	260
Kentucky	6	545	3.31	16.8	410
Louisiana	11	325	1.92	11.3	391
Maine	10	61	2.45	15.2	72
Maryland	10	433	2.27	12.7	457
Massachusetts	9	277	2.14	12.5	345
Michigan	8	908	2.55	12.9	890
Minnesota	6	493	4.55	26.0	343
Mississippi	14	187	1.73	11.8	335
Missouri	12	338	1.88	11.5	550
Montana	10	51	2.03	13.0	73
Nebraska	11	113	2.09	13.0	139
Nevada	14	209	1.73	10.9	284
New Hampshire	10	44	2.11	14.1	64
New Jersey	8	448	2.64	15.2	446
New Mexico	11	178	2.08	11.9	191
New York	8	2,522	2.62	11.2	1,805
North Carolina	12	750	1.75	9.3	846
North Dakota	8	40	3.79	24.3	35
Ohio	8	1,000	2.81	15.7	904
Oklahoma	16	165	1.83	13.0	275
Oregon	10	315	2.37	15.6	373
Pennsylvania	10	978	2.26	11.7	855
Rhode Island	11	80	2.03	10.8	89
South Carolina	11	299	1.82	9.9	369
South Dakota	11	55	2.16	13.5	73
Tennessee	11	385	1.67	8.5	564
Texas	12	2,540	1.95	12.7	3,069
Utah	17	182	1.84	12.9	280
Vermont	5	37	4.10	19.9	27
Virginia	14	293	1.58	10.2	578
Washington	12	504	2.08	12.2	607
West Virginia	8	93	2.18	11.1	111
Wisconsin	9	536	2.49	12.8	474
Wyoming	8	34	2.95	19.1	31

Table 15.4. *State-by-state costs and benefits of a universal prekindergarten program*

State	Government budget benefits in 2050 (millions of 2006 dollars)	Increased compensation in 2050 (millions of 2006 dollars)	Savings to individuals from reduced crime in 2050 (millions of 2006 dollars)	Total budget, compensation, and crime benefits in 2050 (millions of 2006 dollars)	Ratio of total annual benefits to program costs in 2050
National	191,109	431,959	155,736	778,804	8.2
Alabama	1,795	5,019	997	7,812	6.1
Alaska	527	1,502	474	2,503	7.8
Arizona	5,317	11,783	5,866	22,965	7.9
Arkansas	1,526	3,079	1,204	5,809	8.5
California	26,482	64,408	17,927	108,816	8.4
Colorado	3,418	8,183	4,070	15,670	9.4
Connecticut	2,088	5,060	1,257	8,405	9.1
Delaware	311	735	311	1,358	11.2
District of Columbia	591	1,164	505	2,260	8.1
Florida	12,607	24,153	10,499	47,259	7.4
Georgia	7,189	15,396	5,847	28,432	9.0
Hawaii	811	2,066	769	3,646	9.0
Idaho	991	2,286	1,263	4,540	8.7
Illinois	7,673	17,908	6,169	31,750	8.9
Indiana	3,250	8,427	3,168	14,844	7.0
Iowa	1,380	3,402	1,219	6,001	8.4
Kansas	1,616	3,683	1,339	6,638	8.9
Kentucky	2,322	4,599	2,115	9,036	10.0
Louisiana	2,273	5,077	2,317	9,667	8.4
Maine	500	1,180	456	2,136	9.1
Maryland	4,251	10,434	3,061	17,747	8.7
Massachusetts	3,126	8,636	1,461	13,224	7.6
Michigan	5,514	12,800	2,727	21,041	8.1
Minnesota	3,921	9,015	3,901	16,837	10.2
Mississippi	1,326	3,017	1,518	5,862	8.4
Missouri	3,091	7,575	2,433	13,099	8.2
Montana	386	894	418	1,699	8.0
Nebraska	990	2,400	998	4,388	8.6
Nevada	2,174	5,109	2,612	9,895	7.7
New Hampshire	715	2,078	507	3,299	8.6
New Jersey	5,261	13,633	3,362	22,255	10.5
New Mexico	1,037	2,241	1,006	4,284	9.0
New York	12,685	23,184	8,662	44,531	9.4
North Carolina	6,029	12,933	4,746	23,708	6.9
North Dakota	276	616	348	1,240	10.1
Ohio	6,178	13,953	5,204	25,336	8.8
Oklahoma	1,673	4,308	1,609	7,589	8.5
Oregon	2,221	5,174	2,481	9,875	8.2
Pennsylvania	6,447	13,965	5,580	25,992	8.3
Rhode Island	571	1,315	402	2,288	8.0
South Carolina	2,304	5,157	1,770	9,231	7.5
South Dakota	402	936	381	1,718	9.0
Tennessee	3,344	7,721	1,853	12,918	6.4
Texas	17,167	41,978	16,759	75,904	8.0
Utah	2,271	5,776	2,507	10,554	8.8
Vermont	273	668	99	1,040	9.3
Virginia	4,545	13,073	2,332	19,950	7.7
Washington	4,135	10,086	3,120	17,341	7.7
West Virginia	572	1,327	225	2,124	7.9
Wisconsin	3,408	7,486	2,489	13,383	9.5
Wyoming	238	540	317	1,095	11.4

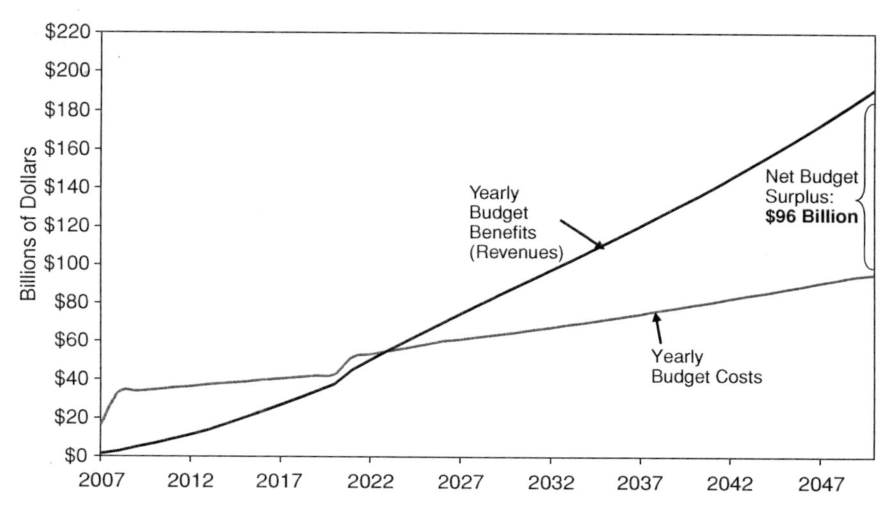

Figure 15.2. Total budget costs and benefits of a universal pre-K program.

Offsetting government budget benefits take a while to outstrip the costs, but the gap becomes substantially favorable over time. For the first 16 years of a universal pre-K program, costs exceed offsetting budget benefits but by a declining margin. By the 17th year of the program, the deficit turns into a surplus that grows every year thereafter, culminating in a net budgetary surplus of some $96 billion in 2050, the last year estimated. Thus, by 2050, every dollar spent on the program by taxpayers would be offset by $2 in budget savings in that year. This pattern is illustrated in Figure 15.2, which shows annual revenue impacts and costs portrayed in real terms.

Approximately 42% of the budgetary benefits from a universal program accrue to the federal government, and 58% go to state governments. If the costs of the pre-K program were divided between the federal government and state governments in proportion to their shares of the budgetary benefits, then for every dollar being spent on the program in 2050, Alabama would experience $1.41 in budget savings and New York would enjoy $2.67 in budget savings. The offsetting budget benefits exceed costs by states in as little as 10 years in Kentucky and New York and in as many as 29 years in Alabama (see Table 15.5).

If the federal government refused to pay for a share of the program costs in proportion to the share of benefits received and only maintained its efforts, allowing states to apply federal savings in Head Start and special education to offset some of the costs of the program (i.e., redistributing federal Head Start commitments equitably among states and holding states harmless from potential losses of federal funds), the program would generate budget surpluses in 46 states by 2050.[3] Collectively, states would experience net budget savings in

[3] In such circumstances, states would pay 95% and the federal government would pay 5% of the net program costs.

Table 15.5. *Government budget effects of a universal program, by state*

State	Additional taxpayer costs in 2008 (millions of 2006 dollars)	Years before annual budget benefits exceed annual costs	Total government surplus in 2050 (millions of 2006 dollars)	Ratio of government budget benefits to program costs in 2050
National	33,338	17	95,605	2.00
Alabama	512	29	518	1.41
Alaska	89	21	206	1.64
Arizona	805	20	2,411	1.83
Arkansas	238	12	844	2.24
California	4,631	17	13,586	2.05
Colorado	560	19	1,749	2.05
Connecticut	349	17	1,159	2.25
Delaware	60	11	190	2.56
District of Columbia	95	12	312	2.12
Florida	1,894	14	6,258	1.99
Georgia	946	13	4,020	2.27
Hawaii	176	20	408	2.01
Idaho	181	19	468	1.90
Illinois	1,392	17	4,101	2.15
Indiana	800	25	1,135	1.54
Iowa	319	19	666	1.93
Kansas	306	16	867	2.16
Kentucky	328	10	1,418	2.57
Louisiana	477	17	1,119	1.97
Maine	95	17	265	2.12
Maryland	668	18	2,212	2.08
Massachusetts	660	22	1,387	1.80
Michigan	1,052	16	2,902	2.11
Minnesota	567	17	2,267	2.37
Mississippi	299	18	629	1.90
Missouri	634	18	1,498	1.94
Montana	88	17	174	1.82
Nebraska	212	19	481	1.94
Nevada	318	22	894	1.70
New Hampshire	135	21	331	1.87
New Jersey	702	14	3,148	2.49
New Mexico	198	14	559	2.17
New York	1,784	10	7,932	2.67
North Carolina	970	21	2,575	1.75
North Dakota	55	16	154	2.26
Ohio	1,203	16	3,287	2.14
Oklahoma	328	21	780	1.87
Oregon	367	19	1,019	1.85
Pennsylvania	1,277	17	3,319	2.06
Rhode Island	114	18	285	1.99
South Carolina	442	17	1,075	1.88
South Dakota	77	16	211	2.10
Tennessee	669	21	1,325	1.66
Texas	2,928	20	7,671	1.81
Utah	393	22	1,069	1.89
Vermont	38	13	160	2.43
Virginia	847	24	1,957	1.76
Washington	673	22	1,888	1.84
West Virginia	120	11	303	2.12
Wisconsin	527	14	2,003	2.43
Wyoming	44	13	142	2.47

23 years, with an average return per state tax dollar expended on the program of $1.26 in 2050. However, the returns per state tax dollar would vary from a low of $0.79 in Alabama to a high of $1.88 in New York in 2050. In addition, in 2050, the federal government would be enjoying a $73 billion budget surplus due to the pre-K investment made largely by states. Including the compensation and crime benefits of the program, the ratio of total state benefits to state program costs in 2050 would vary from a minimum ratio of 5.9 to 1 in Alabama to 11.2 in Wyoming (see Table 15.6).[4]

In addition to budget, earnings, and crime benefits, there are other benefits from high-quality pre-K that have not been evaluated. Some costs may have been omitted from this analysis as well. Some of these omitted costs and benefits are described in the next section.

OMITTED COSTS AND BENEFITS OF TARGETED AND UNIVERSAL PREKINDERGARTEN

The ultimate costs and benefits of a large-scale, nationwide pre-K program could turn out to be higher or lower than what I have estimated. For illustration purposes, this analysis assumed the launch of a pre-K program on a national scale in 2007, with full phase-in by 2008. Yet, for practical purposes, a large-scale pre-K program would have to be phased in over a period longer than 2 years. In general, extrapolating from a relatively small-scale program to a large-scale national program is precarious. Start-up costs, such as the recruitment and training of teachers and staff and the finding of appropriate locations, or benefit reductions may be associated with the scaling up. The quality of teachers and staff may decline, or the teachers and staff may not be as highly motivated as those in the Chicago CPC program. If the pre-K programs increase the number of high school graduates, market wages for higher skilled labor may decline in response to the increased supply of high-skilled workers.

Yet, the estimates provided earlier understate the total benefits of pre-K investment, and the omitted benefits probably far outweigh any omitted costs. For example, the estimates may have omitted some of the value of the future greater productivity of more educated workers. To illustrate how large this omitted benefit might be, consider that between 1973 and 2004, average compensation in the United States increased 46% while average productivity increased 76% (Mishel, Bernstein, & Allegretto, 2006). Thus, the estimated increase in compensation that would occur as a consequence of pre-K investment may reflect less than two-thirds of the actual increase in productivity

[4] The budget benefits, when states pay for most of the program, should perhaps be seen as bonuses that are in addition to the nonbudgetary benefits because the nonbudgetary benefits are by themselves greater than the costs of the program. For example, by 2050, the increase in compensation is estimated to amount to 1.8% of the gross domestic product, or $432 billion, which is more than four times the cost of the program.

Table 15.6. *State-by-state effects of a state-funded universal prekindergarten program with a federal maintenance of effort*

State	Years before annual budget benefits exceed annual costs	State government surplus in 2050 (millions of 2006 dollars)	Ratio of state government budget benefits to program costs in 2050	Ratio of total state benefits to state program costs in 2050	Federal government surplus in 2050 (millions of 2006 dollars)
National	23	23,053	1.26	7.9	72,552
Alabama*		−241	0.79	5.9	760
Alaska*		−34	0.88	7.7	240
Arizona	35	227	1.08	7.6	2,183
Arkansas	16	298	1.48	8.3	546
California	24	2,783	1.23	8.1	10,803
Colorado	24	408	1.27	9.3	1,341
Connecticut	20	366	1.42	8.7	794
Delaware	12	66	1.59	10.9	123
District of Columbia	18	95	1.36	7.8	217
Florida	20	1,876	1.32	7.2	4,381
Georgia	18	1,348	1.46	8.7	2,672
Hawaii	29	63	1.17	8.9	345
Idaho	29	68	1.14	8.5	400
Illinois	21	1,137	1.34	8.6	2,964
Indiana*		−215	0.89	6.8	1,350
Iowa	27	113	1.17	8.2	554
Kansas	22	219	1.32	8.5	648
Kentucky	12	591	1.71	9.8	827
Louisiana	22	275	1.26	8.2	844
Maine	23	60	1.28	8.8	204
Maryland	23	537	1.28	8.4	1,675
Massachusetts	41	60	1.04	7.2	1,328
Michigan	21	805	1.33	7.8	2,097
Minnesota	19	782	1.51	9.9	1,485
Mississippi	28	82	1.13	8.3	546
Missouri	32	164	1.11	7.8	1,335
Montana	25	15	1.08	8.0	159
Nebraska	27	79	1.17	8.3	401
Nevada	41	36	1.03	7.5	858
New Hampshire	44	1	1.00	8.3	331
New Jersey	19	966	1.49	10.1	2,181
New Mexico	18	189	1.44	9.1	370
New York	11	3,882	1.88	9.1	4,050
North Carolina	32	413	1.13	6.7	2,162
North Dakota	19	46	1.41	10.1	108
Ohio	21	932	1.35	8.5	2,355
Oklahoma	35	82	1.10	8.5	698
Oregon	32	105	1.10	8.1	914
Pennsylvania	18	1,075	1.37	8.1	2,244
Rhode Island	23	71	1.27	7.7	214
South Carolina	26	204	1.18	7.3	871
South Dakota	22	44	1.26	8.8	166
Tennessee	41	63	1.03	6.2	1,263
Texas	34	694	1.08	7.8	6,976
Utah	35	125	1.11	8.6	944
Vermont	14	56	1.54	9.0	105
Virginia*		−67	0.97	7.4	2,025
Washington	34	279	1.14	7.5	1,609
West Virginia	13	77	1.31	7.6	226
Wisconsin	17	773	1.59	9.3	1,230
Wyoming	14	47	1.54	11.2	94

* Program budget benefits do not exceed costs within the window of this analysis.

that would take place in the economy. This implies that my estimates of the benefits of the targeted and universal programs in the year 2050 are missing more than $75 billion and $215 billion, respectively, in productivity increases.

I have also not measured the financial savings to families who would place their children in the publicly funded program but who, in its absence, would have paid the costs of private preschool. Because about one-quarter of all families with 3- and 4-year-old children place their children in private preschool programs, the savings to families from the use of publicly funded pre-K are potentially very large, especially for a universal program.

A large pre-K program would have the potential not possible in small programs to improve the school atmosphere for everyone, not just pre-K participants. Raising the academic performance while lowering the criminal activity of the 25% of children who attend high-quality targeted pre-K should benefit the other 75% of children who subsequently attend kindergarten through high school with them. This peer effect may be even greater for a universal program: The reductions in crime and school failure and the boosts to employment, productivity, and earnings may be reinforcing and could produce larger pre-K effects than those I have estimated. Hence, there may be multiplier effects on the economy from the higher skilled, more productive, and higher earning universal pre-K participants.

There is also evidence that a universal program may be more effective than I have estimated if it integrates children from different economic backgrounds more thoroughly than a targeted program could. Schecter (2002) found that low-income children in economically integrated preschools fared better than comparable children in targeted programs that served only low-income children.

I do not calculate the potentially positive effects on the children born to pre-K participants who (as parents) will have higher earnings and employment and lower incarceration rates. Pre-K is an investment in the parents of the future who, as a result of pre-K education, will be able to provide better educational opportunities to their children than they would have without the pre-K program. Hence, the children of pre-K participants may be able to earn more and lead better lives. If this generational effect were accounted for, the benefits of pre-K may be substantially larger than those I have estimated.

Numerous other savings to taxpayers and boons to government budgets may have been omitted. For instance, there is evidence that high-quality pre-K may reduce smoking, which in turn may reduce public health-care expenditures (Schweinhart et al., 2005).

Benefits were further underestimated because I only included benefits for which it was possible to obtain monetary estimates. Thus, I left out benefits such as the intrinsic value of lower drug use, fewer teenage parents, and greater self-sufficiency when pre-K participants become adults. In total, the value of the omitted benefits is likely to swamp the value of the omitted costs, and the total benefits and the benefit-cost ratios of both the targeted and the universal programs are likely to be larger than those presented here.

DIFFICULTIES IN ESTIMATING THE EFFECTS OF PROSPECTIVE PRE-K PROGRAMS

To calculate the effects of a universal program, we must estimate the extent to which the benefits of a high-quality, pre-K program like the Chicago CPC program, which served high-risk children (from low-income families), would apply to medium-risk children (from middle-income families) and low-risk children (from high-income families) who would otherwise attend no preschool. The Chicago CPC program and studies of other high-quality programs found significant long-term benefits for high-risk children, but most of these high-quality programs did not include children from middle- and upper-income families, and thus they do not provide evidence of the long-term effects of high-quality pre-K participation on more advantaged children. Unfortunately, not many studies have examined the benefits of high-quality prekindergarten on medium- and low-risk children.

Differential pre-K benefits for children with different backgrounds manifest themselves in two ways. First, there is a baseline effect: Different populations have different rates of everything from child abuse to special education to criminal behavior. This different baseline can be thought of as a "room for improvement" effect. Second, there may be a differential treatment effect: For reasons not captured fully by the baseline differences, different children may see greater or lesser treatment effects from prekindergarten.

A reasonable expectation is that the benefits of high-quality pre-K will be more positive for less advantaged children than they will be for more advantaged children because there is more room for improvement among poor children. The incidence of academic and social problems is generally higher for high-risk children than it is for more advantaged children. For example, middle- and upper-income children are retained at only about 72% and 50%, respectively, of the rate of poor children. Similarly, children from middle-income and well-to-do families use special education at roughly 67% and 38%, respectively, the rate of low-income children (Karoly & Bigelow, 2005). Likewise, poor children are disproportionately involved in crime and are about four times more likely to be victims of child abuse and neglect than are nonpoor children (Mocan & Rees, 1999; Sedlak & Broadhurst, 1996).

Collectively, these data suggest that high-quality pre-K programs may be able to generate smaller benefits from low-risk than from high-risk children. For example, assuming for illustration purposes that the average low-risk child commits two crimes while the average high-risk child commits four crimes and that a pre-K program cuts crime rates in half for all children, then the criminal justice system will be spared the costs of only one crime per low-risk child but a greater two crimes per high-risk child due to the pre-K program. This is the baseline effect: A higher starting point leaves less room for absolute improvement.

In addition to the fact that room for improvement differs among children from various socioeconomic backgrounds, the empirical research on the measured impacts of pre-K generally shows that lower-, middle-, and upper-income children benefit from high-quality prekindergarten. Yet, it shows mixed findings on how much these groups of children benefit and on which of these groups of children benefits the most.

Larsen and Robinson (1989) found significant gains for boys but not for girls from pre-K participation for children from above-average income and educationally advantaged families. Garces, Thomas, and Currie (2000) found that high-risk children who attended Head Start had some gains relative to comparable children who attended no preschool. In contrast, lower risk children who attended preschool other than Head Start (mostly private preschools) had no significant gains relative to comparable children who attended no preschool.[5]

Analyses of Georgia's state preschool programs (Henry, Gordon, Henderson, & Ponder 2003; Henry et al., 2005) indicated that children from all economic backgrounds benefit from preschool. Children in Georgia attending state preschool made significant gains from the beginning of preschool to the end of first grade on a variety of tests compared to national samples of children their age, of whom only about two-thirds attended some preschool.

Evaluations of Oklahoma's universal pre-K program (Gormley & Gayer, 2005; Gormley, Gayer, Phillips, & Dawson, 2004) also indicated that children from all economic backgrounds benefit from pre-K. Poorer children tended to gain more than richer children, but the differences in gains were not large. In addition, some of the largest gains appear to have been experienced by lower- to middle-income children. It should also be noted that the children who attended the state's universal pre-K were compared to children who had not attended the universal pre-K but who may have attended some other form of preschool. Thus, the gains that were measured reflect the benefits of attending a relatively high-quality public pre-K program compared to the gains of attending, on average, lower quality preschool or no preschool at all.

Studies in Canada and England also found that children who attended pre-K had better academic outcomes than children who did not attend preschool, regardless of their economic background (Lipps & Yipton-Avila, 1999;

[5] The lack of significant benefits from non–Head Start preschool for low-risk children that Garces et al. (2000) found must be considered with caution because we have no data on the quality of the non–Head Start programs the children attended. If their findings for low-risk children reflect the relatively low quality of the private preschools they attended, then low-risk children moving from low-quality private preschools to high-quality public pre-K may get some, all, or nearly all of the benefits associated with a high-quality program.

Sammons et al., 2002, 2003). Likewise, a study of the French pre-K program (Hirsch, 2004) found that children gain from attending additional years of pre-K and that these benefits are similar across income levels.

Barnett, Lamy, and Jung (2005), in an analysis of kindergarten children in five states, found that one year of state-funded, relatively high-quality pre-K significantly raised test scores compared to those of children who did not attend the state-funded program. They found a somewhat stronger effect of pre-K on the print awareness of low-income children, but the improvements in math and vocabulary tests were virtually identical for children from high- and low-income families. Note, too, that many of the children in the comparison groups attended preschool programs other than the relatively high-quality state-funded pre-K. Thus, this study also suggests that higher quality preschool programs provide benefits beyond those achieved by other preschool programs for children from all economic backgrounds.

In a nationwide analysis, Magnuson, Ruhm, and Waldfogel (2004) and Magnuson, Meyers, Ruhm, and Waldfogel (2005) found that children who attended preschool were better prepared and performed better in kindergarten than did students who did not attend preschool, regardless of economic background. However, they found that the greatest math and reading gains were achieved by the most disadvantaged children. In contrast, the reduction in grade retention was roughly the same for high- and non-high-risk children. Magnuson, Ruhm, and Waldfogel (2004) also provided estimates for the effects on reading and math skills of preschool participation relative to nonparticipation for the full sample and a subsample of children living in poverty, which suggested that average-risk children may receive anywhere from 60% to 95% of the benefits of preschool that are received by high-risk children.

Several points are clear. Children from low-, middle-, and upper-income families benefit from preschool. Higher quality pre-K provides greater benefits than lower quality preschool. Studies differ on the degree of impact that preschool has on children from different economic backgrounds. Some studies find that the positive effects of pre-K on children from more and less advantaged backgrounds are nearly identical. Other studies suggest that children from low-income families gain more from pre-K than do children from middle- and high-income families.

Given the mixed results on the relative effects of preschool on children from different economic backgrounds, it is not certain to what extent the benefits of a high-quality, universal program modeled after the Chicago CPC program, which served high-risk children (from low-income families), would apply to medium-risk children (from middle-income families) and low-risk children (from high-income families) who would otherwise attend no preschool. Thus, I offer high-, low-, and intermediate- (intermediate being the most likely) range estimates of these possible effects. Earlier in the chapter, the intermediate-range estimates were used, but the following sensitivity analysis examines the full range of effect estimates.

For the high-end estimate, I assume that the effects of pre-K are virtually identical for children of all economic backgrounds. Thus, I assume that all children in a universal, high-quality pre-K program who would otherwise have attended no preschool would get 100% of the pre-K effects measured in the Chicago CPC program. Moving from the baseline targeted-program estimates to the universal-program estimates, the costs and benefits are attenuated only to account for the lower incidence of academic and social problems experienced by middle- and upper-income children.

For the low-end estimate, I assume that children from middle-income and wealthy families would experience much less improvement from pre-K than did the relatively disadvantaged children in the Chicago CPC program. Thus, for the low estimate, I assume that middle- and upper-income children (who would otherwise have attended no preschool) would experience, on average, only 70% and 40%, respectively, of the improvement observed in the Chicago CPC program.

Finally, for the intermediate estimate, I assume that children from middle-income and wealthy families would experience somewhat lower benefits from pre-K than did the relatively disadvantaged children attending the Chicago CPC program. Thus, for the intermediate estimate, I assume that middle- and upper-income children (who would otherwise have attended no preschool) receive, on average, only 85% and 70%, respectively, of the benefits estimated in the targeted prekindergarten program.

These attenuations are applied on top of adjustments for the baseline or "room for improvement" effect, so the true attenuation for middle- and upper-income children is significantly higher. Thus, the estimating procedure calculates benefits of pre-K per mid- and low-risk children that are far less than 85% and 70% of those for high-risk children, as assumed in the intermediate estimate. For example, with the baseline adjustments, I assume that middle- and upper-income children (who would otherwise attend no preschool) receive, on average, only 21% and 18%, respectively, of the reduction in child maltreatment rates; 61% and 35%, respectively, of the reduction in retention; and 57% and 27%, respectively, of the reduction in special education experienced by relatively disadvantaged children.

The intermediate estimate is consistent with the findings of Gormley et al. (2004) with respect to the relative benefits of the Oklahoma pre-K program for low-income children (those who qualified for free lunch) and financially advantaged children (those who paid full price for lunch).[6] Specifically, on tests of letter identification, spelling, and applied problems, the relatively financially advantaged children experienced improvements that were 78%, 83%, and 64% as great as the improvements experienced by the relatively poor children. I based the most likely intermediate estimates in part on the Oklahoma results because

[6] The intermediate estimates are also reasonably consistent with the findings of Magnuson, Ruhm, et al. (2004), noted earlier, which suggest that average-risk children who attend preschool may get anywhere from 60% to 95% of the benefits received by high-risk children.

the Oklahoma universal pre-K program, which serves most of the 4-year-olds in the state, is similar to although somewhat lower in quality than the Chicago CPC program. In addition, its estimated initial effects on school readiness of high-risk children are similar in size to those estimated for the initial effects of the Chicago CPC program on high-risk children. Thus, for both reasons, it may be reasonable to assume that the effects of the Oklahoma program on middle- and upper-income children will be similar to those of a Chicago CPC-style universal program on middle- and upper-income children. However, it should be noted that the children who attended Oklahoma's universal pre-K were compared to children who had not attended the universal pre-K but who may have attended some other form of preschool. Thus, the gains that were measured for the Oklahoma participants reflected the benefits of attending a relatively high-quality pre-K program compared to the gains of attending, on average, a combination of lower quality and no preschool at all. Because I am trying to measure the impact of a high-quality pre-K program on middle- and high-income children who would otherwise attend no preschool, and given that middle- and high-income children who did not attend the Oklahoma program are more likely to have attended some other preschool, basing my estimate on the outcomes of the Oklahoma program may result in overly conservative estimates of the benefits for mid- and low-risk children.

To calculate the benefits of targeted and universal pre-K, we also must estimate the extent to which the benefits of a high-quality pre-K program like the Chicago CPC program, which compared outcomes for children who attended a high-quality pre-K program to outcomes for children who (for the most part) attended no preschool, will apply to children who would otherwise attend some form of preschool. In the United States, about half of 3- and 4-year-olds are already attending some form of preschool. Hence, if we were to create publicly funded, high-quality pre-K, it is probable that many of the children who would attend such a program would have otherwise attended some form of preschool. As already noted, research suggests that many existing preschool programs provide benefits to participants relative to children who do not attend preschool. In addition, higher quality pre-K programs provide greater benefits than lower quality preschool programs (see Henry, Henderson, et al., 2003; Henry et al., 2005; National Institute of Child Health and Human Development, 2005; and Peisner-Feinberg et al., 2001). Hence, children moving from lower quality preschool to a higher quality pre-K program should gain but not as much as children moving from no preschool to high-quality pre-K. Thus, the estimated positive effects of public, high-quality pre-K must be attenuated to take into account that many of its prospective participants would attend some form of preschool and receive some of the benefits of pre-K in the absence of the public program.

Numerous studies of private preschool programs found their educational quality to be highly variable, often poor, and lower on average than the quality available in existing public programs (Blau, 2001; Cost, Quality, and Child Outcomes Study, 1995; Currie, 2001; Helburn & Bergmann, 2002; Henry, Gordon, et al., 2003; Henry et al., 2005; Phillips, Voran, Kisker, Howes, & Whitebook, 1994; Ripple, Gilliam, Chanana, & Zigler, 1999; Smith, Kleiner, Parsad, Ferris, & Greene, 2003). Magnuson, Meyers, Ruhm, and Waldfogel (2004), Magnuson, Ruhm, et al. (2004), and Magnuson et al. (2005) reported that children in public pre-K had larger gains than children in all other forms of preschool. Some researchers have concluded that the quality of private preschools, on average, is so poor that they offer little or even no benefit to participants (Barnett, Ackerman, & Robin, 2006).

There is some evidence of the effectiveness of existing public pre-K programs relative to high-quality pre-K programs. Barnett (2002, 2005) found that the relatively lower quality programs achieved only about 25% of the reduction in special education and 55% of the reduction in grade repetition achieved by the higher quality programs. However, as Barnett noted, it may be misleading to compare these results because the higher quality programs were serving more disadvantaged children. Similarly, Barnett et al. (2006) found that children attending Head Start experienced only 25% to 35% of the improvement in letter-word identification and spelling that was experienced by poor and nonpoor children in the relatively higher quality Oklahoma universal pre-K program. However, it is not certain whether these differences in initial results will persist.

The bottom line is that there is little quantitative evidence to indicate exactly how much smaller the impacts of existing preschool programs would be compared to a prospective high-quality program. I assume that most existing preschool programs, whether private or public, provide benefits but are not of high quality and as effective as the prospective high-quality pre-K programs proposed in this study. I provide a wide range of estimates of the effectiveness of the proposed programs relative to existing preschools: high, low, and intermediate (or most likely) estimates. In the estimates of the cost effectiveness of a high-quality, public pre-K presented in this chapter, I used the intermediate estimate, but the sensitivity analysis performed later includes the full range of estimates.[7]

My high estimate assumes that children attending high-quality public pre-K who would otherwise have attended some other preschool would receive about 90% of the benefits received by comparable participating children who would have otherwise attended no preschool. This estimate implies that most existing preschool programs are of low quality and not generating many benefits.

[7] In the cost and benefit estimating procedure, when attenuating the potential benefits to account for prior preschool attendance, I do not factor out the fact that 15% of the Chicago CPC program control group attended preschool. Thus, my attenuation for prior preschool attendance may be too great.

At the other extreme, I assume that children who would otherwise have been enrolled in some form of preschool in the absence of a public program reap only 30% of the benefits of comparable children attending the public program who would have otherwise attended no preschool. This implies that existing preschool programs are fairly high quality, generating a substantial portion of the benefits of the prospective high-quality public programs.

Finally, my intermediate estimate assumes that children who would have attended some other preschool in the absence of high-quality public pre-K would experience 60% of the effect experienced by comparable participating children who would otherwise have attended no preschool. This estimate implies that the prospective programs will be of greater quality than existing preschool programs and will generate improvements that are about two and a half times as large as those produced in the average existing preschool program. This estimate may be conservative because the initial effects of high-quality public pre-K programs on the school readiness of nonpoor and poor children may be substantially more than two and a half times as large as the initial effects of medium-quality public preschool programs (Barnett et al., 2006).

In the next section, a sensitivity analysis is performed to demonstrate what effect various estimates of the impacts of high-quality pre-K on children of different socioeconomic backgrounds and attenuation rates that account for current preschool attendance have on estimates of the cost effectiveness of high-quality public pre-K.

SENSITIVITY ANALYSIS FOR TARGETED AND UNIVERSAL PREKINDERGARTEN

For the targeted program in the year 2050, when I allow participants who would have attended some other preschool program in the absence of the high-quality public program to experience as little as 30% and as much as 90% of the impacts experienced by the Chicago CPC participants, the annual budgetary surplus would range from $45 billion to $68 billion, the return per tax dollar invested would vary from $2.83 to $3.51, the increase in compensation would be between $132 billion and $179 billion, and the savings to individuals from less crime would vary from $65 billion to $89 billion.

In addition to accounting for current preschool enrollment, a sensitivity analysis of the universal program must consider that a large-scale universal pre-K program would draw in children from middle- and upper-income families who are at lower risk for educational failure and other problems than those in the targeted program. Such children might (or might not) experience smaller positive impacts from pre-K than those in the targeted program. In the sensitivity analysis that follows, I examine the cost effectiveness of universal pre-K when we account for various impacts of current preschool enrollment; allow middle- and upper-income children to experience as much as 100%

and as little as 70% and 40%, respectively, of the high-quality pre-K effects experienced by low-income children; and adjust for socioeconomic factors.[8]

The lowest estimate of the effects of universal pre-K assumes that participants who would have attended some other preschool program in the absence of the high-quality program would experience only 30% of the impacts experienced by the Chicago CPC participants and that pre-K impacts on middle- and upper-income children are only 70% and 40%, respectively, of those for the Chicago CPC participants. These impacts are then further attenuated to account for socioeconomic factors. The highest estimate of the effects of universal pre-K assumes that participants who would have attended some other preschool program in the absence of the high-quality program would experience 90% of the impacts experienced by the Chicago CPC participants and that pre-K impacts on middle- and upper-income children are 100% of those for the Chicago CPC participants. The high-end impacts are also further adjusted to account for the lower incidence of social and academic problems experienced by middle- and upper-income children.

My lowest and highest estimates of the effects of universal pre-K investment suggest that this investment would generate in 2050 a budgetary surplus of at least $45 billion and as much as $156 billion, a return per tax dollar invested of at least $1.50 and as much as $2.51, an increase in compensation of between $301 billion and $588 billion, and savings to individuals from less crime and child abuse that vary from a low of $109 billion to a high of $210 billion.

To appreciate how conservative the low-end estimate is, consider what it assumes about the benefits of high-quality public pre-K for middle- and upper-income children who, in its absence, would have attended some other form of preschool relative to the benefits experienced by the poor children who participated in the Chicago CPC program. With socioeconomic baseline adjustments, treatment effect attenuations, and attenuations for prior preschool attendance, middle- and upper-income children would experience only 15% and 6%, respectively, of the grade-retention benefit; 14% and 5%, respectively, of the reduction in special education; and 5% and 3%, respectively, of the reduction in child maltreatment (see Table 15.7).

In other words, even adjusting for a very wide range of estimates for the effects of current preschool participation and the impact of high-quality pre-K on children from different economic backgrounds, high-quality universal pre-K has substantial long-term benefits for government budgets, the economy,

[8] In other sensitivity analyses, I also varied the prospective enrollment rate in the universal program from a high of 94% to a low of 68% compared to the 81% assumed in the estimates presented in this chapter. High enrollment rates, by scaling both costs and benefits, produced somewhat larger estimates of budget surpluses, compensation increases, and crime savings. However, they also generated somewhat lower estimates of the ratio of budget benefits to budget costs. Low enrollment rates produced somewhat smaller estimates of budget surpluses, compensation increases, and crime savings. However, they also generated somewhat higher estimates of the ratio of budget benefits to budget costs.

Table 15.7. *Range of treatment effects for middle- and upper-income children relative to poor children accounting for various treatment impacts, preschool attendance, and differences in social and academic experiences*

Experiences	Middle-income children	Upper-income children
Grade retention	15% to 72%	6% to 50%
Special education	14% to 67%	5% to 38%
Child maltreatment	5% to 25%	3% to 25%

and crime reduction. In addition, as noted earlier, the value of the omitted benefits is likely to greatly exceed the value of omitted costs. Thus, although the governmental budget benefit–cost ratio of a national-scale pre-K program (whether targeted or universal) could be somewhat higher or lower than the preferred estimate presented in this chapter, it is improbable that this ratio would be less than the 1:1 ratio necessary for the program to eventually pay for itself.

IMPLICATIONS FOR POLICY

The economic case for public investment in pre-K is compelling. Research demonstrates that investment in high-quality pre-K, even when its benefits are not fully accounted for, is a cost-effective public-policy strategy for enriching children and the nation. A nationwide commitment to high-quality early childhood education would cost a significant amount of money up front, but it would have a substantial payoff in the future because such a program would ultimately reduce costs for remedial and special education, criminal justice, and child welfare, and it would increase income earned and taxes paid. Over time, governmental budget benefits alone outweigh the costs of high-quality pre-K; that is, high-quality pre-K *pays for itself*! It is striking that a national program, either funded jointly by federal and state governments or financed largely by states, will have significant positive effects on the long-term budget outlooks of both federal and state governments. Thus, a national pre-K initiative should be seen as a sound investment on the part of government that generates substantial long-term benefits.

A case for public investment in either a targeted or a universal pre-K program can be made, with the best policy depending in part on whether a higher value is placed on the ratio of benefits to costs (which is higher for a targeted program) or the total net benefits (which are higher for a universal program). However, when policy makers weigh the benefits of investment in a targeted versus a universal program, they should take other criteria into consideration. For example, if public funds are limited, a targeted program may be more attractive because it is less expensive to implement. Likewise, if a large priority is placed on narrowing the achievement gap between children from lower-income and upper-income families, then the targeted program may be more effective in achieving this goal.

In contrast, a universal program available to all children may garner greater public support and thus be more likely to achieve the high quality necessary for optimal results. In addition, children who are not eligible for a targeted program can benefit from high-quality pre-K, and targeted programs are likely to fail to reach many of the children they are designed to serve. A universal program not only benefits middle- and upper-income children but also may have larger effects than a targeted program for the most at-risk children. Given that the positive impacts of pre-K may be larger for at-risk than for more advantaged children, a pre-K program, whether targeted or universal, may help reduce achievement gaps between poor and nonpoor children and ultimately reduce income inequality nationwide.

REFERENCES

Barnett, W. S. (1993). Benefit-cost analysis of preschool education: Findings from a 25-year follow-up. *American Journal of Orthopsychiatry, 63*(4), 500–508.

Barnett, W. S. (2002). *The battle over Head Start: What the research shows.* New Brunswick, NJ: National Institute for Early Education Research.

Barnett, W. S. (2005). Maximizing returns from prekindergarten education. In *Federal Reserve Bank of Cleveland Research Conference: Education and economic development* (pp. 5–18). Cleveland, OH: Federal Reserve Bank of Cleveland.

Barnett, W. S., Ackerman, D. J., & Robin, K. B. (2006, May 18). *California's Preschool for All Act (Proposition 82): A policy analysis.* New Brunswick, NJ: National Institute for Early Education Research.

Barnett, W. S., Lamy, C., & Jung, K. (2005, August). *The effects of state prekindergarten programs on young children's school readiness in five states.* New Brunswick, NJ: National Institute for Early Education Research.

Blau, D. M. (2001). *The child care problem: An economic analysis.* New York: Russell Sage.

Cost, Quality, and Child Outcomes Study Team. (1995). *Cost, quality, and child outcomes in child care centers* (2nd ed.). Denver: University of Colorado Economics Department.

Currie, J. (2001). Early childhood education programs. *Journal of Economic Perspectives, 15*(2), 213–238.

Garces, E., Thomas, D., & Currie, J. (2000). *Longer term effects of Head Start* (Working Paper, series 00–20). Santa Monica, CA: RAND Corporation.

Gormley, W. T., & Gayer, T. (2005). Promoting school readiness in Oklahoma: An evaluation of Tulsa's pre-K program. *Journal of Human Resources, 40*(3), 533–558.

Gormley, W., T., Gayer, T., Phillips, D., & Dawson, B. (2004). *The effects of Oklahoma's universal pre-kindergarten program on school readiness.* Washington, DC: Center for Research on Children in the U.S. Georgetown University. Retrieved from http://www.crocus.georgetown.edu.

Helburn, S. W., & Bergmann, B. R. (2002). *America's child care problem: The way out.* New York: Palgrave.

Henry, G. T., Gordon, C. S., Henderson, L. W., & Ponder, B. D. (2003, May). *Georgia pre-K longitudinal study: Final report 1996–2001.* Atlanta: Georgia State University, Andrew Young School of Policy Studies.

Henry, G. T., Henderson, L. W., Ponder, B. D., Gordon, C. S., Mashburn, A. J., & Rickman, D. K. (2003, August). *Report of the findings from the early childhood study: 2001–02.* Atlanta: Georgia State University, Andrew Young School of Policy Studies.

Henry, G. T., Rickman, D. K., Ponder, B. D., Henderson, L., Mashburn, A., & Gordon, C. S. (2005). *The Georgia early childhood study, 2001–2004: Final report.* Atlanta: Georgia State University, Andrew Young School of Policy Studies.

Hirsch, E. D., Jr. (2004). *Equity effects of very early schooling in France.* Core Knowledge Preschool. Retrieved from http://www.coreknowledge.org/CK/Preschool/FrenchEquity.htm.

Karoly, L., & Bigelow, J. H. (2005). *The economics of investing in universal preschool education in California.* Santa Monica, CA: RAND.

Larsen, J. M., & Robinson, C. C. (1989). Later effects of preschool on low-risk children. *Early Childhood Research Quarterly, 4,* 133–144.

Lipps, G., & Yipton-Avila, J. 1999. *From home to school: How Canadian children cope* (Catalogue # 89F0117XIE). Culture, Tourism and the Center for Education Statistics. Ottawa, Ontario: Statistics Canada.

Lynch, R. G. (2004). *Exceptional returns: Economic, fiscal, and social benefits of investment in early childhood development.* Washington, DC: Economic Policy Institute.

Lynch, R. G. (2007). *Enriching children, enriching the nation: Public investment in high-quality prekindergarten.* Washington, DC: Economic Policy Institute.

Magnuson, K. A., Meyers, M. K., Ruhm, C. J., & Waldfogel, J. (2004). Inequality in preschool education and school readiness. *American Educational Research Journal, 41*(1), 115–157.

Magnuson, K. A., Meyers, M. K., Ruhm, C. J., & Waldfogel, J. (2005). Inequality in children's school readiness and public funding. *Focus, 24*(1), 12–18.

Magnuson, K. A., Ruhm, C. J., & Waldfogel, J. (2004, April). *Does prekindergarten improve school preparation and performance?* (NBER Working Paper 10452). Cambridge, MA: National Bureau of Economic Research.

Masse, L., & Barnett, W. S. (2002). *A benefit-cost analysis of the Abecedarian early childhood intervention.* New Brunswick, NJ: National Institute for Early Education Research, Rutgers University.

Mishel, L., Bernstein, J., & Allegretto, S. (2006). *The state of working America 2006/2007.* Ithaca, NY: ILR Press.

Mocan, H. N., & Rees, D. I. (1999). *Economic conditions, deterrence and juvenile crime: Evidence from micro data* (Working Paper #7405). Cambridge, MA: National Bureau of Economic Research.

National Institute of Child Health and Human Development. (2005). Early child care and children's development in the primary grades: Follow-up results from the NICHD study of early child care. *American Educational Research Journal, 42*(3), 537–570.

Peisner-Feinberg, E. S., Burchinal, M. R., Clifford, R. M., Culkin, M. L., Howes, C., & Kagan, S. L. (2001). The relation of preschool child-care quality to children's cognitive and social development trajectories through second grade. *Child Development, 72,* 1534–1553.

Phillips, D. A., Voran, M., Kisker, E. Howes, C., & Whitebook, M. (1994). Child care for children in poverty: Opportunity or inequity? *Child Development, 65,* 472–492.

Reynolds, A. J. (2000). *Success in early intervention: The Chicago Child-Parent Centers.* Lincoln: University of Nebraska Press.

Reynolds, A., Temple, J., Robertson, D., & Mann, E. (2002, Winter). Age 21 cost-benefit analysis of the Title 1 Chicago Child-Parent Centers. *Educational Evaluation and Policy Analysis, 24*(4), 267–303.

Ripple, C., Gilliam, W., Chanana, N., & Zigler, E. (1999). Will fifty cooks spoil the broth? *American Psychologist, 54*(5), 327–343.

Rolnick, A., & Grunewald, R. (2003, March). Early childhood development: Economic development with a high public return. *Fedgazette.* Federal Reserve Bank of Minneapolis.

Sammons, P., Sylva, K., Melhuish, E., Siraj-Blatchford, I., Taggart, B., & Elliot K. (2002). *Measuring the impact of preschool on children's cognitive progress over the preschool period* (Institute of Education Technical Paper 8a). London: University of London.

Sammons, P., Sylva, K., Melhuish, E., Siraj-Blatchford, I., Taggart, B., & Elliot K. (2003). *Measuring the impact of preschool on children's social/behavioral development over the preschool period* (Institute of Education Technical Paper 8b). London: University of London.

Schecter, C. (2002). *Language growth in low-income children in economically integrated versus segregated preschool programs.* West Hartford, CT: St. Joseph College.

Schweinhart, L. J., Barnes, H. V., & Weikart, D. P., with Barnett, W. S., & Epstein, A. S. (1993). *Significant benefits: The High/Scope Perry Preschool study through age 27* (Monograph No. 10). Ypsilanti, MI: High/Scope Educational Research Foundation.

Schweinhart, L. J., Montie, J., Xiang, Z., Barnett, W. S., Belfield, C., & Nores, M. (2005). *Lifetime effects: The HighScope Perry Preschool study through age 40.* Ypsilanti, MI: HighScope Educational Research Foundation.

Sedlak, A., & Broadhurst, D. (1996). *The Third National Incidence Study of Child Abuse and Neglect (NIS-3).* U.S. Department of Health and Human Services, Administration for Children and Families, Administration on Children, Youth and Families, National Center on Child Abuse and Neglect. Washington, DC: U.S. Government Printing Office.

Smith, T., Kleiner, A., Parsad, B., Ferris, E., & Greene, B. (2003). *Prekindergarten in U.S. public schools, 2000–2001: Statistical analysis report* (NCES 2003–019). Washington, DC: National Center for Education Statistics.

16

The Fiscal Returns to Public Educational Investments in African American Males

CLIVE BELFIELD AND HENRY LEVIN

INTRODUCTION

Among all of the major demographic groups in the United States, African American (Black) males experience the poorest educational outcomes.[1] Whether we measure such outcomes in terms of test scores, high school graduation, postsecondary attendance, or college graduation, African American males lag substantially behind other groups. It is widely recognized that unequal educational outcomes lead to unequal economic consequences throughout the life-course. In particular, individuals with low-attainment and poor-quality education – characteristics that often overlap – can expect to face inferior employment prospects, low wages, poor health, and greater involvement in the criminal justice system.

Educational inequality for Black males is a moral issue, but it is also an economic one: Poor education leads to large social costs in the form of lower societal income and economic growth, lower tax revenues, and higher costs of public services such as health, criminal justice, and public assistance. Thus, it is possible to assess efforts to improve educational outcomes for Black males as a public investment that might yield high returns.

In this chapter, we undertake a comprehensive assessment of the public returns to investments for improving the educational attainments of Black males. We begin by documenting the extent of educational inequality between Blacks and Whites. Next, we identify educational interventions that would increase the rate of high school graduation, and we calculate their public costs. Then we summarize the fiscal and social benefits of increasing the numbers of Black male high school graduates in terms of higher tax revenues, reduced

[1] For brevity, we use "Black" and "African American" interchangeably; "graduation" refers to high school.

This chapter revises and updates a research paper coauthored with Peter Muennig (Columbia University) and Cecilia Rouse (Princeton University).

public costs for health services, and reduced costs of criminal justice services.[2] Finally, we combine these data into estimating net present values and benefit-cost analyses. We show that investing more in education for these individuals is in the economic interest of both the taxpayer and society. If successful, these investments would most likely pay off without an efficiency-equity trade-off.

EDUCATIONAL STATUS OF BLACK MALES

The relative educational status of Black males in the United States is stark. (Unless stated otherwise, the following data are from KewalRamani, Gilbertson, Fox, and Provasnik, 2007.) The disparities are evident across many educational metrics. In a thorough analysis of Black–White skills gaps, Neal (2006) reported significant differences in attainment (and graduation rates). In 2000, Black males aged 26–30 had, on average, 0.72 fewer years of education than White males (the gap for females was 0.62). This gap was closing from the 1950s to 1960s, but the narrowing appears to have stalled since the 1990s.

Test scores show a similar disparity. Reading results from the National Assessment of Educational Progress (NAEP) for 2005 showed that 36% of the total student population scored "below basic" in 4th grade, 27% in 8th grade, and 27% in 12th grade. For all Blacks (male and female), the proportions scoring "below basic" were 58%, 48%, and 46%, respectively. Similarly, 20% of the total student population scored "below basic" on NAEP math tests in 4th grade, 31% in 8th grade, and 39% in 12th grade; for all Blacks, the respective figures were 40%, 58%, and 70%. These gaps are not closing. Although the reading and math Black–White gaps narrowed during the 1980s, they have stabilized since: The 2004 gaps were almost exactly the same as the 1996 gaps. In 1978, male White–Black NAEP math scores were 306/268, a 38-point gap; by 1986, the gap was 29 points, and from 1996 to 2004, it remained at 28 points.

In addition, Black males are found in disproportionate numbers in special education and suspended or expelled from school (Holzman, 2006). This 2006 report indicates that the national K–12 rate of grade repetition is 12.1% for males; for black males, it is 22.6%. For suspension, the national rate is 14.9%; for black males, it is 24.2%; for expulsions, the rates are 2.9% and 6.7%, respectively.

These schooling differences affect college prospects. Blacks are slightly less likely to take the SAT than others, and their verbal scores average 434 compared to the national average of 503; for math, the respective figures are 429 and 518. Blacks are less likely to go to college, more likely to attend a 2-year rather than a 4-year college, and less likely to complete their degrees. Yet, college-level differences are not close to those in the K–12 education system. Whereas 42% of

[2] In other simulations, we have included the costs of reliance on welfare by educational level. However, these amounts are very small: Most welfare is contingent on having children, not being low-income per se, and is time limited.

Whites aged 18–24 are enrolled in college, the rate for Blacks is 32% (National Center for Education Statistics, 2005, Table 184). Whereas almost 25% of all college degrees are associate's degrees, the rate for Blacks is higher, but is only 30%. Overwhelmingly, then, the disparities between Black college students and other college students are much smaller than the disparities evident through elementary and secondary school.

Importantly, these outcome differences do not fully capture differences in educational investment because they do not account for school quality or college quality. Generally, schooling resources that Black children receive are inferior to those of white children (Duncombe & Yinger, 2005).[3] Based on data from the Education Trust (2006), in more than half of all states, government funding in high-minority school districts is *less* than in low-minority districts.[4] Across the United States, the average shortfall in high-minority districts is $900–$1,200 per year. Therefore, as an approximation, total public K–12 educational investment per Black student is $20,000 *less* than per White student.[5] Of course, this disparity is understated by the amount of compensatory expenditure that is needed to equalize educational outcomes of children from disadvantaged families.

We recognize that many of these educational differences have their origins in family circumstance (Jencks & Phillips, 1998; KewalRamani et al., 2007; Neal, 2006, Table 11). Of U.S. families with children in 2005, 67% of children lived with two married parents, 25% with a single mother, and 8% with a single father. For Blacks, only 36% lived with two married parents, 55% lived with a single mother, and 9% with a single father. Whereas 16% of families in the United States lived below the poverty line, the rate was 30% for Black families.[6] However, in their thorough review of the socioeconomic determinants of the Black–White test score gap, Magnuson and Duncan (2006) concluded that family socioeconomic resources explain just under half a standard deviation; thus, a considerable proportion of the gap is attributable to other factors (e.g., school quality). Therefore, a reasonable conclusion is that the effects of low household income and unstable family structure simply compound the effect of low-quality schooling opportunities.

[3] At the college level, Black high school graduates are more likely to attend 2-year colleges than 4-year colleges; the latter have larger state subventions (National Center for Education Statistics, 2005).

[4] This is so for several reasons. Funds are not in practice allocated using equity-driven formulas. Title I includes a factor explicitly allocating more funds to high-spending states. Little information exists on where resources actually flow at the student level. Spending on teachers is higher in wealthier districts.

[5] The calculation is $1,000 per K–12 year plus the cost of 0.8 year of schooling at $8,500 per year.

[6] Interestingly, young Blacks do not drink, smoke, or use drugs at rates higher than those of the rest of the population. In fact, previous-month usage among 12- to 17-year-olds nationally is 18% for alcohol, 12% for cigarettes, and 8% for marijuana; for Black males, the respective figures are 10%, 6%, and 6%.

Table 16.1. *Highest level of educational attainment for those aged 20*

	Black males		White males	
Less than ninth grade	6,000	2%	18,000	1%
High school dropout	67,000	22%	193,000	14%
High school graduate	99,000	33%	402,000	29%
Some college or above	133,000	44%	757,000	56%
Total cohort size	305,000		1,369,000	

Note: Race-specific adjustments are made for institutionalization and GED receipt.
Source: Data from *Current Population Survey*, March 2005.

In this chapter, we focus on the impact of raising the quality of schooling on high school graduation rates. We select this measure because graduation captures both cognitive and noncognitive attributes that are important for success in adulthood. Graduating from high school is usually a minimum requirement for further training and higher education, and it opens up a range of future possibilities. It is also a goal that is far beyond the reach of many young Black males.

Table 16.1 shows highest attainment levels by race/ethnicity for those aged 20 (allowing for those who graduate late).[7] Each age cohort of Black males is approximately 305,000 persons. Of this Black male population, 22% are high school dropouts; the corresponding figure for White males is 14%. College progression rates are lower for Black males also, but much of this difference is explained by lower rates of high school graduation that preclude the opportunity to attend college. Simply equalizing Black and White graduation rates would require an additional 24,000 Black males to graduate each year. Later, we calculate the economic consequences of failing to ensure graduation rates for Black male students equal to that of White male students and for the aggregate situation in which Black male graduation rates are lower than White male graduation rates.

INTERVENTIONS TO INCREASE HIGH SCHOOL GRADUATION RATES FOR BLACK MALES

To identify effective interventions for increasing high school graduation rates for Black males, we undertook a wide literature search.[8] Of the hundreds of

[7] We account for two ways in which the CPS data are less than ideal. First, we adjust for persons who are incarcerated – these are not counted in the CPS – using incarceration-rate data by educational level from Raphael (2004). Second, we adjust for GED receipt, which is not equivalent to a high school diploma, using data from the NELS derived by Rumberger (2004).

[8] This included searches of journal articles, search engines, and Columbia University libraries. We gave special scrutiny to reports from three organizations with substantial experience in educational evaluation: Manpower Development Research Corporation (MDRC), the

articles and reports we retrieved, only five studies met our criteria of using a credible evaluation design and yielding improvements in graduation rates.[9] The interventions in these studies are summarized in Table 16.2.

Two of the selected interventions take place at preschool. The Perry Preschool program (PPP) is a high-quality preschool program that was the focus of an experimental study using random assignment in the 1960s in which follow-up studies of participants and nonparticipants were conducted up to age 40 (see Chapter 7) (Belfield, Nores, Barnett, & Schweinhart, 2006). The Chicago Child-Parent Center (CPC) preschool program was established in 1967 to provide early education and family-support services emphasizing math and reading skills and using high staff:student ratios and parent education (see Chapter 8). The evaluation used a quasi-experimental design to compare the performance of CPC participants with a matched control group of nonparticipants; follow-up studies of members of both groups were conducted up to age 20 (Reynolds, Temple, Robertson, & Mann, 2002).

We included these preschool interventions because they have the strongest evidence in their favor. However, preschool reforms are unlikely to help Black children unless the reforms are focused on upgrades to the quality of existing programs. Black children already enroll in preschool programs at relatively high rates. As of 2005, 57% of poor children aged 3–5 and 63% of nonpoor students were enrolled in center-based preschool programs nationally. The corresponding percentages for Black students were 65% for poor students and 68% for nonpoor students. Many of these children were in Head Start, but Head Start is reasonably effective, and state programs often fail to spend as much as Head Start.

The class size reduction (CSR) intervention is based on the Tennessee Project STAR experimental study in which students were randomly assigned to larger classes (22 students) or smaller ones (15 students) for up to 4 years from kindergarten to third grade (see Chapter 14) (Finn, Gerber, & Boyd-Zaharias, 2005). The teacher salary increase (TSI) study focused on the effects of raising teacher salaries on graduation rates using state data, with a 10-year time lag assumed before graduation rates would increase (Loeb & Page, 2000). The underlying assumption of this study is that higher teacher salaries will attract more qualified and effective teachers to replace those who leave, which will in turn raise graduation rates. Finally, First Things First (FTF) is a high school reform initiative that closely reflects the present wave of urban high

RAND Corporation, and Mathematica Policy Research (MPR). We appreciate the assistance of Fred Doolittle at MDRC and Mark Dynarski at MPR.

9 We were especially interested in studies using experimental or quasi-experimental methods or a strong econometric identification strategy. In some cases, the evaluations of interventions were of very poor quality. In other cases, the evaluations suggested that there was little educational impact.

Table 16.2. *Interventions that demonstrably raise the high school graduation rate*

Intervention		Details of the intervention	Extra high school graduates if intervention is given to 100 students	Program costs per student[a]	Program costs per new high school graduate[b]	Total educational costs per new high school graduate[c]
PPP	Perry Preschool program	1.8 years of a center-based program for 2.5 hours per weekday, child:teacher ratio of 5:1, home visits, and group meetings of parents	19	$12,532	$65,959	$90,694
CSR	Class size reduction	4 years of schooling (grades K–3) with class size reduced from 25 to 15	18	$13,075	$72,638	$97,373
FTF	First Things First	Comprehensive school reform: small learning communities with dedicated teachers, family advocates, and instructional improvement efforts	16	$5,493	$34,331	$59,066
CPC	Chicago Child-Parent Center program	Center-based preschool program: parental involvement, outreach, and health/nutrition services; based in public schools	11	$4,728	$42,979	$67,714
TSI	Teacher salary increase	10% increase in teacher salaries for all years K–12	5	$2,865	$95,503	$120,238

Note: PPP: Belfield et al. (2006); CSR: Finn et al. (2005); FTF: Quint et al. (2005); CPC: Reynolds et al. (2002); TSI: Loeb and Page (2000). Costs are expressed in present values at age 20 using a 3.5% discount rate.

[a] Cost per student counts the costs of delivering the intervention.

[b] Cost per new high school graduate counts the costs of delivering the intervention to 100 students.

[c] Total costs are program costs plus the induced costs from extra attainment in high school and college ($24,735).

school reform with its emphasis on small learning communities, instructional improvement, and teacher advocacy for each student (Quint, Bloom, Black, Stephens, & Akey, 2005). The research design was a discontinuous time-series using data from Kansas City, Kansas – the site that has accumulated the most extensive FTF experience.

Each intervention showed positive impacts on graduation rates. Column 3 of Table 16.2 shows the estimated new high school graduates if the intervention was delivered to 100 students. The educational effectiveness is based on the evaluations of each of the reforms: PPP is the most effective at 19 new graduates; TSI would yield 5 new graduates.[10] All interventions are replicable, and although none are limited only to Black males, all but the TSI address predominantly Black students.[11] Thus, we have reasonable grounds for expecting similar effects if the interventions were implemented today.

We now turn to the public costs of these interventions. Costs were taken from studies that either accounted directly for the resources and their expenses for each intervention or were computed from the additional resources required using the ingredients approach (Levin & McEwan, 2001).[12] In addition to the direct costs of the intervention, the cost of two additional years of schooling for each added graduate was calculated, as well as the state college subsidies for those additional graduates who might be expected to pursue higher education. Because these new high school graduates would be likely to have lower academic achievement and socioeconomic status than existing graduates, we estimated college continuation and completion rates accordingly.[13] Thus, the total public

[10] Because they occur at different educational levels, these interventions may be combined to strengthen their effects. For example, the impact of TSI on student achievement seems to increase as teacher salaries increase. Presumably, higher quality teachers associated with higher salaries are able to use smaller class size more productively (see Peevely, Hedges, & Nye, 2005).

[11] In the PPP and CPC interventions, almost all the participants were Black. In the CSR intervention, we use graduation rates for students on free lunch and populations with a high concentration of Blacks in the experimental setting. In the FTF intervention, about half of the students were Black. The TSI data are based on state averages and may understate the expected improvement in graduation rates for Black males because of their relatively small number in the overall student population (about 3%) and because many reforms have shown larger impacts for minorities.

[12] For example, costs of PPP and CPC were taken directly from the studies and converted to 2004 prices (see table notes). Costing of CSR was based on the need for more teachers and classrooms and, for FTF, on the need for more teachers and counselors. For TSI, we estimated a 10% increase in salaries and benefits. Both PPP and CPC reduced grade retentions and assignments to special education, thus saving public expenditures. These cost savings have been deducted to obtain "net" costs of producing additional high school graduates.

[13] We used the NELS 88 follow-up of eighth-graders to estimate college participation 6 years later. Among Black male graduates in the lowest quartile on reading scores, about 18% and 16% were in 2-year and 4-year colleges, respectively. According to the 1996–2001 Beginning Postsecondary Students Longitudinal Study, 5-year completion rates for students in the bottom third of socioeconomic status were 50%. Thus, for our calculations, 1 of 12 of the new high school graduates is expected to complete a 4-year degree and 1 of 6 a 2-year degree.

cost of raising graduation rates of Black males is the sum of the direct program (intervention) costs and the additional publicly funded schooling and college costs induced by the intervention. To ensure consistent accounting, all money figures are expressed as present values at age 20 with a discount rate of 3.5% and using 2004 prices.[14]

The fourth through sixth columns of Table 16.2 show the program costs per student, the program costs per new high school graduate, and the total educational costs per new high school graduate. The program costs per student refer to all students who receive the intervention but, of course, many of these students would have graduated even in its absence (we assume these persons cannot be identified ex ante). Program costs vary from $2,900 to $13,100. Costs per additional graduate refer to the public costs when divided by only the additional graduates who are produced. These costs vary from $34,300 to $95,500. The final column shows the total public cost when educational progression has been considered.

Assuming that the intervention is delivered to 100 students whose graduation probabilities are unknown, the total public cost per new high school graduate ranges from $59,066 to $120,238. The lowest public cost per additional graduate is found for FTF; because it is implemented in high school, it is the least affected by adjusting to present value at age 20. Although TSI has the highest cost among these alternatives, we remind the reader that the TSI result is an average for all students, and there are good reasons for expecting that success rates might be considerably higher – even double – for Black males. Krueger and Whitmore (2001) reevaluated the Tennessee class size reduction data: They found that the gain for Black students was 7–10 percentile points (versus 3–4 percentile points for Whites) and that during the years of class size reduction, K–3, the test score gap between Blacks and Whites declined by 38% and by about 15% thereafter. If a similar doubling of the average effect were to result from higher salaries for teachers, the TSI cost per additional graduate would fall to among the lowest.

Many alternative interventions may be effective. We do not include them in our analysis, either because they have not been proven to be effective (especially for Black males) or because there is inadequate information on their costs. Interventions not selected include the following: reforms to reallocate teachers or improve the quality of the teaching profession,[15] family engagement

[14] The choice of the appropriate discount rate is a subject of debate. A discussion of the issues and the choice of 3.5% are in Moore et al. (2004). Because the interventions occur at different ages and yet could all be implemented immediately (albeit on a different cohort of children), we choose age 20 as the focal year. Costs or benefits before that age are uprated (inflated) by 3.5% and after that age are discounted by 3.5%.

[15] According to Hanushek (2006), there is simply no reliable evidence on policies that would improve allocation or raise teacher quality.

or involvement programs,[16] policies that would raise family income,[17] privatization reforms,[18] neighborhood interventions,[19] small school reforms,[20] and specific programs (e.g., Advancement Via Individual Determination [AVID]) for which the evidence is inadequate. We do note, however, that some reforms, such as the high school mentoring and advisement program Check & Connect, have been found to be effective and are very likely to be cost effective.

To expand the range of effective interventions, we considered interventions that raise test scores as a mediator for higher graduation probabilities. An analysis of the National Education Longitudinal Study of 1988 (NELS 88) showed that a one-unit standard deviation increase in eighth-grade test scores is associated with an almost 50% decrease in the probability of dropping out (Rumberger & Larsen, 1998). However, our own analysis of NELS 88 revealed this relationship to be sensitive to race, sex, and subject of study (Belfield & Levin, 2009). That is, the association between graduation and test scores for Black males was strongest in reading test scores (for other males, it was in math scores; for females, both subjects were strongly influenced). In addition, there was no correlation between test scores and graduation probabilities for those with test scores above the median. Finally, we are not aware of studies that relate early-grade test scores to subsequent graduation probabilities with the exception of the STAR experiment (Finn et al., 2005).

PUBLIC BENEFITS OF ADDITIONAL BLACK MALE GRADUATES

Increasing the number of Black male high school graduates not only improves those individuals' life chances but also yields public benefits via government savings. Here, we briefly review the methods for deriving these public benefits, and we calculate the effects per graduate (for full details, see Belfield, 2006; Muennig, 2006; and Rouse, 2006).

Additional Tax Revenues

Table 16.3 shows the labor-market outcomes by educational attainment for Black males aged 21–64 using Current Population Survey (CPS) data (see Rouse, 2006). Black male high school dropouts are much less likely to

[16] Family-engagement programs have been found to raise literacy levels in the early grades (Senechal, 2006). Yet, family involvement in school decision making has not been found to be widely effective.

[17] In our review of the literature in Belfield and Levin (2007), we found that increasing family incomes might be effective if the increase in income were permanent or if it were targeted at young families.

[18] Privatization reforms include competition, charter schools, and vouchers. The research in this field is very partisan, but few of the benefits of privatization have been significant.

[19] The Moving to Opportunity program found few benefits to the families involved.

[20] Small schools are probably more efficient (Kuziemko, 2006), but they are expensive to create.

Table 16.3. *Mean labor-market outcomes by educational attainment for Black males aged 21–64*

	High school dropout	High school diploma	High school diploma or more
Employed	48.8%	67.3%	71.9%
Unemployed	10.0%	8.7%	7.8%
Discouraged worker	1.3%	0.9%	0.6%
Not in the labor force – other	39.9%	23.1%	19.7%
Number of weeks worked last year	25.4	35.5	38.0
Employer provides pension plan	33.1%	50.7%	58.0%
Covered by employer/union-provided health insurance	23.2%	42.8%	48.9%
Annual earnings (all persons)	$12,262	$22,199	$31,230

Note: Sample includes men aged 21–64. All means are weighted. Annual earnings includes all persons, working or not.
Source: Data are from March supplement of the *Current Population Survey*, 2003 and 2004.

participate in the labor force or be employed (or work continuously). Across all Black males (regardless of employment status), dropouts report considerably lower earnings than graduates. In addition, graduates are more likely to have health insurance and pension coverage. These differences in labor-market status translate into not only higher earnings but also higher tax revenues as a public benefit over the life-course.

Rouse (2006) used a three-step procedure to estimate the additional tax revenues per new high school graduate. First, she estimated the age-earnings profiles of Black males with different education levels; to obtain an adequate sample size of about 11,000 Black males aged 21–64, she combined data from the 2003 and 2004 CPS. From these data, Rouse estimated the additional lifetime income associated with graduation and higher education (assuming productivity growth of 1.5% per annum). Second, she used the National Bureau of Economic Research TAXSIM model to estimate the federal and state taxes on these incomes. Third, she converted the lifetime figures to present values at age 20, using a 3.5% discount rate.

This method is likely to produce conservative results. Although earlier economic studies assumed that the measured returns to schooling and the schooling coefficient in earnings functions were overstated because of unmeasured differences in ability associated with the schooling variable, a variety of more recent studies do not confirm that expectation. Studies of twins and siblings with different levels of education as well as those using instrumental variables have found that the "naïve" coefficient in earnings functions does not appear to be biased upward.[21] Accordingly, no adjustment is made for

[21] See the review in Rouse (2006). Levin (1972) assumed a 25% downward adjustment in additional earnings for an ability correction.

differential ability in these estimates. Importantly, the CPS data include "high school equivalency" in their definition of high school graduation, meaning that those who passed the GED exam – about 14% of all Black males – are treated as high school graduates.[22] Yet, although the GED is popularly referred to as a "high school equivalency," it is not: GED recipients' earnings profiles have been found to be closer to those of dropouts than to high school graduates (Cameron & Heckman, 1993). Thus, because the presence of GED recipients in CPS data biases downward the additional income that is associated with actual high school completion, CPS data understate the differential earnings associated with high school completion.

The method used by Rouse (2006) yields significant differences in earnings and tax contributions across education levels, which are reported in the top panel of Table 16.4. Whereas the present-value lifetime earnings of Black male dropouts are $292,200 at age 20, the respective figures are $601,800 for high school graduates and $1,479,000 for those with a bachelor's degree or higher. There are correspondingly large differences in tax payments, which are reported in the second two panels of Table 16.4, depending on whether the individual files taxes as a single person or as the head of a household. Using the average of these two tax calculations, a Black male dropout contributes $118,000 in income taxes over his lifetime; the respective figures are $222,400 for high school graduates and $607,000 for college graduates. To these, we add property tax and sales taxes, which increase all values by 5%.[23]

The bottom panels of Table 16.4 show the present-value differences between high school dropouts and persons with higher educational attainment. Assuming that a new high school graduate would have a small probability of going on to college and completing a degree, we can calculate the present-value income and tax gains per new Black male high school graduate. Both are substantial. The individual is anticipated to earn $423,500 more if he graduates from high school (calculated as income differentials multiplied by the probabilities given in footnote 13). (These large earnings figures raise a significant question as to why individuals do not accumulate more education: The implied private discount rate is more than 40%.) Table 16.5 presents the distribution of tax savings. Overall, the present value at age 20 of the extra tax revenue associated with each additional high school graduate would be about $167,600.

[22] The CPS does not adjust for the probability of incarceration. At age 20, about 19% of Black male high school dropouts are incarcerated; for Black male high school graduates, the percentage declines to 8%. All income and tax revenue estimates take this into account.

[23] Sales tax was calculated for each state as per capita tax revenues divided into personal per capita income; a national average was obtained using state population weights. This figure was multiplied by the after-tax difference in incomes between dropouts and graduates (factoring in college progression rates). Sources for these data were the Federation of Tax Administrators, the U.S. Department of Commerce, the Bureau of Economic Analysis, and the Survey of Current Business.

Table 16.4. *Present value of lifetime earnings and taxes paid by Black males*

	High school dropout	High school graduate	Some college	BA degree or more
Earnings	$292,174	$601,845	$858,755	$1,478,989
Taxes paid				
Individual basis	$87,730	$182,922	$265,876	$505,057
Family basis	$148,183	$261,914	$391,305	$708,823
Average	$117,957	$222,418	$328,951	$606,940
		Difference over dropout		
		High school graduate	Some college	BA degree or more
Earnings	baseline	$309,672	$566,581	$1,186,815
Taxes paid				
Individual basis	baseline	$95,192	$178,146	$417,326
Family basis	baseline	$113,731	$243,122	$560,640
Average	baseline	$104,462	$210,634	$488,983

Note: 2004 dollars. Figures corrected for incarceration probabilities. Discount rate is 3.5%. Productivity growth is assumed as 1.5%.

Source: Data from March supplement of the *Current Population Survey*, 2003 and 2004.

This amount alone is more than is currently spent on each student over his or her K–12 schooling.

Projected Savings in Public Health Costs

High school graduates have improved health status, lower rates of mortality, and fewer social problems (Lantz, House, Lepkowski, Williams, Mero, & Chen, 1998). This is true for both Blacks and Whites, but the lower educational levels of Black males contribute to less healthy lifestyles and poorer health status such

Table 16.5. *Total present-value lifetime tax revenue gains*

	Lifetime tax revenue gains
Per expected high school graduate:	
Baseline: income taxes only	$154,200
Baseline + sales and property taxes	$167,623
Baseline without Social Security taxes	
Federal government	$83,434
State/local government	$18,934

Note: An expected high school graduate is one who probabilistically either terminates education after graduation (prob. = 0.75), completes some college (prob. = 0.17), or completes a bachelor's degree (prob. = 0.08). Federal income taxes do not include Social Security taxes. Discount rate is 3.5%.

that their life expectancy is considerably shorter than for White males: Arias, Anderson, Kung, Murphy, and Kochanek (2003, p. 116) reported that as of 2001, Black male life expectancy was 69 years compared to 75 years for White males – a shockingly large gap.

Because of poorer job prospects and low incomes, Black male dropouts are unlikely to have private health-care coverage. By default, they must depend on health care that is publicly or philanthropically financed. The largest insurer for those under age 65, Medicaid, is a means-test program for which eligibility depends on low income. Participation in Medicaid declines as education increases because those with more education are more likely to have higher incomes; this makes them ineligible for Medicaid and more likely to have private health insurance (as shown in Table 16.3). In addition, those who qualify for Social Security Disability Income (SSDI) receive benefits from Medicare. For example, kidney disease is the numerically highest qualifying condition, a condition for which persons with lower educational attainments are especially at risk (Wong, Shapiro, Boscardin, & Ettner, 2002). Functional limitations before age 65 are also criteria for SSDI benefits and are found more often for persons with less education (Cutler & Lleras-Muney, 2006).

The estimates for differences in public costs of health care by educational level are derived from the 2002 Medical Expenditure Panel Survey (MEPS). This is a nationally representative sample of more than 40,000 noninstitutionalized civilians, with oversampling of households with incomes less than twice the poverty line. The MEPS data also contain socio-demographic data as well as medical expenditures, enabling us to measure the health-related quality of life. These estimates were combined with enrollment costs from the National Health Accounts (NHAs) to estimate aggregate health expenditures (Arnett, Blank, Brown, & Cowan, 1990).

We performed two analyses, with Muennig (2006). First, we used a regression analysis to predict coverage by public insurance with controls for age, race, gender, and ethnicity. Second, we estimated per capita public insurance costs for Black males at different educational levels. The latter estimate includes costs not captured in the MEPS, such as government payments to hospitals that serve disproportionately low-income populations.[24] For Black males aged 18–24, the gradients of public coverage are steep: 81% of those with less than 9 years of education have publicly reimbursed care, in contrast to only 28% of college graduates. Table 16.6 shows the differences in expenditure by education level. Whereas African American males with 9–11 years of education consume nearly $110,000 of public health care over their lifetimes, college graduates consume less than $40,000.

Again using the probabilities of college progression, we estimate the lifetime savings in public health costs. As shown in Table 16.7, for each high school

[24] The analysis also calculated health-related quality-of-life scores for Black males, which were shown to be positively related to education and negatively related to age.

Table 16.6. *Lifetime present-value public medical costs by education*

	High school dropout	High school graduate	Some college	College graduate
Absolute				
With differential mortality	$108,585	$83,179	$57,421	$37,346
Without differential mortality	$108,585	$81,268	$56,198	$36,174
Advantage over dropouts				
With differential mortality		$25,406	$51,164	$71,239
Without differential mortality		$27,317	$52,837	$72,411

Note: In all analyses, subjects die at a rate equal to that of nongraduates. In the baseline analysis, high school graduates are assumed to be at 76% the risk of annual mortality of nongraduates. Likewise, college graduates are assumed to have 63% of the risk of nongraduates. Discount rate is 3.5%.

graduate relative to high school dropout, we estimate present-value savings at age 20 to be $33,518. If high school and college graduates have the same risk of death as nongraduates, then savings increase.

Finally, it is possible to calculate the societal burden of low education on public health costs. From the societal perspective, gains are measured in Quality-Adjusted Life Years (QALYs, or years of perfect health), which have a value of roughly $80,000 excluding productivity costs (Muennig, 2006). The average African American male will gain about 1.6 QALYs from an intervention that promotes him to a high school graduate. This amounts to roughly $129,000 worth of additional healthy life per individual.

Projected Savings in Criminal Justice Costs

High school graduates are much less likely to commit crimes than dropouts (Lochner & Moretti, 2004). The average rate of institutionalization for all Black males aged 18–65 is 8%, compared to 19% for Black male dropouts, 8% for Black male graduates, and 1% for Black male college graduates (Raphael, 2004). For younger cohorts, roughly one-quarter of Black male dropouts are incarcerated (Harrison & Karberg, 2003). Based on data for California, over

Table 16.7. *Lifetime present-value public medical cost savings*

	PV cost savings
Per expected high school graduate	
With differential mortality	$33,518
Without differential mortality	$35,253

Note: An expected high school graduate is one who probabilistically either terminates education after graduation (prob. = 0.75), completes some college (prob. = 0.17), or completes a bachelor's degree (prob. = 0.08). For the cohort of Black males aged 20, there are 67,000 high school dropouts. Equating Black and White male graduation rates entails 24,000 additional high school graduates.

the early lifetime up to age 35, a Black male dropout is almost certain to have been incarcerated for some period (Raphael, 2004); nationally, the probability is approximately 60% (Pettit & Western, 2004). For Black male high school graduates, the likelihood is less than 20%.[25] Importantly, overall rates of incarceration for Black males are six to eight times those of White males (Pettit & Western, 2004).

Belfield (2006) divided the economic burden of crime for the public sector into four categories: criminal justice system operation (police, courts); costs of incarceration including parole and probation; public restitution to victims; and crime-prevention expenditures by government agencies. He then examined the relationship between graduation and five types of crime: murder; rape/sexual assault; violent crime (robbery, aggravated assault); property crime (burglary, larceny); and drug offenses. Each of these crime types imposes high public costs and is lower for those with more education. The effect of education on the commission of these crimes is based on results from Lochner and Moretti (2004). Unit costs were estimated from a range of sources, including the Bureau of Justice Statistics and the FBI Uniform Crime Rate data (Belfield, 2006).

The total annual cost savings per new expected high school graduate are reported in Table 16.8. Over a lifetime, the minimum public costs of criminal justice that would be saved by converting a high school dropout to a graduate would be at least $55,500.[26] This figure is large and is just for the year of being 20 and only for generating a new high school graduate (i.e., family resources and local environments are not improved). Importantly, it does not include any beneficial impacts on juvenile crime (which occurs before age 20).

Social Gains From High School Graduation

Taxpayers are not the only ones who would reap economic benefits from increases in educational attainment: Society as a whole would benefit. The social gains to the state include the savings to the taxpayer, but there are three additional components.

First, there is the increase in private income earned by each new graduate. This increase in net income can be calculated as the change in gross income

[25] Bonczar (2003) reported that 9% of Black males aged 18–24 were ever incarcerated in the 1990s; the rate for those aged 25–34 was 20%. Raphael (2004, Table 4) found rates for high school dropouts of 19% (ages 18–24), 114% (ages 25–34), and 123% (ages 35–44); for high school graduates, the rates were 2%, 15%, and 16%, respectively.

[26] This estimate is understated for two reasons and should be viewed as highly conservative because the five specific types of crime listed here account for, perhaps, 80% of the differential costs associated with education. Detailed data on the public costs associated with other crimes are not readily available. In addition, the costs of juvenile crime before the age of 20 are not included. Thus, we believe that the public benefit in reducing the costs of criminal justice through raising educational attainments is even higher than this estimate and should be interpreted in that light.

Table 16.8. *Total present-value lifetime cost savings from reduced criminal activity per Black male expected high school graduate*

	Total fiscal savings
Per expected high school graduate	
Baseline (federal and state)	$55,524
By government agency (baseline model):	
Federal government	$5,634
State/local government	$49,891

Note: Annual criminal activity is reported by Belfield (2006). Criminal activity is assumed to decay to zero by age 65. The decay rate is based on the actual incidence of crime for each age group (Uniform Crime Reports [UCR], 2004, Table 1). Impacts on incarceration reported by Lochner and Moretti (2004); amount reported adjusts for the lower UCR crime figures compared to the National Crime Victimization Survey (NCVS), and it assumes that these estimates account for only 80% of all crimes in value terms.

minus the tax payments. Second, there are savings to society from reductions in crime. The fiscal consequences of inadequate education are a function of the budgets for the criminal justice system but, clearly, the victims of crime bear the largest burden in terms of reduced quality of life and monetary losses (e.g., time off work). Moreover, all persons make private expenditures for insurance and other forms of protection to prevent becoming the victim of crime or to cushion its financial impact. We also note that many victims of crime are of the same race as the perpetrators, and perpetrators' family members also may be included as victims: If fathers are incarcerated, there are more single-parent households, total family income is lower, and welfare dependency is higher.

Unfortunately, these costs are much harder to estimate with precision than fiscal costs: Ludwig (2006) estimated that these social costs are 4.5 times larger than the fiscal costs; data reported by Miller, Cohen, and Wiersema (1996) yielded a factor that is closer to 2.5. Following convention, the more conservative ratio is applied here.

Second, health status has an economic value (Cutler & Lleras-Muney, 2006). Based on calculations by Muennig (2006), the improvement in Black male health per new high school graduate would be as high as 1.47 QALYs. Over a lifetime, this health improvement is valued at approximately $182,000.

Finally, there are externalities from education on economic growth: Workers with more human capital might also make their coworkers more productive and attract investment into the state. Reviewing the literature, McMahon (2006) estimated these externalities to be worth 37% to 61% of the total market returns to education. In contrast, in an extensive review of cross-country evidence, Pritchett (2006) suggested that the effect is quite small and possibly zero. However, this evidence came from countries with very different economic structures from the United States. Therefore, we estimate that the first-best externalities are 37% of the total private-income benefits. Therefore, if the net private earnings advantage is $1,000, the externality is (conservatively) $370.

These are very large numbers, reflecting the facts that the primary beneficiary of additional education is the individual and that the main burden of crime is on the victim and not the taxpayer.

PUBLIC INVESTMENT RETURNS

When we add up the three public benefits to education, they are substantial. Specifically, the value of the public benefits realized by additional tax revenues and reductions in the cost of public health and crime amounts to almost $256,700 per new high school graduate. Yet, these public benefits of investment in better education must be weighed against the public costs to obtain the returns to the investment. Table 16.9 shows the net present values of the lifetime public benefits of graduation for Black males for each of the five potential interventions. The savings are reported in the top panel, with the total costs for each of the five interventions reported just below. The benefit-cost ratio ranges from about 2 to greater than 4 among the alternatives, meaning that for every dollar invested in raising high school completion among this group, there are two to four dollars in public benefits. Even more impressive is the large surplus of benefits over costs for each additional graduate. For each additional Black male high school graduate, the net public benefit in present value at age 20 is between $136,400 and $197,600. Taking the median intervention, the net present value is $166,000, which is more than 10 times the cost of delivering the intervention to one single student.[27]

Social savings are also reported in Table 16.9. These savings total $930,900 and comprise three large elements: fiscal benefits, net private-earnings gains, and externalities. Of course, when these savings are applied, the benefit-cost ratios would be significantly higher and each intervention easily reaches a threshold ratio of 1.

One possible source of underestimation of the benefits is that there are a number of newer, promising interventions. These programs may have even more powerful effects because they reflect a consensus on what is needed to ensure graduation: small school size, high levels of personalization, high academic expectations, strong counseling, parental engagement, extended-time

[27] To give an aggregate picture of the potential for reaping public benefits of educational improvements for Black males, we report the net savings from simply equalizing the graduation rates of Black and White males for a single cohort of 20-year-olds. The net fiscal benefit would range from $3.27 billion to $4.74 billion, with a median figure of $3.98 billion.

Table 16.9. *Estimated fiscal and social net benefits per Black male high school graduate*

	Present values at age 20 per new high school graduate (Discount rate of 3.5%)				
Tax revenues			$167,623		
Health cost savings			$33,518		
Crime cost savings			$55,524		
Total fiscal benefits			**$256,665**		
Net private benefits			$258,000		
Externalities					
Health valuation			$182,000		
Victim costs of crime			$138,800		
Productivity gains			$95,400		
Total social benefits			**$930,900**		
	FTF	**CPC**	**PPP**	**CSR**	**TSI**
Total costs	**$59,066**	**$67,714**	**$90,694**	**$97,373**	**$120,238**
Fiscal benefit:cost ratio	4.35	3.79	2.83	2.64	2.13
Net present value	$197,599	$188,951	$165,971	$159,292	$136,427
Social benefit:cost ratio	15.75	13.75	10.26	9.56	7.74

school sessions, and competent and appropriate personnel.[28] However, they have not yet been rigorously evaluated.

Given our research method, these results are probably understatements of the total public savings. Issues related to the sensitivity of our models are reported in Table 16.10.

In addition, the cost savings do not include public assistance, a full accounting of the criminal justice costs for juveniles, intrafamily benefits such as child health, or the deadweight loss of taxation.[29] They assume that interventions cannot be reasonably targeted to youth on the margin of academic achievement or success but must be given to every student. In fact, minority status is concentrated in the public school system (KewalRamani et al., 2007). Black students comprise 17% of the 48.4 million public-school students.

[28] *Small size* describes a small school in which students and staff are known to each other and accountable. *Personalization* refers to a caring environment in which individual personal and academic needs are addressed. *High academic expectations* call for a demanding level of study that each student is expected to meet. *Strong counseling* refers to the availability of personnel to guide students facing personal challenges. *Parental engagement* enlists parents in support of the educational accomplishments of their child and the school. *Extended time* refers to longer time in school. *Competent and appropriate personnel* refer not only to teaching qualifications of personnel but also to their commitment to the school. These changes should not be done on an individual basis but together to comprise a different schooling experience (Quint, 2006).

[29] Costs of public assistance are difficult to calculate because they are mainly embodied in the Temporary Assistance to Needy Families (TANF) program, which provides support for children in low-income families. Most of this funding goes to single mothers, even though the behavior of fathers is clearly influential.

Table 16.10. *Sensitivity issues*

Factors that would *raise* the benefit:cost ratios	Factors that would *reduce* the benefit:cost ratios
Omitted impacts	**Overstated impacts**
Juvenile crime	Fall in wages with more graduates in the labor market
Intrafamily impacts	No college progression
Teen pregnancy	Marginal graduate not the same as the average graduate
Deadweight loss in collecting taxes	Discount rate too low
Wealth accumulation	
More intensive education for those who would graduate anyway	
Understated impacts	**Increasing average costs**
Interventions can be targeted	Upward-sloping average cost curve for delivery of interventions
Undercounting of persons in poverty	

However, one-third of all students in the 20 largest districts are Black, and 12% of all Black students are in one of six school districts (i.e., New York City, Chicago, Broward County in Florida, Philadelphia, Detroit, and Prince Georges County in Maryland). Thus, it is possible to target reforms to specific districts.

In contrast, there are factors that we have not included that are likely to lower the benefit-cost ratios: (a) increasing the number of graduates will reduce their wages; (b) marginal graduates are not the same as average graduates; (c) an assumption of zero college progression; and (d) a higher discount rate on future benefits. Certainly, a higher discount rate will reduce the net present values of educational investments, but our rate is the "industry standard" recommended by Moore, Boardman, Vining, Weimer, and Greenberg (2004). The assumption of zero college progression is extreme, given the high rates of college attendance even among students in the lowest ability quartiles.

A more considerable concern is whether the expansion of graduates will reduce relative wages. First, we note that we are explicit in representing the marginal graduate rather than an entire cohort change. Given the low quality of schooling that many Black males face, a reasonable assumption may be that some who do not graduate are similar to those who, because they attend better schools, are graduates presently. Second, we note that the annual age cohort of Black males is 300,000 persons in a national labor force with more than 120 million high school graduates. Moreover, among all of the subpopulations, Black males face the biggest challenge in the labor market. Despite the nation's strong economic growth in the 1990s, Black male adults experienced lower employment and labor-force participation rates and significantly higher incarceration rates (Holzer & Offner, 2006). There is also some evidence that economic mobility is lowest for Blacks: Those in the poorest quartile are very unlikely to move up across generations (Isaacs, 2007).

Nevertheless, an increase in the supply of graduates ceteris paribus must reduce wages. Goldin and Katz (2008) reviewed trends in education–earnings premiums over the postwar period. For high school graduates over dropouts, the premium trended sharply downward from 1945 to 1960, was flat from 1960 to 1980, and trended upward from 1980 to 2005. (For college students over high school graduates, the pattern was the same except the most recent upswing was stronger.) Much of this pattern can be explained by changes in (relative) supply: The ratio of graduates to dropouts grew by 5.6% pa from 1960 to 1980 but only by 2.5% pa from 1980 to 2005 (with large-scale immigration). Overall, the trend clearly showed a general increase in the overall education–earnings premiums since 1980. Moreover, changes in relative demand for educated workers are difficult to explain without at least some reference to changes in the education level of the workforce; an increase in the supply of educated workers may in part create the demand for more skilled products (skill-biased technological change). This would imply that the ceteris paribus assumption might be relaxed.

However, if skill prices diverge from wages, the reduction may be masked. Heckman, Lochner, and Taber (1998a) argued that wage compression is likely in the short run as the returns to skill rise because the low-skilled employee works harder (facing an imminent wage cut) and the high-skilled worker trains more (to take advantage of rising returns to skill). Current wage gaps might reflect the same process in reverse: The low-skilled workers are accumulating more skill and the high-skilled employees are not (but instead are cashing in). Although it is possible that current gaps overstate the long-term gap, the secular trend caused by skill-biased technical change is so great that it swamps these effects and any changes in the elasticity of substitution between low-skill and high-skill workers. "A policy that reverses this trend [in rising relative wages from 1979 to 1987 for skilled workers] requires a once and for all increase of approximately 20% in the number of high-skill persons in the workforce.... For a 1990 workforce of 120 million, it is necessary to transform about 5.4 million people to college equivalents to reverse the decade long erosion of real wages" (Heckman et al., 1998a, p. 6). Even if all Black male dropouts were to become graduates, the number of college equivalents would not exceed 200,000 annually.

Finally, we note that there is a further general equilibrium effect to consider. In the model of Heckman, Lochner, and Taber (1998b), if a policy is implemented to increase college enrollment, those who would have otherwise gone to college lose out because they have to pay for the policy (independent of changing skill prices). Yet, this effect would be negated if the policy generated a positive fiscal return, and it was internalized by potential college graduates.

SUMMARY

This chapter calculates the public savings (financial benefits) from greater public investments in the education of African American males. More than one-fifth of each age cohort of Black males in the United States is not a high school graduate. We identify five interventions that would – based on credible research – increase the graduation rate; we also report the public cost of each intervention. We then calculate the lifetime public benefits in terms of increased tax revenues and lower spending on health and crime. In present values for a Black male aged 20, these public benefits amount to $256,700 per new graduate, and the median intervention would cost only $90,700. The benefit:cost ratio is 2.83:1 for each marginal high school graduate. Including the social benefits of graduation, the total benefits are $930,900 per marginal Black male graduate. The benefit:cost ratio for the median intervention then rises to 10.26:1. These results suggest that increased investments in education for Black males at risk of dropping out of high school should be an economic priority. They would also contribute significantly to a more equitable society.

CONCLUSION

In U.S. secondary schools, education levels are currently stagnant and perhaps declining: After a century of growth, the high school graduation rate peaked at just under 80% by 1970; since then, it has trended downward toward 70% (Goldin & Katz, 2008, Figure 9.2), a trend that is also supported by recent research by Heckman and LaFontaine (2008). Black males are heavily represented in the numbers of dropouts, not only because of family and community disadvantage but also because of poor schooling investments. As we showed earlier, transforming high school dropouts into graduates yields a significant private, fiscal, and social benefit.

This is a case in which greater equity produces greater efficiency in the use of public resources. Yet, these high public returns also pose a quandary for financing these educational improvements. More than half of the public benefits accrue to the federal government, but it pays less than 10% of the cost of K–12 schooling. Thus, the incentive structure for reaping the benefits is not well aligned with the tax system.

Other than education, there is a dearth of solutions to this situation; those that are offered tend to be reactive, such as making sure ex-offenders get job training, rather than proactive changes that would avoid involvement in the criminal justice system in the first place (Pouncy, 2006). Given the estimates derived here, showing underinvestment and high returns, it makes economic sense to consider effective educational investments in Black male high school dropouts as a high priority.

REFERENCES

Arias, E., Anderson, R., Kung, H., Murphy, S., & Kochanek, K. (2003). Deaths: Final data for 2001. *National Vital Statistics Reports, 52.*

Arnett, R. H., Blank, L. A., Brown, A. P., Cowan, C. A., et al. (1990). Revisions to the national health accounts and methodology. *Health Care Finance Review, 11*, 42–54.

Belfield, C. R. (2006). *The consequences of raising the graduation rate for black males: The effects on crime* (Working Paper). New York: Teachers College.

Belfield, C. R., & Levin, H. M. (2007). The economic losses from high school dropouts in California. *California Dropout Research Project, University of California Santa Barbara*. Retrieved from http://cdrp.ucsb.edu/dropouts/pubs_reports.htm.

Belfield, C. R., & Levin, H. M. (2009). *Some economic consequences of improving mathematics performance*. New York: Teachers College.

Belfield, C. R., Nores, M., Barnett, S. W., & Schweinhart, L. J. (2006). The HighScope Perry Preschool Program. *Journal of Human Resources, 41*(1), 162–190.

Bonczar, T. P. (2003). *Prevalence of imprisonment in the U.S. population, 1974–2001* (NCJ 197976). Washington, DC: U.S. Department of Justice.

Cameron, S. V., & Heckman, J. J. (1993). The nonequivalence of high school equivalents. *Journal of Labor Economics, 11*(1), 1–47.

Cutler, D., & Lleras-Muney, A. (2006). *Education and health*. Paper presented at the Health Effects of Non-Health Policy Conference, Bethesda, MD.

Duncombe, W., & Yinger, J. (2005). How much more does a disadvantaged student cost? *Economics of Education Review, 24*, 513–532.

Education Trust. (2006). *The funding gap 2005: Low income and minority students short-changed by most states*. Washington, DC: Author.

Finn, J. D., Gerber, S. B., & Boyd-Zaharias, J. (2005). Small classes in the early grades, academic achievement, and graduating from high school. *Journal of Educational Psychology, 97*, 214–223.

Goldin, C., & L. F. Katz. (2008). *The race between education and technology*. Cambridge, MA: Belknap.

Hanushek, E. A. (2006). Alternative school policies and the benefits of general cognitive skills. *Economics of Education Review, 25*, 447–462.

Harrison, P. M., & Karberg, J. (2003). *Prison and jail inmates at midyear 2002* (NCJ 198877). Washington, DC: U.S. Department of Justice.

Heckman, J. J., & LaFontaine, P. (2008). *The declining American high school graduate rate: Evidence, sources, and consequences* (Working Paper). Chicago: University of Chicago.

Heckman, J. J., Lochner, L., & Taber, C. (1998a). Explaining rising wage inequality: Explorations with a dynamic general equilibrium model of labor earnings with heterogeneous agents. *Review of Economic Dynamics, 1*, 1–58.

Heckman, J., Lochner, L., & Taber, C. (1998b, May). Tax policy and human-capital formation. *American Economic Review, 88*(2), 293–297.

Holzer, H. J., & Offner, P. (2006). Trends in employment outcomes of young black men, 1970–2000. In R. B. Mincy (Ed.), *Black males left behind* (pp. 11–38). Washington, DC: Urban Institute.

Holzman, M. (2006). *Public education and black male students: The state report card*. Retrieved from http://www.schottfoundation.org.

Isaacs, J. (2007). Economic mobility of black and white families. Retrieved from http://www.brookings.edu/~/media/Files/rc/papers/2007/11_blackwhite_isaacs/11_blackwhite_isaacs.pdf.

Jencks, C., & Phillips, M. (1998). *The black–white test gap*. Washington, DC: Brookings Institution.

KewalRamani, A., Gilbertson, L., Fox, M., & Provasnik, S. (2007). *Status and trends in the education of racial and ethnic minorities* (NCES 2007–039). Washington, DC: National Center for Education Statistics.

Krueger, A. B., & Whitmore, D. M. (2001). *Would smaller classes help close the black–white achievement gap?* (Working Paper 451). Princeton, NJ: Princeton University.

Kuziemko, I. (2006). Using shocks to school enrollment to estimate the effect of school size on student achievement. *Economics of Education Review, 25*, 63–75.

Lantz, P. M., House, J. S., Lepkowski, J. M., Williams, D. R., Mero, R. P., & Chen, J. (1998). Socioeconomic factors, health behaviors, and mortality: Results from a nationally representative prospective study of U.S. adults. *Journal of the American Medical Association, 279*, 1703–1708.

Levin, H. M. (1972). *The cost to the nation of inadequate education.* Select Senate Committee on Equal Educational Opportunity, 92nd Congress. Washington, DC: U.S. Government Printing Office.

Levin, H. M., & McEwan, P. J. (2001). *Cost-effectiveness analysis: Methods and applications.* Thousand Oaks, CA: Sage Publications.

Lochner, L., & Moretti, E. (2004). The effect of education on crime: Evidence from prison inmates, arrests, and self-reports. *American Economic Review, 94*, 155–189.

Loeb, S., & Page, M. E. (2000). Examining the link between teacher wages and student outcomes: The importance of alternative labor market opportunities and non-pecuniary variation. *Review of Economics and Statistics, 82*, 393–408.

Ludwig, J. (2006). *The cost of crime: Understanding the financial and human impact of criminal activity.* Testimony, U.S. Senate Committee on the Judiciary, September 19, 2006.

Magnuson, K. A., & Duncan, G. (2006). The role of family socioeconomic resources in the black–white test score gap among young children. *Developmental Review, 26*, 365–399.

McMahon, W. W. (2006). Education finance policy: Financing the non-market and social benefits. *Journal of Education Finance, 32*, 264–284.

Miller, T. R., Cohen, M. A., & Wiersema, B. (1996). *Victim costs and consequences: A new look* (NCJ 155282). Washington, DC: National Institute of Justice Research Report.

Moore, M. A., Boardman, A. E., Vining, A. R., Weimer, D. L., & Greenberg, D. H. (2004). Just give me a number! Practical values for the social discount rate. *Journal of Policy Analysis and Management, 23*, 789–812.

Muennig, P. (2006). *The consequences of inadequate education for black males: The effects on health* (Working Paper). New York: Teachers College Equity Symposium.

National Center for Education Statistics. (2005). *Digest of educational statistics.* Washington, DC: Institute of Education.

Neal, D. (2006). Why has black–white skill convergence stopped? In E. Hanushek & F. Welch (Eds.), *Handbook of the economics of education* (pp. 511–576). Amsterdam: Elsevier.

Peevely, G., Hedges, L., & Nye, B. A. (2005). The relationship of class size effects and teacher salary. *Journal of Education Finance, 31*, 101–109.

Pettit, B., & Western, B. (2004). Mass imprisonment and the life course: Race and class inequality in U.S. incarceration. *American Sociological Review, 69*, 151–169.

Pouncy, H. (2006). Toward a fruitful policy discourse about less-educated young men. In R. B. Mincy (Ed.), *Black males left behind* (pp. 293–310). Washington, DC: Urban Institute.

Pritchett, L. (2006). Does learning to add up add up? The returns to schooling in aggregate data. In E. Hanushek & F. Welch (Eds.), *Handbook of the economics of education* (pp. 635–695). Amsterdam: Elsevier.

Quint, J. (2006). *Meeting five critical challenges of high school reform.* New York: Manpower Development Research Corporation.

Quint, J., Bloom, H. S., Black, A. R., & Stephens, L., with Akey, T. M. (2005). *The challenge of scaling up educational reform: Findings and lessons from First Things First.* New York: Manpower Development Research Corporation.

Raphael, S. (2004). *The socioeconomic status of black males: The increasing importance of incarceration* (Working Paper). Berkeley: University of California.

Reynolds, A. J., Temple, J. A., Robertson, D. L., & Mann, E. A. (2002). Age 21 cost-benefit analysis of the Title I Chicago Child-Parent Centers. *Educational Evaluation and Policy Analysis, 24,* 267–303.

Rouse, C. E. (2006). *The economic consequences of inadequate education for black males: The effects on labor market income and tax revenue* (Working Paper). New York: Teachers College Equity Symposium.

Rumberger, R. (2004). Why students drop out of school. In G. Orfield (Ed.), *Dropouts in America* (pp. 267–294). Cambridge, MA: Harvard University Press.

Rumberger, R. W., & Larson, K. A. (1998). Student mobility and the increased risk of high school dropout. *American Journal of Education, 107,* 1–35.

Senechal, M. (2006). *The effect of family literacy interventions on children's acquisition of reading.* Washington, DC: National Institute for Literacy.

Uniform Crime Reports (UCR). (2004). Crime data retrieved from http://www.fbi.gov/ucr/ucr.htm.

Wong, M. D., Shapiro, M. F., Boscardin, W. J., & Ettner, S. L. (2002). Contribution of major diseases to disparities in mortality. *New England Journal of Medicine, 347,* 1585–1592.

17

A New Cost-Benefit and Rate of Return Analysis for the Perry Preschool Program: A Summary

JAMES J. HECKMAN, SEONG HYEOK MOON, RODRIGO PINTO,
PETER SAVELYEV, AND ADAM YAVITZ

INTRODUCTION

The Perry Preschool Program was an early childhood education program conducted at the Perry Elementary School in Ypsilanti, Michigan, during the early 1960s. The evidence from it is widely cited to support the economic argument for investing in early childhood programs.

Only disadvantaged children living in adverse circumstances who had low IQ scores and a low index of family socioeconomic status were eligible to participate in the Perry program. Actual participation was determined by a toss of a coin. Beginning at age 3 and lasting 2 years, treatment consisted of a 2.5-hour preschool program on weekdays during the school year, supplemented by weekly home visits by teachers. The curriculum was based on supporting children's cognitive and socio-emotional development through *active learning* in which both teachers and children had major roles in shaping children's learning. Children were encouraged to plan, carry out, and reflect on their own activities through a plan-do-review process. Follow-up interviews were conducted when participants were approximately 15, 19, 27, and 40 years old. At these interviews, participants provided detailed information about their life-cycle trajectories including schooling, economic activity, marital life, child rearing, and incarceration. In addition, Perry researchers collected administrative data in the form of school records, police and court records, and records on welfare participation.

As the oldest and most cited early childhood intervention, the Perry study serves as a flagship for policy makers advocating public support for early childhood programs. Schweinhart et al. (2005) and Heckman, Moon, Pinto, Savelyev, and Yavitz (2010b) describe the program and its outcomes in detail and report substantial short-term and long-term treatment effects. They report crime reduction as a major benefit.

However, critics of the Perry program point to the small sample size of the study, the lack of a substantial long-term effect of the program on IQ, and the absence of statistical significance for many estimated treatment effects.[1] Anderson (2008) claims that the program does not work for boys, although he examines only a subset of its outcomes using arbitrarily constructed indices of diverse outcomes, and he does not perform a cost-benefit analysis overall or by gender.[2] The existing cost-benefit analyses of the program do little to assuage these concerns, presenting estimates of rates of returns without standard errors, leaving readers uncertain as to whether the estimates are statistically significantly different from zero.[3] In response, Heckman, Moon, Pinto, Savelyev, and Yavitz (2010a) present the first rigorous cost-benefit study of the Perry program that addresses four major challenges: (a) the compromise inherent in the randomization protocol (see Heckman et al. 2010b); (b) the lack of program data past age 40 and the need to extrapolate out-of-sample to obtain earnings profiles past that age to estimate lifetime impacts of the program; (c) missing data for participants before age 40; and (d) the difficulty in assigning reliable values to nonmarket outcomes, such as crime. The last point is especially relevant for any analysis of the Perry program because crime reduction is touted as one of its major benefits. This chapter summarizes the main findings from our study. For more detailed discussion of the results summarized here, see Heckman et al. (2010a).

Table 17.1 presents the range of estimates from our preferred methodology, defended in Heckman et al. (2010a). It reports separate rates of return for benefits accruing to individuals versus those that accrue to society at large. Our estimate of the overall social rate of return to the Perry program is in the range of 7% to 10%. We report a range of estimates because of uncertainty about some components of benefits and costs that cannot be quantified by standard errors alone. These estimates are above the historical return to equity,[4] but generally below estimates reported in previous studies.

PROGRAM COSTS AND BENEFITS

We confine our evaluation to the costs and benefits of education, earnings, criminal behavior, tax payments, and participation in public welfare programs. There are no reliable data on health outcomes, marital and parental outcomes, the quality of social life, and the like. Our estimated rate of return likely understates the true rate of return, although we have no direct evidence on this issue.

[1] See Herrnstein and Murray (1994, pp. 404–405) and Hanushek and Lindseth (2009).

[2] See Heckman et al. (2010b), who use small sample permutation tests and multiple hypotheses-testing methods to establish that there are strong treatment effects for boys and girls, although their life-cycle realizations differ across groups.

[3] See Rolnick and Grunewald (2003) and Belfield et al. (2006).

[4] The post–World War II stock-market rate of return on equity is 5.8% (see DeLong and Magin, 2009).

Table 17.1. *Selected estimates of internal rates of return (%) and benefit-to-cost ratios*

	Return:	To individual			To society[c]			To society[c]		
	Murder cost[a]				High ($4.1M)			Low ($13K)		
IRR	Deadweight loss[b]	All[d]	Male	Female	All[d]	Male	Female	All[d]	Male	Female
	0%	7.6	8.4	7.8	9.9	11.4	17.1	9.0	12.2	9.8
		(1.8)	(1.7)	(1.1)	(4.1)	(3.4)	(4.9)	(3.5)	(3.1)	(1.8)
	50%	6.2	6.8	6.8	9.2	10.7	14.9	8.1	11.1	8.1
		(1.2)	(1.1)	(1.0)	(2.9)	(3.2)	(4.8)	(2.6)	(3.1)	(1.7)
	100%	5.3	5.9	5.7	8.7	10.2	13.6	7.6	10.4	7.5
		(1.1)	(1.1)	(0.9)	(2.5)	(3.1)	(4.9)	(2.4)	(2.9)	(1.8)
Benefit-cost ratios	Discount rate	All[d]	Male	Female	All[d]	Male	Female	All[d]	Male	Female
	0%	–	–	–	31.5	33.7	27.0	19.1	22.8	12.7
		–	–	–	(11.3)	(17.3)	(14.4)	(5.4)	(8.3)	(3.8)
	3%	–	–	–	12.2	12.1	11.6	7.1	8.6	4.5
		–	–	–	(5.3)	(8.0)	(7.1)	(2.3)	(3.7)	(1.4)
	5%	–	–	–	6.8	6.2	7.1	3.9	4.7	2.4
		–	–	–	(3.4)	(5.1)	(4.6)	(1.5)	(2.3)	(0.8)
	7%	–	–	–	3.9	3.2	4.6	2.2	2.7	1.4
		–	–	–	(2.3)	(3.4)	(3.1)	(0.9)	(1.5)	(0.5)

Note: Kernel matching is used to impute missing values for earnings before age 40, and Panel Study of Income Dynamics projection is used for extrapolation of later earnings. In calculating benefit-to-cost ratios, the deadweight loss of taxation is assumed to be 50%. Nine separated types of crime are used to estimate the social cost of crime. Standard errors in parentheses are calculated by Monte Carlo resampling of prediction errors and bootstrapping. Lifetime net benefit streams are adjusted for compromised randomization.

[a] "High" murder cost accounts for statistical value of life, whereas "Low" does not.

[b] Deadweight cost is dollars of welfare loss per tax dollar.

[c] The sum of returns to program participants and the general public.

[d] "All" is computed from an average of the profiles of the pooled sample and may be lower or higher than the profiles for each gender group.

Source: Heckman et al. (2010b).

Initial Program Cost

We use the estimates of initial program costs presented in Barnett (1996), which include both operating costs (teacher salaries and administrative costs) and capital costs (classrooms and facilities). In undiscounted year-2006 dollars, the cost of the program per child is $17,759.

Education

Perry promoted educational attainment through two avenues: total years of education attained and rates of progression to a given level of education. We estimate tuition and other pecuniary education costs paid by individuals, as well as additional social costs incurred by society to educate them. The amount of educational expenditure that the general public spends will be larger if participants attain more schooling or if they progress through school less efficiently. We estimate the cost of regular K–12 education, GED, special education, higher education, and vocational training. Table 17.2 summarizes the components of our estimated educational costs. Treated females received less special education, progressed more quickly through grades, earned higher GPAs, and attained higher levels of education than their control-group counterparts. (For males, however, the impact of the program on schooling attainment was weak at best.) As a result, society spent comparable amounts of resources on individuals during their K–12 years regardless of their treatment experience, albeit for different reasons.

Employment and Earnings

To construct lifetime earnings profiles, Heckman et al. (2010a) solve two practical problems. First, in the original survey, job histories were determined retrospectively only for a fixed number of previous job spells. Thus, data on missing spells had to be imputed by econometric techniques. Second, because the Perry data were not collected after the age-40 interview, it is necessary to predict earnings profiles beyond this age or else to estimate rates of return through age 40. To impute missing values for ages before the age-40 interview, we use four different imputation procedures:

1. We use a simple piecewise linear interpolation, based on weighted averages of the nearest observed data points around missing values.
2. We impute missing values using estimated Mincerian earnings functions fit on the 1979 National Longitudinal Survey of Youth (NLSY79) "low-ability" African American subsample born in the same years as the Perry subjects.[5]

[5] This "low-ability" subsample is selected by initial background characteristics that mimic the eligibility rules used in the Perry program. NLSY79 is a nationally representative longitudinal

Table 17.2. *Summary of lifetime costs and benefits (in undiscounted 2006 dollars)*

		Crime ratio[a]	Murder cost[b]	Male		Female	
				Treatment	Control	Treatment	Control
Cost of education[c]	K-12/GED[d]			107,575	98,855	98,678	98,349
	College, age ≤ 27[e]			6,705	19,735	21,816	16,929
	Education, age > 27[e]			2,409	3,396	7,770	1,021
	Vocational training[f]			7,223	12,202	3,120	674
	Lifetime effect[g]			−10,275		14,409	
Cost of crime[h]	Police/court			105.7	152.9	24.7	53.8
	Correctional			41.3	67.4	0.0	5.3
	Victimization	Separate	High	370.0	729.7	2.9	320.7
		Separate	Low	153.3	363.0	2.9	16.1
		By type	Low	215.0	505.7	2.8	43.3
	Lifetime effect[g]	Separate	High	−433		−352.2	
		Separate	Low	−283		−47.6	
		By type	Low	−364		−74.9	

Gross earnings[i]	Age ≤ 27	186,923	185,239	189,633	165,059
	Ages 28–40	370,772	287,920	356,159	290,948
	Ages 41–65	563,995	503,699	524,181	402,315
	Lifetime effect[g]	145,461		211,651	
Cost of welfare[j]	Age ≤ 27	89	115	7,064	13,712
	Ages 28–40	831	2,701	11,551	5,911
	Ages 41–65	1,533	2,647	6,528	7,363
	Lifetime effect[g]	−3,011		−1,844	

[a] A ratio of victimization rate (from the National Crime Victimization Survey) to arrest rate (from the Uniform Crime Report), where "By type" uses common ratios based on a crime being either violent or property and "Separate" does not.
[b] "High" murder cost accounts for value of a statistical life, whereas "Low" does not.
[c] From National Center for Education Statistics for 1975–1982 (annually).
[d] Based on Michigan "per-pupil expenditures" (special education costs calculated using National Center for Education Statistics, 1975–1982, annually).
[e] Based on expenditure per full-time-equivalent student (from National Center for Education Statistics, 1991).
[f] Based on regular high school costs and estimates from Tsang (1997).
[g] Treatment minus control.
[h] In thousand dollars.
[i] Gross earnings before taxation, including all fringe benefits. Kernel matching and PSID projections are used for imputation and extrapolation, respectively.
[j] Includes all kinds of cash assistance and in-kind transfers.

Source: Heckman et al. (2010b).

3. We use a kernel-matching method that sorts each Perry subject to similar observations in the NLSY79 sample. We match each Perry subject to all observations in the NLSY79 comparison-group sample, but with different weights that depend on the estimated kernel function.
4. We estimate dynamic earnings functions using the method of Hause (1980).

Given the absence of earnings data after age 40, we employ three extrapolation schemes to extend sample earnings profiles to later ages:

1. We use March 2002 Current Population Survey (CPS) data to obtain earnings growth rates up to age 65. Because it was not possible to extract "low-ability" subsamples from the CPS that are comparable to the Perry control group, we use CPS age-by-age growth rates (rather than levels of earnings) of 3-year moving averages of earnings by gender and educational attainment.
2. We use a "low-ability" subsample of the Panel Study of Income Dynamics (PSID). We first estimate a random-effects model of earnings on the PSID and then use the fitted model to extrapolate earnings in Perry data after age 40.
3. We also use individual parameters from an estimated version of the model of Hause (1980).

All methods are conservative in that they impose the same earnings structure on the missing data for treatment and controls.[6] The earnings include all types of fringe benefits listed in Employer Costs for Employee Compensation, a Bureau of Labor Statistics compensation measure. Table 17.2 presents the estimated gross earnings for a selected combination of imputation and extrapolation methods. See Heckman et al. (2010a) for further details.

Criminal Activity

Crime reduction is a major benefit of the Perry program.[7] Valuing the effect of this reduction in terms of costs and benefits is not a trivial issue, given the difficulty of assigning reliable monetary values to nonmarket outcomes. Heckman et al. (2010a) improve on previous studies (e.g., Belfield, Nores, Barnett, & Schweinhart, 2006) by exploring the impact of using a variety of assumptions to obtain the benefit-cost ratios. For each subject, the Perry data provide a full record of arrests, convictions, charges, and incarcerations

survey, whose respondents are almost the same age (birth years 1956–1964) as the Perry sample (birth years 1957–1962). See Heckman et al. (2010a).

6 All profiles used here incorporate survival rates by age, gender, and education, which are obtained from National Vital Statistics Reports (National Center for Health Statistics, 2004).

7 See, for example, Schweinhart et al. (2005) and Heckman et al. (2010b).

for most of adolescence and adulthood obtained from administrative data sources.[8]

The total social cost of a crime can be calculated as a product of the social cost per unit of crime and the incidence. The empirical challenges of evaluating the cost of crime are twofold: obtaining a complete lifetime profile of criminal activities for each person and assigning relevant monetary value to each type of criminal activity. It is difficult to obtain complete lifetime crime profiles because we do not directly observe each person's participation in criminal activity. Instead, we only observe arrests from police records. To fill the gap between the actual level of crime and arrests, we combine three data sets: (a) the Uniform Crime Report (UCR), which provides arrest rates by gender, race, and age for each year; (b) the National Crime Victimization Survey (NCVS), which is a nationally representative household-level data set on criminal victimization that provides information on unreported crime levels across the United States; and (c) Perry crime records. From the first two data sources, we can compute the ratio of the true incidence level to the total arrests for each type of crime; by multiplying this ratio by the number of arrests of each subject in the Perry data and summing them over crime types and subjects, we compute the true incidence level. To assign relevant monetary values to criminal activities, we compute the unit cost of each type of crime, which is broken down into two components – victimization costs and criminal justice system costs – using estimates in existing literature as well as various data sources such as Expenditure and Employment data for the Criminal Justice System (CJEE).[9] Different types of crime are associated with different unit costs. Table 17.2 summarizes our estimated social costs of crime.

Our approach differs from that used by Belfield et al. (2006) in several respects. First, in estimating victimization-to-arrest ratios, police and court costs, and correctional costs, we use local data rather than national figures. Second, we use two different values of the victim cost of murder: an estimate of "the statistical value of life" ($4.1 million) and an estimate of assault victim cost ($13,000). We report separate rates of return for each estimate. Third, we assume that there are no victim costs associated with "driving misdemeanors" and "drug-related crimes." Whereas previous studies have assigned nontrivial victim costs to these types of crimes, we consider them to be "victimless." However, because such crimes could be the proximal causes of victimizations, we separately account for any crimes with victims that result from initially victimless crimes. Our approach results in a substantial decrease in crime cost compared to the cost of crime used in previous studies because victimless crimes account for more than 30% of all crime reported in the Perry study.

8 The earliest records cover ages 8–39 and that of the oldest covers ages 13–44.
9 See Anderson (1999) and Cohen (2005).

Tax Payments and Welfare Dependence

Taxes are transfers from the taxpayer to the rest of society and represent benefits to recipients that reduce the welfare of the taxed unless services are received in return. Conversely, higher earnings translate into higher absolute amounts of income-tax payments (and consumption-tax payments) that are beneficial to the general public, excluding program participants. Although there have been changes in U.S. income tax rates over the period covered by this evaluation, in our work, we simplify the calculation by applying a 15% individual tax rate and 7.5% FICA tax rate to each subject's taxable earnings for each year. Belfield et al. (2006) used the employer's share of FICA tax in addition to these two components in computing the benefit to the general public, but we do not because a recent consensus among economists is that "the employer's share of payroll taxes is passed on to employees in the form of lower wages than would otherwise be paid"[10] (Congressional Budget Office, 2007, p. 3).

Differentials in the use of welfare are another important source of benefits from the Perry program. We distinguish transfers, which benefit one group in the society at the expense of another, from the costs associated with making such transfers. Only the latter should be counted in computing gains to society as a whole. Because of data limitations, we adopt the following method to estimate full lifetime profiles of welfare receipt.[11] First, we use the NLSY79 and PSID comparison samples to impute the amount received from various cash assistance and food-stamp programs in a fashion similar to our method for earnings imputation and extrapolation. Second, to account for in-kind transfers, we employ the Survey of Income and Program Participation data to calculate the probability of participating in specific in-kind transfer programs for a "less-educated" Black population and then convert it to monetary values using the estimates of Moffitt (2003) for real public expenditures on welfare programs. Table 17.2 summarizes our estimated profiles of welfare use. For society, each dollar of welfare involves administrative costs. Based on Michigan state data, Belfield et al. (2006) estimated a cost to society of 38 cents for every dollar of welfare disbursed. We use this estimate to calculate the cost of welfare programs to society.

INTERNAL RATES OF RETURN AND BENEFIT-TO-COST RATIOS

We calculate internal rates of return and benefit-to-cost ratios for the Perry program under various assumptions and estimation methods. We compute the associated standard errors in three steps. In the first step, we use the bootstrap

[10] The Perry data do not provide enough information about receipt of various in-kind transfer programs. Even for cash-assistance programs, we do not have complete lifetime profiles of cash transfers for each individual.

[11] See Heckman et al. (2010a) for further discussion.

to simultaneously draw samples from Perry and other nonexperimental comparison data sets (e.g., the NLSY79 and the PSID). For each replication, we reestimate all parameters used to impute missing value and recompute all components used in the construction of lifetime profiles. In this process, all components of earnings whose computations do not depend on the comparison group data are also recomputed (e.g., social cost of crime, educational expenditure) because the replicated sample consists of randomly drawn Perry participants. In the second step, we adjust all imputed values for prediction errors by plugging in an error term that is randomly drawn from comparison-group data in a Monte Carlo resampling procedure. Combining these two steps allows us to account for both estimation errors and prediction errors. Finally, we compute point estimates of internal rates of return (IRRs) and benefit-to-cost ratios for each replication to obtain bootstrapped standard errors.

Tables 17.1 and 17.3 show estimated IRRs and associated standard errors computed using various methods for estimating earnings profiles and crime costs under various assumptions about the deadweight cost of taxation. We first set the victim cost associated with a murder at $4.1 million, which includes the statistical value of life (column labeled "High"), and then at $13,000, which is set to the victim cost of assault, to avoid the problem that a single murder might dominate the evaluation (columns labeled "Low"). To gauge the sensitivity of estimated returns to the way crimes are categorized, we compare results from two aggregation schemes: "Separated" and "Property Versus Violent Crimes."[12] The estimates reported in these tables account for the deadweight costs of taxation: dollars of welfare loss per tax dollar. For comparison purposes, we select the kernel-matching imputation and PSID projection of missing earnings in Table 17.1. Our estimates are robust to the choice of alternative extrapolation/interpolation procedures. Because, as documented by Heckman et al. (2010b), the randomization protocol implemented in the Perry program is somewhat problematic, we adjust all lifetime cost and benefit streams for the compromise in randomization by conditioning them on relevant preprogram variables. This is a form of matching.

The estimated rates of return reported in Table 17.3 are comparable for all of the imputation and extrapolation schemes. Alternative assumptions about the victim cost of murder affect the estimated rates of return in a counterintuitive fashion. Assigning a high number to the value of a life *lowers* the estimated rate of return because the one murder committed by a treatment-group male occurs earlier than the two committed by males in the control group. The rates of return are not very sensitive to the crime-categorization method, as shown by comparison of the last two sets of columns. Adjusting for deadweight losses of taxes lowers the rate of return to the program. Our

[12] See Heckman et al. (2010a) for further discussion.

Table 17.3. *Internal rate of return (%), by imputation and extrapolation method and assumptions about crime costs assuming 50% deadweight cost of taxation*

Returns		To individual			To society, including the individual (nets out transfers)								
Victimization/arrest ratio[a]					Separated			Separated			Property vs. violent		
Murder victim cost[b]					High ($4.1M)			Low ($13K)			Low ($13K)		
Imputation	Extrapolation	All[c]	Male	Female	All[c]	Male	Female	All[c]	Male	Female	All[c]	Male	Female
Piecewise linear interpolation[d]	CPS	6.0	5.0	7.7	8.9	9.7	15.4	7.7	9.7	9.5	7.7	10.1	10.2
		(1.7)	(1.8)	(1.8)	(4.9)	(4.2)	(4.3)	(2.6)	(3.0)	(2.7)	(3.9)	(4.5)	(3.6)
	PSID	4.8	2.5	7.4	7.3	8.0	15.3	7.6	9.2	10.0	7.2	9.5	10.5
		(1.6)	(1.8)	(1.5)	(5.0)	(4.1)	(3.7)	(2.7)	(3.1)	(2.8)	(3.7)	(4.4)	(3.1)
Cross-sectional regression[e]	CPS	5.0	4.8	6.8	7.3	8.3	14.2	7.4	10.0	8.7	7.2	10.1	9.2
		(1.4)	(1.5)	(1.3)	(4.5)	(4.1)	(4.0)	(2.3)	(2.9)	(2.2)	(3.4)	(4.0)	(3.3)
	PSID	4.9	4.3	5.9	8.6	9.8	14.9	7.2	10.0	7.8	7.2	10.4	8.7
		(1.6)	(1.8)	(1.5)	(2.3)	(3.3)	(5.2)	(2.9)	(3.0)	(1.5)	(3.7)	(4.1)	(1.5)
	Hause	4.8	4.9	6.8	7.3	8.5	14.9	7.2	10.0	8.7	7.1	10.1	9.3
		(1.4)	(1.4)	(1.2)	(4.0)	(4.2)	(3.4)	(2.7)	(2.9)	(2.3)	(3.0)	(4.1)	(3.2)

Kernel matching[f]	CPS	6.9	7.6	6.6	8.1	9.5	14.7	8.5	11.2	8.8	8.5	11.1	9.4
		(1.3)	(1.1)	(1.4)	(4.5)	(4.1)	(3.2)	(2.5)	(2.9)	(2.9)	(3.5)	(4.3)	(3.5)
	PSID	6.2	6.8	6.8	9.2	10.7	14.9	8.1	11.1	8.1	8.1	11.4	9.0
		(1.2)	(1.1)	(1.0)	(2.9)	(3.2)	(4.8)	(2.6)	(3.1)	(1.7)	(2.9)	(3.0)	(2.0)
	Hause	6.3	8.0	7.1	8.4	9.7	14.6	8.8	11.2	9.3	8.5	11.2	9.6
		(1.2)	(1.2)	(1.3)	(4.3)	(4.0)	(4.0)	(2.3)	(2.5)	(2.4)	(3.2)	(4.2)	(3.7)
Hause[g]	CPS	7.1	6.5	6.5	8.0	8.9	14.7	8.5	10.5	8.6	8.3	10.5	9.1
		(2.5)	(2.7)	(2.0)	(4.7)	(4.2)	(4.2)	(2.6)	(2.2)	(2.7)	(3.1)	(4.0)	(3.3)
	PSID	7.0	6.0	6.2	9.7	10.5	14.8	8.8	11.0	7.4	8.8	11.3	8.4
		(3.0)	(2.9)	(2.2)	(3.7)	(3.8)	(5.6)	(3.2)	(3.4)	(2.5)	(3.7)	(3.1)	(3.2)
	Hause	6.5	5.7	6.3	7.8	8.7	14.5	8.2	10.6	8.5	8.2	11.0	9.4
		(2.3)	(2.0)	(1.8)	(4.7)	(4.2)	(3.5)	(2.5)	(3.0)	(2.7)	(3.3)	(4.0)	(3.6)

Note: Standard errors in parentheses are calculated by Monte Carlo resampling of prediction errors and bootstrapping. All estimates are adjusted for compromised randomization. All available local data and the full sample are used unless otherwise noted.

[a] A ratio of victimization rate (from the NCVS) to arrest rate (from the UCR), where "Property vs. violent" uses common ratios based on a crime being either violent or property and "Separated" does not.

[b] "High" murder cost valuation accounts for statistical value of life, whereas "Low" does not.

[c] The "All" IRR represents an average of the profiles of a pooled sample of males and females and may be lower or higher than the profiles for each gender group.

[d] Piecewise linear interpolation between each pair reported.

[e] Cross-sectional regression imputation using a cross-sectional earnings estimation from the NLSY79 Black low-ability subsample.

[f] Kernel-matching imputation matches each Perry subject to the NLSY79 sample based on earnings, job-spell durations, and background variables.

[g] Based on the Hause (1980) earnings model.

Source: Heckman et al. (2010b).

Table 17.4. *Decomposition of benefit-to-cost ratios: Crime versus other outcomes*

Discount	All			Crime			Other outcomes		
rate	All	Male	Female	All	Male	Female	All	Male	Female
"High" murder cost									
0%	31.5	33.7	27.0	19.7	20.7	16.8	11.8	13.0	10.2
	(11.3)	(17.3)	(14.4)	(8.6)	(11.3)	(15.3)	(3.0)	(4.0)	(3.6)
	–	–	–	62.7%	61.3%	62.1%	37.3%	38.7%	37.9%
3%	12.2	12.1	11.6	8.0	7.2	8.3	4.2	4.9	3.3
	(5.3)	(8.0)	(7.1)	(4.0)	(5.1)	(7.6)	(1.1)	(1.4)	(1.4)
	–	–	–	65.3%	59.5%	71.5%	34.7%	40.5%	28.5%
5%	6.8	6.2	7.1	4.5	3.5	5.5	2.3	2.7	1.6
	(3.4)	(5.1)	(4.6)	(2.5)	(3.2)	(5.0)	(0.6)	(0.7)	(0.8)
	–	–	–	66.1%	56.4%	76.8%	33.9%	43.6%	23.2%
7%	3.9	3.2	4.6	2.6	1.6	3.7	1.3	1.6	0.9
	(2.3)	(3.4)	(3.1)	(1.7)	(2.1)	(3.4)	(0.4)	(0.4)	(0.5)
	–	–	–	66.5%	50.5%	80.1%	33.5%	49.5%	19.9%
"Low" murder cost									
0%	19.1	22.8	12.7	7.3	9.8	2.5	11.8	13.0	10.2
	(5.4)	(8.3)	(3.8)	(3.2)	(5.5)	(1.5)	(3.0)	(4.0)	(3.6)
	–	–	–	38.1%	42.8%	19.5%	61.9%	57.2%	80.5%
3%	7.1	8.6	4.5	2.9	3.6	1.2	4.2	4.9	3.3
	(2.3)	(3.7)	(1.4)	(1.5)	(2.6)	(0.7)	(1.1)	(1.4)	(1.4)
	–	–	–	40.2%	42.2%	26.5%	59.8%	57.8%	73.5%
5%	3.9	4.7	2.4	1.6	1.9	0.8	2.3	2.7	1.6
	(1.5)	(2.3)	(0.8)	(1.0)	(1.7)	(0.4)	(0.6)	(0.7)	(0.8)
	–	–	–	41.0%	41.3%	31.9%	59.0%	58.7%	68.1%
7%	2.2	2.7	1.4	0.9	1.1	0.5	1.3	1.6	0.9
	(0.9)	(1.5)	(0.5)	(0.7)	(1.2)	(0.3)	(0.4)	(0.4)	(0.5)
	–	–	–	41.9%	39.1%	36.1%	58.1%	60.9%	63.9%

Note: The categories "Crime" and "Other outcomes" sum up to "All." Standard errors in parentheses are calculated by Monte Carlo resampling of prediction errors and bootstrapping. The percentages reported are the contributions of each component. Kernel matching is used to impute missing values in earnings before age 40, and PSID projection is used for extrapolation of later earnings. In calculating benefit-to-cost ratios, deadweight loss of taxation is assumed at 50%. Lifetime net benefit streams are adjusted for corrupted randomization by being conditioned on unbalanced preprogram variables.

estimates of the overall rate of return hover in the range of 7% to 10%, and they are statistically significantly different from zero in most cases.

The estimated benefit-to-cost ratios under different discount rates presented in Tables 17.1 and 17.4 generally support the rate of return analysis and are substantial for discount rates commonly used in the literature (3% to 5%).[13] Further, as shown in Table 17.4, a considerable portion of benefits is due to crime reduction. Sensitivity analysis establishes that (a) excluding

[13] Note, however, that the higher the assumed value of victim life, the *higher* the benefit-to-cost ratio. This occurs because the discount rates in the benefit-to-cost analyses are lower than the discount rates produced by the IRR analysis. Timing of crime matters less in the benefit-cost analysis. See Heckman et al. (2010a).

some outliers whose educational attainments are exceptionally high has only modest effects on the estimated IRRs; (b) excluding "hard-core" criminal offenders increases the estimated social IRRs obtained from the pooled sample and strengthens the precision of the estimates; and (c) accounting for local costs instead of relying on national figures increases estimated IRRs, given that criminal justice system costs for Michigan are higher than the corresponding national estimates. When we evaluate the Perry program only through age 40 to avoid uncertainty associated with extrapolation, rates of return and benefit-to-cost ratios fall somewhat but still remain substantially above the historical rate of return to equity and are precisely determined (Heckman et al. 2010a). A complete analysis of the rate of return to the Perry program under various assumptions can be found in our source paper.

CONCLUSION

This chapter summarizes the main results from our previous work on estimating the rate of return to the Perry Preschool Program (Heckman et al. 2010a). We account for locally determined costs, missing data, the deadweight costs of taxation, and the value of nonmarket benefits and costs. Our analysis improves on previous estimates by accounting for compromise in the randomization protocol, by developing standard errors for the estimates, and by exploring the sensitivity of estimates to alternative assumptions about missing data and the value of nonmarket benefits. Our estimates are also robust to a variety of alternative assumptions about interpolation, extrapolation, and deadweight losses. In most cases, they are statistically significantly different from zero. This is true for both males and females. In general, the estimated rates of return are above the historical return to equity of about 5.8% but are well below previous estimates reported in the literature. Our benefit-to-cost ratio estimates support the rate of return analysis. Benefits from improvements in health and the well-being of future generations are not estimated due to data limitations. Our analysis likely provides a lower bound on the true rate of return to the Perry Preschool Program.

REFERENCES

Anderson, D. A. (1999). The aggregate burden of crime. *Journal of Law and Economics, 42*(2), 611–642.

Anderson, M. (2008). Multiple inference and gender differences in the effects of early intervention: A reevaluation of the Abecedarian, Perry Preschool, and Early Training Projects. *Journal of the American Statistical Association, 103*(484), 1481–1495.

Barnett, W. S. (1996). *Lives in the balance: Age 27 benefit-cost analysis of the High/Scope Perry Preschool Program.* Ypsilanti, MI: High/Scope Press.

Belfield, C. R., Nores, M., Barnett, W. S., & Schweinhart, L. (2006). The HighScope Perry Preschool Program: Cost-benefit analysis using data from the age-40 follow-up. *Journal of Human Resources, 41*(1), 162–190.

Cohen, M. A. (2005). *The costs of crime and justice.* New York: Routledge.

Congressional Budget Office (2007). *Historical effective federal tax rates: 1979 to 2005.* [Data tables]. Available from Congressional Budget Office Website: http://www.cbo.gov/ftpdocs/88xx/doc8885/12-11-HistoricalTaxRates.pdf.

DeLong, J. B., & Magin, K. (2009). The U.S. equity return premium: Past, present and future. *Journal of Economic Perspectives, 23*(1), 193–208.

Hanushek, E., & Lindseth, A. A. (2009). *Schoolhouses, courthouses, and statehouses: Solving the funding-achievement puzzle in America's public schools.* Princeton, NJ: Princeton University Press.

Hause, J. C. (1980). The fine structure of earnings and the on-the-job training hypothesis. *Econometrica, 48*(4), 1013–1029.

Heckman, J. J., Moon, S. H., Pinto, R., Savelyev, P. A., & Yavitz, A. Q. (2010a). The rate of return to the HighScope Perry Preschool Program. *Journal of Public Economics, 94*(1): 114–128.

Heckman, J. J., Moon, S. H., Pinto, R., Savelyev, P. A., & Yavitz, A. Q. (2010b). A reanalysis of the HighScope Perry Preschool Program. In press, *Quantitative Economics.*

Herrnstein, R. J., & Murray, C. A. (1994). *The bell curve: Intelligence and class structure in American life.* New York: Free Press.

Moffitt, R. A. (2003). The negative income tax and the evolution of U.S. welfare policy. *Journal of Economic Perspectives, 17*(3), 119–140.

National Center for Health Statistics. (2004). *National Vital Statistics Report, 53*(5). Washington, DC: U.S. Department of Health and Human Services.

Rolnick, A., & Grunewald, R. (2003, March). Early childhood development: Economic development with a high public return. *Fedgazette*, Federal Reserve Bank of Minneapolis.

Schweinhart, L. J., Montie, J., Xiang, Z., Barnett, W. S., Belfield, C. R., & Nores, M. (2005). *Lifetime effects: The HighScope Perry Preschool Study through age 40.* Ypsilanti, MI: High/Scope Press.

Tsang, M. C. (1997). The cost of vocational training. *International Journal of Manpower, 18*(1/2), 63–89.

18

Investing in Our Young People

FLAVIO CUNHA AND JAMES J. HECKMAN

INTRODUCTION

It is well documented that people have diverse abilities, that these abilities account for a substantial portion of the variation across people in socioeconomic success, and that persistent and substantial ability gaps across children from various socioeconomic groups emerge before they start school. The family plays a powerful role in shaping these abilities through genetics and parental investments and through the choice of child environments. A variety of intervention studies indicate that ability gaps in children from different socioeconomic groups can be reduced if remediation is attempted at early ages. The remediation efforts that appear to be most effective are those that supplement family environments for disadvantaged children. Cunha, Heckman, Lochner, and Masterov (CHLM; 2006) present a comprehensive survey and discussion of this literature.

This chapter uses a simple economic model of skill formation to organize this and other evidence summarized here and the findings of related literatures in psychology, education, and neuroscience. The existing economic models of child development treat childhood as a single period (see, e.g., Aiyagari, Greenwood, & Seshadri, 2002; Becker & Tomes, 1986; Benabou, 2002). The implicit assumption in this approach is that inputs into the production of skills at different stages of childhood are perfect substitutes. Instead, we argue that to account for a large body of evidence, it is important to build a model of skill formation with multiple stages of childhood, where inputs at different stages are complements and where there is self-productivity of investment. In

This paper was supported by grants from the National Science Foundation (SES-0241858, SES-0099195, SES-0452089, SES-0752699); the National Institute of Child Health and Human Development (R01HD43411); the J. B. and M. K. Pritzker Foundation; the Susan Buffett Foundation; the American Bar Foundation; the Children's Initiative, a project of the Pritzker Family Foundation at the Harris School of Public Policy Studies at the University of Chicago; and PAES, supported by the Pew Foundation.

addition, to rationalize the evidence, it is important to recognize three distinct credit constraints operating on the family and its children. The first constraint is the inability of a child to choose his or her parents. This is the fundamental constraint imposed by the accident of birth. Second is the inability of parents to borrow against their children's future income to finance investments in them. The third constraint is the inability of parents to borrow against their own income to finance investments in their children.

This chapter summarizes findings from the recent literature on child development and presents a model that explains them. A model that is faithful to the evidence must recognize that (a) parental influences are key factors governing child development; (b) early childhood investments must be distinguished from late childhood investments; (c) an equity–efficiency trade-off exists for late investments but not for early investments; (d) abilities are created, not solely inherited, and are multiple in variety; (e) the traditional ability–skills dichotomy is misleading because both skills and abilities are created; and (f) the "nature versus nurture" distinction is obsolete. These insights change the way we interpret evidence and design policy about investing in children. Point (a) is emphasized in many papers. Point (b) is ignored in models that consider only one period of childhood investment. Points (c), (d), and (e) have received scant attention in the formal literature on child investment. Point (f) is ignored in the literature that partitions the variance of child outcomes into components due to nature and components due to nurture.

OBSERVATIONS ABOUT HUMAN DIVERSITY AND HUMAN DEVELOPMENT AND SOME FACTS OUR MODEL EXPLAINS

Any analysis of human development must reckon with three empirically well-established observations about ability. The first observation is that *ability matters.* A large number of empirical studies document that cognitive ability is a powerful determinant of wages, schooling, participation in crime, and success in many aspects of social and economic life. The frenzy generated by Richard J. Herrnstein and Charles A. Murray's 1994 book, *The Bell Curve,* because of its claims of genetic determinism, obscured its real message, which is that cognitive ability is an important predictor of socioeconomic success (see, e.g., Heckman, 1995; and Murnane, Willett, & Levy, 1995).

A second observation, more recently established, is that *abilities are multiple in nature.* Noncognitive abilities (perseverance, motivation, time preference, risk aversion, self-esteem, self-control, preference for leisure) have direct effects on wages (controlling for schooling), schooling, teenage pregnancy, smoking, crime, performance on achievement tests, and many other aspects of social and economic life (Borghans, Duckworth, Heckman, & ter Weel, 2008; Bowles, Gintis, & Osborne, 2001; Heckman, Stixrud, & Urzua, 2006).

The third observation is that *the nature versus nurture distinction is obsolete.* The modern literature on epigenetic expression teaches us that the sharp distinction between acquired skills and ability featured in the early human capital literature is not tenable (see, e.g., Gluckman & Hanson, 2005; and Rutter, 2006).[1] Additive "nature" and "nurture" models, although traditional and still used in many studies of heritability and family influence, mischaracterize how ability is manifested. Abilities are produced, and gene expression is governed, by environmental conditions (Rutter, 2006). Measured abilities are susceptible to environmental influences, including in utero experiences, and also have genetic components. These factors interact to produce behaviors and abilities that have both a genetic and an acquired character.[2,3] Genes and environment cannot be meaningfully parsed by traditional linear models that assign variance to each component.

Taking these observations as established, we develop a simple economic model to explain the following six facts from the recent empirical literature. First, *ability gaps between individuals and across socioeconomic groups open up at early ages, for both cognitive and noncognitive skills.* See Figure 18.1 for a prototypical figure that graphs a cognitive test score by age of child by socio-economic status of the family.[4] CHLM present many additional graphs of child cognitive and noncognitive skills by age showing early divergence and then near parallelism during school-going years across children with parents of different socioeconomic status. Levels of child skills are highly correlated with family background factors like parental education and maternal ability, which, when statistically controlled for, largely eliminate these gaps (see Carneiro & Heckman, 2003, and CHLM). Experimental interventions with long-term follow-up confirm that changing the resources available to disadvantaged children improves their adult outcomes (see the studies surveyed in CHLM or Blau & Currie, 2006). Schooling quality and school resources have relatively small effects on ability deficits and have little effect on test scores by age across children from different socioeconomic groups, as displayed in Figure 18.1 and related graphs (see Heckman, Larenas, & Urzua, 2004; and Raudenbush, 2006).

Second, *in both animal and human species, there is compelling evidence of critical and sensitive periods in the development of the child.* Some skills or traits are more readily acquired at certain stages of childhood than are other traits (see the evidence summarized in Knudsen, Heckman, Cameron, & Shonkoff, 2006). For example, on average, if a second language is learned before age 12,

1 For example, Becker (1993, pp. 99–100) contrasts the implications for the earnings distribution of ability models of earnings and human capital models, claiming the latter are more consistent with the empirical evidence on earnings. The implicit assumption in his analysis and the literature it spawned is that ability is determined by "nature" (i.e., is genetic) and outside the influence of family-investment strategies.

2 There is some evidence that gene expression affected by environment is heritable (see Rutter, 2006).

3 Some recent evidence on gene–environment interactions resulting from child maltreatment was presented in Caspi, McClay, Moffitt, Mill, Martin, Craig, et al. (2002). Rutter (2006) surveyed this evidence.

4 Permanent income is the measure of socioeconomic status in this figure. See CHLM for the source of this figure and the precise definition of permanent income.

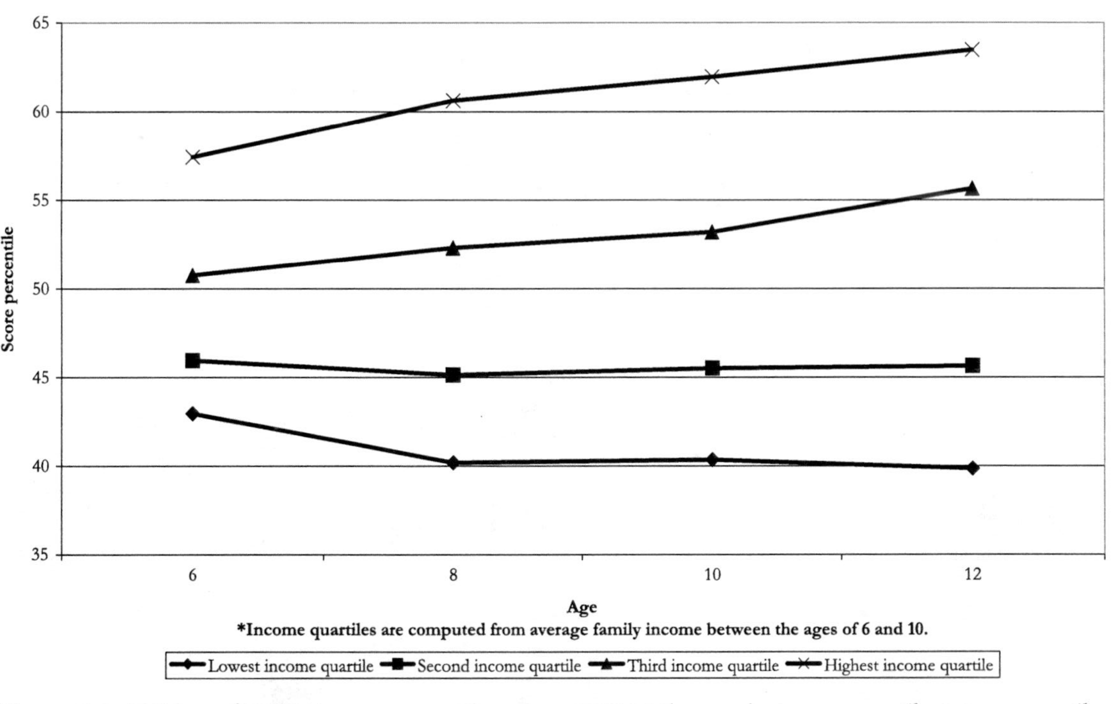

Figure 18.1. Children of NLSY: Average percentile rank on PIAT Math score, by income quartile. Income quartiles computed from average family income between the ages of 6 and 10.

the child speaks it without an accent (Newport, 1990). If syntax and grammar are not acquired early on, they appear to be very difficult to learn later in life (Pinker, 1994). A child born with a cataract will be blind if the cataract is not removed within the first year of life.

Different types of abilities appear to be manipulable at different ages. IQ scores become stable by age 10 or so, suggesting a sensitive period for their formation before age 10 (Hopkins & Bracht, 1975). There is evidence that adolescent interventions can affect noncognitive skills (see CHLM). This evidence is supported by the neuroscience that establishes the malleability of the prefrontal cortex into the early 20s (Dahl, 2004). This is the region of the brain that governs emotion and self-regulation.

On average, the later remediation is given to a disadvantaged child, the less effective it is. A study by O'Connor, Rutter, Beckett, Keaveney, Kreppner, and the English and Romanian Adoptees Study Team (2000) of adopted Romanian infants reared in severely deprived orphanage environments before being adopted supports this claim. The later the Romanian orphan was rescued from the social, emotional, and cognitive isolation of the orphanage, the lower was his or her cognitive performance at age 6. Classroom remediation programs designed to combat early cognitive deficits have a poor track record.

At historically funded levels, public job-training programs and adult literacy and educational programs, like the GED, that attempt to remediate years of educational and emotional neglect among disadvantaged individuals have a low economic return and produce meager effects for most persons. A substantial body of evidence suggests that returns to adolescent education for the most disadvantaged and less able are lower than the returns for the more advantaged (see Meghir & Palme, 2001; Carneiro & Heckman, 2003, and the evidence they cite; Carneiro, Heckman, & Vytlacil, 2006).

The available evidence suggests that for many skills and abilities, later remediation for early disadvantage to achieve a given level of adult performance may be possible, but is much more costly than early remediation (Cunha & Heckman, 2007). The economic returns to job training, high school graduation, and college attendance are lower for less able persons (see Carneiro & Heckman, 2003).

Third, *despite the low returns to interventions targeted toward disadvantaged adolescents, the empirical literature shows high economic returns for remedial investments in young disadvantaged children* (see Barnett, 2004, the evidence in CHLM, and the papers they cite). This finding is a consequence of dynamic complementarity and self-productivity captured by the technology developed in the next section.

Fourth, *if early investment in disadvantaged children is not followed up by later investment, its effect at later ages is lessened.* Investments appear to be complementary and require follow-up to be effective. Currie and Thomas

(1995) document a decline in the performance of Head Start[5] minority participants after they leave the program, return to disadvantaged environments, and receive the low levels of investment experienced by many disadvantaged children.[6]

Fifth, *the effects of credit constraints on a child's outcomes when the child reaches adulthood depend on the age at which they bind for the child's family.* Recent research summarized in Carneiro and Heckman (2002, 2003) and in CHLM demonstrates the quantitative insignificance of family credit constraints in the child's college-going years in explaining a child's enrollment in college. Controlling for cognitive ability, under meritocratic policies currently in place in American society, family income during the child's college-going years plays only a minor role in determining child college participation, although much public policy is predicated on precisely the opposite point of view. Holding ability fixed, minorities are *more likely* to attend college than others despite their lower family incomes (see Cameron & Heckman, 2001, and the references they cite). Augmenting family income or reducing college tuition at the stage of the life cycle when a child goes to college does not go far in compensating for low levels of previous investment.

Carneiro and Heckman present evidence for the United States that only a small fraction (at most, 8%) of the families of adolescents are credit constrained in making college-participation decisions. This evidence is supported in research by Cameron and Taber (2004) and Stinebrickner and Stinebrickner (2008). Permanent family income plays an important role in explaining educational choices, insofar as it is a proxy for the high level of investment in abilities and skills that wealthier families provide, but it is not synonymous with family income in the adolescent years, nor with tuition and fees.

There is some evidence, however, that credit constraints operating in the *early* years have effects on adult ability and schooling outcomes (Dahl & Lochner, 2005; Duncan & Brooks-Gunn, 1997; Duncan & Kalil, 2006; Morris, Duncan, & Clark-Kauffman, 2005). Carneiro and Heckman (2003) show that controlling for family permanent income reduces the estimated effect of early income on child outcomes. Permanent income has a strong effect on child outcomes. The strongest evidence for an effect of the timing of parental income for disadvantaged children is in their early years. The best documented market failure in the life cycle of skill formation in contemporary American society is the inability of children to buy their parents or the lifetime resources that

[5] Head Start is a national program targeted to low-income preschool-age children (ages 3–5) that promotes school readiness by enhancing their social and cognitive development through the provision of educational, health, nutritional, social, and other services to enrolled children and families. There is a new program, Early Head Start, that begins at age 1.

[6] Currie and Thomas (2000) present additional analyses of the Head Start program.

parents provide and not the inability of families to secure loans for a child's education when the child is an adolescent.

Sixth, *socio-emotional (noncognitive) skills foster cognitive skills and are an important product of successful families and successful interventions in disadvantaged families.* Emotionally nurturing environments produce more capable learners. The Perry Preschool Program,[7] which was evaluated by random assignment, did not boost participant adult IQ but enhanced performance of participants on a number of dimensions, including scores on achievement tests, employment, and reduced participation in a variety of social pathologies (see Schweinhart, Montie, Xiang, Barnett, Belfield, & Nores, 2005).

A MODEL OF SKILL FORMATION

We now develop a model of skill formation that can explain the six facts just presented as well as additional findings from the literature on child development. We use the terms *skill* and *ability* interchangeably. Both are produced by environments, investment, and genes.

Agents possess a vector of abilities at each age. These abilities (or skills) are multiple in nature and range from pure cognitive abilities (e.g., IQ) to noncognitive abilities (patience, self-control, temperament, risk aversion, time preference). These abilities are used with different weights in different tasks in the labor market and in social life more generally.[8] Achievement test scores, sometimes confused with IQ scores (e.g., Herrnstein & Murray, 1994), are not pure measures of ability and are affected by cognitive, noncognitive, and environmental inputs (see, e.g., Hansen, Heckman, & Mullen, 2004; and Heckman et al., 2006).

The human skill-formation process is governed by a multistage technology. Each stage corresponds to a period in the life cycle of a child. Although the child development literature recognizes stages of development (see, e.g., Erikson, 1950), the economics of child development does not. Inputs or investments at each stage produce outputs at the next stage. Like Ben-Porath (1967), we use a production function to determine the relationship between inputs and the output of skill. Unlike Ben-Porath, in our model, qualitatively different inputs can be used at different stages, and the technologies can be different at different stages of child development.

[7] The Perry Preschool Program was an intensive family-enhancement preschool program administered to randomly selected disadvantaged Black children enrolled in the program over five different waves between 1962 and 1967. Children were enrolled 2½ hours per day, 5 days a week, during the school year, and there were weekly 1½-hour home visits. They were treated for 2 years, at ages 3 and 4. A control group provided researchers with an appropriate benchmark to evaluate the effects of the preschool program.

[8] CHLM briefly discuss the evidence on this point and suggested a model of comparative advantage in occupational choice to supplement their model of skill formation.

Ben-Porath focused on adult investments in which time and its opportunity cost play important roles. For child investments, parents make decisions and child opportunity costs are less relevant. The outputs at each stage in our technology are the levels of each skill achieved at that stage. Some stages of the technology may be more productive in producing some skills than other stages, and some inputs may be more productive at some stages than at other stages. The stages that are more effective in producing certain skills are called "sensitive periods" for the acquisition of those skills. If one stage alone is effective in producing a skill (or ability), it is called a "critical period" for that skill.

An important feature of our technology is that the skills produced at one stage augment the skills attained at later stages. This effect is termed *self-productivity*. It embodies the ideas that skills acquired in one period persist into future periods and that skills are self-reinforcing and cross-fertilizing. For example, emotional security fosters more vigorous learning of cognitive skills. This has been found in animal species (Cameron, 2004; Meaney, 2001; Suomi, 1999) and in humans (Duncan et al., 2007; Raver, Garner, & Smith-Donald, 2007, who interpret the ability of a child to pay attention as a socio-emotional skill). A higher stock of cognitive skill in one period raises the stock of the next-period cognitive skills. A second key feature of skill formation is *dynamic complementarity*. Skills produced at one stage raise the productivity of investment at subsequent stages. In a multistage technology, complementarity implies that levels of skill investments at different ages bolster each other. They are synergistic. Complementarity also implies that early investment should be followed up by later investment for the early investment to be productive. Together, dynamic complementarity and self-productivity produce multiplier effects that are the mechanisms through which skills beget skills and abilities beget abilities.

Dynamic complementarity, self-productivity of human capital, and multiplier effects imply an equity–efficiency trade-off for late child investments but not for early investments. These concepts, embedded in alternative market settings, explain the six facts from the recent literature summarized in the previous section. These features of the technology of skill formation have consequences for the design and evaluation of public policies toward families. In particular, they show why the returns to late childhood investment and remediation for young adolescents from disadvantaged backgrounds are so low, whereas the returns to early investment in children from disadvantaged environments are so high.

We now formalize these concepts in an overlapping generations model. An individual lives for $2T$ years. The first T years, the individual is a child of an adult parent. From age $T+1$ to $2T$, the individual lives as an adult and is the parent of a child. The individual dies at the end of the period in which he is $2T$ years old, just before his child's child is born. At every calendar year, there are an equal and large number of individuals of every age $t \varepsilon \{1, 2, \ldots, 2T\}$.[9] To simplify the notation, we do not explicitly subscript generations.

A household consists of an adult parent and a child. Parents invest in their children because of altruism. They have common preferences and supply labor inelastically. Let I_t denote parental investments in child skill when the child is t years old, where $t = 1, 2, \ldots, T$. The output of the investment process is a skill vector. The parent is assumed to fully control the investments in the skills of the child, whereas in reality, as a child matures, he or she gains much more control over the investment process.[10] We ignore investments in the child's adult years to focus on new ideas in this chapter. We also keep government inputs (e.g., schooling) implicit. They can be modeled as a component of I_t.

We now describe how skills evolve over time. Assume that each agent is born with initial conditions θ_1. Let h denote parental characteristics (e.g., IQ, education). At each stage t, let θ_t denote the vector of skill stocks. The technology of production of skill when the child is t years old is

$$\theta_{t+1} = f_t(h, \theta_t, I_t), \tag{18.1}$$

for $t = 1, 2, \ldots, T$. We assume that f_t is strictly increasing and strictly concave in I_t, and twice continuously differentiable in all of its arguments.[11]

Technology (18.1) is written in recursive form. Substituting in (18.1) for $\theta_t, \theta_{t-1}, \ldots,$ repeatedly, one can rewrite the stock of skills at stage $t+1$, θ_{t+1}, as a function of all past investments:

$$\theta_{t+1} = m_t(h, \theta_1, I_1, \ldots, I_t), \; t = 1, \ldots, T. \tag{18.2}$$

Dynamic complementarity arises when $\partial^2 f_t(h, \theta_t, I_t)/\partial\theta_t \partial I_t' > 0$ (i.e., when stocks of skills acquired by period $t-1$ (θ_t) make investment in period t (I_t) more productive). Such complementarity explains why returns to educational investments are higher at later stages of the child's life cycle for more able children (those with higher θ_t). Students with greater early skills (cognitive and noncognitive) are more efficient in later learning of both cognitive and noncognitive skills. The evidence from the early-intervention literature suggests that the enriched early preschool environments provided by the Abecedarian,[12]

9 We developed our formal OLG model in Cunha & Heckman (2007).

10 A sketch of such a model was discussed in Carneiro, Cunha, and Heckman (2003).

11 These conditions are sufficient. There is no need for a differentiability requirement for h, and the differentiability requirement with respect to θ_t can be weakened.

12 The Abecedarian Project recruited children born between 1972 and 1977 whose families scored high on a "High Risk" index. It enrolled and enriched the family environments of disadvantaged children beginning a few months after birth and continuing until age 5. At age 5 – just as they were about to enter kindergarten – all of the children were reassigned to either a school-age intervention through age 8 or to a control group. The Abecedarian program was more intensive than the Perry program. Its preschool program was a year-round, full-day intervention.

Perry Preschool Program, and Chicago Child-Parent Center (CPC)[13] interventions promote greater efficiency in learning in school and reduce problem behaviors (see Blau & Currie, 2006, and CHLM).

Self-productivity arises when $\partial f_t(h, \theta_t, I_t)/\partial \theta_t > 0$ (i.e., when higher stocks of skills in one period create higher stocks of skills in the next period). For the case of skill vectors, this includes own and cross effects. The joint effects of self-productivity and dynamic complementarity help explain the high productivity of investment in disadvantaged young children and the lower return to investment in disadvantaged adolescent children for whom the stock of skills is low and, hence, the complementarity effect is lower. These are facts 2 and 3 presented in the previous section.

This technology is sufficiently rich to describe learning in rodents and macaque monkeys. More emotionally secure young animals explore their environments more actively and learn more quickly. This technology also explains the evidence that the ability of the child to pay attention affects subsequent academic achievement. Cross-complementarity serves to explain fact 6. This technology also captures the critical and sensitive periods in humans and animals documented by Knudsen et al. (2006). We now define these concepts precisely.

Period t^* is a critical period for θ_{t+1} if

$$\frac{\partial \theta_{t+1}}{\partial I_s} = \frac{\partial m_t(h, \theta_1, I_1, \ldots, I_t)}{\partial I_s} = 0 \quad \text{for all } h,\ \theta_1,\ I_1, \ldots, I_t,\ s \neq t^*,$$

but

$$\frac{\partial \theta_{t+1}}{\partial I_{t^*}} = \frac{\partial m_t(h, \theta_1, I_1, \ldots, I_t)}{\partial I_{t^*}} > 0 \quad \text{for some } h,\ \theta_1,\ I_1, \ldots, I_t.$$

This condition says that investments in θ_{t+1} are productive in period t^* but not in any other period $s = t^*$. Period t^* is a sensitive period for θ_{t+1} if

$$\frac{\partial \theta_{t+1}}{\partial I_s}\Big|_{h=\bar{h},\theta_1=\theta,I_1=i_1,\ldots,I_t=i_t} < \frac{\partial \theta_{t+1}}{\partial I_{t^*}}\Big|_{h=\bar{h},\theta_1=\theta,I_1=i_1,\ldots,I_t=i_t}.$$

In words, period t^* is a sensitive period relative to period s if, at the same level of inputs, investment is more productive in stage t^* than in another stage $s \neq t^*$.[14]

[13] The CPC was started in 1967 in selected public schools serving impoverished neighborhoods of Chicago. Using federal funds, the center provided half-day preschool program for disadvantaged 3- and 4-year-olds during the 9 months that they were in school. In 1978, state funding became available, and the program was extended through third grade and included full-day kindergarten.

[14] See CHLM for a definition of critical and sensitive periods in terms of technology (18.1).

Suppose for simplicity that $T = 2$. In reality, there are many stages in childhood, including in utero experiences.[15] Assume that θ_1, I_1, and I_2 are scalars.[16] The adult stock of skills, h' $(= \theta_3)$, is a function of parental characteristics, initial conditions, and investments during childhood I_1 and I_2:

$$h' = m_2\left(h, \theta_1, I_1, I_2\right). \tag{18.3}$$

The literature in economics assumes only one period of childhood. It does not distinguish between early investment and late investment. This produces the conventional specification, which is a special case of technology (18.3), where

$$h' = m_2\left(h, \theta_1, \gamma I_1 + (1 - \gamma) I_2\right) \tag{18.4}$$

and $\gamma = 1/2$. In this case, adult stocks of skills do not depend on how investments are distributed over different periods of childhood. For example, take two children, A and B, who have identical parents and the same initial condition θ_1 but have different investment profiles: Child A receives no investment in period 1 and receives I units of investment in period 2, $I_1^A = 0$, $I_2^A = I$, whereas child B receives I units of investment in period 1 and zero units of investment in period 2, $I_1^B = I$, $I_2^B = 0$. According to (18.4), when $\gamma = 1/2$, children A and B will have the same stocks of skills as adults. The timing of investment is irrelevant. Neither period 1 nor period 2 is critical. The polar opposite of perfect substitution is perfect complementarity:

$$h' = m_2\left(h, \theta_1, \min\left\{I_1, I_2\right\}\right). \tag{18.5}$$

Technology (18.5) has the feature that adult stocks of skills critically depend on how investments are distributed over time. For example, if investment in period 1 is zero, $I_1 = 0$, then it does not pay to invest in period 2. If late investment is zero, $I_2 = 0$, it does not pay to invest early. For the technology of skill formation defined by (18.5), the best strategy is to distribute investments evenly, so that $I_1 = I_2$. Complementarity has a dual face. It is essential to invest early to get satisfactory adult outcomes, but it is also essential to invest late to harvest the fruits of the early investment.[17] Such dynamic complementarity helps explain the evidence presented by Currie and Thomas (1995) that for disadvantaged minority students, early investments through Head Start have weak effects in later years if not followed up by later investments. This is fact 4 on our list. Our explanation is in sharp contrast to the one offered by Becker (1991), who explained weak Head Start effects by crowding out of parental investment by public investment. That is a story of substitution against the

[15] Our technology applies to in utero and post-natal investments as well. See Shonkoff and Phillips (2000) for evidence on the importance of such investments.

[16] CHLM analyzed the vector case.

[17] Both periods are critical. Note that in this case, the production function is not strictly differentiable as required in our definition. Our definition can be extended to deal with this limit case.

child who receives investment in a one-period model of childhood. Ours is a story of dynamic complementarity.[18]

A more general technology that captures technologies (18.4) and (18.5) as special cases is a standard constant elasticity of substitution (CES):

$$h' = m_2\left(h, \theta_1, [\gamma (I_1)^{\phi} + (1-\gamma)(I_2)^{\phi}]^{\frac{1}{\phi}}\right) \tag{18.6}$$

for $\phi \leq 1$ and $0 \leq \gamma \leq 1$. The CES share parameter γ is a *skill multiplier.* It reveals the productivity of early investment not only in directly boosting h' (through self-productivity) but also in raising the productivity of I_2 by increasing θ_2 through first-period investments. Thus, I_1 directly increases θ_2, which in turn affects the productivity of I_2 in forming h'. γ captures the net effect of I_1 on h' through both self-productivity and direct complementarity.

The elasticity of substitution $1/(1-\phi)$ is a measure of how easy it is to substitute between I_1 and I_2. For a CES technology, ϕ represents the degree of complementarity (or substitutability) between early and late investment in producing skills. The parameter ϕ governs how easy it is to compensate for low levels of stage 1 skills in producing later skills.

When ϕ is small, low levels of early investment I_1 are not easily remediated by later investment I_2 in producing human capital. The other face of CES complementarity is that when ϕ is small, high early investment should be followed with high late investment if the early investment is to be harvested. In the extreme case when $\phi \to -\infty$, (18.6) converges to (18.5). This technology explains facts 2 and 3 – why returns to education are low in the adolescent years for disadvantaged (low h, low I_1, low θ_2) adolescents but are high in the early years. Without the proper foundation for learning (high levels of θ_2) in technology (18.1), adolescent interventions have low returns.

In a one-period model of childhood, inputs at any stage of childhood are perfect substitutes. Application of the one-period model supports the widely held but empirically unsupported intuition that diminishing returns make investment in less advantaged adolescents *more* productive. As noted in fact 2 of the previous section, the evidence suggests that just the opposite is true. We next embed the technology in a market environment with parental choice of inputs.

THE OPTIMAL LIFE-CYCLE PROFILE OF INVESTMENTS

Using technology (6), we now show how the ratio of early to late investments varies as a function of ϕ and γ as a consequence of parental choices in different market settings. Let w and r denote the wage and interest rates, respectively, in a stationary environment. At the beginning of adulthood, the parent draws the initial level of skill of the child, θ_1, from the distribution $J(\theta_1)$. On reaching adulthood, the parent receives bequest b. The state variables for the parent are

[18] We offer another explanation of the apparently weak Head Start effects later.

the parental skills, h, the parental financial resources, b, and the initial skill level of the child, θ_1. Let c_1 and c_2 denote the consumption of the household in the first and second period of the life cycle of the child, respectively. The parent decides how to allocate the resources among consumption and investments at different periods as well as bequests b', which may be positive or negative. Assuming that human capital (parental and child) is scalar, the budget constraint is:

$$c_1 + I_1 + \frac{c_2 + I_2}{(1+r)} + \frac{b'}{(1+r)^2} = wh + \frac{wh}{(1+r)} + b. \tag{18.7}$$

Let β denote the utility discount factor and δ denote the parental altruism toward the child. Let $u(\cdot)$ denote the utility function. The recursive formulation of the problem of the parent is:

$$V(h, b, \theta_1) = \max \left\{ u(c_1) + \beta u(c_2) + \beta^2 \delta E \left[V\left(h', b', \theta_1'\right)\right]\right\}. \tag{18.8}$$

The problem of the parent is to maximize (18.8) subject to (18.7) and technology (18.6).

When $\phi = 1$, so early and late investment are perfect CES substitutes, the optimal investment strategy is straightforward. The price of early investment is \$1. The price of the late investment is $\$1/(1+r)$. Thus, the parent can purchase $(1+r)$ units of I_2 for every unit of I_1. The amount of human capital produced from one unit of I_1 is γ, whereas $\$(1+r)$ of I_2 produces $(1+\mathrm{r})(1-\gamma)$ units of human capital. Thus, two forces act in opposite directions. High productivity of initial investment (the skill multiplier γ) drives the parent toward making early investments. The interest rate drives the parent to invest late. It is optimal to invest early if $\gamma > (1-\gamma)(1+r)$.

As $\phi \to -\infty$, the CES production function converges to the Leontief case, and the optimal investment strategy is to set $I_1 = I_2$. In this case, investment in the young is essential. At the same time, later investment is needed to harvest early investment. On efficiency grounds, early disadvantages should be perpetuated, and compensatory investments at later ages are economically inefficient.

For $-\infty < \phi < 1$, the first-order conditions are necessary and sufficient given concavity of the technology in terms of I_1 and I_2. For an interior solution, we can derive the optimal ratio of early to late investment:

$$\frac{I_1}{I_2} = \left[\frac{\gamma}{(1-\gamma)(1+r)}\right]^{\frac{1}{1-\phi}}. \tag{18.9}$$

Figure 18.2 plots the ratio of early to late investment as a function of the skill multiplier γ under different values of the complementarity parameter ϕ, assuming $r = 0$. When $\phi \to -\infty$, the ratio is not sensitive to variations in γ. When $\phi = 0$, the function (18.6) is

$$h' = m_2(h, \theta_1, I_1, I_2) = m_2\left(h, \theta_1, I_1^{\gamma} I_1^{1-\gamma}\right).$$

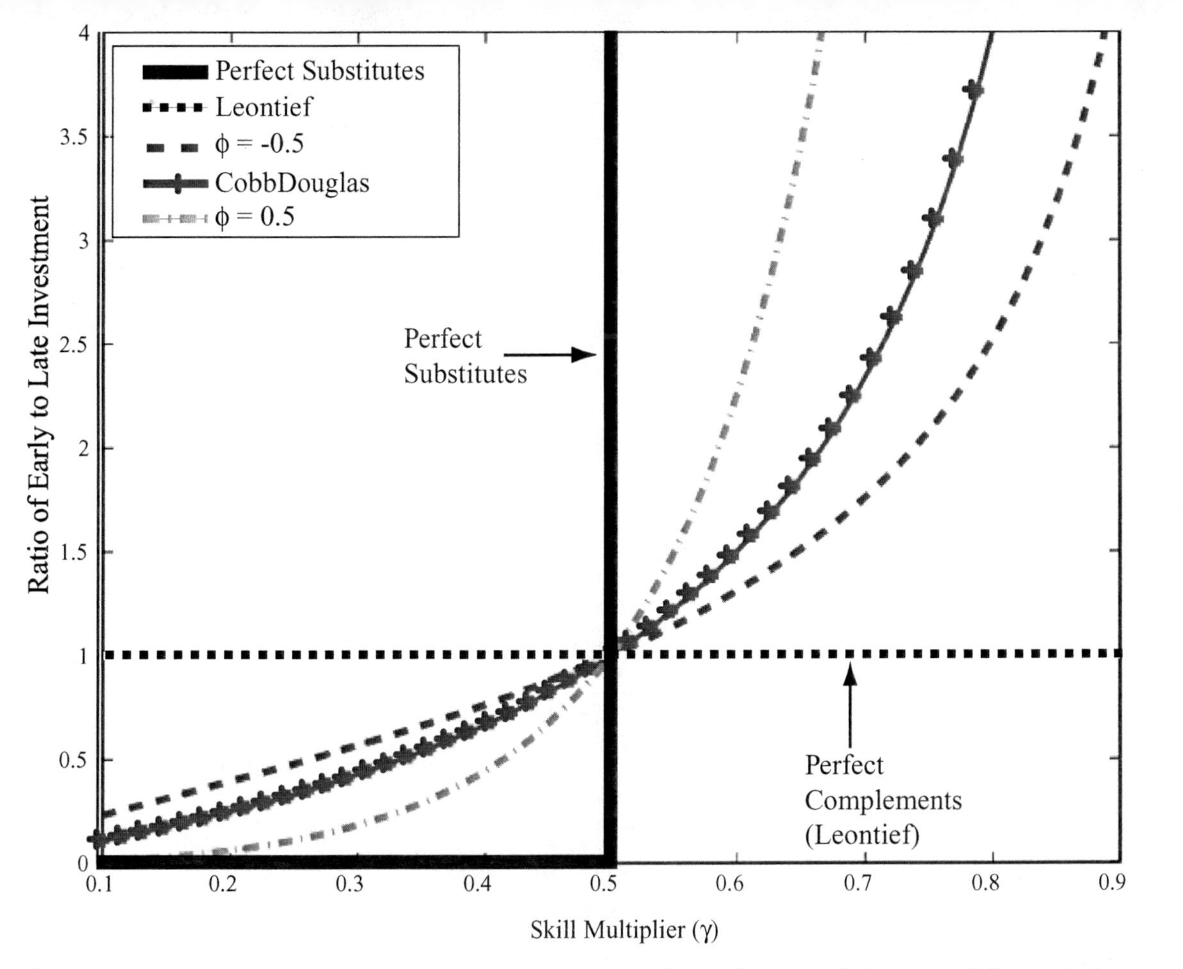

Figure 18.2. Ratio of early to late investment in human capital as a function of the ratio of first-period to second-period investment productivity for different values of the complementarity parameter (assumes $r = 0$).*
Source: Cunha and Heckman (2007).

In this case, from (18.9), the optimal I_1/I_2 is close to zero for low values of γ but explodes to infinity as γ approaches one.

When CES complementarity is high, the skill multiplier γ plays a limited role in shaping the ratio of early to late investment. High early investment should be followed by high late investment. As the degree of CES complementarity decreases, the role of the skill multiplier increases, and the higher the multiplier, the more investment should be concentrated in the early ages.

In a perfect credit market model, optimal investment levels are not affected by parental wages or endowments, or the parameters that characterize the utility function $u(\cdot)$.[19] Note, however, that even in this "perfect" credit market setting, parental investments depend on parental skills, h, because these characteristics affect the returns to investment. From the point of view of the child, this is a market failure due to the accident of birth. Children would like to choose the optimal amount of parental characteristics h to complement their initial endowment, θ_1.[20]

Consider the second credit constraint mentioned in the introduction: Parental bequests must be non-negative (i.e., parents cannot leave debts to their children). The problem of the parent is to maximize (18.8) subject to (18.7), technology (18.6), and the liquidity constraint:

$$b' \geq 0. \tag{18.10}$$

If constraint (18.10) binds, then early investment under lifetime liquidity constraints, $\hat{I}_1$, is lower than the early investment under the perfect credit market model, denoted I_1^*. The same is true for late investment: $\hat{I}_2 < I_2^*$. Under this type of market imperfection, underinvestment in skills starts at early ages and continues throughout the life cycle of the child. This explains fact 1 – that skill gaps open up early and are perpetuated.[21]

In this second case, both early and late investment depend on parental initial wealth b for the families for whom the constraint (18.10) binds. Children who come from constrained families with lower b will have lower early *and* late investment. Interventions that occur at early stages would exhibit high returns, especially if they are followed up with resources to supplement late investment. Once the early-stage investment is realized, however, late remediation for disadvantaged children would produce lower returns if early and late investment are not perfect substitutes, and late investment is more productive the higher the level of early investment. This helps explain fact 5 in the "Observations About Human Diversity and Human Development and Some Facts Our Model Explains" section.

19 We refer to parental resources specific to a given generation.

20 This thought experiment is whimsical. If parents create the child, through genes and environment, the child is not an independent actor. Under a homunculus theory, the child would have an identity independent of the parent.

21 Of course, other reasons why skill gaps open up early and are perpetuated are variations in h and θ_1, the parental environmental, and initial endowment variables, respectively.

The effects of government policies on promoting the accumulation of human capital depend on the complementarity between early and late investment as well as on whether the policies were anticipated by parents or not. For example, the short-run effects of an unanticipated policy that subsidizes late investment will have weaker effects the greater the complementarity between early and late investment. If the technology is Leontief, there is no short-run impact of the policy on adolescent investment. At the time the policy is announced, poor parents have already made their early investment decisions, and in the Leontief case, it is not possible to compensate by increasing late investment as a response to the subsidy.

There is, however, a long-run effect of the policy. If the policy is a permanent change announced before the child is born, new parents will adjust both early and late investment in response to the subsidy to late investment. Note that the same is true for an exogenous increase in the return to education. If there is strong complementarity between early and late investment, in the short run, we would expect weak reactions to the increase in returns to education, as gauged by adolescent investment decisions for the children from very poor family backgrounds, but stronger reactions in the long run. This analysis provides an explanation for why the college-enrollment response to unanticipated increases in the returns to college was initially so strong for adolescents from advantaged families and initially so weak for adolescents from less advantaged families. Adolescents from less advantaged families are more likely to lack the foundational skills that make college-going productive, compared to adolescents from more advantaged families.

There is no trade-off between equity and efficiency in *early* childhood investment. Government policies to promote early accumulation of human capital should be targeted to the children of poor families. However, the optimal second-period intervention for a child from a disadvantaged environment depends critically on the nature of technology (18.6). If I_1 and I_2 are perfect CES complements, then a low level of I_1 cannot be compensated at any level of investment by a high I_2. Conversely, suppose that $\phi = 1$, so the technology (18.6) can be written with inputs as perfect CES substitutes. In this case, a second-period intervention can, in principle, eliminate initial skill deficits (low values of I_1). At a sufficiently high level of second-period investment, it is technically possible to offset low first-period investment, but it may not be cost effective to do so. If γ is sufficiently low relative to r, it is more efficient to postpone investment.

The concepts of critical and sensitive periods are defined in terms of the technical possibilities of remediation. Many noneconomists frame the question of remediation for adverse environments in terms of what is technically possible – not what is economically efficient. Our analysis considers both technological possibilities and costs. From an economic point of view, critical and sensitive periods should be defined in terms of the costs and returns of remediation and not solely in terms of technical possibilities.

Another source of market failure arises when parents are subject to lifetime liquidity constraints and constraints that prevent them from borrowing against their own future labor income, which may affect their ability to finance investment in the child's early years.[22] This is the third constraint considered in the introduction. To analyze this case, assume that parental productivity grows exogenously at rate α. Let s denote parental savings. We write the constraints facing the parent at each stage of the life cycle of the child as:

$$c_1 + I_1 + \frac{s}{(1+r)} = wh + b \qquad \text{(first stage)}$$

$$c_2 + I_2 + \frac{b'}{(1+r)} = w(1+\alpha)h + s \qquad \text{(second stage)}$$

where $s \geq 0$ and $b' \geq 0$. The restriction $s \geq 0$ says that the parent cannot borrow income from his or her old age to finance consumption and investment when the child is in the first stage of the life cycle. Some parents may be willing to do this, especially when α is high. In the case when $s \geq 0$ and $b' \geq 0$ bind, and investments in different periods are not perfect substitutes, the timing of income matters. To see this, note that if $u(\mathrm{c}) = (ca - 1)/\sigma$, the ratio of early to late investment is

$$\frac{I_1}{I_2} = \left[\frac{\gamma}{(1-\gamma)(1+\gamma)}\right]^{\frac{1}{1-\phi}} \left[\frac{(wh + b - I_1)}{\beta((1+\alpha)wh - I_2)}\right]^{\frac{1-\sigma}{1-\phi}}.$$

If early income is low with respect to late income, the ratio I_1/I_2 will be lower than the optimal ratio. The deviation from the optimal ratio will be larger the lower the elasticity of intertemporal substitution of consumption (captured by the parameter σ). Early income would not matter if $\sigma = 1$, which would be the case when consumption in stage 1 is a perfect substitute for consumption in stage 2. Substitutability through parental preferences can undo lack of substitutability in the technology of skill formation.

Our analysis of credit-constrained families joined with a low value of ϕ interprets the evidence presented by Duncan and Brooks-Gunn (1997), Morris et al. (2005), Duncan and Kalil (2006), and Dahl and Lochner (2005) that the level of family income in the early stages of childhood has some effect on the level of ability and achievement of the children. This is fact 5 of the "Observations About Human Diversity and Human Development and Some Facts Our Model Explains" section. Our analysis also interprets the evidence of Carneiro and Heckman (2002) and Cameron and Taber (2004) that, conditioning on child ability, family income in the adolescent years has only a minor effect on adolescent schooling choices.

[22] This type of constraint was also analyzed by Caucutt & Lochner (2004).

COGNITIVE AND NONCOGNITIVE SKILL FORMATION

A large body of research documents the socio-emotional basis of reason (see Damasio, 1994; and LeDoux, 1996). Our analysis goes beyond this literature to formalize a body of evidence that emotional skills promote learning. Mechanisms relating cortisol to stress and the effects of cortisol on the brain development of animals have been documented by Suomi (1999) and Meaney (2001). Duncan et al. (2007) and Raver and colleagues (2007) show that a child's ability to pay attention facilitates later learning.

The framework developed in the "A Model of Skill Formation" section readily accommodates skill vectors. The evidence summarized in the "Observations About Human Diversity and Human Development and Some Facts Our Model Explains" section shows the importance of both cognitive and noncognitive skills in determining adult outcomes. Child development is not just about cognitive skill formation, although a lot of public-policy analysis focuses solely on cognitive test scores. Let θ_t denote the vector of cognitive and noncognitive skills: $\theta_t = (\theta_t^C, \theta_t^N)$. Let I_t denote the vector of investment in cognitive and noncognitive skills: $I_t = (I_t^C, I_t^N)$.We use $h = (h^C, h^N)$ to denote parental cognitive and noncognitive skills. At each stage t, we can define a recursive technology for cognitive skills ($k = C$) and noncognitive skills, ($k = N$):

$$\theta_{t+1}^k = f_t^k\left(\theta_t, I_t^k, h\right), k \in \{C, N\}. \tag{18.11}$$

Note that technology (18.11) allows for cross-productivity effects: Cognitive skills may affect the accumulation of noncognitive skills and vice versa. They also allow for critical and sensitive periods to differ by skill, as is required to account for fact 2.

If cognitive and/or noncognitive skills determine costs of effort, time-preference, or risk-aversion parameters, parental investments affect child and adult behavior. Our analysis of preference formation contrasts with the analyses of Akabayashi (1996) and Weinberg (2001). Those authors build principal–agent models in which the parent (the principal) and the child (the agent) agree on contracts in which parents' financial transfers are conditional on observable measures of effort (e.g., test scores in school). These contracts are designed so that the children are driven toward the level of effort desired by the parents. In our model, parents directly shape child preferences.

Accounting for preference formation enables us to interpret the success of many early childhood programs targeted to disadvantaged children that do not permanently raise IQ but that permanently boost social performance.[23] This is fact 6 of the "Observations About Human Diversity and Human Development and Some Facts Our Model Explains" section. The controversy over Head Start fade-out may have been a consequence of relying only on cognitive measures to gauge performance. The Perry Preschool Program had an IQ fade-out but a

[23] The Abecedarian early intervention program permanently boosted adult IQ. See CHLM.

lasting effect on a variety of participants through age 40. They have been found to work harder, be less likely to commit crime, and participate in many fewer social pathologies than control-group members.[24]

ESTIMATES OF THE TECHNOLOGY

Parametric Specification

We specify the following parametric representation of (18.11). At each age t and developmental stage l, the technology for the production of skill j writes:

$$\theta_{t+1}^j = \left[\gamma_{C,l}^j \left(\theta_t^C\right)^{\phi_l^j} + \gamma_{N,l}^j \left(\theta_t^N\right)^{\phi_l^j} + \gamma_{I,l}^j \left(I_t^j\right)^{\phi_l^j} + \gamma_{P,l}^j \left(\theta_t^P\right)^{\phi_l^j}\right]^{\frac{1}{\phi_l^j}} e^{\eta_{t+1}^j} \tag{18.12}$$

$$1 \geq \phi_l^j, \gamma_{k,l}^j \geq 0, \sum_k \gamma_{k,l}^j = 1 \quad \text{for all} \quad j \in \{C, N\}, l \in \{1, \ldots, L\}, \text{ and } \quad t \in \{1, \ldots, T\}.$$

It is useful to consider a simpler version of (18.12), which one obtains if $\phi_l^j = 0$ or all j and l and if the components of θ_t, I_t, and h are expressed in logs:

$$\theta_{t+1}^j = \gamma_{C,l}^j \theta_t^C + \gamma_{N,l}^j \theta_t^N + \gamma_{I,l}^j I_t^j + \gamma_{P,l}^j \theta_t^P + \eta_{t+1}^j \tag{18.13}$$

Technology (18.13) is estimated by Cunha and Heckman (2008). The main problem that arises in estimating the technology is that vector (θ_t, I_t) is not directly observed. Cunha and Heckman (2008) treat (θ_t, I_t) as a vector of unobserved factors and use a variety of measurements of the latent constructs to proxy these factors. There is a substantial body of econometric work on linear factor models (see, e.g., Aigner, Hsiao, Kapteyn, & Wansbeek, 1984). These models account for measurement errors in the proxies that Cunha and Heckman (2008) find to be quantitatively large. If they are not accounted for, estimates of technology parameters are substantially biased.

In addition to the problem of measurement error, there is the problem of setting the scale of the factors and the further problem that elements of (θ_t, I_t) are likely correlated with the shock η_t. Cunha and Heckman (2008) address these problems by using rich sources of panel data that provide multiple measurements on (θ_t, I_t). They use a dynamic state-space version of a MIMIC model.[25] In the linear setting, it is assumed that multiple measurements on

[24] See Cunha and Heckman (2009). The exact mechanism by which noncognitive skills are boosted is not yet established. It could be that noncognitive skills are created directly in the early years and persist. It could also be that the higher early cognitive skills that fade out foster noncognitive skills that persist. Both channels of influence could be in operation.

[25] See Jöreskog and Goldberger (1975). MIMIC stands for Multiple Indicators and Multiple Causes. Harvey (1989) and Durbin, Harvey, Koopman, and Shephard (2004) are standard references for dynamic state-space models, which generalize MIMIC models to a dynamic setting.

inputs and outputs can be represented by a linear factor setup:

$$Y_{j,t}^{k} = \mu_{j,t}^{k} + \alpha_{j,t}^{k}\theta_{t}^{k} + \varepsilon_{j,t}^{k}, \quad \text{for} \quad j \in \{1, \ldots, M_{t}^{k}\}, k \in \{C, N, I\}, \quad (18.14)$$

where M_t^k is the number of measurements on latent factor k and θ_t^I is latent investment at age t. This approach generalizes to a nonlinear semiparametric framework. Equation (18.12) can be interpreted as a general nonlinear factor model defined in terms of θ_t and I_t.[26] Cunha, Heckman, and Schennach (2010) generalize this framework to a nonlinear setup to identify technology (18.1). They present original results on identification of dynamic-factor models in nonlinear frameworks.

Model Identification

As is standard in factor analysis, Cunha and Heckman (2008) use covariance restrictions to identify technology (18.13). Low-dimensional (θ_t, I_t) (associated with preferences, abilities, and investment) are proxied by numerous measurements for each component.

Treating each of a large number of measurements on inputs as separate inputs creates a problem for instrumental variables analyses of production functions. It is easy to run out of instruments for each input. Such an approach likely also creates collinearity problems among the inputs.

Cunha and Heckman avoid these problems by assuming that clusters of measurements proxy the same set of latent variables. Measurements of a common set of factors can be used as instruments for other measurements on the same common set of factors. Methods based on covariance restrictions and cross-equation restrictions provide identification and account for omitted inputs that are correlated with included inputs. These methods provide an econometrically justified way to aggregate inputs into low-dimensional indices.

Estimates From the Linear Model

Cunha and Heckman (2008) estimate technology (18.13) using a sample of white males from the Children of the National Longitudinal Survey of Youth data (CNLSY). These data provide multiple measurements on investments and cognitive and noncognitive skills at different stages of the life cycle of the child. Table 18.1, extracted from their paper, reports estimates of technology (18.13). The scales of the factors in θ_t are anchored in log earnings.[27] They account for endogeneity of parental investment. Doing so substantially affects their estimates.

[26] Nonlinear factor models are generated by economic choice models in which risk aversion, time preference, and leisure preferences are low-dimensional factors that explain a variety of consumer choices.

[27] See Cunha and Heckman (2008) for a discussion of alternative anchors for θ_t and I_t.

Table 18.1. *Correcting for classical measurement error anchor–log earnings of the child between ages 23–28 White males, CNLSY*

	Noncognitive skill (θ^N_{t+1})			Cognitive skill (θ^C_{t+1})		
Independent variable	Stage 1	Stage 2	Stage 3	Stage 1	Stage 2	Stage 3
Lagged noncognitive skill, (θ^N_t)	0.9849	0.9383	0.7570	0.0216	0.0076	0.0005
	(0.014)	(0.015)	(0.010)	(0.004)	(0.003)	(0.003)
Lagged cognitive skill, (θ^C_t)	0.1442	−0.1259	0.1171	0.9197	0.8845	0.9099
	(0.120)	(0.115)	(0.115)	(0.023)	(0.021)	(0.019)
Parental investment, (θ^I_t)	0.0075	0.0149	0.0064	0.0056	0.0018	0.0019
	(0.002)	(0.003)	(0.003)	(0.002)	(0.001)	(0.001)
Maternal education, S	0.0005	−0.0004	0.0019	−0.0003	0.0007	0.0001
	(0.001)	(0.001)	(0.001)	(0.001)	(0.001)	(0.001)
Maternal cognitive skill, A	0.0001	−0.0011	−0.0019	0.0025	0.0002	0.0010
	(0.000)	(0.000)	(0.000)	(0.001)	(0.000)	(0.000)

Note: Standard errors in parentheses. Cognitive skills are proxied by PIAT math and reading. Noncognitive skills are proxied by the components of the behavioral-problem index. Investments are proxied by components of the home score. Stage 1 is age 6–7 to 8–9; Stage 2 is 8–9 to 10–11; Stage 3 is 10–11 to 12–13.
Source: Cunha & Heckman (2008, Table 11).

Their estimates show strong self-productivity effects (lagged coefficients of own variables) and strong cross-productivity effects of noncognitive skills on cognitive skills (personality factors promote learning; those open to experience learn from it). The estimated cross-productivity effects of cognitive skills on noncognitive skills are weak. Contrary to models in criminology and psychology that assign no role to investment in explaining the life-cycle evolution of capabilities, Cunha and Heckman (2008) find strong investment effects. Remediation and resilience are possible. Capabilities evolve and are affected by parental investment. Investment affects cognitive skills more at earlier ages than at later ages. It affects noncognitive skills more in middle childhood. This evidence is consistent with the literature in neuroscience on the slow maturation of the prefrontal cortex, which governs personality development and expression, and the emergence of more nuanced manifestations of personality with age.

One way to interpret these estimates is to examine the impacts of investment at each age on high school graduation and adult earnings.[28] These outcomes depend differently on cognition and personality. Schooling attainment is more cognitively weighted than earnings.

The estimated effects of a 10% increase in investment are reported in Table 18.2 (see right panel for earnings and left panel for high school graduation). Increasing investment in the first stage by 10% increases adult earnings by 0.25%. The increase operates equally through cognitive and noncognitive skills. Ten percent investment increments in the second stage have a larger effect

[28] Results for high school graduation as an anchor are reported in Cunha & Heckman (2008).

Table 18.2. *Percentage impact of an exogenous increase by 10% in investments of different periods for two different anchors, White males ages 23–28, CNLSY*

Log earnings at age 23–28			Probability of graduating from high school		
Total percentage impact	Percentage impact exclusively through cognitive skills	Percentage impact exclusively through noncognitive skills	Total percentage impact	Percentage impact exclusively through cognitive skills	Percentage impact exclusively through noncognitive skills
	Period 1			Period 1	
0.2487 (0.0302)	0.1247 (0.0151)	0.1240 (0.0150)	0.6441 (0.0789)	0.5480 (0.0672)	0.0961 (0.0118)
	Period 2			Period 2	
0.3065 (0.0358)	0.0445 (0.0052)	0.2620 (0.0306)	0.3980 (0.0466)	0.1951 (0.0229)	0.2029 (0.0238)
	Period 3			Period 3	
0.2090 (0.0230)	0.0540 (0.0059)	0.1550 (0.0170)	0.3565 (0.0389)	0.2366 (0.0258)	0.1198 (0.0131)

Note: Standard errors in parentheses.
Source: Cunha & Heckman (2008, Table 17).

(0.3%) but mainly operate through improving noncognitive skills. Investment in the third stage has weaker effects and operates primarily through its effect on noncognitive skills.

For high school graduation (see left panel, Table 18.2), the effects are more substantial and operate relatively more strongly through cognitive skills than through noncognitive skills. The sensitive stage for the production of earnings is stage 2. The sensitive stage for producing secondary school graduation is stage 1. This reflects the differential dependence of the outcomes on the two capabilities and the greater productivity of investment in noncognitive skills in the second period compared to other periods. This evidence is consistent with other evidence that shows the greater malleability of noncognitive skills at later ages.[29]

Measurement Error

Accounting for measurement error substantially affects estimates of the technology of skill formation. This evidence sounds a note of caution for the burgeoning literature that regresses wages on psychological measurements. The share of error variance for proxies of cognition, personality, and investment ranges from 30% to 70%. Not accounting for measurement error produces downward-biased estimates of self-productivity effects and perverse estimates of investment effects.[30]

Estimates From Nonlinear Technologies

Cunha et al. (2010) estimate nonlinear technologies to identify key substitution parameters.[31] The ability to substitute critically affects the design of strategies for remediation and early intervention.

Cunha et al. (2010) estimate a version of technology (18.12) for general $\phi_l^j, j \in \{C, N\}, l \in \{1, \ldots, L\}$ using the same sample as used by Cunha and Heckman (2008).[32] They estimate a two-stage model of childhood ($L = 2$). Stage 1 is birth through age 4. Stage 2 corresponds to ages 5 through 14.

The major findings from their analysis are as follows:

- Self-productivity becomes stronger as children become older, for both cognitive and noncognitive capability formation.
- Complementarity between cognitive skills and investment becomes *stronger* as children become older. The elasticity of substitution for

[29] See Cunha, Heckman, Lochner, and Masterov (2006); Cunha and Heckman (2007); and Heckman (2008) for a discussion of this evidence.

[30] See Cunha and Heckman (2008), Table 14.

[31] They also account for measurement error and endogeneity of family inputs.

[32] They establish semiparametric identification of their model, including measurement equations.

cognitive inputs is *smaller* in second-stage production.[33] It is more difficult to compensate for the effects of adverse environments on cognitive endowments at later ages than it is at earlier ages. This finding helps explain the evidence on ineffective cognitive remediation strategies for disadvantaged adolescents.

- Complementarity between noncognitive skills and investments becomes *weaker* as children become older. It is easier at *later* stages of childhood to remediate early disadvantage using investments in noncognitive skills.[34]

Cunha et al. (2010) report that 34% of the variation in educational attainment in their sample is explained by the measures of cognitive and noncognitive capabilities that they use.[35] Sixteen percent is due to adolescent cognitive capabilities, 12% is due to adolescent noncognitive capabilities,[36] and measured parental investments account for 15% of the variation. These estimates suggest that the measures of cognitive and noncognitive capabilities that they use are powerful, but not exclusive, determinants of educational attainment and that other factors, in addition to the measures of family investment that they use, are at work in explaining variation in educational attainment.

LESSONS FOR THE DESIGN OF POLICIES

To examine the implications of the estimates of Cunha et al. (2010), consider two social-planning problems that can be solved from knowledge of the technology of capability formation and without knowledge of parental preferences and parental access to lending markets. The first problem we consider determines the cost of investment required to produce high school attainment for children with different initial endowments of their own and parental capabilities. For the same distribution of endowments, the second problem determines optimal allocations of investments from a fixed budget to maximize aggregate schooling for a cohort of children. We also consider a version of the social-planning problem that minimizes aggregate crime.

Suppose that there are H children indexed by $h \in \{1, \ldots, H\}$. Let $\left(\theta^C_{1,h}, \theta^N_{1,h}\right)$ denote the initial cognitive and noncognitive skills of child h. She has parents with cognitive and noncognitive skills denoted by $\left(\theta^P_{C,h}, \theta^P_{N,h}\right)$. Let π_h denote additional unobserved determinants of outcomes. Define $\theta_{1,h} = (\theta^C_{1,h}, \theta^N_{1,h}, \theta^P_{C,h}, \theta^P_{N,h}, \pi_h)$ and let $G(\theta_{1,h})$ be its distribution. We draw H people from the initial distribution $G(\theta_{1,h})$ that is estimated by Cunha,

33 It is 1.5 in the first stage and .56 in the second stage. The estimates are precisely determined.

34 The elasticity of substitution is .54 in the first stage and .77 in the second stage. The estimates are precisely determined.

35 These are the same measures as used in Cunha and Heckman (2008), which we previously discussed.

36 The skills are correlated so the marginal contributions of each skill do not add up to 34%.

Heckman, & Schennach (2010). The price of investment is assumed to be the same in each period and is set at unity.

The criterion adopted for the first problem assumes that the goal of society is to get the schooling of every child to a 12th-grade level. The required investments measure the power of initial endowments in determining inequality and the compensation through investment required to eliminate their influence. Let $v(\theta_{1,h})$ be the minimum cost of attaining 12 years of schooling for a child with endowment $\theta_{1,h}$. Assuming a zero discount rate, $v(\theta_{1,h})$ is formally defined by

$$v\left(\theta_{1,h}\right) = \min\left\{I_{1,h} + I_{2,h}\right\}$$

subject to a schooling constraint $S(\theta^C_{3,h}, \theta^N_{3,h}, \pi_h) = 12$ where S maps end-of-childhood capabilities and other relevant factors (π_h) into schooling attainment, and also subject to the technology of capability formation constraint

$$\theta^k_{t+1,h} = f_{k,t}\left(\theta^C_{t,h}, \theta^N_{t,h}, \theta^P_{C,h}, \theta^P_{N,h}, I_{t,h}, \pi_h\right) \quad \text{for } k \in \{C, N\} \text{ and for } \quad t \in \{1, 2\},$$

and the initial endowments of the child and her parents. Cunha et al. (2009) estimate all of the ingredients needed to perform this calculation. We summarize some of their findings here.

Figure 18.3 plots the percentage increase in investment over that required for a child with mean parental and personal endowments to attain high school graduation. In analyzing the investment required for child endowments, we set parental endowments at mean values. Lighter values correspond to larger numbers. Eighty percent more investment is required for children with the most disadvantaged personal endowments. The negative percentages shown in Figure 18.3 for children with high initial endowments is a measure of their advantage.[37] The empirical analysis of Moon (2009) shows that investments *received* as a function of a child's endowments are typically in reverse order from what is required to attain the goal of universal high school graduation. Children born with advantageous endowments typically receive *more* parental investment than children from less advantaged environments.

A more standard social-planner's problem maximizes aggregate human capital subject to a budget constraint B. We draw H children from the initial distribution $G(\theta_{1,h})$ and solve the problem of how to allocate finite resources B to maximize the average education of the cohort. Formally, the social-planner maximizes aggregate per capita schooling

$$\max \bar{S} = \frac{1}{H} \sum_{h=1}^{H} S\left(\theta^C_{3,h}, \theta^N_{3,h}, \pi_h\right)$$

[37] The corresponding figure for children with the most disadvantaged parental endowments is 95%. See Cunha, Heckman, and Schennach (2010).

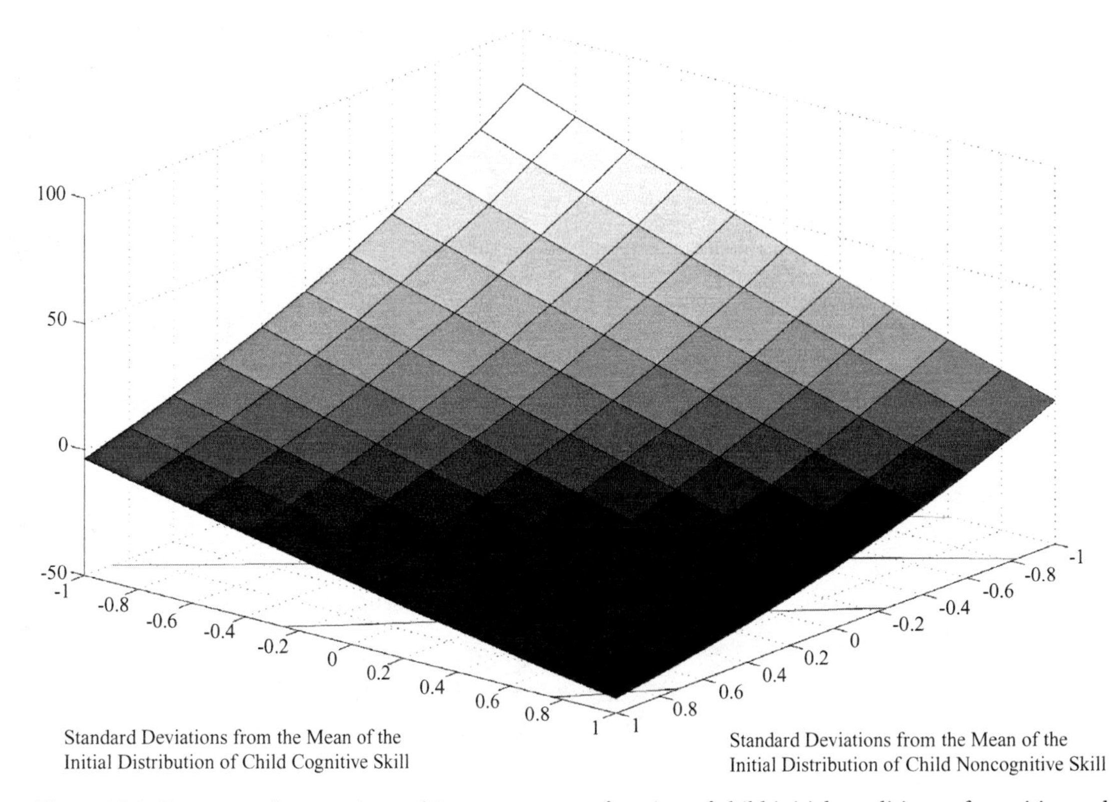

Figure 18.3. Percentage increase in total investments as a function of child initial conditions of cognitive and noncognitive skills.

subject to the aggregate budget constraint,

$$\sum_{h=1}^{H} \left(I_{1,h} + I_{2,h}\right) = B,$$

the technology constraint,

$$\theta_{t+1,h}^{k} = f_{k,t}\left(\theta_{t,h}^{C}, \theta_{t,h}^{N}, \theta_{C,h}^{P}, \theta_{N,h}^{P}, \pi_{h}\right) \quad \text{for} \quad k \in \{C, N\} \quad \text{and} \quad t \in \{1, 2\},$$

and the initial conditions of the child. Solving this problem, we obtain optimal early and late investments, $I_{1,h}$ and $I_{2,h}$, respectively, for each child h. An analogous social-planning problem is used to allocate investments to minimize crime.

Figure 18.4 shows the profile of early (graph on left) and late (graph on right) investment as a function of endowments. For the most disadvantaged, the optimal policy is to invest a lot in the early years. The decline in investment by level of initial advantage is substantial for early investment. Second-period investment profiles are much flatter and slightly favor more advantaged children. This is a manifestation of the dynamic complementarity that produces an equity–efficiency trade-off for later stage investment but not for early investment. It is socially optimal to invest more in the second period of the lives of advantaged children than in disadvantaged children. A similar profile emerges for investments to reduce aggregate crime.[38]

The optimal ratio of early-to-late investment depends on the desired outcome, the endowments of children, and budget B. Figure 18.5 plots the density of the ratio of early-to-late investment for education and crime derived by Cunha et al. (2010).[39] Whereas educational attainment depends strongly on cognitive skills, participation in criminal activities are affected strongly by noncognitive skills. Because compensation for adversity in noncognitive skills is less costly in the second period than in the first period, although the opposite is true for cognitive skills, it is optimal to weight first-period and second-period investments in the directions indicated in the figure. For most configurations of disadvantage, we have that the optimal policy is to invest relatively more on the early years, compared to the later years.

These simulations suggest that the timing and level of optimal interventions for disadvantaged children depend on the conditions of disadvantage and the nature of desired outcomes.[40] Targeted strategies are likely to be effective, especially so if different targets weight cognitive and noncognitive traits differently.

[38] See Cunha, Heckman, and Schennach (2010). They report investment profiles similar to those displayed in Figure 18.4 when they plotted optimal investment against parental endowments.

[39] The optimal policy is not identical for each h and depends on $\theta_{1,h}$, which varies in the population. The densities reflect this variation.

[40] See Cunha, Heckman, and Schennach (2010) for an extensive discussion of these and other simulations.

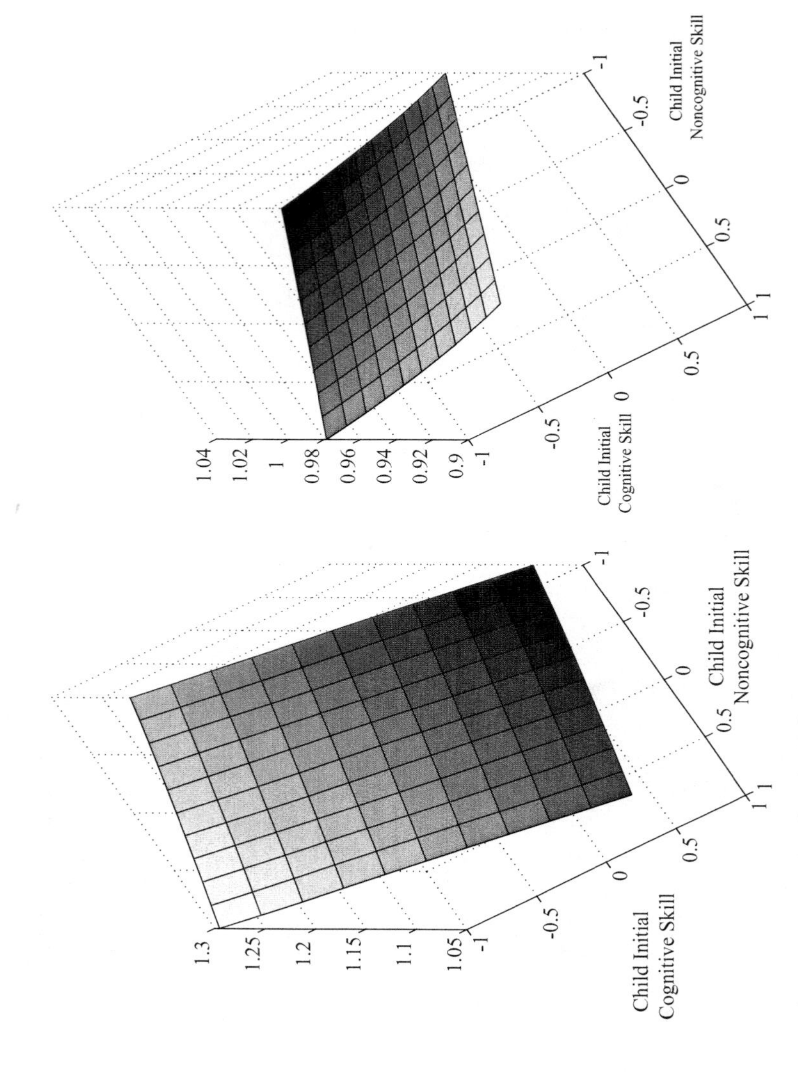

Figure 18.4. Optimal early (*left*) and late (*right*) investments by child initial conditions of cognitive and noncognitive skills maximizing aggregate education.

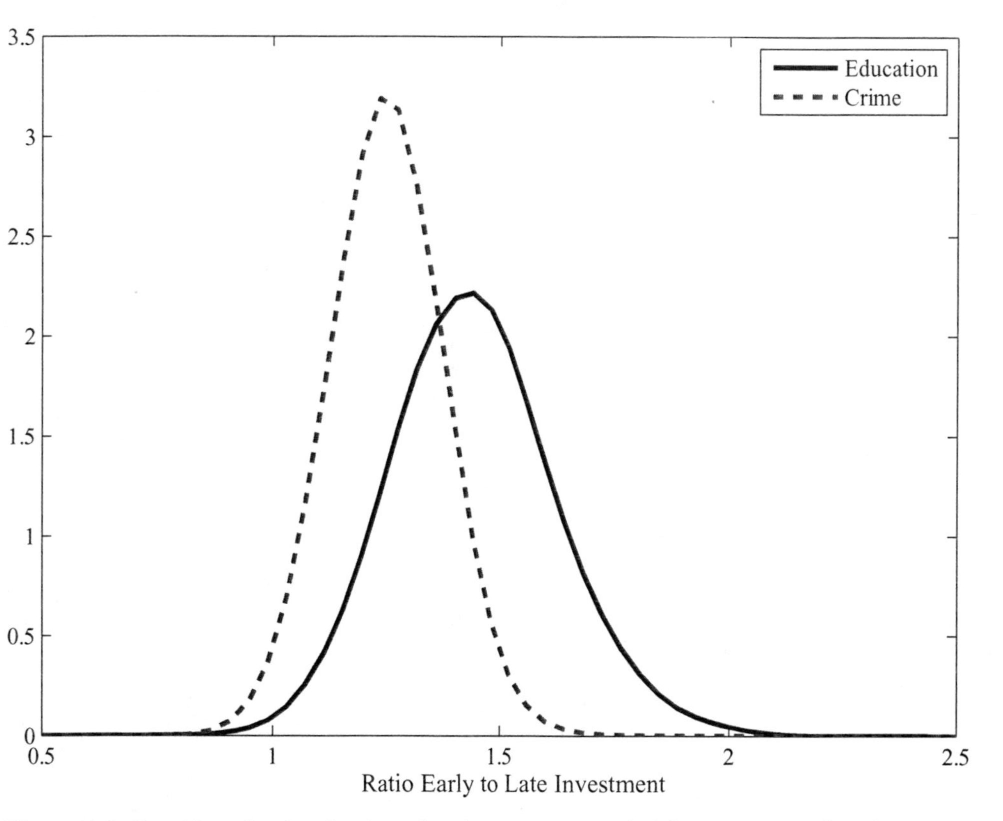

Figure 18.5. Densities of ratio of early to late investments maximizing aggregate education versus minimizing aggregate crime.

SUMMARY AND CONCLUSION

This chapter reviews the evidence from recent research that addresses the origins of inequality and the evolution of the capabilities that partly determine inequality. Both cognitive and noncognitive capabilities are important in producing a variety of outcomes. An emerging literature relates psychological measurements of personality and cognition to economic preference parameters and extends conventional preference specifications in economics.

Comparative advantage is an empirically important feature of economic and social life. The same bundle of personal traits has different productivity in different tasks. Recent empirical work on the technology of capability formation provides an operational empirical framework. Capabilities are not invariant traits and are causally affected by parental investment. Genes and environments interact to determine outcomes. The technology of capability formation rationalizes a large body of evidence in economics, psychology, and neuroscience. Capabilities are self-productive and cross-productive. Dynamic complementarity explains why it is productive to invest in the cognitive skills of disadvantaged young children but why the payoffs are so low for cognitive investments in disadvantaged older children and are even lower for disadvantaged adults. There is no equity–efficiency trade-off for investment in the capabilities of young disadvantaged children. Yet, there is a substantial equity-efficiency trade-off for investment in the *cognitive* skills of disadvantaged adolescents and adults. The trade-off is much less dramatic for investment in the *noncognitive* skills of adolescents. Parental environments and investments affect the outcomes of children. There are substantial costs to uninhibited libertarianism in one generation if the preferences and well-being of the next generation are ignored.[41]

The preferences, motivations, and skill endowments of adults that are created, in part, in their childhoods play important roles in creating inequality. They can be influenced, in part, by policy. But, incentives matter too. Society can reduce crime and promote well-being by operating at both incentive and investment margins.

The right mix of intervention to reduce inequality and promote productivity remains to be determined. The optimal timing of investment depends on the outcome being targeted. The optimal intervention strategies depend on the stage of the life cycle and endowments at each stage. For severely disadvantaged adults with low levels of capabilities, subsidizing work and welfare may be a better response for alleviating poverty than investment in their skills. The substantial heterogeneity in endowments and effects of interventions at different ages suggests that a universal policy to combat the adverse effects of early disadvantage is not appropriate. Optimal investment should be tailored

[41] See Moynihan (2006).

to the specifics that create adversity and to the productivity of investment for different configurations of disadvantage. As research on the economics of capability formation matures, economists will have a greater understanding of how to foster successful people.

REFERENCES

Aigner, D. J., Hsiao, C., Kapteyn, A., & Wansbeek, T. (1984). Latent variable models in econometrics. In Z. Griliches & M. D. Intriligator (Eds.), *Handbook of econometrics* (Vol. 2, pp. 1321–1393). Amsterdam: Elsevier.

Aiyagari, S. R., Greenwood, J., & Seshadri, A. (2002). Efficient investment in children. *Journal of Economic Theory, 102*(2), 290–321.

Akabayashi, H. (1996). *On the role of incentives in the formation of human capital in the family* (Doctoral dissertation, University of Chicago). Retrieved from ProQuest Digital Dissertations. (AAT 9629236).

Barnett, W. S. (2004). *Benefit-cost analysis of preschool education.* Retrieved from http://nieer.org/resources/files/BarnettBenefits.ppt, PowerPoint presentation.

Becker, G. S. (1991). *A treatise on the family* (enlarged ed.). Cambridge, MA: Harvard University Press.

Becker, G. S. (1993). *Human capital: A theoretical and empirical analysis, with special reference to education* (3rd ed.). Chicago: University of Chicago Press.

Becker, G. S., & Tomes, N. (1986). Human capital and the rise and fall of families. *Journal of Labor Economics, 4*(3, Part 2), S1–S39.

Ben-Porath, Y. (1967). The production of human capital and the life cycle of earnings. *Journal of Political Economy, 75*(4, Part 1), 352–365.

Benabou, R. (2002). Tax and education policy in a heterogeneous agent economy: What levels of redistribution maximize growth and efficiency? *Econometrica, 70*(2), 481–517.

Blau, D., & Currie, J. (2006). Preschool, daycare, and afterschool care: Who's minding the kids? In E. Hanushek & F. Welch (Eds.), *Handbook of economics. Vol. 2: Handbook of the economics of education* (pp. 1163–1278). Amsterdam: North-Holland.

Borghans, L., Duckworth, A. L., Heckman, J. J., & ter Weel, B. (2008). The economics and psychology of personality traits. *Journal of Human Resources, 43*(4), 972–1059.

Bowles, S., Gintis, H., & Osborne, M. (2001). The determinants of earnings: A behavioral approach. *Journal of Economic Literature, 39*(4), 1137–1176.

Cameron, J. (2004). *Evidence for an early sensitive period for the development of brain systems underlying social affiliative behavior.* Unpublished manuscript, Oregon National Primate Research Center.

Cameron, S. V., & Heckman, J. J. (2001). The dynamics of educational attainment for black, Hispanic, and white males. *Journal of Political Economy, 109*(3), 455–499.

Cameron, S. V., & Taber, C. (2004). Estimation of educational borrowing constraints using returns to schooling. *Journal of Political Economy, 112*(1), 132–182.

Carneiro, P., Cunha, F., & Heckman, J. J. (2003, October 17). *Interpreting the evidence of family influence on child development.* Paper presented at the conference, "The Economics of Early Childhood Development: Lessons for Economic Policy," Federal Reserve Bank of Minneapolis.

Carneiro, P., & Heckman, J. J. (2002). The evidence on credit constraints in post-secondary schooling. *Economic Journal, 112*(482), 705–734.

Carneiro, P., & Heckman, J. J. (2003). Human capital policy. In J. J. Heckman, A. B. Krueger, & B. M. Friedman (Eds.), *Inequality in America: What role for human capital policies?* (pp. 77–239). Cambridge, MA: MIT Press.

Carneiro, P., Heckman, J. J., & Vytlacil, E. J. (2006). *Estimating marginal and average returns to education.* Unpublished manuscript, University of Chicago, Department of Economics.

Caspi, A., McClay, J., Moffitt, T. E., Mill, J., Martin, J., Craig, I. W., et al. (2002). Role of genotype in the cycle of violence in maltreated children. *Science, 297*(5582), 851–854.

Caucutt, E., & Lochner, L. J. (2004). *Early and late human capital investments, credit constraints, and the family.* Unpublished manuscript, University of Western Ontario, Department of Economics.

Center for Human Resource Research. (2004). *NLSY79 child and young adult data user's guide.* Columbus, Ohio: Ohio State University.

Cunha, F., & Heckman, J. J. (2007). The technology of skill formation. *American Economic Review, 97*(2), 31–47.

Cunha, F., & Heckman, J. J. (2008). Formulating, identifying and estimating the technology of cognitive and noncognitive skill formation. *Journal of Human Resources, 43*(4), 738–782.

Cunha, F., & Heckman, J. J. (2009). The economics and psychology of inequality and human development. *Journal of the European Economic Association, 7*(2–3), 320–364.

Cunha, F., Heckman, J. J., Lochner, L. J., & Masterov, D. V. (2006). Interpreting the evidence on life cycle skill formation. In E. A. Hanushek & F. Welch (Eds.), *Handbook of the economics of education* (pp. 697–812). Amsterdam: North-Holland.

Cunha, F., Heckman, J. J., & Schennach, S. M. (2010). *Estimating the technology of cognitive and noncognitive skill formation. Econometrica, 78*(3), 883–931.

Currie, J., & Thomas, D. (1995). Does Head Start make a difference? *American Economic Review, 85*(3), 341–364.

Currie, J., & Thomas, D. (2000). School quality and the longer-term effects of Head Start. *Journal of Human Resources, 35*(4), 755–774.

Dahl, G. B., & Lochner, L. J. (2005). *The impact of family income on child achievement* (Working Paper 11279). Cambridge, MA: National Bureau of Economic Research.

Dahl, R. E. (2004). Adolescent brain development: A period of vulnerabilities and opportunities. In R. E. Dahl & L. P. Spear (Eds.), *Annals of the New York Academy of Sciences* (pp. 1–22). New York: New York Academy of Sciences.

Damasio, A. R. (1994). *Descartes' error: Emotion, reason, and the human brain.* New York: Putnam.

Duncan, G., & Brooks-Gunn, J. (1997). Income effects across the life span: Integration and interpretation. In G. Duncan, & J. Brooks-Gunn (Eds.), *Consequences of growing up poor* (pp. 596–610). New York: Russell Sage.

Duncan, G., Dowsett, C. J., Claessens, A., Magnuson, K., Huston, A. C., Klebanov, P., et al. (2007). School readiness and later achievement. *Developmental Psychology, 43*(6), 1428–1446.

Duncan, G., & Kalil, A. (2006). *The effects of income in the early years on child outcomes.* Unpublished manuscript, Northwestern University.

Durbin, J., Harvey, A. C., Koopman, S. J., & Shephard, N. (2004). *State space and unobserved component models: Theory and applications: Proceedings of a conference in honour of James Durbin.* New York: Cambridge University Press.

Erikson, E. H. (1950). *Childhood and society.* New York: Norton.

Gluckman, P. D., & Hanson, M. (2005). *The fetal matrix: Evolution, development, and disease.* Cambridge: Cambridge University Press.

Hansen, K. T., Heckman, J. J., & Mullen, K. J. (2004). The effect of schooling and ability on achievement test scores. *Journal of Econometrics, 121*(1–2), 39–98.

Harvey, A. C. (1989). *Forecasting, structural time series models and the Kalman filter.* New York: Cambridge University Press.

Heckman, J. J. (1995). Lessons from *The Bell Curve. Journal of Political Economy, 103*(5), 1091–1120.

Heckman, J. J. (2008). Schools, skills and synapses. *Economic Inquiry, 46*(3), 289–324.

Heckman, J. J., Larenas, M. I., & Urzua, S. (2004). *Accounting for the effect of schooling and abilities in the analysis of racial and ethnic disparities in achievement test scores.* Unpublished manuscript, University of Chicago, Department of Economics.

Heckman, J. J., Stixrud, J., & Urzua, S. (2006). The effects of cognitive and noncognitive abilities on labor-market outcomes and social behavior. *Journal of Labor Economics, 24*(3), 411–482.

Herrnstein, R. J., & Murray, C. A. (1994). *The Bell Curve: Intelligence and class structure in American life.* New York: Free Press.

Hopkins, K. D., & Bracht, G. H. (1975). Ten-year stability of verbal and nonverbal IQ scores. *American Educational Research Journal, 12*(4), 469–477.

Jöreskog, K. G., & Goldberger, A. S. (1975). Estimation of a model with multiple indicators and multiple causes of a single latent variable. *Journal of the American Statistical Association, 70*(351), 631–639.

Knudsen, E. I., Heckman, J. J., Cameron, J., & Shonkoff, J. P. (2006). Economic, neurobiological, and behavioral perspectives on building America's future workforce. *Proceedings of the National Academy of Sciences, 103*(27), 10155–10162.

LeDoux, J. E. (1996). *The emotional brain: The mysterious underpinnings of emotional life.* New York: Simon and Schuster.

Meaney, M. J. (2001). Maternal care, gene expression, and the transmission of individual differences in stress reactivity across generations. *Annual Review of Neuroscience, 24*(1), 1161–1192.

Meghir, C., & Palme, M. (2001). *The effect of a social experiment in education* (Tech. Rep. W01/11). London: Institute for Fiscal Studies.

Moon, S. H. (2009). *Multi-dimensional human skill formation with multi-dimensional parental investment.* Unpublished manuscript, University of Chicago, Department of Economics.

Morris, P., Duncan, G. J., & Clark-Kauffman, E. (2005). Child well-being in an era of welfare reform: The sensitivity of transitions in development to policy change. *Developmental Psychology, 41*(6), 919–932.

Moynihan, D. P. (2006). *The future of the family.* New York: Russell Sage.

Murnane, R. J., Willett, J. B., & Levy, F. (1995). The growing importance of cognitive skills in wage determination. *Review of Economics and Statistics, 77*(2), 251–266.

Newport, E. L. (1990). Maturational constraints on language learning [Special issue]. *Cognitive Science, 14*(1), 11–28.

O'Connor, T. G., Rutter, M., Beckett, C., Keaveney, L., Kreppner, J. M., & the English and Romanian Adoptees Study Team (2000). The effects of global severe privation on cognitive competence: Extension and longitudinal follow-up. *Child Development, 71*(2), 376–390.

Pinker, S. (1994). *The language instinct: How the mind creates language.* New York: Morrow.

Raudenbush, S. W. (2006). *Schooling, statistics and poverty: Measuring school improvement and improving schools.* Inaugural Lecture, Division of Social Sciences, University of Chicago.

Raver, C. C., Garner, P. W., & Smith-Donald, R. (2007). The roles of emotion regulation and emotion knowledge for children's academic readiness: Are the links causal? In R. C. Pianta, M. J. Cox, & K. L. Snow (Eds.), *School readiness and the transition to kindergarten in the era of accountability* (pp. 121–148). Baltimore, MD: Brookes.

Rutter, M. (2006). *Genes and behavior: Nature–nurture interplay explained.* Oxford: Blackwell.

Schweinhart, L. J., Montie, J., Xiang, Z., Barnett, W. S., Belfield, C. R., & Nores, M. (2005). *Lifetime effects: The HighScope Perry Preschool Study through age 40.* Ypsilanti, MI: HighScope Press.

Shonkoff, J. P., & Phillips, D. (2000). *From neurons to neighborhoods: The science of early child development.* Washington, DC: National Academy Press.

Stinebrickner, R., & Stinebrickner, T. (2008). The effect of credit constraints on the college drop-out decision: A direct approach using a new panel study. *American Economic Review, 98*(5), 2163–2184.

Suomi, S. J. (1999). Developmental trajectories, early experiences, and community consequences: Lessons from studies with rhesus monkeys. In D. P. Keating & C. Hertzman (Eds.), *Developmental health and the wealth of nations: Social, biological, and educational dynamics* (pp. 185–200). New York: Guilford.

Weinberg, B. A. (2001). An incentive model of the effect of parental income on children. *Journal of Political Economy, 109*(2), 266–280.

19

Paths of Effects of Preschool Participation to Educational Attainment at Age 21: A Three-Study Analysis

ARTHUR J. REYNOLDS, MICHELLE M. ENGLUND, SUH-RUU OU, LAWRENCE J. SCHWEINHART, AND FRANCES A. CAMPBELL

A hallmark of preschool programs is their capacity to promote lasting effects on child well-being into adulthood. Long-term beneficial effects of early childhood programs have been documented for school performance and achievement, antisocial and criminal behavior, educational attainment, economic well-being, parenting behaviors, health status and behavior, and mental health (Campbell & Ramey, 1995; Karoly, 2001; Karoly, Cannon, & Kilburn, 2005; McLaughlin, Campbell, Pungello, & Skinner, 2007; Reynolds et al., 2007; Schweinhart, Barnes, & Weikart, 1993; Temple & Reynolds, 2007).

The most consistently observed and consequential long-term effects of preschool programs are for educational attainment. Measured by high school completion, years of education, or college attendance, higher educational attainment has been demonstrated in model (Campbell, Ramey, Pungello, Sparling, & Miller-Johnson, 2002; Consortium for Longitudinal Studies, 1983; Schweinhart et al., 1993, 2005) and large-scale programs (Currie & Thomas, 2000; Garces, Thomas, & Currie, 2002; Oden, Schweinhart, Weikart, Marcus, & Xie, 2000; Reynolds, Temple, Robertson, & Mann, 2001). Educational attainment is a key determinant of economic well-being and is a fundamental measure for estimating economic returns in cost-benefit analysis. Although long-term positive effects of preschool have been found for other adult outcomes such as employment and income (Schweinhart et al., 1993), crime prevention (Reynolds et al., 2001; Schweinhart et al., 1993), health status and behavior, and mental health (McLaughlin et al., 2007; Reynolds et al., 2007), they have been demonstrated less consistently.

Although there is now a critical mass of evidence in support of long-term effects on educational attainment, the causal mechanisms that account for these findings are not well understood (Heckman, 2000; Reynolds, Wang, & Walberg, 2003). Among the studies that have found significant increases in educational attainment, comprehensive models have rarely been tested (Ou & Reynolds, 2004; Reynolds, Ou, & Topitzes, 2004). Early studies emphasized the cognitive advantage hypothesis as the major initiator of long-term effects

(Berreuta-Clement, Schweinhart, Barnett, Epstein, & Weikart, 1984; Consortium for Longitudinal Studies, 1983). The second phase of studies added one or two hypothesized mechanisms, such as family support and social adjustment (Reynolds, Mavrogenes, Bezruczko, & Hagemann, 1996; Schweinhart et al., 1993). These studies generally found strong support for cognitive advantage but that family support behavior, motivation, and social adjustment contributed either directly or indirectly to long-term effects. In the Abecedarian Project, the cognitive advantage hypothesis has been the focus of investigations of causal mechanisms (Campbell, Pungello, Miller-Johnson, Burchinal, & Ramey, 2001).

FIVE-HYPOTHESIS MODEL OF CAUSAL MECHANISMS

These and related findings led to the development of the five-hypothesis model of the effects of early childhood intervention (Reynolds, 2000). Derived from the accumulated research on preschool effects over 4 decades, the model posits that the effects of intervention are explained by indicators of five general paths of influence: cognitive advantage, motivational advantage, social adjustment, family support behavior, and school support behavior. Moreover, in the five-hypothesis model, the contribution of any one hypothesis can be accurately assessed only in conjunction with the others. Previous studies have found, based on structural equation modeling, that all five hypotheses contribute to the explanation of the links between Child-Parent Center (CPC) preschool and later outcomes, including school achievement in adolescence, high school completion, and delinquency prevention (Ou, 2003; Reynolds et al., 2004; Zigler, Taussig, & Black, 1992).

For example, Reynolds et al. (2004) found that the five hypotheses together accounted for 58% of the main effect of CPC preschool participation on high school completion and 79% of the main effect of preschool on juvenile arrest. In order of contribution to the model of high school completion, cognitive advantage accounted for 32% of the indirect effect of preschool, school support behavior 28%, and family support behavior 26%. Motivation (measured by school commitment) and social adjustment (measured by teacher ratings of classroom adjustment) accounted for less than 2% of the indirect effect. Nevertheless, the structural model that best fit the observed data included indicators of all five hypotheses. For juvenile arrest, the noncognitive measures made greater contributions.

As documented in the confirmatory impact evaluation approach (Reynolds, 1998, 2005), the identification of mechanisms advances knowledge in three ways. First, it strengthens causal inferences. The identified mechanisms account for, at least in part, the main effect and are the "active" ingredients of change. Because the length of time between the end of the program and outcome assessment is more than 15 years, documenting the process of change is especially important. Even in well-controlled studies, many intervening events and experiences that occur after program completion challenge the capacity to infer causality. If the identified mechanisms lead to a coherent explanation of the main-effect relation, causal inference is strengthened.

Second, the identification of mechanisms increases the generalizability of findings. To the extent that findings across studies share a common mechanism, program replication and expansion in different contexts would be more likely to be successful. In the case of program-specific mechanisms, generalizability would be enhanced for implementation of particular programs.

Finally, clarification of mechanisms of impact helps prioritize program improvement efforts: Program modifications consistent with the identified mechanisms would be supported. For example, if the family-support hypothesis is identified as an important mechanism of effects, greater attention to parental involvement and the provision of family services would be one strategy of program improvement.

PRESENT STUDY

In this study, we used the five-hypothesis model as a framework to test the common paths of influence to educational attainment for studies of three preschool programs: Child-Parent Centers, HighScope Perry Preschool, and the Abecedarian Project. Our study addressed three questions:

1. What is the contribution of each hypothesis to the explanation of the main effect of intervention on years of completed education?
2. Which hypotheses in combination contribute most to the explanation of the main effect of intervention?
3. Are the paths of influence from preschool to years of education similar across the three studies?

We chose these three program studies for several reasons. First, as prospective investigations of life-course development, each study has collected a comprehensive set of postprogram data to assess causal mechanisms. The studies can be matched on indicators of each hypothesis and on ages of measurement. Second, these studies have consistently documented that the estimated links between participation and attainment can be confidently interpreted as program effects. Not only are the studies well controlled but also attrition is low and the pattern of impacts is consistent with the underlying program theory. Third, the studies are heterogeneous in important respects that strengthen generalizability. Although each preschool program provided high-quality educational enrichment to economically disadvantaged families, the programs differed significantly in geographic context, curriculum and services, scale, and implementation history. The CPC program is an established, large-scale intervention in the inner city run by the Chicago Public Schools.

Perry and Abecedarian were research demonstrations implemented in much smaller cities, and Abecedarian was implemented in a university-based child care center. The programs also were implemented in three different decades spanning the 1960s to 1980s. Finally, the programs have demonstrated relatively high economic returns to society that are due, in substantial part, to increased educational attainment (Reynolds & Temple, 2008; Reynolds, Temple, Robertson, & Mann, 2002; Schweinhart et al., 2005; Temple & Reynolds, 2007). Analyses of processes leading to educational attainment will help determine how cost effectiveness is achieved.

FIVE-HYPOTHESIS MODEL FOR YEARS OF EDUCATION

As shown in Figure 19.1, we assessed the contributions of the indicators of five hypotheses leading to years of education completed by age 21 for the three preschool studies. We matched each indicator as closely as possible across studies on both age of measurement and content. We based the sequence of variables on prior research and theory as well as the timing of measurement. For the model, the greater the magnitude of effect of program experiences on a particular pathway or multiple pathways, the more likely that enduring effects would occur.

The cognitive-advantage hypothesis and pathways indicate that the longer term effects of programs are due primarily to the enhancement of cognitive skills broadly defined, including language and numeracy, school readiness, and school achievement. The cognitive-advantage hypothesis was represented by cognitive skills at age 5, which is at the end of program participation; grade retention or special education placement in the elementary grades; and reading-achievement test scores at age 14 or 15. Cognitive skills were assessed at age 5 to test the immediate effect of educational enrichment at school entry, a fundamental tenet of each of the programs.

The family-support hypothesis indicates that impacts on child outcomes derive from greater parental investments in children's development, such as greater parental involvement in education, increased parenting skills, and greater resource supports for parents. We used parental involvement in children's schooling in Grades 1–3 as rated by teachers as the measure of family support.

The school-support hypothesis suggests that longer term effects would occur to the degree that postprogram school experiences reinforce learning gains. Enrollment in higher quality schools and in schools with positive learning environments would strengthen or maintain learning gains, whereas enrollment in schools lower in quality would neutralize earlier learning gains. We used enrollment in relatively high-quality elementary schools as the main measure. In the CPC study, this was enrollment in magnet schools or schools in which 40% or more of the student body were at or above national norms

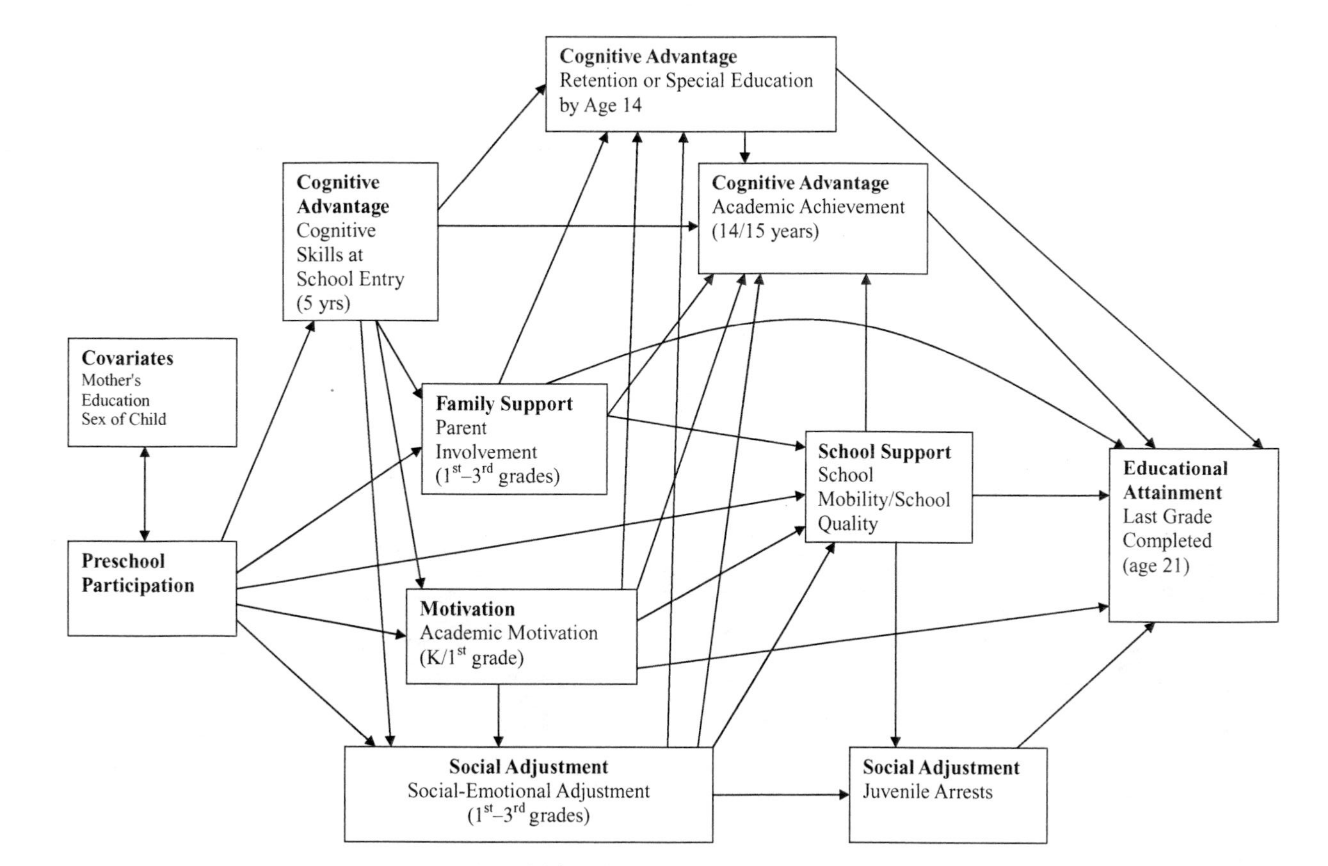

Figure 19.1. Conceptual model for educational-attainment outcomes in early adulthood.

in reading achievement. In the ABC study, enrollment in Chapel Hill public schools was the measure, whereas in the Perry study it was attendance in Ypsilanti schools. Given the potential limitation of the school enrollment variable, we also measured school mobility in the Perry and CPC studies as a secondary measure of school support.

The social adjustment and motivational advantage hypotheses indicate that noncognitive skills can be the mechanism of effects of preschool programs. Common measures include classroom and peer social skills, positive teacher–child relationships, achievement motivation, and school commitment. We measured social adjustment through teacher ratings of classroom adjustment in first to third grades. We also included incidence of juvenile arrest as an adolescent measure of social adjustment. It has been found to be a powerful determinant of educational attainment. In the motivational-advantage hypothesis, the impact of intervention would be dependent on changes in children's self-system attributes such as achievement motivation, school commitment, perceived competence, or educational expectations. We used teacher ratings of achievement motivation as the primary measure of motivation. Although they are proxies for children's perceived motivation, they were measured early enough after the end of the preschool program to assess the short-term effects relative to that of cognitive skills. Because later measures of motivation were available for only the CPC and Perry projects, they were not included.

METHODS

Program and Sample Descriptions

Table 19.1 shows the key features of the three programs and studies. To summarize, each program provided high-quality educational enrichment to children at risk in group settings characterized by small class sizes, a focus on language and cognitive skills, and well-qualified and compensated teachers. Of the three programs, the Carolina Abecedarian Project (ABC) was the most intensive and lengthy, providing full-day, year-round care for 5 years. The HighScope Perry Preschool Program (PPP) provided the most established and structured curriculum, which followed the Piagetian cognitive principle of child-initiated learning. The ongoing Chicago Child-Parent Centers (CPC) provide the most comprehensive services by implementing an intensive parental involvement component, outreach services, and attention to health and nutrition. It also is the only program that became established in public schools.

The HighScope PPP (Schweinhart et al., 1993) was implemented in Perry Elementary School in Ypsilanti, Michigan, from 1962 to 1967. It served 3- and 4-year-old African American children from low socioeconomic status (SES) families. All children had IQ scores in the range of 70–85. The program ran for one half-day (2.5 hours) 5 days a week, with weekly home visits by teachers of 90 minutes. Children enrolled in the program at age 3 or 4. Classes comprised

Table 19.1. *Background and the characteristics of three preschool programs*

Characteristic	Perry Preschool	Abecedarian	Child-Parent Centers
Program and control *N*	58, 65	57, 54	989, 550
Years of implementation	1962–1967	1972–1977	1983–1985
City and context	Ypsilanti, MI Urban	Chapel Hill, NC Rural	Chicago, IL Inner city
Location	Elementary school	University center	Elementary school or adjacent to
Number of sites	1	1	24
Child attributes	Low SES IQs of 70–85	Low SES High risk	Low SES Reside in Title I area
Race/ethnicity	100% Black	96% Black	93% Black 7% Hispanic
Entry age	3 years	1–4 months	3 years
Mean duration	1.8 years	5 years	1.6 years
Length of day	Part-day	Full-day	Part-day
Other components	Weekly home visits	Medical services Nutrition	Parent program Outreach Occasional home visits Health services
Mean class size	22	12 (Infancy) 12 (Preschool)	17
Mean child:staff ratio	5.7 to 1	3 to 1 (Infancy) 6 to 1 (Preschool)	8.5 to 1
Curriculum emphasis	Cognitive and social Child-initiated	Language and social Traditional	Language and social Teacher-directed
Staff compensation	Public school	Competitive with public schools	Public school
School-age services	None	K to Grade 2	K, Grades 1 to 3

an average of 22 children with 4 master's-level teachers for a child:staff ratio of 5.7 to 1.

The impact study included 123 children: 58 children were randomly assigned to PPP in five consecutive cohorts beginning in 1962. With the exception of the first cohort, children attended for 2 years. The control group included 65 children who were in home care. Three families were reassigned to groups after the original assignment. Study children have been followed up to age 40, with intervening follow-ups at ages 9, 15, 19, and 27.

The Abecedarian Project (ABC; Ramey, Campbell, & Blair, 1998; Ramey et al., 2000) was a model educational day care intervention that was implemented from 1972 to 1977 at the Frank Porter Graham Child Development Center at the University of North Carolina–Chapel Hill. Participants entered the program beginning at 6 weeks of age and attended 5 years of full-time, year-round care. The children were almost all African American and were determined to be at high risk of school failure, primarily because of low SES. The focus of the program was to promote optimal child development, with a special emphasis on language. Although there was no family component, medical and nutritional services were provided. Unlike in most early education programs today, teachers were compensated with salaries that were competitive with public schools. The educational levels of the Center's staff varied; some had college degrees, some did not. All had experience as early childhood caregivers or teachers. In year 1, group size was 12 infants with 4 teachers and staff for a child:staff ratio of 3:1. In years 2 and 3, group size was 7 toddlers and 2 teachers for a child:staff ratio of 3.5 to 1. During preschool, classes had 12 children and 2 teachers, a child:staff ratio of 6:1.

The impact study included 111 families. Fifty-seven children were randomly assigned to ABC soon after birth and began the program at an average age of 4 months and continued until the start of kindergarten. Fifty-four children were randomly assigned to the control group; control families could receive many of the same medical and nutritional services as the program group as well as transportation to the center. To investigate the added impact of school-age participation, the study sample was randomly assigned to school-age and control conditions before kindergarten entry. Study participants have been tracked up to age 21, with a 95% sample recovery rate. Follow-up assessments at ages 8, 12, and 15 also were made.

The Child-Parent Center program (CPC; Reynolds, 2000; Reynolds et al., 2001) began in the Chicago public schools in 1967 through federal funding from the Elementary and Secondary Education Act of 1965. Title I of the Act provides grants to local public-school districts serving high concentrations of children from low-income families. The CPC is the nation's second oldest federally funded preschool program. It is a center-based early intervention that provides comprehensive educational and family-support services to economically disadvantaged children and their parents beginning at age 3 and continuing until third grade for up to 6 years of intervention. The 24 centers provide comprehensive services under the direction of the head teacher and in collaboration with the elementary-school principal. Other primary staff members in each center are the parent-resource teacher, the school-community representative, bachelor's-level classroom teachers, aides, nurses, speech therapists, and school psychologists. The cohort attending the preschool program beginning at age 3 in 1983–1984 or at age 4 in 1984–1985 was the focus of the program impact study.

The preschool component is a half-day program for 5 days a week during the school year. Parents are heavily involved in the program through many types of school participation. Preschool classes have 17 children, a teacher, and a teachers' aide for a child:staff ratio of 8.5 to 1. All teachers have bachelor's degrees with certification in early childhood. Most of the children are African American and reside in low-income families. After attending a full- or half-day kindergarten, children can participate in the school-age component in first to third grades.

The Chicago Longitudinal Study (CLS; 1999) of the CPC program has investigated impact for the entire cohort of 989 children born in 1980 or 1979 who attended the preschool program beginning at age 3 and completed kindergarten in the spring of 1986. The comparison group of 550 children in this quasi-experimental design did not attend the CPC program but instead participated in an all-day kindergarten program for children at risk in five randomly selected schools. Because the CPC group was from the highest poverty neighborhoods and the comparison group attended randomly selected schools outside of CPC neighborhoods and also participated in alternative interventions, estimates of impact are likely to be conservative. Study participants have been followed up to age 24, with a sample recovery rate of more than 85% on most outcomes. Follow-up assessments were conducted each year between kindergarten and seventh grade and at ages 15, 17–18, and 22.

Measures

Table 19.2 provides a comparison of measures used for this study across the three programs. The frequencies (including valid and missing data points, range, means, and standard deviations) for each of the variables for each program are provided in Table 19.3. We chose these measures based on two considerations. First, the variables needed to accurately represent the hypothesized mediational model. Second, the outcome measure, covariates, and mediator variables needed to correspond across studies in terms of both the construct and the age range of measurement. We used the highest grade completed by age 21 as an outcome measure for all three studies.

Covariates

Gender of the child, single-parent status, and mother's educational level were included in analyses as covariates. For PPP, the single-parent measure was whether the father was present in the home at program entry; for ABC it was whether the father lived in the home at the birth of the child; and for CPC it was whether the parent was not single at any time from the birth of the child through age 3. We coded mother's educational status for all three studies as 0 = did not complete high school or 1 = graduated from high school.

Cognitive Advantage

We included three measures of the cognitive-advantage hypothesis for each of the programs. At age 5, by kindergarten entry, a measure of IQ or academic achievement was obtained; this measure was the Stanford-Binet (Terman & Merrill, 1960) for PPP; the Weschler Preschool and Primary Scale of Intelligence (WPPSI) (Wechsler, 1967) for ABC; and the Iowa Test of Basic Skills (Hieronymus, Lindquist, & Hoover, 1982), cognitive composite for CPC. A measure

Table 19.2. *Comparison measures for the three preschool programs*

Construct	Variable	Perry Preschool	Abecedarian	Child-Parent Centers
PREDICTOR Preschool Participation	Preschool program enrollment	Preschool vs. no preschool; control group in home care	Educational day care vs. none; control group in home care but received some well-baby care services	Preschool vs. no preschool; 15% of controls enrolled in Head Start and 100% in full-day K (60% for CPC)
COVARIATES	Gender (1 = girls)	Gender	Gender	Gender
	Father present in home	Father in home (study entry – 3 years)	Father in home (birth)	Not single parent (study entry)
	Mother's education – graduated from high school	(study entry – 3 years)	(birth)	(birth or study entry)
OUTCOME Educational Attainment	Last grade completed	21 years	21 years	21 years
MEDIATORS Cognitive Advantage	Cognitive Skills (Kindergarten/5 years)	Stanford-Binet (5 years); standard score	WPPSI IQ (60 mos.); standard score	ITBS cognitive composite (kindergarten entry); standard score
	Reading achievement (14/15 yrs)	California Achievement Tests Reading (age 14; 8th or 7th grade)	Woodcock-Johnson Reading (age 15; 9th or 8th grade)	Iowa Test of Basic Skills Reading Comprehension (age 14; 8th or 7th grade)
	Ever retained or in special education	Through age 15	Through age 15	Through age 15
Social Adjustment	Elementary social adjustment (Teacher rated)	Public Behavior Inventory: socio-emotional adjustment 1–3 averaged	CBI: Social adjustment (newly created variable) 1–2 averaged	SEMAT (socio-emotional maturity) 1–3 averaged
	Adolescent social adjustment: delinquent behavior	Any arrest as juvenile (arrested before age 19)	Arrested before age 19	Any juvenile petition or self-report arrest (arrested before age 18)
Family Support	Parental involvement with school/education	Mother's participation with school (Teacher rating–Ypsilanti Rating Scale) 1–3 averaged	HOME (8 years) New measure of parental involvement 2nd grade	Parent involvement with school (Teacher rating) 1–3 averaged

Construct	Variable	Perry Preschool	Abecedarian	Child Parent Centers
Motivation	Elementary motivation (Teacher rated)	Public Behavior Inventory: Academic motivation (teacher ratings) K/1 averaged	CBI: Newly created motivation variable K/1 averaged	New motivation variable K/1 averaged
School Support	School mobility	# of different schools through 8th grade		# of different schools 4th through 8th grade
	School quality	Ypsilanti vs. non-Ypsilanti school (age 14)	Chapel Hill schools or not (Grades 1–3)	Attended magnet school (Grades 4–8) or 40% + above grade level in reading in 5th grade

of reading achievement at ages 14/15 was also administered to the participants of all three of the studies: PPP – California Achievement Test-Reading Comprehension (Tiegs & Clark, 1963, 1971); ABC – Woodcock Johnson Test of Achievement-Reading Comprehension (Woodcock & Johnson, 1989); and CPC – Iowa Test of Basic Skills (Hieronymus et al., 1982), Reading Comprehension Subscale. In addition, we derived a measure of special education or retention by age 14/15. This variable was coded 0 if the participant had not been retained or received special-educational services at any time between kindergarten and age 14/15 and was coded 1 if the participant had ever been retained or had received special-educational services between kindergarten and age 14/15.

Family Support

All three studies included a measure of parental involvement with school/education between the ages of 7 and 9. A teacher-rated measure of parental involvement with school was averaged across ages 7–9 for PPP. This measure was obtained from the Ypsilanti Rating Scale. For ABC, a measure of parental involvement in education was derived from the Caldwell HOME (Home Observation for Measurement of the Environment) Stimulation Scale (Caldwell & Bradley, 1984), which was given when the children were age 8. Four items were added together to derive a score on parental involvement on education (child has a library card and family arranges for child to go to library once a month; parent reads to, or listens to child read, once a week; child is encouraged to read on his or her own; and parent will offer help if child is frustrated by a task). Parental involvement in school for CPC was obtained from teacher questionnaires completed when the participants were ages 7–9. An average rating was derived from these 3 years.

Table 19.3. *Descriptive statistics for model variables across studies*

Measure	Valid	Missing	Range	Mean	S.D.	Frequency
Outcome						
Highest grade completed at 21 years						
Perry Preschool	123	0	7–16	11.40	1.54	7 = 1 8 = 3 9 = 11 10 = 24 11 = 13 12 = 38 13 = 31 14 = 1 16 = 1
Abecedarian	103	0	8–16	11.92	1.51	8 = 2 9 = 4 10 = 12 11 = 12 12 = 46 13 = 12 14 = 10 15 = 4 16 = 1
Child-Parent Centers	1,296	0	7–14	11.14	1.81	7 = 22 8 = 156 9 = 144 10 = 110 11 = 91 12 = 419 13 = 352 14 = 2
Preschool						
Preschool participation						
Perry Preschool	123	0	0/1	.48		No preschool = 65 Preschool = 58
Abecedarian	103	0	0/1	.52		No preschool = 50 Preschool = 53
Child-Parent Centers	1,296	0	0/1	.66		No preschool = 447 Preschool = 849
Covariates						
Gender						
Perry Preschool	123	0	0/1	.42		Male = 72 Female = 51
Abecedarian	103	0	0/1	.52		Male = 50 Female = 53
Child-Parent Centers	1,296	0	0/1	.52		Male = 630 Female = 666

Measure	Valid	Missing	Range	Mean	S.D.	Frequency
Father present in home						
Perry Preschool	123	0	0/1	.53		No = 58 Yes = 65
Abecedarian	103	0	0/1	.29		No = 74 Yes = 29
Child-Parent Centers	1,296	0	0/1	.23		No = 1,001 Yes = 295
Mother's education at school entry – graduated from high school						
Perry Preschool	123	0	0/1	.22		Non-completion of high school = 97 Graduated high school = 26
Abecedarian	101	2	0/1	.35		Non-completion of high school = 66 Graduated high school = 35
Child-Parent Centers	1,296	0	0/1	.46		Non-completion of high school = 699 Graduated high school = 597
Cognitive advantage						
Cognitive Skills (5 years)						
Perry Preschool (Stanford-Binet)	121	2	60–134	88.31	12.26	
Abecedarian (WPPSI)	93	10	71–125	97.89	12.69	
Child-Parent Centers (ITBS Cognitive Composite)	1,296	0	28–83	47.44	8.79	
Academic achievement 8th grade/age 14						
Perry Preschool (CAT)	95	28	10–59	28.73	11.40	
Abecedarian (Woodcock-Johnson Standard Score)	103	0	69–113	91.60	10.43	
Child-Parent Centers (ITBS Reading Comprehension)	1,227	69	77–212	145.04	21.77	
Either special ed or retained by 8th grade/age 14						
Perry Preschool	112	11	0/1	.63		No = 42 Either special ed or retained = 70
Abecedarian	102	1	0/1	.59		No = 42 Either special ed or retained = 60
Child-Parent Centers	1,296	0	0/1	.35		No = 844 Either special ed or retained = 452

(*continued*)

Table 19.3 *(continued)*

Measure	Valid	Missing	Range	Mean	S.D.	Frequency
Family support						
Parental involvement						
Perry Preschool (average Grades 1–3)	120	3	1–7	4.04	1.68	
Abecedarian (derived from the HOME Stimulation Scale 8 years)	84	19	1–4	3.02	.73	
Child-Parent Centers (average Grades 1–3)	1,242	54	1–5	2.59	1.01	
Social adjustment						
Elementary school social adjustment						
Perry Preschool (PBI socio-emotional adjustment, average Grades 1–3)	116	7	1.25–5.00	3.55	.75	
Abecedarian (Social Adjustment scale derived from the CBI, average Grades 1–2)	89	14	16.00–31.75	24.29	2.68	
Child-Parent Centers (Social Emotional Maturity [SEMAT], average Grades 1–3)	1,251	45	7–30	19.15	4.77	
Adolescent social adjustment						
Perry Preschool (Arrested by age 19)	121	2	0/1	.21		Not arrested = 96 Ever arrested = 25
Abecedarian (Arrested by age 19)	103	0	0/1	.34		Not arrested = 68 Ever arrested = 35
Child-Parent Centers (Arrested by age 18)	1,296	0	0/1	.21		Not arrested = 1025 Ever arrested = 271
Motivation						
Perry Preschool (PBI academic motivation, average grades K–1)	121	2	1.11–4.78	3.07	.78	
Abecedarian (Motivation scale derived from CBI, average K–1)	88	15	25.50–42.00	34.17	3.86	
Child-Parent Centers (Motivation, average K–1, z-score)	1,203	93	−3.17–1.79	.0035	.93	

Measure	Valid	Missing	Range	Mean	S.D.	Frequency
School support						
School mobility						
Perry Preschool (# of different schools through 8th grade)	112	11	0–5	1.64	.97	0 = 4 1 = 60 2 = 26 3 = 17 4 = 4 5 = 1
Child-Parent Centers (# of school moves – Grades 4–8)	1,242	54	0–4	.93	1.00	0 = 522 1 = 410 2 = 194 3 = 103 4 = 13
School quality						
Perry Preschool (School at age 14 – Ypsilanti vs. others)	100	23	0/1	.76		Ypsilanti (1) = 76 Other (0) = 24
Abecedarian (Attended Chapel Hill School any time between 1st and 3rd grades)	91	12	0/1	.94		Did attend Chapel Hill Schools = 85 Did not attend Chapel Hill Schools = 6
Child-Parent Centers (If attended magnet school [Grades 4–8] or 40% or more above grade level in reading)	1,296	0	0/1	.13		Attended magnet school = 162 Did not attend magnet school = 1,134

Note: Means for dichotomous variables are percentages. Missing data for ABC and CPC are among those with outcome data. Original N's are 111 and 1,539, respectively.

Social Adjustment

All three programs included two measures of social adjustment: a measure of socio-emotional adjustment at ages 7–9 and a measure of juvenile arrests. The measure of socio-emotional adjustment used for Perry was the Pupil Behavior Inventory socio-emotional adjustment scale (Vinter, Sarri, Vorwaller, & Schafer, 1966), completed by the participants' teachers at ages 7–9. For each age, the mean of five 5-point items constituted the scale (e.g., isolated, few or no friends). Scale points ranged from very infrequently to very frequently. The analyses used the average of the scores across ages with the negative items reverse-coded to correspond to greater levels of adjustment. Socio-emotional adjustment was derived for ABC by adding together eight 5-point items on the teacher-rated Classroom Behavior Inventory measure (Schaefer, Edgerton, & Aaronson, 1978) obtained at ages 7–8 (e.g., seeks out other children, tries not to do or say anything that would hurt another). The score was then averaged across ages 7–8. A teacher-rated measure of socio-emotional maturity was averaged for ages 7–9 for CPC. Among the items in the 6-item scale were "gets along well with others," "complies with classroom rules," and "completes work according to instructions." Finally, juvenile arrests were rated 0 for no arrests or 1 for any arrests by age 18 or 19. For all three studies, juvenile arrests data were obtained from administrative records.

Motivation

All three studies used an average age 6–7 motivation measure obtained from teacher ratings. PPP used the academic motivation scale of the Pupil Behavior Inventory (Vinter et al., 1966). Questions related to items on the motivation scale of the Pupil Behavior Inventory were identified from the Classroom Behavior Inventory (Schaefer et al., 1978) for ABC and from the teacher questionnaires for CPC. These items were reverse-coded if required, and the item scores were added together. For CPC, some questions were different from kindergarten to first grade, so *z*-scores were derived for both years, and an average z-score was used for analyses. For Perry and ABC, motivation scores were averaged across kindergarten and first grade. Appendix A provides detailed information on the comparison of the motivation measures at the item level across studies.

School Support

Two measures of school support were examined across the studies: school mobility and school quality. The measure of school mobility in Perry was the number of different schools that participants attended from kindergarten through Grade 8 (minus one move from elementary to junior high school). The measure of school mobility for CPC was the number of different schools that participants attended from Grade 4 through Grade 8. School mobility information was not available for ABC.

The PPP study measured school quality by a dichotomous variable indicating whether participants had attended Ypsilanti schools at age 14 or not; similarly, school quality was measured in ABC by whether the participants had attended Chapel Hill schools at any time between Grades 1 and 3. The CPC study measured school quality by a dichotomous variable indicating whether a participant had attended a magnet school at any time between Grades 4 and 8 or if they had attended a school in which 40% or more of the student body were above grade level in reading in Grade 5.

Data Analysis

We used two measures of mediation to assess the contribution of the hypotheses. The difference-in-difference or percent reduction metric describes the proportion of the main effect that is explained by one or more mediators (Mackinnon, 2008). We report the percentage reduction in the main effect associated with each hypothesis separately and with different hypotheses combined. The second measure of mediation is goodness-of-fit of the structural model

Table 19.4. *Main effects of preschool on educational attainment at age 21 controlling for gender, mother's education, and father at home*

	Years of education Mean (S.D.)	Main effects
Perry Preschool		.535 ($p = .049$)
Preschool	11.68 (1.44)	
No-Preschool	11.15 (1.58)	
Abecedarian Project		.567 ($p = .060$)
Preschool	12.22 (1.54)	
No-Preschool	11.65 (1.40)	
Child-Parent Center		.401 ($p = .000$)
Preschool	11.27 (1.75)	
No-Preschool	10.87 (1.90)	

Note: Perry Preschool N = 123; Abecedarian Project N = 103; Child-Parent Center N = 1,296.

estimated in LISREL using full-information maximum likelihood (Jöreskog & Sörbom, 1996a). The models are estimated as a series of nested specifications of direct and indirect effects from those with the fewest parameters (each hypothesis separately) to the greatest number of parameters (all five hypotheses included). Improvement in fit from model to model is indexed by the change in the chi-square value. Goodness-of-fit statistics include chi-square, chi-square change, root mean square error of approximation (RMSEA), root mean square residual (RMR), and the adjusted goodness-of-fit index (AGFI). Based on these indicators, we identified and compared the most interpretable and best-fitting model for each study. We then estimated the standardized indirect effect of preschool participation on years of education from this model. It indicates the extent to which the influence of preschool is mediated by the intervening variables representing the five hypotheses of intervention effects.

RESULTS

Main Effects

The main effects of preschool on educational attainment at age 21 controlling for gender, mother's education, and father present in the home are shown in Table 19.4. These main effects are significant for each of the studies ($p < .10$). The mean number of years of education completed for each of the preschool

Table 19.5. *Percentage reductions in main effect of preschool participation associated with hypothesized mediators for years of education at age 21 (controlling for gender, mother's education, and father at home)*

	Perry Preschool % Reduction	Abecedarian % Reduction	Child-Parent Centers % Reduction
Main effect of preschool	.535	.567	.401
Hypotheses one by one			
Cognitive advantage	77.94%	87.30%	40.15%
Social adjustment	35.51%	46.38%	38.15%
Motivational advantage	32.34%	47.80%	28.69%
Family support	12.20%	24.16%	30.73%
School support	37.01%	1.41%	46.63%
Cumulative models			
Child behavior model Cognitive + Social adjustment + Motivation	77.94%	100.00%	38.15%
Child behavior model + Family support	62.99%	100.00%	46.13%
All 5 hypotheses including School support	57.94%	100.00%	60.34%

groups compared to each of the control groups and standard deviations are also presented in Table 19.4. Across the studies, preschool participation was associated with about a half of a year increase in years of completed education. Effect sizes in standard deviations were 0.35, 0.38, and 0.22, respectively, for Perry, Abecedarian, and CPC programs.

Correlations

For each study, we calculated three sets of correlations: pairwise Pearson correlations, pairwise polychoric correlations, and polychoric correlations using imputed data. Data were imputed in Prelis 2.0 using multiple imputation (Jöreskog & Sörbom, 1996b). The polychoric correlations using imputed data are included in Appendix B.

Mediation Findings

To determine the independent contributions of the hypotheses to the main-effect findings, we first examined the hypotheses one by one. This enabled an assessment of the hypotheses alone without potential confounding or correlation with other hypotheses. For this analysis, we included all indicators of each hypothesis in a hierarchical model after entering program participation and the covariates. As shown in the first section of Table 19.5, the hypotheses accounted for sizable proportions of the estimated main effects across studies. The lone exception was the school-support hypothesis of ABC, which accounted for less than 2% of the effect on years of education. For PPP and ABC, the cognitive-advantage hypothesis accounted for close to 80% of the program impact on educational attainment. For CPC, the school-support hypothesis and cognitive-advantage hypothesis were about equal in accounting for between 40% and 50% of the impact on educational attainment.

In the cumulative models, indicators of more than one hypothesis were assessed simultaneously. For CPC, indicators of all five hypotheses accounted for 60% of the main effect on educational attainment. The school-support hypothesis, for example, uniquely contributed 14% to the explanation of the main-effect relation above and beyond the other four hypotheses.

For PPP and ABC, the model that included three of the hypotheses accounted for the largest share of the main effect (from 70% to 100%), at least in regard to direct effects from the mediator to the outcome and not through other mediators. The addition of the family-support and school-support hypotheses added no unique variance to the main-effect relation above and beyond the child behavior model that included cognitive, social, and motivation measures. The reduction in the percentage of the main effect accounted for by mediators should be interpreted cautiously because it may include random fluctuations from model to model and collinearity among mediators.

Structural Modeling

The percentage-reduction approach estimates only the contribution of the mediator directly on the outcome; it does not assess indirect effects. Based on the sequence of variables displayed in Figure 19.1, we estimated structural models in LISREL for each study and compared model fit and interpretability of the estimates (Jöreskog & Sörbom, 1996a). Figures 19.2–19.4 show the structural path analyses for PPP, ABC, and CPC, respectively. These findings are based on the best-fitting model that included all five hypotheses (final model in Appendix C). Standardized coefficients that are significant at the .05 level are shown (dashed line shows $p < .10$).

In preliminary steps, we found the following results. Model fit for each of the studies was poor when only one or two hypotheses were assessed (see Appendix C). As hypotheses were added and hypothesized paths estimated, model fit improved dramatically. In almost all cases, model fit for each of the studies was best when all five hypotheses were included. The one exception was for the school-support indicator of ABC. Enrollment in Chapel Hill versus other public schools was dropped after model fit was consistently poor. This was primarily due to its lack of contribution to the model. For PPP, enrollment in Ypsilanti schools also did not contribute to the model and was dropped in favor of the lone mobility variable.

The standardized indirect effects on years of education, which measures the total influence of preschool through the mediating variables, were significant

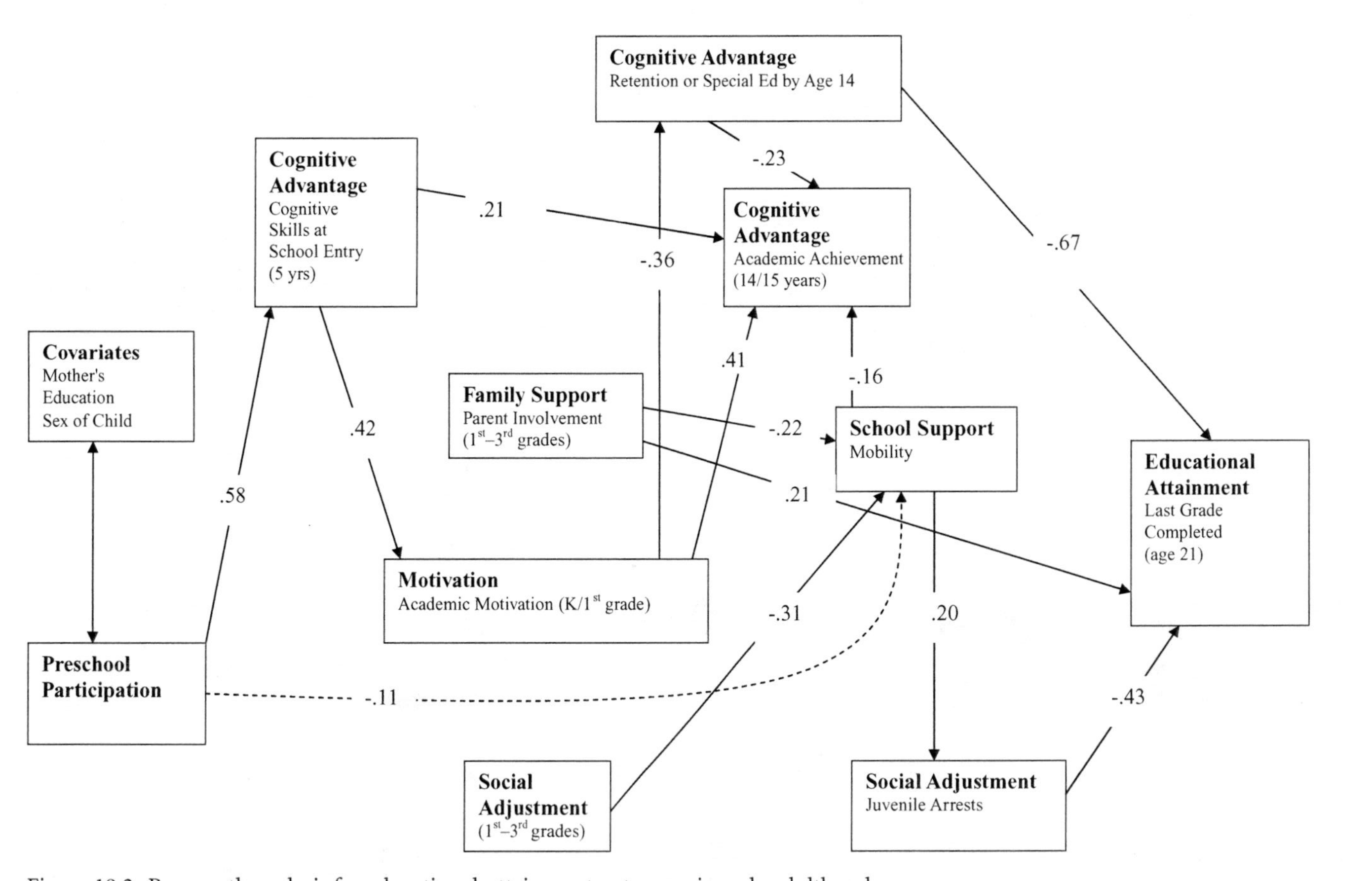

Figure 19.2. Perry path analysis for educational-attainment outcomes in early adulthood.
Note: Coefficients are standardized, significant at the .05 level, and are from the best-fitting model of all five hypotheses. Dashed line is significant at $p < .10$.

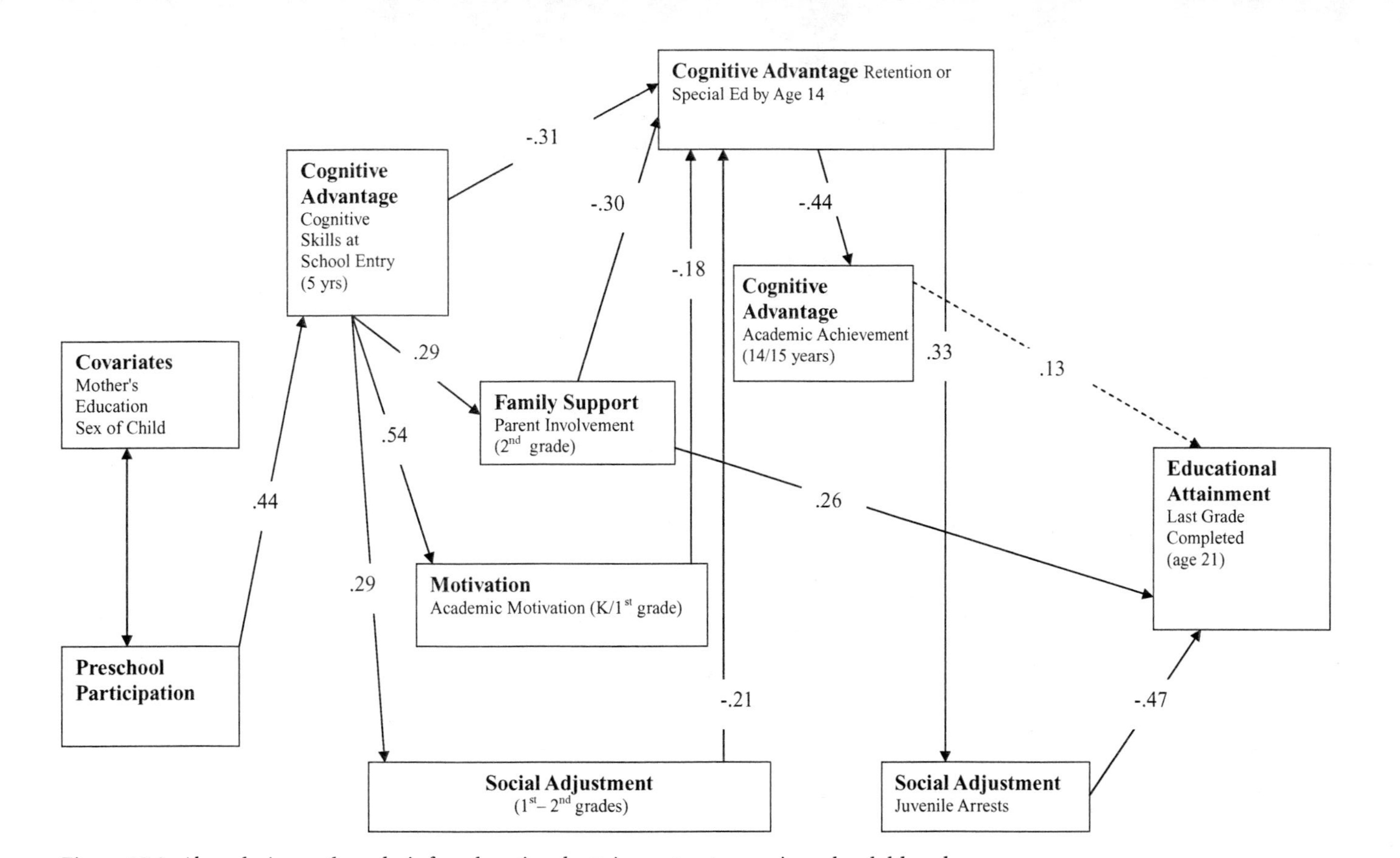

Figure 19.3. Abecedarian path analysis for educational-attainment outcomes in early adulthood.
Note: Coefficients are standardized, significant at the .05 level, and are from the best-fitting model of all five hypotheses. Dashed line is significant at $p < .10$.

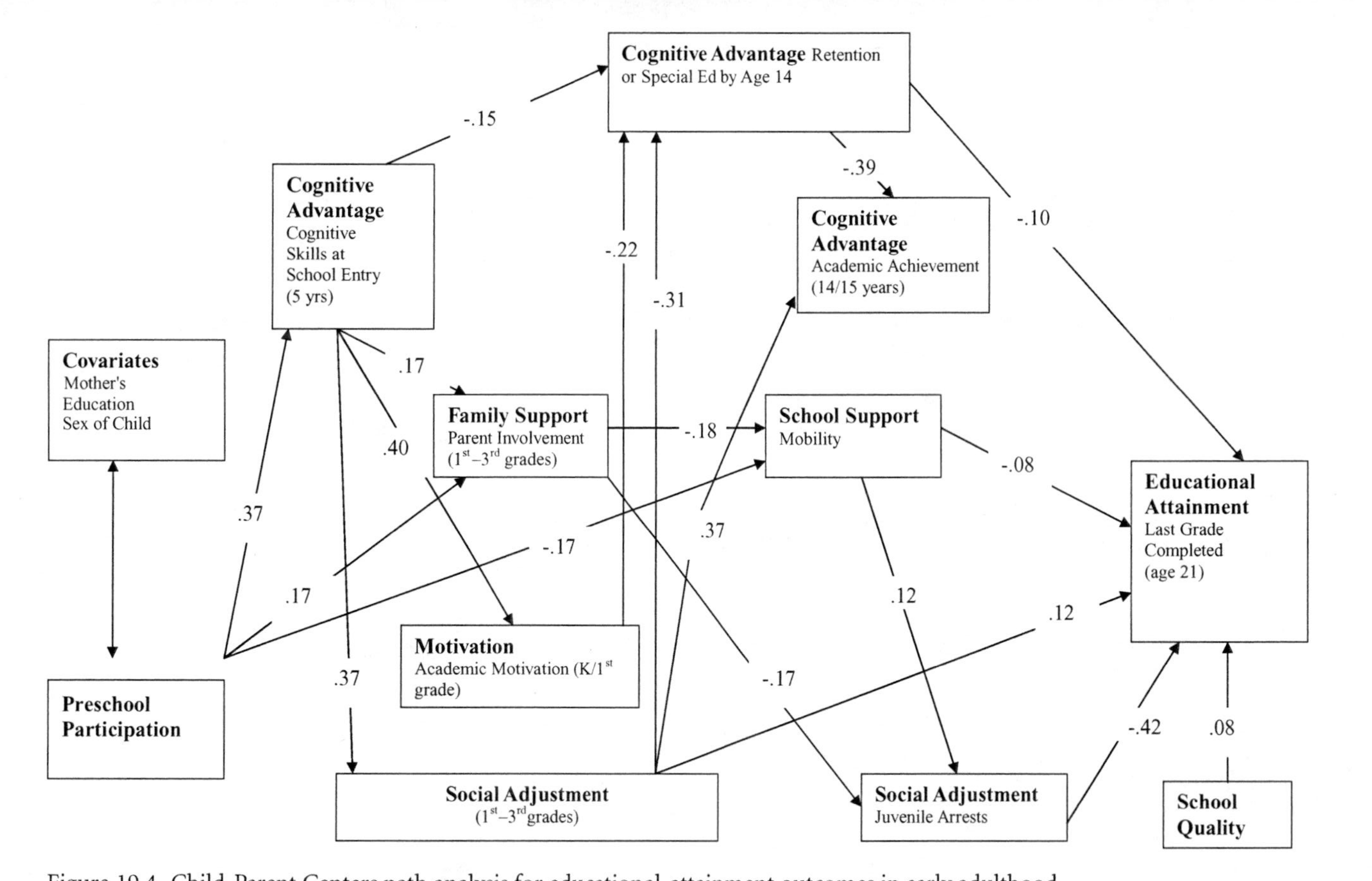

Figure 19.4. Child-Parent Centers path analysis for educational-attainment outcomes in early adulthood.
Note: The following paths are not listed here but are listed in Figure 19.5: Preschool to School Quality (.16), Cognitive 5 years to School Quality (.32), Motivation to School Quality (.11), Parent Involvement to School Quality (.18), School Quality to Arrests (−.14), and School Quality to Academic Achievement age 14 (.23). Coefficients are standardized, significant at the .05 level, and are from the best-fitting model of all five hypotheses.

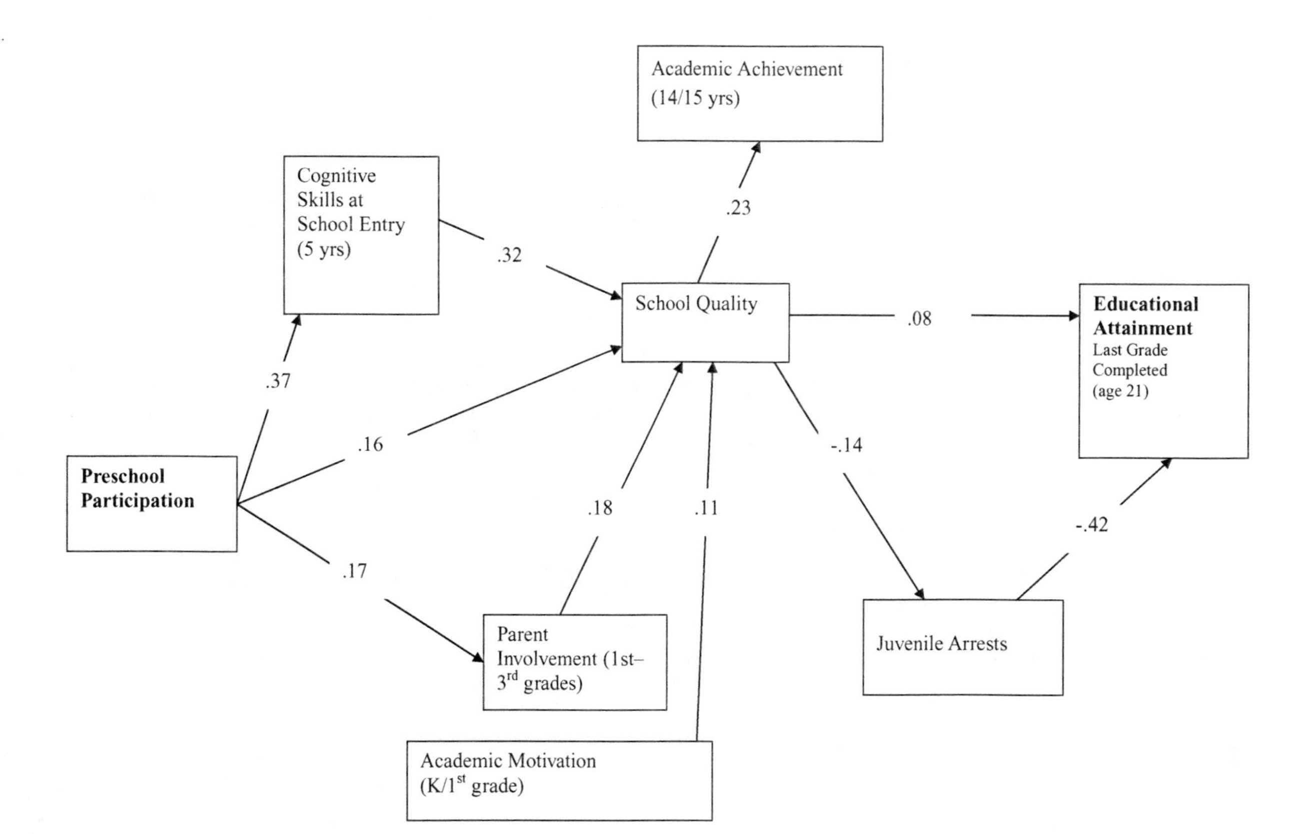

Figure 19.5. Child-Parent Centers path analysis for school quality predicting to educational attainment in early adulthood.

and similar across the studies (0.126 for PPP, 0.144 for CPC, and 0.102 for ABC). This finding indicates that the intervening variables transmitted a relatively large share of the effect of preschool to educational attainment.

A key difference between the paths of influence in CPC versus the other two studies was the greater role of measured school quality in CPC (see Fig. 19.5). Measured as enrollment in magnet schools or in relatively high-performing schools, school quality was a direct outcome of CPC preschool and directly predicted years of education even after controlling for early and later cognitive skills. Age-5 cognitive skills, parental involvement, and academic motivation also predicted school quality directly. School quality also affected years of education through negatively influencing juvenile arrest (school quality to juvenile arrest path = −0.14 and juvenile arrest to educational attainment path = −0.42).

Initiating Paths of Influence

Of particular relevance for program design and modification is the identification of the initial effects of participation. They denote the early mediators leading to longer term effects on educational attainment. As shown in Figure 19.6, each program substantially affected cognitive skills at age 5 as measured by standardized tests. Impacts on motivation, as measured by teacher ratings at ages 6–7, were smaller but were consistent in magnitude across the three programs. Only PPP and CPC showed evidence of positive effects on social adjustment as measured by teacher ratings in elementary school, although neither coefficient was statistically reliable. Only CPC preschool was found to be significantly and meaningfully associated with parental involvement in school measured by teacher ratings. This finding is not surprising given the comprehensive family services in the program. Teacher ratings of parental involvement in PPP and parent ratings of home support in ABC were not affected by program participation. These findings show the strong contribution of cognitive skills in the immediate effects of intervention.

Common Paths

As shown in Figure 19.7, five paths (shown in thicker arrows) were consistently significant and of relatively large size across all three studies. The first was the immediate effect of preschool on cognitive skills at age 5. The standardized coefficients for CPC, ABC, and PPP were 0.37, 0.44, and 0.58, respectively. Two other paths also involved early cognitive skills: cognitive advantage to parental involvement (0.17, 0.29, 0.28) and cognitive advantage to academic motivation (0.40, 0.54, 0.47). These findings indicate that the short-term effects of intervention on social and emotional development are through cognitive skills.

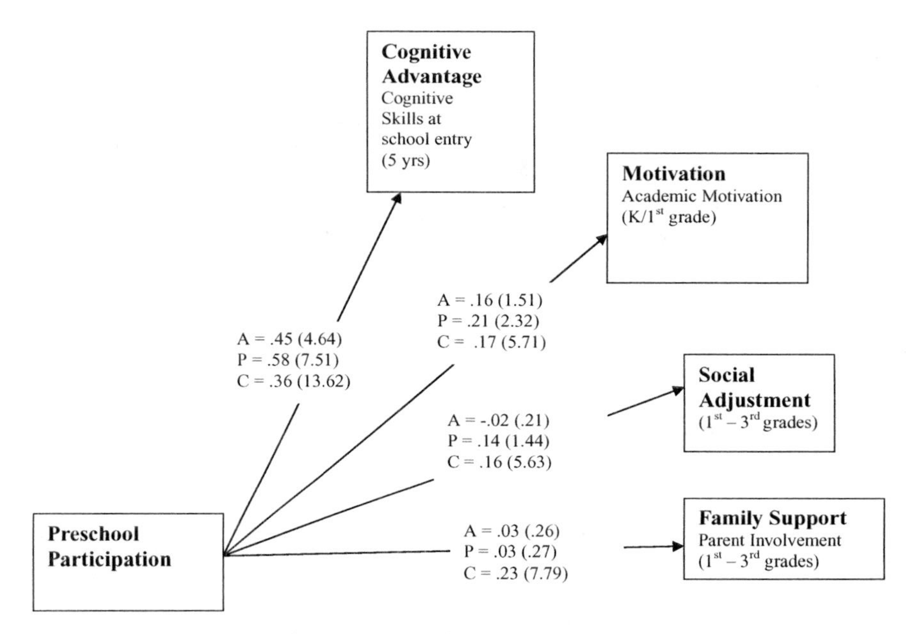

Figure 19.6. Path analysis for initial paths from preschool participation to hypothesized mediators. *Note:* A = ABC, P = Perry, C = CPC. Standardized path coefficients and (t-values) from LISREL corrected for measurement error and controlling for gender and mother's education.

The remaining common and strong paths across studies were from motivation to retention/special education (−0.22, −0.18, and −0.35) and then retention/special education to reading achievement at age 14/15 (−.39, −0.44, −0.21). These findings indicate that the process of effects begins with the enhancement of cognitive skills but continues to later achievement and school performance through, at least in part, motivation.

Uncommon Paths

Several paths were dissimilar across all three studies or were common across only two of the three studies. These latter findings are shown by the thinner arrows in Figure 19.7. Although in all three studies juvenile arrest was negatively associated with years of education, this association was much weaker in PPP (−0.14) than in CPC (−0.42) and ABC (−0.47). As a measure of school support, mobility was predicted by teacher ratings of parental involvement in both PPP and CPC studies (−0.28 and −0.18). In a similar fashion, mobility predicted juvenile arrest (0.20 and 0.12). Mobility was not measured in ABC. As displayed in Figure 19.8, the initial cognitive advantage found in each program was most strongly transmitted to later achievement and to educational attainment in PPP and ABC, but less so for CPC.

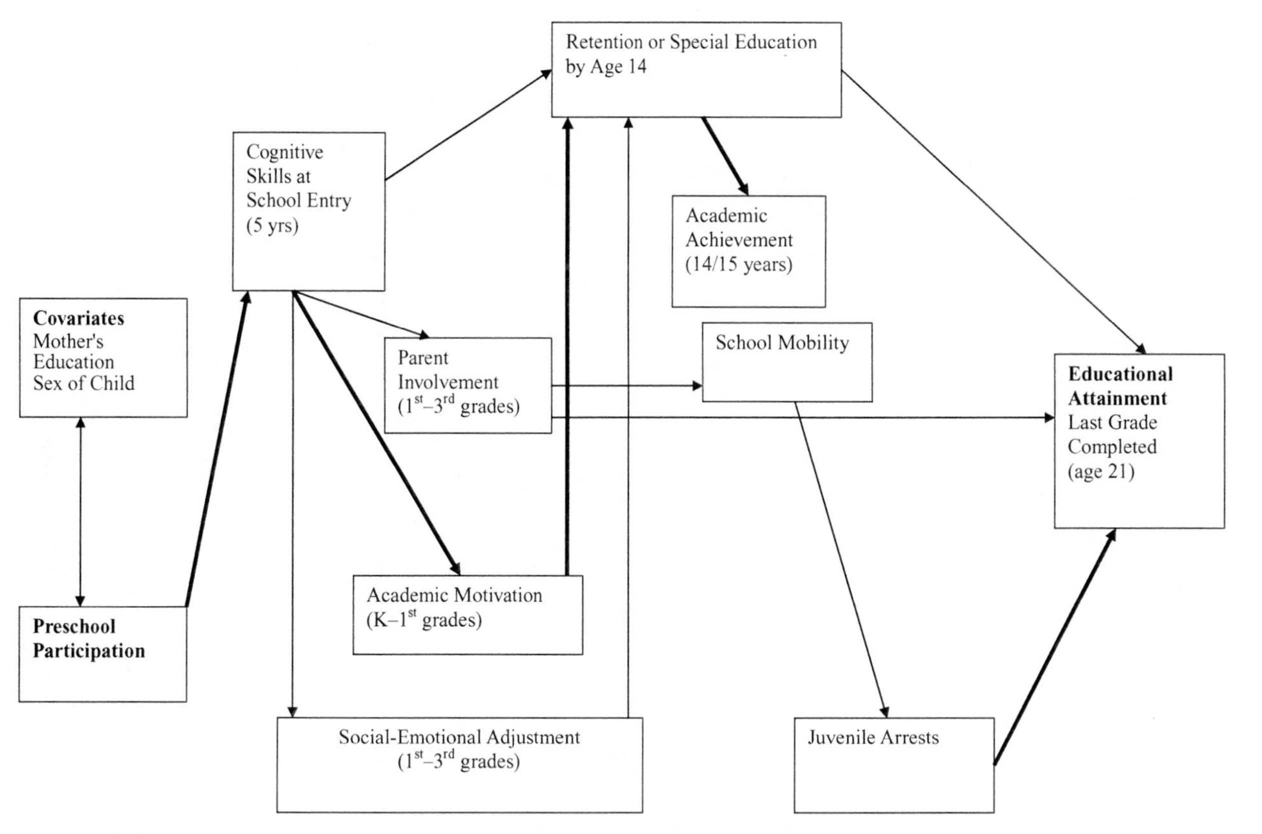

Figure 19.7. Path analysis for educational-attainment outcomes in early adulthood common paths across the three studies. *Note:* Thicker lines indicate consistency across studies; other lines indicate consistency in two studies.

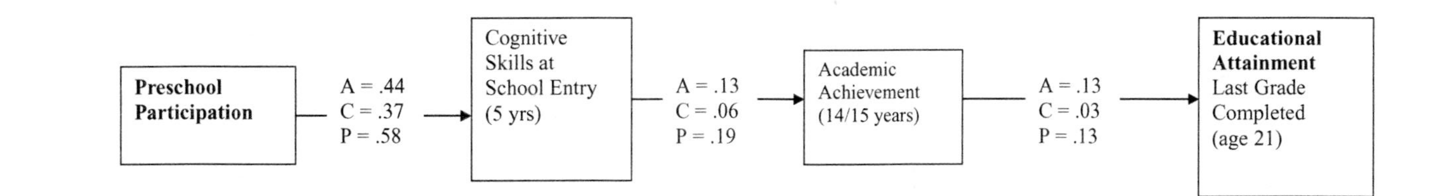

Figure 19.8. Results of path analyses for cognitive paths to educational-attainment outcomes in early adulthood.
Note: A = ABC, C = CPC, P = Perry. For simplicity, paths from cognitive skills at age 5 to retention/special education by age 15 (A = −0.31, C = −0.15, P = 0.04) and from retention/special education by age 15 to educational attainment (A not estimated–addition of path did not add to model fit; C = −0.10, P = −0.67) are not shown.

DISCUSSION

The study findings should be interpreted in the context of three important limitations. First, common measures across studies for the school-support hypothesis were not available. Although school mobility and quality were assessed in the CPC study, direct measures of school quality were not available in the Perry and Abecedarian studies. In addition, as a measure of discontinuity of schooling, the number of school moves was not available in the Abecedarian study. In the percentage-reduction approach to mediation, we included enrollment in Ypsilanti and Chapel Hill schools as proxy measures of school support, but more precise measures are needed to fully assess school quality. For the LISREL models, the school-enrollment measures of Perry and Abecedarian were not included because they worsened model fit and created substantial instability in parameter estimates. Consequently, the contributions of school support to the long-term effects of intervention could not be assessed well across studies.

Second, the measurement of social adjustment and of motivation was not well distinguished across studies. Because the Abecedarian study included only teacher ratings of child adjustment in the early grades, we used teacher ratings from kindergarten to third grade to assess motivation and social adjustment. Although we included measurement errors for these indicators in the structural models and estimated across-equation correlations among the disturbances involving these constructs, it is possible that this measurement approach introduced construct confounding that made it difficult to assess the independent contributions of the teacher-rated measures. Moreover, we detected collinearity in some of the estimated models that produced instability in the regression coefficients. The use of self-reports of motivation would help improve the construct distinction among the social adjustment and motivation measures.

Finally, the relatively small sample sizes of the Perry and Abecedarian studies reduced the robustness and stability of estimates and contributed to relatively poor model fit on some of the fit statistics. Although the sample size was large for the Chicago study, identification of the common mechanisms leading to educational attainment – the major goal of the study – is more difficult. Within-study comparisons of model fit, stability, and parsimony deserve further testing because model interpretability may increase as the number of parameter estimates is reduced.

Contributions of Findings to Understanding the Long-Term Effects of Intervention

The study makes three contributions to knowledge on the effects of early childhood programs. First, the findings support the value of the five-hypothesis model of long-term effects. Although it is the most comprehensive perspective for understanding long-term effects, the model had not been previously tested in the Perry or Abecedarian projects. Not only did most of the hypotheses contribute to the explanation of main effects in the percentage-reduction approach but also the fit of the LISREL models was good only when indicators of all five hypotheses were included. This fit also is reinforced by the significant and substantial indirect effects of preschool found across the three studies. Given the substantial differences among the programs in services, context, and time period, these findings are encouraging for the applicability of the model to other programs. For example, the Perry and CPC programs were prekindergarten programs that implemented different curriculum models. The Abecedarian program provided year-round full-time educational day care for 5 years. The programs also provided different family services. Whereas Perry provided weekly home visits, CPC emphasized school-family involvement in the centers. Abecedarian, alternatively, had no parent component but did include well-baby care services. Despite these differences, the five-hypothesis model provides a framework for documenting the processes of effects of early childhood programs.

Second, paths of influence were complex and involved linkages among different intervening variables. Findings in each of the studies indicated that paths of influence were a chain of links rather than the result of a single mediator. For example, whereas cognitive skills was the initiating path of influence across the three studies, its influence was transmitted by other intervening influences, which, depending on the study, included motivation, social adjustment, remedial education, and school quality. The pathways involving motivation, parental involvement, and social adjustment had similar complex processes. Contrast these patterns of effects with those explained by a sole mediator, such as cognitive skills at school entry. Although the enhancement of cognitive skills is the primary initiating influence of preschool, these skills are dependent on later experiences in contributing to educational attainment at age 21.

Third, the five-hypothesis model can serve as a framework for examining a range of adult outcomes. Although the three programs tested in this study have a direct impact on educational attainment, other outcomes warrant investigation, especially those that are associated with educational attainment. These include economic well-being, health status and behavior, and social behavior. The extent to which the measures of the five hypotheses influence these outcomes when measured later in adulthood will provide key information about the generalizability of the model and mechanisms that affect more general well-being.

Implications

Our study findings have two major implications for improving preschool programs and practices. First, they strengthen confidence in the decision to prioritize investments in early education. Given the general consistency and relative strength of model fit, confidence that high-quality preschool programs promote youth and adult well-being is substantially increased. The impact theories of CPC, Perry, and ABC, which have been empirically corroborated, are that early enrichment of language and social interaction through center-based education strengthens school success, leading to greater educational attainment. One implication is that increasing access to preschool and other early-intervention programs deserves higher priority. Although states have substantially increased investments in preschool programs, only 22% of 4-year-olds across the nation attend state-funded programs (Barnett, Hustedt, Friedman, Stevenson Boyd, & Ainsworth, 2008). Moreover, only 38 states have state-financed programs. The amount of evidence on the positive and enduring effects of high-quality preschool programs is large. There is not only a critical mass of evidence from long-term cost-benefit analyses (Karoly et al., 2005) but also increasing evidence that large-scale programs can improve school readiness and the transition to elementary school.

Second, findings provide key information for strengthening programs and sustaining their effects. Given the importance of entering kindergarten with good literacy skills, improving the quality of preschool programs, and increasing their length and intensity would be expected to strengthen the paths leading to greater educational well-being. As programs located in public schools, for example, Perry and CPC teachers have at least bachelor's degrees with certification in early childhood. Participation begins at age 3, and kindergarten is on-site. The programs were high in quality and structured for a diverse set of learning activities. These features are key to their demonstrated benefits. Likewise, greater opportunities for parental involvement in early interventions also would be expected to strengthen the contribution of the family support hypothesis. As found in CPC specifically, strengthening the quality of elementary schools may also promote the transmission of long-term effects. Structural changes may include reduced class size (Finn, Gerber, Achilles, & Boyd-Zaharias, 2001; Krueger, 2003), preschool to Grade 3 programs that provide comprehensive instructional and family-support services (Reynolds & Temple, 1998), and whole-school reforms such as Schools of the 21st Century (Zigler & Styfco, 1993) and the School Development Program (Comer, Ben-Avie, Haynes, & Joyner, 1999).

In conclusion, our study strengthens support for the generalizability of mechanisms leading from preschool to educational attainment. Whereas the cognitive-advantage hypothesis was the primary initiator of the effects of intervention leading to long-term change, the social-adjustment hypothesis and others contributed in complex ways to the explanation of long-term effects. The extent to which the five-hypothesis model can be used to account for a range of long-term effects into adulthood is an important focus of future research that will continue to inform the development and improvement of early education programs.

SUMMARY

Although there is now a critical mass of evidence in support of long-term effects of high-quality preschool programs, the causal mechanisms that account for these effects are not well understood. This study examined paths of effects from preschool participation to years of education for three program studies: the Chicago Child-Parent Centers, HighScope Perry Preschool, and the Carolina Abecedarian Project. It examined five hypothesized paths: cognitive advantage, family support, social adjustment, motivational advantage, and school support. Findings indicated that five paths of influence from preschool to years of education were consistently significant and of relatively large size across all three studies: (a) the immediate effect of preschool on cognitive skills at age 5, (b) early cognitive skills to parental involvement, (c) early cognitive skills to academic motivation, (d) motivation to retention/special education, and (e) retention/special education to reading achievement at age 14/15. These findings indicate that the process of effects begins with the enhancement of cognitive skills but continues to later achievement and school performance through, at least in part, motivation. Study findings support the value of the five-hypothesis model of long-term program effects. Given the substantial differences among the programs in services, context, and time period, these findings are encouraging for the applicability of the model to other programs.

REFERENCES

Barnett, W. S., Hustedt, J. T., Friedman, A. H., Stevenson Boyd, J., & Ainsworth, P. (2008). *The state of preschool 2007: State preschool yearbook.* New Brunswick, NJ: National Institute of Early Education Research.

Berrueta-Clement, J., Schweinhart, L., Barnett, W. S., Epstein, A., & Weikart, D. (1984). *Changed lives: The effects of the Perry Preschool Program on youths through age* 19. Ypsilanti, MI: High/Scope Press.

Caldwell, B. M., & Bradley, R. H. (1984). *HOME observation for measurement of the environment* (rev. ed.). Little Rock: Center for Child Development and Education, University of Arkansas at Little Rock.

Campbell, F. A., Pungello, E. P., Miller-Johnson, S., Burchinal, M., & Ramey, C. T. (2001). The development of cognitive and academic abilities: Growth curves from an early childhood educational experiment. *Developmental Psychology, 37*(2), 231–242.

Campbell, F. A., & Ramey, C. T. (1995). Cognitive and school outcomes for high-risk African American students at middle adolescence: Positive effects of early intervention. *American Educational Research Journal, 32*, 743–772.

Campbell, F. A., Ramey, C. T., Pungello, E., Sparling, J., & Miller-Johnson, S. (2002). Early childhood education: Young adult outcomes from the Abecedarian Project. *Applied Developmental Science, 6*, 42–57.

Chicago Longitudinal Study. (1999). *Chicago Longitudinal Study: User's guide* (Vol. 6). Madison: Waisman Center, University of Wisconsin.

Comer, J. P., Ben-Avie, M., Haynes, N. M., & Joyner, E. T. (Eds.). (1999). *Child by child: The Comer process for change in education.* New York: Teachers College Press.

Consortium for Longitudinal Studies. (1983). *As the twig is bent... lasting effects of preschool programs.* Hillsdale, NJ: Erlbaum.

Currie, J., & Thomas, D. (2000). School quality and the longer-term effects of Head Start. *Journal of Human Resources, 35*(4), 755–774.

Finn, J. D., Gerber, S. B., Achilles, C. M., & Boyd-Zaharias, J. (2001). The enduring effects of small classes. *Teachers College Record, 103*(2), 145–183.

Garces, E., Thomas, D., & Currie, J. (2002). Longer term effects of Head Start. *American Economic Review, 92*(4), 999–1012.

Heckman, J. (2000). Policies to foster human capital. *Research in Economics, 54,* 3–56.

Hieronymus, A. N., Lindquist, E. F., & Hoover, H. D. (1982). *Iowa Tests of Basic Skills: Manual for school administrators.* Chicago: Riverside.

Jöreskog, K., & Sörbom, D. (1996a). *LISREL 8: User's reference guide.* Chicago: Scientific Software.

Jöreskog, K., & Sörbom, D. (1996b). *PRELIS 2: User's reference guide (3rd ed.).* Chicago: Scientific Software.

Karoly, L. A. (2001). Reducing poverty through human capital investments. In S. H. Danziger & R. H. Haveman (Eds.), *Understanding poverty (314–356).* New York: Russell Sage.

Karoly, L. A., Cannon, J. S., & Kilburn, M. R. (2005). *Early childhood interventions: Proven results, future promise.* Santa Monica, CA: RAND.

Krueger, A. B. (2003). Economic considerations and class size. *Economic Journal, 113,* F34–F63.

MacKinnon, D. P. (2008). *Introduction to statistical mediation analysis.* New York: Lawrence Erlbaum.

McLaughlin, A. E., Campbell, F. C., Pungello, E. P., & Skinner, M. (2007). Depressive symptoms in young adults: The influences of the early home environment and early educational childcare. *Child Development, 78,* 746–756.

Oden, S., Schweinhart, L., Weikart, D., Marcus, S., & Xie, Y. (2000). *Into adulthood: A study of the effects of Head Start.* Ypsilanti, MI: HighScope.

Ou, S. (2003). *The effects of an early childhood intervention on educational attainment.* Unpublished doctoral dissertation, University of Wisconsin–Madison.

Ou, S., & Reynolds, A. J. (2004). Preschool education and school completion. In R. E. Tremblay, R. G. Barr, & R. D. Peters (Eds.), *Encyclopedia on early childhood development* (pp. 1–10). Montreal: Centre for Excellence in Early Childhood Development. Retrieved from http://www.child-encyclopedia.com.

Ramey, C. T., Campbell, F. A., & Blair, C. (1998). Enhancing the life course for high-risk children: Results from the Abecedarian Project. In J. Crane (Ed.), *Social programs that work* (pp. 163–183). New York: Russell Sage.

Ramey, C. T., Campbell, F. A., Burchinal, M., Skinner, M. L., Gardner, D. M., & Ramey, S. L. (2000). Persistent effects of early intervention on high-risk children and their mothers. *Applied Developmental Science, 1,* 2–14.

Reynolds, A. J. (1998). Confirmatory program evaluation: A method for strengthening causal inference. *American Journal of Evaluation, 19,* 203–221.

Reynolds, A. J. (2000). *Success in early intervention: The Chicago Child-Parent Centers.* Lincoln: University of Nebraska Press.

Reynolds, A. J. (2005). Confirmatory program evaluation: Applications to early childhood intervention. *Teachers College Record, 107,* 2401–2425.

Reynolds, A. J., Mavrogenes, N. A., Bezruczko, N., & Hagemann, M. (1996). Cognitive and family-support mediators of preschool effectiveness: A confirmatory analysis. *Child Development, 67,* 1119–1140.

Reynolds, A. J., Ou, S., & Topitzes, J. (2004). Paths of effects of early childhood intervention on educational attainment and juvenile arrest: A confirmatory analysis of the Chicago Child-Parent Centers. *Child Development, 75*, 1299–1328.

Reynolds, A. J., & Temple, J. A. (1998). Extended early childhood intervention and school achievement: Age 13 findings from the Chicago Longitudinal Study. *Child Development, 69*, 231–246.

Reynolds, A. J., & Temple, J. A. (2008). Cost-effective early childhood development programs from preschool to third grade. *Annual Review of Clinical Psychology, 4*, 109–139.

Reynolds, A. J., Temple, J. A., Ou, S., Robertson, D. L., Mersky, J. P., Topitzes, J. W., et al. (2007). Effects of a school-based, early childhood intervention on adult health and well-being: A 19-year follow-up of low-income families. *Archives of Pediatrics and Adolescent Medicine, 161*, 730–739.

Reynolds, A. J., Temple, J. A., Robertson, D. L., & Mann, E. A. (2001). Long-term effects of an early childhood intervention on educational achievement and juvenile arrest: A 15-year follow-up of low-income children in public schools. *Journal of American Medical Association, 285*(18), 2339–2346.

Reynolds, A. J., Temple, J. A., Robertson, D. L., & Mann, E. A. (2002). Age 21 cost-benefit analysis of the Title I Chicago Child-Parent Centers. *Educational Evaluation and Policy Analysis, 24*, 267–303.

Reynolds, A. J., Wang, M. C., & Walberg, H. J. (Eds.). (2003). *Early childhood programs for a new century*. Washington, DC: CWLA Press.

Schaefer, E. S., Edgerton, M., & Aaronson, M. (1978). *Classroom Behavior Inventory, revised*. Chapel Hill: University of North Carolina.

Schweinhart, L. J., Barnes, H. V., & Weikart, D. P. (1993). *Significant benefits: The High/Scope Perry Preschool study through age 27*. Ypsilanti, MI: High/Scope Press.

Schweinhart, L. J., Montie, J., Xiang, Z., Barnett, W. S., Belfield, C. R., & Nores, M. (2005). *Lifetime effects: The HighScope Perry Preschool Study through age 40*. Ypsilanti, MI: HighScope Press.

Temple, J. A., & Reynolds, A. J. (2007). Benefits and costs of investments in preschool education: Evidence from the Child-Parent Centers and related programs. *Economics of Education Review, 26*(1), 126–144.

Terman, L. M., & Merrill, M. A. (1960). *Stanford-Binet Intelligence Scale Form L-M: Manual for the third revision*. Boston: Houghton-Mifflin.

Tiegs, E. W., & Clark, W. W. (1963). *California Achievement Tests: Complete battery* (1957 ed.). Monterey Park, CA: California Test Bureau/McGraw-Hill.

Tiegs, E. W., & Clark, W. W. (1971). *California Achievement Tests* (1970 ed.). Monterey Park, CA: California Test Bureau/McGraw-Hill.

Vinter, R. D., Sarri, R. C., Vorwaller, D. J., & Schafer, W. E. (1966). *Pupil Behavior Inventory*. Ann Arbor: University of Michigan Press.

Wechsler, D. (1967). *Wechsler Preschool and Primary Scale of Intelligence*. New York: Psychological Corporation.

Woodcock, R. W., & Johnson, M. B. (1989). *Woodcock-Johnson Psycho-Educational Battery – Revised*. Allen, TX: DLM Teaching Resources.

Zigler, E. & Styfco, S. J. (1993). *Head Start and beyond: A national plan for extended childhood intervention*. New Haven, CT: Yale University Press.

Zigler, E., Taussig, C., & Black, K. (1992). Early childhood intervention: A promising preventive for juvenile delinquency. *American Psychologist, 47*, 997–1006.

Appendix A: Comparison of Items for Motivation Measures, Kindergarten and First Grade

Perry Preschool (Public Behavior Inventory: (Academic Motivation)	Abecedarian (newly created from Classroom Behavior Inventory)	CPC-K (newly created from teacher questionnaires)	CPC-1 (newly created from teacher questionnaires)
Does not show initiative	Asks questions that show an interest in ideas (CBI-19); tries to figure things out for self before asking questions (CBI-29); wants to know more about things that are presented in class (CBI-36)	Volunteers answers	Displays confidence in approaching learning tasks; participates in group discussions
Is not alert and interested in schoolwork	Often cannot answer a question because mind has wandered (CBI-11); pays attention to what he or she is doing and is not easily distracted (CBI-33)	Concentrates on assigned activities; asks questions about work in an alert way; is inattentive	Shows interest in learning
Learning is not retained well			
Does not complete assignments	Stays with a job until it is finished, even if it is difficult (CBI-15); attends to the task to be done (CBI-40)	Finishes work	Completes work according to instructions
Is not motivated toward academic performance	Works earnestly, doesn't take it lightly (CBI-6); keeps busy for long periods of time without my attention (CBI-21); works carefully and does his or her best (CBI-23)	Is eager to learn	Came to class ready to learn
No positive concern for own education			
Hesitant to try or gives up easily	Tries to do things for self (CBI-3)	Tries hard	
Uninterested in subject matter		Gets bored easily	Reads for enjoyment
Does not show positive leadership			
	Works without asking me for help (CBI-12)	Works independently when required to do so	

Note: Items are from actual instruments. For each study, item responses were based on 5-point scales. Negatively worded items were reverse-coded so that higher scores reflected greater motivation.

Appendix B: Perry Preschool Project Correlation Table (Polychoric correlations-imputed data)

	1	2	3	4	5	6	7	8	9	10	11
1. Preschool participation	–										
2. Cognitive Advantage: Stanford-Binet 5 years	.564	–									
3. Cognitive Advantage: Reading CAT 8th grade (14 years)	.288	.459	–								
4. Either special ed or retained by age 15	−.017	−.193	−.525	–							
5. Family Support: Parent involvement 1–3 averaged	.045	.288	.278	−.306	–						
6. Social Adjustment: Socio-emotional adjustment 1–3 averaged	.130	.242	.439	−.385	.414	–					
7. Social Adjustment: Any juvenile arrest	−.202	−.141	−.119	−.266	−.141	.043	–				
8. Motivation: PBI academic motivation K/1 averaged	.239	.448	.657	−.470	.418	.529	−.082	–			
9. # of different schools through 8th grade	−.077	.037	−.172	.199	−.195	−.205	.160	.025	–		
10. Ypsilanti vs. non-Ypsilanti School at 14 yrs	.397	.084	.036	−.497	−.098	−.101	.070	−.154	.007	–	
11. Highest grade/year of education completed by age 21	.230	.314	.351	−.478	.428	.256	−.252	.307	−.199	.155	–
Means (S.D.)	.472 (.501)	88.309 (12.239)	27.967 (10.692)	.626 (.486)	4.023 (1.664)	3.546 (.737)	.203 (.404)	3.074 (.774)	1.642 (.933)	.211 (.410)	11.40 (1.54)

Abecedarian Project Correlation Table (Polychoric correlations-imputed data)

	1	2	3	4	5	6	7	8	9	10
1. Preschool participation	–									
2. Cognitive Advantage: WPPSI (60 mo.)	.369	–								
3. Cognitive Advantage: Reading Woodcock-Johnson (14 years)	.320	.472	–							
4. Either special ed or retained by age 14	−.272	−.531	−.556	–						
5. Social Adjustment: Child Behavior Index derived scale 1–2 averaged	−.053	.251	.253	−.411	–					
6. Social Adjustment: Any juvenile arrest by age 19	−.133	−.097	−.227	.427	−.138	–				
7. Family Support: Parent involvement scale derived from HOME (age 8)	.035	.230	.021	−.485	.178	−.067	–			
8. Motivation: Child Behavior Index derived scale K/1 averaged	.200	.491	.387	−.530	.270	−.315	.180	–		
9. Chapel Hill School vs. non–Chapel Hill School (1–3 grades)	.024	.200	.080	−.050	−.333	.580	.093	−.016	–	
10. Highest grade completed by age 21	.293	.331	.293	−.446	.078	−.482	.264	.319	.084	–
Means (S.D.)	.515	97.757	91.602	.592	24.471	.340	3.039	34.154	.845	11.922
	(.502)	(12.220)	(10.428)	(.494)	(2.572)	(.476)	(.685)	(3.642)	(.364)	(1.506)

Child-Parent Centers Correlation Table (Polychoric correlations-imputed data)

	1	2	3	4	5	6	7	8	9	10	11
1. Preschool participation	–										
2. Cognitive Advantage: ITBS Cognitive Composite (Kindergarten)	.371	–									
3. Cognitive Advantage: ITBS Reading Comprehension (8th grade)	.195	.417	–								
4. Ever retained or special ed through 8th grade	−.233	−.402	−.633	–							
5. Social Adjustment: SEMAT average Grades 1–3	.183	.375	.602	−.603	–						
6. Social Adjustment: Any juvenile petition or self-report arrest by 18	−.174	−.108	−.335	.325	−.294	–					
7. Family support: Parent Involvement average Grades 1–3	.239	.251	.377	−.397	.526	−.297	–				
8. Motivation: New scale K/1 averaged, z-score	.182	.387	.503	−.564	.747	−.230	.422	–			
9. # of school moves Grades 4–8	−.239	−.177	−.229	.246	−.196	.265	−.255	−.124	–		
10. If attended magnet school (Gr 4–8) or 40% + above grade level reading (5th grade)	.320	.395	.342	−.197	.152	−.285	.249	.175	−.296	–	
11. Educational Attainment: Highest grade completed by age 21	.152	.153	.361	−.355	.348	−.483	.221	.262	−.273	.290	–
Means (S.D.)	.655 (.476)	47.440 (8.794)	145.019 (21.435)	.349 (.477)	19.108 (4.750)	.209 (.407)	2.585 (.996)	.003 (.910)	.936 (.981)	.125 (.331)	11.135 (1.814)

Appendix C: LISREL Goodness-of-Fit Statistics for Tested Pathway Models of Educational Attainment

	Perry Preschool					Abecedarian Project					Child-Parent Centers				
Model	df	χ^2	RMSEA	RMR	AGFI	df	χ^2	RMSEA	RMR	AGFI	df	χ^2	RMSEA	RMR	AGFI
Single-mediator models															
Null	41	395.58	.25	.18	.31	43	559.97	.27	.20	.32	53	2,907.53	.24	.19	.40
Cognitive	33	244.77	.19	.15	.49	35	432.39	.19	.15	.53	45	1,733.98	.17	.16	.64
Motivation	39	384.91	.24	.18	.33	41	551.31	.26	.20	.34	51	2,829.37	.23	.18	.41
Social adjustment	36	379.18	.26	.18	.27	38	534.15	.29	.19	.25	48	2,493.62	.22	.18	.45
Family support	39	374.53	.24	.18	.33	41	553.06	.27	.20	.30	51	2,784.79	.23	.18	.42
School support	39	388.35	.25	.18	.30	41	554.23	.28	.20	.28	49	2,662.08	.23	.28	.42
Cumulative mediator models															
Cognitive + Motivation + Social adjustment	26	199.06	.19	.14	.46	28	410.07	.22	.14	.42	38	1,418.69	.16	.15	.67
All 5 hypotheses together	23	241.86	.22	.13	.33	24	249.44	.23	.51	.35	32	1,177.55	.15	.13	.67
All 5 hypotheses plus cross-hypotheses paths added	14	94.92	.20	.09	.45	11	25.58	.11	.04	.76	10	52.55	.06	.01	.94

Note: RMSEA = Root mean square error of approximation; RMR = root mean square residual, AGFI = adjusted goodness-of-fit index. Null model has no specified mediators for the main effect of preschool.

APPENDIX

Question-and-Answer Sessions

PART I: PRENATAL AND INFANT PROGRAMS

Barbara Devaney, Mathematica Policy Research, "WIC Turns 35: Program Effectiveness and Future Directions" (Chapter 2)

David L. Olds, University of Colorado Health Sciences Center, "The Nurse-Family Partnership: From Trials to Practice" (Chapter 3)

Frances A. Campbell, University of North Carolina, "Carolina Abecedarian Project" (coauthor: Craig T. Ramey, Georgetown University) (Chapter 4)

Q: "Why do the nurses produce larger effects than the paraprofessionals?"

SPEAKER DAVID OLDS:

A: First of all, the families visited by paraprofessionals did not open their doors to the visitors as they did for the nurses. It goes back to this point about families having to believe that this is worthwhile for them to engage in. The result is that the nurses completed more visits than paraprofessionals did. But the differences that we see between nurse-visited families and paraprofessional families are not simply explained by the quantitative results – the number of completed home visits. It looks like on a per-visit basis, the nurses are accomplishing more as well. I think that what we're seeing is that nurses are more successful in eliciting the kinds of behavioral changes and adaptive responses that we all would like to see than paraprofessionals are. I think that goes back to their basic training and clinical competence in being able to manage the complexities that they encounter in dealing with families with multiple issues regarding health, behavior, social contexts, and so forth, that make life hard.

Q: My question is for Barbara. You indicated a range of impacts for WIC, including some impacts on health care access. Most of this seemed positive to me, but I wonder about greater utilization of emergency rooms. Is that a good thing or a bad thing?

SPEAKER BARBARA DEVANEY:

A: WIC children were much more connected to the health care system in every single way. I chose the emergency room as the result because it's one that we obviously would wish that people wouldn't be forced to use by having better preventive care. And that's what we expected to see when we started the study, but the results came across and we must have looked at probably 20 different measures of utilization of diagnosis of health care conditions, utilization of different kinds of health care, and we saw this result where children got more. Perhaps the best example is dental care. WIC children were more likely to have had a preventive dental care visit at every age. They were also more likely to have had a curative dental care visit. So they are using it for prevention, but they're also using it when they need it for treatment. And I think the question we ask is, what's happening to these poor kids who aren't getting their preventive care and also not getting treatment when they need it, which is in this case non-WIC children.

Q: This is about Abecedarian and the dosage. Do you think that it was necessary for Abecedarian to have 5 years to get the effect that you show? In the chart, there's a drop-off in the IQ difference after age 3. So maybe just the general question you could address is: Did it really require 5 years to get many of the effects that you later saw?

SPEAKER FRANCES CAMPBELL:

A: The data won't answer that question. I don't think we can prove that the first 3 years made a difference, but it may very well have. There's no other study with that long lasting of an effect on IQ. You know there's a book called *The Myth of the First Three Years,* and [the author] believes very strongly that the first 3 years of treatment weren't necessary. But I still have an open mind about that.

Q: This is a follow-up to [a previous] question. I'm going to direct it to David. Now that there's all this evidence about the positive effects of home intervention and early programs like this, everybody is jumping on board. Here's my big worry, and I'll be interested in your reaction to this. You have been very careful to make sure when people implement the Nurse-Family Partnership program [that] they do so in the way you originally designed the program. I now worry that these programs are being watered down. Not just yours, but other programs that are being implemented because a lot of communities don't have the money to do it right. I worry if it's not done right, we're going to end up where people start saying, "Well, these programs are like a lot of other programs; they really don't work." Do you have any ideas about how we can assure quality control when we implement these programs across cities and states?

SPEAKER DAVID OLDS:

A: I think that as a field, we need to be really quite circumspect about what's working and what's not. I think we need to ground policy and practice on the basis of replicated randomized controlled trials. This is the standard that the FDA [Food and Drug Administration] requires, and it's the standard the Surgeon General employed in recommending violence-prevention programs. I think that the early intervention field needs to embrace this standard as well. We need to develop interventions that truly show promise, test them, replicate them, and use that as a foundation for policy and practice. Then we need to find ways of creating the infrastructure that's needed to preserve the programmatic integrity of those programs found to work as they get rolled out in the communities.

Q: The problem is children take a long time to grow up. With randomized clinical trials waiting for long-term outcomes, people are going to want to do things earlier. The question I have is, can we mine or have we mined the randomized clinical trials we've already done to identify the short-term changes that are the best predictors of the long-term benefits to use as scientific evidentiary road maps to know when we have a program that works? If we have, is it in the child-behavior outcomes or is it in the parent-behavior outcomes where we find our best predictors?

SPEAKER DAVID OLDS:

A: I don't think we need to wait 15 or 20 years to answer the question about whether [programs are] working or not. I agree with you about that point. We do have enough information about what the relationship between early functioning and later functioning is that will give us some confidence that if we see changes in early risk and protective factors that we'll know that we're on the right track. But we have to look at those early indicators in a rigorous way. Among the things I would want to see would be things like changes in language functioning at the end of the second year of life. Early indicators of child functioning are more important in my view than things like parents' report of their feelings of stress or even their self-reports of parenting because I think those are susceptible to all kinds of equivocal interpretations.

SPEAKER FRANCES CAMPBELL:

A: There are some very early things that we saw, like the changes in IRB ratings where the children appeared to be more engaged with people and their environments. That was very early in life; that was before they were 2. There is a lot of evidence about language development before the age of 2, and if you look way down the road, our effect on intellectual functioning was probably mostly because of our effect on language development. I don't think that we have shown that the first 3 years didn't matter.

SPEAKER BARBARA DEVANEY:

A: I would argue that, on the WIC side, there may have been too much emphasis on some longer term outcomes and not enough emphasis on more proximal impacts affecting the growth and development of children. There are a lot of influences on that. You can see if WIC has effects on whether you're getting the preventive care that you need, the medical care, whether you're eating good foods, etc. I think that goes a long way in itself of showing evidence of program effectiveness. I actually think the short-term effects are the more important ones to be looking at now.

PART I: PRENATAL AND INFANT PROGRAMS

Helen H. Raikes, University of Nebraska, "Early Head Start Impacts at Age 3 and a Description of the Age 5 Follow-Up Study" (coauthors: Rachel Chazan-Cohen, U.S. Department of Health & Human Services; John M. Love, Mathematica Policy Research; and Jeanne Brooks-Gunn, Columbia University) (Chapter 5)

Q: Helen, I was really interested by your findings about the highest risk families and wanted to ask a question – but first share a quick observation that goes back to the question to David [Olds] about what home-visiting programs ought to look like. As we're listening today, we're hearing about interventions that vary somewhat in their likely power or their likely effectiveness. We are looking at the effects of those different-powered interventions across somewhat similar groups of kids. What I'm wondering about is whether there are thresholds that we need to be noticing regarding the sort of intensity of intervention given a particular age of kid, given a particular group or condition of a population that would have public-policy implications. For instance, under what conditions would a home-visiting program need a certain kind of intensity? So let me jump back to the highest risk families that you talked about, Helen. It was interesting to me that there were some good outcomes – as I remember, higher receptive vocabulary scores. Is that right?

SPEAKER HELEN RAIKES:

A: At age 5 we had some positive impacts, sleeper effects, but not at age 3.

Q: And then there are more IEPs [individualized education programs]. And we could look at more IEPs as maybe a bad outcome. There are more kids showing up in special education. But we might imagine that it's actually a good outcome, sort of like the ER visits that we heard about earlier, that kids are in some circumstance where they're being caught by a system that might be prepared to serve them. I'm very curious about how we think about the different programs that were embedded in Early Head Start and how they might vary in terms of intensity; how we look at different home-visiting models and how they might vary in terms of intensity; and how we then turn to thinking about how the relationship between those differences in intensity and the thresholds of effectiveness that we might see in different subgroups.

SPEAKER HELEN RAIKES:

A: One of the wishes that we have in Early Head Start is we can prompt more discussion about this particularly high-risk group. As you were saying, different intervention studies get different kinds of effects for their highest risk group. One study will report we had the greatest impacts on children who had the greatest risk, and another such as ours reported that we did not have an impact on that group. I will suggest to you that there are probably big differences in who we're calling highest risk families. Within Early Head Start, of course, we're starting with a poverty population, and so these are some of the highest of the highest risk that we're putting in our high-risk group. Does that mean somebody else doesn't have them in their sample? I don't know. At the end of age 3, before we had these age 5 findings, we went back to the program and said, this program needs to be more intense for this group of families as, clearly, the program isn't hitting the mark for them yet and the research was designed to help the program improve. That led to a number of new studies – a study of mental health interventions, for example. It led to a study for children who are also in the child welfare system. Those results are yet to come out. The general statement was that Early Head Start as it was first conceived was not intensive enough to meet the needs of those families – except for perhaps changing the trajectories that pertain to those living in very high-risk environments that we didn't measure as well at age 3 as we did at age 5. I can't help but think that Early Head Start was beginning to have an impact at age 3 on whether there was domestic violence in the home, child abuse, and so forth. Hard to measure, and maybe we wouldn't have even seen an effect if we measured it well, but we did see it at age 5, which perhaps rendered families then able to realize the benefits that they were then able to get from Head Start when they got there. I want to add one other thing. We know that the group of families that are most likely to be intermittently served are the most likely to drop out of programs, and so I would suggest to you we know the least about them of all the groups and need to know perhaps the most.

PART II: PRESCHOOL EDUCATION

Ronna Cook, Westat, "Interim Findings of the Head Start Impact Study"

Lawrence J. Schweinhart, HighScope Educational Research Foundation, "How to Take the HighScope Perry Preschool to Scale" (Chapter 7)

Arthur J. Reynolds, University of Minnesota, "Impacts and Implications of the Child-Parent Center Preschool Program" (coauthors: Judy A. Temple and Suh-Ruu Ou, University of Minnesota) (Chapter 8)

Q: Do you have any explanation regarding the finding for Hispanic 3-year-olds that the English-speaking Hispanic 3-year-olds seemed to benefit from Head Start more than the Spanish-speaking 3-year-olds?

SPEAKER RONNA COOK:

A: When we looked at the subgroups of African American, Hispanic, Other, and White, we did find some significant subgroup findings for the Hispanic children. Language was the only area where we didn't find it as much. And so I think it depends on how the subgroups themselves were defined at that particular point. And so I would really like to say that I'd rather give you better information on that in another few months. Can I just say one thing to Larry [Schweinhart]? I mean, if we're going to have a discussion about effect sizes at any point, I think before we can talk about small/medium/large effect sizes, we have to come together on – and I've said this in a number of arenas – how are we going to measure effect sizes. Some use a control group standard deviation, some use a treatment group standard deviation, some use a combination of both, so you can get very different effect sizes. I also worry what the conversation really needs to be about, especially for preschool: Are the measures that we're using really good enough to be able to make some of the statements that we're making? I just put that out to the group and to you.

Q: Art, my question is for you, and it has to do with a parent involvement requirement for the pre-K portion of the Chicago program. When I looked at your book on this intervention, if I recall correctly, the parent-involvement component of the program was a requirement for the pre-K version. I've worried some, and I'm kind of curious about your thoughts about this, whether the pattern of results that you see here could be exacerbated by selection due to the requirement that parents become involved in the program. I'd like to hear your thoughts on that particular issue. I'm also curious about whether you think that some of the ethical issues that have made it difficult to conduct a randomized control trial of the Chicago program when it first began still apply in today's environment.

SPEAKER ARTHUR REYNOLDS:

A: Sure. Parents were expected to be involved in the program on some regular basis that they could define. They signed a home–school agreement. We tried to get reports of how many parents might have been reluctant to get involved because they had to sign some agreement. That answer was maybe 1%, so based on the reflections of teachers and others in the program, no parent refused to be in the program because they had to sign some parent–school agreement. Whether that restricted the pool of people, the families that could participate in the program, absolutely not. The program also conducted canvassing to get the highest risk children involved. You saw all the staff there. These programs were the highlight of the neighborhood. So, did such an agreement or an expectation to get involved turn anybody away? No. If it was any percentage, I'd say 1%; for 99%, it wasn't an issue.

Something you get with Perry and other programs is the challenge of a package effect – researchers are getting the total effect of all the features working simultaneously. It's very difficult to sort out which effect or which part of the program is deriving the other effect. What's the role of the experiments looking further into the program? I would say one option is looking at what parent-involvement programs give the largest effect possible. Do you need a program to look exactly like the CPC model, with everything in there? I'm not sure. I think there's a huge advantage to having a parent resource room, but I think the experimentation in order to do critical analysis of actually the most beneficial type of parent program would be a useful test, such as comparing a home-visitation family-support program to a school-affiliation parent-involvement program. For these kids, I'm not convinced that a home-visitation program would have worked. But I'd like to see comparisons of those approaches.

Q: Ronna, I know that you were talking today about nationally representative Head Start centers, but could you talk a little bit about the distributions of quality across those Head Starts in any of the analyses that are looking at the relations between variations in quality and the Head Start programs, and in the outcomes.

SPEAKER RONNA COOK:

A: Yes. There is definitely a distribution of quality across the Head Start centers. In the next analyses coming out, we are specifically defining Head Start centers based on the higher ECERS [Early Childhood Environment Rating Scale] scores versus lower ECERS scores. We will be looking at differences in terms of the outcomes, including parenting practices. We're also looking at a quality composite score that will likely not be that much different from the ECERS score itself. My guess, then, is that we should see some differences based on the programs, although some of the research this morning said that quality really didn't make the differences in terms of the outcomes, so I don't know. But that is where we're going with the analysis.

SPEAKER LAWRENCE SCHWEINHART:

Q: I have questions for each of my colleagues here. Ronna, what is the subsequent publication schedule for the Head Start Impact Study, and how is the federal government related to that? And for Arthur, I've heard [that the] Chicago Public Schools can't afford the CPC program, and I wonder what the current status is.

SPEAKER RONNA COOK:

A: I can't blame the federal government on how long it's taking us to get the findings out. Our hope is that the final report will be out through first grade in the end of July 2008. Then we have to do the third-grade follow-up, and we're not even done with the data collection there. Some of it, as we said this morning, we started this back in 2000 and each time you start to do analysis, new ways you should be doing things come [into] vogue. As time goes on, one of our big issues is the differences between 1 and 2 years of Head Start. And we did not keep children out of Head Start for 2 years. Initially, it was going to be the 3-year-old cohort who would be out for 2 years; the 4-year-old cohort was only going to get 1 year. One of the things we're really struggling with is, how do you do that analysis of the 1 versus 2 years, especially in reality, I think most people would expect that all kids who went to Head Start as 3s were expecting to be back there at 4s. Well, they don't. Now, how do you look at 1 versus 2 years? So, there are methodological and analytic issues that have delayed the report from coming out.

SPEAKER ARTHUR REYNOLDS:

A: To answer [Lawrence Schweinhart's] other question about Chicago, I think there certainly are fiscal challenges in Chicago with the Child-Parent Center program because it is more expensive than the state pre-K program, and it costs $2,000 more per child than the state of Illinois' prekindergarten program, which is financed by a block grant from the state. So, there are challenges and potentially reductions of funding in some of the centers, but the program is still operating in a way that can be effective, but not at the same level of quality that it used to be when we tracked our samples in the mid-1980s.

Q: I have two questions. Ronna, for you, on the language differences among Hispanics, was their language measured in English, Spanish, or both? When you say, "We didn't see differences for Spanish speaking," was it because you didn't see differences in speaking Spanish or . . . ?

SPEAKER RONNA COOK:

A: No, I was talking about English. In 2002, we measured Spanish-speaking children who were tested completely in Spanish in the fall at baseline with two English subtests. Then in spring of 2003, Spanish-speaking children were measured in English with two Spanish-speaking subtests. I was speaking about the English-speaking subtests.

Q: I wanted to follow up on Art's really good comment about the differences in the parent education and support component, and it was interesting that both Larry and Art identified those aspects as salient features to carry forward in replication. I would like to hear Ronna then respond about the parent support education aspect of Head Start in terms of how it is different from what the two of them described, and all of you to comment on what you think are the relative costs of your three specific approaches, recognizing you may or may not be able to do that last piece.

SPEAKER ARTHUR REYNOLDS:

A: Just a quick thought on the Child-Parent Center. I think it was more costly because there is a parent room in each center that was dedicated for parents to work together, to receive training, to get involved in the program, and to volunteer. That's a big center. What we've learned is that the experience over the last 20 years – and this was since the inception – is that the whole reason why the program was begun in the first place is that kids had low attendance rates. They weren't coming to school, as parents were afraid of the schools because of their own experiences. So parents needed a place to go. Because of the dedicated space for a parent program with a menu option [of] 20 or 30 things that could be done there, more parents came in. Typical rates of parent involvement in Head Start are probably around 50% historically, and the CPC's is probably 80%. The parent program is a large source of the overall program effect. We have documented that probably 20% to 25% of the long-term effect into adulthood can be attributed to improvements in parent involvement through our causal analysis of a five-hypothesis model.

SPEAKER LAWRENCE SCHWEINHART:

A: It drives me a little bit crazy that administrators can't afford programs with high demonstrated return on investment – not only Chicago, but the whole configuration of Head Start. We were looking at a replication of the Perry program, not with Head Start, but with child care centers in West Palm Beach, Florida. They've had some experience with trying to do this kind of program with certified teachers. And we had a well-funded project working with the Center for Study and Prevention of Violence at the University of Colorado that would involve their studying replications, so it would involve all [these] criteria you're talking about. But they were insisting that the research money pay for certified teachers. But once you start trying to take research money and applying it to program costs, you can't do the research. The great puzzle to me right now is whether we can afford to do something that we know is going to have a high return on investment. "Afford" has a funny meaning in that context, but that seems to be where we are. Regarding home visits, the way to do that in existing structures is to have a lot of part-day programs come up with the teacher salaries by doing double sessions – they have one group of kids in the morning and one in the afternoon. You could put extensive parent outreach programs into place by buying out their second session, which means that you're in effect doubling the teacher cost. Of course, then you deal with the fact that teacher salaries have gone up relative to the cost of living and so forth. If they're ahead of inflation, then we've got real puzzles as to whether we can maintain a low teacher:child ratio, extensive parent outreach, and salaries. We've got a real conundrum that can only be solved by the intelligent application of principles regarding trade-offs in which you still hang on to what is most valuable.

SPEAKER RONNA COOK:

A: I think there's a real discrepancy between Head Start performance standards that require many different types of activities for parents, including parent counsels, home visits, and parents working in the centers, but I think there [are] two things that we found. One is that the standards are not necessarily implemented in the same way all across the country. That's very important. Second, what we found, even from interviews with parents, is that more parents are working now; it's much harder to be involved in the Head Start center as originally conceived. It's just not happening the same way. Head Start could be looking at how to pull in that parent involvement more than is happening now. That was one of the reasons I was concerned about what parenting outcomes we were going to be looking at. I wasn't sure how much you should hold Head Start responsible for things that they aren't really implementing in the way that they could or should be implementing.

PART II: PRESCHOOL EDUCATION

William T. Gormley Jr., Georgetown University, "Small Miracles in Tulsa: The Effects of Universal Pre-K on Cognitive Development" (Chapter 9)

Elena V. Malofeeva, HighScope Educational Research Foundation, "Lessons From the Evaluation of the Great Start Readiness Program (GSRP): A Longitudinal Evaluation" (coauthors: Lawrence J. Schweinhart and Marijata Daniel-Echols, HighScope Educational Research Foundation) (Chapter 10)

W. Steven Barnett, National Institute for Early Education Research (NIEER), "Abbott Preschool Program Longitudinal Effects Study (APPLES) Year One Findings" (coauthors: Ellen Frede, Kwanghee Jung, and Alexandra Figueras, NIEER; Cynthia Esposito Lamy, Robin Hood Foundation) (Chapter 11)

Q: This is a question for William. I was interested when you were talking about the gains or the effects of the Tulsa pre-K regarding race, ethnicity, and SES, and you saw gains all across. Are you going to see or are you seeing a change in the achievement gap? You are having gains, but is it narrowing the achievement gap?

SPEAKER WILLIAM GORMLEY:

A: We've tried to look at that, and not very successfully. Remember that even though the gains were somewhat bigger for disadvantaged children, they were still really big for middle-class children. So we are not predicting that universal pre-K in Oklahoma or anywhere else will lower the achievement gap. An interesting question is whether that's the most appropriate goal for public policy. A somewhat different perspective would be John Rawls's perspective, which is that we ought to try to improve conditions for disadvantaged children. If we can do that by also improving conditions for middle-class children, and that has some spillover effects that are good for disadvantaged children, then a Rawlsian perspective would suggest that that's a good outcome. In contemplating these issues, it's important for us to decide what is the most relevant yardstick, and reasonable people will disagree on that.

Q: I've got a question for William also. You present age-equivalent test scores for children exposed to the Tulsa pre-K. Do you also do that age equivalent for the free-lunch status? So the question really is, once you age equivalize, do your results hold up?

SPEAKER WILLIAM GORMLEY:

A: We haven't done that yet. But we could.

Q: Okay, because you're making the assumption that these programs are working for middle-class kids, and it could just be age. Am I correct on that? That is, you've got a bias in there that these kids are younger, and until you do the age equivalent, I don't know how you get rid of that bias.

SPEAKER WILLIAM GORMLEY:

A: I don't think that's right. Essentially, we are making comparisons after a regression–discontinuity point. And so, in effect, we're comparing statistically a student who is exactly 5 years old with a student who is just one day short of being 5 years old.

Q: Is that what you mean by "age equivalent"?

SPEAKER WILLIAM GORMLEY:

A: For the age equivalent, we first have to convert the regression scores into age equivalents using information supplied to us by the Woodcock-Johnson people. And then we focus on the regression coefficient for the child born September 1 and the regression coefficient for the child born on September 2, and that becomes our comparison. Does that make sense?

The step that I didn't explain in my presentation is that Woodcock-Johnson actually tells you for, let's say, a 5-year old, exactly what the expected score for letter-word identification or spelling or applied problems would be. We used that information to calculate that particular table.

Q: Actually, this question is for all three of the panelists, but I'd like to see Bill start. Many in this room differ on what is an optimum setting. Head Start is homogeneously poor kids; I tried to convert it to an integrated program. I ran Head Start, but I did not succeed. Actually, we have way more data now that's consistent with what you reported. I mean, we knew from the Coleman report 40 years ago, and all the data since have demonstrated, that if you want to optimize poor children's performance, integrate them with middle-class children. I'd like you just to respond. I mean, there's a debate, and I might not be able to convince my friends that they ought to go universal. They make a sound argument that the biggest payoff is going to be for poor kids – you get the biggest bang for the buck, which I can understand. How important do you and the other two members think doing integrated programs is compared to continuing in the Head Start model? We've been doing the latter for 42 years, and I just would like to know the panel's opinion.

SPEAKER WILLIAM GORMLEY:

A: There are at least two issues on the table: One is universal versus targeted, and the other is school-based programs versus a mixed-services delivery system. On that second question, I believe in federalism, and I believe that individual states should make choices that suit them. Oklahoma has opted for a public-school–based system, and that works wonderfully in Oklahoma. Georgia has opted for a mixed-services delivery system, and that has produced good results in Georgia. If I were the czar, I would probably prefer the school-based program because I think that that has all sorts of advantages. It makes for smoother transitions into the schools, the quality of people who are recruited by the public schools is usually better, there are more career options for people who get hired by the public schools, and that helps with both recruitment and retention. That's my own preference, but I respect the decisions that other states have made to go in other directions. I do believe it is important that public schools be an important part of the mix, and that's why I have some reservations about the way that Florida's situation is evolving.

SPEAKER ELENA MALOFEEVA:

A: From our studies, we have seen that when we look at program quality – for example, for Head Start separately versus state-funded separately – quality is a lot higher for state-funded pre-K. In a recent study that looked at the variation study, kids attended blended classrooms. The distinction was mixed. I can't give you an answer on how that affected child outcomes now, but that's an interesting shift.

SPEAKER W. STEVEN BARNETT:

A: As Bill said, there are a few separate issues, and we don't take our research in New Jersey or any other state that we've looked at to suggest that a mixed-delivery system versus all public or all private is necessarily preferable – only that we've seen that in a mixed-delivery system, both public and private can perform at the same level. Interestingly, in our state, we did a survey of teachers because many of these teachers were teachers in the private programs before they were part of the public system and acquired the degree of certification to meet the state standards, and we wanted to see what would happen to them, what their experiences were. This survey was carefully stratified to ensure that we had a representative sample of public and private programs. And we got the data back. There were many more public-school teachers than private-program teachers. And we thought, well, what went wrong with this study? Well, it turns out nothing went wrong with the study. The private-program teachers now identify as public-school teachers. So there are hybrids of public/private that may be quite different from what we've seen before and what we've debated about in the past. Those programs may perform differently. I actually think it's an exciting development, certainly for researchers, but maybe for the people being served.

The second question, as Bill pointed out, has an ethical dimension about the choice of serving all kids or just children in poverty. But I think that second question about how much do low-income children gain from being in a program that also serves the middle class has two dimensions. One is more systemic. Will the quality and funding levels and other ways of support be different for a program that has broad participation by the middle class? Then there's the second question: Does having a mix of kids in your classroom result in different or better outcomes for low-income kids? I think we have some evidence on that, but we could use a lot more.

SPEAKER ARTHUR REYNOLDS:

A: To add a point, states are in a position to go to the next step. What policy should states adopt about targeted versus universal? For example, in the state of Minnesota, I think there's a sequence of steps where, in effect, you could have both if you identify a strategy that is going to ultimately get you to universal access for all kids in the state. In Minnesota, for example, there's no standardized state pre-K program. Maybe you start with at-risk kids, like Illinois did, because we know the strong benefits. Then, since we know there are benefits for middle-class kids based on the recent evidence that we have from Oklahoma, so that within 5 years, you get to the universal system. We all have to have an openness to change based on new data that come in that show that all kids are benefiting from preschool.

Q: I was a little puzzled by this comparison of the longitudinal design and the regression–discontinuity design [RDD]. I'm not convinced that they should be the same. It seems to me that they're asking a different question. Maybe I'm not quite getting it right. The longitudinal design is comparing those who had the Abbott preschool versus those who didn't and may have had some other preschool. Whereas the regression–discontinuity design seems to be asking what the effect is of getting this preschool versus those who haven't yet had a chance to get it, but will. So it's almost like getting it versus not, versus getting it versus counterfactual. It seems the counterfactual is different to me. So I just wanted to see if you could clear this up. Are they really answering the same question?

SPEAKER W. STEVEN BARNETT:

A: What we think is that they're answering close to the same question but not exactly the same question. But close.

Q: I want to pick up on a point that Steve made, and this actually isn't a question. Craig Ramey and Sharon Ramey wrote a marvelous article in *American Psychologist* about 10 years ago on characteristics of programs that have enduring impact. And their first two characteristics are number one, developmental timing, which is basically start early; and number two, intensity, which includes a concept of duration. Every one of the presentations I've heard today has a duration aspect to it. We talked about kids who had 2 years instead of 1 year, 3 years instead of 2 years. We really have to address that question systematically. How much of any particular intervention is necessary to have what kind of outcomes? When I talk about class size tomorrow morning, 2 years of a small class have longer enduring impact, stronger impact, than 1 year, and 3 are better than 2, and 4 are better than 3. That's all we have, but with the same kind of reason we have to ask: How much do we want to invest for what level of outcome?

SPEAKER ARTHUR REYNOLDS:

A: Dosage, duration – we often miss this in intervention work. There are several studies now that show that kids with 2 years of preschool do better, at least on school-readiness outcomes early on, than kids with 1 year, and that that could put kids past the threshold of avoiding later need for preventive services. The evidence is increasing that that is the case.

Q: The regression-discontinuity analyses are really interesting. It sounds like they have a lot of potential. What are your concerns about the RDD analyses? What are your concerns about the kinds of possible overstatements that they may produce?

SPEAKER W. STEVEN BARNETT:

A: I'll start with a few. First, you need a much larger sample size than for a randomized trial. I think there's some tendency in our studies for the results to be less robust with respect to different approaches to the analysis, as the sample size is smaller. That already hints at the second issue that I see, which is that it's not clear what you have to do to get the right functional form. We don't have good theoretical guidance on that. If your answers are robust across a bunch of different functional forms, that's great. If they're not, then you sort of scratch your head. There are issues if you had lots of cases that violated the assignment rule. In the New Jersey study, it's a fraction of 1%, so it's trivial. But that's not always true. Then there are other issues if it looks like there are nonlinearities around the cutoff. And again, if you don't have a very large data set, what do you do about that?

SPEAKER ELENA MALOFEEVA:

A: On the issue of sample size, it is true that you do need fewer subjects than if it's a matched comparison group. It can be a positive and negative at the same time. Also, if you use a regression-discontinuity design, how do you track kids longitudinally? Then we go back to your control group. Who are you going to compare your kids to? The other issue is outliers. In regression discontinuity, somehow it's a huge issue, because it matters who you have close to the cutoff. Those two, three kids with data that are out of the range might make a huge difference. You're right because there is no clear guidance. How do we do it when you do have those lines that are not linear?

SPEAKER WILLIAM GORMLEY:

A: We're accumulating a good list here. Before I add a couple of points, I'd just say that my bottom line is that the regression-discontinuity design has a lot of advantages for short-term effects analysis, really big advantages over the leading quasi-experimental alternatives, and that's why we find it so attractive. One nice feature of the design is that you can vary the functional form to suit the data, so there's nothing that says that you have to have a linear model. You can experiment with different nonlinear models. You can try different windows. We prefer in most of our studies to use all of our data points. But we typically present in our published work a variety of different windows in which we look at all the data points, and we look at data points only 6 months to the left and 6 months to the right, data points 3 months to the left and 3 months to the right, and so long as you're not looking at subgroups, you can even do 1 month to the left, 1 month to the right just to see how robust the findings are. That's a nice feature of the regression-discontinuity design, assuming that your sample size is big enough. The best feature of the design is that you have a reality check staring you in the face, just to see if your observables are balancing. And if you have a lot of interesting demographic variables in your database, and they balance, then that suggests that you're home free or close to it. One of my concerns about it, in addition to those that have been expressed: I've sometimes asked myself if it's possible that kindergarten students by virtue of having been tested once or twice before may have an advantage; that is, maybe they feel a little more comfortable with testing processes. They've never been tested using Woodcock-Johnson before, but they may have gotten some diagnostic testing. If that's the case, that might conceivably give them a little boost in contrast to the pre-K entrants, who have never, one suspects, been tested before by anyone. The other concern I have has to do when you shift your focus from dependent variables that tap cognitive skills, which is what we've mainly been talking about, to dependent variables that tap socio-emotional development, where almost inevitably you're relying on people's perceptions. You have to hope that when teachers or parents who are doing the socio-emotional ratings use your instrument that they're not making some mental adjustments for the child's age. This is something I know Steve has thought about; it's something that concerns us. Our remedy to that potential problem is twofold. First, try to choose an instrument that encourages teachers or parents to give a raw assessment rather than some kind of relative assessment with respect to the child's age. That is the first and most important remedy. Second, for socio-emotional outcomes in particular, you ought to use some kind of complementary testing technique, even if it isn't as strong as regression-discontinuity design, in order to make sure that your results are pointing in the same direction.

SPEAKER ARTHUR REYNOLDS:

A: We can probably have a separate conference on some of the methodological issues in intervention and prevention and research; I think it is great to have methodological pluralism so we can learn from the advantages and disadvantages of each technique. We could probably have a conference on that.

Q: I wanted to follow up on your question. We've talked a lot about variation in dosage, in intensity, but no one said anything about part-day versus full-day. And it made me think with your Michigan School Readiness Program, because you had a lot of variation there, what your thoughts are on what we can expect from a part-day program versus a full-day program in both short-term and long-term outcomes.

SPEAKER ELENA MALOFEEVA:

A: We get mixed findings. We did an evaluation of South Carolina First Steps programs. They're across the state, and I think if I'm correct, the finding there is that kids who go to full-day programs get better social skills overall. However, cognitive outcomes are better in part-day programs. We did have a separate study in Michigan that addressed that particular option. We did find that full-day had higher quality as rated by people going into the classrooms. The outcomes were no different for our study. I know that's not the case in general.

SPEAKER WILLIAM GORMLEY:

A: I'm glad you raised that question because some people have quoted us as saying that full-day programs are more effective than half-day programs. Actually, our very first article was based on a homegrown instrument that Tulsa public schools teachers used, and it was a fixed menu, it was not Woodcock-Johnson. We had reason to believe that particular instrument was not particularly good for higher achieving students. In our first report, we did find bigger effects for full-day students than for half-day students, but we cautioned that that might be an artifact on the particular instrument we were using. In our second study, using Woodcock-Johnson, we found big effects for half-day and big effects for full-day. So that's where we stand, at least in Tulsa, as both types of programs were very effective for students.

SPEAKER W. STEVEN BARNETT:

A: We actually have a working paper on our website on a small randomized trial of half-day versus full-day pre-K, followed by full-day versus extended-day kindergarten, with the added wrinkle of extended-year, an extra 2 weeks on either end. So you can't disentangle the extended-year from the extended-day. There are larger impacts of the extended-day extended-year program, and they grow as children move through kindergarten. That's, however, a very high-quality program. We also reviewed the literature when we did that study, and the review looks to us like it really depends on what they do – first what the quality is, because more of something that's not very good doesn't do anything, and second, the extent to which they actually devote the additional time to things that are likely to produce gains in children's learning and development.

Q: I want to ask a question about measurement, but before I do that, I want to make two observations. The first one is that if I'm remembering right, over the course of the day, we've heard a fair amount of evidence of pluralism in how we're assessing outcomes for kids. The common measures are things like the PPBT, the ECERS, and maybe some elements of the Woodcock-Johnson. The other comment is regarding another regression-discontinuity design issue because it's so appealing: the similarity in measurement, in both pre- and post-intervention groups and regression-discontinuity design. A challenge in a traditional RDD design with kids going into kindergarten is assessment of literacy – that the topographies of literacy would be very different for kids in kindergarten and first grade than they might be for kids in 3- and 4-year-old programs. Having an instrument that would allow us to make sensible assessment of what it would look like pre- and post-kindergarten entry would be difficult. I think we can do it, but that leads me to the question. Pluralism is a good thing, except when it's not helpful to research, but all three of these panelists are talking about an intersection between science and practice. I'm wondering if the three of you could comment on where you think we are in terms of measurement around this point of kindergarten entry in terms of both helping researchers, practitioners, and policy makers think about what's working and what we need to do differently.

SPEAKER ELENA MALOFEEVA:

A: Certainly for state-funded pre-K programs, because they have their own peculiarities and their evaluations, this is a huge issue. If you look at the meta-analysis that has been done in the past by [Edward] Zigler, you would see that out of the 33 state evaluations they had, they could only evaluate 13 of them because they had so many methodological issues of all sorts and kinds, starting from measurement to absolutely no comparison group to how long is long, new hypothesis testing, and what is being compared.

SPEAKER WILLIAM GORMLEY:

A: My sense of the field is that we've moved very quickly to a much higher plateau over the past several years, and that's a good thing. I do agree there are advantages when scholars use similar measures. We deliberately selected the CLASS instrument because we think there is growing interest in applying that to pre-K settings in particular, and we're very pleased with how that turned out. A lot of us do use effect sizes, and it might be nice if we used precisely the same kinds of effect size measures, although I'm not sure it would matter that much. The bigger question with effect sizes is not so much what the denominator winds up being, but how appropriate it is to compare effect sizes for very different kinds of interventions and different points in the life cycle. Admittedly, the nice thing about effect sizes is that that's what you can use them for, but there's something to be said for caution in making those kinds of comparisons. The other point I'd make about the state of the art is that we're in a much better position now at assessing short-term program impacts than we are at assessing long-term program impacts.

SPEAKER W. STEVEN BARNETT:

A: We're actually moving at a pretty good clip in terms of the development of measures. We've had big issues with children whose primary language is not English. We've moved to using a variety of assessments of literacy in English and Spanish, and inevitably, as you're doing this, some of them don't work very well. Many of you must have seen the article by Adele Diamond looking at executive function in the current issue of *Science*. That's in one of our Abbott Preschool studies, using a type of measure we've never used before that measures these things in a much more detailed and different way, and yet we're still using the social-skills rating scale, and we're delighted to say that Adele is getting big increases on her measures of executive function, and we're getting a half a standard deviation on the social-skills rating scale.

Q: One of the central themes that came across all three of your presentations and a theme that we've been hearing all day is the value of higher quality programs. In each of the programs that you were looking at, there were variations in quality, and I wonder if you have any advice or suggestions for improving quality in pre-K programs systematically, so we could raise the bar in terms of quality of programs.

SPEAKER W. STEVEN BARNETT:

A: That's substantially the subject of the APPLES paper. You start there with a program that has set high standards and is very well funded, and then you put into place a multilayered system of plan–do–review. It begins with the teacher in the classroom, self-assessing practice, and assessing children in ways that are real to the teacher and connected to the teacher's assessment of her own practice. Then on top of that, you have the system of people who work with the programs who assess children and teachers and coach teachers in the classroom specifically in areas they need to improve. Then you have a larger layer up from there where the state is monitoring district-level: How are the kids doing, how are the districts doing, and what do we need to do to support their improvement? It made remarkable changes in the quality of the program over a period of 5 years. You have to have that kind of patience – that doesn't happen in 1 or 2 years. These things are very difficult to sustain.

Q: Are you seeing the improvement in quality occurring for the particular teachers who are there or are changing out of the staff in the program?

SPEAKER W. STEVEN BARNETT:

A: It's both. Much of it is, these are the same people who were there who've improved their practice. That's certainly true in the public schools, but it's also true in the private programs. We sent them to college in some cases, and we created a special certification program of 15 credits for people who are already teaching and may have a college degree tied to what the state standards are for learning and teaching. Certainly, as a country, we don't pay that kind of attention to what we're doing in higher education or whatever system we're using to prepare teachers. Getting all of that synched together and having adequate resources is an important part of moving quality of programs.

SPEAKER WILLIAM GORMLEY:

A: I would just add that we need to think more about some bottom-up approaches of improving quality in child care. I'm intrigued by North Carolina's system of star ratings, and what we need to know is for those states that have or will soon have these kinds of star rating systems for child care centers or other kinds of preschool organizations, do parents use that information? Do they use it wisely? How many parents need to use that information in order to affect the behavior and incentives of child care centers and pre-K programs? That's an area that is ripe for research.

SPEAKER ELENA MALOFEEVA:

A: Just to add to what the panelists have said, in the state of Michigan, not only do we send monitors into the classrooms or into the Michigan School Readiness Program [MSRP]; we also have teachers do self-reports. And those scores do come up a little higher than what we see, but overall if you look across different types of settings, MSRP classrooms are all high quality. That makes you wonder, is higher quality related partly to the fact that they think about, once they assess themselves, what the different components of quality are? The other activity is happening at the state level. Teachers go and rate themselves on program quality assessment and then participate in specific kickoff activities where teachers help to set up appropriate goals in areas where they're low. They talk about what they can do in terms of teaching children or professional development that would boost their scores. A very separate issue comes up in family child care settings because we certainly do not have a lot of instruments that we can assess quality in those types of settings because they're unique. They can have kids of different ages, they can have infants, and they can have school-aged kids all in the same center. How do you assess quality there? Also, how you make quality information available to parents is going to make a difference.

PART III: KINDERGARTEN AND EARLY SCHOOL-AGE SERVICES AND PRACTICES

Andrew J. Mashburn, University of Virginia, "Opportunity in Early Education: Improving Teacher–Child Interactions and Child Outcomes" (coauthor: Robert C. Pianta, University of Virginia) (Chapter 12)

Vi-Nhuan Le, RAND, "School Readiness and the Achievement Gap: Can Full-Day Kindergarten Level the Playing Field" (coauthors: Sheila Nataraj Kirby, Heather Barney, Claude Messan Setodji, and Daniel Gershwin, RAND) (Chapter 13)

Jeremy D. Finn, University at Buffalo – SUNY, "Small Classes in the Early Grades: One Policy, Multiple Outcomes" (coauthors: Allison E. Suriani, University at Buffalo – SUNY, and Charles M. Achilles, Seton Hall University) (Chapter 14)

Q: Andrew, a couple of questions of clarification. It wasn't clear to me whether you were saying that there were no effects of what might be called "structural characteristics" of classrooms or policies on your measures of child outcomes, or that there were no effects, except through the impact on what happens in classrooms. Second, it seems to me that a policy requirement you have is providing meals to children to address nutritional needs of the small number of children who don't have adequate nutrition at home. You would not expect this policy to have an impact on the general population, nor would you expect it to have an impact on the general population's math scores.

SPEAKER ANDREW MASHBURN:

A: When we talk theoretically about quality and outcomes, the framework has been direct effects. We line up all these different features of preschool programs, we put them into a metric of low and high quality, and we look to see the extent to which they influence children's outcomes. The point of this analysis was to question the theoretical framework of how this research has been conducted over the last 25 years. When we line up these inputs and we don't find that they're related to child outcomes, it's not that we are saying they're not important. We are saying the theoretical way these analyses are being specified and conducted is inaccurate, and that children develop through the mediating mechanism of classroom interactions.

Regarding the point about meals, we're using as our outcome academic, language, social, and emotional skills. We didn't put in physical well-being; we didn't put in psychological well-being – we were limited by the developmental outcomes we had. You can argue that meals should influence academic and social well-being for children who are not well nourished. For those who are well nourished, meals might allow you to be more engaged within classrooms and actually have an influence on development and learning. We were limited by the outcome data that we had.

Q: The first question is just a technical question. The first speaker mentioned the problem of missing data; I think you said you used multiple imputations. But I wasn't really sure, given the kind of pattern that you reported, that there weren't systematically missing data, so you'd have to very carefully model a selection process. I am just curious how you did that. The second question is regarding the paper on classroom size. I've seen a lot of these studies before on STAR. As Jeremy was saying, there are consistent effects of reduced classroom size on performance. The real question though, what you didn't address, was the real rate of return of this compared to some of the other interventions. Studies done by myself and others [show] that the rates of return to classroom size reductions were really quite low. My impression is if you compared these returns to some of the higher returns estimated for early childhood interventions, the rate of return is relatively low, nowhere near 10 to 12%, and at least looking at Krueger and Whitmore's 2001 paper, "Would Smaller Classes Help Close the Black–White Achievement Gap?," it really was very small.

And the third point for the third paper: I wasn't exactly sure how you would model the issue of teacher assignment to students in your analysis. In fact, one way is, because of salary systems in public schools, you can reward better teachers, but you can't really promote them and reward them in the same way with better students. So there's a real assignment issue that happens in advance, and I wonder how you address that. There's some earlier work by Sherman Rosen and others.

SPEAKER VI-NHUAN LE:

A: Kids who had two or more test scores tended to perform lower on the observed scores than kids who had a fuller, complete set of test-score data.

What multiple imputation does – it's a joint vector of observation – so it takes all of the observed variables in every single covariate and predicts the missing value for the particular variables that are missing. We could only condition on the observables that we had. To the extent that those were missing as well, to the set of covariates, we couldn't model that.

SPEAKER JEREMY FINN:

A: On the rate of return question and the cost-benefit analysis, I don't think we can complete the discussion of that issue. You're certainly correct in your reading of Krueger and Whitmore's analysis in that they report rates of return under different economic scenarios of somewhere from 2 to 6%, and you're right, that isn't high. I want to mention a few things. Since Krueger's work, there's been some very extensive work by Hank Levin and others incorporating additional benefits to society of reducing dropout rates. They estimate what each dropout costs us in terms of lost tax revenues, increased crime rates, increased health care costs, and from a different perspective they include other financial benefits. Even at that, the cost-benefit analyses have been incomplete.

Finally, on comparing the rate of return to lower class sizes to preschool programs, I think it's not a comparison to preschool because we're not either going to put youngsters in preschool programs or give them small classes. But what we haven't done is the research that says, "Can some of the problems associated with preschool, namely, the tendency of preschool benefits to drop off over the years, be ameliorated by putting kids in intensive K to 3 programs?" And by "intensive" I would include a small number of students per teacher.

Q: In terms of priority, if you had to spend the first dollar, it would probably return more in the early years rather than the later years, right? [A] 3% return versus, say, [a] 12% return. For policy purposes, since you have a fixed budget, where do you spend the money? The issue is not whether the return is positive; the issue is if you have a fixed budget, you want to know where to allocate it.

SPEAKER JEREMY FINN:

A: All of our previous research led Project STAR to decide that the early grades were where they should start, where it was most likely to have an effect. We don't have data on later grades, but if you look at the data we do have, clearly the kids who started earliest, namely, in kindergarten, had the greatest benefit, and kids who started in third grade had no significant benefit after 1 year in small classes. So there is some argument for starting early.

SPEAKER ARTHUR REYNOLDS:

A: I'm going to give just one quick follow-up. I think in the intervention field, there's an issue with the synergy in research between intervention strategies at different ages. We don't have great research on the synergy. To what extent is there an advantage for kids who have high-quality early environments who then get seamless later interventions, like Early Head Start to Head Start? There seems to be some evidence in the Early Head Start study about possible synergy for high-risk kids. It's the same thing here; we need more research to better understand the conditions. There might be more of a benefit than we see for some experiences. So I think it's a good example, but there's going to be ongoing discussion of that issue, certainly.

Q: I'm a research scientist dealing with programs in brain stimulation and I have a couple comments.

One is that in order to do our program, we really need full-day kindergarten. Daily all-day kindergarten is a piece of the infrastructure; it has to be in place before we can put the quality into the program. I realize that this conference is about policy statements regarding effectiveness that can go to legislatures that will then funnel money to fund this infrastructure, and the same thing with class-size reduction. It's important. I thought Andrew's statements about the quality were just a wonderfully fitting end or a summary of what the missing piece is here, because it seems to me that when you have these large data sets, which legislatures like, you end up with kind of a fruit salad in terms of all the populations that can be sliced and diced. When you use such large data sets, there's a leveling effect, and what you end up with is looking at the mildly effective programs. As Andrew showed, only 14% of these programs are really high quality, so many of the benefits of the infrastructure of class size and all-day kindergarten will wash out. If you can somehow put program quality into the mix here, I think you'll find that these infrastructure changes really provide the platform upon which to mount the effective programs, and then you'll see the kinds of effects that we're seeing here in Minnesota, where we have schools in which all or 90% or more of the children in third grade are proficient in reading. The question is: How much trouble is it going to be to add the quality component to the data sets that you already have? Thank you.

SPEAKER VI-NHUAN LE:

A: I'd like to comment on the statements with which I agree. One of the weaknesses of large-scale data sets such as the ones put out by NCES [National Center for Education Statistics] is that what they make up for in sample size, they lack in richness and quality. As I noted in my own research, one of the big holes is the lack of information on program quality. We'd love to go out there and do what Andrew does and go into the classrooms and see the teacher interactions, but it's unlikely that you could do that with 3,000 classrooms across the United States. What I'd like to see is smaller-scale research where we are able to look at the richness of the data and then do a meta-analysis across these different sites. It is the case that we are making that trade-off. As to whether full-day kindergarten allows for an infrastructure, that's unknown right now. It is said that perhaps Minnesota is having these great effects because they are using the time wisely. We don't know what supports they have that other states don't, but I think that's certainly an avenue for future research.

SPEAKER ANDREW MASHBURN:

A: To address the last point about what it takes to get metrics of quality in our large-scale data systems: It takes going into classrooms. What it takes is observing classroom interactions using standardized observational procedures. Most of the metrics of quality are done by teachers reporting and checking boxes. One of the beauties of working in a center that's affiliated with a school of education is that you realize that classrooms aren't black boxes. Classrooms are people, and they're interactions, and they're relationships, and you can measure and assess the quality of them. We're only going to have a full understanding of what works for which children when we go and measure the things that are directly responsible for their development. So I think getting that information in the data system is simply a matter of spending the money to send a person to a classroom to make these observations.

SPEAKER ARTHUR REYNOLDS:

A: I don't want to go into a lot of extra detail, but there's been a lot of recent research on the cost effectiveness of full-day kindergarten versus half-day kindergarten. [Steve] Aos at the Washington State Institute for Public Policy just did a meta-analysis of 23 studies of full-day versus half-day kindergarten over the last 20 years. I've done independent analysis on our own study in Chicago, which is reported in a review of Pre-K–3 interventions that is going to be available next year for publication. All of those studies show decisively that the impact of full-day kindergarten versus half-day kindergarten is a one-year effect; there are no enduring effects that have been detected in any of those studies on academic achievement. Researchers haven't looked at socio-emotional outcomes, but that evidence leads to the conclusion that the benefit-cost ratio is close to zero or even negative, based on the achievement for full-day kindergarten versus half-day kindergarten.

Q: As some of you know, I've been very interested in the academic achievement of homeless and highly mobile children, and I believe they're affecting a lot of research I've heard about the past couple of days because they're not missing at random from these studies. I have two issues. First, how are these highly mobile children affecting a lot of the research we've been hearing about? Second, how are their needs going to be addressed by even the most amazing quality in a given classroom because no matter how wonderful it is, these kids keep moving around, which undermines their academic achievement over time? Have you analyzed the data from the point of view of highly mobile children?

SPEAKER ANDREW MASHBURN:

A: That's a very important question and a very difficult question, as you can imagine. I mean, I think the way that we as a field handle children who move from one study site to one that's not a site is that we treat them as missing data and we impute their missing values. Whether that's accurate or not is probably an important question. From a theoretical perspective, children who are at risk, we could say, maybe not transient or mobile, but just who experience risk factors, which could be considered a proxy for transience and mobility, the idea that the quality of interactions affect children and how children development is proposition one. Proposition two is that the extent to which these interactions have effects on children depend upon other things, like the individual characteristics of the child. So what we might consider is that high-quality interactions may have a different effect on different kids, and in fact we might suggest that higher quality interactions would have a stronger positive effect on risky kids. I don't think it really answers your question about transience and mobility, but I think it shows that when we think about high-quality interactions and we can get children to experience that consistently, it might have different effects for the group of kids that you're talking about compared to other groups of kids.

SPEAKER VI-NHUAN LE:

A: Perhaps it hasn't been addressed directly in this conference because for the most part, kids don't drop out before seventh grade, so it's more of an adolescent phenomenon. I agree with you that it would be difficult to track them, especially if they are homeless. Depending on whether they stay within the state or the district, it's possible to track them, but I agree, mobile kids are the ones who tend to be most in need and actually drop out of the system and then just fall out.

SPEAKER JEREMY FINN:

A: I've thrown up my hands many times in frustration about our inability to handle student mobility, especially as researchers. Routinely, they weren't included in studies, students who even change schools once. I have no other comment except frustration about that. I also wanted to take this opportunity to agree with something that Arthur said a minute ago, about what it takes to get ideas that we know and have demonstrated empirically work into common practice. I started out in class size when I first went to Tennessee. My first trip in life to Tennessee was for this reason. I went there and told them I was slightly familiar with the research on small classes up to that point and they would never find a positive effect; the research was just too mixed. If I hadn't analyzed the data, I probably still wouldn't believe it. But I think back on all of the teachers who say they would prefer a small class to a large class and are even willing to strike in some areas on behalf of small classes, and all of the parents who want their kids to be in a smaller class and will even pay to have them go to a private school and when you ask them why, they say it's because my children need small classes. Every program we've talked about here, every preschool program and continuing, starts with the premise that the class will be small. If we have that, and we have fairly hard data (as least hard data as far as education data go) on academic benefits and long-term benefits, what do we have to do to go the next step to get this to be common practice? I also want to say while I have the microphone that I disagree with some of my colleagues abut universal small classes. I would not vote for a referendum that put more tax dollars into small classes in my neighborhood because I don't think it would be worth it. We have good schools, and we have a highly educated community, but when I look at the tremendous benefits to kids in poorer areas, I'm astounded at the resistance to paying for that.

SPEAKER ARTHUR REYNOLDS:

A: Good point. I'd echo [a previous] comment. I think we've addressed the issue of mobility very seriously in the field for a long time, especially homelessness, which maybe includes the highest risk kids. The one thing I might say in the afternoon session is that there's going to be some research presented from the [Pritzker] Consortium [on] Early Childhood Development [University of Chicago] about some of the mechanisms leading from early childhood education to later child well-being. In one of the studies, the Chicago study, for example, we find that one of the mechanisms by which the CPC program affects later outcomes, such as educational attainment and lower crime, is to reduce mobility. Kids who go to Child-Parent Centers change schools less frequently as a result of their participation in the program because of the learning environment that's created, which then lowers the risk for later behaviors.

PART IV: ECONOMIC SYNTHESES OF EARLY CHILDHOOD INVESTMENTS

James J. Heckman, University of Chicago, "A New Cost-Benefit and Rate of Return Analysis for the Perry Preschool Program: A Summary" (coauthors: Seong Hyeok Moon, Rodrigo Pinto, Peter Savelyev, and Adam Yavitz, University of Chicago) (Chapter 17)

Flavio Cunha, University of Pennsylvania, "Investing in Our Young People" (coauthor: James J. Heckman, University of Chicago) (Chapter 18)

Arthur J. Reynolds, University of Minnesota, "Paths of Effects of Preschool Participation to Educational Attainment at Age 21: A Three-Study Analysis" (coauthors: Michelle M. Englund and Suh-Ruu Ou, University of Minnesota; Lawrence J. Schweinhart, HighScope Educational Research Foundation; and Frances A. Campbell, University of North Carolina) (Chapter 19)

Q: Question for Flavio, with two parts. In your estimates of the productivity of investments, I think there is a tendency to interpret the pattern as reflecting biology. But if I understand it correctly, the estimated productivity of these investments is of a marginal investment so that they're contingent on the current pattern of investments. So, if we're already investing heavily in K–12 relative to the first 5 years, part of the difference in productivity is due to the pattern of investments that's already there. This might look different if you were to go to countries that have different investment patterns. Second, for all of your estimates, the assumption is that they are smoothly continuous. Have you looked to see if they are not monotonically increasing, if there are reasons to think, for example, the first year of life might be different, and whether there are some discontinuities or more turns in the road than the monotonic increase might imply?

SPEAKER FLAVIO CUNHA:

A: Let me start with the second question because it is easier. We estimated many different versions of the model. The first version was only one stage, assuming that the impact of the investment was the same at all years up to the point that you estimate one technology per year. In this case, you don't get a monotonic shape. The big problem, however, is sample size. It turns out that you do not have a large enough sample, so the method is very flexible because it's not assuming that the technology is linear. It can be highly nonlinear. The investment can be discontinuous for that matter. There is almost no assumption about the structure of the error terms. It is not really nonparametric, but it is very flexible. With few observations, these error terms become much larger. To answer your question, it is not monotonic, but there is almost no evidence that they would be increasing, for example, but it was always the case that the earliest was higher. So, for example, the impact on investment around age 0, 1, and 2 was higher than 5 and 6, but not necessarily the case that the impact of the investment at 3 and 4 was higher than 5 and 6, which begs the question that maybe measurements at different stages have different reliability. We made different assumptions on the structure of the measurement error. We started with one in which measurement error was classical, we moved to another one in which measurement error was correlated across different equations, and then we moved to another one in which it was uncorrelated across equations but correlated over time. We never actually found different results on that extent. The other question is more difficult. If there is some variation in investments, say, that are unexpected by parents, that could actually trigger some form of readjustment, potentially, that could change the optimal behavior. Although I don't know information I could use to check that. It could be the case, as you were saying, that the technology may be different for Scandinavia. And it may be different because of many reasons, including biological reasons and the institutional setting.

A few years ago, I presented this research in Brazil, where I went through details of the evidence from Perry and Abecedarian and the CPC. At the end of the conference, two leaders approached me and told me, "You are nuts; you don't know what you're saying." And I asked them, "Why are you saying that?" And they told me, "Look, in our town, we actually set up an early childhood center where mothers could take their children, and in the middle of the game, the federal Brazilian government gave a subsidy for poor parents and their children." The subsidy was really large for a Brazilian context, about $50 a month. If you are a poor mother and you get $50 per month subsidy, and there is a center that will take care of the child for you, you can think of what happened. They showed some very interesting evidence that one year after the center opened, and they already had the federal money, there was an increase in fertility. And one year after they closed, there was a decline in fertility. So I completely agree with you that what we see in the real data in terms of investments is in part reaction to the institutional setting. But I would say that's exactly why we need to put this evidence from the treatment effect in a social context. How will the policies we are discussing have an effect? Another case is child mobility. If we improve access to high-quality early childhood programs, how will that affect parental decisions to live nearby and perhaps stabilize the household? That may have positive impacts. So it is exactly variations around the model that I think we need to address.

Q: My questions and comments are addressed toward the first presentation, the Perry reanalysis. First, let me begin by saying that I'm glad to see somebody working on reanalyzing the existing data as well as issues that my forthcoming paper addresses. I believe there was some discussion before lunch about some differences between my own analysis of these data and the current analysis that was presented. My impression was that the papers were construed as having very different conclusions, but that doesn't seem to be the case, as far as I can tell. I think there are a lot of similarities that we agree on. I think that both of our analyses agree that there are definitely more significant effects for females. It seems to me that the main discrepancies include some disagreements on the male crime results. In terms of crime, if I interpreted the slides correctly, it seemed like there was a stronger absolute effect for females on violent crimes. So the crime effect doesn't appear to survive the multiplicity adjustment or to replicate in Abecedarian. My interpretation of the presentation here is that these crime effects have large benefits, but given that it didn't seem to survive the multiplicity adjustment and replicating the Abecedarian, are we really so confident of that? Also, I think there's an important point for external validity. Most of the explanations I've heard for reconciling this result with the lack of result in the Abecedarian are related to the fact that Abecedarian has lower crime rates, and the statistics I know of are that around age 20, about 51% of the Perry kids have a criminal record and about 43% of the Abecedarian kids. So there is some difference there, but it's not all that large, and if going down to only 40% of the kids having a criminal record really eliminates the scope for crime reductions, then what is your feeling on the external validity of these results to other populations?

SPEAKER RODRIGO PINTO:

A: I think we have to think linearly. We do not base our results on only 40% of criminal records. We saw each one of the criminal files that the police have. Of course, we couldn't see any names and other IDs, but we reviewed the files on employment and knew for sure. We do not address any questions based on 40% of criminal records. We have a lot of data on criminal records, and the violent crime I put here is just to pick some variable that resembles what we have, but the real analysis of crime is much denser. I have to say I like Anderson's paper a lot – it's one of the few papers that tries to address the question of small sample data, and actually to do resampling. The way we modify our work to yours is based on the sample procedure. Instead of flipping a coin and addressing the label of treatment control, we address the randomization protocol as well.

SPEAKER ARTHUR REYNOLDS:

A: It's very difficult to make generalizations from two studies about the relationship of gender to outcomes and crime. Interestingly, in the Chicago sample, for example, we find the exact opposite the Perry project found, we found much higher rates of high school graduation for males who attended preschool compared to males who did not attend preschool whereas Perry found that their program favored females. So I think [with regard to] the external validity of findings, we have to be very careful about making inferences based on the analysis of two studies for the field. So I'd encourage you to look at other launchings of those studies like Chicago's and others to get a better picture of the whole kind of context going on for both crime and for education.

Q: Just to clarify the difference in the rates of return that you found in the reanalysis of the Perry school, I caught 10% as an overall rate of return. Did you divide that into participant and nonparticipant amounts?

SPEAKER SEONG HYEOK MOON:

A: I showed the private return rate and the total return rate for the society together: 10% is the total return rate. And for the individual return, that was about a 5% return for males and about a 7 or 8% return for females.

Q: I would like to ask my question to all the researchers. All the analysis that I heard all day and I think yesterday is based on a few programs that were built a long time ago. I can see the validity, why we have to use them in terms of the analysis, because you can follow the children all the way to high school. But are you thinking about the horizon? These programs were built a long time ago. The demographics of America have changed. I think some of the programs were created because African Americans were the main target, but things are changing in America, and I'm just wondering if all of you are following other programs.

SPEAKER ARTHUR REYNOLDS:

A: I just want to clarify, the CPC program is an ongoing intervention today in Chicago public schools. I think many of the points of the analysis here look at the mechanisms, long-term effects, and cost effectiveness. You have to, in a sense, wait for 20 years to see what the effects are in order to calculate cost-benefit estimates. Many of the principles of the programs, the actual workings of the program in Chicago, still exist today, so I think that it's quite relevant to the programs today.

Q: Just to follow up, when we began a longitudinal study in the late 1970s here in Minneapolis public schools, we had a participation rate in our small study of 29% ethnic minority students, which was very similar to the 27% rate in Minneapolis public schools. Today, that rate is over 80%, and we have English-language learners in something like 90 languages. We have wave upon wave of immigrants and refugees that have transformed Minneapolis public schools in ways that I think are important to consider. It's a very important point that we are changing, and of course these longitudinal studies and long-term effectiveness examinations have to address that in some way. We don't want to just wait 20 years. But I think it's a really important question that's been raised.

SPEAKER ARTHUR REYNOLDS:

A: The point of the causal and mechanism analysis, you have to realize, is that among the Perry, Abecedarian, and Chicago Child-Parent programs, they differed by three decades. One was in the early sixties, one was in the early seventies, [and] one was in the early eighties, respectively. The programs were different. Samples were different in some ways. Yet, there were commonalities, the same findings in both cognitive and noncognitive dimensions. If the process is common among those three decades, there's a lot of relevance of those findings to today. That's why the commonality strengthens the point that there's a lot to learn from these studies. If we were to compare studies or analysis with samples of today, the kinds of populations, levels of risk that are available, and contexts might change the tenor or strength of the relationships. But I still think we would find a number of things in common.

SPEAKER FLAVIO CUNHA:

A: In our study, we did not use any of these studies to show the estimation, although we did use the insights of these studies to build the model. And I think that we have to move on to better understanding what the causal mechanisms are, and how the treatment actually interacts with the social context. I can't emphasize that enough. It's not only saying, "Early childhood matters, and here is the return to Perry Preschool," but it's also that if there's such and such change to society at such and such times, watch out for possible fertility effects. Watch out for possible changes in mobility because they may come as well. And the other thing is, progress is not just understanding and documenting the impacts, but it's also using that knowledge to create new models that can give us better ideas on how to proceed later on in life. I would use a lot of these studies to give me better ideas about what theoretical models can reconcile that.

Q: I'm going to skip over a couple of other things I'd love to say about school quality and how we might measure that, and the interesting lack of paths from academic achievement to educational attainment. But this is more of a challenge to all of you, but particularly to Arthur – that is, your model identified a number of very fascinating elements, and a lot of those elements appear in the achievement-gap literature as well. It's a slightly different question, but what I would really like to see all of us do is, say, what percent of the achievement gap at *X* point – high school graduation, for example, for Blacks, for Whites, for Hispanics, and so forth – can early childhood education make a contribution to reducing the gap? How much of it can be reduced, and what percent can be attributed to some of these other movable elements that might be out there? I think legislators are looking for this type of information as they make their state investments.

SPEAKER ARTHUR REYNOLDS:

A: The interaction here is going to causal mechanisms, how they interact and give us information about [the] percentage of different gaps and differential performance. We can attribute certain things – cognitive, noncognitive – for a school context and a family context, and break down those percentages in a more precise way as kids progress through school. It's hard to get precise numbers for that, but I think I would totally agree that we need to have more precision about getting those percentages. It's a challenging enterprise to try to take into account, and getting independent contributions and all of those things.

Q: I just want to make another comment, because Abecedarian doesn't have high school graduation effects. Where we have an effect is whether or not you go past high school. That's important to keep in mind, so I want this audience to take that message home. The other thing is, we've got a paper out under review right now where we put the amount of early risk in early childhood together with early intervention to see what predicts later outcomes. Early risk predicts not graduating from high school irrespective of early treatment.

SPEAKER ARTHUR REYNOLDS:

A: As your paper just showed in *Child Development* a few months ago, participation in the Abecedarian intervention was associated with lower rates of depressive symptoms in adulthood, which also was found in the CPC study.

Q: First, in light of the last set of comments, congratulations on the set of papers that you folks have put together, because I think they help us address many of the issues that have been brought up. We had papers yesterday on Head Start, Early Head Start, our study in New Jersey, Bill Gormley's studies in Oklahoma, that addressed new interventions, new populations. We haven't had the time to do very long-term analyses, but as we begin to get a greater understanding of the causal relationships through the older analyses, that can help us figure out which of these interventions have the magnitude and the types of impacts that are really important for long-term outcomes. This really highlights the strengths of looking at the whole literature, not just at an individual study, to try to draw conclusions. The other thing it made me think about was the subgroup analyses. I think we have to be very cautious there because it seems to me it is not appropriate, even with the larger studies, although there's less risk there, to simply pick subgroups and analyze them separately and then say, well, they look different. The appropriate way to do it is in fact to include tests of whether there are treatment interactions by the subgroup characteristics. Many of these, I think, probably wouldn't be statistically significant. And yet we look at them in parallel, as if they are. But that's an analysis that in many cases hasn't been conducted.

Q: Two quick comments. One thing I really liked about this panel, and particularly the idea of technology for the formation of skills, is that it begins to sound developmental. Over the past 2 days, there has not been a very strong developmental flavor to what we've been hearing, even though the organization of the 2 days had a developmental character to it. We started with early kinds of intervention. But what I mean by "developmental" is that developmental data, knowledge, theory are growing by leaps and bounds at multiple levels of analysis, from epigenetic to neurobehavioral and so forth, and it's likely that there are going to be windows of vulnerability and opportunity for leverage and change that we're probably going to want to be smarter and more strategic about.

The other comment is that we're nationally about to spend a huge fortune studying 100,000 children longitudinally in the national children's study. And I'm just hoping that some of you in this room who have been involved in these important studies are advising or thinking about the possibility of parallel supplemental research that is going to take advantage of that. We're going to have normative data on 100,000 children. The recruitment of those families will begin or has already begun. That's a really important opportunity, and I'm just curious if anybody is going to take advantage of it.

SPEAKER FLAVIO CUNHA:

A: I would say a little bit more. Up to this point, we have made all the effort in the world to make sure that choices don't contaminate our analysis, but I am proposing that we should embrace choices. They're very informative about real life. As social scientists, we should be able to understand and predict and forecast how people are going to react once these programs are done in real life, not with 123 people.

SPEAKER ARTHUR REYNOLDS:

A: Certainly. [A previous speaker] emphasized the point about developmental continuity. I couldn't agree more that the research needs to try to mirror or map on as much as possible what life-course development really looks like in terms of developmental continuity. We need to make sure it's embedded in our research models.

SPEAKER JAMES HECKMAN:

Q: I have a comment. I just want to amplify the point that was made earlier by Steve [Barnett] and by several people and also what Flavio [Cunha] was saying, and that is that these schemes essentially allow us to go beyond the treatment-control mentality. I see it in this conference in the last few days. A lot of people see the randomized trial as being the only source of human knowledge. That's a very crippling idea, because we do have these developmental mechanisms. What's been exciting is that we actually can understand. So we can take, for example, the Perry data and hopefully the Abecedarian data and the CPC data and actually blend it in with nonexperimental data, because we have a common algorithm. Cognitive and noncognitive skills are just shorthand for much bigger developmental issues. I want to add health and other dimensions. Then you can use science to integrate these studies. I heard some people around the room over the last few days suggesting that if it wasn't a randomized trial of a particular study, then you couldn't start making policy. It's a huge mistake; it's very inhibiting. I think we always have to make policies. No program that's ever been tried is going be the best program that we can put in place tomorrow. So the way we establish external validity, and actually do serious policy analysis, is by understanding these causal mechanisms. That's why I'm so pleased with Arthur's paper, and I'm happy with the work that we're doing here in these reanalyses. But I do think it's something that we could talk a lot more about today or in the future, which is to go beyond this notion that "if it isn't an experiment, then it's worthless." In the Perry case, the experiment was contaminated. But when you actually use some principles and actually use some social science, and use a little statistics, you get an even stronger result once you recognize that. But it's not just Perry, it's not just Abecedarian, it's not just CPC, it's also NLSY, it's CNLSY, it's going to be all these other studies. I think that's how we're going to build this into a science and use development.

SPEAKER ARTHUR REYNOLDS:

A: I know a quote about validity: "Validity is a property of knowledge claims and not research methods." We need a critical analysis of evidence across regardless of what the design is. That's how we get validity.

Q: Just following up on my earlier question that it wasn't clear that it was answered, at least to my satisfaction, was that the Anderson study as I read it found virtually no effect relative to a placebo for males yet significant effects for females, which really has significant implications for these huge returns to these programs.

SPEAKER ARTHUR REYNOLDS:

A: In the case of the CPC, the opposite is the case. The CPC program found gigantic effects, a 16-percentage point difference for African American males' high school graduation that can't be explained away. So we need a broader analysis of different interventions.

NAME INDEX

SUBJECT INDEX